The Wisdom of Egypt

Jewish, Early Christian, and Gnostic Essays in
Honour of Gerard P. Luttikhuizen

Edited by

Anthony Hilhorst
and
George H. van Kooten

BRILL
LEIDEN · BOSTON
2005

This book is printed on acid-free paper.

Photograph frontispiece by Elmer Spaargaren

Library of Congress Cataloging-in-Publication Data

The wisdom of Egypt : Jewish, early Christian, and gnostic essays in honour of Gerard P.
  Luttikhuizen / edited by Anthony Hilhorst, George H. van Kooten.
      p. cm. — (Ancient Judaism & early Christianity, ISSN 0169-734X = Arbeiten zur
  Geschichte des antiken Judentums und des Urchristentums ; 59)
      Includes bibliographical references and indexes.
      ISBN 90-04-14425-0 (alk. paper)
      1. Egypt—Religion. 2. Bible. O.T.—Criticism, interpretation, etc. I. Hilhorst, Anthony.
  II. Kooten, Geurt Hendrik van, 1969- III. Luttikhuizen, Gerard P. IV. Arbeiten zur
  Geschichte des antiken Judentums und des Urchristentums ; Bd. 59.

BL2441.3.W57 2005
200′.93—dc 22

BL
2441.3
.W57
2005

                                                                                        2005042196

ISSN   0169-734X
ISBN   90 04 14425 0

The Wisdom of Egypt

Ancient Judaism
and
Early Christianity

Arbeiten zur Geschichte des Antiken Judentums und des Urchristentums

VOLUME 59

CONTENTS

PART TWO

EARLY CHRISTIANITY & EGYPT

PART THREE

GNOSTICISM & EGYPT

PREFACE

On the exact day that this volume will be offered to Gerard Luttikhuizen, he will pass the milestone of an academic career spanning
some four decades, for the latter part of which he held the chair in
New Testament and Early Christian Studies at the University of Groningen. Educated at the Catholic University of Nijmegen, where he
had the good fortune to have Professor Bas van Iersel as his teacher
for the New Testament, he developed a keen scholarly interest in
the life and message of Jesus of Nazareth and its early reception,
which would have resulted in a thesis on Mark's Gospel but for his
appointment to the theological faculty in Groningen. That faculty's
engagement in Jewish Christian literature eventually led him to tackle
the Book of Elchasai, the study of which resulted in his 1984 thesis,
*The Revelation of Elchasai: Investigations into the Evidence for a Mesopotamian
Jewish Apocalypse of the Second Century and its Reception by Judeo-Christian
Propagandists*, supervised by Professor Freek Klijn. The widening of his
field of investigation had begun earlier than this, however, and gained
a solid foundation from his study of Coptic in Münster. In Groningen
his teaching duties comprised both the New Testament and Coptic.
His initial love of the former area by no means diminished; in addition
to the synoptic Gospels he delighted in studying the letters of Paul, to
which he dedicated his inaugural lecture, and the book of Revelation.
With regard to Coptic, this not only satisfied his love of linguistics but
also enabled him to study that monument of Gnostic literature, the
Nag Hammadi Library. In point of fact, he was—and, of course, still
is—fascinated by Gnosticism, which, he never tires of stating, is so
important in early Christianity. It comes as no surprise that almost
all of his students have either written their theses on Coptic Gnostic
texts, or at least when writing them used the proficiency in Coptic
they had acquired from Gerard's lessons. His own interests can be
surmised from the bibliography at the end of this Festschrift, and are
well reflected by the titles of volumes to which he has contributed,
and by the titles of his monographs, including his *Gnostic Revisions of
Genesis Stories and Early Jesus Traditions* (Brill, forthcoming), and his *De
veelvormigheid van het vroegste christendom*, a book in Dutch on the diversity
of earliest Christianity.

Nag Hammadi and the Coptic language naturally point to Egypt,
which Gerard first visited in 1976 and which interests him not just as

an object of academic study. Indeed, not every tourist can say that
they hired a bike in Luxor and visited the villages and their inhabitants in the neighbourhood instead of just gazing at the antiquities, as
he did. Thus, both scholarship and life seemed to suggest Egypt as a
focus for the present volume, which colleagues and students wish to
offer Gerard as a token of their admiration and friendship. It proved
in fact surprisingly easy to gather together a number of papers dealing
with subjects that might interest the honorand.

A number of the contributions are concerned with Egypt and Judaism. These papers, in part one of this volume, deal with Jewish writings
whose provenance and/or subject matter scholarly consensus relates
to or situates in Egypt: the Greek translation of Genesis, compared
with the transformative interpretation of Genesis in Rabbinic and
Qumranic circles (GARCÍA MARTÍNEZ); the rewriting of the account of
Moses' birth in Egypt in the *Book of Jubilees* (VAN RUITEN); the rewriting
of the Moses story by Artapanus, an Egyptian Jew of the Ptolemaic
era (KUGLER); the Egyptian setting of *Joseph and Aseneth* (BOLYKI); the
Wisdom of Solomon, taken as an example of Alexandrian Judaism and
compared with later Gnostic Wisdom speculation (LIETAERT PEER-
BOLTE); the last Ptolemaic ruler, Cleopatra VII, and her dealings with
Herod the Great according to Josephus (VAN HENTEN); and the pagan
magical use of the Jewish formula 'The God who drowned the King
of Egypt' (VAN DER HORST). This part starts with the opposite of a
positive understanding of the 'Wisdom of Egypt'—Joshua's mention
of 'the disgrace of Egypt', an enigmatic expression which seems to
highlight the ambivalent character of the relationship between Egypt
and Israel (NOORT).

Part two contains studies of the relations between Egypt and Early
Christianity. This part opens with a discussion of the Hosea quotation
at the beginning of Matthew's Gospel: 'Out of Egypt I have called my
son' (MENKEN). The title of the Festschrift is not only inspired by the
utterance of 1 Kings 5.10 (MT) to the effect that Solomon's wisdom
surpasses 'all the wisdom of Egypt', but also by Acts 7.22, where Moses
is said to have been 'instructed in all the wisdom of the Egyptians'.
This passage receives separate treatment (HILHORST). Other papers deal
with the expectations of Nero's return in the Egyptian *Sibylline Oracles*
(book 5), the study of which is brought to bear on a reinterpretation of
the setting of Paul's Second Letter to the Thessalonians (VAN KOOTEN);
the notion of 'the condemning heart' in 1 John, seen from an ancient
Egyptian perspective (TE VELDE); the Egyptian-Jewish background of

one of the Eucharistic prayers in the *Didache* (VAN DE SANDT); the setting of the *Letter of Barnabas* in early second-century Egypt (LOMAN);
the interpretation of Paul's rapture to paradise in early Christian
writings, among which several from Egypt (ROUKEMA); the Egyptian
symbol *par excellence*, the sphinx, and its theological interpretation by
Plutarch and Clement of Alexandria (HERRMANN & VAN DEN HOEK);
the critical portrayal of two 'foolish Egyptians', Apion and Anoubion,
in the *Pseudo-Clementines* (BREMMER); the martyrdom of the Christian
Alexandrian Potamiaena, put in the context of the persecutions of
Emperor Severus (BAKKER); and the attitude towards women within
ascetic circles in early Christian Egypt (PESTHY).

Finally, Gnostic writings, in most cases Coptic Gnostic literature
from Egypt, are dealt with in part three. This part begins with
a paper devoted to Alexandrian Gnosticism at the beginning of
Christianity, emphasizing the peaceful coexistence of Gnostic and
non-Gnostic Christians within the Christian communities (JAKAB).
Other papers address the eschatology of the *Gospel of Thomas* in the
context of scholarly debate about the historical Jesus (HOGETERP); the
Gnostic Basilides of Alexandria and his sources of inspiration (BOS);
the apocrypha genre, applied in Gnostic literature, against the background of the secret book in ancient Egypt (VAN DIJK); the references
to antediluvian patriarchs such as Adam and Enoch in the Cologne
Mani Codex, which is believed to have been translated into Greek in
Egypt (TIGCHELAAR); the anthropology of the *Acts of Andrew* and other
Gnostic literature (ROIG LANZILLOTTA); the *Acts of Peter and the Twelve*,
passed down among the Nag Hammadi writings, with regard to both
the supposed itineraries of the apostles (TUBACH) and the identity of
Lithargoel whom they meet on their journey (CZACHESZ). The volume
concludes with papers on *The Holy Book of the Great Invisible Spirit*, or
The Egyptian Gospel, discussing its concepts of *gnōsis* and *mageia* (MEYER),
and on fate, magic, and astrology in the encyclopaedic work entitled
Pistis Sophia, and written by an Egyptian author (VAN DER VLIET).

All the papers together highlight the Egyptian subject matter, background or provenance of many Jewish, Early Christian and Gnostic
texts. Covering a broad spectrum of themes, genres and traditions,
they show that Egypt was a vibrant point of reference, sometimes even
a focal point and cradle for Jews, Christians and their thought. They
impressively demonstrate the extent to which Egypt was involved in
the formative stages of Judaism and Christianity and, at the same
time, that it was far from isolated from the wider developments in
the ancient world.

Issues like these stirred the scholarly imagination of Gerard Lut-tikhuizen, and we all hope that Gerard will continue his scholarly concerns. There is much that still needs to be said about the origins of Gnosticism, most Nag Hammadi texts are still waiting for a Dutch translation directly from Coptic, and several PhD students hope for his continued coaching. But there is no denying that he has many other interests. He likes travelling with his wife Marleen. He is a gifted painter, and both creating works of art and enjoying those of others, especially contemporaries, will take up much of his time. And without a shadow of doubt he will continue to listen to the music of Bach, Johann Sebastian of course, of whom he is a devotee and on whom an expert, even if he is not an active musician himself. So we will just have to wait and see, and wish him a wonderful *otium cum dignitate*.

Groningen, January 2005   Anthony Hilhorst
                                                        George van Kooten

PART ONE

JUDAISM & EGYPT

THE DISGRACE OF EGYPT: JOSHUA 5.9A
AND ITS CONTEXT

Ed Noort

1. *Introduction*

Egypt, Israel and the Hebrew Bible are interrelated in many ways[1] and linguistic, literary, and cultural influences are not hard to detect.[2] For example, Egyptian architecture, art and iconography are still visible in the material culture of Ancient Israel, especially in the coastal plain. The title of this collection of studies for our colleague Gerard Luttikhuizen is derived from 1 Kings 5.10. Here, the legendary wisdom of Solomon surpasses 'all the wisdom of Egypt'. The image of Egypt is that of a powerful, prosperous and highly educated country with plenty of food (Gen 12.10; 42.1ff.; Exod 16.3; Num 11.5).[3] In times of political crisis Egypt served as a shelter (1 Kings 11.26ff., 40 [Jeroboam]; Isa 20; 2 Kings 25.26 [murderers of Gedaliah]) and Judean kings sought Egyptian military assistance several times. However, the overall picture of Egypt in the Hebrew Bible is a negative one.

Due to the infiltration of the Exodus tradition in almost all literary compositions[4] of the Hebrew Bible, the foremost image is that of an

---

[1] For a general introduction see D.B. Redford, *Egypt, Canaan and Israel in Ancient Times*, Princeton, NJ 1995[2]; M. Görg, *Die Beziehungen zwischen dem Alten Israel und Ägypten: Von den Anfängen bis zum Exil* (Erträge der Forschung 290), Darmstadt 1997. F.V. Greifenhagen, *Egypt on the Pentateuch's Ideological Map: Constructing Biblical Israel's Identity* (Journal for the Study of the Old Testament Supplement Series 361), Sheffield 2003, reconstructs the image of Egypt in the Pentateuch as a part of the ideological map of the Jewish Diaspora within Egypt during the Persian period. B.U. Schipper's dissertation *Israel und Ägypten in der Königszeit: Die kulturellen Kontakte von Salomo bis zum Fall Jerusalems* (Orbis Biblicus et Orientalis 170), Göttingen 1999, challenges the antiquity of the relationship between Egypt and Israel. In his opinion the historical contacts start only in the late monarchical period of Judah.

[2] R.J. Williams, 'Ägypten und Israel', in: *Theologische Realenzyklopädie* (Berlin 1977), i, 492-505 (Bibl.).

[3] H. Ringgren, מצרים, in: *Theologisches Wörterbuch zum Alten Testament* (Stuttgart 1984), iv, 1099-111.

[4] W. Zimmerli, *Grundriß der alttestamentlichen Theologie* (Theologische Wissenschaft 3), Stuttgart 1978[3], I § 2: 'Jahwe, der Gott Israels von Ägypten her', 16-20.

oppressor. Egypt is the 'house of slavery' (Exod 13.3; Deut 6.12; 7.8 etc.) and in the summa of ethical thinking, the Decalogue, YHWH presents himself not as the God of Heaven and Earth, nor as the Creator, but as the God 'who brought you out of Egypt' (Exod 20.2; Deut 5.6). How deeply this image was rooted in Israel's reflections on the past, in its thinking about its own identity, may be demonstrated by a small detail. Isa 19.25 reads 'Blessed be Egypt, my people, and Assyria the work of my hands, and Israel my heritage', a stunning eschatological vision in which the former enemies are called 'my people' and 'the work of my hands'. The blessing is framed by the contention that there will be an altar to YHWH in the land of Egypt. The LXX did not accept such a vision and introduced a prepositional 'in' to read 'Blessed be my people that is *in* Egypt …' The object now is Israel in slavery. Israel is now blessed, rather than the Egyptians! Translation can be a deadly weapon.

2. *The ambivalence of the role of Egypt and the crux interpretum of Josh 5.9*

Without doubt, the praise of the wisdom of Egypt will be sung in this collection of studies. There is ample reason for this in the book of Proverbs, in the Psalms and in the narratives of the wisdom traditions. However, in this paper I would like to stress the ambivalent character of the relationship between Egypt and Israel by studying an enigmatic expression from Joshua 5.9a, the famous crux interpretum חרפת מצרים.[5] The divine speech to Joshua in 5.9 reads:

היום גלותי את־חרפת מצרים מעליכם
ויקרא שם המקום ההוא גלגל עד היום הזה

Today I have rolled away the חרפת מצרים from upon you, and he called the name of this מקום Gilgal until the present day.

The translation of חרפת מצרים depends on the interpretation. Common

---

[5] M.N. van der Meer has recently intensively studied Joshua 5.2-12 in his dissertation *Formation and Reformulation: The Redaction of the Book of Joshua in the Light of the Oldest Textual Witnesses*, Leiden 2001, 219-352, with an excellent survey of the history of research of the passage on 223-51. Two other important studies of Joshua 5.2-12 are K. Bieberstein, *Josua-Jordan-Jericho: Archäologie, Geschichte und Theologie der Landnahmeerzählungen Josua 1-6* (Orbis Biblicus et Orientalis 143), Göttingen 1995, 194-223; G.C. den Hertog, *Studien zur griechischen Übersetzung des Buches Josua*, Diss. Gießen 1996.

Bible translations read: 'the reproach of Egypt' (American Standard Version; Jewish Publication Society; King James Version; New King James Version; Revised Standard Version), 'the disgrace of Egypt' (New Revised Standard Version; Jewish Publication Society Tanakh), 'die ägyptische Schande' (Einheitsübersetzung) or 'die Schande Ägyptens' (Elberfelder Bibel; Revidierte Lutherübersetzung); the Dutch translations read almost in unison 'de smaad van Egypte' (Leidsche Vertaling; NBG 1951; Statenvertaling; but cf. NBV 2004: 'de schande van Egypte'). The interpretations of the meaning of the חרפת מצרים differ greatly. The most important suggestions are either the uncircumcised state of the people who left Egypt and their offspring born on the way through the wilderness, or the humiliation of the slavery in Egypt, depending on the interpretation of the context.

3. *The early history of reception: the LXX*

The situation is further complicated by the LXX, which reads:

> καὶ εἶπεν κύριος τῷ 'Ιησοῖ υἱῷ Ναυη· ἐν τῇ σήμερον ἡμέρᾳ ἀφεῖλον τὸν ὀνειδισμὸν Αἰγύπτου ἀφ' ὑμῶν. καὶ ἐκάλεσεν τὸ ὄνομα τοῦ τόπου ἐκείνου Γαλγαλα.

> The Lord said to Iesous, son of Naue: On this very day I took away the disgrace of Egypt from you. And he called the name of that place Galgala.

A minor difference between MT and LXX is the patronymic plus υἱὸς Ναυη after Joshua. A second one, the stress on 'this very day', is not unusual.[6]

The more important difference in LXX is the lack of עד היום הזה in MT 5.9bβ together with ויחנו in v. 10. The most frequent explanation is that the entire phrase ויחנו בני-ישראל בגלגל from MT is missing in LXX. In that case a homoioteleuton from גלגל...גלגל can easily be reconstructed. Presupposing this, the LXX translator, however, had to find a new subject for ἐποίησαν ...τὸ Πασχα (5.10) and he chose οἱ υἱοὶ Ισραηλ, which was exactly the same as in MT.

---

[6] Contra Van der Meer, *The Redaction of the Book of Joshua*, 288. For Josh 5.9 ἐν τῇ σήμερον ἡμέρᾳ, see Jer 1.18, var. Josh 22.29 ἐν ταῖς σήμερον ἡμέραις; 1 Sam 17.10 σήμερον ἐν τῇ ἡμέρᾳ ταύτῃ; Judith 7.28; 8.12, 18;13.17 ἐν τῇ ἡμέρᾳ τῇ σήμερον. As an aetiological formula ἕως τῆς σήμερον ἡμέρας used in Joshua 4.9; 6.25; 9.27; 10.27; 13.13; 22.3; 24.31.

For this reason—the accidental choice of the same expression[7]—a homoioteleuton is an unlikely solution. The differences between MT and LXX cannot be attributed to a technical mistake; we have to look for an intended change in one or the other direction.

Van der Meer has come up with the following ingenious solution. Because of the Qal of the verb קרא corresponding to ἐκάλεσεν in the LXX, the subject must be either YHWH or Joshua. Between 5.3 Βουνὸς τῶν ἀκροβυστιῶν, 'the Hill of the Foreskins', and 5.8f. there is no change of location, so, in the eyes of the LXX translator, Gilgal and the Hill of the Foreskins must be the same place. After 4.19 the name of Gilgal was already known by the people. Therefore, Van der Meer presumes a divine subject in 5.9: 'in Josh 5.9 [the place] receives its proper name "Gilgal" from the mouth of the Deity himself.'[8] The consequence of this choice is that in his eyes the phrase 'until the present day' 'would not have been very appropriate'.[9] The LXX thus intentionally removed the phrase from the Vorlage. The presupposition of this reasoning is that the formula 'until the present day' is only used after human action and name-giving. In Ezek 20.29, however, there is human name-giving but the context is a divine speech and the argumentation is based on word play just as in Josh 5.9. Ezek 20.29 reads:

> And I (YHWH) said to them: 'What is the high place about, to which you go up? Thus its name has become "high place" to the present day.'

The word play around במה using the elements מה and בוא demonstrates that it is not inappropriate to connect a divine subject or speech with the formula 'to the present day.

Thus, more possibilities are available as there is no decisive reason why LXX should shorten the text. The aetiological formula is therefore probably an expansion produced by MT. MT stresses both the connection between the divine interpretation of Joshua's action and the divine name-giving, as well as the fact that this toponym is still known to the present reader.

Is it possible to propose that the phrase ויחנו בני־ישראל בגלגל is indeed an expansion of the MT and not a shortening by the LXX

---

[7] It may be argued, however, that this choice is in line with the naming of the whole chapter. The phrase οἱ υἱοὶ Ισραηλ appears in 5.1([2x]), 2, 3, 4, 10, 12.

[8] Van der Meer, *The Redaction of the Book of Joshua*, 335.

[9] Ibid.

translator? With regard to the frequency of both expressions, בני־ישׂראל in MT and υἱοὶ Ισραηλ in LXX appear roughly the same number of times. בני־ישׂראל[10] appears 69 times and υἱοὶ Ισραηλ 73 times in the Book of Joshua. Given the varying lengths of both texts, this is not an appreciable difference.

In four cases, however, there is an expansion of the MT vis-à-vis the LXX. In these four cases LXX does not read any form of υἱοὶ Ισραηλ or its equivalents. MT 1.2 specifies the receiving party of the promise of the land: 'to them, *to the sons of Israel*'. MT 3.1 shifts from the first person singular 'Joshua got up' to the plural 'they set out' by inserting 'he *and all the sons of Israel*'. Here too, the aim is to bring in the Israelites, the group, rather than to solve a syntactical problem. The opening sentence of the conquest of Jericho reads MT 6.1: 'Now Jericho was totally sealed off *in the face* of *the sons of Israel*. No-one could leave or enter.' And, finally, MT has a remarkable plus in 18.10. After the lot casting in Shiloh, MT reads: 'And Joshua apportioned there the land to *the sons of Israel* in accordance with their portions.' Again there is no reason why LXX should have shortened the text here. However, an expansion of MT can be explained. MT stresses the fulfilment of the divine commands of Josh 13.6, 7. Everything happened as YHWH and Moses ordered. So apart from MT 5.10, we have four more cases where the text in MT has been expanded for reasons of clarifying or stressing the role of the Israelites.

In several cases LXX reads 'Israel' or a personal pronoun, unlike the MT where the בני־ישׂראל are mentioned, for example in 11.19 in the summing up of the war in the north, and in the particular note of the killing of Balaam, the son of Beor. Josh 13.22 reveals a long tradition of exegetical interpretation within the Hebrew Bible itself.[11] LXX reads καὶ τὸν Βαλααμ τὸν τοῦ Βεωρ τὸν μάντιν ἀπέκτειναν ἐν τῇ ῥοπῇ. The subject refers to the Reubenites, whose territory is discussed in 13.15-23. Related to those territorial claims, traditions about Balaam are referred to. In Num 22-24 MT, Balaam—reluctantly—functions

---

[10] בני־ישׂראל is by far the most used expression in Joshua MT; כל־ישׂראל) appears only 41 times.

[11] H. Donner, 'Balaam pseudopropheta', in: H. Donner, R. Hanhart, and R. Smend (eds), *Beiträge zur alttestamentlichen Theologie: Festschrift für Walther Zimmerli zum 70. Geburtstag*, Göttingen 1977, 112-23.

as a prophet of YHWH. The overall picture is a positive one. This is changed in Deut 23.3-5 and radicalized in the late text of Num 31.8 where not only the kings of Midian are killed, but also Balaam. Depending on Num 31.8, Josh 13.22 pictures Balaam as a קוסם, a diviner, and after the laws of Deut 18 and 13 such a false prophet is put to death. What LXX claims for the Reubenites, MT claims in its presumed orthodoxy for the totality of all Israelites. Under the guidance of Moses the בני־ישראל killed the dangerous false prophet.

Further, it can be observed that in expressions in MT 7.23; 19.51 and 21.1, LXX mentions 'Israel' where MT offers combinations with 'the sons of Israel'.[12]

In conclusion, we have some indications that the MT has been consciously expanded by mentioning בני־ישראל to stress the particular role of the Israelites in the book of Joshua. There is no need to assume that the LXX has been systematically shortened.

But how can we explain the encampment at Gilgal itself: ויחנו בני־ישראל בגלגל? The encampment at Gilgal is first mentioned in 4.19: 'The people came up out of the Jordan [on the tenth day of the first month] and camped at Gilgal on the eastern border of Jericho.' Most exegetes[13] agree that the verse itself originally belonged to one of the older versions of the crossing narrative. The solemn date formula 'on the tenth day of the first month', however, is understood as a priestly insertion preparing for the Passover of 5.10-12. Indeed, the priestly instructions for Passover from Exod 12.3, 6 refer to the tenth and the fourteenth day of the first month. The two dates link Josh 4.19 and 5.10. Within this framework the encampment of 5.10 is regarded as a repetition of 4.19, which LXX 5.10 with its supposed

---

[12] The opposite can also be seen. In 3.7, 17; 6.18; 8.35; 10.10; 21.45 and 23.2, LXX reads υἱοὶ Ισραηλ. Here υἱοὶ Ισραηλ is read as כל־ישראל (3.7, 17; 23.2), מחנה ישראל (6.18), כל־קהל ישראל (8.35), לפני ישראל (10.10), בית ישראל (21.45). In most cases—about fifty times—there is a one-to-one translation: בני־ישראל with υἱοὶ Ισραηλ.

[13] M. Noth, *Josua* (Handbuch zum Alten Testament 1.7), Tübingen 1953², 39; T.C. Butler, *Joshua* (Word Biblical Commentary 7), Waco, Texas 1983, 50-1; V. Fritz, *Das Buch Josua* (Handbuch zum Alten Testament 1.7), Tübingen 1994, 48; R.D. Nelson, *Joshua* (Old Testament Library), Louisville 1997, 70; J.L. Sicre, *Josué* (Nueva Biblia Española), Estella 2002, 142. More critically: Bieberstein, *Josua-Jordan-Jericho*, 184f. For an overview of the history of research see E. Noort, *Das Buch Josua: Forschungsgeschichte und Problemfelder* (Erträge der Forschung 292), Darmstadt 1998, 147-64; Sicre, *Josué*, 147-54: Excurso 5: 'Distintas aproximaciones a Jos 3-4'.

systematizing character correctly removed.[14] In this case a longer MT is presupposed, shortened by LXX.

Two problems[15] have to be solved here: the date formula and the chronological system behind it, and the geographical marker Gilgal.

The following chronological remarks are made in the final text of the first chapters of Joshua:

1.11 Joshua's instruction to the officers: the crossing of the Jordan will take place *within three days*: בעוד שלשת ימים[16] (A).[17]

2.2 The scouts sent out by Joshua stay overnight[18] in the house of the prostitute Rahab (B).

2.16 Rahab to the scouts: 'hide yourselves in the hill country for three days' (B).

2.22 The scouts return to Joshua and report after hiding for three days (B).

3.1 Itinerary: From Shittim to the Jordan: one day and a stay overnight. The crossing will take place the next day (C).[19]

3.2 Preparations *at the end of three days* for crossing on the fourth day: מקצה שלשת ימים[20] (A).

3.5 Speech: Joshua to the people: '*Tomorrow* YHWH will do wonders among you' (C).

3.7 Divine speech: YHWH to Joshua: '*Today* I will begin to make you great' (D).

---

[14] E. Otto, *Das Mazzotfest in Gilgal* (Beiträge zur Wissenschaft vom Alten und Neuen Testament 107), Stuttgart 1975, 61 note 1: 'So dürfte wohl V. 10aα als neben Jos 4,19 überflüssig angesehen und gestrichen worden sein.'

[15] The remarkable conjunction of Passover with eating the produce of the land and the Feast of the Unleavened Bread could be a third problem. The conjunction, however, is not so remarkable when Joshua 5.10-12 is recognized as the entry into the land where the laws of Lev 23 are observed. Josh 5 is a practical exercising of Lev 23.

[16] The same expression in Joseph's explanation of the dreams of Pharaoh's chief cupbearer and baker: Gen 40.13, 19.

[17] The symbols A-F systematize the different chronological remarks.

[18] LXX does not mention 'this/that night' in v. 2 but refers to it in the speech of the king's servants to Rahab in v. 3. MT adds 'that night' in v. 2 to try to avoid the sexual connotations of the simple 'they lay down there'.

[19] The chronology of 3.1 may fit with 3.2 if necessary, but is not related to the time scheme of 1.11 and 3.2. For an overview of the positions in the literary-historical debate, see Bieberstein, *Josua-Jordan-Jericho*, 171 note 141.

[20] The expression only appears for a second time in Josh 9.16.

4.19 Narrative: the people came up out of the Jordan *on the tenth day of the first month* (E).

5.10 Narrative: the Israelites celebrated Passover *on the fourteenth day of the month* (E).

5.11 Narrative: the Israelites ate the produce of the land *the day after*[21] Passover (E).

6.14 Narrative: *six days* of encircling Jericho (F).

6.15 Narrative: *on the seventh day*, the walls of Jericho came down (F).

A first look at the texts reveals that Josh 2 has its own chronology (B), fitting with its character as an isolated story in the composition of Josh 1-12. In the overall scheme the chronology of this narrative is not related to the crossing story. The scouts return on the fifth day of their adventure. They report to Joshua after the crossing has occurred. Though belonging to different literary layers, Josh 1.11; 3.2, 5, 7 all focus on the crossing of the Jordan and its meaning for Joshua and Israel. The general time expressions, 'within three days', 'at the end of three days', 'the next day' and 'this very day', stress the enigmatic role of the crossing. This specific use of the date formulas is often seen in (travel) narratives or itineraries. Especially the span of three days leads to a decisive turn of the events: Gen 22.4 (Abraham – Isaac); 31.22 (Laban – Jacob); 34.25 (Dinah – Shechem); Exod 19.16 (theophany); Josh 9.16, 17 (Gibeon); Judg 20.30 (Israelites – Benjaminites) etc. The tension-building function for a transition from old to new, here from the wilderness to the Promised Land, is expressed by the date formulas. Their general and symbolic content cannot be used for a precise time scheme. They draw attention to a point of decision.

These general expressions differ significantly from the (post-)priestly time formulas in 4.19 and 5.10, 11 where an exact day is meant and given because of the relation with Exod 12.3, 6. The central item is the Passover celebration connected with the Feast of Unleavened Bread. The horizon of this redactor is not only Exod 12, but first and foremost Lev 23. Lev 23.5, 6 connects the Passover offering on the fourteenth day of Nisan with the Feast of Unleavened Bread on the fifteenth day of the same month. Lev 23.14 forbids eating bread, parched grain or fresh ears before the first offering. Dealing with these

---

[21] According to MT, explicitly contrary to LXX.

combinations, MT specified its text vis-à-vis the LXX. The story about the manna in Exod 16.35 explicitly states that manna belongs to the gifts of the desert and stops as soon as Canaan has been reached. For LXX Josh 5.11, 12 manna stops on the very same day the Passover meal is eaten, i.e. the fourteenth day.[22] MT, however, knowing Lev 23, has to separate Passover, the eating of the unleavened bread and the cessation of manna. ממחרת הפסח, 'the day after Passover', is added to its text. The chronological remark is thus again an expansion of MT, not a shortening of LXX. MT constructs a Passover which will pass the examination of the strictest Deuteronomists as demonstrated by 2 Kings 23.21-23. In the eyes of this author there are only two regular Passovers celebrated in the Promised Land: the Passover of Joshua and the Passover of Josiah. Up until this point we have noticed expansions of MT, not shortenings of LXX. These expansions are clearly painted in deuteronomistic colours.

Looking back at the different chronological formulas representing different aspects and used in the first chapters of Joshua, it is no longer possible to reconstruct a single chronological scheme for the crossing of the Jordan, which is what Wilcoxen[23] did in the days when exegesis reconstructed many festivals as a background for the supposed cultic character of the text:

> The legend covers events of *two seven-day periods*, one containing a ritual or symbolic crossing of the Jordan river by the Ark and the people and commemorating the entry into the land, and one repeating, during the festival period, the miraculous conquest[24] by the people and the Ark of the great Canaanite city of Jericho.[25]

Wilcoxen presumes a seven-day period for the crossing by reckoning inclusively, 'so that "three days" actually means "part of today, tomorrow, and part of the next day"' (62). However, his combination is an

---

[22] For the relation between Josh 5 and Lev 23 see Nelson, *Joshua*, 80 and more importantly M. Fishbane, *Biblical Interpretation in Ancient Israel*, Oxford 1985, 145-51, who refers to Num 33.3 and the connection between Sabbath, Akkadian *šapattu* and the full moon on the fifteenth of the month. Extensive coverage by Van der Meer, *The Redaction of the Book of Joshua*, 275-6.

[23] J.A. Wilcoxen, 'Narrative Structure and Cult Legend: a Study of Joshua 1-6', in: J.C. Rijlaarsdam (ed.), *Transitions in Biblical Scholarship* (Essays in Divinity 6), Chicago 1968, 43-70.

[24] The seven-day scheme of Josh 6 is clear in spite of multiple reworkings of the text. The walls of Jericho come tumbling down on the seventh day of the encircling.

[25] Wilcoxen, 'Narrative Structure and Cult Legend', 64.

unlikely solution considering the different character of the chronological formulas in this part of the book of Joshua.

The second problem is the geographical setting of the encampment at Gilgal, which is missing in the LXX. However, Gilgal is not the only toponym in the text. The celebration of Passover has a second geographical marker in v. 10: בערבות יריחו, already known from Josh 4.13 and probably the original stage for Passover. We have seen that Lev 23 and Exod 12 were in the background for the combination of Passover and the Feast of the Unleavened Bread. Now Bieberstein[26] has drawn attention to the fact that Exod 12.48-50 requires every participant of the Passover meal to be circumcised. This is the rationale for the circumcision narrative of Josh 5.2-8. It is here that circumcision enters the stage. As soon as Passover was combined with the condition of circumcision and this combination functioned as the 'Vorlage' for Josh 5, the narrative of Josh 5.2-8 introduced the circumcision ceremony. Josh 5.2-8 is Exod 12 in action. The *conditio sine qua non* for the Passover of 5.10 is the fact that every Israelite should be circumcised. In fulfilling this command, however, MT and LXX[27] each go their own way.

MT states explicitly that the older generation, coming out of Egypt, was circumcised. They had died in the desert (5.4, 6).[28] The younger generation, however, those Israelites born in the desert and who would enter the Promised Land, were not circumcised (5.5). Obviously the narrator needs an explanation for this. His references to Numbers and Deuteronomy are introduced by the phrase 'This is the reason why' (5.4), stressing the necessity of circumcision.

The main difference between LXX and MT is the group which is circumcised: according to LXX, not only those who were born on the way through the desert but also those who were uncircumcised when they left Egypt were circumcised (5.4).[29] This differs from MT, which states that every man going out of Egypt had been circumcised and that this entire generation had died by the time the Promised Land was reached. This is generally not regarded as a complete contradiction

---

[26] Bieberstein, *Josua-Jordan-Jericho*, 408.
[27] Discussed in detail by Van der Meer, *The Redaction of the Book of Joshua*, 255-64, 287-329.
[28] Reference: Num 14.21-35; 32.13 and Deut 1.34-36, 39.
[29] καὶ ὅσοι ποτὲ ἀπερίτμητοι ἦσαν τῶν ἐξεληλυθότων ἐξ Αἰγύπτου.

because Num 14.29 is aimed at men older than twenty years of age who have to die. Some of the group who were younger than twenty could be survivors of the group which had left Egypt. Van der Meer has demonstrated that the Greek translator had a special concern for the fate of the younger generation.[30] Although not every point in Van der Meer's argument is convincing, one thing is clear. The MT version with its emphasis on the death of an entire generation is replaced in LXX by a more thoughtful exegesis of the Pentateuch passages about Israel in the wilderness, the participants of the conquest and the entry into the Promised Land. Whereas MT goes for totality, LXX prefers to be the better student of Scripture. The same tendency towards specificity can be seen in the fact that LXX describes the time in the wilderness as a period of forty-two years (Josh 5.6) instead of forty (MT), based on Num 10.11, 12; 12.16; 14*.[31]

Both LXX and MT stress the fact that the circumcision is performed with flint knives. There is no reason to assume that the rendering 'sharp flint knives' (LXX) demonstrates the purpose of the text showing that 'the painful operation on the adult population was at least performed by sharp knives', and that the aim of the addition in LXX in Josh 24.31a where the flint knives are buried with Joshua is the reassurance that 'the crude practice of circumcising men with these stones was restricted only to the time of Joshua.'[32] Flint knives can be as sharp and useful as iron ones. Here in 5.2 , in the final text of MT, it is said that in the narrator's opinion circumcision is a very old practice and that circumcision, Joshua, Passover and the entry into the new land belong together. To combine all the elements, the 'Hill of the Foreskins', the circumcision and the Passover in the plains of Jericho, the MT author repeated the encampment at Gilgal from 4.19. Contrary to what we have seen in Josh 5.4-7, it was LXX, not MT, that intended to expand, to include more refined scriptural references.

In and around Josh 5.9 it is MT that stresses the role of the Israelites, reminds readers of Gilgal's name and repeats the encampment of 4.19. MT watches over the correct chronology of Passover and the Feast of the Unleavened Bread by constructing the fifteenth day. LXX goes its own way with the addition of the circumcision scene.

---

[30] Van der Meer, *The Redaction of the Book of Joshua*, 315-23.
[31] Two years before and forty years after the Kadesh events.
[32] Van der Meer, *The Redaction of the Book of Joshua*, 290-1.

By means of scriptural exegesis, the author/translator reconstructs a
second group of uncircumcised Israelites. The developments within
the different versions referring to circumcision demonstrate a growing
refinement of inner-biblical exegesis. As Fishbane puts it:

> They (the text and traditions) were…subject to redaction, elucidation,
> reformulation, and outright transformation. Accordingly, our received
> traditions are complex blends of *traditum* and *traditio* in dynamic interac-
> tion, dynamic interpretation, and dynamic interdependence.[33]

4. *A survey of explanations*

Having surveyed the context of 5.9 and the variations between
MT and LXX, the question of the meaning of v. 9 and especially of
חרפת מצרים is still open. This exegetical crux can be solved in the
following ways:

1. It is frequently proposed that the disgrace of Egypt describes
    the state of slavery during the time the Israelites dwelt in Egypt.
    This slavery did not end with the Exodus but with the entry
    into the new land.[34] The difficulty, however, is that nowhere
    it is stated that the state of slavery was maintained during the
    period in the desert. On the contrary, in the Ten Command-
    ments YHWH presents himself as the God who liberated Israel
    from Egypt: 'I am YHWH, your God, who brought you out
    of Egypt, out of the house of slavery' (Exod 20.2). Bringing
    the Israelites out of Egypt has brought an end to slavery. Not
    the conquest of Canaan but the Exodus was the central item
    of Israel's creed. Therefore YHWH reveals his own, previously
    unknown and hidden name to Moses at the beginning of the
    Exodus narrative (Exod 3.13-15; 6.2-8). Such examples, the
    number of which can be increased easily, demonstrate the
    immense importance of the Exodus theme as the liberation
    from slavery.
2. The most obvious solution within the context of 5.2-9 seems to
    be that the 'disgrace of Egypt' refers to a state of uncircumcision

---

[33] Fishbane, *Biblical Interpretation in Ancient Israel*, 543.
[34] According to the newer commentators: Butler, *Joshua*, 59; Fritz, *Das Buch
Josua*, 59.

either in Egypt or during the period in the wilderness.[35] Gen 34.14 refers to uncircumcision as a 'disgrace'. For 5.9 'today I rolled away the disgrace of Egypt' is the ultimate divine approval of what happened in 5.2-8. Egyptians, however, practised circumcision, so the reproach can only refer to a state of not being circumcised. According to MT this is the case only during the wilderness time, but during that time a reproach of Egypt does not make any sense.

3. Apart from the main positions of nos. 1 and 2, a great number of variants can be observed. K. Galling refers to the פסילים in Judg 3.26 and the twelve stones set up in Gilgal (Josh 4.20) and concludes: 'Vielleicht hängt der doch nur gezwungen mit der Beschneidung zu verbindende Ausdruck von dem "Abwälzen der Schmach Ägyptens" mit einem Abrenuntiationsritus (Gen 35; Josh 24) zusammen.' The 'Hill of the Foreskins' refers to the place where foreigners were circumcised.[36] However, besides the difficult combination of texts, which allows speculation, we do not know anything about an 'Abrenuntiation' at Gilgal.

4. A *non liquet* is defended several times. It is no longer possible to determine the exact meaning of 'I have rolled away the disgrace of Egypt', because the original story included in the conclusion of 5.9 is replaced by the later circumcision narrative. This narrative, however, cannot be the background to 5.9.[37]

5. The 'disgrace of Egypt' means the state of slavery in Egypt, but it has a function in the preparation of Passover. Crossing the Jordan is repeating the enigmatic wonder of Exod 14 as reflected in Josh 4.23. The Exodus and the wondrous crossing of the Red Sea end the disgrace of Egypt, but it is represented here, in the new land, after the crossing of the Jordan.[38] The difficulty with this approach is a literary-historical one. The link between the two crossings of the Red Sea and the Jordan belongs to the latest layers of the text. This combination only plays a role in a final text reading.

---

[35] L. Koehler and W. Baumgartner, *Hebräisches und aramäisches Lexikon zum Alten Testament*, Leiden, i, 1967, 342b.

[36] K. Galling, 'Das Gemeindegesetz in Deuteronomium 23', in: W. Baumgartner, O. Eissfeldt, K. Elliger, and L. Rost (eds), *Festschrift für Alfred Bertholet zum 80. Geburtstag*, Tübingen 1950, 176-91, esp. 190.

[37] Noth, *Josua*, 25.

[38] M.A. Beek, *Jozua* (POT), Nijkerk 1981, 66.

6.   The crossing of the Jordan and the erection of the stones are the real end of the disgrace of Egypt, understood here as the state of slavery. Situated after the circumcision, however, it is the wrong text in the wrong place. 5.9 originally belonged to the conclusion of 4.19 and should be read directly after that verse.[39]

7.   The 'disgrace of Egypt' should be related to the presumed mockery of the Egyptians in Num 14.13-16 if YHWH would eventually fail to bring his people to Canaan after he had brought them out of Egypt.[40] 'Israel's bondage, which at the Exodus had been broken in principle, was finally and definitively removed now that the people were safely on Canaan's side, no longer subject to the words of shame of which Num 14.13-16; Deut 9.28 speak hypothetically'.[41]

8.   Josh 5.9 belongs to the latest layers of chap. 5. Its background is the post-exilic situation. During the exile, circumcision became the ultimate sign of Jewish identity in uncircumcised Babylonian surroundings. After the return to Judah, circumcision was related to the (re)conquest/resettlement of the land. In retrospect, uncircumcision during the Babylonian exile was the disgrace mentioned in 5.9. Egypt stands for Babylonia.[42] In the same way C.G. den Hertog explains the role of circumcision in the LXX of Josh 5. During the revolts of the Maccabees, circumcision was a major bone of contention between Hellenized and orthodox Jews. 'Gerade in einer stark von hellenistischem Geist geprägten Stadt wie Alexandrien müssen wir solche Tendenzen vermuten... Jos[Ubs] wird die Gelegenheit erkannt haben, seine "liberalen" Volksgenossen auf die Notwendigkeit der Beschneidung hinzuweisen, damit auch sie τὸν ὀνειδισμὸν Αἰγύπτου (v. 9) ablegen.'[43] Egypt means Alexandria, not Babylon.

---

[39] J.H. Kroeze, *Het boek Jozua* (COT), Kampen 1968, 70.
[40] K.A. Deurloo, 'Spiel mit und Verweis auf Torah-Worte in Jos 2-6; 9', *Dielheimer Blätter zum Alten Testament* 26 (1989/90[1992]) 70-80.
[41] M. Woudstra, *The Book of Joshua* (The New International Commentary on the Old Testament), Grand Rapids 1981, 102.
[42] Bieberstein, *Josua-Jordan-Jericho*, 190-1, 420.
[43] Den Hertog, *Zur griechischen Übersetzung des Buches Josua*, 148.

With an eye to this wide variety of possibilities, the first question must be how חרפה, 'disgrace', 'shame' is used in the Hebrew Bible. The closest parallel to the enigmatic expression חרפת מצרים, 'the disgrace of Egypt', is Zeph 2.8a חרפת מואב, 'the disgrace of Moab'. The continuation of this verse in 2.8b, 'with which they put my people to shame', illustrates that the expression refers to the humiliation caused by the Moabites. The same can be concluded for Josh 5.9: it concerns a disgrace effected or executed by Egypt. In social and political relations childlessness is a חרפה (Gen 30.23), as is mutilation as a condition for a peace treaty (1 Sam 11.2). Being raped is a disgrace for the victim (2 Sam 13.13), as are widowhood (Isa 54.4) and famine (Ezek 36.30). The same is the case for living in the ruins of Jerusalem (Neh 1.3; 2.17) and the mockery of the Samarians and Sanballat (Neh 4.4). Social injustice in Judah is a reason for taunting the outsiders (Neh 5.9). Towns, states and nations may become objects of shame (Bozrah: Jer 49.13; Jerusalem: Lam 5.1; Ezek 5.14, 15; 16.57; 21.33 by the Ammonites; 22.4).

חרפה has its own place in the Psalms, especially in the psalms of lament. The awful state of the prayer is a disgrace for the people around him (Pss 22.7; 31.12; 44.14; 79.4; 89.42; 89.51; 109.25), for God (Ps 69.8, 11) and for the prayer him/herself (Ps 69.21).[44] The prayer does not want to be victimized, he wants his adversaries to be in a state of disgrace (Pss 71.13; 79.12). In self-accusation Ephraim speaks of 'the disgrace of my youth' (Jer 31.19).

In the relationship between God and man, the impious and the nations or Judah/Ephraim are able to shame God (2 Kings 19.4; Hos 12.15; Joel 2.17; Pss 74.10, 18, 22; 79.12). In return, God shames his adversaries (Ps 78.66) or confers everlasting disgrace on the Judean community (Jer 23.40) and on the remnants of Jerusalem (Jer 24.9; 29.18 [insertion vis-à-vis LXX]). On the other hand, it is YHWH who takes away the disgrace of his people (Isa 25.8 חרפת עמו; Ezek 36.15 חרפת עמים). His prophets or the prayer in general suffer from disgrace on YHWH's account (Jer 15.15; 20.8).

In relation to circumcision it was a disgrace for the sons of Jacob to

---

[44] C. de Vos, *Klage als Gotteslob aus der Tiefe: Der Mensch vor Gott in den individuellen Klagepsalmen* (Diss. Groningen 2004), 144, 147, with the observation about the mixture of social death and the mockery of a helpless God: 'Damit schließen die Mitmenschen den Betroffenen nicht nur aus ihrer Gemeinschaft aus, sie zweifeln dazu noch über die Zuwendung, die er von Gott erwarten kann' (147).

give Dinah away to one who was uncircumcised (Gen 34.14). Goliath's cursing is a reproach on Israel, in David's view the words of an uncircumcised Philistine (1 Sam 17.26).[45] The uncircumcised ears of the remnant of Israel cannot listen. Therefore the word of YHWH is a disgrace for them (Jer 6.10). חרפה in relation to Egypt is mentioned in texts referring to the murder of the governor Gedaliah and groups fleeing to Egypt to escape the revenge of the Babylonians. Fleeing to Egypt will bring disgrace (Jer 42.18) for the remnant of Judah among all nations (Jer 44.8, 12). The notion that the disgrace is *rolled away* (גלל) by God occurs in Ps 119.22.[46]

5. *Conclusions*

To sum up, the disgrace of Egypt is a unique formulation in the Hebrew Bible. In the context of Josh 5.9 it means malicious pleasure on the side of Egypt at the expense of Israel. It refers neither to the slavery in Egypt nor to circumcision in the original setting of Josh 5.2-8. There is no reason for mockery, either for the bondage in Egypt or for a supposed state of uncircumcision during or after the Egypt period.

Now it is YHWH who explicitly 'rolls away' the disgrace of Egypt, a common expression as Ps 119.22 proves. This expression was chosen here to enable a pun on Gilgal. The reason for the Egyptian mockery should be situated in the time between the exodus from Egypt and the arrival at Gilgal. It is not the desert period itself to which the חרפה refers, but the active role of YHWH in it. In the scheme of Numbers he condemned Israel to forty years of wandering in the wilderness until the entire Exodus generation had died. In the eyes of the Egyptians, however, YHWH, who had delivered Israel from the hands of Pharaoh, was not able to bring his people into the Promised Land. This is the main argument of Moses in Num 14.13-16 and Deut 9.25f. YHWH is blamed, therefore he himself takes away the disgrace.

The arrival at Gilgal grows theologically into an absolute new beginning where everything important is present. 4QJoshua[a] reads Josh 8.30-35 MT after the crossing of the Jordan and before the

---

[45] Van der Meer, *The Redaction of the Book of Joshua*, 269 has drawn attention to the fact that 'it is not the state of being uncircumcised *per se* that is the object of humiliation, but rather the humiliating subjection of Israel to *uncircumcised* foreigners.'

[46] גל מעלי חרפה Var. Ps 119.39.

circumcision scene of 5.2-8.[47] Even Deut 27.2-8 is executed directly after the crossing. The Torah is written and recited. After the arrival in the Promised Land, Sinai, the symbol for the Torah, once given in the wilderness, repeated in Moab on the threshold of Canaan, has come home.[48]

The whole scenery of the disgrace of Egypt so far is firmly in deuteronomistic hands. Starting with eating the produce of the land, however, the feasts of Passover and the Unleavened Bread are introduced. In an exegetical refining of the relation between the laws of the Pentateuch and the new beginning, late priestly hands make circumcision the ultimate condition for a life *coram Deo* in the land. Now the circumcision and the 'Hill of the Foreskins' appear. Without circumcision there can be no life in the Promised Land.

This means that from the history of research, nos. 7 and 2 with some aspects of 8 in a *diachronical* script offer the best possibilities for understanding the final text of Josh 5.9 and the history behind it. Egypt plays the role of the scapegoat in this text. Here, with the 'disgrace of Egypt', the Egyptians were accused of something they were only assumed to have done. There was no judicial proof, accusations were made solely on the basis of collective memory, of an one-sided image of Egypt. As we have seen in the introduction, changing this negative image was difficult. The blessing of Egypt from Isa 19.25, with which we began our discussion, was 'Lost in Translation'. Perhaps that is the tragedy of a small country with a mighty neighbour.

---

[47] E. Noort, '4QJoshua[a] and the History of Tradition in the Book of Joshua', *Journal of Northwest Semitic Languages* 24 (1998) 127-44.

[48] E. Noort, *Een plek om te zijn: Over de theologie van het land aan de hand van Jozua 8.30-35*, Kampen 1993, 18.

LA GENÈSE D'ALEXANDRIE, LES RABBINS ET QUMRÂN

Florentino García Martínez

Dans les écrits de la tradition rabbinique nous trouvons toute une série de listes qui énumèrent les changements du texte biblique qui auraient été faits intentionnellement par les traducteurs au moment de la traduction en grec de la Bible hébraïque. Ces listes se trouvent dans les midrashim tannaïtiques (comme la *Mekilta de Rabbi Ismael*, dans le commentaire à Exode 12.40), dans les talmudim (*b. Meg.* 9a-b; *y. Meg.* 71d, traité *Sopherim* 1.7-8), ainsi que dans des collections de midrashim plus tardives, comme *Abot de Rabbi Nathan* (version B, chap. 37), *Tanhuma Exod* (para. 22) ou le *Midrash Hagadol* (Exod 4.20), en dans d'autres compositions postérieures comme le *Yalkut Shimoni* (Gen 3).[1]

Evidemment, ces listes ne sont pas uniformes, ni dans le nombre de corrections faites, ni dans les lieux du Pentateuque concernant les corrections. Certaines listes indiquent en tête le total de ces corrections, bien que souvent le nombre des corrections enregistrées ne corresponde pas au nombre effectif de corrections transmises dans le texte. Ainsi, la version B de l'*Abot de Rabbi Natan* nous dit «Cinq anciens [pas soixante-dix ou soixante-douze] écrivirent la Torah en grec pour le Roi Ptolémée. Ils y changèrent dix choses. Ce sont, etc.» Mais quand on compte le total des changements on arrive à onze. *Tanhuma* parle aussi de dix corrections, mais ne nous rapporte pas moins de quatorze passages, et *Exodus Rabbah* (5.5) nous dit que les changements faits furent de 18, sans spécifier lesquels. Il est vrai que dans le cas de *Abot*, les

---

[1] L'étude la plus complète de ces listes est le chapitre «Die Devarim für Talmai» dans le livre de Giuseppe Veltri, *Eine Tora für den König Talmai: Untersuchungen zum Übersetzungsverständnis in der jüdisch-hellenistischen und rabbinischen Literatur* (Texte und Studien zum antiken Judentum 41), Tübingen 1994, 22-112. Plus compact, mais aussi fondamental, est l'article d'Emanuel Tov, «The Rabbinic Tradition concerning the 'Alterations' Inserted into the Greek Pentateuch and Their Relation to the Original Text of the LXX», *Journal for the Study of Judaism* 15 (1984) 65-89, réédité avec quelques modifications dans Id., *The Greek and Hebrew Bible: Collected Essays on the Septuagint* (VTSup 72), Leiden 1999, 1-18 (les citations de cet article proviennent toujours de la version publiée dans le *JSJ*.)

corrections se trouvent dans des sections du livre qui énumèrent des listes de dix choses (comme un procédé mnémonique). Après les dix corrections *Abot* énumère les dix choses planifiées depuis le début du monde, les dix choses créées à l'aurore du monde, les dix noms avec lesquels on nomme la prophétie, les dix personnes qui furent appelées 'hommes de Dieu', et beaucoup d'autres listes de dix, pour finir avec les dix fois où le mot 'générations' apparaît dans la Torah et desquelles il ne nous donne que sept. Ce qui nous fait penser que le numéro dix est tout à fait artificiel. D'autres listes (comme la *Mekilta* ou *b. Meg*), par contre, ne mentionnent pas le nombre total des corrections mais donnent simplement les passages corrigés, dont le total oscille entre 13 et 15. Dans les listes il n'y a pas non plus d'uniformité totale dans la transmission des passages corrigés, bien que les variations ne soient pas trop grandes, et en ce qui concerne la Genèse on trouve une forte consistance. En plus, presque la moitié des corrections concernent le texte de la Genèse.

Dans cette contribution, écrite pour honorer la passion «alexandrine» de Gerard Luttikhuizen, collègue et très cher ami dès les premières heures à Groningen, qui m'a tant appris non seulement sur la pluriformité du christianisme dans son contexte grec, mais sur les interprétations et transformations de la Genèse dans les écrits gnostiques, je voudrais regarder ces corrections dans une perspective qumrânienne, où le texte de la Genèse est souvent interprété et transformé. En vue des limites imposées à nos contributions, uniquement les quatre premières des sept corrections concernant la Genèse seront ici présentées.

Ma première intention était d'examiner les manuscrits *bibliques* qumrâniens de la Genèse pour voir si on pouvait découvrir quelques traces de ces corrections. Je ne m'attendais pas à trouver la forme grecque de ces corrections à Qumrân, parce que nous n'avons pas trouvé de manuscrits de la Genèse en grec à Qumrân,[2] mais je pensais

---

[2] La Genèse n'est pas présente parmi les manuscrits grecs trouvés à Qumrân. Dans la grotte 4 on a trouvé deux copies du Lévitique (4Q119 = 4QLXXLeviticus[a] et 4Q120 = pap4QLXXLeviticus[b]), une copie du Nombres (4Q121 = 4QLXXNumbers) et une copie du Deutéronome (4Q122 = 4QDeuteronomy), voir P.W. Skehan, E. Ulrich, J.A. Sanderson, *Qumran Cave 4.IV: Palaeo-Hebrew and Greek Biblical Manuscripts* (Discoveries in the Judaean Desert 9), Oxford 1992, 161-97, et dans la grotte 7 un fragment de l'Exode (7Q1) et un fragment de la Lettre de Jérémie (7Q2), voir M. Baillet, J.T. Milik, R. de Vaux, *Les 'Petites Grottes' de Qumrân* (Discoveries in the Judaean Desert of Jordan 3), Oxford 1962, 142-3. Sur les manuscrits bibliques en grec trouvés à Qumrân voir A.R.C. Leaney, «Greek Manuscripts from the Judaean

que dans les nombreux manuscrits hébreux de la Genèse des diverses grottes[3] il aurait pu rester des traces avec lesquelles nous pourrions déterminer si ces corrections correspondaient à des formes anciennes du texte biblique, comme Tov le présume,[4] ou si elles étaient le produit de l'activité exégétique des rabbins, comme en conclut Veltri, sans qu'elles aient aucune valeur textuelle.[5]

Mais, malheureusement les accidents de conservation des manuscrits ne m'ont pas permis de développer cette ligne de recherche. De tous les versets de la Genèse corrigés selon les rabbins, seulement Gen 1.1 a été conservé partiellement dans deux manuscrits (4Q2, 4Q7, et dans 4Q8c qui semble être le titre du livre) dans la forme représentée tant par le texte massorétique que par la LXX. Il m'a fallu donc changer

---

Desert», dans J.K. Elliott (éd.), *Sudies in New Testament Language and Text*, Leiden 1976, 283-300; E. Ulrich, «The Septuagint Manuscripts from Qumran: A Reappraisal of Their Value», dans G.J. Brooke–B. Lindars (éds), *Septuagint, Scrolls and Cognate Writings: Papers Presented to the International Symposium on the Septuagint and Its Relations to the Dead Sea Scrolls and Other Writings* (Septuagint and Cognate Studies 33), Atlanta 1992, 48-80; Id., «The Greek Manuscripts of the Pentateuch from Qumran: Including Newly Identified Fragments of Deuteronomy (4QLXXDeut)», in A. Pietersma et al. (éds), *The Septuagint: Studies in Honour of John William Wevers*, Mississauga, ON 1984, 71-82; L.J. Greenspoon, «The Dead Sea Scrolls and the Greek Bible», dans P.W. Flint–J.C. VanderKam (éds), *The Dead Sea Scrolls After Fifty Years: A Comprehensive Assessment*, I, Leiden 1998, 101-27.

[3] Pas moins de 19 exemplaires, voir E. Tov, «Categorized List of the 'Biblical Texts'», dans E. Tov et al., *The Texts from the Judaean Desert: Indices and An Introduction to the* Discoveries in the Judaean Desert *Series* (Discoveries in the Judaean Desert 39), Oxford 2002, 167-8.

[4] «If our analysis up to this point is correct, it is difficult to avoid the unconventional assumption that the nine biblical passages which do not agree with the transmitted text of the LXX reflect another textual form of the translation. This other text of the LXX evidently contained the original text of the translation which differs from its form which has been handed down in all manuscripts.» «Accordingly, in view of this situation, we may presume that the biblical passages mentioned in this list of alterations reflect the original text of the LXX, while the archetype of all manuscripts known to us was corrected to MT.» Tov, «The Rabbinic Tradition concerning the 'Alterations'», respectivement 74 et 76.

[5] Veltri, *Eine Tora für den König Talmai*, 112: «Die *Devarim* sind keine textkriti-sche Liste. Vielmehr stellen sie eine 'fiktive Überlieferung' dar, mit deren Hilfe die Rabbinen/Redaktoren Schwierigkeiten der Bibelexegese auszuräumen versuchen. Mit Ausnahme von Num 16,15 sind die *Devarim* keine 'Lesarten' des hebräischen Textes; wären sie 'Lesarten', so spräche dies für ihren textkritischen Ursprung. In der Mehrzal aber sind sie *exegetische* Änderungen und setzen den MT voraus. Die *Devarim erklären* ihn, sie stellen keine *Alternative* dar! Das rabbinische Verständnis der 'Tora für Talmai' läßt sich also *in nuce* folgendermaßen definieren: eine Tora, bei der die Erklärung des Textes *im Text* stattfindet—und zwar dadurch, daß er *verändert* wird.»

de perspective et approcher ces corrections depuis la perspective des textes *non-bibliques* de Qumrân, dans l'espoir que ces textes nous apporteront quelque lumière, sinon sur la Genèse d'Alexandrie, au moins sur les pourquoi de ces corrections rabbiniques.

Ces corrections ont été transmises, évidemment, en hébreu; mais selon les rabbins elles auraient été faites en grec, au moment de la traduction alexandrine. Le fait que seulement une partie des corrections corresponde au texte de la LXX connu,[6] a mené un certain nombre d'auteurs (comme Shemaryahu Talmon)[7] à penser que ces corrections ont été faites sur le texte hébreu et que ces listes seraient donc semblables aux listes des *tiqquné sopherim* ou corrections des scribes qui énumèrent des changements faits sur le texte hébreu lui-même.[8]

La référence à la traduction grecque pour le Roi Ptolémée dans les introductions qui précèdent les listes de corrections est trop constante, trop explicite et trop emphatique, pour qu'elle puisse être complètement accidentelle. Elle s'explique uniquement si les corrections ont été réalisées sur la traduction grecque, c'est-à-dire si le texte hébreu a été rendu intentionnellement en grec d'une manière qui ne corresponde pas au texte hébreu des massorètes. Le texte le plus clair dans ce sens est *b. Meg* 9a qui commence ainsi:[9]

> Cela concerne la narration d'un incident en rapport avec le Roi Ptolémée, selon qu'il a été enseigné: On raconte du Roi Ptolémée qu'il avait réuni soixante-douze anciens et les avait placés dans soixante-douze chambres, et il ne leur révéla pas pourquoi il les avait rassemblés; et il s'adressa à chacun d'eux et il leur dit: 'écris pour moi la Torah de Moïse ton Maître.' Le Saint, il soit bénit, mit du conseil dans le cœur

---

[6] Les auteurs ne sont pas d'accord ni sur le nombre des corrections ni sur quelles corrections précisément correspondent au texte de la LXX connu. Pour Tov (art. cit., 73), Gen 2.2, Exod 4.20; 24.5 et 24.11, Nomb 16.15 et Lév 11.6 seraient identiques avec les passages de la LXX, et Exod 12.14 assez proche. Pour Veltri (op. cit., 98) seulement Gen 2.2, Exod 12.40, Lév 11.6 et Nomb 16.15 pourraient être considérés comme des retraductions du grec, «Die übrigen Textänderungen zu den Bibelversen spiegeln lediglich textkritische und exegetische Schwierigkeiten eines schon fixierten hebräischen Textes wider.»

[7] Sh. Talmon, «The Three Scrolls of the Law that were found in the Temple Court», *Textus* 2 (1962) 14-27 (p. 26).

[8] Voir D. Barthélemy, «Les tiqquné sopherim et la critique textuelle de l'AT», dans *Congress Volume Bonn 1962* (Vetus Testamentum Supplements 9), Leiden 1963, 285-300, et C. McCarthy, *The Tiqqune Sopherim and Other Theological Corrections in the Masoretic Text of the OT* (Orbis Biblicus et Orientalis 36), Freiburg 1981.

[9] Toutes les traductions, sauf indication du contraire, sont propres.

de chacun, et eux tous s'accordèrent et ils écrivirent pour lui … (la suite est la liste en question).

En plus, certaines de ces corrections ont été préservées dans les textes grecs tels que nous les connaissons. Mais l'exemple le plus clair est la correction à propos de Lev 11.6 (11.5 dans la LXX), parce qu'elle est explicitée dans la tradition rabbinique et ne laisse aucun doute.

Dans le texte massorétique de Lev 11.6 (LXX 11.5) se trouve un *hapax* (employé uniquement là et dans Deut 14.7), le mot ארנבת, un mot de signification incertaine comme les mots employés pour d'autres animaux mentionnés dans ce chapitre, mais qui est traduit généralement par «lièvre». Dans la LXX ce mot est traduit par δασύποδα (δασύπους) et non pas par λαγών (λαγώς).[10] Comme nous l'explique une note sur le grec du Pentateuque alexandrin de Michel Casevitz, δασύπους veut dire «qui a les pieds velus» et appartient au vocabulaire technique, «le mot est déjà attesté chez les Comiques de l'époque classique et chez Aristote et remplace le plus ancien et banal λαγώς».[11] Cette dernière précision nous donne la clef du changement. Dans la liste de *b. Meg* (et aussi dans *y. Meg*, le traité *Sopherim*, *Mekilta*, et *Abot de Rabbi Nathan*) ארנבת est en fait changé en צעירת הרגלים, que l'on traduit usuellement par «léger de pieds» (en comprenant l'expression comme שעירת הרגלים due au changement phonétique du ש en צ)[12] une expression assez exactement traduite par δασύποδα. Le changement aurait été donc fait afin d'éviter l'emploi du nom dynastique de Ptolémée.[13] Ce que nous dit expressément le texte du Talmud:

---

[10] Aquila traduit ארנבת précisément par λαγών dans ce cas.

[11] *Le Pentateuque. La Bible d'Alexandrie*, sous la direction de C. Dogniez et M. Harl, Paris 2003, 638. Dans *La Bible d'Alexandrie 3: Le Lévitique*, Paris 1988, 128, les auteurs P. Harlé et D. Pralon soulignent «Le choix de *dasúpous* préféré à celui de *lagõs* ne poserait aucun problème si la tradition rabbinique n'avait relevé ici un cas d'évitement délibéré de la part des LXX … Il nous paraît plus vraisemblable que le nom *lagõs* a été évité par les LXX parce qu'il évoquait le nom du père du premier Ptolémée, *Lâgos*, fondateur de la lignée des Lagides.»

[12] Veltri, *Eine Tora für den König Talmai*, 101-2, a justement remarqué que *tous* les témoins manuscrits sauf le manuscrit München 117 de la *Mekilta* portent la lecture צעירת הרגלים, littéralement «'junge/kleine' oder 'schnelle' (?) Füsse» et note «Der Ausdruck ergibt zwar einen Sinn, der aber weder im biblischen noch im rabbinischen Sprachgebrauch geläufig ist und überdies keine Parallele zur LXX von Lev 11,6(5) aufweist» et par conséquence «daß der Fehler zwar früh in den rabbinischen Schriften auftrat, nicht aber zur selben Zeit, da die Änderung festgestellt wurde.»

[13] E. Tov, «The Rabbinic Tradition concerning the 'Alterations'», 89 laisse la

> Et eux n'écrivirent pas pour lui את הארנבת parce que le nom de la
> femme de Ptolémée était הארנבת (c'est à dire λαγώς) afin qu'il ne dise
> pas: 'les juifs se sont moqué de moi et ils ont placé le nom de ma femme
> dans la Torah.'

Selon *y. Meg* celle qui portait le nom de *Lagos* aurait été la mère de
Ptolémée, et nous savons qu'en réalité c'était le nom du père, duquel
provient le nom dynastique des Lagides. Mais cela n'a aucune importance. Ce qui compte est que le texte du Talmud nous prouve sans
aucun doute que dans ce cas le changement a été fait sur le texte grec
et non pas sur le texte hébreu.

La tradition rabbinique affirme donc qu'au moment de la traduction
en grec du texte biblique un certain nombre de corrections auraient
été faites, notamment au texte de la Genèse. Et je crois que dans
cette tradition pourrait se trouver un noyau de vérité historique, dont
l'étendue est impossible à préciser mais qui permet de considérer ces
corrections comme témoins de l'effort fait pour imposer une certaine
exégèse du texte biblique déjà à l'époque de la première traduction
grecque. L'examen de ces corrections à la lumière des traditions
exégétiques attestées à Qumrân (dans un cadre chronologique donc
beaucoup plus proche de la Genèse d'Alexandrie que le monde des
rabbins) peut nous aider à comprendre les motifs et la portée de ces
corrections.

1. *Gen 1.1*

La première correction nous la trouvons dans la première phrase
de la Genèse.[14] Il n'est pas question dans ce cas d'un changement
des mots, mais d'un changement dans l'ordre des mots. Les premiers traducteurs de la LXX auraient traduit le texte massorétique

---

chose en suspens: «It may be that this claim is nothing but a *post factum* explanation;
on the other hand, it is just possible that λαγωόν is the original translation of ארנבת
which was later supplanted by δασύποδα.»

[14] Cette phrase a donné lieu à des interprétations innombrables, anciennes et
modernes, tant dans le judaïsme que dans le christianisme. Dans notre perspective,
voir P. Schäfer, «Berešit bara' 'Elohim: Zur Interpretation von Gen 1,1 in der
rabbinischen Literatur», *Journal of Jewish Studies* 2 (1971) 161-6; G. Anderson, «The
Interpretation of Gen 1.1 in the Targums», *Catholic Biblical Quarterly* 52 (1990) 21-9;
F. García Martínez, «Interpretación de la creación en el Judaísmo antiguo», dans
M.L. Sánchez León (éd.), *Religions del món antic: La creació*, Palma 2001, 115-53.

אלהים ברא בראשית «Au commencement créa Dieu» par בראשית ברא אלהים «Dieu créa au commencement», nous disent les listes; c'est-à-dire par ὁ θεὸς ἐποίησεν ἐν ἀρχῇ, au lieu du familier ἐν ἀρχῇ ἐποίησεν ὁ θεός de la LXX.[15] Un tel changement semble tout à fait innocent, mais, à mon avis, il n'est pas innocent du tout.

Pour E. Tov ce changement d'ordre aurait pu être motivé par le désir du traducteur de commencer la Torah avec le nom de Dieu.[16] Il dit: «In this instance the inversion of the word order can be ascribed to the exegetical motivation of the translator who, it seems, wanted to begin the Pentateuch with ὁ θεός.»[17] La correction serait donc plutôt d'ordre littéraire, une anticipation en quelque sorte de la très belle *disputatio* que nous raconte l'*Alphabet de Rabbi Aquiva* et dans laquelle chaque lettre de l'alphabet intervient devant Dieu pour le convaincre (avec les arguments tirés de l'Ecriture!) à commencer par elle à écrire la Torah et qui est finalement gagnée par la lettre *bet* parce qu'avec elle tout le monde «bénira» le Seigneur.[18] On ne peut pas exclure, évidemment, cette interprétation, ni que le changement d'ordre soit purement stylistique. Mais je crois qu'il y a beaucoup plus que ça derrière ce changement d'ordre des paroles.

Pour Hüttenmeister, dans sa traduction du traité *Megilla* du Talmud Yerushalmi,[19] la correction aurait pour finalité de rendre impossible l'interprétation de la phrase dans laquelle בראשית aurait été considéré comme le sujet de la phrase et אלהים l'objet («Bereshit créa Dieu») et ainsi de couper court à toute interprétation polythéiste. Mais cette interprétation ne fonctionne pas en grec, à moins d'imaginer qu'à la place de ὁ θεός on aurait traduit «Dieu» par un nom indéclinable.

Pour Veltri, le motif de la correction serait d'affirmer sans ambages une *creatio ex nihilo* et d'éviter l'impression que donne la Genèse (quand

---

[15] Aquila préserve le même ordre des mots de l'hébreu, mais il change la traduction grecque de בראשית par κεφάλαιον, reprenant ainsi le lien étymologique du mot hébreu avec 'la tête', et celle du ברא qu'il traduit par κτίζω: Ἐν κεφαλαίῳ ἔκτισεν θς.

[16] Une explication que l'on peut trouver déjà dans *Tanhuma B* Bereshit 4, où l'humilité de Dieu est contrastée (avec référence à Gen 1.1) avec la superbe des rois qui font précéder de leurs noms la mention de leurs œuvres.

[17] Tov, «The Rabbinic Tradition concerning the 'Alterations'», 87.

[18] Voir L. Ginzberg, *The Legends of the Jews*, Philadelphia 1968[12], I, 5-8. La même tradition se trouve dans *y. Hag.* 2,77c, *b. Ber.* 55a et dans *Genesis Rabbah* 1.10.

[19] F.G. Hüttenmeister, *Megilla: Schriftrolle* (Übersetzung des Talmud Yerushalmi II/10), Tübingen 1987, 56.

on lit 1.1-2 comme une seule phrase qui sert d'introduction à 1.3) qu'avant la création de la terre il y avait déjà quelque chose.[20] C'est vrai que dans le monde grec les opinions sur la *creatio ex nihilo* étaient divisées, de sorte que Sagesse 11.17 dit «elle qui a créé le monde d'une matière informe (ἐξ ἀμόρφου)» en reprenant l'expression platonicienne du *Timée* 51a, et que 2 Mac 7.28 semble réagir précisément contre cette idée: «regarde le ciel et la terre et vois tout ce qui est en eux, et sache que Dieu les a faits de rien (οὐκ ἐξ ὄντων)», mais les auteurs sont divisés sur l'interprétation précise de ces allusions,[21] et l'idée d'une matière préexistante ne semble pas avoir joué aucun rôle dans les plus anciennes interprétations de la Genèse.

Moi, je crois plutôt que la correction implique une affirmation polémique et emphatique que c'est Dieu, et Dieu seul, le créateur du tout, sans l'aide de personne, et que sa finalité est celle de couper court à une interprétation instrumentale du *bet* ('par' ou 'avec'). La première note de *La Bible d'Alexandrie*,[22] souligne admirablement l'ambiguïté profonde du grec et de l'hébreu:

> *Au commencement:* cette initiale du récit, en grec (*en arkhêi*) comme en hébreu (littéralement 'en tête'), a donné lieu à d'innombrables interprétations juives ou chrétiennes. Pour les lecteurs grecs, l'expression prise au sens temporel indique un début, mais peut aussi indiquer, en un sens instrumental, que Dieu a créé 'par son principe', 'par son pouvoir', autres sens possibles du mot *arkhê*.

Que cette deuxième interprétation n'était pas quelque chose d'imaginaire est facile à prouver. Un hymne trouvé dans un manuscrit de la grotte 11[23] nous dit expressément: ברוך עושה ארץ בכוחו מכין תבל

---

[20] Veltri, *Eine Tora für den König Talmai*, 30: «Demnach wird die Umstellung in der 'rabbinischen' LXX wohl eine deutliche Antwort auf die Frage der *creatio ex nihilo* bzw. der seit den Anfängen wähnenden Existenz des Urstoffes dargestellt haben. Den Rabbinen zufolge ist die Interpretation der griechischen Tora eine eindeutige Stellungnahme für eine Schöpfung ohne Urstoff, und zwar insofern, als die Umstellung von בראשית an die dritte Stelle im Satz einen Temporal- bzw. Modalsatz unmöglich macht. Somit ist die Absolutheit des göttlichen Schaffens festgeschrieben.»

[21] Voir J. Goldstein, «The Origins of the Doctrine of Creation Ex Nihilo», *Journal of Jewish Studies* 35 (1984) 127-35 and D. Winston, «Creatio Ex Nihilo Revisited», *Journal of Jewish Studies* 37 (1986) 88-91.

[22] *Le Pentateuque: La Bible d'Alexandrie*, 694.

[23] 11Q5 col. XXVI 9-15, publié par J.A. Sanders, *The Psalms Scroll of Qumran Cave 11* (Discoveries in the Judaean Desert of Jordan 4), Oxford 1963, 47. Sur ce poème, connu comme «Hymne au Créateur», voir F. García Martínez, «Creation in the Dead Sea Scrolls», dans G.H. van Kooten (éd.), *The Creation of Heaven and Earth:*

בחוכמתו, «Béni soit celui qui créa la terre par son pouvoir, qui établit le monde avec sa sagesse!»[24] Cette phrase nous prouve clairement la possibilité de l'interprétation au sens instrumental du *bet* de בראשית, et elle nous aide aussi, avec sa mention de «avec sa sagesse» (בחוכמתו), à comprendre le développement exégétique qui mena à l'interprétation du texte hébreu que la correction essaie de bloquer.

Dans un très beau poème du livre des Proverbes, cité ici dans la traduction de la Bible de Jérusalem, quelque peu modifié pour serrer de plus près le texte hébreu, la Sagesse personnifiée dit d'elle-même:

> YHWH m'a créée (קנני),[25] principe (ראשית) de son chemin,
> la première de ses œuvres les plus anciennes.
> Dès l'éternité je fus formée,
> dès le commencement (מראש), avant l'origine de la terre. (Prov 8.22-23)

Et la même sagesse nous dit dans un texte de Ben Sirach (24.9), malheureusement pas conservé en hébreu, mais dont la traduction grecque a circulé à Alexandrie: πρὸ τοῦ αἰῶνος ἀπ' ἀρχῆς ἔκτισέν με «avant les siècles, dès le commencement il m'a créée.»

Si la Sagesse donc avait été créée la première, avant tout autre réalité, si elle avait été créée comme «principe», comme «commencement» (ראשית) de tout, il était donc possible de considérer le mot ראשית comme le nom de la Sagesse, et de traduire en conséquence בראשית non par «au commencement» mais par «avec la sagesse». C'est effectivement cela la traduction que nous donne l'hymne trouvé à Qumrân, dont la composition peut remonter au troisième ou deuxième siècle (l'hymne n'est pas une composition qumrânienne). Et c'est aussi la traduction que nous trouvons dans certaines traductions du Pentateuque en araméen du premier verset de la Genèse.[26] Les manuscrits fragmentaires

---

Re-interpretations of Genesis I in the Context of Judaism, Ancient Philosophy, Christianity, and Modern Physics (Themes in Biblical Narrative 8), Leiden 2005, 49-70; dans la note 78 de cet article se trouve une abondante bibliographie sur cet hymne.

[24] 11Q5 XXVI 13-14.

[25] La signification précise du verbe קנה ('créer' ou 'acquérir') a été très discutée, parce que le verbe fut employé pour prouver l'éternité de la Sagesse, identifiée au Verbe; mais la suite ne laisse aucun doute que la Sagesse est présentée comme étant créée, et ainsi a été comprise par la traduction de la LXX: Κύριος ἔκτισέν με ἀρχὴν ὁδῶν αὐτοῦ.

[26] Pour les textes, voir *Biblia Polyglotta Matritensia. Series IV: Targum Palaestinense in Pentateuchum. L. I. Genesis*, Editio critica sub directione Alexandri Diez Macho, Madrid 1988.

du targum palestinien 110, 240 et 440, traduisent Gen 1.1, «Avec la sagesse (בחוכמה) créa Dieu les cieux et la terre.» Le targum Neofiti hésite apparemment et nous donne une double traduction: «Dès le commencement (מלקדמין), avec sagesse (בחוכמה) acheva la *memra* de Yahveh les cieux et la terre».

Dans le monde grec, transi de platonisme, la création de la sagesse avant les cieux et la terre, devait exercer une attraction particulière. Aristobule n'avait-il pas déjà dit (dans le frag. 5 cité par Eusèbe dans sa *Praeparatio Evangelica*)[27] que «un de nos ancêtres, Salomon, avait dit mieux et plus clairement que la sagesse existait avant les cieux et la terre, ceci s'accorde avec ce que disent les philosophes grecs»? Et Philon d'Alexandrie ne dira-t-il plus tard que *Arkhê* est un des noms de la sagesse? Dans son *Legum Allegoriae* I § 43, en commentant Gen 2.8, nous lisons, dans la traduction de Claude Mondésert: «La sagesse élevée et céleste a, comme il l'a montré, des noms multiples (πολυώνυμος): il l'a appelée principe (ἀρχή), image (εἰκών) et vision de Dieu (ὅρασις θεοῦ).»[28]

Je crois donc pouvoir conclure que cette première correction visait précisément à éviter ce type d'exégèse et à souligner que Dieu, et Dieu tout seul, est le créateur.

2. *Gen 1.26*

La deuxième correction de nos listes correspond à Genèse 1.26, et elle a une portée théologique évidente. Le texte massorétique lit נעשה אדם בצלמנו כדמותנו «Faisons l'homme à notre image, comme notre ressemblance.» A la différence de la correction précédente qui implique un simple changement dans l'ordre des mots, dans ce cas le texte lui-même aurait été corrigé. Bien qu'il y ait quelques petites différences parmi les témoins (la deuxième préposition est supprimée dans *Abot* בצלמנו ודמותנו, et dans la *Midrash Hagadol* une citation modi-

---

[27] Les fragments attribués à Aristobule sont facilement accessibles dans A.M. Denis, *Fragmenta pseudepigraphorum quae supersunt graeca* (PVTG 3), Leiden 1970, 217-28. L'étude fondamentale reste N. Walter, *Der Thoraausleger Aristobulos: Untersuchungen zu seinen Fragmenten und zu pseudepigraphischen Resten der jüdisch-hellenistischen Literatur* (TU 86), Berlin 1964.

[28] Claude Mondésert, *Legum Allegoriae I-III* (Les œuvres de Philon d'Alexandrie 2), Paris 1962, 60-3. Dans la note, Mondésert suggère que Philon a pu s'inspirer du texte de Prov 8.22, qu'il cite dans *Ebr.* 31.

fiée de Gen 1.27 est ajoutée) ils sont tous d'accord dans le double changement du texte: le pluriel «faisons» aurait été traduit par le singulier אעשה «Je vais faire», et les pronoms suffixes pluriels «notre» auraient été supprimés. Le texte aurait donc était changé en אעשה אדם בצלם ובדמות «Je vais faire l'homme en image et en ressemblance», c'est-à-dire ποιήσω ἄνθρωπον ἐν εἰκόνι καὶ ἐν ὁμοιώσει au lieu de ποιήσωμεν ἄνθρωπον κατ' εἰκόνα ἡμετέραν καὶ καθ' ὁμοίωσιν de la LXX.[29]

Cette correction élimine d'un trait non seulement le risque d'une interprétation polythéiste du pluriel «faisons» mais aussi les pronoms encore plus troublants et avec le risque évident d'anthropomorphisme. La LXX que nous connaissons avait déjà supprimé le deuxième pronom en traduisant בצלמנו par κατ' εἰκόνα ἡμετέραν, mais כדמותנו simplement par καθ' ὁμοίωσιν, sans pronom, mais avait conservé la signification de l'original par l'introduction d'un καί qui ne se trouve pas dans le texte hébreu et qui permet de relier l'image et la ressemblance avec un seul pronom.[30]

Que le texte hébreu se soit prêté à des interprétations de toutes sortes, est facile à prouver dans le contexte alexandrin. Dans le livre de la Sagesse de Salomon nous rencontrons dans 9.1-2 cette interprétation: «Oh Dieu de nos pères et Seigneur de miséricorde, Tu as tout fait avec ta parole et avec ta Sagesse tu as formé l'homme.» Et chez Philon (dans son *De confusione linguarum* 179)[31] nous pouvons lire:

> Dans ces conditions, il était normal que Dieu rende ses subordonnés solidaires de la création de l'homme. Il dit: «Faisons l'homme», afin qu'on Lui rapporte les seules bonnes actions de l'homme, et les fautes à d'autres. En effet, il n'a pas semblé convenable à Dieu, au Chef Suprême, que la voie, qui à l'intérieur même de l'âme raisonnable, conduit au mal, soit Son œuvre. C'est pourquoi Il a confié aux êtres qui Lui sont

---

[29] La traduction au grec de Tov est ποιήσω ἄνθρωπον κατ' εἰκόνα καὶ καθ' ὁμοίωσιν, parce que, malgré qu'il reconnaisse que la LXX a probablement lu les prépositions ב et כ du TM comme כ et כ, «it is impossible to be precise in regard to this type of grammatical phenomena». «The Rabbinic Tradition concerning the 'Alterations'», 78.

[30] C'est peut-être à cause de cela que *La Bible d'Alexandrie*, 94, traduit le texte de la LXX par «Faisons un homme selon notre image et selon *notre* ressemblance» (souligné FGM) malgré l'absence du deuxième pronom. Les autres versions conservent les deux pronoms pluriels, et Aquila fait même la distinction des prépositions: ἐν εἰκόνι ἡμῶν καὶ καθ' ὁμοίωσιν ἡμῶν.

[31] J.G. Kahn, *De confusione linguarum* (Les œuvres de Philon d'Alexandrie 13), Paris 1963, 142-5.

inférieurs la création de cette partie de l'homme. Car il fallait bien que le volontaire qui fait pendant à l'involontaire, et qui a été institué pour remplir complètement l'univers, fût révélé.

L'exégèse chrétienne, où la Sagesse sera identifiée avec le Christ, exploitera savamment ces ambiguïtés. Déjà dans l'*Epître de Barnabé* (5.5) nous pouvons lire en parlant de Jésus-Christ: «Si le Seigneur a supporté de souffrir pour nous, alors qu'il était le Seigneur du monde entier, Lui à qui Dieu dit à la création du monde: 'Faisons l'homme à notre image et ressemblance' ...»[32] La même idée se trouve exprimée d'une manière très concise dans un beau poème d'Ephrem le Syrien: «Le Père ordonna avec sa voix, mais c'est le Fils qui fit le travail.»[33]

Les targumim nous offrent une traduction littérale du texte hébreu, sans changer les pluriels. Neofiti et le manuscrit 110 évitent l'emploi du mot «image» (צלם) et traduisent par «à notre ressemblance, comme semblable à nous» (נברא בר נש בדמותן כד נפק בן), alors que Pseudo-Jonathan évite l'emploi de «ressemblance» (דמות) et traduit «à notre image, selon notre icône» (בצילמנא כדייוקננא). Pseudo-Jonathan est le seul qui essaie d'éviter le danger du polythéisme des pluriels en introduisant une conversation de Dieu avec ses anges, auxquels évidemment se réfèrent les pluriels problématiques: «Et Dieu dit aux anges qui servent devant lui qui furent crées dans le deuxième jour de la création du monde: Faisons Adam etc.»[34]

Dans la littérature rabbinique nous rencontrons, évidemment, beaucoup d'explications soit du pluriel du verbe «faisons» (y compris celle du Pseudo-Jonathan) soit des formes plurielles des suffixes, toutes orientées à sauvegarder l'idée que c'est Dieu, et lui tout seul, qui créa l'homme (le huitième chapitre de *Bereshit Rabba* en rassemble une longe série), face à des interprétations moins orthodoxes. Mais aucune n'arrivera à la radicalité des corrections qui résolvent le problème simplement en changeant le texte. *Bereshit Rabba* 8.8 nous raconte comment Moïse lui-même se troubla au moment d'écrire ce verset:

---

[32] P. Prigent–R.A. Kraft, *L'Epître de Barnabé* (Sources Chrétiennes 172), Paris 1971, 108-9. Voir F.R. Prostmeier, *Der Barnabasbrief* (Kommentar zu den Apostolischen Vätern 8), Göttingen 1999, 242.

[33] Cité par T. Kronholm, *Motifs from Genesis1-11 in the Genuine Hymns of Ephrem the Syrian* (Coniectanea biblica; Old Testament Series 11), Lund 1978, 40.

[34] Voir M. Pérez Fernández, «Targum y midrás sobre Gen 1,26-27; 2,7; 3,7.21: La creación de Adán en el Targum de PseudoJonatan y en Pirqe de Rabbi Eliezer», dans D. Muñoz León (éd.), *Salvación en la Palabra: Targum–Derash–Berith. En memoria del profesor Alejandro Díez Macho*, Madrid 1986, 471-87.

Rabbi Shemuel bar Nachman dit au nom de Rabbi Jonathan: «Quand Moïse écrivait la Torah et devait consigner l'œuvre de chaque jour, en arrivant au verset 'Et Dieu dit: faisons l'homme à notre image, etc.', il s'exclama: «Seigneur de l'univers, pourquoi veux-tu donner un prétexte aux hérétiques?» «Moïse, tu écris!—lui répondit-il—celui qui veut se tromper qu'il se trompe!»»

J'ai déjà mentionné que la version de la liste transmise dans le *Midrash Hagadol* préserve ici une forme plus longue que tous les autres témoins, et dans laquelle la citation de Gen 1.26 est directement suivie par le début du Gen 1.27. En traduction, cette forme de la correction dit: «Je vais faire l'homme selon image et ressemblance, et Dieu créa Adam selon l'image et selon la ressemblance» (ויברא אלהים את האדם בצלם ובדמות). Je suis convaincu que cette addition est secondaire et plus tardive parce qu'elle nous donne en plus de la correction l'explication, selon le principe rabbinique que les difficultés du texte biblique s'expliquent par la suite du texte. Dans ce cas, le verbe au singulier de la correction s'explique par l'emploi du verbe au singulier dans Gen 1.27 (ויברא, 'et créa'). Dans un dialogue entre Rabbi Shimlay et des hérétiques dans *Bereshit Rabba* 8.9 nous pouvons lire:

Rabbi Shimlay dit: Dans chaque lieu où tu trouves un argument (תשובה dans l'édition) pour les *minim*, tu trouves à côté sa guérison (רפואתה). Eux (les hérétiques) lui demandèrent à nouveau: Pourquoi est-il écrit: 'Et Dieu dit: faisons l'homme, etc.' Lisez ce qui suit, leur répondit- il. Il n'est pas écrit: 'Et créèrent (ויבראו) dieux l'homme', mais 'Et créa (ויברא) Dieu l'homme.'

A Qumrân nous ne trouvons pas d'élaborations exégétiques sur ce texte de la Genèse, mais nous trouvons à sa place l'affirmation explicite et emphatique que c'est Dieu, et Dieu tout seul (רק) qui créa l'homme, à l'occasion le juste. Dans le *Rouleau des Hymnes*, dans la colonne VII.17-18 de la nouvelle numérotation[35] (XV.14 de Sukenik) nous pouvons lire: ואיכה יוכל כול להשנות דבריכה רק אתה בראתה צדיק «Comment quelqu'un pourrait changer tes paroles? Toi seul, tu as créé le juste.»

Par contre, il n'est nulle part question dans les manuscrits conservés, de l'homme comme image de Dieu. Le mot «image» צלם se trouve seulement employé deux fois dans le *Document de Damas* (et dans deux

---

[35] F. García Martínez–E.J.C. Tigchelaar, *The Dead Sea Scrolls Study Edition*, I, Leiden/Grand Rapids 2000, 154-5.

copies de la grotte 4) qui cite et interprète la mention des «piédestaux de vos images» d'Amos 5.26. Et le mot דמות, si cher à Ezéchiel, se trouve une seule fois (hors des *Cantiques pour le Sacrifice du Sabbat* où il a une signification particulière) dans 4Q504 frag. 8, une collection de prières qui porte le titre de *Paroles des Luminaires*. Dans la prière pour le premier jour de la semaine qui est centrée sur la création, nous pouvons lire à la ligne 4 «[Adam] notre [pè]re, Tu (l')as façonné à la ressemblance de [Ta] gloire» אדם אבינו יצרתה בדמות כבודכה.[36] L'emploi du verbe יצר et non pas des verbes ברא ou עשה nous indique que l'auteur pense plutôt à la deuxième création, celle de Gen 2, où Dieu façonna l'homme avec de l'argile. Mais ce qui est intéressant c'est la substitution du pronom par la référence à la gloire de Dieu qui permet à l'auteur d'introduire le thème de la gloire d'Adam (un thème fréquent à Qumrân) comme un reflet de la gloire de Dieu.

Ces deux textes qumrâniens, donc, nous prouvent que cette «correction» de Gen 1.26 était parfaitement compatible avec l'interprétation tout à fait orthodoxe de ce texte biblique à Qumrân.

3. *Gen 1.27*

La troisième correction de nos listes concerne le texte qui se trouve dans Gen 1.27 et aussi dans Gen 5.1. Le texte massorétique lit זכר ונקבה ברא אתם dans Gen 1.27 et זכר ונקבה בראם dans Gen 5.1, c'est-à-dire «mâle et femelle il les créa», ce qui est traduit par la LXX dans les deux cas par ἄρσεν καὶ θῆλυ ἐποίησεν αὐτούς «mâle et femelle il les fit.» A la place de ce texte les listes présentent comme correction un texte qui est constant dans l'élément essentiel, le changement du pluriel au singulier de l'objet, soit il écrit comme suffixe בראו (comme dans Gen 5.1), ou comme un pronom séparé ברא אתו (comme dans Gen 1.27), mais qui varie dans l'élément que précise la modalité exacte de l'idée de base générale que l'on essaie d'introduire dans le texte avec la correction.

Une partie des témoins[37] donne comme correction: זכר ונקבה בראו «mâle et femelle il le créa». Le résultat de la correction nous

---

[36] Edition et traduction de M. Baillet, *Qumrân Grotte 4.III (4Q482-4Q520)* (Discoveries in the Judaean Desert 7), Oxford 1982, 162-3.
[37] Pour une liste complète de toutes les variantes dans les manuscrits, voir Veltri, *Eine Tora für den König Talmai*, 37.

donne en grec la phrase ἄρσεν καὶ θῆλυ ἐποίησεν αὐτόν, et cette phrase, comme la phrase en hébreu, veut dire tout simplement que le premier homme fut créé par Dieu à la fois homme et femme, l'être androgyne de la tradition et de la pensée grecque. Evidemment, la finalité de la correction vise à résoudre l'incongruité du TM, qui dans le vers 27 change directement du singulier au pluriel, mais elle sert aussi à accentuer que le texte biblique parle de l'homme primordial et à introduire dans le texte les conceptions sur l'homme primordial, à l'occasion l'idée de l'androgyne importée de la pensée grecque. Que nous ayons à faire à une importation directe, me semble prouvé par le fait que dans *Genesis Rabbah* 8.1, dans une explication de Gen 5.1-2 attribuée à Rabbi Yirmeyah (et dans laquelle est dit explicitement «Quand le Saint, béni soit-Il, créa le premier homme, il le créa androgyne»), il emploie le mot grec ἀνδρόγυνος transcrit en hébreu אנדרוגינס.

Dans l'autre partie des témoins de la liste le mot ונקבה est remplacé par ונקביו or ונקבו, un mot donc au pluriel et avec le suffixe masculin qui se rapporte au mâle que Dieu créa, c'est-à-dire au premier homme. Le mot désigne des orifices, et il est normalement traduit par les organes génitaux féminins (Saldarini, par exemple, dans sa traduction de la version B de l'*Abot* traduit «A male with corresponding female genitals he created him»;[38] Lauterbach traduit la version de la *Mekilta* «A male with corresponding female parts created He him».[39] Cette interprétation voit donc dans cette variante une confirmation du caractère androgyne du premier homme. Même Tov indique dans une note «It appears that ונקביו/נקביו refers to the female orifices of the primeval man who was thus androgynos»[40] malgré qu'il reconnaisse que נקב/נקוב «in rabbinic literature is used only in connection with the male sexual organ».

Et pourtant, tant dans l'hébreu rabbinique que dans l'araméen, le mot a la signification générale d'un orifice, un trou, également quand on parle des orifices de l'homme. Le pluriel employé avec le suffixe masculin doit se traduire simplement par «ses orifices». La correction selon ces témoins de la liste est זכר ונקוביו בראו «un mâle et ses orifices il créa». Ce que Dieu créa dans Gen 1.27 donc est seulement l'homme,

[38] A.J. Saldarini, *The Fathers According to Rabbi Nathan (Abot the Rabbi Nathan): Version B* (Studies in Judaism in Late Antiquity 11), Leiden 1975, 215.
[39] J.Z. Lauterbach, *Mekilta de-Rabbi Ishmael*, i, Philadelphia 1976, 111-12.
[40] Tov, «The Rabbinic Tradition concerning the 'Alterations'», 87.

lui tout seul, avec ses orifices, non pas l'homme et la femme, et non
plus l'androgyne, homme et femme à la fois. Il me semble que la
correction, dans la forme qui nous a été transmise par la moitié des
témoins représente une négation du caractère androgyne du premier
homme, et par conséquent une négation de tout élément féminin dans
la divinité dont l'homme (avec ses orifices) est l'image.

Pour Veltri[41] la signification de la correction dans cette forme serait
celle d'introduire dans le texte la création de l'homme primordial
comme *prototype* formé (selon les conceptions gnostiques) d'un élément
céleste et d'un autre terrestre: d'une part «image et ressemblance»
de Dieu (la composante divine, en commun avec les êtres célestes)
et d'autre part «mâle avec ses orifices» (la composante terrestre, en
commun avec les animaux). Veltri emploie le texte de *Bereshit Rabba*
8.11, et la discussion des rabbins qui suit la citation prouve certainement que la correction est ainsi comprise, parce que la connexion
avec ובדמות בצלם est explicite dans les mots de R. Tiflai. Mais ce
texte est le seul qui unisse Gen 1.27 et 5.2, et le seul qui donne cette
explication. Dans la version que nous offre *b. Meg* la correction lit:
זכר ונקבה בראו ולא כתבו בראם «mâle et femelle il le créa, et ils n'écrivirent pas il les créa». Ce détail final, nous indique que le motif de
la correction est l'harmonisation de la phrase avec la forme du verbe
qui précède directement dans le texte massorétique de Gen 1.27
בצלם אלהים ברא אתו, «à l'image d'Elohim il le créa», ou il est question
aussi de l'image de Dieu, mais sans que cela ait aucune importance
vis-à-vis de la «correction». Le premier homme est donc «mâle et
femelle» et cela parce qu'il a été créé à l'image de Dieu.

Chez Philon (*De opificio mundi* 134)[42] le même type de réflexion sur le
premier homme comme image de Dieu le mènera à nier sa corporalité
et à le considérer plutôt comme une idée, ni homme ni femme:

> Moïse dit ensuite: «Dieu façonna l'homme en prenant une motte de terre
> et il souffla sur son visage un souffle de vie» (*Gen.* 2,7). Il montre par là
> très clairement la différence du tout au tout qui existe entre l'homme
> qui vient d'être façonné et celui qui avait été précédemment engendré
> à l'image de Dieu. Celui-ci, qui a été façonné, est sensible; il participe
> désormais à la qualité; il est composé de corps et d'âme; il est homme
> ou femme, mortel par nature. Celui-là, fait à l'image de Dieu, c'est une

---

[41] Veltri, *Eine Tora für den König Talmai*, 42.
[42] Roger Arnaldez, *De Opificio mundi* (Les œuvres de Philon d'Alexandrie 1), Paris
1961, 230-1.

idée, un genre ou un sceau; il est intelligible, incorporel, ni mâle ni femelle (ἀσώματος, οὔτ᾽ ἄρρεν οὔτε θῆλυ) incorruptible de nature.

A Qumrân le texte de Gen 1.27, dans la forme transmise par les massorètes, a été employé pour justifier une opinion légale toute particulière et propre à la secte. Dans le *Document de Damas* les «constructeurs du mur» sont condamnés pour être tombés dans les filets de Bélial, et pour avoir forniqué «en épousant deux femmes pendant leur vie (c'est-à-dire la vie d'eux), alors que le principe de la création est: mâle et femelle Il les créa; et ceux qui entrèrent dans l'arche: deux par deux ils entrèrent dans l'arche». (CD IV 20-21)[43] Ce texte a été fortement discuté,[44] parce que pris dans le sens littéral il propose une norme de vie censée contredire tout ce que nous savons du judaïsme de l'époque. Pour cela, une grande majorité de savants ont proposé de changer le pronom masculin en féminin (Dupont-Sommer, par exemple, dit «Entendons sans doute: de leur vivant *à elles deux*»[45]) et comprendre en conséquence que le texte interdirait soit la bigamie ou tout autre mariage après divorce, ou simplement la bigamie, ou un mariage nouveau pendant que la première épouse est encore en vie. Mais ce que le texte en réalité interdit est tout deuxième mariage, même après le décès de la première épouse.[46] Le texte de la Genèse est interprété en donnant toute la force au singulier זכר ונקבה. Dieu créa donc un seul homme et une seule femme, et cette interprétation est considérée comme «la fondation de la création», et Dieu fit aussi rentrer dans l'arche un seul mâle et une seule femelle de chaque espèce. Alors que les «constructeurs du mur» croient que l'homme peut avoir successivement plusieurs femmes, soit parce que l'épouse est morte, soit parce qu'ils ont divorcé, le texte de la Genèse signifie pour les membres de la communauté de Damas que la loi de la créa-

---

[43] La meilleure édition du texte est celle de E. Qimron dans M. Broshi (éd.), *The Damascus Document Reconsidered* (The Israel Exploration Society), Jerusalem 1992; le texte est à la p. 17.

[44] Les études les plus importantes sont recueillies dans F. García Martínez, «Damascus Document: A Bibliography of Studies 1970-1989», dans M. Broshi (éd.), *The Damascus Document Reconsidered*, 63-83.

[45] A. Dupont-Sommer, *Les écrits esséniens découverts près de la Mer Morte* (Bibliothèque historique), Paris 1983, 144.

[46] Voir F. García Martínez, «Man and Woman: Halakhah Based upon Eden in the Dead Sea Scrolls», dans G.P. Luttikhuizen (éd.), *Paradise Interpreted: Representations of Biblical Paradise in Judaism and Christianity* (Themes in Biblical Narrative 2), Leiden 1999, 95-115.

tion exige une monogamie absolue: l'homme ne peut avoir qu'une femme pendant toute sa vie; il peut, bien sûr, divorcer d'elle, mais ni après le divorce ni après l'éventuel décès de sa femme, il ne peut en prendre une autre.

A Qumran donc il n'y a pas de place pour la correction du pluriel ברא אתם dans ברא אתו, et נקבה est toujours la femme.

4. *Gen 2.2*

La quatrième correction de nos listes concerne la Genèse 2.2. Le texte massorétique lit: ויכל אלהים ביום השביעי «Et Dieu conclut au septième jour (l'ouvrage qu'il avait fait)». Le texte hébreu a occasionné beaucoup de difficultés parce que Dieu même semble transgresser le repos du Sabbat, vu qu'il conclut son ouvrage le septième jour. Les listes sont concordes dans l'essentiel: le changement du septième jour pour le sixième: ויכל ביום השש «et conclut au jour sixième» (la majorité des témoins omet «Dieu»). Dans ce cas, nous sommes sûrs de la traduction grecque, parce que dans la Septante (comme dans la version samaritaine et dans la version syriaque) nous trouvons l'ordinal six et non pas sept: καὶ συνετέλεσεν ὁ θεὸς ἐν τῇ ἡμέρᾳ τῇ ἕκτῃ «Et Dieu acheva le sixième jour ses œuvres, qu'il avait faites».

La présence de la même lecture dans d'autres témoins comme le Pentateuque samaritain pourrait nous faire penser que nous nous trouvons ici devant une vraie variante textuelle. D'autre part, l'affirmation explicite d'Exode 20.11 «Car en six jours Yahveh a fait le ciel, la terre, la mer et tout ce qu'ils contiennent, mais il a chômé le septième jour», et réitérée dans 31.17 «Car en six jours, Yahveh a fait les cieux et la terre, mais le septième jour, il a chômé et repris haleine» porterait plutôt à penser que la «correction» vise à harmoniser le texte biblique discordant et à mettre en accord les deux visions sur le repos sabbatique.[47]

Etienne Nodet, qui n'est jamais à court d'idées originales, suggère que derrière ce changement se trouve une polémique sur le début du sabbat, le vendredi après-midi selon le texte massorétique, et le samedi

---

[47] Sur les diverses interprétations rabbiniques, voir B. Grossfeld, «Targum Onqelos and Rabbinic Interpretation to Genesis 2:1,2», *Journal of Jewish Studies* 24 (1973) 176-8.

matin pour les autres témoins.[48] Mais je pense plutôt que nous avons ici aussi une «correction» exégétique motivée par une intensification de la rigueur dans l'observance du sabbat,[49] dont le repos ne saurait être troublé par aucune œuvre (מלאכה), soit-elle divine.

Plusieurs des témoins anciens du monde hellénistique, qui mentionnent le nombre six à la place du sept, vont dans ce sens. Ainsi, Flavius Josèphe, dans ses *Antiquités* 1 § 35 nous dit:[50]

> Ainsi, selon Moïse, le monde avec tout ce qu'il contient fut fait en un total de six jours; et le septième jour, Dieu se reposa et suspendit ses travaux. Pour cette raison, nous aussi nous passons ce jour-là dans le repos de nos labeurs et l'appelons *sabbat*, mot qui en hébreu veut dire 'repos.'

Et Philon dit que le monde fut achevé en six jours (*De opificio mundi* 89) et parle de l'*hexaeméron* de la création (*Leg. Alle.* 2.12). Ou encore l'*Epître de Barnabé* 15.2-3:[51]

> Si mes fils gardent le sabbat, alors je répandrai sur eux ma miséricorde. Il mentionne le sabbat au commencement de la création: Et Dieu fit en six jours les œuvres de ses mains. Il les acheva au septième jour pendant lequel il se reposa et qu'il sanctifia.

Mais ce fait, est plus clair dans les deux écrits palestiniens qui nous ont le mieux préservé les discussions sur le sabbat: le *Livre des Jubilés* et le *Document de Damas*.[52] Or dans *Jub* 2.1 nous pouvons lire:[53]

> L'ange de la Face parla à Moïse selon la Parole du Seigneur, en ces termes: «Ecris le récit complet de la création, comment le Seigneur Dieu accomplit en six jours tout Son ouvrage, tout ce qu'Il a créé, et le septième jour a célébré le sabbat, l'a sanctifié pour tous les âges et l'a institué comme un mémorial de tout Son ouvrage.»

---

[48] E. Nodet, «Josephus and the Pentateuch», *Journal for the Study of Judaism* 28 (1997) 154-94 (p. 179).
[49] Suggéré comme une possibilité par Veltri, *Eine Tora für den König Talmai*, 48-9.
[50] Dans la traduction d'Etienne Nodet, *Flavius Josèphe: Les Antiquités juives. Livres I à III*, II, Paris 1990, 9.
[51] Dans la traduction de Pierre Prigent, *Epître de Barnabé* (Sources Chrétiennes 172), Paris 1971, 182-5.
[52] Pour le sabbat dans *Jubilés* et à Qumrân, voir Lutz Doering, *Schabbat* (Texts and Studies in Ancient Judaism 78), Tübingen 1999, 43-118 (*Jubilés*) et 119-282 (Qumrân).
[53] Selon la traduction d'André Caquot dans *La Bible: Ecrits intertestamentaires*, Paris 1987, 641.

Et avant de décrire en détail le sabbat et ses lois, il répète dans 2.16-17:

> Il a achevé le sixième jour tout son ouvrage, tout ce qui est dans les cieux et sur la terre, dans la mer et dans les abîmes, dans la lumière et dans les ténèbres, partout. Il nous a donné un grand mémorial, le jour du sabbat, afin que nous soyons six jours au travail et que nous nous reposions de tout travail le septième jour.

Du *Livre des Jubilés* (auparavant connu surtout à travers la traduction éthiopienne) nous avons trouvé à Qumrân pas moins de quinze copies dans la langue originale, distribuées dans cinq grottes,[54] et l'œuvre est citée en plus comme une composition ayant autorité dans le *Document de Damas*.[55] Rien d'étonnant donc que dans le code sur le sabbat du *Document de Damas*[56] et dans d'autres textes qumrâniens nous retrouvions la même rigueur d'interprétation des lois bibliques du repos pendant le sabbat.

A Qumrân, nous n'avons trouvé aucun témoin de Gen 2.2, ni dans les manuscrits bibliques ni dans des citations dans les manuscrits non bibliques; mais je suis convaincu que si le verset avait été préservé nous y trouverions la «correction» dûment attestée, parce qu'à Qumrân où l'on n'hésitait pas à changer le texte biblique en fonction de l'interprétation que l'on considérait comme la seule vraie, et les normes qumrâniennes sur le sabbat nous montrent une rigueur comparable à celle du *Livre des Jubilés*.

Mais si cette correction a été introduite dans le contexte des polémiques sur le repos sabbatique, pourquoi est-elle mise en rapport avec le Roi Ptolémée? Est-ce que les disputes sur le sabbat étaient «a hot item» à Alexandrie? Je ne saurais donner une réponse concluante. Mais peut-être est-ce significatif que Aristobule (qui adressa son œuvre à Ptolémée), dans le fragment sur le sabbat transmis par Eusèbe, cite le texte biblique avec la «correction» incluse («Il est dit clairement dans notre loi que Dieu se reposa le septième jour... Parce que la loi dit qu'Il fit les cieux et la terre dans six jours ...»). Dans le *Genesis Rabbah* 10.9, nous trouvons une référence isolée à cette «correction»

---

[54] 1Q17-18 publiés dans *DJD* 1; 3Q19-20 et 3Q5 publiés dans *DJD* 3; 4Q176a publié dans *DJD* 5; 4Q216-224 publiés dans *DJD* 13, et 11Q12 publié dans *DJD* 23.

[55] Dans CD XV 2-4.

[56] CD X 14—XI 18.

(«Celui-ci est l'un des textes qu'ils modifièrent pour le Roi Ptolémée: Et il conclut au jour sixième et se reposa le jour septième»), mais nous trouvons aussi le commentaire suivant:

> Le Roi Ptolémée demanda aux anciens de Rome: 'Dans combien de jours créa le monde le Saint, bénit soit-il?' 'Dans six', lui répondirent-ils. 'Et depuis ce temps là brûle la Gehenna pour les méchants? Malheur au monde qui a un tel juge!'

En tout cas, la polémique sur le sabbat continuera longtemps, et le texte biblique continuera à être employé contre les juifs encore à une époque plus tardive. Jérôme, en commentant Gen 2.2, nous donne un bon exemple:[57]

> Pro die sexta in Hebraeo diem septimam habet. Artabimus igitur Iudaeos qui de otio Sabbati gloriantur, quod iam tunc in principio sabbatum dissolutum sit, dum Deus operatur in sabbato, complens opera sua in eum, et benedicens ipsi diei quia in illo universa compleverit.

Rien d'étonnant donc que le changement de sept en six fusse déjà introduit au temps du Roi Ptolémée, et qu'à la différence des autres changements que nous avons examinés, celui-ci nous pouvons le trouver encore aujourd'hui dans *La Bible d'Alexandrie*.[58]

---

[57] CCL 72,4 cité par Veltri, *Eine Tora für den König Talmai*, 51.

[58] Une version préliminaire de cette contribution fut lue à l'Ecole Normale Supérieure de Paris en présence du groupe de recherche sur *La Bible d'Alexandrie*, dirigé par M. Harl. Je remercie très sincèrement tous les participants à la discussion qui ensuivit la conférence pour leurs précieuses observations.

THE BIRTH OF MOSES IN EGYPT ACCORDING TO THE *BOOK OF JUBILEES* (*JUB* 47.1-9)

Jacques T.A.G.M. van Ruiten

1. *Introduction*

The *Book of Jubilees* consists of a rewriting of the biblical narrative of the book of Genesis: the primeval history and the history of the patriarchs, with a special emphasis on Jacob. For this reason, one of the traditional names of the book is *The Little Genesis*.[1] Despite its emphasis on Genesis, however, the *Book of Jubilees* also deals with the book of Exodus. One can point to the beginning of chapter 1, where the author combines Exodus 19.1 (the arrival of the people of Israel in the wilderness of Sinai) and Exodus 24.18-21 (the ascension by Moses of the mountain to receive the tablets of stone) to describe the scene for the revelation.[2] Moreover, the narrative of Exodus 1-14 is represented at the end, in *Jubilees* 46.1-48.19. It is a very condensed rendering, however. Some passages are omitted and other passages are significantly abbreviated, for example the story of the plagues (Exodus 7-12), which the author deals with in just four verses (*Jub* 48.5-8). The passage immediately preceding the story of the plagues (Exod 2.23-7.9), and following the period of Moses in Midian, is also dealt with very briefly (*Jub* 48.1-4). The theophany at the burning bush, the commission of Moses, and

---

[1] This name occurs in four different forms ἡ Λεπτὴ Γένεσις (e.g., Epiphanius); ἡ Λεπτογένεσις (e.g., Didymus of Alexandria); τὰ Λεπτὰ Γενέσεως (Syncellus); ἡ Μικρογένεσις (Jerome). All forms probably reflect an original Hebrew form: בראשית זוטא. Cf. H. Rönsch, *Das Buch der Jubiläen: oder die Kleine Genesis; unter Beifügung des revidirten Textes der in der Ambrosiana aufgefundenen lateinischen Fragmente*, Leipzig 1874 (repr. Amsterdam 1970), 461-8; R.H. Charles, *The* Book of Jubilees *or the Little Genesis: Translated from the Editor's Ethiopic Text*, London 1902, xvi.

[2] Exod 19 and 24 are parallel versions of the episode on Mount Sinai, which supplement each other in many ways. *Jub* 1.1-4 may be an example of a text that reflects a version in which elements of both chapters have been combined. According to E. Tov, '4Q364: 4QReworked Pentateuch[b]', in: H.W. Attridge et al., *Qumran Cave 4-VIII: Parabiblical Texts. Part 1* (DJD 13), Oxford 1994, 221-2, the text of 4Q364 (Frg. 14) also shows a combination of elements of both chapters (i.e., Exod 19.17 and Exod 24.12-14).

the revelation of the Name is dealt with in just one phrase ('You know who spoke to you at Mt Sinai'). Although the rewriting in this part of the book is very concise, the author nevertheless takes the opportunity to present his world view. The narratives about Moses in Exodus 3-14 are in fact being rewritten in *Jubilees* as a battle between Mastema and the Angel of God. The world is under the control of the creator God, all-powerful and good, yet He permits the forces of evil to have some influence on mankind. Mastema is the leader of this host of evil powers. The Egyptian magicians are on the side of Mastema, whereas Moses is on the side of the Angel of God.

As far as the first two chapters of the Book of Exodus are concerned, a few passages are omitted altogether (Exod 1.1-5, 13-21; 2.16-22), whereas the text of Exod 1.6-8 is quoted merely as the basis for an extensive addition in the *Book of Jubilees* (*Jub* 46.1-11), which serves mainly as a transition between the Jacob episode and that of Moses. It explains why the prosperous situation for Israel in Egypt changed into a situation of slavery. The only passages that are followed quite extensively are Exod 1.9-12 (cf. *Jub* 46.12-16), which describes the situation of distress for the children of Israel, Exod 2.1-10 (cf. *Jub* 47.1-9), which describes the birth of Moses, and Exod 2.11-15 (cf. *Jub* 47.10-12), which describes the first period of his life until his flight to Midian. In the context of this contribution, I shall restrict myself to *Jubilees* 47.1-9, which can be considered as the rewriting of Exod 2.1-10, the story of Moses' birth.

2. *Exodus 1.22-2.10*

In contemporary exegetical literature, most exegetes assume that Exod 2.1-10 is a literary unit,[3] but a few exegetes consider Exod 1.22-2.10,[4] 1.15-2.10,[5] or 1.8-2.10[6] as a unit. Exod 2.11-15 is regarded as part

---

[3] E.g., C. Houtman, *Exodus* (COT), Kampen 1986, i, 254-77; J.I. Durham, *Exodus* (WBC 3), Waco, Texas 1987, 13-17; W.H. Schmidt, *Exodus*, vol. i: *Exodus 1-6* (BKAT II.1), Neukirchen-Vluyn 1988, 49-64. According to some, Exod 2.1-10 is part of larger unity, either Exod 2.1-22 (e.g., G. Beer, *Exodus mit einem Beitrag von K. Galling* [HAT], Tübingen 1939), or 2.1-15 (e.g., F. Michaeli, *Le livre de l'Exode* [CAT], Neuchâtel 1974).

[4] So W.H.C. Propp, *Exodus 1-18* (AB 2), New York 1998, 142-60.

[5] Cf. I. Willi-Plein, 'Ort und literarische Funktion der Geburtsgeschichte des Mose', *Vetus Testamentum* 41 (1991) 110-18.

[6] Cf. B.S. Childs, *Exodus*, London 1977[2], 7.

of a larger entity, e.g., Exod 2.11-22 or Exod 2.11-25, whereas Exod 1.22 belongs to Exod 1.(8)15-22. I agree with the majority, and consider Exod 2.1-10 as a unit, although I think that it is only possible to understand this passage in close connection with Exod 1.15-22.[7] The command of Pharaoh to kill every Hebrew male child (Exod 1.15-22) forms the background to the story of the birth of Moses (Exod 2.1-10).[8]

Exodus 2.1-10 can be considered as a kind of a marriage and birth report, which strengthens the unity of the passage. The basic structure is as follows: 1. A man knew[9] / took[10] a woman; 2. The woman conceived; 3. The woman gave birth to a son; 4. The woman or the man named this son; 5. Finally, an explanation of the name is given. Stages 3 and 4 are often taken together: the woman gave birth to a named son. The text of Exodus 2.1-10 can be considered as an extended form of this report: 1. A man from the house of Levi *went and took to wife* a daughter of Levi (2.1); 2. The woman conceived (2.2a); 3. She gave birth to a son (2.2b); 3b. *Interlude in which it is made clear that the son of the biological mother becomes the son of his adoptive mother* (2.2c-10c); 4. The adoptive mother named him Moses (2.10d); 5. Because she said (explanation of the name) (2.10ef).

In comparison with the basic structure of the marriage and birth report, it is striking in the first place that it is said in the beginning that the man 'went', and, secondly, that after the mention of the birth (2.2b), the giving of the name does not follow immediately but

---

[7] Cf. Childs, *Exodus*, 7; Willi-Plein, 'Ort', 110-18.

[8] The connection between Exod 1.15-22 and Exod 2.1-10 is stressed by the fact that the root ילד ('to give birth to') occurs often in both passages: eleven times in Exod 1.15-22 (1.15, 16, 17 (2x), 18 (2x), 19 (2x), 20, 21), mostly in the form of מילדת ('midwifes'), and nine times in Exod 2.1-10 (Exod 2.2, 3, 6 [2x], 7, 8, 9 [2x], 10). The relative independence of Exod 1.15-22 is expressed by the resemblance between the beginning (1.16) and the end (1.22) of the passage.

[9] For ידע in the meaning of 'having intercourse', see *Theologisches Handwörterbuch zum Alten Testament (THAT)*, i, Munich etc. 1971, 682-701, esp. 691; *Theologisches Wörterbuch zum Alten Testament (TWAT)*, iii, Stuttgart 1982, 479-512, esp. 494.

[10] לקח means literally 'to take'. Cf. *THAT*, i, 875-9; *TWAT*, iv, 588-94. It can be used in the meaning of 'take to wife', as is the case in Exod 2.1. With the preposition—it is used in Exod 21.10 and other texts, e.g., Gen 4.19; 11.29; 22.19; 25.20 (cf. also Exod 34.16: 'to take a wife for'). Cf. J. Scharbert, 'Ehe und Eheschliessung in der Rechtssprache des Pentateuch und beim Chronisten', in: G. Braulik (ed.), *Studien zum Pentateuch: Walter Kornfeld zum 60. Geburtstag*, Wien 1977, 213-25.

is postponed until the end of the story (2.10d). Moreover, it is not the biological father or mother who gives the child its name, but another, i.e. the adoptive mother of the child, the daughter of Pharaoh. Between the report of the birth and the giving of the name, the text explains how a newborn son becomes an adopted son of a new mother. At the same time, the text makes clear that he was initially brought up by his own mother.

The story of the birth of Moses can also be considered as a tale.[11] The exposition consists of the command by Pharaoh that all Hebrew-born sons are to be executed (1.[15-]22). In Exod 1.16, they are to be killed by the midwives, in Exod 1.22, they are to be thrown into the Nile. Generally speaking, Moses would have had no chance of living. He would have remained without a name. Then the story introduces the first complication. A Levite marriage produces a son (2.1-2b). Because of the death penalty, this son brings crisis. Moses' mother then decides to save her child. She puts the baby into a basket prepared for the river and places it in the grass at the riverbank (Exod 2.3). The mother gives up her child in order to give him a chance of life.[12] The baby's sister watches to determine what happens to the child (Exod 2.4). However, this act by the mother heightens the tension of the story. A female member of the royal house, a person who has no relationship with the children of Israel, finds him (Exod 2.5). The daughter of Pharaoh recognizes him as a Hebrew, a boy condemned to death by the decree of her father. She has the power to condemn the baby to immediate death. This can be considered as the climax of the story. After this point the dénouement starts, because the storyteller develops the account in such a direction, that the princess does not condemn the child to his death. Instead, 'she took pity on him' and cared for him (Exod 2.6). After this act, the sister of Moses approaches the daughter of Pharaoh and the biological mother acts as Moses' nurse (Exod 2.7-9) and the infant is given his name (Exod 2.10).

The story of the birth of Moses is often compared to stories known

---

[11] For the genre of a tale, see, e.g., C. Westermann, *Die Verheißungen an die Väter: Studien zur Vätergeschichte* (Forschungen zur Religion und Literatur des Alten und Neuen Testaments 116), Göttingen 1976; G.W. Coats, *Genesis with an Introduction to Narrative Literature* (FOTL 1), Grand Rapids, MI 1983, 7-8 *et passim*. For the following see also G.W. Coats, '2 Samuel 12.1-7a', *Interpretation* 40 (1986) 170-4.

[12] Cf. A. Brenner, 'Female Social Behavior: Two Descriptive Patterns within the 'Birth of the Hero' Paradigm', *Vetus Testamentum* 36 (1986) 257-73, esp. 269.

to other people in the Ancient Near East. The 'birth of the hero' myth is a well-known and widely used model.[13] The difficult circumstances attending the birth and childhood of a hero are almost universal. One need only point to the Legend of Sargon of Akkad.[14] He was also set afloat on a river in a reed basket, rescued by a water-drawer, nurtured, and became in time a mighty hero and king. The specific modelling in Exod 2.1-10, however, deviates in many respects from the general motif.[15] The descent of the child is not completely anonymous and socially insignificant in that his Levitical origin is mentioned. In Exodus, nothing is written about a clear career at the royal court. After the explanation of the name, the narrative ends abruptly. The report of the birth has priority over the motif of the abandonment. It is not the aim of the author to tell the story of the earliest youth of Moses, he explains how a Levitical child becomes an Egyptian child. Moreover, it seems striking that the actors in Exod 2.1-10 are nearly exclusively women.[16]

3. *Blanks in the biblical text*

On several points, the text is open for interpretation or is unclear.[17] Who were this man and woman (Exod 2.1ab)? What is meant by the statement that the man 'went' (Exod 2.1a)? Why does Moses'

---

[13] Cf. H. Gressmann, *Mose und seine Zeit*, Göttingen 1913; J. Campbell, *The Hero with a Thousand Faces*, Princeton 1933; O. Rank, *The Myth of the Birth of the Hero and Other Writings*, New York 1964; A. Dandes, *The Study of Folklore*, Englewood 1965; D.B. Redford, 'The Literary Motif of the Exposed Child', *Numen* 14 (1967) 209-28; Brenner, 'Female Social Behavior', 257-73; Schmidt, *Exodus*, i, 55-57.

[14] The Legend of Sargon can be found in W. Beyerlin (ed.), *Religionsgeschichtliches Textbuch zum Alten Testament*, Göttingen 1975, 123-4; J.B. Pritchard (ed.), *Ancient Near Eastern Texts relating to the Old Testament*, Princeton 1955, 119.

[15] Cf. Willi-Plein, 'Ort', 110-18. According to Durham (*Exodus*, 15) the form of the story of the birth of Moses is dictated by the larger theological purpose governing Exod 1 and 2.

[16] With the exception of the action of the father (Exod 2.1ab: 'a man from the house of Levi') who has to play his role in the procreation, and the son (2.10a: 'the child'), only women are the subjects of the verbs used in this passage: Moses' biological mother (2.2a-3e, 9ef); Moses' sister (2.4, 7); Moses' adoptive mother, the daughter of Pharaoh (2.5-6; 8ab, 9a-d, 10b-f). In the genealogy (Exod 6.20; cf. Num 26.57-59) the father is named (Amram), as is his wife (Jochebed).

[17] For the following see S.C. Reif, 'Classical Jewish Commentators on Exodus 2', in: M. Bar-Asher (ed.), *Studies in Hebrew and Jewish Languages Presented to Shelomo Morag*, Jerusalem 1996, *73-*112.

birth follow immediately upon the reference to his parents' marriage (Exod 2.2ab), given the fact that he also has a sister (Exod 2.4, 7) and a brother (cf. Exod 4.14)? Why was it possible to hide him for the specific period of three months (Exod 2.2cd)? Why could she no longer hide him (Exod 2.3a)? Why did she use asphalt and pitch? Why did she place the basket in the grass at the riverbank (Exod 2.3e)? How long did it stay there until the daughter of Pharaoh found it? Where did Pharaoh's daughter and her servants go and how and why was the baby fetched (Exod 2.5)? How could Pharaoh's daughter see that Moses was a Hebrew child (Exod 2.6)? It is mentioned that the child grew and that his mother brought him to Pharaoh's daughter (Exod 2.10ab), but how long did Moses' mother nurse him and how old was Moses at that time? Why was it not possible for an Egyptian woman to nurse him (Exod 2.7c)? These are questions which readers in subsequent generations have tried to answer in their commentaries and rewritings.[18]

4. *An overall comparison between Exodus 1.22-2.10 and* Jubilees *47.1-9*

In this contribution, I shall thus confine myself to one of the rewritings of Exod 1.22-2.10, i.e., *Jub* 47.1-9. In this part of his narrative, the author of *Jubilees* is concerned with the birth of Moses and the first twenty-one years of his life. The author struggles with some of the questions just mentioned. He tries to answer them with his rewriting.

As far as the overall structure is concerned, the text of Exodus 1.22-2.10 can be considered both as a marriage and birth report and as a tale. It is surprising that *Jubilees* does not follow the structure of the marriage and birth report of the biblical text, as it does elsewhere.[19] As can be seen in the following table, the only element of the basic structure of a marriage and birth report that is taken over is the men-

[18] E.g., D.J. Harrington, 'Birth Narratives in Pseudo-Philo's Biblical Antiquities and the Gospels', in: M.P. Horgan (ed.), *To Touch the Text: Biblical and Related Studies in Honor of Joseph A. Fitzmyer, S.J.*, New York 1989, 316-24, esp. 319. For an anthology of the interpretation in rabbinic and mediaeval Jewish literature of Exodus 1.22-2.10, see M.M. Kasher, *Encyclopedia of Biblical Interpretation, VII: Exodus*, New York 1967, 35-58. See also A. Rosmarin, *Moses im Lichte der Agada*, New York 1932, 45-59.

[19] For an overview of the structure of the genealogies of *Jubilees* in comparison to the genealogies in Genesis, see J.T.A.G.M. van Ruiten, *Primaeval History Interpreted: The Rewriting of Genesis 1-11 in the Book of Jubilees* (JSJSS 66), Leiden 2000, 113-24.

tion that Moses was born. The other elements that are taken over
from Exodus are elements that do not belong to the basic structure
of the birth report.

Exodus 2.1-10	*Jubilees 47.1-9*
1. A man from the house of Levi went (2.1a)	1. Your father came (47.1a)
2. He took to wife a daughter of Levi (2.1b)	2. –
3. The woman conceived (2.2a)	3. –
4. She gave birth to a son (2.2b)	4. You were born (47.1b)
5. Interlude (2.2c-10c)	5. Interlude (47.2-9)
6. The adoptive mother named him Moses (2.10d)	6. –
7. Because she said (explanation of the name) (2.10ef)	7. –

The story of the birth of Moses can also be considered as a tale. In
this respect the narrative structure runs more or less parallel in both
versions. However, there are some striking differences, as one can see
in the following table.

Exodus 2.1-10	*Jubilees 47.1-9*
1. *Exposition*: Pharaoh's command that all Hebrew sons born are to be executed (1.15-22).	1. *Exposition*: return of Moses' father and his birth in a time of distress (47.1).
2. *First complication*: A Levite marriage produces a son (2.1-2b).	2. *First complication*: Pharaoh's command that all Hebrew sons born are to be executed (47.2).
3. *Second complication*: Moses' mother puts the baby into a basket prepared for the river and places it in the grass at the riverbank (2.3).	3. *Second complication*: Moses' mother puts the baby into a basket prepared for the river and places it in the grass at the riverbank (47.3-4).
4. *Climax*: Pharaoh's daughter recognizes him as a Hebrew (2.5-6c).	4. *Climax*: Pharaoh's daughter finds him (47.5).
5. *Dénouement*: The princess 'took pity on him' and cared for him (2.6d). After this act, Moses' sister can go to Pharaoh's daughter, the biological mother acts as Moses' nurse (2.7-9).	5. *Dénouement*: The princess 'took pity on him' (47.6). After this act, Moses' sister can go to Pharaoh's daughter, the biological mother acts as Moses' nurse (47.7-8).
6. *Conclusion*: Moses was brought to Pharaoh's daughter and is given his name (2.10).	6. *Conclusion*: Moses educated by his father, and brought to the royal court (47.9).

The arrival of Moses' father and Moses' birth bring about a complication in the narrative of Exodus, because he was born in a situation of death penalty for every male who was born. In *Jubilees*, however, this is explicitly mentioned as part of the exposition. The complication there starts with the decree of the death penalty. As far as the conclusion is concerned, the name-giving is left out by *Jubilees*, whereas his education by his father and his bringing to the royal court is given more importance.

Although the narrative structure is parallel in both texts, there are only a few *verbatim quotations*. However, many *variations* strengthen the similarity between both texts. The variations are partly caused by the fact that the story of Exod 1-2 is told in *Jubilees* to Moses by the angel of the presence. Several elements in the story of Exodus which are told in the third person singular are put in the second person singular in *Jubilees* (*Jub* 47.1a, b, 3c, 4a, d, 5c, 6b, 7a, 8b, d, 9a, b). In addition to the verbatim quotations and the variations, there are many *additions* and some *omissions*.

In the following synoptic overview, I have tried to present a classification of the similarities and dissimilarities between Exodus 1.22-2.10 and *Jubilees* 47.1-9. I have used small caps and square brackets to highlight those elements of Exodus which do not occur in *Jubilees*, and vice versa, i.e., the omissions and additions. Small caps in one text correspond to square brackets in the other. I have used normal script for the corresponding elements between both texts, i.e. the verbatim quotations of one or more words from the source text in *Jubilees*. I have used italics to indicate the variations between Exodus and *Jubilees*, other than additions or omissions. Sometimes there is a rearrangement of words and sentences. I have underlined those elements.[20]

---

[20] Quotations from the biblical text follow the Revised Standard Version, with slight modifications, whereas quotations from *Jubilees* are according to J.C. VanderKam, *The Book of Jubilees*, vol. ii (CSCO 511; Scriptores Aethiopici 88), Louvain 1989. *Jub* 47.1-9 is nearly completely preserved in Latin. Both the Latin and the Ethiopic translations go back to a Greek translation of the Hebrew original. Cf. VanderKam, *Book of Jubilees*, vol. ii, vi-xxxi; K. Berger, *Das Buch der Jubiläen* (JSHRZ II.3), Gütersloh 1981, 285-94. The edition of the Latin text of *Jub* 47.1-9 can be found in J.C. VanderKam, *The Book of Jubilees*, vol. i (CSCO 510; Scriptores Aethiopici 87), Louvain 1989, 298. The text-critical value of the Latin text of *Jub* 47.1-9 is discussed in the notes to the translation of the Ethiopic text of *Jub* 47.1-9 in VanderKam, *Book of Jubilees*, ii, 305-8.

Exodus 1.22-2.10   *Jubilees* 47.1-9

1.22a Pharaoh [ ] *commanded* ALL HIS PEOPLE   [cf. Jub *47.2a-3b*]
       [ ],
    b *'Every son that is born to the Hebrews you
       shall throw into the Nile,*
    c BUT YOU SHALL LET EVERY DAUGHTER
       LIVE'.
       [   ]
                                                    1a DURING THE SEVENTH WEEK, IN
                                                        THE SEVENTH YEAR, IN THE FORTY-
                                                        SEVENTH JUBILEE,
                                                        your father came FROM THE LAND OF
2.1a *A man from the house of Levi went*   CANAAN.
      [   ]   [   ]

    b AND TOOK TO WIFE A DAUGHTER OF
       LEVI.
   2a THE WOMAN CONCEIVED
    b *and bore a son;* [   ]   b *You were born* DURING THE FOURTH
                                                        MONTH, IN ITS SIXTH YEAR, IN THE
                                                        FORTY EIGHTH JUBILEE,
                                                     c WHICH WAS THE TIME OF DISTRESS
                                                        FOR THE ISRAELITES.
      [cf. *Exod 1.22*]   2a Pharaoh, THE KING OF EGYPT *had
                                                        given orders* [   ] REGARDING THEM
                                                     b *that they were to throw their sons–every
                                                        male who was born–into the river.* [   ]
                                                    3a THEY CONTINUED THROWING (THEM
                                                        IN) FOR SEVEN MONTHS
                                                     b UNTIL THE TIME WHEN YOU WERE
                                                        BORN.
                                                        [   ]
    c AND WHEN SHE SAW THAT HE WAS A
       GOODLY CHILD,
    d *she* hid *him* for three months.   c *Your mother* hid *you* for three
                                                        months.
   3a *When she could hide him no longer*   d *Then they told about her.*
    b she *took* for *him* a box MADE OF   4a She *made* a box [   ] for *you,*
       BULRUSHES,
    c covered it with asphalt and pitch;   b covered it with pitch and asphalt,
    d and she put *the child* in it [   ]
    e and put it in the grass at the   c and put it in the grass at the
       riverbank.   riverbank.
                                                    d She put *you* in it FOR SEVEN DAYS.
      [   ]   e YOUR MOTHER WOULD COME AT
                                                        NIGHT
                                                    f AND NURSE YOU,
   4a And [ ] *his* sister *stood at a distance, to*   g and DURING THE DAY *your* sister
       know what would be done to him.   MIRIAM *would protect you from the
                                                        birds.*
   5a [ ] The daughter of Pharaoh went   5a AT THAT TIME TARMUTH, the
       out to bathe at the river,   daughter of Pharaoh, went out to
                                                        bathe in the river
    b AND HER MAIDENS WALKED BESIDE THE   [   ]
       RIVER;
    c SHE SAW THE BOX IN THE GRASS

Exodus 1.22-2.10		*Jubilees 47.1-9*	
d	and *sent* her *maid* to bring *it*.	b	*and heard you crying*.
	[ ]	c	She *told* her *slaves*[21] to bring *you*,
6a	WHEN SHE OPENED IT	d	SO THEY BROUGHT YOU TO HER.
b	SHE SAW THE CHILD;		[ ]
c	*and lo, the babe was crying*.		
	[ ]	6a	SHE TOOK YOU OUT OF THE BOX
d	She took pity on *him*	b	and took pity on *you*.
e	AND SAID:		[ ]
f	'THIS IS ONE OF THE HEBREWS' CHILDREN'.		
7a	Then *his* sister said to *the daughter of Pharaoh:*	7a	Then *your* sister said to *her*:
b	'Shall I go	b	'Shall I go
c	and call for you *a woman, a nurse*, from the Hebrew women,	c	and call for you *one* of the Hebrew women *who will care for*
	to nurse the child for you?'	d	*and nurse this infant* for you?'
8a	*The daughter of Pharaoh* said to her:	e	[*She* said to her:
b	'Go'.	f	'Go'.][22]
c	*The girl* went	8a	*She* went
d	and called *the child's* mother.	b	and called *your* mother JOCHEBED.
9a	AND PHARAOH'S DAUGHTER SAID TO HER:		[ ]
b	'TAKE THIS CHILD AWAY,		
c	AND NURSE HIM FOR ME,		
d	*I will give you* YOUR *wages*'.	c	*She* gave *her* wages
e	THE WOMAN TOOK THE CHILD		[ ]
f	*and she nursed him*.	d	*and she took care of you*.
	[ ]	9a	AFTERWARDS,
10a	*And the child grew*,		*when you had grown up*,
b	and *she brought him* to Pharaoh's daughter,		*you were brought* to Pharaoh's daughter
c	and *he* became her son;	b	and *you* became her son.
d	AND SHE NAMED HIM MOSES,		[ ]
e	FOR SHE SAID:		
f	'BECAUSE I DREW HIM OUT OF THE WATER'.		
	[ ]	c	YOUR FATHER AMRAM TAUGHT YOU (THE ART OF) WRITING.
		d	AFTER YOU HAD COMPLETED THREE WEEKS (= 21 YEARS),
		e	HE BROUGHT YOU INTO THE ROYAL COURT.

---

[21] Most of the Ethiopic manuscripts read 'Hebrew women', while Latin has 'slave'. For text-critical reasons, most translations opt for 'slaves'. Cf. VanderKam, *Book of Jubilees*, ii, 306.

[22] With the exception of one manuscript, these words from Exod 2.8 have fallen from the Ethiopic manuscripts. Cf. VanderKam, *Book of Jubilees*, ii, 307.

5. *An analysis of the rewriting of Exodus 1.22-2.10 in* Jubilees *47.1-9*

a. *Dating the events*

The first difference between *Jubilees* and Exodus that strikes the eye is the dating of the events. The author of *Jubilees* attaches great significance to a chronological system within which he frames his rewriting.[23] He puts the biblical narratives in a continuous chronological system, from the creation of the world until the entrance into the promised land, which took place 2450 years after the creation. This system is characterised by its heptadic arrangement: years, weeks of years, and jubilees of years. The history is divided into periods of jubilees. Each jubilee consists of seven weeks of years, i.e. seven times seven years. Moses' father arrived in Egypt in the 7th year of the 7th year-week of the 47th jubilee (cf. *Jub* 47.1a), which is *a.m.* (*anno mundi*) 2303. Moses was born in the 4th month of the 6th year-week of the 48th jubilee, which is *a.m.* 2330. Between the arrival of Amram and the birth of Moses is a period of 27 years. Moreover, Moses remained 21 years in his parental house (*Jub* 47.9d: 'three weeks'). Later it is said that he remained 21 years in the royal court (*Jub* 47.10a). So Moses was 42 years when he ran away and arrived in Midian. This was during the 6th year of the 3rd year-week of the 49th jubilee, which is *a.m.* 2372 (cf. *Jub* 48.1). He lived for another 36 years in Midian, and then returned to Egypt in the 2nd year of the 2nd year-week of the 50 jubilee, which is *a.m.* 2410 (cf. *Jub* 48.1).

b. *Naming the characters*

A second difference is the naming of the characters. Exodus speaks about 'a man from the house of Levi' and 'a daughter of Levi' (Exod 2.1), about 'his sister' (Exod 2.4, 7a), the daughter of Pharaoh (Exod 2.5-10), and of 'Moses' (Exod 2.10). All the characters are anonymous, with the exception of Moses who is given his name at the end of the story. By contrast, *Jubilees* names all characters with the exception of Moses. The narrative starts with 'your father' (*Jub* 47.1a), who had already been named 'Amram' in the preceding chapter (cf. *Jub* 46.9). Moses' mother is called by her name 'Jochebed' (cf. *Jub* 47.8), his sister

---

[23] Cf. J.C. VanderKam, 'Das chronologische Konzept des Jubiläenbuches', *Zeitschrift für die alttestamentliche Wissenschaft* 107 (1995) 80-100.

by her name 'Miriam' (*Jub* 47.4g), and the daughter of Pharaoh by her name 'Tarmuth' (*Jub* 47.5a).

Although Amram, Jochebed and Miriam are not called by their names in Exodus 1-2, their names are in accordance with the biblical data. In the genealogy of Exod 6.14-25, it is said that Amram married his aunt Jochebed (Exod 6.20: 'Amram took to wife Jochebed his father's sister'), and that she bore to him Aaron and Moses. In this genealogy, it is made clear that Amram is from the house of Levi. He is one of the sons of Kohath (Exod 6.18), who is one of the sons of Levi (Exod 6.16). This shows that the author of *Jubilees* uses also passages from the book of Exodus that he skips over in his rewriting. As we will see later on, the author of *Jubilees* could not stress the fact that Amram married his aunt.[24] In the genealogy of Num 26.57-59, it is mentioned that Jochebed, who was born to Levi in Egypt, bore to Amram not only Aaron and Moses, but also Miriam their sister. In Exod 15.20, Miriam is called the sister of Aaron. In contrast with the biblical books, Aaron does not occur at all in the Book of *Jubilees*. This is probably due to the choice of Levi as the prototypical priest rather than Aaron who carries that role in Exodus-Numbers.[25] The name 'Tarmuth', the name of Pharaoh's daughter, is not found in biblical literature. Flavius Josephus calls her almost identical 'Thermouthis' (*Jewish Antiquities* 2.24). In rabbinic literature, she is called 'Bithiah' (cf. *b. Meg* 13a; *Lev r* 1.3).

c. *The stay of Amram in Canaan*

In *Jub* 47.1, the author mentions that Moses' father Amram comes 'from the land of Canaan'. This is nowhere stated in the biblical literature. In the preceding chapter of the *Book of Jubilees*, it had been explained how Moses' father had left Egypt and had gone on a journey to Canaan (cf. *Jub* 46.10). This was connected with the burial of the bones of all Jacob's sons, except those of Joseph, in Hebron (*Jub* 46.9-10). The transfer of these bones is linked up with a battle between the king of Egypt and the king of Canaan:

---

[24] Cf. notes 32 and 33.

[25] Cf. J.C. VanderKam, *The Book of Jubilees* (Guides to Apocrypha and Pseudepigrapha), Sheffield 2001, 142. According to Ravid, in omitting any reference to Aaron in the *Book of Jubilees*, the author intended to undermine the legality of the Zadokites' right to act as High Priests. See L. Ravid, 'Purity and Impurity in the Book of Jubilees', *Journal for the Study of the Pseudepigrapha* 13 (2002) 61-86, esp. 84.

(5) Before he (= Joseph) died he ordered the Israelites to take his bones along at the time when they would leave the land of Egypt. (6) He made them swear about his bones because he knew that the Egyptians would not again bring him out and bury him on the day in the land of Canaan, since Makamaron, the king of Canaan—while he was living in the land of Asur—fought in the valley with the king of Egypt and killed him there. He pursued the Egyptians as far as the gates of Ermon. (7) He was unable to enter because another new king ruled Egypt. He was stronger that he, so he returned to the land of Canaan and the gates of Egypt were closed with no one leaving or entering Egypt (8) Joseph died in the forty-sixth jubilee, in the sixth week, during its second year. He was buried in the land of Egypt, and all his brothers died after him. (9) Then the king of Egypt went out to fight with the king of Canaan in the forty-seventh jubilee, in the second week, during its second year. The Israelites brought out all the bones of Jacob's sons except Joseph's bones. They buried them in the field, in the double cave in the mountain. (10) Many returned to Egypt but a few of them remained on the mountain of Hebron. Your father Amram remained with them. (*Jub* 46.6-10)

It is difficult to interpret the events and characters mentioned in *Jub* 46.6-10. The kings of Canaan and Egypt might reflect the conflicts between the Seleucides who controlled Palestine and the Ptolemies in Egypt.[26] The description of this conflict, which has no parallel in the biblical text, seems to serve a few goals. In the first place, it refers to a saying of Joseph at the end of the book of Genesis:

> And Joseph said to his brothers: 'I am about to die; but God will visit you, and bring you up out of this land to the land which he swore to Abraham, to Isaac, and to Jacob'. Then Joseph took an oath of the sons of Israel, saying: 'God will visit you, and you shall carry up my bones from here' (Gen 50.24-25).

The text does not make clear why Joseph did not ask for his bones to be taken up to Canaan right away, as Jacob had asked (cf. Gen 47.29-30). The author of *Jubilees* suggests an answer to this question. A war had caused the border between Egypt and Canaan to be closed. It is for this reason that his bones could not be transported immediately to Canaan. Therefore, Joseph asked his brothers to make sure that he would be buried in Canaan.[27] In the biblical text, this request is executed during the exodus from Egypt (cf. Exod 13.19).

In the second place, according to the author of *Jubilees*, the victory

---

[26] VanderKam, *Book of Jubilees*, 81-2. Cf. Charles, *Book of Jubilees*, 245-6.
[27] Cf. J.L. Kugel, *The Bible As It Was*, Cambridge, Mass. 1997, 282-3.

of the king of Egypt enabled the Israelites to transport the bones of
the sons of Jacob outside Egypt in order to bury them in Canaan,
'in the field, in the double cave in the mountain' (*Jub* 46.9), which is
'the mountain of Hebron' (*Jub* 46.10). According to the biblical data,
the bones of Joseph were to be kept in Egypt. However, they were
taken along by Moses and the Israelites at the time of the exodus
from Egypt (Exod 13.19). Nowhere in the biblical literature does it
state that the bones of the brothers of Joseph were also to be buried
in Canaan. According to the author of *Jubilees*, this must have been
obvious. He makes it possible by using a tradition that is not found
in the Bible and that connects the transport of the bones with a war
between Egypt and Canaan.

The same tradition can be found in the *Testaments of the Twelve
Patriarchs*. There, too, it is said that the bones of all the patriarchs were
buried in Hebron.[28] In the case of Simeon and Benjamin, a war is
also mentioned. In the *Testament of Simeon* 8.2, it is said that the bones
of Simeon were carried by his sons 'in secret' up to Hebron 'during
a war with Egypt'. The sons of Benjamin also carried the bones of
their father in secret to Hebron, 'because of a war with Canaan'
(*Test. Benj.* 12.3). They returned afterwards: 'They returned from the
land of Canaan and resided in Egypt until the day of the departure
from Egypt' (*Test. Benj.* 12.4). It is not clear whether, according to the
Testaments of the Twelve Patriarchs, the bones of all patriarchs, with the
exception of Joseph, were transported at the same time to Hebron, as
Jubilees puts it, or at different times. Whereas with regard to Simeon
and Benjamin the text speaks about a war, with regard to Gad, the
text speaks about a period of five years after his death before his bones
were transported (*Test. Gad* 8.4), whereas in the case of Levi, Zebulon,
and Dan, it is said that they were transported 'later' (cf. *Test. Levi* 19.5;
Test. Zebulon 10.6; *Test. Dan* 7.2).[29]

The tradition that the bones of Joseph's brothers were brought from
Egypt to Canaan before the bones of Joseph is also found in Flavius
Josephus, although no war is mentioned:

> His brothers also died in Egypt, after a rich and prosperous life. Their
> bodies were taken later by their descendants and buried in Hebron. The

---

[28] Cf. *Test. Reuben* 7.1-2; *Test. Simeon* 8.1-2; *Test. Levi* 19.5; *Test. Judah* 26.4; *Test.
Zebulon* 10.6; *Test. Dan* 7.2; *Test. Naftali* 9.1-2; *Test. Gad* 8.3-4; *Test. Asher* 8.1; *Test.
Benjamin* 12.1-4.
[29] Cf. Charles, *Book of Jubilees*, 245.

bones of Joseph were carried away to Canaan much later, when the
Hebrews moved away from Egypt (*Jew. Ant.* 2.199-200).

Acts also speaks about the transport of the bones, but does not mention a war:

> And Jacob went down into Egypt. And he died, himself and our fathers,
> and they were carried back to Shechem and laid in the tomb that
> Abraham had bought for a sum of silver from the sons of Hamor in
> Shechem (Acts 7.15-16).[30]

According to the author of *Jubilees*, the burial of the bones of the
patriarchs enabled Amram, one of the descendants of Levi, to go to
Canaan in the company of many other Israelites. After the burial of
the patriarchs, most of the Israelites returned to Egypt. A few of them,
however, remained on the mountain of Hebron, among whom was
Moses' father Amram. The reason why these few stayed in Canaan is
not made clear. It may possibly have been because after some time the
king of Canaan prevailed over Egypt: 'The king of Canaan conquered
the king of Egypt and closed the gates of Egypt' (*Jub* 46.11). It is not
said for how long the gates of Egypt remained closed. In any case,
Amram stayed for 40 years in Canaan. He arrived in Canaan in the
2nd year of the 2nd year-week of the 47th jubilee, which is *a.m.* 2263
(cf. *Jub* 46.9), and he arrived back in Egypt in the 7th year of the 7th
year-week of the 47th jubilee, which is *a.m.* 2303 (cf. *Jub* 47.1a).

   The additions about a war between Egypt and Canaan were possibly also motivated by the wish to explain why the people of Egypt
were afraid of the people of Israel. The king of Egypt conceived an
evil plan against Israel because he was afraid of them (cf. *Jub* 46.12).
When war came they would also fight against Egypt and unite with
the enemy, i.e. the king of Canaan, because their minds were oriented
towards Canaan (cf. *Jub* 46.13). The slavery imposed on them was
meant to stop them multiplying and to make them weaker.

d. *Marriage report*

The marriage report (Exod 2.1b: 'He took to wife a daughter of
Levi') and the reference to the subsequent intercourse (Exod 2.2a:

---

[30] Likewise, in rabbinic literature it is said that the bones not only of Joseph but
also of his brothers were eventually brought for burial in Hebron. Cf. *Mekhilta de Rabbi
Ishmael, Beshallah*, Introduction; *Mekhilta de Rabbi Shimon bar Yohai* 14; *Gen r* 100.11.

'The woman conceived') is omitted in *Jubilees*. The narrative passes on directly from 'your father came' to 'you were born'. There is of course a period of 27 years between Amram's return (*a.m.* 2303) and Moses' birth (*a.m.* 2330). Since *Jub* 47.4g (cf. Exod 2.4) presupposes the birth of a sister prior to Moses' birth, the marriage between Amram and Jochebed must have taken place at least some years before Moses' birth. Since Jochebed was born in Egypt (cf. Num 26.59), and it is not said that she went with Amram to Canaan, nor that she came back with him to Egypt, it seems most probable that the marriage took place in Egypt between *a.m.* 2303 and some years before *a.m.* 2330.

The omission of the marriage report is quite unusual because it is an important issue for the author of *Jubilees*.[31] He even adds a marriage into reports of events where the biblical text does not have a marriage report. The author is very interested in genealogical affairs. The reason for the omission may have been that Amram, grandson of Levi, married Jochebed, daughter of Levi, i.e., he married his aunt (cf. Exod 6.20). According to Halpern-Amaru, the relationship between Amram and Jochebed is too well documented in the Bible to rework it into another kind of relationship.[32] This might otherwise have been preferable inasmuch as a marriage between an aunt and a nephew is not permitted according to Levitical law (Lev 20.19: 'You shall not uncover the nakedness of your mother's sister or of your father's sister, for that is to make naked one's near kin; they shall bear their iniquity').[33] The author of *Jubilees* was indeed unwilling to confirm that an impure marriage had produced Moses. Therefore, he just omitted the marriage report between Amram and Jochebed. According to rabbinic literature, before Sinai this Levitical law was only concerned with maternal relationships. In their eyes, Levi had married two different women, one of whom was the mother of Kohath, and the other of Jochebed (cf. *b. Sota* 58b).[34]

---

[31] Cf. note 19.
[32] Cf. B. Halpern-Amaru, *The Empowerment of Women in the* Book of Jubilees (JSJSS 60), Leiden 1999, 122-4.
[33] The *Jubilees* genealogies avoid this kind of relationship between husband and wife also elsewhere. Cf. Halpern-Amaru, *Empowerment*, 123.
[34] Cf. Halpern-Amaru, ibid.

e. *Three months of hiding*

The author of *Jubilees* also omits the phrase: 'And when she saw that
he was a goodly child' (Exod 2.2c).[35] The subsequent mention of a
period of hiding, i.e., three months (Exod 2.2d), has produced a tradition in aggadic literature about a premature birth of Moses, i.e., in
the sixth or seventh month of the pregnancy of Jochebed.[36] There is
another example of this in *Targum Pseudo-Jonathan*, on Exod 2.2: 'The
woman conceived and bore a son *at the end of six months*. When she saw
he was *viable*, she hid him for three months, *which gives a total of nine*'.
Also in the *Mekhilta* can be read: 'The Egyptians counted nine months
for her, but she bore *in six months*'.[37] The clue to this tradition is that
it is written in Exod 2.2 that Jochebed hid Moses for three months.
This would make sense only if the Egyptians expected the baby three
months earlier than the actual birth.

In another, probably later, tradition it is said that Moses was born

---

[35] I do not know the reason for the omission. Ezekiel the Tragedian (*Exagoge* 14)
and Flavius Josephus (*Jew. Ant.* 2.218) also omit the phrase, although the excellence
of Moses is revealed to his father in a dream (*Jew. Ant.* 2.210-217). The word טוב
can be applied to moral qualities as well as to physical appearance. The Septuagint
translates ἀστεῖον ('fine', 'handsome') which can refer to physical qualities. *Targum
Pseudo-Jonathan* translated with 'viable' (בר קיומי). Moses' mother sees that her son
is healthy despite his premature birth (see below). Therefore she tries to keep him.
Rabbinic literature tries to explain the significance of the description: 'The woman
conceived and bore a son and she saw that he was fine. R. Meir taught: His name
was Tob. R. Joshia: His name was Tobiah ('The Lord is good'). R. Judah: He was
worthy of the prophecy. The others say: he was born circumcised' (*Exod r* 1.20; cf.
b. Sotah 12a). Some rabbis connected it with the beginning of Genesis: 'When Moses
was born the house was filled with light. For here it is written: 'She saw him, that
he was good', and elsewhere we read that 'God saw the light, that is was good' (Gen
1.4)'. Cf. Rosmarin, *Moses*, 50; Kasher, *Encyclopedia*, 39-40; G. Vermes, *Scripture and
Tradition in Judaism* (SPB 4), Leiden 1973, 184-5; A. Salvesen, *Symmachus in the Pentateuch*
(JSSM 15), Manchester 1991, 67.

[36] P. van der Horst, 'Seven Month's Children in Jewish and Christian Literature
from Antiquity', *Ephemerides Theologicae Lovanienses* 54 (1978) 346-60, esp. 234-5 (reprint
in Id., *Essays on the Jewish World of Early Christianity* [NTOA 14], Göttingen 1990,
233-47). Cf. also L. Ginzberg, *The Legends of the Jews*, v, 397 note 44; E.B. Levine,
'Parallels to Exodus of Pseudo-Jonathan and Neophyti I', in: A. Diez Macho (ed.),
Neophyti I, iii, Madrid-Barcelona 1971, 424; R. Bloch, 'Moïse dans la tradition rabbinique', in: H. Cazelles et al. (eds), *Moïse, l'homme de l'alliance*, Paris 1955, 102-18;
D. Daube, *The New Testament and Rabbinic Judaism*, London 1956, 7; J. Heinemann,
'210 Years of Egyptian Exile', *Journal of Jewish Studies* 22 (1971) 19-30; M. Abraham,
Légendes juives apocryphes sur la vie de Moïse, Paris 1925, 49.

[37] J.N. Epstein and E. Z. Melamed, *Mekhilta de Rabbi Shim on bar Yohai*, Jerusalem
1955, 6, 17.

six months after the remarriage of Amram and Jochebed. After the decree of Pharaoh to throw all newborn Hebrew boys into the river, Amram divorced Jochebed, who was at that moment already three months pregnant (cf. *Exod r* 1.13, 20). However, Miriam rebuked her father, and after this he remarried immediately. The Egyptians considered the return of Jochebed as the beginning of the pregnancy.[38]

Jubilees does not explicitly mention either of these traditions with regard to the birth of Moses. However, what should one think of the addition in *Jub* 47.3ab: 'They continued throwing the Hebrew sons into the river *for seven months, until the time when you were born*'? This seems to imply that there is a relationship, whatever it may be, between the commandment of Pharaoh to kill every male who was born, and the expectation of the birth of Moses.[39] The rearrangement of the decree and the conception in *Jubilees* not only clears Amram and Jochebed of the accusation that they had intercourse in a time when the decree was already proclaimed, it also makes a connection between the decree and the birth of Moses. It is possible that, according to the author of *Jubilees*, the decree was issued at the conception of Moses. In this case, too, 'seven months' then implies that Moses was born too early.

f. *Moses at the riverside (Exodus 2.3-10 // Jub 47.3d-9)*

In the continuation of the narrative, the author of *Jubilees* follows more or less the storyline of Exodus. There are a few additions, some omissions and several variations, as can be seen in the synoptic overview.

The story in Exod 2.3a about the end of Moses' period of hiding merely reads: 'when she could hide him no longer'. It gives no reason why she could hide him no longer. *Jub* 47.3d has a variation on the biblical text and reports that after she hid the infant for three months, they, i.e. unidentified informers, told on her. It gives a reason why Moses' mother could no longer hide him. The Egyptians were tracing her. In a certain way, it gives her an excuse. This variation matches other aggadic elaboration, for example that in *Targum Pseudo-Jonathan*:

---

[38] Cf. Rosmarin, *Moses*, 45-6.
[39] Flavius Josephus mentions the fact that a priest reports to the king that in the near future a child will be born among the Israelites who will, when he has grown up, end the dominion of the Egyptians, and who will bring the Israelites to power (*Jew. Ant.* 2.205). However, this started before the conception of Moses.

'It was no longer possible for her to hide him, because the Egyptians had noticed her' (*Tg Ps J* Exod 2.3).[40]

Exodus continues with the report that Moses' mother gets herself a box made of bulrushes, and covered it with asphalt and pitch. In *Jubilees*, the mother makes the box herself, and the material is not specified. The materials asphalt and pitch are reversed in *Jubilees*. In Exodus, the mother first puts the child in the box, and then leaves the box on the riverbank. In *Jubilees*, the mother first puts the box on the riverbank, and then puts the child in it. It indicates perhaps something of the special care and tenderness Moses receives, which we find also in the continuation of the text.

Exodus is not explicit about how long the basket stayed there until the daughter of Pharaoh found it, nor does it state what happened with the baby before it was found. The biblical text only reads that 'his sister stood at a distance to know what would be done to him' (Exod 2.4). *Jubilees*, however, is more specific. In line with its stress on the number seven, it relates that Moses stayed in his basket for seven days. Moreover, he was taken special care of by his mother and his sister. At night, his mother would come to nurse him, whereas during the day his sister kept an eye on him. Unlike the biblical text, according to which Moses' sister stood some distance away (Exod 2.4), Miriam did not watch at a distance;[41] she protected him from the birds.[42]

---

[40] So also in *b. Sotah* 12a; *Exod r* 1.20; *Song of Songs r* 2.15.2. See also Ezekiel the Tragedian: 'When she could no longer escape detection' (*Exagoge* 15); cf. Philo, *De Vita Mosis* 1.9-10.

[41] See also Ezekiel the Tragedian, *Exagoge* 18: 'My sister Mariam stood guard nearby'. See also Philo, *De Vita Mosis* 1.12.

[42] According to Halpern-Amaru, *Empowerment*, 123 note 52, the reference to the birds appears to be a subtle indicator of Mastema for its recalls the young Abram combating the work of Mastema in Chaldea (*Jub* 11.11-13, 18-21). It is true that apart from the reference to the Prince of Mastema in Abraham's words to Jacob, he occurs after the binding of Isaac only in the Exodus story. With regard to Abram, the Prince of Mastema sent crows and birds so that they might eat the seed which was being sown in the earth. In this way, he reduced the inhabitants of Babylon to poverty (*Jub* 11.9-13). Then the birth of Abram is recounted, and the mention that his father taught him writing (*Jub* 11.14-17). As a young boy, Abram protected the seed (*Jub* 11.18-22). In the story about the binding of Isaac, Prince Mastema questioned the nature of Abraham's faithfulness, and suggested that he should be tested by offering his son (*Jub* 17.16). With regard to Moses, his birth and his education by his father is recounted (*Jub* 47.1-9). However, it is his sister who protected Moses from the birds. Later on, the Prince of Mastema wanted to kill Moses and save the Egyptians (*Jub* 48.3-4), and he empowered the magicians (*Jub* 48.9).

The princess comes to the Nile to bathe. The narrative is slightly changed in *Jubilees* at this point. The biblical text mentions that the princess was accompanied by her maidens. When she saw the box, she sent her maid to bring the box. Only after she had opened the box does she see the child and hear him crying (cf. Exod 2.5-6c). In *Jubilees* it is not said that Pharaoh's daughter was accompanied by her maidens, although they are presupposed. Exodus uses four verbs before arriving at the crying of the child ('she saw', 'she sent', 'she opened', 'she saw', and only then she heard the child crying). In *Jubilees*, it is said immediately that she heard Moses crying (*Jub* 47.5b). This is probably what arouses her compassion. Thereafter, she ordered her slaves to bring Moses to her, and they did so. Then she took Moses out of the box (*Jub* 47.5-6).

When the princess saw the baby, she recognized him as a Hebrew child, in the biblical text (Exod 2.6f). The text does not explain how she knows this. This might be the reason for the omission of this identification in *Jubilees*.[43]

Furthermore, there is no direct conversation between Moses' mother and Pharaoh's daughter in *Jubilees*. The text simply says that the princess gave wages to Moses' mother, and that she took care of him (*Jub* 47.8ab).

In Exodus, Moses is brought by his mother to the royal palace. It is not said in the biblical text how long his mother took care of him (Exod 2.9e-10b: 'The woman took the child, she nursed him, the child grew, she brought him to Pharaoh's daughter'). In *Jubilees*, it is said twice that Moses was brought to Pharaoh's daughter, without the mother being mentioned in this respect. The first time an indefinite formulation is used: 'Afterwards, when you had grown up, *you were brought* to the Pharaoh's daughter'.[44] Shortly after this, the father is named explicitly as the one who brought Moses to the court: 'He (= your father Amram) brought you into the royal court' (*Jub* 47.9e). Moreover, the text makes clear at what age Moses went to Pharaoh's daughter. He was 21 years old (*Jub* 47.9d: 'after you had completed three weeks'). This makes clear that, according to *Jubilees*, Moses got

---

[43] In rabbinic literature, it is said that she saw that he was circumcised (*b. Sotah* 12a). According to others, an angel told her that Moses was a Hebrew son (*b. Sotah* 12b).

[44] In fact a plural form of the verb is used: 'they brought you'. This functions as an indefinite plural. Cf. VanderKam, *Book of Jubilees*, ii, 307.

his earliest education not in the palace of Pharaoh, but in his own house, by his own father (*Jub* 47.9c: 'your father Amram taught you the art of writing'). This resolves a problem that the biblical text does not answer, namely how does Moses become aware that he was one of the Israelites?[45] But there is something more. He could use his skill to write the *Book of Jubilees*.[46] Moreover, the notion that Moses' father Amram taught him the art of writing seems to be at odds with a tradition that reports on Moses' education in Egyptian wisdom.[47] However, it is consistent in the *Book of Jubilees*, and it puts Moses on one line with all the patriarchs.

The art of writing is an important issue in the *Book of Jubilees*. Fathers teach their sons the art of writing (cf. *Jub* 8.2; 11.16; 47.9; cf. 19.14). In addition, it was Enoch who was the first on earth to learn the art of writing, instruction, and wisdom (*Jub* 4.17). Abraham learned to write from his father (*Jub* 11.16), although it was the Angel of the Presence who taught him Hebrew (*Jub* 12.25-27). When Jacob and his brother grew up 'Jacob learned the art of writing, but Esau did not learn it' (*Jub* 19.14).

The art of writing and reading is often connected with *halakhic* instruction of one type or another that is written down by the fathers in a book (*Jub* 4.17; 7.38-39; 10.13-14; 10.17; 12.27; 21.10; 39.6-7; 45.16) and handed down to their sons. In this way, the author of *Jubilees* creates a chain of tradition which is quite distinctive: Enoch, Methuselah, Lamech, Noah, Shem, Abram, Isaac, Jacob, (Joseph), Levi. In *Jub* 19.24, the chain of tradition is traced back to Adam: Adam, Seth, Enos, Malaleel, Enoch, Noah, Shem.[48] It is interesting to note that some links in the chain have been omitted. I would point to the generations between Shem and Abram (Arpachsad, Kainan, Shelah, Eber, Peleg, Ragew, Serug, Nahor, Terah), which the author of *Jubilees*

---

[45] Cf. Jacobson, *Exagoge*, 78. Ezekiel the Tragedian recounts that it was his mother who told Moses about his descent: 'My mother brought me to the princess' palace, after telling me all about my lineage and God's gifts' (*Exagoge* 33-35).

[46] VanderKam, *Book of Jubilees*, 118-20.

[47] E.g., Ezekiel the Tragedian, *Exagoge* 37; Philo, *De Vita Mosis* 1.20-24; Acts 7.22. Cf. Berger, *Jubiläen*, p. 539. See also the article by A. Hilhorst in this collection.

[48] Cf. K. Müller, 'Die hebräische Sprache der Halacha als Textur der Schöpfung: Beobachtungen zum Verhältnis von Tora und Halacha im Buch der Jubiläen', in: H. Merklein, K. Müller, and G. Stemberger (eds), *Bibel in jüdischer und christlicher Tradition* (BBB 38), Frankfurt 1993, 157-76, esp. 161 note 6.

sees as being erratic, troubled generations.[49] This could be seen in conjunction with the fact that during these generations, the earth was divided (cf. *Jub* 8.9-9.15; 10.27-36), the Tower of Babel was built (cf. *Jub* 10.19-26), and evil spirits began to have an influence on Noah's grandchildren (*Jub* 10.1-15). As a consequence of the collapse of the Tower, the knowledge of the Hebrew language was lost (*Jub* 12.25; cf. *Jub* 10.26). The antediluvian patriarchs Kenan and Jared are also omitted from the chain of tradition. This is possibly due to the fact that Kenan was associated with Cain, and Jared is associated with the Watchers, because in his days they came down to earth.

The *halakhic* instructions that are written in the books of the fathers are about several subjects. Enoch wrote down 'the signs of the sky in accord with the fixed pattern of their months so that mankind would know the seasons of the years according to the fixed patterns of each of their months' (*Jub* 4.17). He also taught the law of the first fruits (*Jub* 7.38-39; cf. *Jub* 7.35-37). Noah wrote down all the kinds of medicine which would preclude the evil spirits from pursuing Noah's children (*Jub* 10.12-14). When he was in the house of Potiphar, Joseph remembered Abraham's words 'that no one is to commit adultery with a woman who has a husband' (*Jub* 39.6). The purpose of linking the *halakhic* instructions to the chain of tradition was obviously to anchor those instructions that are important for the author of *Jubilees* in the time of the Patriarchs.[50] In fact the *halakhah* of *Jubilees* is immanent to the creation.[51] The *halakhah* written in the books of the Patriarchs is on various occasions said to be derived from the teachings of the angels. Enoch wrote down his testimony 'as we [the angels] had told him' (*Jub* 4.18). Noah wrote 'everything (just) as we [the angels] had taught him' (*Jub* 10.13; cf. *Jub* 10.10) in a book. It was the Angel of the Presence who taught Abraham Hebrew in order to enable him to study the books of his fathers (*Jub* 12.25-27). Joseph himself

---

[49] Cf. Halpern-Amaru, *Empowerment*, 21.

[50] K. Berger, *Das Buch der Jubiläen* (JSHRZ 5.3), Gütersloh 1981, 279; S. Rosenkranz, 'Vom Paradies zum Tempel', in: S. Lauer and H. Ernst (eds), *Tempelkult und Tempelzerstörung (70 n. Chr.): Festschrift für Clemens Thoma zum 60. Geburtstag* (Judaica et Christiana 15), Bern 1995, 27-131, esp. 36; B. Ego, 'Heilige Zeit—heiliger Raum—heiliger Mensch: Beobachtungen zur Struktur der Gesetzesbegründung in der Schöpfungs- und Paradiesgeschichte des Jubiläenbuches', in: M. Albani, J. Frey, and A. Lange (eds), *Studies in the Book of Jubilees* (TSAJ 65), Tübingen 1997, 207-19, esp. 207.

[51] Cf. *Jub* 12.25-27, where Hebrew is called 'the language of the creation'. Müller, 'Hebräische Sprache', 165.

remembered that for committing adultery, heaven had ordained the death penalty (*Jub* 39.6). This means that the *halakhah* was ultimately anchored in the order of heaven.[52]

Moses is placed within the authoritative written tradition that began with Enoch before the flood and extended through the patriarchal period to Moses' time. All patriarchs contributed to this written tradition and they transmitted it to their favourite sons. The full law would be recorded in Moses' time.[53]

6. *Final remarks*

The comparison between *Jub* 47.1-9 and Exod 1.22-2.10 showed that the narrative structure runs more or less parallel in both versions. However, the structure of the marriage and birth report is not taken over. As far as the wording is concerned, the author of *Jubilees* sometimes reproduces the text of Exodus quite literally, but he also changes his model at other places. He omits certain phrases and passages, and he adds others, while he also modifies passages that run parallel. The author of *Jubilees* is a careful reader of the biblical text. This text poses some difficulties to him (e.g., blanks, inconsistencies). With his rewriting he tries to solve these problems. I point to the relocation of Exod 1.22, the omission of the marriage report, the naming of the characters, the stay of Amram in Canaan, and several of the variations in the report of the abandonment of Moses (Exod 2.3-10; cf. *Jub* 47.3-9). Sometimes the alterations in the rewriting are in line with biblical data (e.g., the naming of the characters). However, sometimes they are not, and in these cases the author of *Jubilees* is able to put his own bias in the text. I point not only to the periodization of history, but also to the omission of the marriage report, and Moses' education by his father.

---

[52] This is, in fact, in line with the mention of the 'heavenly tablets' in *Jubilees* at other places (*Jub* 3.10; 4.5; 5.13-14; 6.31, 35; 16.3, 9; 19.9; 23.32; 24.33; 30.19-22; 31.32; 32.21-22). Several *halakhot* can be found on the heavenly tablets. For a study on the heavenly tablets see F. García Martínez, 'The Heavenly Tablets in the Book of *Jubilees*', in: Albani, Frey, and Lange, *Studies in the Book of Jubilees*, 243-60.

[53] Cf. VanderKam, *Book of Jubilees*, 120.

HEARING THE STORY OF MOSES IN PTOLEMAIC EGYPT: ARTAPANUS ACCOMMODATES THE TRADITION

Rob Kugler

Although hardly an all-sufficient explanation for the violence committed in recent years by some minority religious groups, literalist readings of sacred texts in the face of culturally pluralistic challenges have long played a part in engendering extremism in the name of God. Knowing that obliges those of us who study the compositional and interpretive histories of religious texts to identify and lift up the constructive ways religionists have wielded their sacred texts in the face of the threat of hegemonic pluralism. This essay, offered in honor of Prof. Gerard Luttikhuizen, points to one such instance, the rewriting of the Moses story from a Ptolemaic-era Egyptian Jew called Artapanus.

1. *Artapanus on Moses: An overview of the account and its genre, provenance and date*

Eusebius's *Praeparatio Evangelica* and Clement's *Stromata* preserve fragments of this striking work. Three portions survive.[1] The first two provide an etymology for the name Jews and an overview of the sojourns of Abraham and Joseph in Egypt.[2] The third fragment, our focus, is the longest.

---

[1] Fragment 1 appears in *Praep. Ev.* 9.18.1; fragment 2 is found in *Praep. Ev.* 9.23.1-4; and fragment 3 is taken from *Praep. Ev.* 9.27.1-37 (with parallel material to 23-25 in Clement, *Stromata* 1.23.154.2-3). Note that Alexander Polyhistor (mid-first century BCE) provided the summaries recited by Eusebius; thus we have no verbatim extracts of Artapanus' own work. The edition used in preparing this essay is that of Holladay 1983.

[2] The first fragment only provides a (mostly inexplicable) etymology for the name Jews ('Hermiouth') and an account of Abraham's journey to Egypt where he taught Pharaoh astrology and remained for twenty years, after which time he returned to Syria while others who traveled with him there remained to enjoy Egypt's prosperity. Fragment 2 tells Joseph's story, repeating elements of Genesis 37.39-47. It describes his rise to power in Egypt and his accomplishments as a cultural patron in ancient Egypt.

The account rehearses Moses' story according to Exodus but adds much to it. It begins by explaining that Merris, a barren daughter of Pharaoh betrothed to an Egyptian named Chenephres, took as her own a child of the Jews and named him Moses. As an adult he earned the name Mousaios (the mythical Greek poet of Thrace), but according to Artapanus he was the *teacher* of Orpheus, not his son or disciple as was normally the case according to Greek literature. The fragment then notes that Moses was a cultural benefactor, giving Egypt ships, means for lifting stones, water-drawing and fighting devices, philosophy and the division of land in Egypt. He also gave sacred writings to the priests of Egypt and assigned gods as animals. Moses did these things to maintain the stability of Pharaoh's rule, who by this point in the story was Merris' husband, Chenephres. As a result the masses loved Moses, the priests gave him 'divine honor,' and he was called Hermes because of his skill at interpreting the scriptures. Chenephres became jealous and sought to destroy Moses by sending him as the commander of an army of ill-prepared and poorly-equipped farmers against the advancing Ethiopians. Moses and his army, however, endured successfully a ten-year war. In Moses' honor the army founded a city and consecrated the ibis to it. The Ethiopians themselves were won over by Moses and it is he who taught them circumcision. Chenephres continued to be jealous of Moses, and when Moses suggested in Memphis that Egypt adopt a breed of oxen for its tilling capacity, Chenephres sought to take credit for the innovation by naming a bull of the breed Apis and dedicating a temple to it, and having the beasts consecrated by Moses buried in Memphis 'to conceal the [good] ideas of Moses.' This too only created more honor for Moses: as any reader in Egypt would have known, the slain bull was honored by the Memphites with the Apis necropolis. Thus Chenephres plotted again to kill Moses by sending him with the assassin Chanethothes to bury the body of the now-deceased Merris. Aaron learned of the plot and warned Moses so that he was able to slay Chanethothes instead.

Thus Moses fled to Arabia where he met Raguel and married Raguel's daughter. Then Moses foiled Raguel's wish to make war on Egypt out of concern for the safety of his countrymen. Meanwhile, Chenephres died for his opposition to the Jews. Back in Arabia Moses was confronted in the wilderness by God and commanded to set the Jews free from Egyptian rule. When Moses came to Pharaoh with his brother Aaron and his intentions became known, Pharaoh imprisoned him, but God opened the prison to release Moses and he went to the palace where he met with the king. When at the king's command Moses whispered the name of God in the ear of the king, the king died, only to be immediately revived by a generous Moses. After writing the name of God and sealing it to keep it from harming others, Moses used the rod provided by God to direct against Egypt the full range of plagues to gain his people's release. After the requisite series of plagues Pharaoh let the people go and they left Egypt with legitimately procured supplies from the Egyptians. They then miraculously passed through the sea dry-shod under Moses' leadership while Pharaoh's pursuing army suffered a fiery-watery death. Fleeing into the wilderness Moses and the people were sustained there with manna from heaven.

For obvious reasons there is little disagreement that this is the work of an Egyptian Jew.[3] Its intense interest in Egyptian religious traditions suggests an origin in the Memphite region,[4] and its apparent respect for religious boundaries and balances reflects a conscious appreciation of the Ptolemaic policy of religious tolerance.[5]

It is also generally agreed that the work was likely in circulation among the Jews of Egypt by around the middle of the second century BCE.[6] This was a period of relative political stability in the Ptolemaic empire, but of considerable political uncertainty for the Jews within the imperial realm. This unease was the result of Onias having sided with Philometor's widow, Cleopatra II, in her struggle for the throne with Physcon (who assumed power as Ptolemy VIII Euergetes II in 145 BCE). Only because Physcon had the wisdom to marry Cleopatra, his brother's widow, did the crisis end and were the parties to it spared further punishment, the Jews under Onias' command included. The result, in any case, for Jews throughout Egypt was renewed concern to appease the new Ptolemaic ruler; one obvious way to do so was to

---

[3] This in spite of the observation that Artapanus' name 'is of Persian origin, and this may point to a mixed descent' (Holladay 1983, 189).

[4] That the work comes not from Alexandria, but from the *chora*, is in any case widely accepted; see, for example, Collins 2000, 39. On the importance of Memphis for Egyptian religious traditions, see Thompson 1988.

[5] On the Ptolemaic openness to the cultures of others, see especially Samuel 1983, and further comments below.

[6] The text's dependence on the LXX places it after the middle of the third century BCE and Polyhistor's acquaintance with it requires it to have gained some breadth of distribution before 60 BCE. A handful of other indicators have assured most observers that the work was completed before the last third of the second century BCE. For a summary of arguments regarding the treatise's date of composition, see Collins 2000, 38-9.

seek the stability and prosperity of his kingdom lest he hold Onias'
mistaken allegiance against them.

With respect to genre, although it does not evince every one of the
elements of a biography or romance, the Moses account is perhaps best
described as a mixture of the two. Like a romance it entails the pairing
of two partners (here Moses and the people of Israel), travel toward
a destination while under threat, and a denouement that brings the
partners to the fulfillment of their happy fate. At the same time, the
tale evokes the biographical genre in that it relates Moses' life history
with the added effect of cultivating in auditors a virtue ascribed to the
story's hero, notably Moses' concern for the stability and prosperity
of the state in which one dwells.[7]

2. *Constructing the receptive context for Artapanus' account of Moses*

What in the experience of Jews in Egypt might have prompted an
author to compose this sort of account of Moses' life? What does the
account indicate about its implied audience? Thanks to the enormous
wealth of papyri unearthed in the Egyptian *chora* over the last century
and a half we may answer this question with considerably more detail
than is usually the case in speculating about ancient audiences. Indeed,
the broad range of papyrological and archaeological evidence provides
material first for some basic insights into the life of all ethnicities
resident in Ptolemaic Egypt.[8] On the strength of that evidence the

---

[7] This view of the genre of Artapanus' work is surely to be regarded as unusual,
but it simply joins an already long line of commentators who, reflecting the difficulty
of the matter, offer sharply competing proposals on this topic. See, for example
Holladay 1977, 215-18 (and Holladay 1983, 190-1) for a description of it as a 'historical romance'; Collins 2000, 39-40 has dubbed it 'competitive historiography';
and Koskenniemi 2002, 18 note 3 regards it as a 'romantic history.' What all of
these commentators seem to overlook or underplay is the distinctly biographical
character of the Moses account, and the possibility that audiences may have sensed
in this the contours of a Greco-Roman romance narrative, even without a pairing of
two individuals as lovers. That such genre-bending and genre-blending was actually
intended by an author can hardly be certain, but it does seem quite possible, even
likely, that receptors of the text would have observed these genre elements just as
we do. That such an authorial strategy or audience perception gives rise in part to
a text's capacity to move an audience and endure over time is the insight of Hans
Robert Jauss (1982).

[8] For the Jewish experience in particular see the papyri presented in Tcherikover
and Fuks 1957-64 (henceforth *CPJ*); inscriptions which add to the evidentiary base

classical historian Alan Samuel has observed that all ethnicities living under Ptolemaic rule in Egypt were subject to and beneficiaries of the Ptolemies' conservative commitment to maintaining the status quo in the local economy, and likewise to permitting without interference the perpetuation of ethnic literatures, religions, and art.[9] Samuel's analysis of economic policy in Ptolemaic Egypt reveals the pursuit of stasis as the basic principle behind the rulers' actions and thought in all areas of human endeavor.[10] With respect to religious matters, for instance, the Ptolemies confined their adaptation of Greek divinities to Egyptian norms to matters of appellation alone; otherwise they preserved the native religious practices and encouraged Egyptians and other resident aliens to do likewise.

This policy is unsurprising given the widely-held conviction in the ancient world that goods of all kinds were limited in nature.[11] The

---

are provided in Horbury and Noy 1992 (henceforth *CIJ*). This body of evidence is due for reassessment, since especially Tcherikover and Fuks applied principles of selection that we now know too narrowly defined the pool of papyri that pertain to Jewish life in Egypt.

[9] Samuel 1983. Note that Samuel thinks—probably correctly—that this basic principle is rooted, in turn, in the Macedonians' appreciation of Aristotelian and Platonic notions of the state as an entity that flourished best when it was static and the individual lived in subordination to the state and its goal of maintaining a steady status quo.

[10] Samuel 1984, 48-9, observes (chiefly on the basis of the *Revenue Laws* of Ptolemy Philadelphus) a resistance to pursuing economic expansion even when population growth required it or technological advances permitted it. In pursuing a policy of maintaining static agricultural outputs the Ptolemies either eschewed technical advances or used them only to reach the goals established by the productivity levels they discovered upon conquering Egypt. For instance, Samuel notes that although a number of advances were available throughout the period, only a handful actually appear in the sources (e.g., the Archimedian screw as an aid to a pumping device, and this is datable only to the late Hellenistic period at best). Likewise, when growing populations challenged the limits of their existing local economies, the Ptolemaic solution was not to expand that local economy, but to relocate a portion of the populace to another region where their needs could be met without economic expansion.

[11] For the classic study of the notion of 'limited good,' see Foster 1965. That the concept was more generally dispersed in the ancient human imagination is apparent from quotes like the following from Aristotle in *Nichomachean Ethics* 1106b29: 'Again, it is possible to fail in many ways (for evil belongs to the class of the unlimited, as the Pythagoreans conjectured, and good to that of the limited), while to succeed is possible only in one way (for which reason also one is easy and the other difficult—to miss the mark easy, to hit it difficult); for these reasons also, then, excess and defect are characteristic of vice, and the mean of virtue.' For more extensive proof of the power of this notion in the Greek social and political philosophy that shaped Ptolemaic policy, see *Nichomachean Ethics*, Book V and *Politics*, Book I, as suggested by Samuel himself in a related vein (16)!

state, the economy, culture, and religion were all natural organisms of limited scope, determined in their natures. The proper goal of human interaction in these areas of life was therefore to maintain the balances already in place among them. So in economic life to increase inordinately one's wealth or to expand an existing economy were actions that violated the natural order of things and harmed the common good. Likewise, to adjust the 'religious economy' through hegemonic claims which actually reduced allegiance to one god for the sake of another disturbed the natural order. Obviously, this basic principle had enormous implications for religious thought and practice in a pluralistic context like the Memphite region, and concomitantly, for the sort of challenges that in particular a Jewish community might have faced in that context with its sense of being chosen by the one God.

The Herakleopolis papyri support this general observation about the Ptolemaic concern for stasis, and they add nuance and detail to it. The papyri are the correspondence between Jewish citizens of Herakleopolis and the leaders of the municipality's Jewish *politeuma*.[12] They confirm that at least the Jews in this part of Egypt—close to Memphis and its religious center—embraced the notion of limited good and the Ptolemaic passion for economic, cultural, and religious stasis. In almost all cases the appeals from citizens to the rulers of the *politeuma* had to do with the failure of a party to meet his or her contractual obligations, whether they be pecuniary interests or the apparently more consuming passion for maintaining proper balance in human relationships. In *P. Köln* Inv. 21038 (date to June or July 134) the complainant asks the rulers to require a family, two of whose members he cared for during an illness, to recompense him with time-limited household assistance from one of their daughters. In *P. Köln* Inv. 21046 (date to March 134) the petitioner seeks the assistance of the *politeuma*'s rulers in settling the case of an unsolved death or murder of a servant. The concern is not so much to achieve justice for the deceased as to provide the survivors some remuneration from the responsible parties for the loss.[13] Without any economic interests, in *P. Heid.* Inv. G 4927 (dated 7 October 135) 'Andronicus of the *politeuma*' petitioned the rul-

---

[12] See Cowey and Maresch 2001 for the papyri. Throughout this essay the papyri are cited by their titles and numbers as they are presented in Cowey and Maresch.

[13] The petitioner bids the rulers to take the matter in hand ὡς ἡμεῖς μὲν τευξό-μεθα τοῦ δικαίου, 'so that we achieve justice' (lines 29-30).

ers to call before them Nicharcus, a non-Jew and inhabitant of the wharf area. Andronicus wanted the leaders of the *politeuma* to enter a judgment against Nicharcus for having publicly cursed Andronicus before other citizens of the *politeuma* and non-Jews as well. Andronicus clearly sees this slight by a non-Jew of low status (indicated by Nicharcus' residence in the wharf area) as a violation of his honor and seeks remediation of the imbalance created by the affront. A similar concern apparently lies behind *P. Vindob.* 57700 (dated 30 September 142): this records the appeal of a *politeuma* ruler in Peempasbytis to the ruler in Herakleopolis for help in settling an honor dispute between parties who fell into an alcohol-induced public cursing contest. A final piece of evidence that the Jewish community embraced the value of social stability and equitable distribution of honor appears in *P. Heid.* Inv. G 4877 (from *ca.* 135). Here the petitioner appeals from the local jail to the rulers of the *politeuma* for release. His argument is not that he was unjustly imprisoned, but that incarceration has accomplished its goal of drawing from him recompense for the wrong done to his neighbors. The imbalance his wrongdoing caused, whatever it may have been, has been corrected and he feels that there is no further purpose in his confinement.

That this shared commitment in the *chora* to stasis and stability likewise entailed respect for existing religious affiliations is also well attested by the Herakleopolis finds. Of first order significance is the very fact of the *politeuma* papyri, testifying as they do to the existence of this Jewish political-social organization in the cities and villages of Ptolemaic Egypt. The details reported in the papyri also bear witness to the freedom of religious groups to adhere to their ways in the *chora*. *P. Heid.* Inv. G 4931 (dated 12 January 134) shows that Jews observed their own marriage laws in lieu of those imposed on Greek citizens living in Egypt. *P. Köln* Inv. 21041 (dated 15 March 133), though demonstrating that the Jewish community adapted on occasion to Ptolemaic loan laws, reminds the reader that nonetheless the Ptolemies left the enforcement of such laws to the leaders of the separate Jewish community. *P. Vindob.* G 57704 (dated 6 July 135), though introducing the notion of swearing an oath, does say that the obliged party stands under compulsion according to the ancestral customs (see also *P. Köln* Inv. 21031, lines 7-8, 40). And *P. Vindob.* 57700 (dated 30 September 142) records the correspondence between rulers in Peempasbytis and Herakleopolis, indicating that we may speak of Jewish *politeumata* throughout the Memphite region, not just a single such community (see also *P. Vindob.* G 57706 [Penei] and *P. Münch.* III 1, 149 [Tebetnoi]).

Finally, we should also take into account the work of Dorothy Thompson on the religious character of the city of Memphis under the Ptolemies and its influence on the surrounding region.[14] By means of a much-to-be-emulated comparative and multicultural approach Thompson not only reveals the diverse religious economies that existed alongside the dominant Egyptian cults in the Memphite region; she also documents further the Ptolemaic policy of offering and requiring from others respect for the religious boundaries and balances the Ptolemies encountered upon asserting hegemony over the region and created by importing new populations into the area.

All in all then, a target or receiving audience in the Memphite region for Artapanus' account of Moses consisted of at least a few Jews who lived cheek to jowl with Egyptian neighbors and their cultural and religious claims; who saw themselves as engaged in a social, religious and cultural economy of limited goods and honor; and who were themselves permitted, and even encouraged, to pursue their own religious beliefs and practices in this larger context. But they were also compelled by Onias' opposition to Physcon to be particularly mindful—even publicly appreciative—of the different cultures around them, that of their neighbor Egyptians in particular.[15]

Here, however, is where Jews most closely associated with the native Egyptian population may have experienced tension with their environment. While the Ptolemaic and general limited-good ancient worldview depended on all parties in a pluralistic context adopting a laissez-faire stance vis-à-vis the alternative religious and ethnic claims of the neighbor, Judaism's monotheism and its scripturally-based self definition as the chosen people of the one God were intrinsically hegemonic. Reconciling these central notions of the Jewish faith with the demands of life in the pluralistic context of Ptolemaic Egypt—especially in one potentially hostile to Jews thanks to Onias' misplaced support of Philometor—must have presented a serious challenge to many Jews trying to make their way in Ptolemaic Egypt. Indeed, it could have promoted a religious extremism not unlike what we often witness in

---

[14] In introducing Memphis to her readers, Thompson quotes *P. Oxy.* 2332.531, which describes Memphis as the city 'which gave birth to the gods' (4).

[15] See Appendix for further discussion of the profile of Egyptian Jews who were most inclined to appreciate Artapanus' account.

the contemporary context, including rigid readings of sacred traditions as a defense against the dominant culture's or plural cultures'
hegemony.

3. Receiving Artapanus in mid-second century BCE Herakleopolis

Extremism, though, was not Artapanus' response. His solution for
Andronicus-of-injured-pride and the rulers of the *politeumata* in Peempasbytis and Herakleopolis was not to offer refuge in rigid inerrantist
or literalist readings of their sacred traditions, but to provide instead
a bold, clever adaptation of those traditions to the new, demanding
circumstances, an adaptation that nonetheless did not surrender the
core of Jewish belief.

First, whether Artapanus intended it as such or not, the curiosity
of the work's mixed genres would almost certainly have earned it an
attentive audience from the outset. Literary theorists have long observed
that from antiquity to the present, texts that use familiar genres in
innovative ways are the works most likely to succeed in captivating
their audiences. So while an ancient audience in Herakleopolis, for
instance, might have expected to be entertained inasmuch as the plot
hints at a *romance*, they surely also were aware that as a *biography* it meant
also to persuade them to a particular virtue; that is, charmed by the
account's appeal they were likewise made captive to its argument.[16]

And at its most basic level, that argument was that recipients should
emulate Moses, a hero of the faith. The deviations from the Exodus
narrative especially see to this as they work consistently to burnish
Moses' image: as Mousaios he is not the student of Orpheus, but
his teacher instead; for all of his effort on Egypt's behalf the masses
loved him and the priests deemed him worthy of divine honor; for his
ability to interpret texts he earned the honorific name Hermes. And
what would one do to emulate Moses? Seek the stability and well-
being of one's Egyptian neighbors and respect and appreciate their
religious practices. After all, acting on the authority of their sovereign
God, Moses, a founder of their tradition established those religious
realities for Egypt.[17] He brought to Egypt the skills it needed for its

---

[16] As noted above, for this understanding of how genre-mixing and genre-bending functions, see Jauss 1982.

[17] Holladay 1977, 226 says of Moses as he appears in Artapanus' sights: 'It

glory: shipping to profit from the Nile; machines for lifting stones to
create the pyramids; the weapons unique to Egyptian war-making;
tools for drawing water for irrigation; and philosophy (thought by
many in the ancient world to have originated in Egypt).[18] He established the nomes of the land of Egypt that permitted it structure and
prosperity. He assigned to the nomes their respective gods to watch
over them and guard their success. He assigned the sacred writings
of the Egyptians to their priests. And he established the cults of the
dog, cat, and ibis for the Egyptian people. And all of these things he
did for the sake of guarding the stability of the monarchy and the
kingdom as a whole. And even after Pharaoh unreasonably became
his enemy, Moses continued to prosper Egypt by his own actions as
well as by those taken against him. He inspired his soldiers to found
a city and name it Hermes and under his influence they consecrated
the ibis to it. His suggestion of a breed of cattle to the Pharaoh for its
agricultural usefulness moved Pharaoh to institute the Apis cult and
Pharaoh's murder and burial of the bulls chosen by Moses established
the all-important animal necropolis in Memphis. After he was driven
from Egypt by the plot against his life, Moses thwarted his father-in-
law's plan to attack Egypt, and this out of regard for the people of the
land. And when upon returning to Egypt he whispered the name of
the God whom he served in the ear of Pharaoh and Pharaoh expired
at the sound of it Moses graciously revived Pharaoh. His flooding of
the Nile established for the first time the river's eternal pattern of
overflowing its banks to make fertile the surrounding alluvial plain.
And the rod he used to enact the plagues on Egypt inspired the rod
present in each Isis temple. Indeed, the narrative encouraged recipients
to accept the boundaries imposed on them by life in the Egyptian
chora under Ptolemaic rule, to live uncomplainingly within the limited
good world they were fated to inhabit, for it was one created by God
through Moses for that world's own good.

But with this Moses narrative Artapanus would have also reminded

---

becomes obvious that Artapanus' list [of Moses' benefactions for Egypt] has been
compiled to fit with the rest of his portrait of Moses as cult benefactor and political
leader who establishes *harmonia* successfully.'

[18] Holladay 1977, 223, observes that the list of cultural benefactions provided by
Moses is not so long as to make him an equal of Prometheus, thus a divine being,
but rather reveals his care for Egypt inasmuch as each is 'singularly beneficial to
Egypt.'

recipients that in spite of the legitimacy of their neighbors' religious choices and traditions, their God was still sovereign. This is especially true of the latter half of the fragment where it behaves most like biblical historiography and hews most closely to the Exodus narrative. Again, here the deviations from that well-known account were likely particularly formative of their recipients' imagination. The latter half of the fragment shows that not only did the God of Israel sponsor the religions of Egypt; when the practitioners of those religions were hostile to the people of Israel this God did not hesitate to take action against the perpetrators. Even in this limited good, static world that required respect for the neighbors' beliefs, the God of Israel remained master of the universe. It is the God of Moses who was in charge and who benefited or destroyed Egypt, its people, and its leader. This is the God who killed Chenephres for his abuse of the Jews. This is the God who answered Moses' prayer for a respite for the people from a fire without fuel. This is the God who commanded Moses to make war against Egypt to set the people free. This is the God who, at least according to Clement's fragment of Artapanus, opened the doors of the prison in which Moses was restrained by Pharaoh. This is the God whose name, when whispered in someone's ear or disdained in its written form, can slay them. This is the God who provided Moses with a rod that had power over Isis, the Egyptian divinity of earth and water. This is the God who subordinated and shamed Egypt's priests when they thought to challenge him. And this is the God who delivered the people led by Moses through the miracle of the parted sea. Here, in subtle changes to and embellishments of the scriptural narrative, the audience would have encountered a story that assures the absolute superiority of the God of Israel over all other powers and religious realities.[19] Although they may be legitimate—indeed their sponsorship by the God of Israel through Moses assures the recipient that they are—Egyptian religions and their demands remain subordinate to the God who made them in the first place.

---

[19] Among the changes the most significant might be use of the rod as the instrument of control throughout (to subordinate Isis). Among the embellishments one in particular stands out, though it has not, to my knowledge, been recognized as yet. The relationship between Moses and Pharaoh seems to be modeled on that between David and Saul, as if to say that this is not a contest between one who is of God and one who is not, but between two who are both under God's control. It goes the hegemonic claim of the Exodus narrative that Pharaoh is subject to God one better.

In short it seems quite likely that Artapanus' work, often sold short
by commentators as naïve, pagan, or at least syncretistic, in fact worked
powerfully to assuage Egyptian Jews' natural anxieties relative to the
legitimacy of their own self understanding as the chosen people of the
one God. By following the example of Moses they could happily grant
legitimacy to their Egyptian neighbors' religious practices and even
put their shoulder to the plow that prospered Egypt as a whole. But
at the same time they could rest assured that, within the boundaries
of their own community and imaginations, they remained the chosen
people of the one God, the master of all the universe. They could be
certain that push-come-to shove, their God would see to them in a
pinch. Thus Artapanus' response to a stiff cultural challenge was not
an inerrantist or literalist retreat into his sacred texts that might have
engendered religious extremism in his audience. Instead, he offered a
richly interpretive reading of his people's most revered traditions that
authorized them to adapt to the competing, dominant culture while
remaining faithful to their own tradition. I suspect we could learn
from this ancient Jew, were we to listen to him well.

APPENDIX

The evidence permits us to speak even more specifically of who among
the Jews of Egypt would have been inclined to concern themselves with
the sentiments of their non-Jewish neighbors, that is, who might have
found Artapanus' account particularly suggestive. Those least inclined
to accommodate the Egyptian neighbors would have been Jewish soldiers of all ranks who often received cleruchies and reduced tax burdens
from the Ptolemies for their services. As a result of their nearly exclusive
affiliation with the Greek rulers they did not integrate well with local
Egyptian culture (see *CPJ* 18-32; *CIJ* 1531, cited in Barclay 1996, 23
note 9). The remaining groups, however, *were* probably entangled with
Egyptian culture and life and so were likely target or receiving audiences for Artapanus' work. Poor farm workers—from day laborers to
peasant owners of small plots of land—had many opportunities to integrate with their Egyptian neighbors with whom they shared the lowest
rungs on the socioeconomic status ladder (see *CPJ* 9, 13, 14, 36, 38,
39, 133, cited in Barclay 1996, 24 for evidence of this wide association
between Jews and Egyptians). Another group included administrators
for the Ptolemaic government and some artisans (e.g., potters) who,
in spite of their close association with the Ptolemies, were oriented in

their daily activities mostly to the local population, and so were also particularly 'deeply enmeshed in Egyptian society' (Barclay 1996, 24; in support of this claim Barclay cites *CPJ* 12; 25; *CPJ* 1 section V, and *CIJ* 1443, and especially *CPJ* 46 which indicates a Jewish family [two members of which have Egyptian names] shared its crockery with an Egyptian family; among the bureaucrats we find police officers and chiefs as well as tax farmers for the Ptolemaic government). Lastly, of course, there may have been some Jewish slaves still on the scene in mid-second century BCE Egypt (in spite of the story in *Letter of Aristeas* 12-27 that suggests Ptolemy II Philadelphus freed the Jewish slaves). These Jews, too, would have had reason for intimacy with aspects of the culture native to their home.

The recent papyri finds at Herakleopolis support this taxonomy of Jewish groups in Egypt. One text, *P. Vindob.* G 57701, dated to 135/34 BCE, is an appeal to the rulers of the *politeuma* for help in a marriage-related real estate transaction from 'Polyktor . . . of the Macedonians and a member of the cavalry of Demetrius.' This soldier was clearly a Jew inasmuch as he sought judgment from the Jewish *politeuma*. Yet he made certain to identify himself explicitly by his regimental associa-tion—the Macedonians—and to name his commander, Demetrius, likely a Greek himself. With this language Polyktor unmistakably telegraphed his desire to link himself to his Ptolemaic masters and to disassociate himself from his Jewish roots. Given this, there is little left to the imagination regarding his view of local Egyptians. On the other hand two papyri (*P. Köln* Inv. 21031, dated 20 June 132; *P. Vin-dob.* G 57704, dated 6 July 135) indicate that Jews made legal oaths, a practice not easily attributed to Ptolemaic influence and unusual among Jews, but more frequently observed among Egyptians (see, for example, *P. Duke* Inv. 754 R [scriptorium.lib.duke.edu/papyrus/records/ 754r.html]; *P. Duke* Inv. 11 R [scriptorium.lib.duke.edu/papyrus/records/ 11r.html]). Unfortunately the social status of the parties to the disputes is not entirely clear, but the casual use of oaths indicates their assimilation of some Egyptian practices, and thus close association with their Egyptian neighbors.

Bibliography

Barclay, J.M.G. 1992. 'Manipulating Moses: Exodus 2.10-15 in Egyptian Judaism and the New Testament,' in: R. Carroll (ed.), *Test as Pretext: Essays in Honour of Robert Davidson* (JSOTSup 138), Sheffield, 28-46.

Barclay, J.M.G. 1996. *Jews in the Mediterranean Diaspora: From Alexander to Trajan (323 BCE-117 CE)*, Edinburgh.

Collins, J.J. 2000. *Between Athens and Jerusalem: Jewish Identity in the Hellenistic Diaspora* (2nd edition), Grand Rapids, MI.

Cowey, J.M.S. and K. Maresch (eds). 2001. *Urkunden des Politeuma der Juden von Herakleopolis (144/3-133/2 v. Chr.) (P. Polit. Iud.): Papyri aus Sammlungen von Heidelberg, Köln, München und Wien* (Papyrologica Coloniensia 29), Wiesbaden.

Foster, G.M. 1965. 'Peasant Society and the Image of Limited Good,' *American Anthropologist* 67 (1965) 293-315.

Holladay, C.L. 1977. *Theios Aner in Hellenistic Judaism: A Critique of the Use of this Category in New Testament Christology* (SBLDS 40), Missoula, MT.

Holladay, C.L. 1983. *Fragments from Hellenistic Jewish Authors*, i, *Historians* (SBL Texts and Translations Pseudepigrapha Series 10/20), Chico, CA.

Horbury, W. and D. Noy. 1992. *Jewish Inscriptions of Graeco-Roman Egypt*, Cambridge.

Jauss, H.R. 1982. *Toward an Aesthetic of Reception* (Theory and History of Literature 2), Minneapolis, MN.

Koskenniemi, E. 2002. 'Greeks, Egyptians and Jews in the Fragments of Artapanus,' *Journal for the Study of the Pseudepigrapha* 13 (2002) 17-31.

Samuel, A. 1983. *From Athens to Alexandria: Hellenism and Social Goals in Ptolemaic Egypt* (Studia Hellenistica 26), Louvain.

Tcherikover, V. and A. Fuks. 1957-64. *Corpus Papyrorum Judaicarum*, 3 vols., Cambridge, MA.

Thompson, D. 1998. *Memphis Under the Ptolemies*, Princeton.

EGYPT AS THE SETTING FOR *JOSEPH AND ASENETH*: ACCIDENTAL OR DELIBERATE?

János Bolyki

The Jewish Hellenistic romance *Joseph and Aseneth*[1] is set in Egypt, its protagonists are mostly Egyptians, and its heroine is the daughter of the chief priest of Heliopolis. The plot is based on Gen 41.45: 'Pharaoh gave Joseph the name Zaphenath-paneah; and he gave him Asenath daughter of Potiphera, priest of On, as his wife.' In this famous Old Testament narrative, Joseph is a slave thrust into prison, but Pharaoh, impressed by his ability to interpret dreams, appoints him as his counsellor and charges him with the task of collecting the harvest for seven years and distributing it for the following seven years, and finally he also marries him to Aseneth. We have little information about when the romance was composed,[2] the exact intentions of its author[3] or its targeted readership;[4] consequently, any information that helps to define its provenance will facilitate a better understanding of the book. All suggestions are important, whether they concern historical, statistical or material evidence, the period of writing, the religious historical background, or the literary character of the work. Such information, however, will only shed light on the circumstances of the composition, and then only from the perspective of provenance.

Our object in this paper goes beyond this. Not only do we want to demonstrate that this romance was certainly written in Egypt, but also that it must have been written in Egypt on account of its deepest level of meaning. We will first address traditional issues, such as vocabulary statistics, material evidence, authorial intent, situation of the first read-

---

[1] References are to the chapter and verse division of Philonenko's edition: M. Philonenko, *Joseph et Aséneth*, Leiden 1968. The expansions by C. Burchard, *Joseph und Aseneth*, Gütersloh 1983, are specifically noted. Henceforth referred to as *JosAsen*.

[2] Researchers have dated it to between 150 BC (G. Bohak) and AD 3-400 (R.S. Kraemer), reflecting uncertainty.

[3] We shall duly see the differences in explaining authorial intent, i.e. as a 'roman à clef', a missionary tract, a family saga, a treatise serving the internal affirmation of the community, a writing of solar epiphany and mystery.

[4] Most students believe the Egyptian Jewish Diaspora as the targeted readership, though some think it might have been meant for proselytes.

ers, and literary analogies; we will then examine the existential motifs
of the romance, proceeding from a study by Gerard Luttikhuizen.[5]

Overview of the history of research

Although most scholars believe that the romance was written in Egypt,
there are exceptions. Let us first consider the majority opinion. C.
Burchard, who edited the text and is one of its major experts, addresses
the question of provenance in several of his works.[6] He believes that
the book was written in Egypt because the plot is set in Egypt, the
heroine, the circumstances, and several recurring expressions ('the gods
of Egypt', 'Egyptian idol gods') are Egyptian; finally, the romance's
material concerning Joseph's presence in Egypt is identical with that
of Gen 37.39-50. 'Eine jüdisch-hellenistische Missionsschrift, die von
einer Ägypterin handelt, die sich von den ägyptischen Göttern zu dem
einen Gott bekehrt, sollte in Ägypten entstanden sein.'[7] He notes that
other alternative localisations have to date not been proven. 'Egypt
is the most likely birthplace of a tale extolling the conversion of an
Egyptian chief priest's daughter and showing the children of Israel
involved in local political strife.'[8] M. Philonenko, another editor of
the text, agrees with Burchard with regard to the provenance of the
romance. He claims that the story of Joseph and Aseneth is a 'roman à
clef' that was written in the Jewish Diaspora of Egypt by a 'Juif d'origine
égyptienne'.[9] However, he locates the romance not in Alexandria but
in rural Egypt. D. Sänger, who considers the romance as a writing
composed in order to reinforce the identity of a community of Jews and
those Egyptian proselytes who had joined them, as well as to regulate
the possibilities of mixed marriages between them, agrees with the
theory of an Egyptian provenance.[10] G. Bohak takes the firmest stand

---

[5] G.P. Luttikhuizen, 'The Hymn of Jude Thomas, the Apostle, in the Country of
Indians (*ATh* 108-113)', in: J. Bremmer (ed.), *The Apocryphal Acts of Thomas*, Louvain
2001, 101-14. Let me here acknowledge all that I have learned from the scholar
being honoured, and that I very much appreciated the hospitality of the Luttikhuizens
during my stays in Groningen.

[6] C. Burchard, *Untersuchungen zu Joseph und Aseneth*, Tübingen 1961; Id., *Gesammelte
Studien zu Joseph und Aseneth*, Leiden 1996.

[7] Burchard, *Untersuchungen*, 142.

[8] Burchard, *Gesammelte Studien*, 307.

[9] Philonenko, *Joseph et Aséneth*, 61ff., 101, 109.

[10] D. Sänger, 'Bekehrung und Exodus: Zum jüdischen Traditionshintergrund von

behind the Egyptian provenance,[11] dating the book between 160 and 145 BC, a decisive period in the history of the Egyptian Jews. Finally, we can refer to R. Chesnutt, who studied *JosAsen* from the perspective of mystery religions with reference to the motifs of 'conversion and rebirth' or 'heavenly food' (in chapters 10-17). In his opinion, 'virtually all specialists who have commented on the provenance of *JosAsen* have pointed to Egypt (...) Nothing militates against the idea that *JosAsen* was written in Egypt.'[12]

Let us now turn our attention to the minority opinion. P. Batiffol, who published *JosAsen* at the end of the nineteenth century, was not primarily interested in the provenance of the romance but its Christian background. He suggested the northern part of Asia Minor as a place of origin. Accepting several of Batiffol's points, E.W. Brooks nevertheless preferred Syria. V. Aptowitzer, who claimed that *JosAsen* was written originally not in Greek but in Hebrew, believed that it was composed in Palestine.[13] Recently, R.S. Kraemer has published a profound study based on a wide range of sources.[14] She implies that the author was a Christian living in Syria in Late Antiquity, and in particular in a monastery where the spiritual influence of Ephraem Syrus could be felt. However interesting Kraemer's hypothesis is, I cannot subscribe to it because (as I have tried to demonstrate in a former study) the ethical attitudes in *JosAsen* are typically Hellenistic Jewish and not Christian.[15]

Statistics and the use of words

The noun 'Egypt' and its derivative adjective 'Egyptian' occur twenty-one times in the text of the romance. Nine of them refer to Joseph's

---

"Joseph und Aseneth"', *Journal for the Study of Judaism* 10 (1979) 11-36 at 35.

[11] G. Bohak, *Joseph and Aseneth and the Jewish Temple in Heliopolis*, Atlanta, Georgia 1996, 27-30.

[12] R. Chesnutt, *From Death to Life: Conversion in Joseph and Aseneth*, Sheffield 1995, 78-9.

[13] Chesnutt, *From Death to Life*, 76-80.

[14] R.S. Kraemer, *When Aseneth Met Joseph: A Late Antique Tale of the Biblical Patriarch and His Egyptian Wife Reconsidered*, New York/Oxford 1998, 286-93.

[15] J. Bolyki, '"Never Repay Evil with Evil": Ethical Interaction between the Joseph Story, the Novel *Joseph and Aseneth*, the New Testament and the Apocryphal Acts', in: F. García Martínez and G.P. Luttikhuizen (eds), *Jerusalem, Alexandria, Rome: Studies in Ancient Cultural Interaction in Honour of A. Hilhorst*, Leiden 2003, 41-53.

commission (collecting and distributing corn) or his wedding ceremony and the guests invited; in five cases, 'Egyptian' refers to the gods of Egypt, always derisively, from the point of view of the Jewish Diaspora in Egypt. As far as Joseph is concerned, it was part of his duty 'to go round the whole land of Egypt' (1.1). His rank was the 'ruler of all the land' of Egypt (ἄρχων, 4.8).[16] He had to ensure that no one in Egypt would die of famine (26.3). Though eating in the same room with Egyptians, he could sit at a separate table (7.1). He calls Pharaoh 'my father', who appointed him 'the supervisor of all the land of Egypt' (20.7 in Burchard's text). All leaders of Egypt were invited to his wedding banquet, and no work was allowed in the country until the celebration was finished (21.6-7). After Pharaoh's death, Joseph ruled (ἐβασίλευσεν) as a regent for Pharaoh's son; when he ascended to the throne, Joseph became the 'father' (foster father) of the new ruler. The young Joseph was so extraordinarily handsome that distinguished Egyptian women suffered much, 'indeed pushing' to make love with him, but Joseph rejected them out of hand (7.3-5).

Aseneth was also very beautiful, but was quite unlike the daughters of the Egyptians (1.7). In the same chapter, the text claims that the fame of her beauty spread through the land (looking at Egypt from without, vv. 9 and 13) as well as all around the land (looking at Egypt from within, including the countries maintaining contacts with Egypt). 'Egypt' and 'all the world' (οἰκουμένη) are used synonymously: in 1.13, Philolenko's shorter text has 'all the world', while Burchard's text has 'all Egypt'. As already mentioned, the romance often speaks of the gods of Egypt, though always derisively. Made of gold or silver, their effigies can be hung on walls (2.4). Their names and images can be inscribed on jewels (3.10); furthermore, they can be destroyed (11.3). Those that eat from the sacrifices offered to the gods 'transgress the law' and 'act impiously' (12.5).

To sum up, the use of words and imagery are closely related to Egypt; although they render its Egyptian provenance probable they do not exclude all other possibilities.

---

[16] References to chapter and verse divisions follow the (shorter) Philonenko edition.

Material evidence

We will begin our survey by referring to R.S. Kraemer, who is of the opinion that *JosAsen* was probably not written in Egypt. As a fair debater, she lists the material evidence that supports the views of her opponents rather than her own.[17] These she divides into two groups: (1) calendar references and (2) agricultural data. As far as calendar data are concerned, the events of 1.1 and 3.1 take place at the time of the summer solstice, which the author connects with the encounter between the young hero and heroine, the main event of the romance. On the basis of several facts, it is best to define the time of the plot of *JosAsen* as the period of autumn harvest. The reason is that Aseneth's parents bring dates, figs, pomegranates, and grapes from their land (4.4). This squares with ancient Egyptian produce. The rite, which is described in Greek tracts of magic, and which was practised at the time when the Nile inundation began to retreat, i.e. in the autumn, is roughly identical with the calendar date of *JosAsen* (1.1 and 3.1). Kraemer also refers to the fact that the fruit brought by Aseneth's parents appear in the mosaics of several synagogues, as part of the allegorical representation of autumn. The observation that certain army units in the battle scene of the romance lay in ambush in the bed of a brook—possibly because they dried out in the autumn—might be relevant here (24.16, 26.5). Also in relation to the agricultural produce listed in the romance (4.4), G. Bohak came to the conclusion that the recurring expression 'land of our heritage' (3.7, etc.) is also used for the area Pharaoh gave to the chief priest Onias IV for the purposes of the temple and as property. This supports an Egyptian provenance for the romance, because the author and his readers used the story about the patriarchs as a literary justification of their claims to the areas mentioned.[18]

The arguments in support of an Egyptian provenance proposed by C. Burchard are more theological in nature, although he does propose an argument of material and historical character worth considering: the firstborn son of the Pharaoh in the romance is betrothed to the daughter of the King of Moab (1.9). 'Moab' had by then long ceased to exist, and it actually refers to the Nabatean kingdom; based on

---

[17] Kraemer, *When Aseneth Met Joseph*,, 292 note 6, cf. ibid., 107 note 35.
[18] Bohak, *Joseph and Aseneth and the Jewish Temple in Heliopolis*, 64-7.

this piece of information, the story can be dated to around 100 BC, which fits in well with the Egyptian conditions. R. Chesnutt argues for an Egyptian provenance on the basis of the following material data: 'architecture, landscape, seasons, agriculture, furniture, and hygiene'.[19]

Clarification of a 'scandalous' biblical issue and its consequences

This issue is related to the purpose of writing the book. Gen 41 and following are unbiased about the marriage of the patriarch Joseph with an Egyptian, i.e. Gentile, girl. Such a relationship is exceptional even in the narratives of the patriarchs (e.g. Gen 24.41) because the Egyptians were not only Gentiles, but also the descendants of Ham whom Noah had cursed (Gen 9.22-27). History justified the practice, since endogamy was necessary for the survival of the Jewish Diaspora after the captivity (Tob 4.12). This was particularly so in Egypt where, in the period of Hellenism, a significant Jewish community lived, joined by a large number of Gentile proselytes.

In his book on Aseneth, V. Aptowitzer discusses the three answers Jewish theology gives to these issues.[20] (1) Aseneth was the daughter of Dinah, who had been raped (Gen 34). She was sent away from home and ended up in Egypt, where chief priest Pentephres and his wife adopted her. She was thus a descendant of Jacob, Joseph's niece in fact. (2) Aseneth saved Joseph from Pharaoh, disproving the accusations of Potiphar's wife. (3) Aseneth is a pious and upright woman who, like Ruth the Moabite, was accepted in the community of Israel. The problem is that the Aseneth in Genesis existed long before the romance itself, and the 'solutions' listed by Aptowitzer were devised even later, in Haggadic literature. *JosAsen* was written between the two, and sought answers to problems typically arising from the Egyptian Diaspora situation. To put it simply: those Egyptian Gentiles who, denying their gods, sought protection under the wings of the God of Israel[21] could fit into the community of Israel and join Israel as proselytes; marriage

---

[19] Chesnutt, *From Death to Life*, 80.
[20] V. Aptowitzer, 'Asenath, the Wife of Joseph: A Haggadic Literary-Historical Study', *Hebrew Union College Annual* 1 (1924) 239-306, especially 242-3.
[21] Aseneth herself is given the honorary title of 'City of Refuge' (15.6) by the prince of the angels, meaning that she became the prototype and ancestral mother of Gentile-proselytes joining the God of Israel. Cf. Burchard, *Gesammelte Studien*, 307.

with such partners was legal. In R. Chesnutt's opinion, the 'target community' for the romance cannot be defined rigidly or one-sidedly; it has something to say to both God-fearing Gentiles drawn to Jewish monotheism and Jews wanting to be reassured of the values of their faith. Nevertheless, an important punch line of the ancient author is that converted Gentiles should have equal rights with ethnically born Jews in the Jewish community.[22] Consequently, it is clear that the marriage of Joseph and Aseneth was no mere academic or abstract theological question for either the ancient author or his readers, but a daily and practical problem. Finally, one should be aware that this issue was especially important for the rather numerous Jewish Diaspora in Egypt; this, too, renders an Egyptian provenance probable.

Aspects of Egyptian religion

According to some scholars, the complexity of the romance is partly caused by elements of Hellenised Egyptian religion that appear in it with varying degrees of intensity. With respect to the relationship between astrology and religion, M. Philonenko regards it as a 'roman à clef'.[23] In his opinion, on the one hand, the name Aseneth contains the name of the Egyptian goddess Neith, and means 'belonging to Neith'.[24] According to Philonenko, this figure was later assimilated into the goddess Isis. On the other hand, Joseph personified the sun god, Helios. Pharaoh was considered to be the son of Re, the sun god, and he adopted Joseph as his son.[25] This is what Aseneth says as Joseph visits her: 'behold the sun is come to us from heaven in his chariot and has come into our house today' (6.5). Thus Philonenko believes that the romance is 'an astrological allegory'[26] reporting the encounter between Helios (represented by Joseph) and the goddess Neith (represented by Aseneth) at a certain point of time defined by Egyptian astrology. He also calls attention to the fact that the sun, moon and the eleven stars feature as an allegory of Joseph and his family in Joseph's dream in the Genesis story itself. Kraemer notes

---

[22] Chesnutt, *From Death to Life*, 264.

[23] Philonenko, *Joseph et Aséneth*, 61-79.

[24] Sänger, 'Bekehrung und Exodus', 13ff.

[25] 20.7 according to the longer version by Burchard.

[26] Philonenko, *Joseph et Aséneth*, 79ff. Chesnutt speaks of a 'solar epiphany' when discussing Philonenko's view (*From Death to Life*, 79).

that the seven virgins attending Aseneth (2.10-11; 17.4-5) represent the cosmos. This imagery occurs in Sumerian and Babylonian sources as well as the Mithraic cult, and was known and applied by Jews in Egypt, as the example of Philo demonstrates (*On the Creation of the World* 112).[27] *JosAsen* also notes that the virgins attending Aseneth 'were very beautiful, like the stars of heaven' (2.11). This also suggests an Egyptian provenance.

JosAsen, however, not only contains elements of Hellenised Egyptian religion, but could also be related to some Gnostic features. Philonenko therefore calls it not only a 'mystical' romance and 'roman à clef', but also 'a Gnostic drama'.[28] Thus the God of Israel is the 'Most High', who blesses Aseneth, the representative of the personification of Wisdom (17.5; 21.3). Aseneth thus becomes the daughter of the Most High (21.3). Her contrition, spiritual suffering and prayer parallel the conversion and prayer of the Gnostic Sophia or Pistis Sophia. And Joseph, whom the text calls Saviour (σωτήρ) (25.6), saves Aseneth/ Sophia. Philonenko himself admits that it is not 'pure' Gnosis that is present in the romance, rather a type of Gnosis related to the Old Testament and the consciousness of faith among the Egyptian Jewish community. As a matter of fact, the majority of scholars do not accept Philonenko's 'Gnostic drama' hypothesis. Luttikhuizen, for instance, does not even regard certain parts of Hermetic literature as Gnostic; in his view 'they belong to the Platonic *koine* of late antiquity.'[29]

All this concerns us insofar as the part of Gnostic literature related to Hermetic literature is demonstrably Egyptian in origin, and renders an Egyptian provenance for *JosAsen* probable. This is why K.-W. Tröger approaches the rebirth scenes of *JosAsen* through a review of the rebirth tract in Hermetic Gnosis (*Corpus Hermeticum* XIII). He considers this tract as certainly Egyptian: 'Ägypten ist ihr Ursprungsort (…) Vielleicht ist die Hermetik aus den ägyptischen Mysteriengemeinden entstanden. Gerade der Wiedergeburtstraktat (*Corpus Hermeticum* XIII).'[30]

---

[27] Kraemer, *When Aseneth Met Joseph,*, 118ff.
[28] Philonenko, *Joseph et Aséneth*, 83-9.
[29] Luttikhuizen, 'The Hymn of Jude Thomas', 101.
[30] K.-W. Tröger, 'Die hermetische Gnosis', in: Id., *Gnosis und Neues Testament: Studien aus Religionswissenschaft und Theologie*, Berlin 1973, 101.

Hellenistic Jewish narratives and Deuterocanonical wisdom literature

If we study the romance from the perspective of Hellenistic Jewish narratives and Deuterocanonical wisdom texts, we come to interesting results concerning provenance again. It can be observed that these writings always summarize their conclusions in a confession, which can inform the reader about life in the Hellenistic Jewish Diaspora. Without attempting to be complete, let us consider a few examples. In the *Book of Tobit*, the author has the angel Raphael state the lesson: 'Now therefore, when thou (= Tobit) didst pray, and Sara thy (future) daughter-in-law, I did bring the remembrance of your prayers before the Holy One: and when thou didst bury the dead, I was with thee likewise' (12.12). This sentence was probably interesting for those Diaspora Jews who practised their faith only within the family. What means would they have otherwise had, lacking not only a Temple but also a synagogue? The angelic apophthegm mentions two: private prayer and the proper burial of the members of one's family. The book of *Judith* was written in the period of the Maccabean wars, its readers were Jews who had returned to Palestine and even took up arms to fight the enemy. The main message of the book (its confession, as it were) is as follows: 'Woe to the nations that rise up against my kindred! The Lord Almighty will take vengeance of them' (16.17). The *Wisdom of Solomon* is a masterful work of wisdom literature influenced by Hellenism; it is addressed to those who want to hold on to the Old Testament traditions in a new intellectual climate. To this end, a knowledge of the new intellectual environment had to be coupled with its critique from the perspective of Jewish religion. This is why the author summarizes the essence of his book in this way: 'As for Wisdom, what she is, and how she came up, I will tell you, and will not hide the mysteries from you.' *Sirach*, another document of wisdom literature, was written from a somewhat more conservative point of view than the *Wisdom of Solomon*, but certainly with a view to the future of Israel. This is what it advises the reader: 'And put thy feet into her [Wisdom's] fetters, and thy neck into her chain' (6.24). The book of *Baruch* can be regarded as a prophetic sermon, exhorting the people to maintain the Wisdom/Torah: 'Hear, Israel, the commandments of life. (...) Thou hast forsaken the fountain of wisdom. (...) Learn where is wisdom (...) that thou mayest know also where is length of days' (3.9, 14). Finally, here is an example of heroism choosing martyrdom in the face of tyranny from an apocryphal writing, the *Martyrdom of*

Isaiah, which is part of the *Ascension of Isaiah*: 'You can take away from me nothing but the skin of my flesh' (5.10).

These observations may prove useful for understanding *JosAsen*. Our romance also contains didactic summaries. The summaries can be divided according to the two parts of the book: the marriage of Joseph and Aseneth (chapters 1-21) and the struggle between Joseph's brothers for and against him (chapters 22-29). The two apophthegms of the first part are about the roles of the protagonists: Joseph 'is ruler of all the land of Egypt' (4.8); and 'you shall no more be called Aseneth, but "City of Refuge" shall be your name (...) and within your walls those who give their allegiance to God in penitence will find security' (15.6). The important message of the second part is that the brothers of Joseph must not be hostile to one another in the land of Egypt: 'Do not repay evil for evil' (23.9; 28.4,14; 29.3). The Jewish Diaspora living there must not forget that they were not always oppressed there, but rather that they once had a leading role. Joseph is a symbol of political-economic leadership; Aseneth is the prototype of the Gentile-turned-Jewish proselytes. This, however, needs solidarity between the brothers; they cannot allow some of them to join with the evil son of Pharaoh against Joseph, the chosen one of God. All this is related to Egypt, and makes an Egyptian provenance probable.

Scholars who believe that an Egyptian origin for *JosAsen* is probable or certain on the basis of examining the Jewish Diaspora in Egypt find three ways of explaining the author's intention and the readers' anticipated response. The first explanation is that life in the Jewish Diaspora was *threatened*. D. Sänger[31] sees the political situation of Egyptian Jewry in the first century AD reflected in the romance, and this is how he infers the date of its composition. In his opinion, in order to understand the motive behind writing the romance we need to find serious conflicts between the Egyptian indigenous population, the Roman authorities, and the Jews living there, following periods of relative peace. In this respect, the period between 100 BC and AD 117 can come under consideration. On this basis, Sänger relates the writing of the Aseneth romance to three historical events: (1) the persecution beginning in 88 BC; (2) the pogrom that broke out in AD 38 and (3)

---

[31] Sänger, 'Bekehrung und Exodus', 11-36; Id., 'Erwägungen zur historischen Einordnung und zur Datierung von "Joseph und Aseneth"', in: A. Caquot (ed.), *La Littérature Intertestamentaire*, Paris 1985, 181-202.

the clashes of AD 66 during the reign of Emperor Caligula. Sänger thinks the year 38 AD the most probable.[32] Whichever date is true, the Egyptian origin and setting is certain, according to this hypothesis.

The second explanation for the provenance of *JosAsen* that derives from the situation of the Jewish Diaspora in Egypt has a *religious* character. It is based on the *missionary* or *proselyte-reassuring* purpose of the novel. According to Philonenko, *JosAsen* was written with the twofold intention of spiritually strengthening the members of the Jewish Diaspora in Egypt and winning sympathizers.[33] According to Aptowitzer, the romance has an analogy in the conversion of Queen Helena of Adiabene—of which Josephus was so proud to write. Aseneth is the high-ranking Gentile lady who is happy to serve the God of Israel and his Law.[34] G.W.E. Nickelsburg thinks that the book was written for people interested in Judaism and who had been acquainted with it, in other words for those for whom 'Judaism is made attractive and understandable through the use of motifs and elements to which Gentiles are accustomed'.[35] In his study of ancient romance, Szepessy argues that *JosAsen* should not be thought of as a love story, for we have good reason to deem it a work 'of religious propaganda (...) with a missionary purpose'.[36]

We know that works meant for those interested in Judaism (the proselytes) sought to prove that monotheistic Jewish religion was not alien to the Hellenistic world and were often written in Egypt, more particularly in Alexandria. We just have to think of the works of Philo and Pseudo-Phocylides. Would it not be only self-evident to mention the intentions of *JosAsen* among these, with the difference that the former are wrapped in philosophical and ethical argument, while the latter in a narrative?

It is particularly interesting how G. Bohak connects *JosAsen* with the *ancestral myth of a Jewish settlement in Egypt*.[37] In his opinion, the book

---

[32] Sänger is certainly justified in believing that political conflicts are reflected in the romance, but it must not be forgotten that they are mainly about the feuds between the sons of Jacob and not conflicts with outsiders. The only enemy the sons of Jacob have in the romance is the son of Pharaoh.

[33] Philonenko, *Joseph et Aséneth*, 53-61 and 106-7.

[34] Aptowitzer, *Asenath*, 305-6.

[35] G.W.E. Nickelsburg, 'Joseph and Aseneth', in: Id., *Jewish Literature Between the Bible and the Mishnah*, Philadelphia 1981, 262.

[36] T. Szepessy, *Héliodoros és a görög szerelmi regény*, Budapest 1987, 46.

[37] Bohak, *Joseph and Aseneth and the Jewish Temple in Heliopolis*, 88ff.

was written in Egypt between 160 and 145 BC by a Jewish author who maintained close links with the temple in Heliopolis. This was built by Onias IV, the exiled high priest with Egyptian (i.e. Ptolemaic) permission, and rivalled the Jerusalem temple for a while. By naming Aseneth the 'City of Refuge', the angel suggested that Jewish refugees would settle where the girl lived. This settlement, which Josephus, with a tinge of exaggeration, calls the 'country of Onias' (*The Jewish War* 7.430), actually did exist: Jewish inscriptions and tombstones have been found in the area.[38] Bohak thus explains the writing of *JosAsen* not by the fact that the community was threatened, nor by the faith-reassuring or missionary intentions of the author, but on the basis of the need for the Jewish community to prove, to both themselves and to outsiders, that they did have the right to settle and build a temple in Egypt, and this even had primacy over the temple and congregation of Jerusalem. This was why they resorted to 'correcting' the text of Exod 1.11 by inserting the name of their city (On = Heliopolis) after Pithom and Ramesses, and thus it 'turned out' from the context that they had built it. This was the purpose of using the figures of Joseph and Aseneth. The latter, in spite of being an Egyptian girl of rank, joined them according to Gen 41.45. She 'was a perfect peg on which hang any claims for the city'.[39] Both the method of approach and the diligent researches of Bohak demonstrate an Egyptian provenance for the book.

Ancient romance

We also find signs referring to Egypt if we study *JosAsen* from the perspective of *ancient romance*. On the basis of the text of one of the best-known ancient romances in Greek, Heliodorus' *Aethiopica*, and relying on the discussion by T. Szepessy,[40] we can establish the following arguments. Since most of *Aethiopica* takes place in Egypt, we can compare it with the Egyptian features of *JosAsen*. Considering the material analogies, the descriptions of Egyptian foodstuffs show

---

[38] Ibid., 84-7. By 'ancestral' or 'self-interpretation myth' we mean a story whereby a community justifies its existence through an old story.

[39] The popularity of Joseph in their circles is witnessed to by the fact that they often gave the name of Joseph to their sons, ibid., 92.

[40] Szepessy, *Héliodoros és a görög szerelmi regény*.

a conspicuous similarity. The protagonists of *Aethiopica* eat walnuts, figs, freshly picked dates and other fruits. We have seen that *JosAsen* 4.4 lists almost the same diet. Second, it might be interesting to note that both romances mention the bellicose shepherds' hiding in the marshy Nile delta, whom Szepessy calls 'semi-barbarian'.[41] We know that Joseph's herdsman brothers rising up against him hid in the reed bed of a brook[42] when they wanted to abduct Aseneth and turn her over to the son of Pharaoh (24.16-17). Although the herdsmen in Heliodorus are called βούκολος (cowherd), not ποιμήν ('shepherd', the usual Biblical expression), they nevertheless remind us of the fact that Joseph's brothers were permitted by Pharaoh to settle in the Nile delta area, and that they could easily be involved in scuffles with one another or the representatives of the state (chapters 24-29). It might seem unlikely that Joseph's faithful brothers (Levi, Simeon, Benjamin) confronted the soldiers of Pharaoh in *JosAsen*, but this becomes more plausible if we realize that, in Heliodorus' romance, the leader of the cowherds returning from a round of marauding is received 'as a king' by the ones who remained in the hideout.[43]

Similarities of content between the two romances also direct our attention to Egypt. As far as their genre is concerned, they are both love stories, or, to be more precise, 'family sagas'. Adopted from Euripides' play *Helene*, the theme became central to the ancient novel. The plot of the novels focuses on the encounter between the young people, their immediate falling in love, separation, and their reunion after many adventures. As Euripides' play takes place in Egypt, many of the much later romances follow suit. 'Greek writers had a predilection for having their heroes and heroines travel to the land of Egypt',[44] but there was no need to 'have' Joseph or Aseneth 'travel' to Egypt, as the basic story already took place there. One of Heliodorus' protagonists says: 'In the poetry of Homer, the deepest secrets are blended with the most wondrous beauty in an Egyptian way' (Heliodorus, *Aethiopica*

---

[41] *JosAsen* 24-29 and Heliodorus, *Aethiopica* 2, *passim*; cf. Dio Cassius 7.71.4.1-2. Szepessy, *Héliodoros és a görög szerelmi regény*, 107-8.

[42] The same sort of ambush tactic is described in Heliodorus, *Aethiopica* 8.16.1: the Ethiopian scouts hide in the reeds on the banks of the Nile and suddenly attack their enemies (Chariclea at the Stake).

[43] Ibid., 101.

[44] Ibid., 107.

3.15.1; Calasiris' divine commissioning). This may well be equally true of *JosAsen.*

Literary motifs and psychological archetypes

We have left our most cogent reason for an Egyptian origin of *JosAsen* to the last. In this respect, we are no longer using the word origin in its geographical sense but, to borrow Luttikhuizen's nice expression, as a 'network of allusions'.[45] We wish to prove, on the basis of Luttikhuizen's study mentioned above, that *the Egyptian character of Joseph and Aseneth is a necessary consequence of its literary motifs and psychological archetypes.* In other words, the Egyptian setting is not accidental but deliberate. In his study, Luttikhuizen reviews and discusses the famous Hymn of the Pearl in the *Acts of Thomas.* The Hymn is about a Parthian prince who is sent to Egypt by his royal parents to fetch the precious pearl that is guarded by an evil dragon.[46] If he succeeds, he will inherit the kingdom. The prince undertakes the task, forgetting his valuable robe 'that gave him his princely identity and dignity'. Arriving in Egypt, he begins to adopt Egyptian customs and clothing and eat Egyptian food. He forgets about his mission and falls into a deep sleep. Then his parents send him a letter reminding him of his dignity and obligation. He recovers the pearl from the dragon, and sets out for home. On the way he finds his royal robe, which helps him find his way. Luttikhuizen suggests that this is a poetic image of the Hellenistic idea of the descent of the soul into matter and its ascent after receiving divine warning.

   It was not only the Parthian prince who lost his genuine home in Egypt. There are many similar elements in *JosAsen.* For the contrite Aseneth, Egypt is under the power of the dragon, which thrusts her into a deep spiritual dream, and from whom she has to flee (12.10). Upon the advice of the angel, Tobias drives the demon to Egypt, its actual home (Tob 8.3). In these narratives, however, Egypt is not only the place of spiritual descent but also that of dream. Awoken by the letter from his parents, the Parthian prince remembers his royal

---

[45] Luttikhuizen, 'The Hymn of Jude Thomas', 114: 'A coherent story provoking a network of allusions'.

[46] See recently A.F.J. Klijn, *The Acts of Thomas: Introduction, Text, and Commentary,* Leiden 2003[2], 182-98.

home. However, Joseph is led to Egypt by his ambitious dreams (Gen 37.1-11) where, after interpreting Pharaoh's dreams, they come true (Gen 41.1-36).

The 'network of allusions' is further tightened by the motif of dress. The Parthian prince left behind his robe 'shot with gold', as he set out for Egypt, but it was sent to him by his parents on his way home. The robe here stands for man's real, divine self. What a lot of dress symbols there are in both the biblical stories of Joseph and in *JosAsen*! His brothers envy his many-coloured coat (Gen 37.3-4). The brothers make their father believe that a beast killed his son by clothes dipped in blood (Gen 37.31-35). Pharaoh gives Joseph, the slave freed from prison, fine linen vestments and a gold chain around his neck (Gen 41.42). Joseph visits Aseneth for the second time 'wearing a marvellous white tunic, and the robe wrapped around him was Byssus purple' (5.6). And we have not even mentioned all the dresses Aseneth wears and changes! Having met Joseph, she throws her royal, gold-laced robe away, changes, and sprinkles herself with ashes (10.9-13 and 13.1-3). But, upon the command of the angel, she takes her mourning attire off, and puts on the best, as yet untouched garments. All this reminds us of the importance of dress, the taking off of poor-slavish rags, and putting on the new clothing symbolizing our 'genuine' self and lifting us into the higher spheres. The New Testament clearly states that putting off our old clothes means leaving behind our old nature, and, with the new clothes, we put on our new existence (Eph 4.22-24).

The archetypal nature of Egypt and its related motifs are quite obvious from the above. According to K. Kerényi, the heroes of all ancient romances can be traced back to the legend of Isis and Osiris; they are variations of the archetypal couple, expressing some general human sense of life and self-interpretation.[47] It is an everlasting human desire 'to be freed from the Egypt of sin' and to rise to a higher sphere. In this respect, what is interesting is not the influence that one text exerted upon the other, but the relationship between archetypes present in all. Nonetheless, we must realize that the thought-world of the Jewish Diaspora of Egypt was not so much dominated by the Old Testament 'Exodus motif', the desire to be delivered from Egypt, as

---

[47] K. Kerényi, *Die griechisch-orientalische Romanliteratur in religionsgeschichtlicher Betrachtung*, Darmstadt 1962², 229; Thomas Mann and Karl Kerényi, *Gespräch in Briefen*, Zürich 1960, quoted by Szepessy, *Héliodoros és a görög szerelmi regény*, 218 note 40; cf. R. Merkelbach, *Roman und Mysterium in der Antike*, Munich 1962, 53-5.

rather the purpose of ensuring the right to live there. This was not the expression of an individual desire but an archetypal expression of the desire of a community. The author of *JosAsen* fortuitously combined the psychological archetypes of individual and collective unconscious in the heroes, personifying basic historical claims and aspirations. It is this very feature of the romance that justifies the conclusion that the Egyptian setting is not accidental but essential, getting to the heart of the matter.

THE *WISDOM OF SOLOMON* AND THE GNOSTIC SOPHIA

Bert Jan Lietaert Peerbolte

Over the years Gerard P. Luttikhuizen has drawn attention to the many varieties in early Christianity as well as to the importance of Hellenistic Judaism to the diverging beliefs of these groups.[1] Especially his study of Gnostic literature forms an important contribution to our understanding of the formative period of Christianity.[2] The present contribution is offered to Luttikhuizen on the occasion of his 65th birthday as a token of gratitude for his role as teacher in the first years of my theological education in Groningen and his continuing friendship after these years.

On the occasion of the retirement of his predecessor A.F.J. Klijn, Luttikhuizen argued that the Sophia myth, which is so prominent in Gnostic writings, e.g. the *Apocryphon of John*, was not influenced directly by Jewish wisdom speculations.[3] According to Luttikhuizen, 'the personified Wisdom of Jewish Wisdom literature and the Sophia of the Gnostic myth are quite different figures.'[4] Notwithstanding the many similarities in terminology that can be found between Jewish wisdom speculations and the Gnostic Sophia myth, Luttikhuizen points to two important differences. Firstly, the Gnostic myth does

---

[1] Luttikhuizen has summarized his views recently in Dutch: *De veelvormigheid van het vroegste christendom*, Delft 2002.

[2] See especially his PhD dissertation, which was published as *The Revelation of Elchasai: Investigations into the Evidence for a Mesopotamian Jewish Apocalypse of the Second Century and its Reception by Judeo-Christian Propagandists* (Texte und Studien zum antiken Judentum 8), Tübingen 1985, and numerous other contributions after that.

[3] G.P. Luttikhuizen, 'The Jewish Factor in the Development of the Gnostic Myth of Origins: Some Observations', in: T. Baarda, A. Hilhorst, G.P. Luttikhuizen, and A.S. van der Woude (eds), *Text and Testimony: Essays in Honour of A.F.J. Klijn*, Kampen 1988, 152-61. Luttikhuizen develops his argument in contrast to G. MacRae, 'The Jewish Background of the Gnostic Sophia Myth', *Novum Testamentum* 12 (1970) 86-101. On the *Apocryphon of John*, see among many other publications also G.P. Luttikhuizen, 'Intertextual References in Readers' Responses to the Apocryphon of John', in: S. Draisma (ed.), *Intertextuality in Biblical Writings* (FS Van Iersel), Kampen 1989, 117-26.

[4] Luttikhuizen, 'Jewish Factor', 160.

not describe Sophia in terms of Jewish wisdom speculation as either the first helper or emanation of the highest God, nor is Sophia characterised as companion and helper of the creator-god as she is in Jewish wisdom speculations. Secondly, Luttikhuizen points out that the fall of Sophia in the Gnostic myth cannot be compared with the descent of wisdom in Jewish literature. According to Luttikhuizen, the similarities between the Gnostic Sophia myth and Jewish wisdom speculation do not imply that the spiritual and intellectual milieu in which the Gnostic Sophia myth originated was that of Hellenistic Judaism. In search of this milieu, Luttikhuizen more recently focused on the *Apocryphon of John* to conclude that '(its) authors (…) were second-century Christians with an intellectual background in popular Greek-Hellenistic philosophy.'[5]

A Jewish writing in Greek that contains an extensive description of Wisdom and for that reason is relevant to the Gnostic Sophia myth is the *Wisdom of Solomon*. Many scholars regard this writing as a clear example of Alexandrian Judaism in which the Jewish religion was described in terms of popular Greek philosophy. It is the aim of this contribution to check Luttikhuizen's argument by looking into both the Gnostic Sophia myth as found in the *Apocryphon of John* and the portrayal of wisdom in the *Wisdom of Solomon*. If Luttikhuizen is right, it means that the Sophia myth found in e.g. the *Apocryphon of John* does not necessarily indicate a Jewish origin. In order to test Luttikhuizen's view, I will first briefly treat the description of Sophia in the *Apocryphon of John* and two other Gnostic writings, and next discuss the role of wisdom in the *Wisdom of Solomon*, especially Wis 7.22-8.1. That pericope will be discussed as a case study, the outcome of which may be extrapolated to the *Wisdom of Solomon* as a whole.

1. *The Sophia myth in the* Apocryphon of John

The *Apocryphon of John* is a Gnostic writing that describes the origin of the world and the cosmos as a whole. It is cast in the narrative framework of a revelatory speech by the risen Christ to John, son of

---

[5] G.P. Luttikhuizen, 'The Rewriting of Genesis', in: F. García Martínez and G.P. Luttikhuizen (eds), *Jerusalem, Alexandria, Rome: Studies in Ancient Cultural Interaction in Honour of A. Hilhorst* (SJSJ 82), Leiden/Boston 2003, 187-200 at 199; see also his discussion of the *Apocryphon of John* in FS Van Iersel.

Zebedee. Irenaeus' reference to it in his *Adversus Haereses* 1.29 indicates that some form of this writing must have been in use by 185 CE. The writing is found in four manuscripts, three of which belong to the Nag Hammadi codices (NH), whereas the fourth is part of the Berlin Codex (BG).[6]

In its crucial passage the *Apocryphon of John* describes how Sophia, the lowest of twelve aeons, haughtily tries to bring forth an emanation by herself. In the Gnostic theogony this is depicted as an act of haughtiness, because only 'the Monad [is a] monarchy with nothing above it' (NH II.1.2.26-27).[7] The aeons can only produce offspring in a male-female combination, but Sophia brings forth a thought all by herself, and this thought turns into a being: the creator-god Yaldabaoth (NH II.1.9.25-10.19). This is the evil deity who in the end is responsible for the creation of the cosmos as a whole. The unauthorised way in which Sophia brings forth her offspring results in a gradual loss of the light: eventually the cosmos created by Yaldabaoth is characterised by darkness.

The *Apocryphon of John* thus accounts for the problem of evil in the world by interpreting it as intrinsically connected with the creation of the cosmos.[8] The whole process of creation was eventually triggered by Sophia's decision to generate Yaldabaoth all by herself. This Yaldabaoth is the one who creates the cosmos, but since he himself was not the result of a pairing of two aeons, his creation fails. Yaldabaoth was cast out of the divine light-world, and did not share the light with his creation. Ultimately, Sophia is presented as responsible for the creation of the cosmos, but also for the lack of light that characterises it.

The description found in the *Apocryphon of John* is perhaps the most explicit, but not the only account of Sophia's part in the process of creation. In the tractate *On the Origin of the World* (NH II.5 and XIII.2) Sophia is described as the creator of the stars and the heavenly luminaries:

---

[6] For an introduction, edition, translation and synopsis of the *Apocryphon of John*, see M. Waldstein and F. Wisse, *The Apocryphon of John: Synopsis of Nag Hammadi Codices II,1; III,1; and IV,1 with BG 8502,2* (Nag Hammadi and Manichean Studies 33), Leiden 1995. See also the discussion in R. Roukema, *Gnosis and Faith in Early Christianity: An Introduction to Gnosticism*, London/Harrisburg 1999, 36-49.

[7] Transl. F. Wisse, in: J.M. Robinson (ed.), *The Nag Hammadi Library*, Leiden 1996[4].

[8] On this, see Luttikhuizen, *De veelvormigheid van het vroegste christendom*, chap. 7, 119-28.

> Now when she wished, the Sophia who was in the lower heaven received authority from Pistis, and fashioned great luminous bodies and all the stars. And she put them in the sky to shine upon the earth (...) (NH II.5.112.1-5).[9]

It is noteworthy that the creation process in the *Apocryphon of John* results in a cosmos devoid of light, whereas *On the Origin of the World* describes Sophia as the creator of heavenly luminaries. In *The Sophia of Jesus Christ* (NH III.4 and BG 8502.3) Sophia is even introduced as the consort of the First Man. The risen Christ, also described as 'the Holy One' or the 'Saviour', explains to Bartholomew:

> I want you to know that First Man is called 'Begetter, Self-perfected Mind'. He reflected with Great Sophia, his consort, and revealed his first-begotten, androgynous son. His male name is designated 'First Begetter Son of God'; his female name 'First Begettress Sophia, Mother of the Universe'. Some call her 'Love' (NH III.4.104.5-20).[10]

There is an obvious difference between the picture of Sophia in the *Apocryphon of John* and that in *On the Origin of the World* and *The Sophia of Jesus Christ*. In both these texts Sophia is depicted in a less negative way than in the *Apocryphon of John*. Furthermore, *The Sophia of Jesus Christ* describes her as acting in conjunction with First Man, and *On the Origin of the World* depicts her as responsible for the creation of the lights of heaven. The picture of Sophia in the Gnostic writings referred to above is that of the creator-deity who played a leading role in the origin of the cosmos.

Many scholars have argued that this view of Sophia was generated by Jewish wisdom speculations.[11] Since perhaps the most explicit description of wisdom is found in the *Wisdom of Solomon*, the remainder of this article will consist of an analysis of the most important features of this description.

---

[9] Transl. H.-G. Bethge and B. Layton in: Robinson, *Nag Hammadi Library*.

[10] Transl. D.M. Parrott, in: Robinson, *Nag Hammadi Library*; see also *Eugnostos the Blessed* (NH III.3.8.31-9.5).

[11] See especially MacRae, 'The Jewish Background', 97: 'The Jewish contribution to the myth is already clear from the large number of points of contact between the two traditions ...'

2. *The* Wisdom of Solomon *and its picture of Wisdom*

The *Wisdom of Solomon* is usually dated either to the third or second century BCE or to the decades around the beginning of the Common Era.[12] The more recent date of the writing is argued in a very convincing manner by Giuseppe Scarpat in a number of articles and in his three-volume commentary on the writing.[13] According to Scarpat, the κράτησις of Wis 6.3 is a reference to the capture of Alexandria by Augustus Caesar in 30 BCE. Scarpat elaborates his argument with reference to the language of the *Wisdom of Solomon*. Since the vocabulary shows a remarkable similarity to texts that supposedly were written in Alexandria, Scarpat concludes that the provenance of the *Wisdom of Solomon* should indeed be located there. The evidence he mentions from *P. Fayum* 22 is indeed a strong indication that the writing should be dated somewhere after 30 BCE.[14] This means that the writing originated around the beginning of the Common Era.[15]

The *Wisdom of Solomon* is an implicit pseudepigraphon using the genre of a *protreptikos*.[16] Its author purports to be King Solomon, but he does not explicitly identify himself as such. Only in the references to his status as king and his special relation to wisdom does the implied author state his identity.[17] Hence, the implied reader has to be familiar with the figure of Solomon to identify the narrator of the book with this king. This, in combination with the Greek language in which the

---

[12] For a discussion of the textual tradition of *Wisdom*, the date of origin, its provenance and other introductory questions, see C. Larcher, *Le livre de la Sagesse ou la Sagesse de Salomon*, i, Paris 1983, 53-161. According to Larcher (141-61) *Wisdom* was originally composed in three different parts that were combined into the present form.

[13] G. Scarpat, *Libro della Sapienza: Testo, traduzione, introduzione e commento*, 3 vols (Biblica 1, 3, 6), Brescia 1989-99.

[14] *P. Fayum* 22 speaks of 'the thirty-eighth year of the κράτησις by Caesar, son of god' to date an event that apparently took place in 8 CE. Cf. Scarpat, *Libro della Sapienza*, i, 17 (ἔτους ὀγδόου καὶ τριακοστοῦ τῆς καίσαρος κρατήσεως θεοῦ υἱοῦ, μῆνος κτλ.). The identification of Alexandria as the place of origin is likely, although there is no solid evidence to prove it.

[15] For this date, see C. Larcher, *Le livre de la Sagesse ou la Sagesse de Salomon* (Études Bibliques 1), i, Paris 1983, 141-61. Larcher argues in favour of a date around 15/10 BCE.

[16] For this definition of the genre of the *Wisdom of Solomon* see G.J. Boiten, *Wijsheid in context: Een onderzoek naar de retorische opbouw van het boek Wijsheid van Salomo en naar de betekenis van Vrouwe Wijsheid* (PhD-diss. Groningen 1996), 53-4.

[17] See esp. *Wisdom* 8.17-21.

writing is cast, defines the intended audience as a Hellenistic Jewish audience.[18]

a. *Wisdom and righteousness*

The figure of wisdom in the *Wisdom of Solomon* is not a new literary creation, but part of a longer tradition of a personified portrayal of wisdom. Other texts witnessing to this tradition are e.g. Proverbs 1-9; Job 28; Wisdom of Sirach; *1 Baruch*; and *1 Enoch*. According to L.L. Grabbe, this tradition on wisdom as a person takes two main forms, viz. that of wisdom as a goddess-like figure or a seducer, lover or erotic figure.[19] Both types of personification can be found in the *Wisdom of Solomon*.

There is reason to divide the *Wisdom of Solomon* into three parts: (1) 1.1-6.21; (2) 6.22-11.1; (3) 11.2-19.22.[20] The first part of the *Wisdom of Solomon* defines σοφία in terms of δικαιοσύνη. The opening statement of the writing is an appeal to the rulers of the earth to love righteousness (1.1), which is further elaborated by the remarks on 'goodness' and 'sincerity of heart'. The three characteristics mentioned here are presented as preconditions for the entrance of wisdom into a person's life: 'wisdom does not enter into a deceitful soul' (1.4). After the relationship between wisdom and justice has been postulated in this way, it is further explained in the following parts. In 1.6 wisdom is explained as a 'kindly spirit' (φιλάνθρωπον πνεῦμα) that is apparently synonymous with the Spirit of God that fills the entire earth (1.7; πνεῦμα κυρίου πεπλήρωκεν τὴν οἰκουμένην[21]). Verses 1.14-15 subsequently describe God as the creator of everything and conclude that 'righteousness is immortal'.

---

[18] Scarpat, *Libro della Sapienza*, i, 13-29.

[19] L.L. Grabbe, *Wisdom of Solomon* (Guides to the Apocrypha and Pseudepigrapha 3), Sheffield 1997, 68.

[20] This division has been proposed by H. Hübner, *Die Weisheit Salomos, Liber Sapientiae Salomonis* (Das Alte Testament Deutsch; Apokryphen 4), Göttingen 1999. It is clearly not the only option. Scarpat chooses a division in two parts: 1.1-6.21 and 6.22-19.22. For Larcher, see note 12. G. Gilbert also proposed a division in three parts, but it differs from that of Hübner—I. chaps 1-6; II. chaps 7-9; III. chaps 10-19; see G. Gilbert, 'Wisdom Literature', in: M.E. Stone (ed.), *Jewish Writings of the Second Temple Period: Apocrypha, Pseudepigrapha, Qumran Sectarian Writings, Philo, Josephus* (Compendia Rerum Iudaicarum ad Novum Testamentum, section 2), Assen/Philadelphia 1984, 301-13.

[21] The perfect tense is used here as a 'resultative perfect'; cf. J.H. Moulton and N. Turner, *A Grammar of New Testament Greek*, iii, *Syntax*, Edinburgh 1963, 84-5.

The main section of the first part of *Wisdom* (1.16-6.21) depicts the opposition between the ungodly and the righteous, in which the ungodly are portrayed as cruel oppressors who do not care about the widow and the orphan, whereas the righteous are described as oppressed, but still safe with God. Especially the description of the fate of the suffering righteous in 3.1-9 is of great importance for the early responses to Jesus' ministry. But for the present purpose it is of greater interest to see that the first six chapters of the *Wisdom of Solomon* depict wisdom as closely related to God's Spirit who enables humans to distinguish between ungodly and righteous behaviour. After the remark in 1.6 on wisdom as a 'kindly spirit', and the apparent equation of that spirit with the 'Spirit of God' (1.7), the first mention of wisdom follows in 6.9, where the rulers of the earth are again (cf. 1.1-4) called upon to learn wisdom by the practice of righteousness. Thus, wisdom is implicitly defined as the God-given ability to distinguish between righteousness and ungodliness. This ability starts with the correct attitude, viz. the willingness to be instructed (6.17), which eventually leads to immortality, and thus brings people near to God (6.18-19).

Two observations in particular should be made here. Firstly, the closeness of wisdom to righteousness is related to the view of the *Wisdom of Sirach*, and yet there is an important difference. Whereas it is Ben Sira's view that wisdom is intertwined with knowledge and obedience of the Torah (cf. Sir 15.1; 19.20; 21.11), this connection is not explicitly made in the *Wisdom of Solomon*. As we said above, the first part of the *Wisdom of Solomon* presents wisdom as the attitude of distinguishing between righteousness and ungodliness. The examples of righteous behaviour mentioned in chaps 1-6 are indeed cast in traditional terms that can also be found in the Torah, but nowhere is the Law mentioned explicitly. Thus, there is an obvious difference between the descriptions of wisdom in the *Wisdom of Sirach* and the *Wisdom of Solomon*.

Secondly, although wisdom is presented as an attitude, it is also depicted in the guise of a personification. Especially the image of 6.13-14 is telling. There wisdom is described as sitting by the door of those who rise early to meet her. This description is an inversion of the situation depicted in Prov 8.34, which contains a blessing of those who meet wisdom at her doors or gate. Already this single example points out that the personification of wisdom in the *Wisdom of Solomon* is part of a longer tradition.

The remarks in 6.22-25 indicate that the implied author, 'Solomon', will continue the writing with a description of wisdom and her actions. Read from this perspective, part two (6.22-11.1) is a eulogy on wisdom and a presentation of Solomon as the king who received wisdom after he had prayed for it. The remainder of the writing (part three, 11.2-19.22) is a Midrash-like exposition of the Exodus narrative in which 'wisdom' is hardly mentioned anymore.[22] Nevertheless, 6.22-25 indicates that this third part of the writing should probably be read as a description of the liberating effects of wisdom. Hence, regardless of whether the three parts of the writing were originally intended as a unity or not,[23] the present text of the *Wisdom of Solomon* describes wisdom in terms of righteousness and the history of Israel. It is presented as active throughout this history, and it is even equated with the Spirit of God. God is presented as present in Israel's history through his Spirit, his Wisdom. The fact that this specific description of God's liberating presence in Israel's history originated in Alexandria around the beginning of the Common Era indicates that the author must have had a special hermeneutical interest.[24] The re-telling of the Exodus narrative should be read as a reflection upon the actual situation of Jewish residents of Alexandria. This specific narrative, with its heavy accent on liberation from the bonds of Egypt, must have formed a means of encouraging Jewish readers in a difficult social context.[25]

In part three (11.2-19.22) of the *Wisdom of Solomon* the role of wisdom is stated in a more implicit manner. Part one (1.1-6.21) more or less equates wisdom with the ability to learn and practice righteousness, and part two focuses on the description of wisdom itself. For this reason, it is important to take a closer look at this second part of the *Wisdom of Solomon*. In doing so I shall limit myself to a central passage, viz. the encomium of wisdom in 7.22-8.1.

---

[22] Although 18.14-15 does mention the λόγος.

[23] See the discussion in Larcher, *Le livre de la Sagesse*, mentioned above in note 12.

[24] This is elaborated by S. Cheon, *The Exodus Story in the Wisdom of Solomon: A Study in Biblical Interpretation* (Journal for the Study of the Pseudepigrapha Supplement Series 23), Sheffield 1997.

[25] The situation of the Jews in Alexandria at this time is clearly described in Philo's *Embassy to Gaius*. For a discussion of this situation, see E.M. Smallwood, *The Jews under Roman Rule from Pompey to Diocletian: A Study in Political Relations*, Leiden 1981, esp. 220-55.

b. *A case study: Wis 7.22-8.1*

The passage 7.22-8.1 contains a eulogy on wisdom presented by the author as a description of her character and her relationship to God. This passage is crucial to the understanding of the writing as a whole, since it is here that 'Solomon' explicitly gives the description he has previously announced. In the opening lines of the second part of the book (6.22-25) 'Solomon' states that he will reveal the character of wisdom to his readers, who have been addressed in 6.1 as the 'kings' and 'judges of the ends of the earth'. The announcement is that the history of wisdom will be described 'from the creation onward' (6.22).

The next pericope presents 'Solomon' as a mortal man (7.1-6). Especially the remark in 7.5 (οὐδεὶς γὰρ βασιλέων ἑτέραν ἔσχεν γενέσεως ἀρχήν—'none of the kings had a different start of his origin') appears to be polemical against the Hellenistic ideology of the divine king.[26] In contrast to the divine rulers of the Hellenistic world, Solomon is portrayed here as a man who has received wisdom as a gift from God (7.7-21). God is mentioned as the 'guide of wisdom' (αὐτὸς καὶ τῆς σοφίας ὁδηγός ἐστιν; 7.15), who is able to grant wisdom to human beings. It is God who is depicted as the one who gave wisdom to Solomon (7.17), and this wisdom is explained as the knowledge of all existing things (τῶν ὄντων γνῶσις). Thus, σοφία is defined here in terms of γνῶσις, and the objects of this knowledge are mentioned: the cosmic order, the structure of time, the essentials of all living creatures, the spiritual and the human world, and the effects of plants and roots (vv. 17-21). Solomon is hence depicted as an initiate of wisdom with great knowledge of astrology, physics, demonology, and alchemy. The *Testament of Solomon* proves that this perception of Solomon as a great initiate in esoteric secrets brought about speculations on his power over demons and his knowledge of magic and medicine.[27] Solomon's knowledge is summarised in his remark in Wis 7.21: 'Both hidden things and those that are clear I have learned, because the fashioner of all things, wisdom, has taught me' (ὅσα τέ ἐστιν κρυπτὰ καὶ ἐμφανῆ ἔγνων· ἡ γὰρ πάντων τεχνῖτις ἐδίδαξέν με σοφία).

The translation 'fashioner of all' (also in NRSV) is used for the words

---

[26] As found in e.g. *P. Fayum* 22; cf. above, note 14.
[27] See especially the introduction by D.C. Duling, in: J. Charlesworth (ed.), *The Old Testament Pseudepigrapha*, i, New York 1983, 935-59.

ἡ ... πάντων τεχνῖτις. For the present purpose it is important to find the exact meaning of these words, because they may ascribe the role of creator to wisdom, and thus reduce the parallel to the picture of Sophia in the *Apocryphon of John*. At first sight, it is likely that wisdom is indeed portrayed as the creator here: the masculine form of the noun (τεχνίτης) is used in Wis 13.1 as a metaphorical reference to God. There, it is stated that human beings can know God from his works as they can know the artisan from what he creates. This verse indicates the usual meaning of the noun as 'artisan', and the metaphor clearly refers to God's work as the creator of all. Human beings are able to acknowledge the creator through the creation. Notwithstanding the clear parallel with the words used in 13.1 (ἐπέγνωσαν τὸν τεχνίτην), however, Scarpat argues that the use of τεχνῖτις for wisdom does not indicate that wisdom is depicted as the creator of all in 7.21. According to him, this would not agree with the logic of the writing as a whole.[28] Scarpat's argument is important for a comparison of the portrayal of wisdom in the *Wisdom of Solomon* with the Gnostic Sophia myth and therefore deserves some attention.

Scarpat argues that 7.21 first of all characterises wisdom as the knowledge of all things 'hidden and manifest'.[29] The parallel in LXX Dan 2.47 indicates for Scarpat that 7.21 does not speak of visible and invisible things, but of occult and well-known truths. Next, Scarpat argues that the noun τεχνῖτις does not designate wisdom as the creator of all things, but as the most important of the *artes liberales*. Among a number of other texts, Scarpat refers to Philo's *De Ebr.* 88, where wisdom is characterised as the first of the crafts (σοφία τέχνη τεχνῶν). John of Damascus (8th century) even refers to philosophy as the 'τέχνη of all arts'. Thus, the expression used in 7.21 (ἡ πάντων τεχνῖτις) does not necessarily identify wisdom as the creator of all things, but as the artisan who was involved in the process of crafting. Wisdom is depicted as the most important of the *artes liberales*.

Scarpat's analysis is clearly important, and yet it is difficult not to see a connection between 7.15-21 and 6.22. In the latter verse, 'Solomon' had announced that he would speak about the history of wisdom

---

[28] Scarpat, *Libro della Sapienza*, ii, 61-2: 'Dunque πάντων τεχνῖτις non vorrà dire "creatrice del mondo", anche perché non si capisce la logica di un tale appello all'aspetto creativo della Sapienza.'

[29] For this paragraph see Scarpat, *Libro della Sapienza*, ii, 59-61.

'from the creation onward'. Furthermore, the designation τεχνῖτις immediately after 7.17-20 implies an involvement of wisdom in the 'structure of the world', the 'activity of the elements', and all other natural, cosmological, spiritual, and physical objects mentioned. These observations urge us to read 7.21 as a statement on the involvement of wisdom in the genesis of all there is, even though σοφία may not be presented explicitly as the creator. Apparently the *Wisdom of Solomon* does relate σοφία to creation but does not explicitly state its role as that of the creator. And yet wisdom is depicted as somehow involved in the origin of all things. This ambivalence indicates an important difference between the role of wisdom in the *Wisdom of Solomon* and Sophia in the *Apocryphon of John*: the latter is explicitly described as ultimately responsible for the process of creation (even though Yalda-baoth is eventually the creator), whereas the former is only implicitly depicted as present in the process of creation. In the *Wisdom of Solomon* it is clearly God who is depicted as the creator. Another difference is formed by the fact that the whole process of creation is regarded as negative in the *Apocryphon of John* and other Gnostic writings, whereas the *Wisdom of Solomon* does not view it as such.

Many parallels have already been mentioned by others to clarify Wis 7.21.[30] To mention but one: the *Corpus Hermeticum* (fragment 23, §§64-65) contains a passage in which Isis describes the Monarch God as the τεχνίτης of all:[31]

καὶ ἐκ τούτου εἶπεν Ὧρος· Ὦ τεκοῦσα, πῶς οὖν τὴν θεοῦ ἀπόρροιαν ἔχειν εὐτύχησεν ἡ γῆ; καὶ εἶπεν Ἶσις· Παραιτοῦμαι γένεσιν ἱστορεῖν· οὐ γὰρ θεμιτὸν σῆς σπορᾶς καταλέγειν ἀρχήν, ὦ μεγαλοσθενὲς Ὧρε, ὡς μήποτε ὕστερον εἰς ἀνθρώπους ἀθανάτων ἔλθῃ γένεσις θεῶν· πλὴν ὅτι γε ὁ μόναρχος θεός, ὁ τῶν συμπάντων κοσμοποιητὴς καὶ τεχνίτης, [...] τὸν μέγιστόν σου πρὸς ὀλίγον ἐχαρίσατο πατέρα Ὄσιριν καὶ τὴν μεγίστην θεὰν Ἶσιν, ἵνα τῷ πάντων δεομένῳ κόσμῳ βοηθοὶ γένωνται.

And, at that, Horus said: 'O Mother, how was the earth so fortunate as to receive the emanation of God?'
And Isis answered: 'I refuse to tell you the beginning, because it is not permitted to describe the origin of your procreation, o Greatest Horus, lest the beginning of the immortal gods would become known later to humans. Only this can I say, that the Monarch God, the maker and

---

[30] See e.g. the discussion in Scarpat, *Libro della Sapienza*, ii, 60-2.
[31] A.D. Nock and A.J. Festugière, *Corpus Hermeticum*, iv, Paris 1954, 20-1.

> fashioner of all that is, [...] for some time he graciously favoured Osiris,
> your father, and the greatest goddess Isis, so that they should become
> helpers for the world that is lacking in all.

Here, the 'Monarch God' is depicted as responsible for the creation
of life itself. The situation resembles the one reflected in the *Wisdom
of Solomon*, in that the Highest God is presented as the creator of the
cosmos. For this, he is characterised as κοσμοποιητής and τεχνίτης.
Isis' role, at best, is that of an assistant. And yet the similarity to the
Apocryphon of John may even be more important, since the Highest God
is mentioned as ὁ μόναρχος θεός. In NH II.2.26-27 the reconstructed
text describes this deity as 'The Monad', who 'is a unity with nothing
above it' (ΤΗΟΝΑϹ ϵΟΥΜΟΝΑΡΧΙΑ Τϵ ϵΜΗ ΠϵΤϢΟΟΠ ϨΙΧϢϹ).[32] Many
other examples could be mentioned, but already this single passage
from the *Corpus Hermeticum* indicates that both the *Wisdom of Solomon* and
the *Apocryphon of John* show a proximity to pagan religious language.
Therefore, this language, notably from the Isis religion, but also from
other deities worshipped as creators, should be taken into account in
any further comparison of the two sources.[33]

The most explicit description of wisdom in the *Wisdom of Solomon* is
given in the eulogy of 7.22-8.1 (quoted from NRSV):

22   There is in her a spirit that is intelligent, holy,
            unique, manifold, subtle,
            mobile, clear, unpolluted,
            distinct, invulnerable, loving the good, keen,
            irresistible,
23   beneficent, humane,
            steadfast, sure, free from anxiety,
            all-powerful, overseeing all,
            and penetrating through all spirits
            that are intelligent, pure, and altogether subtle.
24   For wisdom is more mobile than any motion;
            because of her pureness she pervades and penetrates
            all things.

---

[32] For this reconstruction, see Waldstein & Wisse, *Apocryphon of John*, 20-1.

[33] Also Boiten, *Wijsheid in context*, 131-42, points at the many similarities between
the description of wisdom in the *Wisdom of Solomon* and the cult of Isis. She indicates
that the use of images and words known from the cult of Isis implies that the author
of the *Wisdom of Solomon* was familiar with that imagery, but also wanted to present
the Jewish religion as superior to the cult of Isis.

25   For she is a breath of the power of God,
          and a pure emanation of the glory of the Almighty;
          therefore nothing defiled gains entrance into her.
26   For she is a reflection of eternal light,
          a spotless mirror of the working of God,
          and an image of his goodness.
27   Although she is but one, she can do all things,
          and while remaining in herself, she renews all things;
          in every generation she passes into holy souls
          and makes them friends of God, and prophets;
28   for God loves nothing so much as the person who lives
          with wisdom.
29   She is more beautiful than the sun,
          and excels every constellation of the stars.
          Compared with the light she is found to be superior,
30   for it is succeeded by the night,
          but against wisdom evil does not prevail.
8.1   She reaches mightily from one end of the earth to the
          other, and she orders all things well.

Many scholars have pointed out that this description of the character of wisdom has been heavily influenced by Hellenistic philosophical vocabulary, and it is not necessary to repeat their argument here in detail.[34] The fact that verses 22-23 list 21 characteristics of wisdom is no coincidence: this number equals 3 times 7, two symbolic numbers that are often found in numerical speculations of the Hellenistic period.[35] What is especially important in this passage is the fact that wisdom is described as a positive force in the world that acts on behalf of God. Since it is impossible to discuss all details of the passage in the present contribution, I will limit myself to three important features: the epithets for wisdom mentioned in vv. 22-23, the cosmological terminology used in the passage as a whole, and the relation to God described in vv. 25-26.

1.   It has been noted that the twenty-one epithets of wisdom given in vv. 22-23 agree to a certain extent with descriptions found in several

---

[34] See e.g. D. Winston, *The Wisdom of Solomon: A New Translation with Introduction and Commentary* (The Anchor Bible 43), New York 1979,178-83; also Boiten, *Wijsheid in context*, 79-90.

[35] For a discussion and numerous Hellenistic parallels to this passage, see also Larcher, *Livre de la Sagesse*, ii, 479-93; Scarpat, *Libro della Sapienza*, ii, 112-28.

pagan Hellenistic texts.[36] Comparison of Wis 7.22-23 with contemporary pagan texts shows that the genre applied here was not unknown in the Hellenistic world. One of the texts that is often mentioned as evidence is the Hymn of Cleanthes. This hymn has been preserved by Clement of Alexandria, and describes Zeus in a large number of epithets that are given in similar fashion to those of wisdom in the passage under discussion:[37]

> Τἀγαθὸν ἐρωτᾶς μ᾿ οἷον ἔστ᾿; ἄκουε δή·
> τεταγμένον, δίκαιον, ὅσιον, εὐσεβές,
> κρατοῦν ἑαυτοῦ, χρήσιμον, καλόν, δέον,
> αὐστηρόν, αὐθέκαστον, αἰεὶ συμφέρον,
> ἄφοβον, ἄλυπον, λυσιτελές, ἀνώδυνον,
> ὠφέλιμον, εὐάρεστον, ἀσφαλές, φίλον,
> ἔντιμον, ὁμολογούμενον *****
> εὐκλεές, ἄτυφον, ἐπιμελές, πρᾶον, σφοδρόν,
> χρονιζόμενον, ἄμεμπτον, αἰεὶ διαμένον.

> You ask me what the good is like—listen:
> well ordered, just, holy, pious,
> self-controlled, useful, beautiful, necessary,
> austere, blunt, always profitable,
> fearless, painless, advantageous, harmless,
> beneficial, pleasurable, secure, friendly,
> honoured, of one mind *****
> famous, not puffed up, careful, gentle, strong,
> lasting, blameless, everlasting.

It is immediately clear that this hymn uses the same genre as Wis 7.22-23 does in its enumeration of the epithets of wisdom, although the number of characteristics mentioned differs. In the Cleanthes Hymn the number probably even amounts to thirty (depending on the reconstruction in line 7 of *****), and in that case consists not of 3 x 7 but of 3 x 10 epithets. A relationship of literary dependence of the Cleanthes Hymn on the *Wisdom of Solomon* is improbable, and cannot be substantiated. Furthermore, the date of attestation for the hymn is later than that of the *Wisdom of Solomon*. For these reasons

---

[36] The Stoic philosopher Cleanthes mentions 26 divine attributes; cf. E. des Places, 'Épithètes et attributs de la "Sagesse" (Sg 7,22-23 et SVF I 557 Arnim)', *Biblica* 57 (1976) 414-19.

[37] Clement, *Strom.* 5.110.2; also *Protr.* 72.2. For the text, see O. Stählin (ed.), *Clemens Alexandrinus*, ii, *Stromata Buch I-VI*, Berlin 1985.

the use of the same genre and comparable epithets in the description of Zeus rather indicates that the presentation of wisdom in Wis 7.22-23 has been put in words that the author must have known from his pagan environment.

2.   The cosmic characteristics of wisdom as described in 7.22-8.1 entail a comparison of wisdom with the sun, the stars and the light. The characterisation in 7.26-27 clearly presents wisdom in a cosmological metaphor as the ἀπαύγασμα ... φωτὸς ἀιδίου, and this cosmological terminology is also used in vv. 29-30. There, wisdom is mentioned as εὐπρεπεστέρα ἡλίου and ὑπὲρ πᾶσαν ἄστρων θέσιν. And in 8.1 the encomium concludes with a description of the cosmic power of wisdom, who 'reaches mightily from one end of the earth to the other' and 'orders all things well'.

The characteristics of wisdom mentioned here are put in terms of 'sun', 'light' and 'stars'. This characterisation recalls the description of Sophia in e.g. the Gnostic tractate *On the Origin of the World* (cf. above), where it is said that 'she created great luminaries and all the stars'. Indeed, Wis 7.29-8.1 describes wisdom as superior to the sun, the stars, and the heavenly luminaries, but this is also the point where the comparison stops: Sophia is mentioned as the creator of these heavenly lights, but the *Wisdom of Solomon* does not say this of wisdom. It is evident that in this regard the description of the Gnostic Sophia does use the same vocabulary as that of wisdom in the *Wisdom of Solomon*, but that there is also an important difference. The *Wisdom of Solomon* does not describe wisdom as the creator of these cosmic elements. Again, it is likely that descriptions of Isis and other Hellenistic deities who were worshipped for their creative power constitute the *tertium comparationis*. The language of these pagan cults should be seen as the prime source for the vocabulary, style, and metaphors used both in the *Wisdom of Solomon* and in the Gnostic Sophia myth.

The closeness to this pagan religious vocabulary is made evident, for instance, by a comparison with what is commonly known as the Isis Aretalogy found in Kyme, Thessaloniki, and Ios, also described by Diodorus (I,27).[38] In this text, Isis is depicted as proclaiming her power

---

[38] M. Totti, *Ausgewählte Texte der Isis-Serapis-Religion* (Studia Epigraphica 12), Hildesheim 1985, 1-4.

by an enumeration of her most important deeds. She is presented as
the creator of the cosmos in §§12-14:

ἐγὼ ἐχώρισα γῆν ἀπ᾽ οὐρανοῦ
ἐγὼ ἄστρων ὁδοὺς ἔδειξα
ἐγὼ ἡλίου καὶ σελήνης πορείαν συνεταξάμην

I have separated earth from heaven
I have pointed out the paths of the stars
I have assembled the course of the sun and the moon

It is remarkable that the relation between Isis and the sun recurs in
the same Aretalogy in §§44-45:

ἐγὼ ἐν ταῖς τοῦ ἡλίου αὐγαῖς εἰμί
ἐγὼ παρεδρεύω τῇ τοῦ ἡλίου πορείᾳ

I am there in the rays of the sun
I am present in the course of the sun

The parallel to the role of wisdom in the *Wisdom of Solomon* is evident, but again it is also clear that the picture of Isis as the creator
of the sun, the moon and the stars is closer to that of Sophia in the
Apocryphon of John than to the picture in the *Wisdom of Solomon*.

Given the many other similarities between Isis and wisdom in the
Wisdom of Solomon, John S. Kloppenborg is correct in concluding that
this work has been thoroughly influenced by the language of Isis
worship.[39] It was probably this same language that later played a formative role in shaping the picture of Sophia in the Gnostic myth.

3.   The relationship of wisdom to God in the *Wisdom of Solomon* is
relatively vague throughout the writing, but 7.25-26 describes wisdom as
a 'breath of the power of God', an 'emanation' of his glory, a 'spotless
mirror of the working of God', and 'image of his goodness'. These are
poetic images reminiscent of neo-Platonic descriptions.[40] The relation
of wisdom to God is described in these metaphors as close, and it is
clear that God is the one who brings forth wisdom. Wisdom is not a
separate person or entity, apart from God, but a power of God himself.
This resembles the situation in the *Apocryphon of John*. There, Sophia
is one of the aeons emanating from the Monad, and for that reason

---

[39] J.S. Kloppenborg, 'Isis and Sophia in the Book of Wisdom', *Harvard Theological Review* 75 (1982) 57-84.
[40] Cf. Winston, *Wisdom of Solomon*, 184-90.

she is also depicted as stemming from the highest God. Nevertheless, Sophia's position is that of the lowest of the aeons, whereas wisdom in Wis 7.25-26 is mentioned as the sole emanation of God. Again, the concepts of wisdom in the *Wisdom of Solomon* and Sophia in the *Apocryphon of John* appear related, but they are also distinct. Again the two sources share the same vocabulary. In this respect it is important to note that the *Apocryphon of John* uses the same terminology as Wis 7.25-26, but applies it to the 'only-begotten One', the Son of Barbelo and the Father, and not to Sophia. The Father is described as the 'pure light' into which Barbelo looks (NH III.9.10-12; ⲁⲩⲱ ⲁⲥϭⲱϣⲧ ⲉⲛⲁϣⲟ ⲛ̄ϭⲓ ⲧⲃⲁⲣⲃⲏⲗⲟⲛ̄ ⲉϩⲟⲩⲛ ⲉⲡϩⲓⲗⲓⲕⲣⲓⲛⲉⲥ ⲛ̄ⲟⲩⲉⲓⲛ—'And Barbelo gazed intently into the pure light'). The same metaphor is used for the Supreme God as in Wis 7.25 (εἰλικρινής). After turning to the Father, Barbelo 'gave birth to a spark of light resembling the blessed light, but he is not equal in greatness.' This smaller light is described as 'the only-begotten One, who came forth from the Father, the divine Self-Generated, the first-born Son of all the Father's (sons), the pure light' (NH III.9.16-19). The last characterisation ('the pure light' ⲡⲓⲗⲓⲕⲣⲓⲛⲉⲥ ⲛ̄ⲟⲩⲉⲓⲛ) refers to the Father. Here, again it is obvious that the *Apocryphon of John* uses the same metaphors as the *Wisdom of Solomon*, but in a different context. A relation of literary dependence cannot be substantiated, and therefore the link must be considered traditio-historical in character.

Conclusion

The case study presented here supports the conclusion that the picture of wisdom as described in the *Wisdom of Solomon* is similar to that of Sophia in the Gnostic myth, but differs from it on a number of decisive points. The language used in the *Wisdom of Solomon* is comparable to that of the *Apocryphon of John*, but the differences should not be overlooked. Both sources have been influenced by pagan Hellenistic terminology, in which especially the cult of Isis and other creator-deities must have played an important role. The picture of Sophia in the *Apocryphon of John* is probably somehow related to Jewish wisdom speculations as found in the *Wisdom of Solomon*, but this relation cannot be substantiated as one in which concepts or ideas are directly borrowed. Instead, the conclusion should be that the Gnostics who described the myth of Sophia and the theogony in the *Apocryphon of John* were thoroughly influenced by the pagan Hellenistic milieu in which the *Wisdom of Solomon* was also written. Within this Hellenistic milieu they expressed their views in terms that are reminiscent of, but also different from, Jewish wisdom speculations. Hence, Luttikhuizen's view that the Gnostic Sophia myth differs in an important manner from Hellenistic Jewish wisdom speculations does hold true when put to the test in the case of one of the most important sources in which these speculations are found, the *Wisdom of Solomon*.[41]

---

[41] I sincerely thank Prof. Riemer Roukema for his critical remarks on an earlier version of this article.

CLEOPATRA IN JOSEPHUS: FROM HEROD'S RIVAL TO THE WISE RULER'S OPPOSITE

Jan Willem van Henten

Introduction

Cleopatra VII was the last Ptolemaic ruler, who for some time partly restored the huge Ptolemaic empire by using her unorthodox partnerships with powerful Romans. Roman authors murdered her character after her and Antony's demise at Actium in 31 BCE. Cleopatra VII became world-famous as a most clever seductress through Shakespeare's *Antony and Cleopatra*, which was strongly inspired by Plutarch's biography of Antony. Elizabeth Taylor's part of Cleopatra in Joseph L. Mankiewicz's 1963 movie *Cleopatra* made her even more famous in our own age.

Josephus is one of the most negative ancient sources about Cleopatra. He goes beyond the usual contempt for Cleopatra's sexual immorality, greed and perverted hunger for power, and portrays her in *Against Apion* as the ultimately wicked foreign ruler. Josephus' Cleopatra passages show an increasing tendency to blacken the famous and intelligent queen; so much so that Michael Grant concludes in his biography of Cleopatra that Josephus 'is savagely biased against the queen'.[1]

Why is a separate discussion of the Cleopatra passages in Josephus useful? First, Cleopatra's dealings with Herod the Great, as reported by Josephus, show two client rulers in action, fighting for Roman support and benefactions in very different ways. Second, the various Cleopatra passages have been treated before as one coherent cluster,[2] but this approach does not do justice to the changes of Cleopatra's image in Josephus' works. Third, although Josephus' descriptions show many parallels with statements by non-Jewish authors, there are some issues in his works that arc remarkable if not altogether unique, and deserve further discussion. This contribution, therefore, aims at giving a survey

---

[1] M. Grant, *Cleopatra*, London 1972 (repr. London 2001), 240.
[2] I. Becher, *Das Bild der Kleopatra in der griechischen und lateinischen Literatur*, Berlin 1966, 63-8.

of all Cleopatra passages in an ongoing discussion, while highlighting the differences between Josephus' works.[3]

1. *Cleopatra in the* Jewish War

Parallel passages that appear in the *Antiquities* and show only minor differences in comparison to the *Jewish War* will also be discussed in this section when relevant.[4] Cleopatra is first mentioned in the *Jewish War* in connection with one of the unsuccessful Jewish delegations coming to Antony in order to protest against Herod and his brother Phasael, who took over the rule from Hyrcanus II (*War* 1.243//*Antiquities* 14.324). According to the *Jewish War* the location of Antony's hearing of this delegation was Daphne near Antioch, upon the Orontes. The *Antiquities* passes over the location in silence, but briefly indicates its context by hinting at Antony and Cleopatra's first meeting in Cilicia, with the famous seduction scene on a golden barge in Tarsus in 41 BCE.[5] The important thing for us here is Josephus' note in the margin that Antony 'was already enslaved by his love for Cleopatra' (Ἀντώνιον ἤδη τῷ Κλεοπάτρας ἔρωτι δεδουλωμένον) at this very early stage, whereas Roman authors suggest that Antony fell in love with Cleopatra at a much later date.[6] Josephus' not at all flattering statement about Antony, which anticipates Cleopatra's attempts to make Antony act against Herod, is, in fact, only partly warranted by further events as told by Josephus. Antony was certainly extremely generous to Cleopatra, but there are clear cases where he did not give in to her when it did not match his or Rome's interests (cf. below).[7] Several Roman authors also suggest that Antony was Cleopatra's slave.[8] The

---

[3] The relevant passages are: (1) *Jewish War* 1.243-4; 1.277-9; 1.359-61; 1.362-3; 1.365-7; 1.389-90; 1.396-7; 1.439-40; 7.300; (2) *Antiquities* 14.324; 14.374-6; 15.24, 28, 32, 45-6, 48, 62-3, 65, 75-9; 15.88-95; 15.96-103; 15.104-5; 15.106-7; 15.110; 15.115-7; 15.131-2; 15.140; 15.191-2; 15.215, 217; 15.256-7; (3) *Against Apion* 2.56-61.

[4] *War* 1.243//*Antiquities* 14.324; *War* 1.361//*Antiquities* 15.94-5; *War* 1.363 //*Antiquities* 15.104; *War* 1.365//*Antiquities* 15.110; *War* 1.367//*Antiquities* 15.115-7, 140; *War* 1.396-7//*Antiquities* 15.215, 217.

[5] Plutarch, *Ant.* 26.1ff.; Strabo C 673f.; Appian, *Bell. civ.* 5.8; Cassius Dio 48.24.2. Many biographies of Cleopatra, more or less popular, have appeared, but the most balanced is still H. Volkmann, *Kleopatra: Politik und Propaganda*, Munich 1953. Cf. H. Schalit, *König Herodes: Der Mann und Sein Werk*, Berlin 2001², 69.

[6] Livius, *Periocha* 130: 36 BCE; Velleius Paterculus 2.82.3f.: 34 BCE.

[7] With Schalit, *Herodes*, 120.

parallel passage in *Antiquities* 14.324 formulates it slightly differently, focusing upon Cleopatra as actor: 'she laid her hands on him by love' (δι' ἔρωτος αὐτὸν ἐκεχείρωτο).[9]

The second Cleopatra passage in the *Jewish War* concerns Herod's return to Egypt in a rather difficult situation during his struggle for power against Antigonus and the Parthians (*War* 1.277-9//*Antiquities* 14.374-6) in the winter of 40-39 BCE. The *War* reports that Herod was respectfully escorted to Alexandria by Cleopatra's commanders, and was even splendidly received by the queen herself. She tried to persuade Herod to become one of her military commanders for an upcoming campaign (*War* 1.279). Josephus does not elaborate her motives, but the offer to become a commander in her army is quite probable, not only because there was a tradition of Jewish commanders in the Ptolemaic army, but also because Herod managed to make an excellent impression on foreign rulers.[10] Josephus even suggests an eagerness on Cleopatra's part by using the plural παρακλήσεις ('requests', 'exhortations'). However, Herod declined her offer and sailed for Rome despite the winter and the disorder in Italy.

The *War*'s next passage about Cleopatra (*War* 1.359-62//*Antiquities* 15.89-103 contains a cluster of very negative information about her. It

---

[8] Becher, *Kleopatra*, 64-5, whose view of Josephus' description of Antony's relationship with Cleopatra is contradictory. On the one hand she states: 'Die Gestaltung des Verhältnisses Antonius-Kleopatra entspricht in die Einzelheiten hinein (Zauber- und Liebesmittel) dem Tenor der römischen, besonders augusteischen Interpretation (ant XIV 324, xv 93; bell I 243.359; Ap. II 58)' (p. 64), on the other hand she notes that Josephus' suggestion that Antony behaved as Cleopatra's slave is a correction of the usual Roman view (p. 65). Yet, several Roman others suggest the same (Florus 2.14.4; Dio 50.5.25-6; Appian, *Bell. civ.* 5.8-9), and Antony's behaviour towards his sweetheart was by no means considered 'un-Roman' by all Romans: J. Griffin, *Latin Poets and Roman Life*, London 1985, 32-47. Cf. the defence of Antony in R. Syme, *The Roman Revolution*, Oxford 1939, 104-5: 'The memory of Antonius has suffered damage multiple and irreparable. The policy which he adopted in the East and with the Queen of Egypt were vulnerable to the moral and patriotic propaganda of his rival. ... Many of the charges levelled against the character of Antonius—such as unnatural vice or flagrant cowardice—are trivial, ridiculous or conventional' (p. 104).

[9] Cf. also *Antiquities* 15.93 (Antony totally overcome by Cleopatra), 15.101 and 15.131 concerning the Arabs.

[10] Grant, *Cleopatra*, 128. P. Richardson, *Herod: King of the Jews and Friend of the Romans*, Columbia 1996, note 131, has doubts about the offer because of the later tensions between Herod and Cleopatra. Schalit, *Herodes*, 83 and 104 note 26, assumes that Cleopatra would have murdered Herod if she would have known that he intended to become king of Judea, because she herself wanted to incorporate Syria and Phoenicia again in the Ptolemaic territories.

concerns Antony's grants of important and partly Judaean territories
to Cleopatra (37-6 or 34 BCE). It is introduced by Josephus' statement
that Antony was already corrupted by his love for Cleopatra and
overcome in every respect by his desire for her (ἤδη γὰρ Ἀντώνιος
τῷ Κλεοπάτρας ἔρωτι διεφθαρμένος ἥττων ἦν ἐν πᾶσιν τῆς ἐπιθυμίας,
1.359), and that she had murdered all her relatives. Both points do
appear in other sources,[11] but Josephus focuses on the consequences
for the client kings in Egypt's periphery, and not on those for Rome.
He also highlights these points by putting them at the beginning of
this passage, as a signal for his readers to understand that Cleopatra's
murderous plans—getting rid of high-ranking officials in Syria as well
as the kings of Judaea and Arabia, and taking over their territories (cf.
War 1.365)—were partly successful because Antony behaved as her
slave. The passage emphasizes Cleopatra's greed (πλεονεξία, 360) for
more possessions and territories, and mentions her murderous intentions several times (*War* 1.359, 360, 361; cf. 440). Antony refrained
from killing officials according to *War* 1.359-360, but Josephus mentions in passing, in connection with a fabricated accusation of Mariamme by Herod's sister and mother (below), that both king Lysanias
of Chalcis and the 'Arab' (i.e. Nabataean) king Malchus died because
of Cleopatra's 'cleverness' (δεινότης, perhaps a *double entendre*), and
that Herod feared for his life as well (*War* 1.439-40).[12] *War* 1.359-60
tells us that Antony behaved not very loyally towards his client king
Herod.[13] He granted Cleopatra all the cities 'this side of the River
Eleutherus [*Antiquities*: between the River Eleutherus and Egypt] except
Tyrus and Sidon'[14] as well as the balsam plantation of Jericho (*War*
1.361//*Antiquities* 15.95), which was leased back from Cleopatra by
Herod (*War* 1.362//*Antiquities* 15.96).[15] The *Antiquities*' description of

---

[11] Velleius Paterculus 2.85.6 notes that Cleopatra ruined Antony. Cf. Becher,
Kleopatra, 62. For Cleopatra's murdering her siblings, see below pp. 127, 131.

[12] The death of Lysanias is confirmed by *Antiquities* 15.92, that of Malchus (56-
28 BCE) not; this must be a mistake, because other sources confirm that he outlived
Cleopatra, Richardson, *Herod*, 165 note 62.

[13] Josephus suggests that the client kings mentioned lost their status as 'friends'
(*War* 1.361), but Schalit, *Herodes*, 774 suggests that τὸ δὲ τούτων ἔγγιον φίλους is
corrupt.

[14] *Antiquities* 15.95 explains the exception of Tyrus and Sidon by their being free
cities from the time of their ancestors onwards.

[15] Jericho's profits because of the balsam, used as a medicine against headache
and eyesight problems, and palm wine production were enormous. The lease that

Antony's gift of territories to Cleopatra suggests that there had been earlier grants, and that Antony tried to satisfy Cleopatra by giving her Coele-Syria[16] instead of Judaea (*Antiquities* 15.79). *Antiquities* 15.92 refers to the gift of Lysanias' kingdom of Chalcis to Cleopatra.[17] Both gifts are not mentioned in the *Jewish War*.

Herod had to pay Cleopatra equalled half of his annual income in 4 BCE. Cf. Richardson, *Herod*, 166.

[16] The reference 'Coele-Syria' ('Hollow Syria') in this period is unclear, because it was associated with several areas, including the Decapolis area with, perhaps, Damascus as its capital, Chalcis as well as the area between the Lebanon and Anti-Lebanon Mountains. Cf. E. Bickerman, 'La Coelé-Syria: Notes de géographie historique', *RB* 54 (1947) 256; H. Buchheim, *Die Orientpolitik des Triumvirs M. Antonius: ihre Voraussetzungen, Entwicklung und Zusammenhang mit den politischen Ereignissen in Italien*, Heidelberg 1960, 16 note 28; Richardson, *Herod*, 70 note 74; Schalit, *Herodes*, 775-7, and for a later period F. Millar, *The Roman Roman Near East: 31 BC - AD 337*, Cambridge, MA 1993, 121-3.

[17] Josephus seems to date Antony's grants of territories to Cleopatra at least in the *Antiquities* to 35-34 BCE, after Herod's giving account to Antony about the death of Aristoboulos (*Antiquities* 15.64-79). This chronology does not match with Plutarch's and Porphyrius's date for the grants in 37 BCE (Eusebius, *Chron.* ed. Schoene 1.170) and the latter date should be preferred. Cf. Buchheim, *Orientpolitik*, 68-74; Grant, *Cleopatra*, 240; G. Hölbl, *Geschichte des Ptolemäerreiches: Politik, Ideologie und religiöse Kultur von Alexander dem Grossen bis zur römischen Eroberung*, Darmstadt 1994, 217; Schalit, *Herodes*, 120, 773-4. Schalit, *Herodes*, 773-7, suggests that there may have been three successive grants of territories to Cleopatra. The first grant (37-36 BCE) consisted of Lysanias' Kingdom of Chalcis, Coele-Syria (either the area between Lebanon and Antilebanon that traditionally carries that name, or, following Schalit [p. 775] and Buchheim [p. 101 note 28] the region of the Decapolis in Jordan), Cilicia, Cyprus and the cities between the Eleutherus and Egypt (i.e. the coastal area of Phoenicia south of the Eleutherus and Palestine). Gaza may have been a separate grant in 35 BCE, and the third grant (34 BCE) would consist of Jericho and certain Nabataean areas. The separate grant of Gaza is doubtful. *Antiquities* 15.217, 254 implies that Gaza was taken away from Herod in the thirties and given to Cleopatra, *Antiquities* 15.254 states that Herod, on his accession to the throne in 40 BCE, appointed Costobarus as governor of Gaza, and 15.217 notes that Octavian returns it to Herod as part of Cleopatra's former territory. Dio 49.32.4-5 and Plutarch, *Ant.* 36, mention most of Antony's gifts together, confirming a huge grant of territories to Cleopatra in 37 (36) BCE, but referring to Phoenicia instead of the cities between the Eleutherus and Egypt. Schalit's identification (p. 777) of 'Phoenicia' in Dio and Plutarch with Josephus's 'cities between the Eleutherus and Egypt' is not entirely accurate, because Dio (loc. cit.), contrary to Plutarch, does not refer to Phoenicia only, but to 'large parts of Phoenicia and Palestine'. This phrase probably equals Josephus' reference to 'the cities between the Eleutherus and Egypt' in *Antiquities* 15.95. In that case, Josephus and Dio refer to the same, large coastal area. Assuming that Josephus' and Dio's geographical references are correct and Plutarch's account deficient, a separate grant of Gaza becomes improbable, because it was part of the coastal area included in Antony's grant in 37 (36) BCE. That would leave us with two grants only, one in 37 (36) BCE and one in 34 BCE. Strabo reports Antony's gifts of Korakesion and Amaxia

In *War* 1.362 Josephus moves on to a campaign of Antony against the Parthians, which was, in fact, directed at the Armenians (34 BCE).[18] He notes without further comments that Cleopatra accompanied Antony up to the Euphrates, and then came to Herod in Judaea, returning via Apamea and Damascus. Herod behaved as if he was her client king, mollifying her hostility (δυσμένειαν, cf. *Antiquities* 15.65) with huge presents and leasing the territories that Antony had taken away from his kingdom for an annual sum of 200 talents. *Antiquities* 15.106 notes that Herod faithfully paid this sum 'because he considered it unsafe to give Cleopatra a reason for hating him'.[19] At the end of her visit he escorted her to Pelusium, treating her with the highest respect (cf. *Antiquities* 15.103, 132). After Antony's victorious return from Armenia Cleopatra got the Armenian king Artabazes, as well as the money and all the booty, as spectacular presents from Antony (*War* 1.363//*Antiquities* 15.104).[20] Josephus consistently refers to Parthians in *War* 1.362-3, but other sources confirm that it was the Armenian king who was brought to Alexandria as prisoner of war.[21]

The next episode (*War* 1.365-85//*Antiquities* 15.110-60) precedes the

---

(C 669, 763), but does not mention Jericho. He also recalls that Cleopatra owned the island Elaiussa, but does not mention Antony's gift of it (C 671). Becher, *Kleopatra*, 40-1; E. Schürer, *The History of the Jewish People in the Age of Jesus Christ (175 BC-AD 135): A new English Version*, rev. and ed. by G. Vermes, F. Millar, and M. Goodman, i, Edinburgh 1973, 298, 300 with note 36.

[18] Schalit, *Herodes*, 774, is not persuasive in arguing that this is not a mistake of Josephus, referring to Dio 49.33.3, where it is noted that Antony tried to fool the Armenian king by pretending that he marched out against the Parthians; Josephus even refers to the Parthians after Antony's return (*War* 1.363). The parallel passage in *Antiquities* 15.96 correctly refers to Armenia.

[19] The *Antiquities* offers more information about Herod leasing back the territories given to Cleopatra (15.96, 106-7, 132) and reports that Herod leased the Nabataean parts in turn to Malchus, who had to pay him 200 talents (15.107). Richardson, *Herod*, 166 note 74 with references, doubts that the annual sum that Herod had to pay to Cleopatra was 400 talents (as implied by *Antiquities* 15.132), and argues that 15.106-7 implies that Herod had to pay 200 talents all in all, and, therefore, got Jericho for free (receiving 200 talents from the Nabataean king). But the *Antiquities* reports that Malchus was very lax in paying Herod (15.107), and the 200 talents for Malchus' lease is as improbably high as the total sum for Herod of 400 talents. From 'Arabia' Cleopatra got the enclave at the southern section of the Dead Sea that produced bitumen. The lease of Jericho and the Dead Sea section must have been an important contribution to Cleopatra's enormous wealth at the end of her life (Dio 51.15.4).

[20] *Antiquities*'s formulation is slightly different and adds that Artabazes' sons and satraps accompanied him as prisoner of war.

[21] Josephus, *Antiquities* 15.104; Dio 49.31-40; Plutarch, *Ant.* 50.7. Buchheim, *Orientpolitik*, 90-1; Becher, *Kleopatra*, 29.

definitive battle between Antony and Octavian at Actium (31 BCE). As most loyal client king Herod prepared himself to support and join Antony, but Cleopatra's scheming spiked his guns. In a cunning plan of divide and rule she persuaded Antony to order Herod to fight 'the Arabs' (i.e. Nabataeans),[22] so that she could take over the kingdom from the king who would lose this war (*War* 1.365 // *Antiquities* 15.110).[23] A theme obvious in other sources, that Cleopatra wanted to play the first fiddle in assisting Antony's decisive battle against Octavian, is not mentioned by Josephus at all.[24] A series of confrontations between Herod and the Nabataeans follow, with Herod finally gaining a great victory.[25] The treacherous and disastrous interference of Athenion, one of Cleopatra's generals, in a second battle (*War* 1.367, 369, 375; *Antiquities* 15.115-7, 140), matched, of course, Cleopatra's plan for both kings.[26]

In the aftermath of Actium Herod persuaded Octavian, during a meeting at Rhodes in the Spring of 30 BCE, to allow him to become his client king. In his impressive speech, Herod suggests to Octavian that he had advised Antony to get rid of Cleopatra by murdering her:

> I told him that the death of Cleopatra was the only remedy for his misfortunes, and I promised him, once he killed her, money, walls for his safety, an army, and myself as an ally in war against you (καὶ ἐμαυτὸν ὑπισχνούμην κοινωνὸν τοῦ πρὸς σὲ πολέμου). However, his passionate love for Cleopatra (οἱ Κλεοπάτρας ἵμεροι), as well as God, who wanted to grant you victory, stopped up his ears (*War* 1.389-90 // *Antiquities* 15.190-2).

The assumption that this rather improbable statement flowed out of Josephus' own pen, as most of the information about speeches in his works seems to do, is supported by the observation that it links up with

---

[22] The pretext for the war, the treachery of the Nabataean king, is only provided by *Antiquities* 15.110; cf. 15.107.

[23] Josephus' description of Cleopatra's successful scheming to keep Herod away from Antony in his final battle against Octavian is trustworthy in the opinion of Becher, *Kleopatra*, 67-8, because it matches descriptions of similar performances by her.

[24] Herod, one of her serious enemies, could have complicated that. Cf. Grant, *Cleopatra*, 196. Cleopatra's role in the Battle of Actium has been much discussed by ancient authors. Cf. Becher, *Kleopatra*, e.g. 32, 75-7, 108-10, 182-3.

[25] About the battles and Herod's commander speech, see Richardson, *Herod*, 166-8; Schalit, *Herodes*, 122-4; J.W. van Henten, 'Commonplaces in Herod's Commander Speech in Josephus' *Antiquities* 15.127-46' (in print).

[26] See esp. *Antiquities* 15.116. Josephus explicitly refers to his treachery in *War* 1.369.

Josephus' earlier point, that Antony's deeds resulted out of his love for Cleopatra (*War* 1.243, above).[27] It also cleverly notes in passing that Herod saw himself as the much better alternative for Cleopatra: if Antony had killed Cleopatra, he would have had Herod as ally in the battle against Octavian.

Thus, the statement makes explicit what has been presupposed in several of the passages discussed: Herod and Cleopatra were competitors, both fighting for benefits from Antony. Octavian's decision to maintain Herod as client king must have been motivated mainly by his strong expectation that the relationship was going to be mutually beneficial.[28] Herod's statement about Cleopatra in the parallel passage in *Antiquities* 15.191-2 is rather different:

> For, he [Herod] said, if she had been got out of the way earlier, he [Antony] would have had the possibility to maintain his rule and would have found it easier to make his arrangements with you rather than be enemies. But he did not take thought of any of these considerations, unfortunately for him but profitably for you, and preferred his ill-advisedness.

Here Herod suggests that Antony and Octavian would have not become enemies without Cleopatra's interference, turning Cleopatra—not Antony—into Rome's real enemy, in line with Augustean propaganda.[29]

War 1.396-7 // *Antiquities* 15.215, 217 notes the deaths of Antony and Cleopatra without any details, and Octavian's return to Herod of the territory that had been given to Cleopatra as well as his generous grant of Gadara, Hippus, Samaria, Gaza, Anthedon, Joppa and Straton's Tower, and his transfer of Cleopatra's four hundred bodyguards from Gaul.[30] These grants were made during a visit of Herod to Alexandria in 30 BCE, after Octavian had secured his control over Egypt. Finally, the note in *War* 7.300 suggests that Herod prepared the fortress of

---

[27] Schalit, *Herodes*, 127-9 argues, with W. Otto, that the speech derives from Herod's memoirs and that it is probable that Herod did make such a statement, trying to show in this way that he was loyal to the Roman people, in line with the legal argument that Cleopatra and not Antony was Rome's enemy at Actium. W. Otto, 'Herodes', *PRE*, Supplementband II (1913), 1-158 at 1.

[28] Cf. Becher, *Kleopatra*, 68; Schalit, *Herodes*, 129.

[29] P. Zanker, *The Power of Images in the Age of Augustus*, Ann Arbor 1988, 58-60.

[30] See for details about these grants Schalit, 2001, 130, 162 and 776, who argues that Gaza and Samaria also had been transferred by Antony from Herod's territory to Cleopatra.

Masada as a refuge specifically because of his fear of Cleopatra (τὸν μείζω δὲ καὶ χαλεπώτερον ἐκ τῆς βασιλευούσης Αἰγύπτου Κλεοπάτρας), apart from the possible threats from the Jewish people. The weapons and food supplies would be used a hundred years later by the Zealots at Masada (*War* 7.295-9).[31]

In short, the information about Cleopatra in the *Jewish War* is brief and mostly in passing, apart from *War* 1.359-67, which mentions her frequently. With his strongly negative statement at the beginning of this passage Josephus emphasizes Antony's love for her and her use of her sexuality, as well as her greed and murderous intentions. He creates the impression that Antony was ruined by this evil woman, which is very much in line with her portrait in several Roman sources. Cleopatra and Herod appear as each other's natural enemies in the *War*, because both were extremely ambitious and strongly dependent on Antony's favours.[32]

2. *Cleopatra in* Jewish Antiquities *14-15*

The *Antiquities'* version of Herod's visit to Alexandria at the beginning of his career (*War* 1.277-9 // *Antiquities* 14.374-6) differs in two ways from the report in the *War*. Cleopatra's reception of Herod is rephrased in more neutral terms: Herod was 'held by Cleopatra' and she could not persuade him to stay (... ὑπὸ Κλεοπάτρας κατείχετο. πεῖσαι μέντοι μένειν αὐτὸν οὐκ ἠδυνήθη ..., 375-6). Herod's splendid reception in the *War* and the offer to become one of her commanders are both left out, which implies that one of the very rare positive portrayals of Cleopatra in the *War* is retouched in the *Antiquities*.

In the *Jewish War* the next event in which Cleopatra is involved concerns Antony's transfer of territories, including Jericho, to Cleopatra (*War* 1.359-61 // *Antiquities* 15.88-103), but the *Antiquities* inserts an important cluster of references to Cleopatra before this transfer. Mariamme's mother Alexandra addresses Cleopatra several times as an intermediary to Antony and a protector against Herod, her son-in-law (*Antiquities* 15.24, 28, 32, 45-6, 62). Cleopatra was not only the woman with the

---

[31] Becher, *Kleopatra*, 66.
[32] Grant, *Cleopatra*, 139-41, 158-60. After Antony's gift of Jericho and the cities of Coele Syria up to the Eleutherus river to Cleopatra, she must have become Herod's worst enemy. Cf. Becher, *Kleopatra*, 65-6.

greatest status (ἀξίωμα, *Antiquities* 15.101) in the ancient world,[33] but also the person closest to Antony when they were together, and as a consequence a powerful help for manipulating Antony. Josephus' description suggests the existence of a complicated web of competing royal persons and factions, all dependent on Antony as the ultimate *patronus*. They could use Cleopatra as broker, by entering into a client relationship with her as well. Costobarus uses such a strategy during his defection from Herod (*Antiquities* 15.256-8).[34] He proposes in a message that Idumaea should be 'returned' to her and that he would gladly serve under her rule.

Alexandra does something similar. First, she secretly writes to Cleopatra in order to get her son Aristoboulos appointed as high priest instead of Ananel (15.24), hoping, in fact, that he could be Herod's successor (15.42). When Antony's friend Dellius visits her, he persuades Alexandra to send portraits of her exceptionally beautiful children to Antony in order to make sure that her wish would be fulfilled, but decides against taking Mariamme with him to Alexandria: 'he feared summoning the girl, who was married to Herod, and also wanted to avoid accusations passed on to Cleopatra because of such an affair' (15.28).[35] This passage, hinting at Antony as somebody indulging in sexual pleasures (cf. 15.27), points at a dangerous trait of Cleopatra in Josephus' portrait of hers: she accused whoever she could in order to gain something out of it and everybody was afraid of her accusations, including Herod (15.48, 65, 77). When Alexandra writes a second time to Cleopatra, the queen advises her to come over secretly to Alexandria with her son (15.45-6), obviously undermining Herod's power by supporting someone who could take over the rule from him. Alexandra's clever plan to escape together with Aristoboulos in two coffins ultimately fails because Herod discovers it, but the king refrains from punishing her as well as from blaming Cleopatra: 'He thought that Cleopatra, out of hatred towards him (ἐπὶ τῷ πρὸς αὐτὸν μίσει), would not bear to receive the blame' (15.48). When Herod finally succeeds in having Aristoboulos murdered in the swimming pool of

---

[33] B. Mayer-Schärtel, *Das Frauenbild des Josephus: Eine sozialgeschichtliche und kultur-anthropologische Untersuchung*, Stuttgart/Berlin 1995, 86.

[34] Details: Schalit, 2001, 142-4, 777.

[35] Schalit, *Herodes*, 104-7, argues that the *Antiquities*' version of this portrait story (cf. *War* 1.439-40) is highly improbable, but that the manufacture itself of portraits was not uncommon within the Herodian family.

his palace in Jericho (36 BCE),[36] Herod almost overplays his hand. Cleopatra jumps to the case after receiving Alexandra's complaint, and urges Antony to avenge the murder:

> She [Cleopatra] was for a long time already eager to help her [Alexandra] with her request and felt pity for Alexandra's mishaps. She made the entire thing her own business and did not let Antony go, urging him to punish the murder of the boy. For it was not right that Herod, who was king through him over a territory that in no way belonged to him, displayed such unlawful matters to the ones who were real kings (15.63).

Cleopatra's contempt for Herod as a self-made king of non-Judean origin is obvious,[37] and the situation becomes very dangerous for him because of Cleopatra's interference. Antony demands from him to render an account, and Herod has to obey:

> Since he was afraid of the accusation and Cleopatra's hostility (ὁ δὲ τήν τε αἰτίαν δεδοικὼς καὶ τὴν Κλεοπάτρας δυσμένειαν), because she did not cease working to achieve that Antony became hostile to him, he decided to obey (15.65).

This delicate power game between Herod and Cleopatra, both trying to get Antony to do what would support their interest, temporarily ends with the king as winner—at least this is what a letter from Herod to his relatives, paraphrased by Josephus, implies (*Antiquities* 15.74-9). Herod apparently won Antony over with his gifts from Jerusalem and satisfying explanations: 'Cleopatra's words meant little in comparison to the favours coming from Herod' (15.76; cf. 15.131). Cleopatra was even warned by Antony not to interfere in the rule of the Judaean kingdom (15.77). The letter also explains Cleopatra's behaviour, anticipating, in fact, the next Cleopatra episode in the *Antiquities* narrative:

> He [Herod] also wrote that he gained these honours [i.e. participating in Antony's legal decisions and feasting with him] all the same despite Cleopatra's giving him a hard time with her accusations of him. Cleopatra desired his country and demanded that his kingdom would be given in addition to her, doing her very best in every way to get him out of the way (ἡ πόθῳ τῆς χώρας ἐξαιτουμένη τὴν βασιλείαν αὐτῇ προσγενέσθαι πάντα τρόπον ἐκποδὼν αὐτὸν ἐσπουδάκει ποιεῖσθαι) (15.77).

---

[36] Aristoboulos had been appointed high priest by Herod around the turn of the year 37-36 BCE, Schalit, *Herodes*, 111.
[37] Becher, *Kleopatra*, 67.

Cleopatra's strategy of eliminating rival kings in order to take over their territories becomes obvious in the *Antiquities*' next episodes (below). Whether or not by means of this strategy, as emphasized by Josephus, Cleopatra did in fact manage to restore most of the Ptolemaic kingdom and its huge territories outside Egypt.[38] At this moment, however, Herod's letter in the aftermath of Aristoboulos' death notes that Antony partly satisfied Cleopatra by giving her Coele-Syria instead of Herod's territory (15.79, above).

Antiquities 15.88-103 variously expands the *War*'s rather compact passage about Cleopatra's murderous attitude towards Antony's client kings, and Antony's grant of cities and territories to her (*War* 1.359-61); it also changes the sequence of the events somewhat. First, Josephus anticipates Cleopatra's attempt to kill Herod and take over his territory by noting beforehand that she wished for his death and territory (*Antiquities* 15.77, 79; cf. 15.92). *Antiquities* 15.88 links up with these passages and notes that Cleopatra kept pressing Antony for giving her the dominions (δυναστείας) of neighbouring rulers after murdering them and that Antony gave in to her in most cases 'out of his passion for her' (ἐκ τῆς ἐκείνου πρὸς αὐτὴν ἐπιθυμίας, 15.88). Yet, Antony did not give Cleopatra the main territories of Herod and Malchus, probably because that did not fit in with his general policy concerning these kingdoms, which provided important extra support for his wars against the Parthians and Armenians.

Second, Josephus offers his own shorthand commentary on Cleopatra with a brief excursus (*Antiquities* 15.89-91), which surpasses the parallel comment in *War* 1.359 in its repetitive negative vocabulary and devastating characterization. Josephus emphasizes Cleopatra's greed (πλεονεξία; 15.89, 90; perhaps also 15.79)[39] and her lawlessness (παρανομία; 15.89; cf. 15.90). Her greed for money is exemplified by making her into a robber of temples and tombs in general:

> For temples and tombs were violated (καὶ ναοὶ καὶ τάφοι παρενομήθησαν) for the sake of money, if it was only hoped for somehow. No sacred place seemed so inviolable to her that it could not be stripped of its valuables, no secular place would not suffer any forbidden act whatsoever, if it only was bound to enhance the abundance fuelled by the greediness of this wrong-doing lady (15.90).

---

[38] Hölbl, *Geschichte*, 217-18.
[39] The Greek in 15.79 is ambiguous and can be translated by 'hope for a greater advantage' or 'hope of satisfying her greediness'.

This statement perhaps echoes Cleopatra's desperate attempt to collect whatever money she could lay her hands on after the defeat at Actium,[40] but it closely corresponds to the stereotypic image of the godless foreign tyrant as applied to Antiochus IV and Nero in other sources.[41] Josephus also elaborates the general reference about murdering her relatives in *War* 1.359 with specific information about the murder of her brother Ptolemy XIV with poison and her sister Arsinoe in Ephesus with Antony's help (15.89).[42] Josephus final criticism of Cleopatra in this passage bluntly disqualifies her as a ruler: she was intemperate and totally lacked self-control:

> In short, nothing at all was sufficient for this woman, who was extravagant and a slave of her desires as well (τὸ δ' ὅλον οὐδὲν αὔταρκες ἦν γυναικὶ καὶ πολυτελεῖ καὶ δουλευούσῃ ταῖς ἐπιθυμίαις). Everything thinkable was deficient of the things she was craving for (15.91).

Incidentally, Josephus suggests here that Cleopatra's greed was related to an addiction to extravagant luxury, which is also a prominent motif in Plutarch, Fronto and Lucan (*Phars.* 10.109-10, 139-40).[43]

Third, the case of Lysanias, the king of Chalcis is proof that Cleopatra's murderous plans to have rulers killed and take over their territories succeeded. She accused him of siding with the Parthians and had him killed (*Antiquities* 15.92), whereupon Antony gave her Lysanias' kingdom.[44]

Fourth, one element of Cleopatra's character, her use of seduction as strategy, gets special attention in *Antiquities* 15.88-103. Like

---

[40] Cf. *Against Apion* 2.60. After the disaster of Actium Cleopatra executed wealthy Egyptians, confiscated their possessions and plundered temples as well (Dio 51.5.4). Becher, *Kleopatra*, 68, following T. Reinach, assumes that Josephus' exaggerated reproach originates in the bitterness of Alexandrian Jews about Cleopatra's aggressive behaviour towards them (cf. *Against Apion* 2.60).

[41] J.C.H. Lebram, 'König Antiochus im Buch Daniel', *VT* 25 (1975) 737-72; J.W. van Henten, 'Antiochus IV as a Typhonic Figure in Dan. 7', in: A. S. van der Woude (ed.), *The Book of Daniel in the Light of New Findings* (BETL 106), Louvain 1993, 223-43; Id., 'Nero Redivivus Demolished: the Coherence of the Nero Traditions in the Sibylline Oracles', *Journal for the Study of the Pseudepigrapha* 21 (2000) 3-17.

[42] Cf. for the murder of Cleopatra's siblings Appian, *Bell. civ.* 5.1.9, who wrongly gives Miletus in stead of Ephesus as location of Arsinoe's death. The *Antiquities* also delivered Serapion to Cleopatra. The poisoning of Cleopatra's brother Ptolemy XIV is only attested by Josephus, Becher, *Kleopatra*, 64.

[43] Becher, *Kleopatra*, 119, 134-45, 181.

[44] This happened in 37-6 or 34 BCE. See Schürer, *History*, i, 253, 287-8 with notes 5 and 565.

the *War*, the *Antiquities* states that Cleopatra had a huge influence on Antony because of his love and desire for her (ἐπιθυμία in *War* 1.359 and *Antiquities* 15.88; cf. *Antiquities* 15.93, 101), but the *Antiquities* refers explicitly to her sexual relationship with him[45] and also adds her use of drugs in order to make him obey her (μὴ μόνον ἐκ τῆς ὁμιλίας, ἀλλὰ καὶ φαρμάκοις, *Antiquities* 15.93). Cleopatra's use of drugs or sorcery in her attempts to seduce men is well known from other sources, and her success with males was attributed to her beauty in later sources only.[46] The *Antiquities* adds a detailed report about Cleopatra's attempt to seduce Herod (15.96-103), when she visits Herod in Jericho after having received the territories including Jericho from Antony and having returned from escorting him on his campaign against the Armenians. This was first and foremost a business meeting, in which Herod leased back parts of Arabia and Jericho from her. Josephus suggests that Cleopatra enjoyed her visit and stretched it, and tried to seduce Herod. Josephus is ambiguous about her motive: he notes that she was used to enjoy sexual pleasures with other men and hints that she was attracted to Herod, but also suggests that it was a trap:

> Being in this region and meeting Herod frequently, she kept trying to have sex with the king. By nature she enjoyed the pleasures from this without disguise. Perhaps she did experience some erotic desire for him, or, which is more plausible, she was secretly preparing the outrageous act that was going to be done to her as the beginning of a trap. Altogether she kept showing herself as having been overcome by desire (15.97).

Ironically, when Herod considers murdering her while she was in Judaea, he condemns her licentiousness and notes that she would not even be faithful to Antony (*Antiquities* 15.98-9), and Herod's friends, who advise him not to murder her, imply that giving in to her was a sin (*Antiquities* 15.102).

This seduction passage, which links up with Josephus' characterization of Cleopatra in 15.89-91 through the repetition of 'by nature' (φύσει, 15.89, 97), turns her into a most audacious killer queen. But to whom should we attribute this tradition? Otto and Schalit consider it absolutely possible that Cleopatra did try to seduce Herod

---

[45] Grant, *Cleopatra*, XVII, states that Cleopatra's sexuality dominated her character.

[46] Cleopatra's ravishing beauty is a later motif, which arises for the first time in Lucan's *Pharsalia*. Cf. Becher, *Kleopatra*, 108-10.

because she could be trusted to do such a thing,[47] but in that case it would probably have been incorporated already in the *War*. Another explanation of the story's origin is that it came from Herod's memoirs, which were incorporated in the *Antiquities* according to 15.174.[48] Whether Herod has invented it himself or not, it definitely turns him, in the light of the developments after Actium, into a friend of the Roman people, and it anticipates his advice, which he said to have given Antony, to kill her, as reported to Octavian after Antony and Cleopatra's death (*War* 1.389-90//*Antiquities* 15.191-2). Finally, the story about Cleopatra's attempt to seduce Herod and Herod's inclination to murder her could also be Josephus' own invention, perhaps taking Herod's discussion with Octavian (*War* 1.389-90//*Antiquities* 15.191-2) as point of departure.[49]

Thus, in the *Antiquities* Josephus consistently expands the Cleopatra materials from the *War* and blackens her image, probably by incorporating contemporary traditions about her that circulated in Rome. One example of this tendency is that the *War*, in line with other earlier sources, suggests that Cleopatra's use of sexual relationships served to accomplish political goals, whereas in the *Antiquities* (15.97) her image becomes more negative in this respect and lines up with suggestions by several contemporaneous authors that it was a goal in itself.[50] Cleopatra's attempt to seduce Herod, only described by the *Antiquities*, emphasizes her shameless use of sexuality, which reminds one of the dangerous strange woman of Proverbs 7. Cleopatra's portrait in the *Antiquities* is a key example of Josephus' distrust of women in general,[51] and also shows him applying a double standard: promiscu-

---

[47] Otto, 'Herodes', 47; Schalit, *Herodes*, 121. Grant, *Cleopatra*, 159-60, considers both Cleopatra's attempt to seduce Herod and Herod's plan to murder her as certainly untrue, because both would have made Antony extremely angry.

[48] Otto, 'Herodes', 46; Schalit, *Herodes*, 121.

[49] Another possibility is that Josephus constructed Cleopatra's attempt to seduce Herod in order to suggest a parallel to her well-known unsuccessful attempt to seduce Augustus, reported in Cassius Dio 51.12 and Florus 2.21.9, Becher, *Kleopatra*, 34. Of course, Herod would have loved such an association, so we should not exclude the possibility that the story ultimately derives from his memoirs.

[50] Plinius, *Nat. hist.* 9.119, who characterizes her as a whoring queen (*regina meretrix*); Lucan, *Phars.* 10.358-60, 369-70, 374-5. Becher, *Kleopatra*, 181-2.

[51] Mayer-Schärtel, *Frauenbild*, esp. pp. 184-91. A. Brenner, 'Are we Amused? Small and Big Differences in Josephus' Re-Presentations of Biblical Female Figures in the *Jewish Antiquities* I-VIII', in: A. Brenner (ed.), *Women and Humour in the Bible and*

ous behaviour by women was a horror for him, who seems to have advocated the *univira* ideal for women;[52] but male rulers like Herod could display similar behaviour without any criticism. Josephus' own comment, especially in 15.89-91, offers a totally negative portrait of Cleopatra, which becomes close to the stereotypic image of wicked tyrants, displaying enormous greed, lawlessness, murder of their own family, robbing of temples and tombs, and total lack of self-control.

3. *Cleopatra in* Against Apion

The one passage about Cleopatra in *Against Apion* (2.56-61) relates to Apion's accusations against the Jewish people, which apparently included an accusation of Cleopatra ('... apparently reproaching *us* for her ungracious treatment of us', 2.56).[53] Josephus bounces back Cleopatra's accusation without reporting any detail of it, and it is hard to avoid the impression that he constructed a pretext to present his condensed catalogue of Cleopatra's crimes, which deals specifically with the Jews just at one point, at the end. Most of the information in the catalogue of Cleopatra's crimes is Rome centred, but remains brief and not very specific. Only readers with considerable knowledge of the queen's deeds and her reputation in Rome would have understood its *finesses*. The passage introduces Cleopatra as the last queen of the Alexandrians (*ultima Alexandrinorum regina*), and this phrase may have been triggered by the fact that Apion was an Alexandrian; it is derogatory for Cleopatra nevertheless. Interestingly, the first part of the passage (2.57-8) shows a partial overlap with *Antiquities* 15.88-90, implying that the image in *Against Apion* is closest to the queen's pitch-black image in the *Antiquities*. I present this section as a list, with the parallel passages in the *Antiquities* (and the *War*) indicated in brackets:

(2.57) *cui nihil omnino iniustitiae et malorum operum defuit*	(*Antiquities* 15.89)
uel circa generis necessarios	(*War* 1.359)
uel circa maritos suos,	(*Antiquities* 15.89)

Related Literature (The Bible in the 21st Century 2), London 2004, 90-106.

[52] J.W. van Henten, 'The Two Dreams at the End of Book 17 of Josephus' Antiquities', in: J.U. Kalms and F. Siegert (eds), *Internationales Josephus-Kolloquium Dortmund 2002* (Münsteraner Judaistische Studien 14), Münster 2003, 78-93, esp. 83-4 with references.

[53] The translations from *Against Apion* derive from H.S.J. Thackeray, *Josephus: The Life. Against Apion*, Cambridge, Mass. 1926.

qui etiam dilexerunt eam,
uel in communi contra Romanos omnes et
benefactores suos imperatores,
quae (2.58) etiam sororem Arsinoen occidit in templo
nihil sibi nocentem,   (*Antiquities* 15.89)
peremit autem et fratrem insidiis   (*Antiquities* 15.89)
paternosque deos et sepulcra progenitorum depopulata est, (*Antiquities* 15.90)
percipiensque regnum a primo Caesare eius filio
et successori rebellare praesumpsit,
Antoniumque corrumpens amatoriis rebus   (*War* 1.359 etc.)
et patriae inimicum fecit
et infidelem circa suos amicos instituit
alios quidem genere regali spolians,
alios autem demens et ad mala gerenda compellens.

The opening of the catalogue in 2.57, 'who committed every kind of injustice and crime' (*cui nihil omnino iniustitiae et malorum operum defuit*) sets the tone and echoes *Antiquities* 15.89 ('Taking pleasure in greediness by nature she left no unlawful deed undone'), although the 'greediness' comes only later in *Against Apion*. The cluster of correspondences with the *Antiquities* is confirmed by the fact that both passages continue with Cleopatra's crimes against her relatives. *Against Apion* 2.57 has the general phrase *uel circa generis necessarios*, which matches *War* 1.359 most closely, but it is articulated in 2.58 in a similar way as in *Antiquities* 15.89. Cleopatra's brother remains anonymous in both passages (above). The phrase *uel circa maritos suos qui etiam dilexerunt eam*, 'and her devoted husbands', can be explained in several ways. The passage may be repetitious if we assume that it was inspired by the assumption that the murdered Ptolemy XIV was not only Cleopatra's younger brother but also her husband, as Cassius Dio 42.44.1-2 apparently does.[54] Marriages of brothers and sisters within the royal family were a well-known practice. If *Against Apion* hints at this, did Josephus indeed make the most out of Cleopatra's murders of her brother and her sister. Ancient readers could, however, easily link these phrases to the stereotype of evil tyrants like Nero (above). And finally, the general phrasing of the passage also allows an association to Antony's fate (see below).

The next reference, 'the Romans in general, and their emperors, her benefactors', implies that Cleopatra was the archenemy of all

---

[54] References in Hölbl, *Geschichte*, 212 with note 71.

Romans. Strictly speaking, 'emperors' is anachronistic, but the passage is written in a post-Actium perspective. Augustus's propaganda tried to turn Cleopatra, instead of Antony, into the actual enemy of the Roman people; but Josephus formulates it a little differently: he blames Cleopatra of making Antony into the enemy of his fatherland, thus causing civil war between Antony and Octavian.[55] The reference may also hint at Cleopatra's treachery towards Antony, in general (cf. *Antiquities* 15.98-9) or specifically at her role during the battle at Actium, which is mentioned in *Against Apion* 2.59, or after the defeat, when she tried to switch camps.[56] Or, it may refer to her infidelity in sexual relationships, mentioned by Josephus in *Antiquities* 15.97. *Against Apion* 2.58, 'plundered her country's gods and the sepulchres of her ancestors' (*paternosque deos et sepulcra progenitorum depopulata est*), corresponds with Cleopatra's violation of temples and tombs in *Antiquities* 15.90, but the minor additions of *paternosque* and *progenitorum* make her image even worse because these changes turn Cleopatra into an enemy of her own people too. There is hardly evidence for this Josephan statement in indigenous sources. The next phrase (*percipiensque* ...) makes Cleopatra's role as antagonist of Augustus explicit, and is ironic as well: 'who owing the throne to the first Caesar, dared to revolt against his son and successor'. Julius Caesar did come to rescue Cleopatra's rule, but Octavian/Augustus was his adoptive son, while Cleopatra and Caesar had a son, Caesarion, whom Cleopatra presented as co-ruler in Egypt after her plan to make him Caesar's heir failed because of Caesar's murder.[57] As indicated in the list above *Antoniumque corrumpens amatoriis rebus* 'and who corrupted Antony by sensual love' parallels *War* 1.359 most closely, but Antony's servility to Cleopatra because of his love for her, and the disastrous result of the relationship, are hinted at several times in both the *War* and the *Antiquities* (above). Several mouthpieces of Augustus emphasized that Cleopatra made Antony into an enemy of the Roman people (*et patriae inimicum fecit*; see above about *War* 1.365-85).

The continuation of the catalogue in *Against Apion* 2.59 is more specific and not paralleled by other Josephus passages, but the picture

---

[55] Several other ancient authors have done the same, Becher, *Kleopatra*, 67 and 182.

[56] Cleopatra may have fallen for Octavian's secret declaration of love for her after Actium (Dio 51.8.6-7; 51.9.5; 51.10.6-9).

[57] Hölbl, *Geschichte*, 207-14.

remains extremely negative. Cleopatra would have deserted Antony during the Battle at Actium, and compelled him, dramatically named as the father of her children, to surrender his army and his title. This is a distortion of what really happened at Actium, but fits in with certain Roman views about Antony's defeat. The tradition about Cleopatra's 'treason' at Actium was apparently triggered by her breaking Octavian's blockade with her ships and sailing home.[58] *Against Apion* 2.60 brackens Cleopatra's suicide after Octavian had taken control over Alexandria together with her refusal to give corn to the Alexandrian Jews during the famine in 43-42 BCE.[59] The Romans probably could not care less about this reproach of her maltreatment of the Alexandrian Jews. However, this must have been a significant point for Jewish readers, not only because some of their ancestors may have suffered from this famine, but also because this claim contrasted Cleopatra with other rulers who did provide food to Jews in case of a famine, like Joseph according to the Jewish Bible, Herod himself and Helena of Adiabene. Josephus presents Herod's measures during the famine of 28-7 or 25-4 BCE in a favourable light (*Antiquities* 15.299-314), and Helena of Adiabene is highly praised because she bought grain in Alexandria for a large sum and dried figs in Cyprus to relieve the famine in 46-7 CE for the Jerusalemites (*Antiquities* 20.51-3). The most appealing counter example for Jewish readers, however, was probably Joseph, who took care of his father and brothers' families in Egypt during the years of famine (Gen 41.53-47.27; *Antiquities* 2.93-193), who did not succumb to the seduction of Potiphar's wife (Gen 39; *Antiquities* 2.39-63), and who was for Josephus a prime model of the prudent statesman, exemplifying a ruler's most important virtue, self-control (σωφροσύνη).[60] Finally, Josephus briefly notes in *Against Apion* 60 that Cleopatra's end was what she deserved, like every wicked ruler who turned against the Jews, as one could add on the basis of parallels from Josephus' own works.

---

[58] Plutarch, *Ant.* 66; Cassius Dio 50.33.2-3; Orosius 6.19.11. Cf. Becher, *Kleopatra*, 32, 75-7.

[59] Appian, *Bell. civ.* 4.108; Seneca, *De malo belli civilis* (= *Anth. Lat.* no. 462). Becher, *Kleopatra*, 65-6, 87, 116. Grant, *Cleopatra*, 219, does not consider *Against Apion* 2.60 trustworthy, referring to Thackeray and Smallwood.

[60] M. Niehoff, *The Figure of Joseph in post-Biblical Jewish Literature* (Arbeiten zur Geschichte des antiken Judentums und des Urchristentums 16), Leiden 1992; L.H. Feldman, 'Josephus' Portrait of Joseph', *Revue Biblique* 99 (1992) 379-417 and 504-28.

Thus, in *Against Apion* 2.56-60 the transformation of Cleopatra into a wicked ruler has been completed. The catalogue of her crimes partly overlaps her portrayal in the *Antiquities*, but details make her picture even worse. She becomes the archenemy of the Roman people but also turns into the enemy of her own people by violating Egypt's gods and the tombs of her ancestors. The additional material focusing on Actium and its aftermath supports her extremely negative image and the final cut is her refusal to supply corn to the Alexandrian Jews, which contrasts her in Josephus' own works with Herod, Helena of Abiadene and Joseph, the model of the wise ruler.[61]

---

[61] I thank Prof. Athalya Brenner and Luuk Huitink for many most helpful suggestions.

'THE GOD WHO DROWNED THE KING OF EGYPT': A SHORT NOTE ON AN EXORCISTIC FORMULA

PIETER W. VAN DER HORST

In the middle of the third century CE, the Christian scholar Origen wrote in his apologetic work *Contra Celsum* that

> the formula 'the God of Abraham, the God of Isaac, and the God of Jacob' is used not only by members of the Jewish nation in their prayers to God and in their exorcisms of demons, but also by almost all others who deal in magic and spells. For in magical treatises it is often to be found that God is invoked by this formula (4.33).[1]

He then goes on to say that

> furthermore, 'the God of Israel', and 'the God of the Hebrews', and 'the God who drowned the king of Egypt and the Egyptians in the Red Sea', are formulae which are often used to overpower demons and certain evil powers (4.34).[2]

Pagan use of originally biblical or Jewish formulae, including the above-mentioned, is indeed widely attested.[3] It is upon the formula last mentioned by Origen, 'the God who drowned the king of Egypt and the Egyptians in the Red Sea', that I want to focus here. To begin with, it is to be observed that this is not a literal quote from Scripture. In Exod 15.4 LXX we read that God 'cast Pharaoh's chariots and

---

[1] As a matter of fact, the formula 'the God of Abraham, the God of Isaac, and the God of Jacob' indeed occurs more often in the Greek Magical Papyri than the other formulae mentioned by Origen (see below in the text). For references and literature see R. Kotansky, *Greek Magical Amulets: The Inscribed Gold, Silver, Copper, and Bronze Lamellae*, i, *Published Texts of Known Provenance*, Opladen 1993, 291.

[2] Translation (slightly modified) by H. Chadwick, *Origen: Contra Celsum*, Cambridge 1965, 209-10. On Origen's own belief in the efficacy of magic see G. Bardy, 'Origène et la magie', *Recherches de science religieuse* 18 (1928) 126-42, and N. Brox, 'Magie und Aberglaube an den Anfängen des Christentums', *Trierer Theologische Zeitschrift* 83 (1974) 157-80, esp. 161-6.

[3] See, *inter multos alios*, W.L. Knox, 'Jewish Liturgical Exorcism', *Harvard Theological Review* 31 (1938) 191-203, and Id., *St. Paul and the Church of the Gentiles*, Cambridge 1939, 208-11 ('Jewish Influences on Magical Literature') and M. Smith, 'The Jewish Elements in the Magical Papyri', in his *Studies in the Cult of Yahweh* (ed. by S.J.D. Cohen), ii, Leiden 1996, 242-56.

his army into the sea, he sunk (κατεπόντισεν) his picked officers in the Red Sea.' And in Deut 11.3-4 LXX Moses says to the people of Israel that they have to remember

> all [God's] signs and the miracles that he did in Egypt to Pharaoh, the king of Egypt, and to all his land, and what he did to the army of the Egyptians, to their chariots and their cavalry, how he made the water of the Red Sea flow over (ἐπέκλυσεν) them as they pursued you.

All the ingredients of the formula are found in these two biblical passages, so although it is not a quote, the contents are there. The wording of the formula—ὁ θεὸς ὁ καταποντώσας ἐν τῇ ἐρυθρᾷ θαλάσσῃ τὸν Αἰγυπτίων βασιλέα καὶ τοὺς Αἰγυπτίους—is reminiscent of both passages, καταποντώσας being closer to κατεπόντισεν in Exod 15.4 than to ἐπέκλυσεν in Deut 11.4, but 'the king of the Egyptians' being closer to 'the king of Egypt' in Deut 11.3 than to 'Pharaoh' in Exod 15.4. Be that as it may, the important thing is that the formula captures in a nutshell the essence of the most dramatic story of Israel's past, its liberation by God from Egypt and the consequent destruction of its enemies.

In the framework of a magical spell such a formula has the function of a *historiola*, a mini-history[4] about the great deeds of a deity in the past, told in order to induce the deity concerned to remain true to its reputation and repeat its powerful act(s) in the present. As Fritz Graf has aptly said about *historiolae*, they are 'in magische Rezepte eingebaute knappe Erzählungen (...), die einen mythischen Präzedenzfall für eine magisch wirksame Handlung liefern.'[5] And in the same framework David Frankfurter writes about *historiolae* in terms of 'the idea that the mere recounting of certain stories situates or directs their "narrative" power into this world'.[6] Of this phenomenon we have many pagan, Jewish, and Christian instances.[7]

In the famous exorcistic charm called the *Hebraïkos logos* in the great

---

[4] D. Aune, 'Magic in Early Christianity', *Aufstieg und Niedergang der Römischen Welt* II.23.2 (1980), 1547, aptly calls it a 'mini-aretalogy.'

[5] F. Graf, 'Historiola', *Der Neue Pauly* 5 (1998) 642.

[6] D. Frankfurter, 'Narrating Power: The Theory and Practice of the Magical *Historiola* in Ritual Spells', in: M. Meyer and P. Mirecki (eds), *Ancient Magic and Ritual Power*, Leiden 1995, 457-76, here 457.

[7] See T. Hopfner, 'Mageia', *Pauly-Wissowa* 14.1 (1928), 343, and A.A. Barb, 'The Survival of Magic Arts', in: A. Momigliano (ed.), *The Conflict Between Paganism and Christianity in the Fourth Century*, Oxford 1963, 122. Frankfurter's is the best treatment to date.

magical papyrus from Paris (PGM IV 3007-3086), we find the following adjuration: 'I adjure you by the great god Sabaoth, through whom
the Jordan river drew back and the Red Sea, which Israel crossed,
became impassable' (3053-3055).[8] This passage makes reference to
both Joshua 3.13-14 (or Ps 113.3) and Exod 14.27. Here we do not
find the exact formula 'the god who drowned the king of Egypt' but
the idea is implied clearly in the words about the Red Sea becoming
impassable. In spite of the biblical language and echoes, this spell most
probably is not of Jewish origin but is a case of pagan borrowing of
Jewish motifs.[9] This pagan magician had no qualms about evoking
powerful biblical scenes; the only thing that mattered to him was that
his spell was effective. What could be more effective in chasing away
a demon than invoking the deity who made the Red Sea impassable
to the king of Egypt and drowned him in it? One can observe that in
general the imagery of the plagues of the exodus is strongly emphasized
in this spell. This should not surprise us. Morton Smith has figured
out that out of the roughly 560 spells found in the corpus of pagan
Greek magical papyri, some 200 show biblical or Jewish material one
way or another.[10] This is strong evidence of the pervasive influence
of biblical and post-biblical Jewish traditions in the international and
interdenominational world of late ancient magic. A striking instance,
which is very similar to the case under discussion, is PGM XXXVI
295-311, a love spell in which the magician evokes the image of the
angels of God descending and overturning the five cities of Sodom,
Gomorrah, Admah, Zeboiim, and Segor, and of the God who rained
down sulphur on these cities. Here Genesis 19 is taken into service
in order that the woman desired by the client may come to him and
'fulfil the mystery rite of Aphrodite' (306), i.e., have sex with him!

Although it is to be expected that the magical use of the motif of
'the God who drowned the king of Egypt' started its career in Jewish
circles, there are hardly any Jewish examples prior to the pagan ones
attested by Origen (third cent.).[11] From the third century CE we have

---

[8] Translation by W.C. Grese, in: H.D. Betz (ed.), *The Greek Magical Papyri in Translation*,
Chicago/London 1986, 97. For the Greek text see K. Preisendanz (and A. Henrichs),
Papyri Graecae Magicae: Die griechischen Zauberpapyri, i, Stuttgart 1973,170-2.

[9] See my 'The Great Magical Papyrus of Paris (PGM IV) and the Bible' (forthcoming), and Smith, 'Jewish Elements', 250.

[10] Smith, 'Jewish Elements', 246-7. The only 'purely Jewish' spell found in PGM
is no. XXIIb 1-26, the 'Prayer of Jacob'.

[11] Those scholars who regard the 'Hebrew logos' as a Jewish document dating

a Jewish lead tablet from Hadrumetum in Tunisia containing a love charm in which the sorcerer casts a spell in the name of him 'who created the heaven and the sea' (10) and 'who split the sea with his staff' (12).[12] In view of the parallelism with 'who created the heaven and the sea', there can be no doubt that the subject of 'who split ... the sea' is here God, not Moses. Here we do not find the drowning of the pharaoh explicitly mentioned, but it is certainly implied. Also from later centuries we only find instances that do contain the motif but not the exact wording of the formula, as was also the case in PGM IV (4th cent.). Among the magic bowls from late ancient Babylonia we find a few instances. In bowl 21 published by Naveh and Shaked,[13] we read the following adjuration:

> He who places a crown for the kingship, and makes dominion in the sky, and who has subdued Goliath by the hand of David, and Pharaoh by the hand of Moses, and Egypt by the hand of Joseph, and the wall of Jericho by the hand of Joshua bar Nun, may he ... (10-11).

This string of *historiolae* briefly lists some of the main mighty deeds of the God of Israel, of which the drowning of the king of Egypt is only one in a series. In the second instance, the largest Aramaic incantation bowl known so far,[14] the exorcism starts with the words, 'In the fullness of thy triumph thou overthrowest thy adversaries, thou send-

---

from before 70 CE, will of course take exception to this. On that matter see my forthcoming 'The Great Magical Papyrus of Paris (PGM IV) and the Bible'.

[12] For the text see G. Maspéro, 'Sur deux *tabellae devotionis* de la nécropole romaine d'Hadrumète', *Bibliothèque Égyptologique* 2 (1893) 303-11. It is also to be found in A. Deissmann, 'Ein epigraphisches Denkmal des alexandrinischen Alten Testaments', in his *Bibelstudien*, Marburg 1895 (repr. 1977), 29; L. Blau, *Das altjüdische Zauberwesen*, Budapest 1898 (repr. 1970), 97; A. Audollent, *Defixionum tabellae*, Paris 1904, 373-7, no. 271 (cf. ibid., 323, no. 241, line 26: χωρίσας τὴν θάλασσαν Ἰαώ); and R. Wünsch, *Antike Fluchtafeln*, Bonn 1912, 21-6, no. 5. For an English translation and commentary see J.G. Gager, *Curse Tablets and Binding Spells from the Ancient World*, New York/Oxford 1992, 112-15 (no. 36). Gager doubts its Jewish provenance, unrightly so; see R. Kotansky, 'Greek Exorcistic Amulets', in: Meyer & Mirecki, *Ancient Magic and Ritual Power*, 274. Literally the text reads, 'who split his staff with the sea', but this is obviously an error; so rightly Deissmann, 'Ein epigraphisches Denkmal', 38, and P.S. Alexander, 'Jewish Elements in Gnosticism and Magic', in: W. Horbury et al. (eds), *The Cambridge History of Judaism*, iii, Cambridge 1999, 1075 with note 51.

[13] J. Naveh and Sh. Shaked, *Magic Spells and Formulae: Aramaic Incantations of Late Antiquity*, Jerusalem 1993, 127-30.

[14] J. Naveh and Sh. Shaked, *Amulets and Magic Bowls: Aramaic Incantations of Late Antiquity*, Jerusalem/Leiden 1985, 198-9, no. 13 line 2.

est forth thy fury, it consumes them like stubble' (Exod 15.7). To be sure the pharaoh and his army are not mentioned here explicitly, but these words, quoted from the Song at the Sea, are almost a direct continuation of the words 'Pharaoh's chariots and his army he cast into the sea' (Exod 15.4), and there is no doubt that it was exactly these adversaries the magician had in mind. So again we see how important the evocation of this mighty deed of God was for exorcists, just as Origen mentioned, the parallel between the two—exorcism and exodus—of course residing in the element of liberation from an evil power.[15]

No wonder that in Christian circles, both in Egypt and elsewhere, many of these originally Jewish elements were adopted for exorcistic purposes.[16] Typically Christian elements were added, however, the cross and the resurrection of course foremost among them, being the Christian counterparts of the exodus from Egypt. Hence they could serve the same purpose.[17] In his *Dialogue with Trypho* 85.2 Justin quotes a summary of the Creed which has been taken over from an exorcistic formula, as Knox has convincingly argued.[18] And in *Contra Celsum* 1.6, Origen says that Christian exorcists subdue demons 'by the name of Jesus with the recital of the histories about him'. What else is the Creed than a recital of the histories (*historiolae*) about Jesus? 'These credal exorcisms are surely formed on the earlier Jewish model of reciting the *historia* of the God of Israel.'[19] There is abundant evidence indeed that in exorcistic formulae Christian *historiolae* very soon began to be added to those of Jewish origin, or to supplant them.[20] But that is another story.

---

[15] I did not find any instances in the three volumes *Magische Texte aus der Kairoer Geniza*, edited by P. Schäfer and S. Shaked, Tübingen 1994-99.

[16] E.g., the death of the Egyptians at the exodus is mentioned (as part of a long series of *megaleia tou theou*, all from the OT) in an exorcistic formula said to have been composed by Gregory Thaumatourgos; see for the Greek text Th. Schermann, *Griechische Zauberpapyri und das Gemeinde- und Dankgebet im 1. Klemensbrief*, Leipzig, 1909, 20. Note that the motif occurs also in Hebrews 11.29; and cf. Justin, *Dialogus* 131.3 and the prayer in *Constitutiones Apostolicae* 8.12.12.

[17] See K. Thraede, 'Exorzismus', *RAC* 7 (1969) 44-117, esp. 109-14.

[18] *St. Paul*, 209. After the quote it is added that in this name (sc. of Jesus Christ whose life has just been summarized) every demon will be defeated and conquered.

[19] Kotansky, 'Greek Exorcistic Amulets', in: Meyer & Mirecki (eds.), *Ancient Magic and Ritual Power*, 263 note 47. Also Kotansky, *Greek Magical Amulets*, 174-80.

[20] See Aune, 'Magic', 1547-8. See also W. Heitmüller, *'Im Namen Jesu': Eine sprach- und religionsgeschichtliche Untersuchung zum Neuen Testament, speziell zur altchristlichen Taufe*, Göttingen 1903, 334-6 ('Die Entstehung des Tauf-Symbols').

PART TWO

EARLY CHRISTIANITY & EGYPT

'OUT OF EGYPT I HAVE CALLED MY SON': SOME OBSERVATIONS ON THE QUOTATION FROM HOSEA 11.1 IN MATTHEW 2.15

Maarten J.J. Menken

At the beginning of Matthew's Gospel we find, after the genealogy (1.1-17), a chain of five narratives on the birth and the early years of the hero of the story, Jesus. The narrator first relates how Jesus is born (1.18-25). Magi come to visit the newborn King of the Jews, whose birth frightens King Herod (2.1-12). Because Herod intends to kill the child, Joseph flees to Egypt with the child and his mother (2.13-15). Herod then has all boys of two years and under in Bethlehem and its surroundings killed (2.16-18). When Herod has died, Joseph returns with the child and his mother to the land of Israel, and they settle in Nazareth (2.19-23). A remarkable trait of the chain is that all five stories contain a quotation from the Old Testament. One of these occurs in the mouth of the scribes who inform Herod of what Scripture says on the place of birth of the Messiah (2.5-6), the four others belong to the characteristically Matthean series of fulfilment quotations (1.22-23; 2.15, 17-18, 23).[1] These quotations are part not of direct discourse but of the words of the narrator, and are introduced by a more or less standardized formula in which the fulfilment of prophetic words is emphasized. The formula basically runs as follows: ἵνα πληρωθῇ τὸ ῥηθὲν διὰ τοῦ προφήτου λέγοντος ..., 'that what was said by the prophet might be fulfilled, when he said ...'. In the fulfilment quotations, the narrator shows *post factum* that in what he has just told, God's plan as revealed by the prophets has been realized. Fulfilment quotations normally occur at the end of a narrative; in Matthew 1-2, this is clearly the case with the final three quotations.

---

[1] See further Matt 4.14-16; 8.17; 12.17-21; 13.35; 21.4-5; 27.9-10. The editorial character of the fulfilment quotations is obvious: some have been inserted in Markan materials (I presuppose the two-document hypothesis), all can be omitted without a loss of flow of the story line, and the introductory formula shows several Matthean traits; see Menken 2004, 2-3.

The position of the quotation

Nevertheless, there is something odd about the first of these three, the quotation from Hos 11.1 in Matt 2.15. It reads: ἐξ Αἰγύπτου ἐκάλεσα τὸν υἱόν μου, 'out of Egypt I have called my son'. In the Matthean application to Jesus, these words must refer to Jesus' return out of Egypt to Israel, not to his leaving Israel for Egypt: God has called his son out of Egypt, not into Egypt. However, at the point in the story where the quotation has been appended, Joseph, Mary and the child have left Israel and are in Egypt; the return out of Egypt occurs later, when after the massacre of the innocents (2.16-18) and the death of Herod (2.19a), Joseph returns on God's command to the land of Israel (2.19-21). One could say that the quotation from Hos 11.1 would be better at home after 2.21.

Scholars have of course been looking for explanations for the odd position of the quotation. According to some, Matthew would focus in 2.21 not on the return out of Egypt but on the journey to Israel.[2] In the view of others, the point of the quotation would be that God preserves Jesus from Herod's violence.[3] Against the former view, it should be said that a journey to Israel is in the present case still a return out of Egypt; moreover, this view might explain why the quotation does not follow after 2.21, but it still leaves its position in 2.15 unexplained. Against the latter view, it should be said that the quotation speaks of calling out of Egypt, not of preserving from danger. Both explanations look like efforts at circumventing the difficulty. Assuming that the source materials used by Matthew in the composition of 2.13-23 roughly consisted of vv. 13-15a, 16, 19-21,[4] we must say that Matthew was at liberty to arrange his text differently, for instance by placing the Hosea quotation after v. 21, or by inserting another prophetic passage after v. 15a.[5] In fact, however, he has arranged his

---

[2] So Strecker 1966, 58; Soares Prabhu 1976, 217; Brown 1993, 219-20; Gnilka 1986, 51; Davies & Allison 1988, 262-3; Fuß 2000, 203-4.

[3] So Gundry 1994, 34; Miler 1999, 47-51.

[4] The fulfilment quotations are due to Matthew's editing, and Matt 2.22-23a was composed by the evangelist: it is very similar to Matt 4.12-13, which is the result of Matthew's rewriting of Mark 1.14a. Matthew no doubt edited his source materials. See Menken 2004, 261-2.

[5] If Matthew had the intention to emphasize that God preserves his Christ from danger, he could have quoted from many other prophetic passages (e.g., Isa 41.8-13; 50.7-9).

text in such a way that a quotation on God's calling his son out of Egypt is appended to a narrative on God's Son going to and being in Egypt, while a narrative on his return out of Egypt follows later. Is there a reasonable explanation for the apparently unusual position of the quotation, preferably an explanation that is consistent with Matthew's editorial habits?[6]

To answer this question, it is useful to take a look at the two instances in Matthew's Gospel where a fulfilment quotation does not occur at its usual place at the end of the episode but at an earlier point: the narratives of the birth of Jesus and of the entry into Jerusalem (Matt 1.18-25; 21.1-11). Some decades ago, Rudolf Pesch carefully analyzed them, and his view has rightly been accepted by many scholars.[7] In the two narratives, we find the following sequence: (1) somebody with divine authority gives an order: an angel to Joseph in 1.20-21, Jesus to the disciples in 21.1-3; (2) a fulfilment quotation follows (1.22-23; 21.4-5); (3) the person or persons to whom the command has been given, respond to it; the evangelist states, by means of an *alttestamentliche Ausführungsformel*, that the order is executed ('he did as the angel of the Lord had commanded him', 1.24; 'they did as Jesus had directed them', 21.6), and the execution is related in detail (1.24-25; 21.6-7). The pattern also occurs in Matthew's narrative on the preparation for the Last Supper (26.18-19; cf. also 28.15), but without a fulfilment quotation. In the case of 21.1-7 and 26.18-19, comparison with Mark (11.4-6; 14.16) shows that the *Ausführungsformel* ('as Jesus had directed them', 21.6; 26.19) is due to Matthew. So we may assume that in the birth narrative, not only the fulfilment quotation in 1.22-23 but also the execution formula in 1.24 comes from the evangelist in his role of editor. The fulfilment quotations in 1.22-23 and 21.4-5 are the only ones in Matthew's Gospel where the introductory formula is preceded by the words '(all) this happened in order that' (1.22; 21.4). The reason for this addition may well be that without it, the OT quotation might

---

[6] The quotation has other problematic aspects as well, such as its textual form or the circumstance that a statement on Israel's exodus out of Egypt has become a prophecy on the Christ's flight to and return from Egypt. On the former, see Menken 2004, 133-42; on the latter, see Miler 1999, 47-55.

[7] See Pesch 1966-67, and for the acceptance of his view, e.g., Nellessen 1969, 27, 33, 50; Soares Prabhu 1976, 55-6, 232-4; Brown 1993, 144-5; Luz 1992, 100; Davies & Allison 1988, 218; Miler 1999, 15, 208.

be mistaken for part of the direct discourse of the order.[8] In any case, it is striking that the command is immediately followed by the fulfilment quotation. It is even more striking that in these two instances the quotation precedes its realization, for the real fulfilment of the quotation now follows, in the events of Jesus' birth (1.24-25) and of his entry into Jerusalem (21.6-11).

By arranging the narratives of Jesus' birth and his entry into Jerusalem in the way just described, Matthew has achieved a double effect. Firstly, the command issued by the angel of the Lord or by Jesus and the words of the prophet in the quotation which immediately follows, are put on a par: both have the same divine authority. Secondly, the execution of the order also implies the fulfilment of the words from Scripture. This is even perceptible in the wording: Matthew has taken care that the same words return in order, quotation and execution (see 1.21, 23, 25: τίκτειν υἱόν, καλεῖν τὸ ὄνομα αὐτοῦ; 21.2, 5, 7: ὄνον καὶ ... πῶλον).

The peculiar position of the fulfilment quotation from Hos 11.1 in Matt 2.15 can, I think, be explained plausibly on the basis of the Matthean pattern detected by Pesch in Matt 1.20-25 and 21.1-7. The pattern is not directly present in the context of our quotation, but a sequence of command, fulfilment quotation, and execution of the command which implies fulfilment of the scriptural word, is to be found here, and all three (command, quotation and execution) concern Jesus' return out of Egypt. To perceive the pattern, we have to take the scene 2.13-15 together with the very similar scene 2.19-21, in which the return out of Egypt is narrated: the two scenes together constitute a sequence of command and execution, with the Hosea quotation in between.[9]

To demonstrate this, I start with a comparison of the two scenes:

---

[8] See Rothfuchs 1969, 33-6.
[9] The scene 2.13-15 displays in itself, just as the scene 2.19-21, a pattern of command (by the angel) and execution (by Joseph), but this cannot explain the position of the quotation: the execution in v. 14 consists in the journey *to* Egypt.

Matt 2.13-15

13 ἀναχωρησάντων δὲ αὐτῶν
ἰδοὺ ἄγγελος κυρίου φαίνεται
κατ᾽ ὄναρ τῷ Ἰωσὴφ
    λέγων·
ἐγερθεὶς παράλαβε τὸ παιδίον
καὶ τὴν μητέρα αὐτοῦ
καὶ φεῦγε εἰς Αἴγυπτον
καὶ ἴσθι ἐκεῖ ἕως ἂν εἴπω σοι·
μέλλει γὰρ Ἡρῴδης ζητεῖν τὸ παιδίον
    τοῦ ἀπολέσαι αὐτό.
14 ὁ δὲ ἐγερθεὶς παρέλαβεν τὸ παιδίον
καὶ τὴν μητέρα αὐτοῦ νυκτὸς
καὶ ἀνεχώρησεν εἰς Αἴγυπτον,
15 καὶ ἦν ἐκεῖ ἕως τῆς τελευτῆς
    Ἡρῴδου.

Matt 2.19-21

19 τελευτήσαντος δὲ τοῦ Ἡρῴδου
ἰδοὺ ἄγγελος κυρίου φαίνεται
κατ᾽ ὄναρ τῷ Ἰωσὴφ ἐν Αἰγύπτῳ
    20 λέγων·
ἐγερθεὶς παράλαβε τὸ παιδίον
καὶ τὴν μητέρα αὐτοῦ
καὶ πορεύου εἰς γῆν Ἰσραήλ·
τεθνήκασιν γὰρ οἱ ζητοῦντες τὴν ψυχὴν
    τοῦ παιδίου.

21 ὁ δὲ ἐγερθεὶς παρέλαβεν τὸ παιδίον
καὶ τὴν μητέρα αὐτοῦ
καὶ εἰσῆλθεν εἰς γῆν Ἰσραήλ.

The parallelism between the two scenes is very strict: in both, the narrator first indicates the situation by means of a genitive absolute, he then describes, in nearly identical wording, the appearance of the angel of the Lord to Joseph in a dream and the command to move elsewhere with the child and his mother, with the reason for the move given in a γάρ-clause, and he finally depicts Joseph's execution of the command in terms that almost literally agree with those of the command. Apart from details, there are two major differences between the two scenes. In the first one, the words of the angel to Joseph do not just end with the command to move, but with a command to stay at the place where he is ordered to go until the angel will tell him. The other difference corresponds with this: the first scene does not just close with Joseph's move but with the statement that Joseph stays in Egypt until the death of Herod.

Now the correspondence between the command to stay and its execution is not complete in 2.13-15: the command ends with the words ἕως ἂν εἴπω σοι, 'until I tell you', but the corresponding words in the execution are ἕως τῆς τελευτῆς Ἡρῴδου, 'until the death of Herod'. This lack of correspondence can be understood in the light of the explanation which the angel gives for the command ('for Herod is about to search for the child, to destroy him'), but the fact remains that with the words ἴσθι ἐκεῖ ἕως ἂν εἴπω σοι, 'be there until I tell you', the angel actually gives a command that is not yet completely executed within the scene 2.13-15, for the angel does not appear to

Joseph a second time in this short narrative to tell him that the time has come to go back.

The angel returns in the scene 2.19-21, to command Joseph to go back to the land of Israel, and this intervention of the angel is the realization of what was announced in the words 'until I tell you'. Only now, after the command of 2.20, can Joseph completely execute the final one of the three imperatives of 2.13, for now the angel has told him to leave Egypt and to go back to the land of Israel. The command 'be there until I tell you' is fully obeyed by Joseph when he leaves Egypt at another command of the angel.

We have here a sequence of (1) an order, (2) a fulfilment quotation and (3) an execution of the order which also implies the realization of the quotation: (1) Joseph is ordered to stay in Egypt until the angel tells him, (2) then follows the fulfilment quotation from Hos 11.1, and, after the intervening episode of the massacre of the innocents, (3) the angel commands him to leave Egypt, and Joseph does so. By doing so, Joseph obeys the command 'be there until I tell you', and at the same time Hosea's prophetic word 'out of Egypt I have called my son' is realized, for through the angelic command to Joseph to go back to the land of Israel God calls his Son Jesus out of Egypt.

So the pattern of Matt 1.20-25 and 21.1-7 is present here in a somewhat modified form. What makes the instance under consideration complex, is that the execution of the command 'be there until I tell you' necessarily consists of two things: first, the angel must tell Joseph (he does so with the command of 2.20: 'get up, take the child and his mother, and go to the land of Israel'), and second, Joseph must obey this order and thereby end his stay in Egypt. To execute the first command, a second command plus its execution are required. An *Ausführungsformel* ('he did as the angel had directed him', or something to that effect) would not make sense because of this complexity. We may surmise that Matthew's possibilities to introduce here the pattern of 1.20-25 and 21.1-7 were limited by the narrative materials that were available to him.

In any case, the pattern of command, fulfilment quotation and execution is there, and it explains the apparently odd position of the quotation. The quotation could of course have been placed after 2.21, but in its present position it emphasizes that God's plan with his Messiah as expressed by Hosea is realized by Joseph obediently staying in Egypt until the angel tells him to go to the land of Israel.

The introductory formula

It is not only the position of the quotation in Matt 2.15 that is strange and requires explanation. The formula with which the quotation is introduced also displays an odd feature, although this is a feature it shares with the introduction to one other fulfilment quotation. In the standard introductory formula, Matthew speaks of τὸ ῥηθὲν διὰ τοῦ προφήτου, 'what was said by the prophet',[10] but in 2.15 and also in 1.22, he speaks of τὸ ῥηθὲν ὑπὸ κυρίου διὰ τοῦ προφήτου, 'what the Lord said by the prophet'. The addition of ὑπὸ κυρίου emphasizes that God, 'the Lord', is the ultimate source of the prophetic word and that the prophet is only his medium. In the usual wording, these aspects are implicitly present in the 'theological passive' ῥηθέν[11] and in διά with the genitive indicating agency,[12] but in 1.22 and 2.15, they are made explicit. The question is: why?

Again, it is Rudolf Pesch who has given an answer to this question in the sixties of the twentieth century. In this case as well, his answer has been adopted by many scholars,[13] but, at least to my mind, wrongly. According to Pesch, Matthew would have added the words ὑπὸ κυρίου in these two cases because the quotations in question (Isa 7.14 in Matt 1.23; Hos 11.1 in Matt 2.15) contain the words υἱός or υἱός μου; Matthew would have recognized his Son of God-Christology in these OT passages, and would have emphasized this aspect by expanding the introductory formula. Pesch is right in stating that Matthew is interested in a Son of God-Christology, although one should perhaps not exaggerate its importance.[14] However, if it were Matthew's intention to highlight the Son of God in the quotation, one would expect him to do so by inserting into the introductory formula the words ὑπὸ τοῦ θεοῦ (as he does when introducing an OT quotation in 22.31), not ὑπὸ κυρίου, for Matthew speaks consistently of Jesus as ὁ υἱὸς τοῦ θεοῦ,

---

[10] In several cases, Matthew adds the name of the prophet (2.17; 4.14; 8.17; 12.17; 27.9), and once, he has the plural 'the prophets' (2.23). In 13.35, the longer text with the name 'Isaiah' should be preferred as the *lectio difficilior*, see Menken 2004, 90-2.

[11] See Zerwick 1963, §236; Blass, Debrunner & Rehkopf 1990, §130.1.

[12] See Turner 1963, 267; Blass, Debrunner & Rehkopf 1990, §223.

[13] See Pesch 1967, and for the acceptance of his view, e.g., Nellessen 1969, 93; Vögtle 1972, 176; Soares Prabhu 1976, 52-3; Nolan 1979, 222; Gundry 1994, 34; Luz 1992, 105, 129; Schenk 1987, 287; Davies & Allison 1988, 212; Knowles 1993, 31 note 2; Miler 1999, 20-1; Fuß 2000, 200.

[14] See Beaton 2002, 91 note 17 with the literature mentioned there.

'the Son of God', not as ὁ υἱὸς τοῦ κυρίου, 'the Son of the Lord'.[15] Besides, the son mentioned in the quotation from Isa 7.14 in Matt 1.23 is not the son of God but the son of the pregnant virgin, and the fulfilment quotation from Isa 42.1-4 in Matt 12.17-21, in which the sonship of Jesus figures prominently (ἰδοὺ ὁ παῖς μου[16]), is introduced by a formula which lacks the words ὑπὸ κυρίου. If Pesch's explanation for the words ὑπὸ κυρίου in Matt 1.22 and 2.15 does not satisfy, can we find a better one?

To my mind, a simple and convincing explanation can be found in the context of the two fulfilment formulae in question. Both quotations which Matthew presents as spoken ὑπὸ κυρίου occur immediately after the appearance of an ἄγγελος κυρίου, an 'angel of the Lord', to Joseph (1.20; 2.13).[17] Moreover, we have seen above that in both cases Matthew has arranged his narrative in such a way as to emphasize that the command of the angel of the Lord and the word spoken by the prophet are of equal authority and are fulfilled at the same time. Matthew reinforces this emphasis by inserting the words ὑπὸ κυρίου in the formula introducing the two fulfilment quotations that follow a command of an ἄγγελος κυρίου.

The end of Matthew 2 yields some negative corroboration for this view. There, we also find a fulfilment quotation ('for he will be called a Nazorean', 2.23),[18] which is fulfilled by Joseph settling in Nazareth in Galilee after having been warned in a dream (2.22-23a). This time, however, there is no mention of an angel of the Lord in connection with Joseph's dream (cf. 2.12), and the words ὑπὸ κυρίου are missing in the formula introducing the quotation. It seems indeed that in 1.22 and 2.15, the presence of these words depends on the appearance of an angel of the Lord whose command is equivalent to the scriptural word.

---

[15] See Matt 4.3, 6; 8.29; 14.33; 16.16; 26.63; 27.40, 43, 54.

[16] In the light of the divine identification of Jesus as 'my beloved Son, in whom I find pleasure' at Jesus' baptism (3.17) and transfiguration (17.5), with its obvious allusion to Isa 42.1, Matthew very probably understood the ambiguous παῖς ('servant' or 'son') as 'son'; see Menken 2004, 59-60, 83. Pesch 1967, 408, draws attention to the difficulty that 12.17 constitutes to his theory, but he then tries to solve the problem by making an unconvincing distinction between a 'παῖς-Christologie' and a 'Gottessohnchristologie'.

[17] Cf. Rothfuchs 1969, 40-1; Gnilka 1986, 20.

[18] On the extent and the sources of this quotation, see Menken 2004, 161-77.

Matthew does not tell us what Jesus and his parents did during their stay in Egypt. Soon after Matthew, both pious Christian and hostile Jewish and pagan fantasy started to fill in the gaps of Matthew's succinct story on Jesus' stay in Egypt.[19] At the beginning of the twentieth century, this fantasy, now mixed with a dose of rationalism, led to the obvious forgery of the so-called Letter of Benan, an alleged old friend of Jesus.[20] Pieces of information supplied by this Benan are that Jesus' parents gave their son to an Egyptian astronomer to have the child educated, that Jesus was instructed in the wisdom of the Egyptians, especially in their medicine, had erudite theological conversations with sages such as Philo of Alexandria, and was loved by an Egyptian woman (but without answering her love). For our evangelist, it is sufficient that his readers know that, because of the commands of the angel of the Lord and Joseph's faithful execution of them, Jesus came to Egypt and returned out of Egypt, and that in this way God called him, as the true representative of Israel, out of Egypt. Literary form and details of Matthew's text as analyzed above, are meant to serve this message.[21]

Bibliography

Beaton, R. 2002. *Isaiah's Christ in Matthew's Gospel* (Society for New Testament Studies Monograph Series 123), Cambridge.

Blass, F. and A. Debrunner. 1990[17]. *Grammatik des neutestamentlichen Griechisch*, ed. F. Rehkopf, Göttingen.

Brown, R.E. 1993[2]. *The Birth of the Messiah: A Commentary on the Infancy Narratives in the Gospels of Matthew and Luke* (The Anchor Bible Reference Library), New York (1977[1]).

Davies, W.D. and D.C. Allison. 1988. *A Critical and Exegetical Commentary on the Gospel according to Saint Matthew*, i, *Introduction and Commentary on Matthew I-VII* (The International Critical Commentary), Edinburgh.

Fuß, B. 2000. *'Dies ist die Zeit, von der geschrieben ist …': Die expliziten Zitate aus dem Buch Hosea in den Handschriften von Qumran und im Neuen Testament* (Neutestamentliche Abhandlungen, Neue Folge 37), Münster.

Gnilka, J. 1986. *Das Matthäusevangelium*, i: *Kommentar zu Kap. 1,1-13,58* (Herders Theologischer Kommentar zum Neuen Testament 1.1), Freiburg.

Gundry, R.H. 1994[2]. *Matthew: A Commentary on His Handbook for a Mixed Church under Persecution*, Grand Rapids (1982[1]).

Heiligenthal, R. 1999[2]. *Der verfälschte Jesus: Eine Kritik moderner Jesusbilder*, Darmstadt (1997[1]).

---

[19] For a discussion of relevant texts, see Luz 1992, 128, 133.

[20] See Schmidt & Grapow 1921; Heiligenthal 1999, 97-9.

[21] I thank Dr J.M. Court for his correction of my English idiom.

Knowles, M. 1993. *Jeremiah in Matthew's Gospel: The Rejected-Prophet Motif in Matthaean Redaction* (Journal for the Study of the New Testament Supplement Series 68), Sheffield.

Luz, U. 1992³. *Das Evangelium nach Matthäus*, i, *Mt 1-7* (Evangelisch-Katholischer Kommentar zum Neuen Testament 1.1), Zürich/Neukirchen-Vluyn (1985¹).

Menken, M.J.J. 2004. *Matthew's Bible: The Old Testament Text of the Evangelist* (Bibliotheca Ephemeridum Theologicarum Lovaniensium 173), Louvain.

Miler, J. 1999. *Les citations d'accomplissement dans l'Évangile de Matthieu: Quand Dieu se rend présent en toute humanité* (Analecta Biblica 140), Rome.

Nellessen, E. 1969. *Das Kind und seine Mutter: Struktur und Verkündigung des 2. Kapitels im Matthäusevangelium* (Stuttgarter Bibelstudien 39), Stuttgart.

Nolan, B.M. 1979. *The Royal Son of God: The Christology of Matthew 1-2 in the Setting of the Gospel* (Orbis Biblicus et Orientalis 23), Fribourg/Göttingen.

Pesch, R. 1966-67. 'Eine alttestamentliche Ausführungsformel im Matthäus-Evangelium: Redaktionsgeschichtliche und exegetische Beobachtungen', *Biblische Zeitschrift*, Neue Folge 10 (1966) 220-45; 11 (1967) 79-95.

Pesch, R. 1967. 'Der Gottessohn im matthäischen Evangelienprolog (Mt 1-2): Beobachtungen zu den Zitationsformeln der Reflexionszitate', *Biblica* 48 (1967) 395-420.

Rothfuchs, W. 1969. *Die Erfüllungszitate des Matthäus-Evangeliums: Eine biblisch-theologische Untersuchung* (Beiträge zur Wissenschaft vom Alten und Neuen Testament 88), Stuttgart.

Schenk, W. 1987. *Die Sprache des Matthäus: Die Text-Konstituenten in ihren makro- und mikrostrukturellen Relationen*, Göttingen.

Schmidt, C. and H. Grapow. 1921. *Der Benanbrief: Eine moderne Leben-Jesu-Fälschung des Herrn Ernst Edler von der Planitz* (Texte und Untersuchungen 44.1), Leipzig.

Soares Prabhu, G.M. 1976. *The Formula Quotations in the Infancy Narrative of Matthew: An Enquiry into the Tradition History of Mt 1-2* (Analecta Biblica 63), Rome.

Strecker, G. 1966². *Der Weg der Gerechtigkeit: Untersuchung zur Theologie des Matthäus* (Forschungen zur Religion und Literatur des Alten und Neuen Testaments 82), Göttingen (1962¹).

Vögtle, A. 1972. 'Die matthäische Kindheitsgeschichte', in: M. Didier (ed.), *L'Évangile selon Matthieu: Rédaction et théologie* (Bibliotheca Ephemeridum Theologicarum Lovaniensium 29), Gembloux, 153-83.

Turner, N. 1963. *Syntax*, vol. iii of J.H. Moulton, *A Grammar of New Testament Greek*, Edinburgh.

Zerwick, M. 1963. *Biblical Greek, Illustrated by Examples*, ed. J. Smith, Rome.

'AND MOSES WAS INSTRUCTED IN ALL THE WISDOM OF THE EGYPTIANS' (ACTS 7.22)

Ton Hilhorst

In his speech to the Sanhedrin, which forms the seventh chapter of the Acts of the Apostles, Stephen offers a summary of the history of Israel. Not surprisingly, the facts narrated usually come from the Old Testament, but there are also amplifications vis-à-vis the source text. This is notably the case in the account of Moses' childhood. Thus, whereas Exodus 2.10 describes Moses' adoption by Pharaoh's daughter simply by saying 'and he became her son', Acts 7.21-22 expands this to

> ^{21} ἀνείλατο αὐτὸν ἡ θυγάτηρ Φαραὼ καὶ ἀνεθρέψατο αὐτὸν ἑαυτῇ εἰς υἱόν. ^{22} καὶ ἐπαιδεύθη Μωϋσῆς ἐν πάσῃ σοφίᾳ Αἰγυπτίων, ἦν δὲ δυνατὸς ἐν λόγοις καὶ ἔργοις αὐτοῦ.

> ^{21} Pharaoh's daughter adopted him and brought him up as her own son.
> ^{22} And Moses was instructed in all the wisdom of the Egyptians, and he was mighty in his words and deeds.[1]

In this paper, we will take a closer look at this expansion, in particular at Moses' instruction 'in all the wisdom of the Egyptians'. What does the expression 'the wisdom of the Egyptians' mean? Indeed, what could Moses learn from the oppressors of his people, mere idol worshippers at that? Our approach will be threefold. First of all, we will investigate the ideas that may have shaped the picture in Acts. We will ask what can have been meant by 'wisdom', what image the author may have had of Egypt and its culture, and what link there was, if any, between Moses' Egyptian education and his might in words and deeds. Secondly, we will review what early Jewish literature had to say about Moses receiving an Egyptian education; maybe the author of Acts was indebted to traditions voiced there. And finally we will study our topic 'downstream', and ask what Acts 7.22 meant to

---

[1] English translations are taken from the Revised Standard Version for biblical passages and the Loeb Classical Library for classical passages, unless otherwise indicated.

Christian readers in the first four centuries. Besides being interesting
from the point of view of reception history, their views may possibly
also contribute to shedding light on the verse.

1. *The wisdom of the Egyptians in Acts 7.22*

Some centuries ago, Acts 7.22 played a crucial role in discussions about
the origin and history of civilizations. Indeed, as Jan Assmann puts it
in his *Moses the Egyptian*, 'the Moses discourse in the seventeenth and
eighteenth centuries almost exclusively based its image of Moses not on
Moses' elaborate biography in the Pentateuch, but on this single verse in
the New Testament'.[2] A fatal blow to speculations about ancient Egypt
was inflicted by Champollion's decipherment of the hieroglyphs in 1822,
and the consequences also made themselves felt in biblical studies. As a
result, the question of what is meant by 'the wisdom of the Egyptians'
in Acts 7.22 has barely attracted modern New Testament scholarship.
Bibliographies fail to mention any title on the subject,[3] monographs
focus on other aspects of Acts[4] and commentaries are usually content to
repeat earlier commentaries referring to Lucian, *Philopseudes* 34, and so
merely transfer the problem.[5] The only commentary that has shown
interest in the statement is, to the best of our knowledge, the one by
Eugène Jacquier, which appeared in 1926 in the 'Études Bibliques'
series.[6] But there seems to be more that can be said.

Let us begin by tackling the term 'wisdom', or rather the Greek term
σοφία. In ancient Greek, the *Lexicon* of Liddell and Scott informs us, it
denotes (1) properly cleverness or skill in handicraft and art, in music
and singing, in poetry, in driving, in medicine or surgery, in divination;

---

[2] Assmann 1999, 10; cf. ibid., 56.

[3] Thus the only title Langevin 1985 provides for Acts 7.22 is Gonzalo Maeso
1974, in which we are told that since Moses, witness Acts 7.22, was instructed in all
the wisdom of the Egyptians, we have to study Egyptian culture thoroughly in order
to understand the Old Testament!

[4] Such as Kastner 1967 and Lierman 2004. The same is true for Bovon 1978.

[5] Lucian speaks of 'a man from Memphis, one of the scribes of the temple, won-
derfully learned, familiar with all the culture of the Egyptians' (θαυμάσιος τὴν σοφίαν
καὶ τὴν παιδείαν πᾶσαν εἰδὼς τὴν Αἰγύπτιον). The 'culture of the Egyptians' here
amounts to magical skill, cf. the sequel to the words cited: 'He was said to have lived
underground for twenty-three years in their sanctuaries, learning magic from Isis'.

[6] Jacquier 1926, 215-16; cf., furthermore, Barclay 1992, 41.

only then is it (2) skill in matters of common life, sound judgement, intelligence, practical wisdom; and finally it is used for (3) learning, wisdom, especially speculative wisdom but also of natural philosophy and mathematics.[7] In the first sense it appears from Homer onward, in the second from Theognis in the sixth and Herodotus in the fifth century BC, and in the third from Euripides in the fifth and Plato in the fourth century BC. Needless to say, these meanings do not succeed each other, the earlier ones coexist alongside the later ones.[8] Thus, the meaning of skill in handicraft and art is used in the Septuagint version of Exodus 31.3, 35.26 and other passages,[9] and Paul in 1 Corinthians 3.10 says about himself ὡς σοφὸς ἀρχιτέκτων θεμέλιον ἔθηκα, 'like a skilled master builder I laid a foundation'. The context in Stephen's speech, however, is not such that we can confidently establish which of these shades of meaning is used in v. 22. We seem to have a choice of two alternatives. On the one hand, σοφία may be a generic term denoting competence in any skill or science. Then πάσῃ σοφίᾳ Αἰγυπτίων would mean all the things the Egyptians were good at and suggests the all-round schooling Moses would need as a leader of his people, as a lawgiver, as an author. On the other hand, it may denote what we would call wisdom, i.e. the state of being wise, the goal of philosophy. The qualification 'of the Egyptians' then suggests a special brand of wisdom typical of the Egyptians.[10] Maybe the former view is preferable because of the absence of the article, πάσῃ σοφίᾳ meaning 'all sorts of wisdom',[11] against πάσῃ τῇ σοφίᾳ, 'all the well-known wisdom'. But

---

[7] Cf. also Stephanus 1848-54, s.v. σοφία; Von Paula Eisenmann 1859; Schmid 1893, 152; 1896, 227-8; Snell 1924, 5-18; Dimitrakos 1950, s.v. σοφία 1; Wilckens 1964, 467-75, and the abundant bibliography in Boned Colera and Rodríguez Somolinos 1998, 465. Clement of Alexandria has an interesting chapter on σοφία in *Stromateis* 1.25-27.

[8] The statement in Goetzmann 1971, 1375 that σοφός and σοφία denote extraordinary skill and knowledge 'in der Frühzeit auch im praktischen Bereich' but are 'später auf das theoretische Wissen konzentriert' is misleading. The claim by Wilckens 1964, 497 note 2 that σοφία was too strongly theological a term to always render חכמה 'technical ability' is also untenable.

[9] Wilckens 1964, 497 note 2; Muraoka 2002, s.v.; see also, e.g., Wisdom 14.2; Josephus, *Ant.* 2.286; Aelian, *Anim.* 10.29.

[10] Thus Hegermann 1983, 618 thinks of sapiential traditions held by the Egyptians. For Egyptian philosophy see, e.g., Artapanus in Eusebius, *Praeparatio Evangelica* 9.27.4 (as an invention by Moses!); Diogenes Laertius 1.10-11; Hopfner 1922-25, 891.

[11] Cf. Springhetti 1966,196, who points out that πᾶς in Acts 7.22 (and in a number of other New Testament passages including Acts 13.10) '= fere παντοῖος'.

'all sorts of wisdom' can also be taken as spiritual wisdom in its several facets. Thus the dilemma remains.

What, however, are we supposed to think of the addition 'of the Egyptians'? In other words, what ideas did the author of Acts foster about Egypt, its inhabitants and its civilization? To answer this question, we should bear in mind that Acts is the work of a Christian who combined commitment to the Bible (roughly what we call the Old Testament) with a drive to be heard by a Hellenistic reading public.[12] We have to ask, therefore, both what his Bible said about Egypt and what reputation Egypt had in the Hellenistic world.

In the Scriptures, the prevailing image of Egypt is negative.[13] This is due to the overwhelming importance of the Exodus from Egypt. To Israel, Egypt is 'the house of bondage' (Exodus 20.2; Deuteronomy 6.12). The Egyptians are idolaters (Deuteronomy 29.17-18; Isaiah 19.1,3; Jeremiah 43.12-13; Ezekiel 20.7; 30.13), and the book of Wisdom scoffs at their worship of animals (11.15-16; 12.24; 15.18-19).[14] Nevertheless, there are positive points like the hospitality offered to Abraham (Genesis 12.10-20), to Joseph and his father and brothers (Genesis 39-50), to the subsequent generations of Israelites (cf. Exodus 16.3: the fleshpots of Egypt) and, eventually, to Jesus, provided the story in Matthew 2.13-15 was known to the author of Acts. Solomon married Pharaoh's daughter (1 Kings 3.1). Even the reputation of wisdom is not denied to Egypt. Isaiah 19.11-15 makes sport of the wise men of Egypt, which is an unintended recognition of their existence. Solomon's wisdom is said to surpass even 'all the wisdom of Egypt' (1 Kings 5.10 [4.30]), which amounts to the same thing; in the Septuagint the passage reads: καὶ ἐπληθύνθη Σαλωμων σφόδρα ὑπὲρ τὴν φρόνησιν πάντων ἀρχαίων ἀνθρώπων καὶ ὑπὲρ πάντας φρονίμους Αἰγύπτου, 'And Solomon abounded greatly beyond the wisdom of all the ancients, and beyond all the wise men of Egypt'. But if we want to know what exactly this wisdom implies, the Bible is sparing in its information.[15] Exodus 7.11 mentions that Pharaoh's wise men and sorcerers changed rods into serpents, so they were expert magicians, and Exodus 7.19 and 8.5 speak of the canals of the Egyptians, an

---

[12] See Plümacher 1972.

[13] Cf. Smelik and Hemelrijk 1984, 1906-7, and Ed Noort on pp. 3–4 of this volume.

[14] For the attitude of Hellenistic Judaism to Egyptian zoolatry, cf. ibid., 1910-20 (add *Sibylline Oracles* 5.77; frg. 3.22, 27-28); for Wisdom cf. ibid., 1913-14.

[15] For an idea of Solomon's wisdom, cf. Wisdom 7.17-21.

acknowledgment of their expertise in water management.[16]

In the Greek world, we frequently meet with an awe of the old age and wisdom of Egyptian civilization.[17] Homer is the first to mention one of its abilities: in Egypt 'every man is a physician, wise above humankind; for they are of the race of Paeëon' (*Odyssey* 4.231-2). Many authors inform their readers about Egypt, notably the historians Herodotus in the fifth and Diodorus Siculus in the first century BC.

Herodotus of Halicarnassus, the 'father of history', records the great wars between the Greeks and the Persians in the first decades of the fifth century BC. While studying the causes and previous history of these wars, his curiosity is roused to investigate the character and manners of the peoples directly or indirectly involved. Thus, the second book of his *Histories* is devoted to Egypt, which he travelled across in order to inspect objects of interest personally and to consult authorities, mainly priests (ἱρέες in his Ionic Greek).[18] Herodotus has no objection to calling the Egyptians the cleverest of all men: λογιώτατοί εἰσι μακρῷ τῶν ἐγὼ ἐς διάπειραν ἀπικόμην (2.77.1); τοὺς σοφωτάτους ἀνθρώπων Αἰγυπτίους (2.160.1).[19] They are a very ancient people, and King Psammetichus found by experiment (itself a sign of an inquiring disposition!) that although the Phrygians are older than the Egyptians, the latter are older than all other people (2.2.1). The Greeks have borrowed various things from the Egyptians: divination (2.49.2; 2.57.3); names of gods (2.50.1); days and months belonging to specific gods (2.82.1); horoscopes (2.82.1); geometry (2.109.3); metempsychosis (2.123.3); preference for military activity over manual work (2.167.1, although Herodotus is not sure of that); the women's festival in honour of Demeter (2.171.3); laws (2.177.2). Among their achievements he mentions that they are the first inventors of the year, of the names of the twelve gods, of altars, images and temples, and of pictures of gods carved in stone (2.4.1-2). They have a remarkable interest in history (2.77.1; 2.91.5) and they record important events (2.82.2; 2.100.1; 2.145.3). Their calendar is

---

[16] The Septuagint introduces the notion of διῶρυξ also in Isaiah 19.6; 27.12; 33.21.

[17] For Greek and Roman views of Egypt see Von Gutschmid 1889, 150-65; Hopfner 1922-25; Iversen 1993[2] (I consulted 1961[1]); Smelik and Hemelrijk 1984, 1869-79 and 1945-55.

[18] Cf. M. Kaiser in Morenz 1968, 201-47; Froidefond 1971, 115-207; Smelik and Hemelrijk 1984, 1873-6.

[19] Cf. also 2.3.1 and 2.121.ζ.2.

more sophisticated than the Greek one (2.4.1). Herodotus was impressed
by the huge buildings he saw in Egypt, not only pyramids but also
temples and labyrinths (2.124-8, 134-8, 148-9, 175-6). Their regulation
of the Nile by digging canals (διώρυχες; 2.108, 137-8, 158) led them
to a practical use of geometry (2.109). Furthermore, we read about
their use of letters (2.36, 106, 124-5, 136, 148). And finally there is
their medical expertise; they do not even have generalists but instead
specialists for every single disease (2.84).

Diodorus Siculus is a representative of the Hellenistic age, when
much more was known about Egypt if only because it was governed
by a Greek upper class. He is the author of a World History in forty
books, many of them preserved only fragmentarily. Although he is
not an independent researcher, his work is valuable to us because it
transmits traditions which are otherwise unknown. His first book, from
§11 onwards, deals with Egypt, its gods, country, history and, finally, its
laws and customs.[20] Like Herodotus, he supplemented his knowledge
of the country by visiting it personally.[21] Even more than his illustrious
predecessor, he states that Egyptian priests were his informants; they
were obviously the scholars of the nation. But unlike Herodotus, he is
anxious to adopt the air of a unprejudiced reporter who notes what he
has heard rather than expressing admiration. Thus, he declares he will
begin his account of history with Egypt because *mythology has it* that the
gods were born there, because *people say* the earliest observations of the
stars were carried out there and because many memorable actions by
great men *are stated* to have been accomplished there (1.9.6). Likewise,
when introducing his exposition on the laws and customs of Egypt,
he recounts a number of glorious achievements (invention of writing,
astronomy, geometry and many other arts, as well as excellent laws)
not as facts but as claims by the Egyptians, adding that they pretend
that Egypt would not have been reigned over by kings for over 4,700
years nor been the most prosperous country in the world had it not
had the very best customs and laws, and ways of living supporting all
sorts of learning (τοῖς κατὰ πᾶσαν παιδείαν ἐπιτηδεύμασιν) (1.69.6).
But in actual fact he seems to agree with all of these claims. The
outstanding qualities of the Egyptians that he reports are roughly the
same as those we find in Herodotus; thus we need not enumerate

---

[20] See Burton 1972; Smelik and Hemelrijk 1984, 1895-903.
[21] 1.4.1; 1.44.1; 1.46.7; 1.83.9; 3.11.3.

them again. Like Herodotus, he stresses Greek indebtedness to the Egyptians.[22]

Although Plato, of course, is not a historian or an ethnographer like Herodotus and Diodorus Siculus, with some reservations he shares their favourable opinion of the Egyptians.[23] In *Phaedrus* 274c-d, he makes Socrates narrate a myth on an Egyptian, Theuth, a man later to become the god Thoth, who came to King Thammous with a number of highly important inventions: arithmetic, geometry, astronomy, backgammon, dice-playing and writing. Also, in the *Timaeus* (21e-25d), Plato brings Egypt to the fore with due respect. According to Diodorus 1.96.2 and 1.98.1 Plato visited Egypt, and Hippolytus, *Haer.* 6.22.1, points out that Plato's *Timaeus* contains wisdom of the Egyptians (σοφία Αἰγυπτίων).

Plato was not the only Greek to visit Egypt. Indeed, a picture of Egypt through Greek eyes is incomplete if it does not touch on the theme of its Greek visitors. Instead of enumerating the diverse authors who have spoken about the subject,[24] let us directly point to one of the most complete lists of visitors, in the Diodorus Siculus book we have just discussed. In 1.96.2 he mentions the following cultivated Greeks as having travelled in Egypt: Orpheus, Musaeus, Melampus, Daedalus, Homer, Lycurgus, Solon, Plato, Pythagoras, Eudoxus, Democritus, and Oenopides, to which in 1.98.5 he adds the names of Telecles and Theodorus. These people included singers (Orpheus, Musaeus), physicians (Melampus), architects (Daedalus), poets (Homer), legislators (Lycurgus, Solon), philosophers (Plato, Pythagoras, Democritus), mathematicians (Eudoxus), astronomers (Oenopides), and sculptors (Telecles, Theodorus). The list is telling in its diversity of fields represented; it shows that the Greeks felt that Egypt excelled at a variety of skills. This lends credibility to the interpretation of 'all the wisdom of

---

[22] Dionysia 1.22.7; 1.23.2-7, heroes and gods 1.23.8-24.1, Eleusinian mysteries 1.29.2.

[23] Cf. Froidefond 1971, 267-342.

[24] See Jüthner 1923, 10-11; Smelik and Hemelrijk 1984, 1878, 1897, 1955; Riedweg 2002, 20-1, 42-3, 64; Krause and Hoheisel 2001, 22-3. Patristic passages include Clement of Alexandria, *Strom.* 1.15.66-69; Hippolytus, *Haer.* 9.17.2; Pseudo-Justin, *Or. Gr.* 14.2. The issue played a role in the discussion about the priority of Jewish / Christian versus Greek culture. Thus, Pseudo-Justin, *Or. Gr.* 14.2; 20; 22.1; 24.1; 27.3-28.6 argues that Homer and many others took advantage of Moses' learning while staying in Egypt, cf. Pépin 1955, 110; Droge 1989, 1; also, Ridings 1995, 103.

the Egyptians' in Acts 7.22 as a body of divergent skills and disciplines rather than a specific kind of speculative wisdom, without, of course, excluding the latter interpretation.

A further feature we have to mention for our portrait of 'Egyptian wisdom' is its secrecy. There was no such a thing as making knowledge and craftsmanship available to whoever might be interested. Knowledge implies power, and power was jealously guarded. The use of hieroglyphs was, in a manner of speaking, a graphic expression of that esotericism.[25] Thus, it was a real privilege to be deemed worthy of an introduction, or rather initiation, into some discipline. This enhances the value of Moses' education in Egypt.

All these traits contributed to the positive conception of Egypt and its culture. Nevertheless, as Smelik and Hemelrijk point out in their study of Egyptian animal worship, the attitude of Greeks and Romans was ambivalent. Although Egypt's antiquity and wisdom may have been imposing, the Egyptians they met in everyday life contrasted markedly with this idealized image, especially to Roman eyes. The situation recalls more or less the Roman appreciation of the Greeks: examples to admire as far as the classical period of Greek civilization was concerned, but called *Graeculi* when their degenerated offspring in the early imperial period had to be described.[26] For our passage in Acts this ambivalence is irrelevant: the 'wisdom of the Egyptians' can only refer to Egypt as the cradle of superior culture. What this Egyptian wisdom stands for precisely, however, remains almost as elusive as it was in the Bible.

Finally, we would like to spend some time studying the statement in Acts 7.22 following the one on the wisdom of the Egyptians. Reading the verse as a whole: 'And Moses was instructed in all the wisdom of the Egyptians, and he was mighty in his words and deeds', we might gather that the latter half of this verse expresses the consequence of the former; in other words, that it was Moses' Egyptian education that enabled him to be powerful both in his words and his actions. Up to a certain point, this may be what was meant. After all, what

---

[25] See on this subject Iversen 1961, 45; Van der Horst 1998, 317-25; Assmann 1999, 83-4.

[26] Smelik and Hemelrijk 1984, 1878-9, 1926 note 470, 1938, 1944, 1954-5, 1999-2000. The difference between both conceptions is that whereas the borderline between both specimens of Greeks is that between past and present, the appreciation of the Egyptians is also diverse for those in the present.

would be the point of mentioning Moses' Egyptian education if he had not profited from it in later life? On the other hand, ultimately we must suppose it was God who gifted him thus, the God who 'sent him as both ruler and deliverer' (Acts 7.35). As for 'words', it is often claimed that this flatly contradicts the account in Exodus 4.10-16, where precisely Moses' 'slowness of speech and of tongue' is an important issue. However, even if Moses lacked the flow of words of his brother Aaron, he may nevertheless be powerful through the things he said, witness his firm leadership of the Israelites, his authoritative exposition in Deuteronomy 5-31, his victorious song (32) and his blessing of the people (33).[27] If we trace back his 'power in words' to his Egyptian training, then once again it is clear that eloquence is not meant. Rhetoric, according to general conviction in the Greek world, was an exclusively Greek quality; 'barbarians' lacked it, not only because Greeks felt their language to be the only language suited for the art of speaking well, but also because that art could only develop in a democracy, which was absent outside the Greek world.[28] As we will see presently, it is not for nothing that in Philo's description of Moses' education it was the Greeks who were summoned 'under promise of high reward' to teach him grammar, rhetoric, and dialectic. Acts 7.22, then, does not claim that Moses was a slick talker. Rather, he was 'mighty in his words and deeds', just like Jesus, according to the men of Emmaus, 'was a prophet mighty in deed and word before God and all the people' (Luke 24.19). It was not the eloquence but the authority of their words which counted.

2. *Moses' Egyptian education in Hellenistic Judaism*

The sober information the book of Exodus provides about Moses' early years has stirred the imaginations both of Jewish and Gentile readers.[29] On the Jewish side, interests are diverse. The aspect which interests us here, Moses' education in Egyptian wisdom, is either conspicuously absent in Hebrew and Aramaic texts of the Second Temple

---

[27] See also Jacquier 1926, 216.

[28] See Jüthner 1923, 6, 8, 35, 128 note 37 and 132 note 93; Diodorus Siculus 1.2.5-6. Curiously, Diodorus 1.76.1 reports that trials in Egypt were held in written form lest the plaintiff or the defendant were to overwhelm the judges with their glibness of tongue.

[29] For the former, see Barclay 1992, 30-40, for the latter, Gager 1972.

and rabbinic literature, or it is denied there outright. Thus *Jubilees*, preserved integrally in Ethiopic but originally a Hebrew composition, makes Moses learn writing from his father (47.9), and assures us that what Moses knew about the creation of the world and the early history of mankind was revealed to him directly by an 'angel of the Presence' who, in his turn, drew his information from the 'heavenly tablets'. In Hellenistic Jewish literature, on the other hand, we find interesting material.

Leaving aside, for the sake of brevity, the peculiar ideas of Artapanus (third or second century BC),[30] our earliest witness is Ezekiel the Tragedian (third or second century BC). In his *Exagoge* 36-8, Moses himself declares:

ἕως μὲν οὖν τὸν παιδὸς εἴχομεν χρόνον,
τροφαῖσι βασιλικαῖσι καὶ παιδεύμασιν
ἅπανθ᾽ ὑπισχνεῖθ᾽, ὡς ἀπὸ σπλάγχνων ἐῶν.

Throughout my boyhood years the princess did,
for princely rearing and instruction apt,
provide[31] all things, as though I were her own

(trans. R.G. Robertson).

The word 'wisdom' does not occur here, but it is clear that Moses was trained in a variety (indeed 'all things') of the skills needed by a king. The passage does not stress the typically Egyptian character of the skills, although the reader will be aware that they are imparted to Moses at the Egyptian court and by Egyptians. We encounter a similar view in Josephus, *Antiquities* 2.236, where Moses, adopted by the princess, is said to have been 'educated with the utmost care, the Hebrews resting the highest hopes upon him for their future, while the Egyptians viewed his upbringing with misgiving'.[32] Obviously, Moses acquires a set of abilities that will enable him to perform mighty deeds on behalf of the Jewish people.

---

[30] See Schürer 1986, 521-5; Barclay 1992, 31-4; also the contribution by Rob Kugler to this volume.

[31] 'Provide' seems to be a fitting rendering here, although it is not a current meaning. Liddell & Scott, s.v. ὑπισχνέομαι 1a, have doubts about the reading here, noting 's.v.l.' (si vera lectio), possibly because of the awkward datives in the second line. But the two texts that transmit our passage, Clement of Alexandria, *Strom.* 1.155.3 and Eusebius, *Praep.* 9.28.3, read either ὑπισχνεῖθ᾽ or ὑπισχνεῖτο. The datives may be of reference: 'as regards royal upbringing and education'.

[32] Cf. Feldman 1991-92, 303-7.

But the most extensive description of Moses' education comes from Philo's *Life of Moses*.[33] Moses, we learn, was given a royal education (1.8), due to his adoption by the king's daughter (1.19-20). The content of his education is described in 1.21-24, from which we quote what is relevant to our enquiry:

> [21]Teachers at once arrived from different parts, some unbidden from the neighbouring countries and the provinces of Egypt, others summoned from Greece under promise of high reward … [23]Arithmetic, geometry, the lore of metre, rhythm and harmony, and the whole subject of music as shown by the use of instruments or in textbooks and treatises of a more special character, were imparted to him by learned Egyptians. These further instructed him in the philosophy conveyed in symbols, as displayed in the so-called holy characters and in the regard paid to animals, to which they even pay divine honours. He had Greeks to teach him the rest of the regular school course, and the inhabitants of the neighbouring countries for Assyrian letters and the Chaldean science of the heavenly bodies. [24]This he also acquired from Egyptians, who give special attention to astrology. And, when he had mastered the lore of both nations, both where they agree and where they differ, he eschewed all strife and contention and sought only for truth. His mind was incapable of accepting any falsehood.[34]

The educational programme described here seems to be a blend of Egyptian and Greek elements, and Moses' teachers are not solely Egyptians but also Greek, Assyrian and Chaldean scholars. But as Alan Mendelson observes, despite the 'international' character of Moses' education, 'the actual disciplines studied are so reminiscent of those mentioned in [Plato's] Book vii of the *Republic* (522c ff.) that the Greek stamp of the studies is clear'.[35] We may add that this stamp is so important to Philo that he ignores that in Moses' time there were hardly any Greeks to teach him the encyclia.[36] The anachronism is

---

[33] For a commentary, see Robbins 1947, 53-6 (of modest use); Graffigna 1999, 262-3; Feldman 2002; Geljon 2004.

[34] Translation by F.H. Colson in the Loeb series; but his rendering of ἱεροῖς γράμμασιν with 'holy inscriptions' I have changed to 'holy characters', in accordance with Van der Horst 1998, 281. The French edition of the *Life of Moses* by R. Arnaldez et al. renders 'dans ce qu'ils appellent leurs textes sacrés', which is also inadequate; likewise, Graffigna 1999, 35 'libri sacri', Feldman 2002, 274 'holy writings'.

[35] Mendelson 1982, 5; cf. Feldman 2002, 273-5.

[36] According to Tatian 38, the Egyptian priest, Ptolemy of Mendes, cited by Apion (early first century AD), said that Moses was a contemporary of Inachus, the first king of Argos, cf. Stern 1974, 379-81; Schürer 1986, 606; Feldman 2002, 272 note 45.

further enhanced by the detail that, whereas teachers from the neighbouring countries and the provinces of Egypt came 'unbidden', the
Greeks had to be attracted 'under promise of high reward', a possible
allusion to the Sophists, who gave instruction for a fee. From them,
he learned grammar, rhetoric and dialectic, for if we regard the disciplines of grammar, rhetoric, dialectic, geometry, arithmetic, music,
and astronomy as the components of an encyclical education,[37] the
first three are taught by Greeks, since Moses learns geometry, arithmetic and music from Egyptian teachers, and astronomy jointly from
Egyptians and teachers 'of the neighbouring countries'.

As regards Moses' training in the art of eloquence, this disagrees
with the account in Exodus 4.10-16, where he is a poor speaker. But
let us not take this contradiction too seriously. In the passage under
discussion, Philo's purpose is to extol Moses' universal learning, but
when he has to deal with Moses' encounter with Pharaoh (*Life of Moses*
1.83), he does not bother to repeat from Exodus Moses' slowness of
speech and of tongue. Josephus is more consistent in that in *Antiquities* 2.271 he is vague about Moses' speech difficulties in order to be
able in *Antiquities* 4.49 to mention his gift 'in speech and in addresses
to a crowd'.

In spite of its international and indeed predominantly Greek character, Moses' education is by no means without its Egyptian elements.
As we have already seen, Moses learnt geometry, arithmetic and music
from Egyptian teachers, and astronomy jointly from Egyptians and
teachers 'of the neighbouring countries'. Furthermore, Egyptians
trained him in 'the philosophy conveyed in symbols, as displayed in
the so-called holy characters and in the regard paid to animals, to which
they even pay divine honours'. The 'philosophy conveyed in symbols'
refers to the secret ideas about the gods and divine matters known
exclusively to the Egyptian priests, who recorded them in hieroglyphs
to keep them secret.[38] Philo even mentions animal worship, and in a
much more lenient way than he usually does.[39] But in case his readers
might think Moses was a worshipper of animals himself, Philo adds

---

[37] See Mendelson 1982, 4.
[38] See note 25. I take the σύμβολα to denote hieroglyphs except those which
simply represented consonants. Cf. Vergote 1939, 208-9.
[39] Cf. Smelik and Hemelrijk 1984, 1915-18; Feldman 2002, 275. Philo's mildness
may be explained by the fact that his *Life of Moses* was meant for non-Jewish readers
whom he did not want to offend by being too scornful.

a statement about Moses' superior gifts as a learner: abhorring lies, if his teachers disagreed with each other, he established for himself what was truth. No doubt, in the same manner he rejected doctrines he felt to be false, including animal worship.

How far may these Hellenistic Jewish texts be regarded as precedents to the statement in Acts? With Acts, they share the idea of Moses' education at the Egyptian court. However, the royal character of this upbringing, stressed by Ezekiel the Tragedian, Philo and Josephus, is left unnoticed in Acts. Josephus keeps silent about the subject matter of the teaching, whereas Ezekiel and Philo evoke its many-sidedness, and Philo adds to that its mixed Greek, Egyptian and Near Eastern character. The author of Acts is the only one to represent it as a strictly Egyptian affair. This is his personal contribution and not just a summary of all that has been said by Philo, as has been repeated since Clement of Alexandria in *Strom.* 1.23.153.3.

3. *Patristic readings of Acts 7.22*

The book of Acts may be characterized as a slow starter when it comes to its popularity in the Early Church. In the first Christian generations, we find hardly any traces of its being read, and it is centuries before the first commentaries on it were written. The earliest series of homilies on Acts is by Origen in the third century, while the earliest commentary is that by Didymus the Blind in the fourth century; both writings survive only in fragments.[40] Nevertheless, the topic of Acts 7.22, Moses' training in Egypt, which was a minor feature after all, was dealt with in a good number of passages in patristic literature. Of course it was possible to develop this topic solely from the passage in Exodus, without referring to Acts 7.22; the witness of Philo proves that. But more often than not the picture in Exodus was combined with the information in Acts in order to gain a complete portrayal, much against the spirit of modern biblical scholarship but quite in accordance with 'pre-critical' Bible study, for which the Scriptures were a unity and cannot contradict each other. Limiting our enquiry to the Fathers down to the end of the fourth century, we shall deal

---

[40] For early quotations of Acts see Haenchen 1968, 1-13 ('Die ältesten kirchlichen Zeugnisse für die Apostelgeschichte und ihren Verfasser'); for patristic commentaries Stuehrenberg 1987.

with observations by Clement of Alexandria, Pseudo-Justin, Origen, Eusebius, Amphilochius, Basil, Gregory of Nyssa, Didymus the Blind, and Chrysostom on the Greek side, and of Hilary, Ambrose, and Ambrosiaster on the Latin.[41] We shall not discuss them one by one, but rather after analysing Clement's exposition, the earliest in time, we will deal with the remaining authors thematically.

Clement, in the first book of his *Stromateis* (1.23.153.2-3), has the following to say about Moses' youth and upbringing:

> [2] When he came of age, he studied with the leading Egyptian savants and learned arithmetic, geometry, rhythm, harmony, meter, music, and symbolic philosophy expressed in hieroglyphic script. Greeks in Egypt taught him the rest of the normal educational curriculum, as a royal child. So Philo says in his *Life of Moses*. [3] In addition, he learned from Chaldean and Egyptian teachers Assyrian script and knowledge of the heavenly bodies. This is why he is said in Acts 'to have been educated in all the wisdom of the Egyptians' (trans. J. Ferguson).

He gives here a detailed summary of Philo, *Life of Moses* 1.21-4, in which he assigns the teaching to Egyptians, Greeks and Chaldeans, and even repeats the 'Assyrian letters' of Philo.[42] He echoes Philo's anachronism of involving Greek teachers, which is the more remarkable since in the same first book of the *Stromateis* he emphasises the chronological priority of the 'philosophy of the barbarians' over Greek philosophy (1.15.66-73) and explicitly makes Moses a contemporary of Inachus (1.21.101.5).[43] Furthermore, Clement is the first and, for the time being, the only author to express the view that Acts 7.22 is a summary of the picture in Philo; Origen, for example, in his *Against Celsus* 3.46, surmises that Stephen has the information about Moses' Egyptian education from old and not widely known books, by which he can hardly have meant Philo. There is no hint that teaching is understood as an initiation into an esoteric lore, except that he identifies Philo's ἱερὰ γράμματα with hieroglyphs (ἱερογλυφικὰ γράμματα). Somewhat later in chapter 23, Clement quotes lines 7 to 40 of Ezekiel the Tragedian, as another description of Moses' youth (1.23.155.2-7). Thus, Clement offers a full collection of traditions about Moses'

---

[41] Our collection of passages is based on the seven volumes of Allenbach 1975-2000 and the survey in Stuehrenberg 1987.

[42] Cf. Van den Hoek 1988, 54.

[43] On the question of the priority see Pépin 1955; Ridings 1995 (2-139 on Clement of Alexandria).

education, both from Hellenistic Jewish and early Christian sources. Many aspects found here will continue to play a role in patristic literature, to which we will now turn.

The chief question is, of course, what does 'the wisdom of the Egyptians' mean. Unfortunately, a clear answer is hampered by the vagueness both of the pictures given and the terms used by the authors. To clarify matters, we can discern three possible meanings of the designation: (1) abstract thought, philosophy of the Egyptians, (2) the liberal arts and sciences, being the subject matter of the Greek encyclical education (ἐγκύκλιος παιδεία), or (3) specifically Egyptian skills or disciplines. The inadequacy of this arrangement is immediately obvious, for the picture in Philo and Clement fits (2) as well as (3). Nevertheless, let us try to work with this classification.

The first option, the wisdom of the Egyptians as their philosophy, applies relatively rarely. In his *Commentarii in Esaiam* 1.75 (128.30 GCS), Eusebius gives a double interpretation of Isaiah 19.7-8, the second of which is that it denotes 'the philosophy that formerly flourished with the Egyptians, of which it has been said "And Moses was instructed in all the wisdom of the Egyptians"'. Thus, from the statement in Acts alone, the existence of an Egyptian philosophy is deduced—a wicked philosophy for that matter, according to Eusebius. Ambrose, *De Abraham* 2.10.73, takes the same view, but he is slightly more positive about the wisdom, even if it is the 'wisdom of this world' and therefore inferior to the 'spiritual wisdom'.[44] Similarly, the unknown author we have given the name Ambrosiaster, in his *Liber quaestionum* 106.1, uses Acts 7.22 as a proof of Egyptian philosophy, a mistaken philosophy, to be sure, which had suggested wrong ideas on the origin of the world and so prompted Moses to present the correct vision in the first chapters of the book of Genesis. Interestingly, the wrong ideas Ambrosiaster alludes to include such Gnostic teachings as the creation of this world by Saclas through his evil angels.[45]

The second meaning, the wisdom of the Egyptians as the encyclical education, is more widespread. As we have just seen in the passage of Clement of Alexandria, this idea was adopted from Philo. Philo allocates the Egyptian teachers geometry, arithmetic, music and astronomy (the

---

[44] In *Exameron* 6.2.8, however, Ambrose describes the wisdom Moses learned from the Egyptians as *inanem illam et usurpatoriam philosophiae doctrinam*.

[45] On Saclas cf. also Ambrosiaster, *Quaest.* 3; Augustine, *De haeresibus* 46; Barc 1981; Böhlig 1989, 425-6.

last-mentioned discipline jointly with other non-Greek teachers), while Greeks took grammar, rhetoric and dialectic upon themselves, but in fact the first four disciplines have nothing un-Greek about them and could have been taught by Greeks as well. Clement repeats that picture. And Origen, refuting Celsus' claim of the Christians' want of education in *Contra Celsum* 6.14, remarks that if Celsus asserts that the Christians have no command of the sciences of the Greeks (τὰ τῶν Ἑλλήνων μαθήματα), he is obviously unaware of the fact that 'our wise men' since far-off days have also been instructed in the profane sciences (τοῖς ἔξωθεν μαθήμασιν), for instance Moses, who was trained 'in all the wisdom of the Egyptians'. Gregory of Nyssa, in his *Life of Moses* 1.18, says the same directly of Moses: during his royal education, he was παιδευθεὶς τὴν ἔξωθεν παίδευσιν. In these and similar contexts, the adjectival adverb ἔξωθεν, 'outside', does not denote Egyptian (non-Greek), but secular (non-Christian[46]) education. Similar observations occur elsewhere in Gregory's œuvre, and in Basil, Didymus the Blind, and, in the West, Ambrose.[47]

Thirdly, there are passages in which the wisdom of the Egyptians stands for specifically Egyptian skills or disciplines. Traditionally, geometry ranks as a Egyptian speciality; we see this in Herodotus, Plato, Diodorus Siculus, and Philo, and many more authors could be mentioned. In patristic literature, there are some rare references to it after Clement of Alexandria. Origen, in his *Second Homily on Genesis* 2.20, defends himself against an allegation by Marcion's disciple, Apelles, who denied the sacred and inspired character of Moses' writings, since, Apelles argued, an ark of 300 by 50 by 30 cubits cannot contain all the animals (Exodus 6). Origen retorts that it would be frankly absurd that someone who was instructed in all the wisdom of the Egyptians, people unrivalled at geometry, would not have realized that four elephants with sufficient food for a year could not be held in an ark of those dimensions. Origen's solution is simple: Moses meant the squares of the numbers mentioned.[48] For Basil, *Commentary on Proverbs*

---

[46] Cf. Geljon 2002, 87 note 41. Didymus, *Fragmenta e catenis in Actus Apostolorum* (112.22 Cramer) has the more explicit expression ἡ τῶν ἔξωθεν τῆς γραφῆς παίδευσις.

[47] Gregory of Nyssa, *Life of Basil* GNO X.1, pp. 110 and 126; *Life of Gregory Thaumaturgus*, GNO X.1, p. 10; Basil, *Oratio ad adolescentes* 3.3; Didymus, *Fragmenta e catenis in Actus Apostolorum* (112.22 Cramer); *Fragmenta e catenis in Psalmos* 540 (372.4 Mühlenberg); Ambrose, *Exameron* 1.2.6 (CSEL 32,1); *De officiis ministrorum* 1.26.123.

[48] We quote the Greek text according to the edition by Doutreleau 1975, 38. Origen similarly refers to Moses' Egyptian education in his *Commentary of John* 28.1.4, where

6, and Ambrose, *De officiis ministrorum* 1.26.122, on the other hand, geometry is just one of those pointless disciplines which keep people from what is really important, Christian wisdom.

There is, however, a quite different Egyptian specialism yet to be discussed, and that is magic. To the standards of Greek culture, geometry is a respectable pursuit, but here we have a much more questionable practice. Consequently, the account in Exodus 7.8-12, where Moses and Aaron outdo the magicians of Egypt, may have embarrassed many a Church Father, as it had embarrassed the Hellenistic Jewish authors.[49] Origen, however, in *Against Celsus* 3.46 courageously faces the biblical facts. Moses, he argues, had acquired a variety of disciplines from the Egyptians, as Stephen witnesses in Acts, and exactly for that reason Pharaoh suspected him of working his miracles as a magician. He therefore summoned his own sorcerers, who were, however, miserably beaten. But Pharaoh was mistaken, Origen adds, in thinking that Moses was a magician: Moses wrought his wonders not by following the lessons of the Egyptians, but in accordance with the promise that he was sent by God. We find essentially the same thought in Gregory of Nyssa in the *Panegyric on his brother Basil*, *Gregorii Nysseni Opera* x.1, p. 112. Origen, *Homily in Exodus* 8.3, furthermore explains that Moses, precisely because of his intimate knowledge of Egyptian learning, including of hidden things, legislated against conjuring 'any likeness of anything that is in heaven above' (Exodus 20.4), another form of magic. Finally, we should mention under our third category the religion of the Egyptians. The only author in our collection of passages to allude to it is, again, Origen. Celsus, he remarks in *Against Celsus* 1.20, speaks highly of the Egyptians who informed him of the myth of conflagrations and floods, but they are poor sages, who have their worship of animals as a proof of their wisdom. Thus, the 'wisdom of the Egyptians' could be conceived of in different ways, even by one and the same author, such as Ambrose, who in *De Abraham* 2.10.73 took it to be philosophy and in *Exameron* 1.2.6 and *De officiis ministrorum* 1.26.123 the encyclia.

There is, however, a further question to be dealt with: how did

---

he alludes to Exodus 26.2, concerning the length of the tabernacle's curtains.

[49] See the illuminating essay by Gager 1994 and, in this volume, Bremmer p. 325 note 83 and Van der Vliet p. 533 note 41.

Christian readers value Moses' training in the wisdom of the Egyptians? Let us begin by quoting two extremes, appearing straight after one another in the *Chain on Acts* on Acts 7.22:

> Ammonius: Neither Moses nor Ananias, Daniel and his comrades would have learned the outside education but for the compulsion and force of despots. For indeed, they have not used it for anything, unless someone might say that it would be well to learn in order to overthrow their frauds.
> Didymus: From the present verse is it clear that the education outside that subject matter of Scripture is not altogether to be thrown away. For it is said by way of praise that Moses was instructed in all the wisdom of the Egyptians, and about Daniel and his Hebrew comrades that they surpassed all people in the philosophy and cognate sciences of the Chaldeans (my trans.).

The fifth-century exegete, Ammonius,[50] with whom this passage starts, is of the opinion that the secular disciplines served no purpose, unless they helped to beat the enemy with his own weapons. This idea has been aired before; we have already seen Origen hinting at it in *Homily in Exodus* 8.3, and Gregory of Nyssa in his *Life of Gregory Thaumaturgus*, *Gregorii Nysseni Opera* x.1, p. 10, suggests that Moses through his Egyptian education knows its weaknesses.[51] Didymus, on the other hand, argues from the immediate context. Whereas we would tend to agree with his vision that Moses' Egyptian education was mentioned 'by way of praise', he is quite alone in this opinion; even if some Church Fathers had a positive opinion of the encyclical education, no-one concludes from the context that this must have been meant. Curiously, for all their dissimilarity, both authors concur in combining the examples of Moses and Daniel, as several exegetes do before them.[52]

The appreciation of Egyptian wisdom varies according to circumstances. Understandably, in apologetic texts, Moses' education at the Egyptian court is mentioned to extol him.[53] In other cases, Moses is pictured as making good use of the lessons at court when he had to deal with issues involving geometry; we have seen this in Origen.[54]

---

[50] Cf. Stuehrenberg 1987, 108.

[51] The same idea is found in Theodoret, *Quaest. Ex.* 2.

[52] Origen, *Against Celsus* 614; *Strom.* PL 26.435B; Basil, *Oratio ad adolescentes* 3.3-4; Didymus, *Commentary on Ecclesiastes* 40.8-10; *Commentary on Psalms* 540.

[53] This applies to Pseudo-Justin, *Cohortatio ad Graecos* 10.1; Origen, *Against Celsus* 3.46; 6.14.

[54] Origen, *Second Homily on Genesis* 2.20; *Commentary of John* 28.1.4.

Some passages simply take for granted that being instructed in all the wisdom of the Egyptians means being exceedingly wise. Thus in the *Commentary on Isaiah* 1.16 (PG 30.221) by Basil, the usefulness of a counsellor is proven by the example of Moses, who, although 'instructed in all the wisdom of the Egyptians', did not hesitate to take the advice of his father-in-law (cf. Exodus 18.24).[55] Gregory of Nyssa praises his brother Basil, *Panegyric on Basil* GNO X.1, p. 110, as someone who, like Moses, is well versed both in secular and Christian wisdom.

But the prevailing appreciation is a comparative one. Even if the wisdom of the Egyptians is useful, it pales before the true wisdom, which is the wisdom of the Christian mysteries, or whatever other name is given to it. The story of Moses departing from the presence of Pharaoh and moving to the land of Midian (Exodus 2.15) was a helpful means to make this clear. Philo, *Life of Moses* 1.32, already pointed out that Moses did not neglect the education of his parents and ancestors for his temporary prosperity at Pharaoh's court. A New Testament passage accentuates the contrast, Hebrews 11.24-7:

> [24] By faith Moses, when he was grown up, refused to be called the son of Pharaoh's daughter, [25]choosing rather to share ill-treatment with the people of God than to enjoy the fleeting pleasures of sin. [26] He considered abuse suffered for the Christ greater wealth than the treasures of Egypt, for he looked to the reward. [27]By faith he left Egypt, not being afraid of the anger of the king; for he endured as seeing him who is invisible.[56]

Eusebius, in his *Life of Constantine* 1.12.1, interprets Moses' departure as a liberation from the tyrant's palace, which enabled him to distance himself from the deeds and words of the tyrant's family which had educated him and to devote himself to the will of the Mightier. Amphilochius, *Iambi ad Seleucum* 221-33, places the emphasis rather on his asceticism. Moses' education in all the wisdom of the Egyptians had been enjoyed in a life of luxury—now he abandoned all that, preferring an austere life to the glory of tyrants. And so he was granted the honour to hear God's voice and to be entrusted with the task of removing the yoke from his people. Basil, in the first chapter of his *Homilies on the Hexaemeron*, evokes the same image, adding to it the feature of Moses' forty years of dedication to the contemplation

---

[55] See Didymus, *Commentary in Job* 107.28 for comparable case. I take for granted that the *Commentary on Isaiah* is a genuine work by Basil, cf. Lipatov 1993.

[56] For this passage cf. Barclay 1992, 43-6.

of the realities (τῇ θεωρίᾳ τῶν ὄντων). The full development of the image as a symbol of the pursuit of secular and spiritual wisdom, respectively, is to be found in Gregory of Nyssa, *Life of Moses* 2.11-12 and Ambrose, *De officiis ministrorum* 1.26.122-3. The latter admits that Moses had occupied himself with such worthless studies as astronomy and geometry, for he was 'instructed in all the wisdom of the Egyptians'. 'But', the bishop continues, 'he judged that wisdom to be detrimental and stupid. Turning away from it, he sought God with his whole heart and so saw Him, interrogated Him, and heard Him speaking.'

Finally a word on Moses' slowness of speech. In the first section of this essay, we discussed the apparent contradiction between Exodus 4.10, where Moses is 'slow of speech and of tongue', and the second half of Acts 7.22, where he features as 'mighty in his words and deeds'. We do not know whether Origen saw a contradiction between both passages. In any case, he seems somewhat uneasy about Moses' deficient speaking ability. This inspires him to the following observation at the beginning of his *Third Homily on Exodus* (*Hom. in Ex.* 3.1):

> As long as Moses was in Egypt and 'was educated in all the wisdom of the Egyptians', he was not weak in speech and slow-tongued nor does he say he was ineloquent. Indeed, he was, compared to the Egyptians, gifted with a sonorous voice and an incomparable eloquence. But when he began to hear God's voice and to catch the divine utterances, then he became aware his voice was thin and weak and realized his tongue was hampered.

Here a preacher is speaking, who both whitewashes Moses of any imperfection and stresses God's overwhelming superiority to any human achievement. Origen's interpretation resurfaces in several later authors, Amphilochius, Basil, Didymus and Ambrose, and as little as Origen do they confront Moses' difficulty in speech of Exodus with his power of words in Acts.

3. *Conclusion*

The results of our investigation can be summarized as follows. As appears from its context, the statement in Acts about Moses' Egyptian upbringing was meant as a positive point. The memory of the bad time the Israelites had in Egypt and the idolatry of its inhabitants obviously played no role. On the contrary, the author is as impressed by the prestige of Egypt as his pagan contemporaries. Acts is, however, not explicit about the purport of the expression 'the wisdom of the Egyptians'; we can as well narrow it down to what we would call philosophy as broaden it to comprise all sorts of skills and disciplines the Egyptians were good at. In any case, the common assertion that Acts summarizes Philo's portrayal of Moses receiving an education in the Greek encyclia cannot be correct: Acts speaks of the wisdom of the Egyptians, thus the wisdom is specifically Egyptian, whatever may be meant by that. As for the apparent discrepancy between Moses' hampering tongue in Exodus and his power of words in Acts, this turns out to be unfounded: the speech disease in Exodus did not prevent Moses from being authoritative in the utterances alluded to in Acts.

If we compare these findings with patristic interpretations of Acts 7.22, one difference we could anticipate is that the Church fathers treated the Bible as a whole in which there are no contradictions. Thus, Acts 7.22 could be used to supplement the picture in Exodus 2.10. On the other hand, at least three aspects are in agreement with our opinion of the text. First of all, just like us, our distant predecessors did not find any trace of resentment against the Egyptians as oppressors or idolaters in the verse. If the ecclesiastical authors had a negative view of Egyptian wisdom at all, it had nothing to do with biblical considerations. Furthermore, then as now, no obvious interpretation of the concept 'the wisdom of the Egyptians' imposed itself. Some of the Church fathers thought only of wisdom in a philosophical sense, others included the several disciplines of the Egyptians, notably those for which they had a reputation, such as geometry. Often Moses' education at the Egyptian court is viewed as a preparatory study, hardly, or not at all, differing from the secular education the Christians deemed necessary for the study of Scripture or, as they expressed with predilection, of the divine mysteries. Where Moses is adduced as a standard example of studying first secular and then true, i.e. Christian, wisdom, he is often accompanied by the example of Daniel who was as expert in Chaldean wisdom as Moses was in Egyptian. Finally, the ancient authors agree with our view that Moses' powerful words can coexist perfectly with a slowness of speech.

Is there anything to be learned from the ideas aired by the Church fathers? I think there is. We have argued that the wisdom of the Egyptians in Acts 7.22 must indeed be specifically Egyptian. Nowhere in early Jewish literature have we found a statement comparable with the one in Acts; thus, we inferred, Acts was evidently unique in stressing the Egyptian character of the wisdom concerned. However, not only Philo represented Moses' instruction at the Pharaoh's court as

an initiation in the Greek encyclia, Clement of Alexandria, who knew
Acts, also held that view and, what is more, declared explicitly that
Acts 7.22 had to be read in the light of Philo's description. Many
other patristic authors shared that view; they obviously saw no need
to conceive of the wisdom of the Egyptians as something specifically
Egyptian, something definitely non-Greek. Against this background,
our reasoning may well have been too rigid. If Hellenistic near-con-
temporaries of the author of Acts such as Philo and Clement could
interpret Moses' education in Egypt as a Greek affair, why could he
not have had the same intention himself?[57]

Bibliography

Editions

Arnaldez, R., C. Mondésert, J. Pouilloux, and P. Savinel 1967. *De Vita Mosis I - II: Introduction, traduction et notes* (Les Œuvres de Philon d'Alexandrie 22), Paris.
Colson, F.H. 1935. *Philo with an English Translation*, vi (Loeb Classical Library), Cambridge, Massachusetts/London.
Cramer, J.A. 1838. *Catena in Acta SS. Apostolorum e cod. Nov. Coll. Descripsit et nunc primum edidit adjecta lectionis varietate e cod. Coislin*, Oxford = Hildesheim 1967.
Doutreleau, L. 1975. 'Le fragment grec de l'homélie II d'Origène sur la Genèse: Critique du texte', *Revue d'Histoire des Textes* 5 (1975) 13-44.
Mühlenberg, E. 1975. *Psalmenkommentare aus der Katenenüberlieferung*, i (Patristische Texte und Studien 15), Berlin/New York.

Monographs, reference works, and articles

Allenbach, J., et al. 1975-2000. *Biblia Patristica: Index des citations et allusions bibliques dans la littérature patristique*, 7 vols., Paris.
Assmann, J. 1999. *Moses the Egyptian: The Memory of Egypt in Western Monotheism*, Cambridge, Massachusetts/London (first printing 1997).
Barc, B. 1981. 'Samaèl - Saklas - Yaldabaôth: Recherche sur la genèse d'un mythe gnostique', in: Id. (ed.), *Colloque international sur les textes de Nag Hammadi (Québec, 22-25 août 1978)* (BCNH Études 1), Québec/Louvain, 123-50.
Barclay, J.M.G. 1992. 'Manipulating Moses: Exodus 2.10-15 in Egyptian Judaism and the New Testament', in: R.P. Carroll (ed.), *Text as Pretext: Essays in Honour of Robert Davidson* (Journal for the Study of the Old Testament Supplement Series 138), Sheffield, 28-46.
Böhlig, A. 1989. *Gnosis und Synkretismus: Gesammelte Aufsätze zur spätantiken Religionsgeschichte* (Wissenschaftliche Untersuchungen zum Neuen Testament 47-48), Tübingen.

[57] I am grateful for help in preparing this essay towards Annewies van den Hoek, Ed Noort, Stefan Radt and, particularly, George van Kooten. Florentino García Martínez and Lautaro Roig Lanzillotta kindly provided me with publications not available in Dutch libraries.

Boned Colera, P., and Rodríguez Somolinos, J. 1998. *Repertorio bibliográfico de la lexicografía griega (RBLG): Diccionario griego-español, Anejo III,* Madrid.

Bovon, F. 1978. 'La figure de Moïse dans l'œuvre de Luc', in: R. Martin-Achard et al., *La figure de Moïse: Ecriture et relectures* (Publications de la faculté de théologie de l'université de Genève 1), Geneva, 47-65.

Burton, A. 1972. *Diodorus Siculus, Book I: A Commentary* (Études préliminaires aux religions orientales dans l'empire romain 29), Leiden.

Dimitrakos, D. 1950. Μέγα Λεξικὸν τῆς Ἑλληνικῆς γλώσσης 8, Athens/Thessaloniki.

Droge, A. J. 1989. *Homer or Moses? Early Christian Interpretations of the History of Culture* (Hermeneutische Untersuchungen zur Theologie 26), Tübingen.

Feldman, L.H. 1991-92 and 1992-93. 'Josephus' Portrait of Moses', *Jewish Quarterly Review* 82 (1991-92) 285-328; 83 (1992-93) 7-50 and 301-30.

Feldman, L.H. 2002. 'Philo's View of Moses' Birth and Upbringing', *Catholic Biblical Quarterly* 64 (2002) 258-81.

Froidefond, C. 1971. *Le mirage égyptien dans la littérature grecque d'Homère à Aristote,* Paris.

Gager, J.G. 1972. *Moses in Greco-Roman Paganism* (Society of Biblical Literature Monograph Series 16), Nashville/New York.

Gager, J.G. 1994. 'Moses the Magician: Hero of an Ancient Counter-Culture', *Helios* 21 (1994) 179-88.

Geljon, A.C. 2002. *Philonic Exegesis in Gregory of Nyssa's* De Vita Moysis (Brown Judaic Studies 333; Studia Philonica Monographs 5), Providence.

Geljon, A.C. 2004. 'Philo van Alexandrië over de jeugd van Mozes: De vita Moysis 1.1-24', *Hermeneus* 76 (2004) 182-91.

Goetzmann, J. 1971. 'σοφία', in: L. Coenen, E. Beyreuther and H. Bietenhard (eds), *Theologisches Begriffslexikon zum Neuen Testament II/2,* Wuppertal, 1375-9.

Gonzalo Maeso, D. 1974. 'Moisés y la antigua cosmogonía egipcia', *Cultura Bíblica* 31 (1974) 97-9.

Graffigna, P. 1999. *Filone di Alessandria, La vita di Mosè: Introduzione, traduzione e apparati: Testo greco a fronte,* Milan.

Haenchen, E. 1968[6]. *Die Apostelgeschichte* (Kritisch-exegetischer Kommentar über das Neue Testament 3), Göttingen.

Hegermann, H. 1983. 'σοφία', in: H. Balz and G. Schneider (eds), *Exegetisches Wörterbuch zum Neuen Testament,* iii, Stuttgart, 616-24.

Hopfner, T. 1922-25. *Fontes Historiae Religionis Aegyptiacae* (Fontes historiae religionum 2), 5 vols, Bonn.

Iversen, E. 1961[1]. *The Myth of Egypt and its Hieroglyphs in European Tradition,* Copenhagen (Princeton 1993[2]).

Jacquier, E. 1926. *Les Actes des Apôtres* (Études Bibliques), Paris.

Jüthner, J. 1923. *Hellenen und Barbaren: Aus der Geschichte des Nationalbewußtseins* (Das Erbe der Alten NF 8), Leipzig.

Kastner, J.M. 1967. *Moses im Neuen Testament,* Diss. Munich.

Krause, M., and K. Hoheisel 2001. 'Aegypten II (literaturgeschichtlich)', *Reallexikon für Antike und Christentum: Supplement-Band I,* Stuttgart, 14-88.

Langevin, P.-É. 1985. *Bibliographie Biblique III: 1930-1983,* Quebec.

Liddell, H.G., R. Scott, H.S. Jones, and R. MacKenzie. 1940[9]. *A Greek-English Lexicon,* Oxford.

Lierman, J. 2004. *The New Testament Moses: Christian Perceptions of Moses and Israel in the Setting of Jewish Religion* (Wissenschaftliche Untersuchungen zum Neuen Testament 2.173), Tübingen.

Lipatov, N.A. 1993. 'The Problem of the Authorship of the *Commentary on the prophet*

Isaiah Attributed to St. Basil the Great', *Studia Patristica* 27 (1993) 42-8.

Mendelson, A. 1982. *Secular Education in Philo of Alexandria* (Monographs of the Hebrew Union College 7), Cincinnati.

Morenz, S. 1968. *Die Begegnung Europas mit Ägypten: Mit einem Beitrag von Martin Kaiser, Herodots Begegnung mit Ägypten* (Sitzungsberichte der Sächsischen Akademie der Wissenschaften zu Leipzig, Philologisch-historische Klasse 113.5), Berlin.

Muraoka, T. 2002. *A Greek-English Lexicon of the Septuagint: Chiefly of the Pentateuch and the Prophets*, Louvain.

Pépin, J. 1955. 'Le «challenge» Homère-Moïse aux premiers siècles chrétiens', *Revue des Sciences Religieuses* 29 (1955) 105-22.

Plümacher, E. 1972. *Lukas als hellenistischer Schriftsteller: Studien zur Apostelgeschichte* (Studien zur Umwelt des Neuen Testaments 9), Göttingen.

Ridings, D. 1995. *The Attic Moses: The Dependency Theme in Some Early Christian Writers* (Studia Graeca et Latina Gothoburgensia 59), Göteborg.

Riedweg, C. 2002. *Pythagoras: Leben, Lehre, Nachwirkung: Eine Einführung*, Munich.

Robbins, W.J. 1947. *A Study in Jewish and Hellenistic Legend with Special Reference to Philo's Life of Moses*, Diss. Brown University.

Schmid, W. 1893 and 1896. *Der Atticismus in seinen Hauptvertretern von Dionysius von Halikarnass bis auf den zweiten Philostratus*, iii, Stuttgart = Hildesheim 1964; iv, Stuttgart = Hildesheim 1964.

Schürer, E., G. Vermes, and F. Millar. 1986. *The History of the Jewish People in the Age of Jesus Christ (175 BC - AD 135)*, iii.1, Edinburgh.

Smelik, K.A.D., and E.A. Hemelrijk 1984. '"Who knows not what monsters demented Egypt worships?": Opinions on Egyptian animal worship in Antiquity as part of the ancient conception of Egypt', *Aufstieg und Niedergang der römischen Welt*, ii.17.4, Berlin/New York, 1852-2000 and 2337-57.

Snell, B. 1924. *Die Ausdrücke für den Begriff des Wissens in der vorplatonischen Philosophie* (σοφία, γνώμη, σύνεσις, ἱστορία, μάθημα, ἐπιστήμη) (Philologische Untersuchungen 29), Berlin.

Springhetti, A. 1966. *Introductio historica - Grammatica in graecitatem Novi Testamenti*, Rome.

Stephanus, H., C.B. Hase, G. Dindorfius, and L. Dindorfius. 1848-54. *Thesaurus Graecae linguae*, vii, Paris.

Stern, M. 1974. *Greek and Latin Authors on Jews and Judaism*, i, Jerusalem.

Stuehrenberg, P.F. 1987. 'The Study of Acts before the Reformation: A Bibliographic Introduction', *Novum Testamentum* 29 (1987) 100-36.

Van den Hoek, A. 1988. *Clement of Alexandria and His Use of Philo in the* Stromateis: *An Early Christian Reshaping of a Jewish Model* (Vigiliae Christianae Supplement 3), Leiden etc.

Van der Horst, P.W. 1998[2]. 'The Secret Hieroglyphs in Ancient Literature', in: Id., *Hellenism - Judaism - Christianity: Essays on Their Interaction* (Contributions to Biblical Exegesis and Theology 8), Louvain, 317-25.

Vergote, J. 1939. 'Clément d'Alexandrie et l'écriture égyptienne: Essai d'interprétation de *Stromates*, V, iv, 20-21', *Le Muséon* 52 (1939) 199-221.

Von Gutschmid, A. 1889. 'Scriptorum rerum Aegyptiacarum series ad temporum rationem exacta', in: Id., *Kleine Schriften*, i, Leipzig, 150-65.

Von Paula Eisenmann, F. 1859. *Über Begriff und Bedeutung der griechischen ΣΟΦΙΑ von den ältesten Zeiten an bis auf Sokrates: Programm des Königlichen Wilhelms-Gymnasiums zu München am Schlusse des Studienjahres 1858/59*, Munich.

Wilckens, U., and G. Fohrer 1964. 'σοφία, σοφός, σοφίζω', *Theologisches Wörterbuch zum Neuen Testament*, vii, Stuttgart, 465-529.

'WRATH WILL DRIP IN THE PLAINS OF MACEDONIA': EXPECTATIONS OF NERO'S RETURN IN THE EGYPTIAN *SIBYLLINE ORACLES* (BOOK 5), 2 THESSALONIANS, AND ANCIENT HISTORICAL WRITINGS

George H. van Kooten

In this paper, dedicated in honour of my close colleague Gerard Luttikhuizen, I argue that one book of the collection of *Sibylline Oracles*, book 5, which is of Egyptian provenance, is of particular importance in re-interpreting the setting of the Second Pauline Letter to the Thessalonians (2 Thess). In this fifth book, the figure of Nero plays a dominant role, as I shall show in §1. Even more importantly for the present purpose, the book also mentions Nero's intentions with regard to Macedonia, the Roman province whose capital is Thessalonica. If one could indeed demonstrate a specific connection between Nero and Macedonia, it might become somewhat clearer why eschatological tensions rose so high in Thessalonica, as is evident from 2 Thess. This suggestion only works, however, if the threatening figure in 2 Thess 2 can plausibly be identified with Nero. I shall give fresh evidence in favour of this identification with the help of Greco-Roman sources in §2. This case will be built particularly on the fact, often overlooked, that Suetonius' report that Nero was expected to leave for the East and receive the sovereignty of Jerusalem (*Lives of the Caesars, Nero* 40.2) runs parallel with the expectation of 2 Thess that the adversary will take up residence in God's temple (2.4) in Jerusalem. If, then, Nero and the adversary of 2 Thess are one and the same, the coupling made between Nero and Macedonia in book 5 of the *Sibylline Oracles* becomes highly relevant for a proper understanding of the circumstances of the community in the Macedonian capital which formed the primary readership for 2 Thess.

That book 5 of the *Sibylline Oracles* entertains such a great interest in Nero, as do other books in the Sibylline collection, is no surprise. The Sibyl had an intimate connection with Rome, and the widespread interest in Sibyls and Sibylline prophecy throughout the Mediterranean area probably stems from this fact.[1] In Rome, the books of the *Sibylline Oracles* were consulted at the command of the Senate in times of crisis. This still happened in crises which occurred in Nero's time. According to Tacitus, after the fire of Rome in AD 64, 'Means were sought for appeasing the gods, and application was made to the Sibylline books, at the injunction of which public prayers were offered' (*Annals* 15.44).[2] These books were the official books, only consulted by order of the Senate. However, according to Dio Cassius, the populace, too, referred to the Sibyl in this eschatological time of crisis:

> they (...) proceeded to repeat another oracle, which they averred to be a genuine Sibylline prophecy, namely: 'Last of the sons of Aeneas (ἔσχατος Αἰνεαδῶν), a mother-slayer shall govern.' And so it proved, whether this verse was actually spoken beforehand by some divine prophecy, or the populace was now for the first time inspired, in view of the present situation, to utter it. For Nero was indeed the last emperor of the Julian line, the line descended from Aeneas (*Roman History* 62.18.4-5).[3]

When the authors of the *Sibylline Oracles*, and in particular those of book 5, made extensive reference in their prophecy to events of Roman history, including those concerning Nero, this was very much in accordance with the general atmosphere of the time. In the Jewish *Sibylline Oracles*, Nero features first and foremost as the figure of 'Nero Redivivus', as it is somewhat misleadingly called in scholarly literature. This is misleading, because on his death in AD 68, many considered Nero not to have died, but merely to have fled to the East, from where he was expected to return. Nero, therefore, was not initially regarded as 'he who lives again' (redi-vivus),[4] as though he were to return from the dead, but he was expected to return from the East in order to take vengeance on those who had risen against him and forced him out of the West. 'Nero Rediturus' would be a more appropriate term

---

[1] See Pease & Potter 1996, 1401.

[2] As a rule, English translations of classical texts are taken from the Loeb series, with some modifications if necessary; the *Sibylline Oracles* are quoted in the translation of Collins 1983. The New Testament is normally quoted in the Revised English Bible translation.

[3] Cf. Dio Cassius, *Roman History*: 'Of the descendants of Aeneas and of Augustus he was the last (ἔσχατος τῶν ἀπὸ τοῦ Αἰνείου καὶ ἀπὸ τοῦ Αὐγούστου γεγονότων), as was plainly indicated by the fact that the laurels planted by Livia and the breed of white chickens perished shortly before his death' (63.29.3).

[4] As is said of Christ in Christian writings; see, e.g., Prudentius, *Cathemerinon* 3.204.

for this phenomenon.[5] In modern-day terms, the supposed disappearance of Nero is comparable with the vanishing of Saddam Hussein during the first stage of the Iraq war before he was arrested on 13 December 2003; the feelings of anxiety and hope Saddam's disappearance caused among different people are also noticeable in the ancient sources about Nero.

The expectations regarding Nero Rediturus in classical sources help us to understand his occurrence in the *Sibylline Oracles* and 2 Thess. It seems that the expectations of Nero's return emerged because of the secretive circumstances of Nero's death, the existence of various rumours about him departing for the East, and Nero's exceptionally young age as emperor.

(a) First of all, the fact that Nero committed suicide at the villa of his freedman Phaon during the night (Dio Cassius, *Roman History* 63.27-29), created a mysterious atmosphere which did not convince all people that he was in fact dead.

(b) Secondly, the idea that Nero had fled Italy was in line with his latest plans. According to Dio Cassius, when Nero 'heard about Galba having been proclaimed emperor by the soldiers (…), he fell into great fear (…); (…) he began forming plans to kill the senators, burn down the city, and sail to Alexandria'; Nero even suggested that he would be able to earn his living by playing the lyre (*Roman History* 63.27.1-2; cf. Suetonius, *Nero* 40.2). Moreover, Suetonius reports that 'some of the astrologers (…) had promised Nero the rule of the East when he was cast off, a few expressly naming the sovereignty of Jerusalem' (*Nero* 40.2).

(c) Finally, the idea that Nero had in fact managed to escape to the East, either to Egypt, Jerusalem, or to another Eastern destination, from where he would return in due course, was perfectly possible in view of Nero's young age. Nero was seventeen when he became emperor and, in AD 68, which we know to be the year of his death, despite

---

[5] This alternative term was coined by Prof. Ruurd Nauta during the discussion of a preliminary version of this paper in the Groningen Ancient World Seminar and could offer more precision in future scholarly debates. See also Collins 1974, 188 note 47: 'It should be noted that Nero was not expected to rise from the dead, at least in the earliest accounts, so the term *redivivus* is inappropriate. The figure expected was the historical Nero, thought to be still alive.' Cf. also Van Henten's discontent with this term with regard to the *Sibylline Oracles* in Van Henten 2000, 17: 'it seems inappropriate to speak of *Nero redivivus* in the context of the *Sibylline Oracles* since the oracles do mention Nero's return, but do not refer to his death in this connection.'

having been emperor for fourteen years, he was still only thirty (Dio Cassius, *Roman History* 61.3.1 and 63.29.3; cf. Suetonius, *Nero* 57.1: 'in the thirty-second year of his age'). According to Tacitus, six years before his death Nero had told Seneca: 'I myself am but entering the first stages of my sovereignty' (*Annals* 14.56).

These factors gave rise to vivid expectations of Nero's return. Such expectancy is attested in reports on popular feelings to this effect and also in reports on the sightings of pseudo-Neros. According to Suetonius,

> There were some who for a long time decorated his tomb with spring and summer flowers, and now produced his statues on the rostra, and now his edicts, as if he were still alive and would shortly return and deal destruction to his enemies. (…) In fact, twenty years later (…) a person of obscure origin appeared, who gave out that he was Nero (*Nero* 57.1-2).

These popular feelings are confirmed by Dio Chrysostom who, in a discourse probably dating from the reign of Domitian (AD 81-96),[6] writes the following about Nero:

> There was nothing to prevent his continuing to be emperor for all time, seeing that even now everybody wishes he were still alive. And the great majority do believe that he is (21.9-10).[7]

As Suetonius already suggested, these widespread expectations in turn gave rise to the appearances of false Neros. Several reports about such pseudo-Neros in the decades after Nero's death have survived. The appearances occurred in AD 69, 79, and 88, took place in Greece, Syria, and Asia, and were often supported by the Parthians, with whom Nero had been on strategic, friendly terms ([a] Dio Cassius 64.9.3: AD 69 under Otho, name unknown; = probably identical with the pseudo-Nero in Tacitus, *Histories* 2.8-9; [b] Dio Cassius 66.19.3: AD 79 under Titus, 'an Asiatic named Terentius Maximus', supported by the Parthians; and [c] Suetonius, *Nero* 57.1-2: AD 88 under Domitian, 'a person of obscure origin', supported by the Parthians).[8] The fact that so many impostors came to the fore is testimony to the widespread

---

[6] See J.W. Cohoon's introduction to this discourse in the Loeb edition of Dio Chrysostom, vol. 2 (1939), p. 271.

[7] For an analysis of this passage, see Klauck 2001, 683-5.

[8] Cf. also Lucian, *The Ignorant Book Collector* 20, with a reference to 'the false Nero in our grandfathers' time'. On the false Neros of the first century AD, see Tuplin 1989.

popular expectations of Nero's return to power. It is this expectancy that also informs the Jewish *Sibylline Oracles*.

1. *The return of Nero in the Egyptian Sibylline Oracles*

1.1. *Introduction*

The notion of Nero as an important adversary is prominent throughout the *Sibylline Oracles*. In book 4, for instance, Nero's return is expected after the eruption of Mount Vesuvius in AD 79:

> But when a firebrand, turned away from a cleft in the earth in the land of Italy, reaches to broad heaven, it will burn many cities and destroy men. (...) Then the strife of war being aroused will come to the West, and the fugitive from Rome will also come, brandishing a great spear, having crossed the Euphrates with many myriads (4.130-139).[9]

Also in books 3 and 5, Nero figures as the eschatological tyrant. Book 5, whose contents point at an Egyptian background of its oracles and/or redactors and which general consensus dates to the period between AD 80 and 130,[10] is particularly concerned with Nero.[11] As Collins has pointed out, however, there is a interesting difference in the actual concept of Nero Rediturus in books 3 and 5.[12] Book 3 possibly identifies Nero with Beliar (Belial), the leader of the forces of

---

[9] According to Collins 1983, 382 it dates from between the destruction of the Jerusalem temple (4.116) and the period following the eruption of Vesuvius in AD 79 (4.130-134); all scholars agree that it was written shortly after the last datable event mentioned—therefore about AD 80.

[10] The likelihood is that the book should be dated before the end of the first century AD. See, for example, Collins 1974, 75: 'The conviction (...) that the destruction of the temple marked the beginning of the final age, makes it probable that the central oracles were written closer to AD 70 than to the time of Hadrian (...). In all, we seem to have a group of Jewish oracles from the end of the first century AD but collected under Hadrian'; Collins 1983, 390; Goodman 1986, 644: 'a date before the end of the first century AD is likely'; Barclay 1996, 225. For precise methods of dating, see Felder 2002, esp. 373-4, 377, 384: 'Starting with the hypothesis that the verses containing laments for the destruction of the Temple, the Nero *redivivus*, and strong anti-Roman sentiments are newer, we can see that almost the entire fifth Sibylline oracle was composed by redactors working in the last decade of the first century CE' (p. 373).

[11] Cf. Jakob-Sonnabend 1990, 140: 'Im fünften Buch der Oracula Sibyllina (...) finden sich die zahlreichsten und ausführlichsten Bemerkungen der sibyllinischen Sprüche zu Nero.'

[12] Collins 1974, 80-7; esp. 86.

darkness in biblical and early Jewish writings, and stresses his super-human behaviour in strongly mythological terms (3.63-74).[13] The mythologizing of the Nero Rediturus notion is in any case visible in the *Ascension of Isaiah*, whose author also identifies Nero and Beliar: 'And after the world has come to its consummation, Beliar, the great prince, the king of this world who has ruled it since it came into being, shall descend; he will come down from his firmament in the form of a man, a lawless king, a slayer of his mother' (4.1-18 at 4.2).[14] Book 5 of the *Sibylline Oracles*, on the other hand, portrays Nero as a human protagonist who remains on the historical scene.

This difference between the *Ascension of Isaiah* and book 3 of the *Sibylline Oracles*, on the one hand, and book 5, on the other, might be relevant to the present discussion, as it poses the question of whether the eschatological opponent in book 5 and in 2 Thess is primarily a human, historical protagonist. Before assessing the behaviour of the Nero Rediturus figure in book 5 of the *Sibylline Oracles*, I shall first devote some attention to the relation between Nero and Egypt, since in this book of the Egyptian *Sibylline Oracles* Nero is also expected to visit Egypt.

1.2. *Nero and Egypt*

The relationship between Nero and Egypt is a strong one, according to the ancient historians. Suetonius mentions that 'Nero planned but two foreign tours, to Alexandria and Achaia' (*Nero* 19.1). Although Nero made it to Greece, his visit to Egypt never took place. According to Tacitus, before visiting Greece in AD 66-68 (Dio Cassius 63.8-19), Nero was secretly 'occupied with the Eastern provinces, Egypt in particular'. Having made every preparation, he nevertheless abandoned his project due to a bad omen (Tacitus, *Annals* 15.36; Suetonius, *Nero* 19.1).[15] We have already seen that some astrologers had promised

---

[13] This passage, 3.63-74, together with its immediate context (3.1-96), was not originally part of book 3. See Goodman 1986, 630, 633, 639-41; for a brief discussion of 3.63-74, see 640-1 and Collins 1974, 86-7.

[14] Translation taken from Müller & Wilson 1992, 609.

[15] Dio Cassius shows that preparations in Egypt were already in a very advanced state, as the governor of Egypt, Caecina Tuscus, had even constructed a bath for the emperor's intended visit to Alexandria. In AD 67 Nero banished this governor for bathing in this bath (*Roman History* 63.18.1). On Nero and Egypt, cf. Schumann 1930, chap. 1.1, 7-21.

that Nero would reign over the East once he had been cast off in the West (Suetonius, *Nero* 40.2), and at the beginning of the Spanish revolt in AD 68, Nero is indeed said to have formed plans to sail to Alexandria (Dio Cassius 63.27.1-2). Without exaggeration, it can be said that Egypt remained at the forefront of Nero's mind. For that reason, it is highly understandable that the Egyptian authors of book 5 of the *Sibylline Oracles* expected that Nero, on his return, would visit Egypt at last.[16]

1.3. *Nero Rediturus in the Sibylline Oracles, book 5*

This expectation is evident from a passage in book 5 in which the authors warn the Egyptians that 'the Persian will come onto your soil like hail, and he will destroy our land and evil devising men' (5.52-98 at 5.93-94); ... 'the one who obtained the land of the Persians will fight (...). He himself will rush in with a light bound from the West' (5.101-105).[17] As Collins rightly assumes, the authors suggest that Nero Rediturus will have reconquered the West first.[18]

In other passages, the authors lay much weight on the fact that Nero Rediturus regards himself as god: 'Even when he disappears he will be destructive. Then he will return declaring himself equal to God' (5.33-34). This characterization of Nero is highly relevant, as the act of declaring oneself equal to God is explicitly mentioned in classical

---

[16] In this regard, I disagree with Van Henten 2000, 16, according to whom 'The association of Nero with Egypt, after all, can hardly be supported by historical data.' This view constitutes an important reason for Van Henten's belief that *Sibylline Oracles* 5.93-110 is not concerned with the figure of Nero Rediturus (see Van Henten 2000, 14-16); 'the details given by the Sibyl about this return may have been, to a considerable extent, recycled traditions about earlier rulers—such as Xerxes—who had undertaken a sustained attack on the West *from the East*' (Van Henten 2002, 16; italics mine). However, given (a) the references to Nero and Egypt in ancient historical authors mentioned above and (b) the fact that this figure is explicitly said to rush in, into Alexandria (5.88), 'with a light bound *from the West* (ἐκ δυσμῶν)' (5.104; cf. 5.371), it seems valid to reckon this passage among the Nero Rediturus passages of book 5. Van Henten at least grants this possibility: 'On the other hand, it is obvious that traditions about malicious Persian rulers may have been combined with elements of the negative stereotype of Nero' (Van Henten 2000, 16).

[17] The allusion to the destruction of 'the city of the blessed ones', Jerusalem, in 5.106-107 shows that this passage is a chronologically distorted blend of *ex eventu* prophecy with regard to the events of AD 70 and future expectations; Nero was of course the emperor who ordered the submission of the Judean revolt in AD 66, which ended with the destruction of Jerusalem after Vespasian was proclaimed emperor.

[18] Collins 1983, 395 note b2.

sources on Nero and in 2 Thess, as we shall see in due course. It also occurs in yet another passage in book 5, where the Sibylline authors describe Nero as 'a godlike man from Italy'; 'him, they say, Zeus himself begot and Lady Hera' (5.138-140).

The most important passage on Nero, for our present purposes, is found in 5.361-396. We have already seen that, in the authors' view, Nero was to return to the West, after which he would also visit and ravage Egypt (5.52-110). In the passage now under consideration, the authors write:

> A man who is a matricide will come from the ends of the earth in flight (…). He will immediately seize the one because of whom he himself perished.[19] (…) There will come upon men a great war from the West. Blood will flow up to the bank of deep-eddying rivers. Wrath will drip in the plains of Macedonia, an alliance [to the people][20] from the West, but destruction for the king (5.363-374).[21]

Nero is portrayed as returning and 'seiz(ing) the one because of whom he himself perished,' i.e. Rome. The encounter between Nero, who returns from the East, and Rome, which represents the West, is apparently envisaged to occur 'in the plains of Macedonia'. It is indeed very striking that Macedonia is singled out as the place 'where West meets East.' The rationale behind this springs easily to mind, when one recalls that the Roman province of Macedonia, with Thessalonica

---

[19] The word 'perished', the translation of ὤλετό (5.367), does not necessarily imply that Nero was thought to have actually died; ὄλλυμαι means 'perish, come to an end, die'. See Liddell & Scott, 1216-17 s.v. ὄλλυμι B.I. To me, it seems most likely that this word is used in the sense that Nero's first period of rule had come to an end. Cf. the discussion of this verse by Van Henten 2000, 9: '"Perished" could refer to Nero's death, but it can also indicate his deposition. Since the *Oracles* do not mention Nero's death and return together elsewhere, the latter interpretation seems to be much more plausible.'

[20] On this text-critical problem in 5.374, see Geffcken 1902, 122, followed by Collins 1983, 402 note u3, but cf. Nikiprowetzky 1987, 1131, note on 5.374. Niki-prowetzky proposes the following translation of 5.373-374: 'Le courroux ruissellera dans les plaines de la Macédoine, [   ] alliance de l'occident et au roi le désastre.' However, the following verses in 5.375-376, which talk of the war being resumed, seem to imply that *the people* had experienced the peace-producing effects of this alliance.

[21] 'Wrath' in 5.373 probably means 'divine wrath'. See Geffcken 1902, 122, note on 5.373-374: 'Gott lässt also seinen Zorn triefen und bringt dem Volke im Westen Hilfe.' This notion of divine wrath is not alien to the Roman world, given the remark by Tacitus in his *Annals* 16.16 on 'the tale of Roman deaths [i.e. suicides, enforced by Nero], honourable perhaps, but tragic and continuous. (…) It was the anger of Heaven against the Roman realm' ('Ira illa numinum in res Romanas fuit').

as its capital, is located on the via Egnatia, the main route from the East to Rome.[22]

2. *2 Thessalonians*

If the above assertion about the battle taking place in Macedonia is true, the relevance of this passage from the Egyptian *Sibylline Oracles* for the interpretation of 2 Thess also becomes clear. This passage draws our attention to the particular atmosphere in Thessalonica at the time of Nero's disappearance in AD 68. This is not to suggest that book 5 of the *Sibylline Oracles* records factual historical information about the actual fears and anxieties in Thessalonica after Nero's supposed disappearance. Rather, it gives us an insight into logical assumptions at the time: that Thessalonica and Macedonia, being at the interface between East and West, would run a high chance of being confronted with Nero on his return to the West. The assumption that Thessalonica's centrality would attract military traffic in times of crisis had, moreover, already been proven right in previous civil wars during the first century BC; both the civil war between Julius Caesar and Pompey and that between Augustus and Antony had taken place in the vicinity of Thessalonica and had threatened and affected the city.[23] The unique position of Thessalonica within the Roman Empire between West and East explains why anxiety could increase rapidly here in times of crisis. This seems to have occurred when the revolts against Nero culminated in another period of civil war known as the 'year of the four emperors'.

The question which remains, however, is whether the threatening figure of 2 Thess 2 can be identified with Nero. This identification used to be common in scholarship from the first half of the nineteenth century onwards, but, as Trilling states in his overview of recent scholarship on the Thessalonian correspondence, now represents 'eine Auffassung, die ... allgemein als unhaltbar abgewiesen wird'.[24] Modern consensus can be summarized in the words of Malherbe:

---

[22] On Thessalonica and the via Egnatia, see Vom Brocke 2001, chap 2.1.3, esp. 108-9; and chap. 3.1.1-3.1.2, 188-99, with maps on 189 (via Egnatia between West and East), 194 (via Egnatia in Thessalonica's vicinity), and 198 (detail: the via Egnatia does not pass through Thessalonica, but passes along the city's edges). See also Rathmann 2002, with a map on 1155-6.

[23] See Vom Brocke 2001, chap. 2.5.4, 178-83, esp. 179.

[24] Trilling 1987, 3395.

The Man of Lawlessness has been identified with various historical figures, such as one or another Roman emperor, particularly Nero (...). All such *historical identifications* fail because Paul has in mind an *eschatological personification* of lawlessness, the ultimate representative of those in whom lawlessness comes to expression (italics mine).[25]

Yet, I would argue again in favour of the identity of this Man of Lawlessness and Nero, not only on the grounds of the light which book 5 of the *Sibylline Oracles* throws on the pivotal location of Thessalonica as the place where the West meets Nero Rediturus on his return from the East, but also because the set of characterizations of the opponent in 2 Thess 2 can be matched with those of Nero in ancient historians. On these grounds, it seems far more likely that the author of 2 Thess had a historical figure in mind, and not a kind of de-historicized, mythologized, personified or literary figure.[26] It seems that Malherbe's antithesis between 'historical identification' and 'eschatological personification' does not work here. As Wilson has argued in a similar case concerning the Book of Revelation and the Book of Daniel, 'in fact most apocalyptic writers are extremely concerned with history'.[27]

As is commonly known, 2 Thess provides an answer to the Thessalonians who have been alarmed by prophetic utterances and pronouncements within the community to the effect that 'the day of the Lord is already here' (2.1-2). Instead of agreeing with this imminent eschatology, the author develops a three-stage eschatology, his clear message being that this eschatology is only in its first stage. In his view, history will unwind as follows. First, in the present, there is a restraining power—both understood as an impersonal, collective neuter and as a personalised, masculine being—which still restrains the appearance of the eschatological oppressor (2.6-7). Secondly, this oppressor, who is already secretly at work (2.7), will be revealed (2.8a). He is characterized as lawless and destructive, as one who raises himself up against

---

[25] Malherbe 2000, 431-2. Cf., however, a more balanced view in Menken 1994, 104-7, who still takes Nero into consideration.

[26] It is only in later sources that the return of Nero becomes chronologically awkward and is therefore placed on a mythical level. See, e.g., *Sibylline Oracles* 8.68-72 on the return of Nero in the time of Marcus Aurelius. As I wish to show in this paper, however, like the authors of books 4 and 5 of the *Sibylline Oracles*, the author of 2 Thess still expects a non-mythical, historical return.

[27] Wilson 1993, 602.

every so-called god or object of worship, enthrones himself in God's temple, and claims to be God; his appearance will be attended by powerful signs, portents, and omens (2.3-4). Thirdly, when he makes his threatening appearance, he will be finally met by Lord Jesus, with whose victory the end will come (2.8).

In this section, I would like to suggest that the characterizations of the adversary fit the figure of Nero, and that one of these features in particular points more precisely to the period after Nero's disappearance in AD 68. If this is correct, the Thessalonians' heightened fear has to do with the prospective return of Nero from the East along the Egnatian Road which passes along the edge of their city. In order to establish this, I shall first discuss the various characterizations of the eschatological opponent and point out their congruence with the image of Nero in classical sources. This is not necessarily to claim that the image is historically correct, but only that such characterizations of Nero did exist at the time.

Another proviso is that not all characteristics mentioned in 2 Thess relate exclusively to the figure of Nero. Some features may be regarded as general, stereotypical attributes derived from the ancient topos of the tyrant, such as his lawlessness (§2.1), thirst for destruction (§2.2), impiety (§2.3a), and claim to be God (§2.3c).[28] Familiar rhetorical topoi as these characteristics may be, some of them strongly contributed to the imagery surrounding Nero in particular. They not only fit Nero in general, insofar as he was regarded to be a tyrannical emperor, they fit him particularly well. However, the possibility of identifying the tyrant of 2 Thess positively with Nero lies in another characteristic: the expectation of the author of 2 Thess that he will take up residence in God's temple (§2.3b). If the author of 2 Thess has the temple of Jerusalem in mind, his expectation is shared by those astrologers whom Suetonius reports to have predicted to Nero that he would become ruler in the East and receive the sovereignty of Jerusalem (*Nero* 40.2). This very precise anticipation of Nero's future career is a very strong indication of Nero's identity with the threatening figure of 2 Thess and makes it more plausible that the stereotypical features of the tyrant mentioned in 2 Thess apply to Nero as well.[29] The parallel between

---

[28] Cf. Cobet 2002 on the tyrant in classical sources. That stereotypical images of tyrants are used in the *Sibylline Oracles*, is argued by Van Henten 2000.

[29] Cf. Van Henten 2000, 11: 'In the Nero passages (...), we can distinguish between motifs that seem to be a blow up of evil deeds that can be laid at the his-

2 Thess and Suetonius is central for this identification, and will be discussed below. The discussion will address the tyrant's characteristics in the order in which they occur in 2 Thess.

2.1. *The man of lawlessness*

The threatening figure is called, first of all, 'the man of lawlessness' (2.3). This is to be taken as a grammatical construction which uses a *genitivus qualitatis* to express the fact that the person in question is lawless, as he is referred to further on: the lawless one (2.8).[30] In classical sources, Nero is viewed as utterly lawless. Alluding to Nero's fondness for playing the lyre, Philostratus complains that 'instead of carrying on the work of making laws, Nero has taken to singing, and strolls like a player outside the gates within which the Emperor ought to take his seat on his throne' (*The Life of Apollonius of Tyana* 5.7). Distinguishing between two types of tyrants, those who put their victims to death without trial, and those who at least bring them before a court of law, Philostratus takes 'Nero as an example of the impetuous disposition which does not trouble about legal forms' (ibid., 7.14). Dio Chrysostom, in turn, takes Nero as an example of those human beings in whom unlimited power leads to unlawful behaviour: 'Take Nero for instance. We all know how in our own time he not only castrated the youth whom he loved,[31] but also changed his name for a woman's' (*Discourses* 21.6). Nero's lawless conduct is under constant criticism in the ancient historians, particularly his aggressive behaviour in the streets, brothels, and wine shops of Rome (Tacitus, *Annals* 13.25), the incest with his mother (14.2) and his murder of her (14.8-9; Dio Cassius, *Roman History* 61.11-14) and his wife Poppaea (Tacitus, *Annals* 16.6). Both Suetonius and Tacitus draw a picture of a gradually declining Nero (Suetonius, *Nero* 27.1; Tacitus, *Annals* 14.13). According to Suetonius, Nero became so shameless, that he even

---

torical Nero's door, and between motifs seemingly inspired by older traditions, for example about earlier tyrannical rulers.'

[30] On this mode of expression, which seems characteristic of a Semitic style which was also preserved in the Greek Septuagint, see Hilhorst 1976, 144-7 at 145: 'Nous devons en chercher la raison dans le nombre restreint d'adjectifs dont disposent ces langues. Là où les Grecs pouvaient désigner des qualités avec des adjectifs, l'hébreu et l'araméen devaient avoir recours à des substantifs.' See also Hilhorst, 146 with reference to 2 Thess 2.3.

[31] I.e. Sporus (see Suetonius, *Nero* 28 and Dio Cassius, *Roman History* 63.12-13).

sarcastically boasted: 'It's likely that I am afraid of the Julian law' (*Nero* 33.2), afraid, that is, of Sulla's law against assassination which was renewed by Julius Caesar.[32]

Yet, there is also some evidence to the contrary. Elsewhere Suetonius seems to stress that 'during Nero's reign many abuses were severely punished and put down, and no fewer new laws were made' (*Nero* 16.2; cf. also Tacitus, *Annals* 13.50-51). Dio Cassius, however, claims that at least some of this legislation was apparently due to Seneca and Burrus,

> who were at once the most sensible and the most influential of the men at Nero's court (...); (...) they took the rule entirely into their own hands and administered affairs in the very best and fairest manner they could (...). [They] made many changes in existing regulations, abolished some altogether, and enacted many new laws, meanwhile allowing Nero to indulge himself, in the expectation that when he had sated his desires (...), he would experience a change of heart (61.3.3-4.2).

According to Dio, this lasted for only a very limited period (61.4.5-5.1).

2.2. *The son of destruction*

The eschatological adversary is also called 'the son of destruction' (2.3). Taking this phrase again as a construction involving a *genitivus qualitatis*, it seems to highlight the figure's destructive character. In classical sources, Nero, as no other Roman emperor, is held responsible for destruction on a enormous scale.

First of all, this consisted of the destruction of Rome in fire in the summer of AD 64. According to Suetonius, Nero interpreted the line 'When I am dead, be earth consumed by fire' (the classical equivalent of 'After me, the deluge') differently: 'Nay, rather while I live', and set fire to the city. 'For six days and seven nights destruction raged' (Suetonius, *Nero* 38.1-2). As Tacitus tells, 'the report had spread that, at the very moment when Rome was aflame, Nero had mounted his private stage, and (...) had sung the destruction of Troy' (*Annals* 15.39); the fire, as Tacitus stresses, also caused the destruction of many temples (*Annals* 15.40).[33] In this way, in the view of Dio Cassius, 'Nero

---

[32] Thus J.C. Rolfe in the Loeb edition of Suetonius, vol. 2 (1914; revised 1997), 136 note *b*, with reference to Sulla's *Lex de sicariis*.

[33] There is a difference in emphasis among the ancient historians with regard to

set his heart on accomplishing what had doubtless always been his desire, namely to make an end of the whole city and realm during his lifetime' (*Roman History* 62.16). Dio also describes the apocalyptic mood at Rome after the fire, where the populace quoted oracles about Rome perishing by the strife of her people, and about a mother-slayer as the last of the sons of Aeneas to govern (62.17-18). According to Dio Cassius, at the beginning of the Spanish revolt in AD 68, Nero was even believed to be contemplating setting fire to the city again before setting sail to Alexandria (*Roman History* 63.27.1-2).

Secondly, Nero's drive for destruction was not confined to Rome. Dio Cassius, as we have already seen, attributed to Nero the desire to make an end not only to the whole city, but also to the entire realm during his lifetime (*Roman History* 62.16). Although Nero was also surrounded by sycophants who predicted the dissolution of the empire should Nero die (Tacitus, *Annals* 14.47), those who participated in the Pisonian conspiracy against him in AD 65 were convinced that the crimes of Nero would bring about the dissolution of the empire, and spoke of the need to hasten to the aid of society (*Annals* 15.50). Not only the authors of book 5 of the *Sibylline Oracles* and 2 Thess, but also Romans entertained an almost apocalyptic fear of Nero's destructive behaviour.[34]

This destruction also affected individual lives. After suppressing the Pisonian conspiracy, Nero took advantage of the situation by 'procuring the destruction of great and guiltless citizens from motives of

---

Nero's participation in causing the fire. Cf. Lichtenberger 1996, 2169-70. Lichtenberger, commenting on Tacitus, *Annals* 15.38: 'There followed a disaster, whether due to chance or to the malice of the sovereign is uncertain (forte an dolo principis incertum), for each version has its sponsors', remarks: 'While Suetonius [*Nero* 38] and Cassius Dio (62.16.1) openly blame Nero for the fire, Tacitus, at the most, hints at such guilt: already here in the first sentence there is only the alternative *forte* or *dolo principis*' (Lichtenberger 1996, 2169). Cf. also Tresch 1965, 33: 'Tacitus möchte (...) überall seine streng historische Auffassung wahren, indem er auch die Gegenseite zu Wort kommen lassen will und so das einseitig negative Bild eines Sueton and Dio vermeidet'.

[34] Cf. Bell 1979, 102, with reference to Tacitus, *Histories* 1.11: 'This was the condition of the Roman State when Servius Galba, chosen consul for the second time, and his colleague Titus Vinius entered upon the year that was to be for Galba his last *and for the State almost the end*' (cf. 1.2: 'The history on which I am entering is that of a period rich in disasters, terrible with battles, torn by civil struggles, horrible even in peace'); and 4.54: 'the end of our rule was at hand'. Since the previous civil war, that between Augustus and Antony, which ended in 31 BC, 'the Roman world had known internal peace' (Bell, 102).

jealousy or of fear' (Tacitus, *Annals* 15.73). Dio Cassius was convinced that Nero 'brought great disgrace upon the whole Roman race and committed many outrages against the Romans themselves' (*Roman History* 61.5.2). The victims also included notable philosophers, poets, and senators, like Seneca (Tacitus, *Annals* 15.56; 15.60-64), Lucan (15.70), and Thrasea (16.21-35), who was executed because he refused to make sacrifices to Nero (16.22; Dio Cassius, *Roman History* 62.26.3). After Nero had returned from his tour through Greece (AD 66-68) to face the final conspiracy against him, for some people 'the very fact that they had prayed and hoped that Nero might perish furnished a motive for their destruction' (63.20.1). Given this widespread terror, it becomes understandable that the expectation of the return of Nero also entailed the belief that he would 'deal destruction to his enemies' (Suetonius, *Nero* 57.1).

Thirdly, and with particular relevance for the present article, Christians too fell victim to Nero's destructive behaviour, as Tacitus emphasizes. When even the public prayers offered at the injunction of the Sibylline books and all other modes of placating heaven could not dispel the belief that the fire of Rome had taken place by Nero's order, finally, 'to scotch the rumour, Nero substituted as culprits, and punished with the utmost refinements of cruelty, a class of men, loathed for their vices, whom the crowd styled Christians'. According to Tacitus, the cruelty inflicted on them caused a sentiment of pity to arise among the Romans, 'due to the impression that they were being sacrificed not for the welfare of the state, but to the ferocity of a single man' (*Annals* 15.44).

No doubt, then, the apocalyptic fear of the Thessalonians would have started to rise at the moment that Nero, after the fire of Rome and the punishment of the Roman Christians, set off on his great Greek Tour of AD 66-68, which brought him to the relative vicinity of Macedonia. Strikingly, there are some remarks in classical sources about Nero's alleged misbehaviour towards Greece. According to Tacitus, after the fire of Rome, the provinces too were financially burdened, but 'in Asia and Achaia, not offerings alone but the images of the gods were being swept away, since Acratus and Carrinas Secundus had been despatched into the two provinces' (*Annals* 15.45). Dio Cassius describes Nero's behaviour whilst in Greece as devastating 'the whole of Greece precisely as if he had been sent out to wage war, notwithstanding that he had left the country free; and he slew great numbers of men, women and children' (63.11.1; cf. Philostratus, *The Life of Apollonius of Tyana* 5.7).

He is also said to have taken away particular territories from Apollo and to have 'also abolished the oracle, after slaying some people' (Dio Cassius, *Roman History* 63.14.2). According to Dio Chrysostom, Nero 'did not keep his hand off of even the treasures of Olympia or of Delphi (…) but went still farther and removed most of the statues on the Acropolis of Athens' (*Discourses* 31.148).

If there is any truth in these statements, they reflect the turmoils surrounding Nero's Greek Tour which might also have created unrest among the Thessalonians. In addition, the Jews in the Christian community of Thessalonica will also have been particularly concerned about the suppression of the Judean revolt against Rome, which Nero also ordered whilst in Greece (Dio Cassius, *Roman History* 63.22). Moreover, as we know from Josephus, following the defeat of Tarichea in Galilee in September 67, six thousand Jewish prisoners of war were sent by Vespasian to Greece and put to work in Nero's project to dig a canal through the Isthmus of the Peloponnesus (*The Jewish War* 3.539-540).[35] In all respects, then, the image of a particularly destructive emperor must have been widespread throughout the Roman world.

2.3. *The one who raises himself up against every god, enthrones himself in God's temple, and claims to be God*

Not only the characterizations of lawlessness and destruction (2 Thess 2.3) fit the figure of Nero. The description of the coming opponent as he who raises himself up against every so-called god or object of worship, enthrones himself in God's temple, and claims to be God (2.4) also seems to hint at Nero.

As has often been argued, these features are clearly reminiscent of the description of Antiochus IV Epiphanes in the Book of Daniel. According to the Septuagint text of Daniel, this figure will utter words against the Most High and will aim to change times and law (7.25). He will magnify himself to the host of heaven, disturb the sacrifice in the Jerusalem temple, and make the holy place desolate (8.9-12). He will destroy the city of Jerusalem and its sanctuary and take sacrifice and offerings away (9.26-27). And in close parallel with 2 Thess, Daniel

---

[35] On this project, see Suetonius, *Nero* 19; Dio Cassius, *Roman History* 63.16: 'As a secondary achievement connected with his sojourn in Greece he conceived a desire to dig a canal across the isthmus of the Peloponnesus' (cf. Philostratus, *The Life of Apollonius of Tyana* 4.24 and 5.7).

expects the figure under discussion to exalt and magnify himself against every god (ἐπὶ πάντα θεόν), and to speak great swelling words; 'he will not regard any gods of his fathers (…), neither will he regard any deity; for he will magnify himself above all. And he will honour the god of fortresses (…): and a god whom his fathers knew not he will honour' (11.36-39). Without doubt, as Malherbe observes, 'it is still the figure of Antiochus IV Epiphanes as described in Daniel that is behind Paul's language here. (…) Paul uses this language apocalyptically.'[36]

Yet, in my view, this does not preclude the probability that the author of 2 Thess uses this description from Daniel to point to Nero as a historical figure. In the second century AD, Clement of Alexandria explicitly identifies the figure from Daniel with Nero (*Stromateis* 1.21.126; 1.21.146). As a matter of fact, the actual resemblance between the wording of 2 Thess and Daniel is limited to Daniel's characterization of the threatening figure as exalting and magnifying himself 'against every god' (Dan 11.36 LXX: ἐπὶ πάντα θεόν), a phrase which runs parallel with 2 Thess 2.4, where the opponent is said to raise himself up 'against every *so-called* god *or object of worship*' (2 Thess 2.4: ἐπὶ πάντα λεγόμενον θεὸν ἢ σέβασμα). Moreover, whereas according to 2 Thess the opponent claims to be God, this is never explicitly stated in Daniel. Although the author of 2 Thess drew on Daniel, there is more to be said in view of the way he applied the Book of Daniel to his own historical circumstances. As I will argue, all characterizations apply neatly to the figure of Nero as perceived by Greco-Roman eyes.

(a) The one who raises himself up against every so-called god or object of worship

In a passage very relevant to our present concerns, Suetonius says that Nero

> utterly despised all cults, with the sole exception of that of the Syrian Goddess [Atargatis], and even acquired such a contempt for her that he made water on her image, after he was enamoured of another superstition, which was the only one to which he constantly clung (*Nero* 56).

This superstition consisted of his veneration of a little image of a girl, the receipt of which had been immediately followed by the detection of a conspiracy against him. For that reason, Nero

---

[36] Malherbe 2000, 420.

continued to venerate it as a powerful divinity and to offer three sacrifices to it every day, encouraging the belief that through its communication he had knowledge of the future (*Nero* 56).

The fact that Nero had a contempt for all cults except for this anonymous image corresponds with the coming opponent's objection against every so-called god or object of worship.

Nero's contempt for all cults is also apparent from his sacrilegious behaviour. According to Tacitus, Nero had entered and swum in the springs of the Aqua Marcia; bathing there was considered as an act of profanation of the sacred waters and the holiness of the site and, Tacitus adds, 'The divine anger was confirmed by a grave illness which followed' (Tacitus, *Annals* 14.22). Furthermore, as Suetonius has it, Nero did not shrink away from stripping many temples of their gifts and melting down the golden and silver images, including those of the Penates, to pay for his extravagant life-style and expensive building programme (*Nero* 32.4).

This behaviour comes to the fore particularly during the fire of Rome, which so well suited Nero's plans for the foundation of a new capital. Tacitus describes how many temples in Rome were ruined:

> It would not be easy to attempt an estimate of the (...) temples, which were lost; but the flames consumed, in their old-world sanctity, the temple dedicated to Luna by Servius Tullius, the great altar and chapel of the Arcadian Evander to the Present Hercules, the shrine of Jupiter Stator vowed by Romulus, the Palace of Numa, and the holy place of Vesta with the Penates of the Roman people (*Annals* 15.41).

After the fire, however, to pay for the capital's rebuilding,

> The gods themselves formed part of the plunder, as the ravaged temples of the capital were drained of the gold dedicated in the triumphs of the vows, the prosperity or the fears, of the Roman nation at every epoch. But in Asia and Achaia, not offerings alone but the images of the gods were being swept away (*Annals* 15.45).

That this was indeed considered to be sacrilege is confirmed by the reaction of Seneca who, 'to divert the odium of sacrilege from himself, had asked leave to retire to a distant estate in the country' (15.45).

According to Dio Cassius, Nero's disrespect for the gods was also noticeable on his Greek Tour during the years AD 66-68. This disrespect particularly applied to Apollo: Nero

> gave 400,000 sesterces to the Pythia for uttering some oracles that suited him (...). But from Apollo, on the other hand, whether from vexation at the god for making some unpleasant predictions to him or because

he was merely crazy, he took away the territory of Cirrha and gave it to the soldiers. He also abolished the oracle, after slaying some people (*Roman History* 63.14.2).

Yet, on the authority of Suetonius we learn that Nero also showed some signs of conscience, insofar as 'in his journey through Greece he did not venture to take part in the Eleusinian mysteries, since at the beginning the godless and wicked are warned by the herald's proclamation to go hence' (*Nero* 34.4). This, however, does not outweigh the widespread evidence of Nero's contempt for gods and objects of worship.[37]

(b) Enthroning himself in God's temple
According to 2 Thess, the figure in question is not only particularly sacrilegious, but will also enthrone himself in God's temple (2.4). In my view, it seems most probable that the author of 2 Thess has the temple of Jerusalem in mind here, in the state before its destruction in August AD 70 (Josephus, *The Jewish War* 6.249-270). It would have been very problematic for the author of 2 Thess to have predicted that the threatening figure would go to the ruined temple after AD 70. After this date, it would have been commonly known that the temple had been destroyed. In Rome, the Temple of Peace, dedicated in AD 75, housed a collection of cultic items from the former temple in Jerusalem (Josephus, *The Jewish War* 7.158-162; Dio Cassius 66.15.1). Their transfer to Rome was depicted on the Arch of Titus, built in memory of Titus after his death in AD 81. Rebuilding of the temple in Jerusalem was rendered impossible as the Romans turned the Jewish temple tax into the *Fiscus Judaicus*, which funded the rebuilding of the Temple of Jupiter on the Capitol at Rome (Dio Cassius, *Roman History* 66.7.2; cf. 66.10.2).[38] For these reasons, if the author of 2 Thess had the Jerusalem temple in mind as the place in which a concrete, historical tyrant would take up residence, it seems most natural to assume that he wrote before the temple's destruction in AD 70. The assumption that, knowing that the temple was in ruins, he would have expected it to be first replaced with a new temple before it could act as the historical stage for the threatening figure seems implausible.

---

[37] Cf. also Nero's misuse of religion by decreeing offerings after exiles and murders (Tacitus, *Annals* 14.64), and by deifying Claudius, whom he had murdered (Dio Cassius, *Roman History* 60.34-35).
[38] On the practice of collecting the *Fiscus Judaicus*, see Goodman 1989.

This means that the threatening figure must have been expected to visit the temple of Jerusalem prior to AD 70 and to take up his seat and reside there.

There is a highly relevant but neglected passage in Suetonius to which I have already referred briefly and which concerns Nero's destiny after his supposed disappearance in AD 68. According to Suetonius, 'Some of the astrologers (...) had promised Nero the rule of the East (Orientis dominationem), when he was cast off, a few expressly naming the sovereignty of Jerusalem (regnum Hierosolymorum)' (*Nero* 40.2).[39] Apparently Jerusalem is regarded as a genuine possible destination in the East to which Nero could go before returning to the West. Alexandria would have been another possibility in the East, and indeed Dio Cassius mentions the fact that, at the beginning of the Spanish Revolt, after Nero had heard about Galba having been proclaimed emperor, Nero formed plans to sail there (Dio Cassius, *Roman History* 63.27.2). According to the prediction of some astrologers to Nero, however, Jerusalem is a destination of equal standing in the East. This comes as no surprise, if one takes into account that Pliny, in his *Natural History* (an encyclopaedia of all contemporary knowledge, dedicated to Titus), deemed Jerusalem to be 'by far the most brilliant of the cities of the East' (5.70: 'longe clarissima urbium Orientis'), whilst Tacitus called it a 'famous city' (*Histories* 5.2: 'famosa urbs'). Even though both authors wrote this in writings dating from after the

---

[39] A possible reason for astrologers to link Nero with Jerusalem has been offered in several publications by Michael Molnar. His suggestion is based on the supposed control of Aries the Ram over Coele Syria, Idumea and Judaea according to Ptolemy, *Tetrabiblos* II.3.65-66, and the prominence of this sign in Nero's astrological chart. See Molnar 1998, esp. 140 (Ptolemy) and 147-8 (Nero's horoscope); Molnar 1999, 109-16; and Molnar 2003. The astrologers' prediction in Suetonius, *Nero* 40.2 might also be related to the 'old and established belief' mentioned in Suetonius, *Vespasian* 4.5, which, according to Suetonius, had spread over all the Orient and entailed the opinion 'that it was fated at that time for men coming from Judaea to rule the world' (cf. Tacitus, *Histories* 5.13: 'this was the very time when the East should go strong and that men starting from Judaea should possess the world'); cf. Bradley 1978, 248 and Klauck 2001, 684 note 5. A publication specifically devoted to the passage in Suetonius, *Nero* 40 is Firpo 1993. Following Mazzarino, and improving on his arguments, Firpo connects this passage from Suetonius with 2 Thess. See Firpo 1993, esp. 255-9 and Mazzarino 1973, vol. 1, §22, 189-95 and §23, 209-10. The passage from Suetonius is also referred to by Barclay 1996, 226, in connection with the speculation on Nero's return from the East in book 5 of the *Sibylline Oracles*; Nero's 'threatening potential has been magnified by his role in the Jewish War and by his rumoured ambitions on Judaea (5.104-10, 150-54; cf. Suetonius, *Nero* 40.2).'

destruction of Jerusalem under the rule of the Flavian emperors, the brilliance and renown of Jerusalem was still remembered. The city's status might have been due, at least partly, to the fame of Herod's Hellenistic building programme,[40] of which the temple of Jerusalem was an important example.

In short, Jerusalem was indeed a respectable choice for an emperor leaving for the East. This makes the astrologers' specification of Jerusalem as the place in the East where Nero would rule quite logical in some sense. The expectation of the author of 2 Thess that the threatening figure would take his seat in God's temple in Jerusalem and reside there seems to be a reflection of this wider conviction among Nero's contemporaries as attested in Suetonius.

Of course, apart from their congruence, Suetonius and the author of 2 Thess also differ in some respects. Whereas Suetonius says that astrologers predicted to Nero that, after he had been cast off, he would receive the sovereignty of Jerusalem, the author of 2 Thess specifically mentions that he will take up residence *in God's temple*. In 2 Thess, the expectation of Nero's ascension to office in Jerusalem is not described in neutral terms, but wholly from the perspective of Nero's impiety and claim to be God. For the Christian author of 2 Thess, Nero's taking up residence in the temple of Jerusalem is the actual or intended result of his objection to every so-called god or object of worship, and by this action he aims to demonstrate that he is a god (2.4). In contrast with Suetonius, the author of 2 Thess would have expected Nero not to move into the large buildings of Jerusalem (Herod's palace and the residences and magnificent houses of high priest and aristocracy in the Upper City, for instance), but into the temple itself. This difference from Suetonius arises, without doubt, from the religious mind-set of the author of 2 Thess. His picture of the events to unfold will have been moulded by his assessment of Nero's character; if Nero was expected to go to Jerusalem, the author of 2 Thess could not envision him stopping short of taking up residence in the temple itself, in its inmost part (ναός).

Despite this difference in emphasis, Suetonius and the author of 2 Thess basically agree in their report on Nero's expected move to Jerusalem in the East with the aim of taking up residence there. This

---

[40] Cf. Roller 1998.

is a peculiarity of Nero's career which is not matched by any other ruler. One might at first, perhaps, think of Antiochus IV Epiphanes or Caligula as similar to Nero in this respect. Yet, Antiochus is only said to have been interested in changing the cult of the temple in Jerusalem, not in residing there.[41] Likewise, Caligula was determined only to erect his own image (ἀνδριάς) in the temple of Jerusalem, not to move there.[42] Nero, however, is explicitly reported to have been expected to move to the East and to receive the sovereignty of Jerusalem (Suetonius) and to take up his seat and reside in God's temple (2 Thess 2.4b: ὥστε αὐτὸν εἰς τὸν ναὸν τοῦ θεοῦ καθίσαι).[43] This expectation is part of the specific course of events of Nero's life and, for that reason, does not correspond with the lives of other tyrants. It is, in other words, not a stereotypical feature of the general rhetorical imagery of tyrants, but unique to Nero.

The passage from Suetonius, thus, seems to be pivotal for a proper understanding of the historical context of 2 Thess. It also turns the other, more general characteristics of the tyrant of 2 Thess into features which depict the tyranny of Nero. As a matter of fact, Nero is the only one who unites *all* the characteristics mentioned in 2 Thess. The tyrant of 2 Thess and Nero are one and the same.

(c) Claiming to be God

The characterization in 2 Thess that the opponent claims to be God (2.4) makes a great deal of sense if he is identical with Nero. The ancient sources are replete with references to Nero's claim to divinity. They tell us that Nero, fond of music and theatrical performance, 'put on the mask and sang tragedies representing gods and heroes and even heroines and goddesses, having the masks fashioned in the likeness of his own features' (Suetonius, *Nero* 21.3). This seems to imply that Nero fused his identity with those of the gods, as is evident from acclamations which Nero received during such performances. In Greece, 'he was acclaimed as the equal of Apollo in music and of the Sun in driving a

---

[41] See Daniel 7-12; 1 and 2 Maccabees; Josephus, *The Jewish War* 1.31-37 and *Jewish Antiquities* 12.234-359, esp. 12.248-256.

[42] See Josephus, *The Jewish War* 2.184-203; *Jewish Antiquities* 18.257-309; and Philo, *The Embassy to Gaius* 186-348.

[43] The infinitive καθίσαι is taken in its intransitive meaning of 'take one's seat' (Liddell & Scott, 853-4 s.v. καθίζω II.1), 'reside' (II.4).

chariot', Suetonius reports (*Nero* 53; cf. Tacitus, *Annals* 14.14).

In Rome, too, Nero was acclaimed as god when he performed on the lyre; a company of Roman knights, the so-called Augustiani, planted among the audience, 'thundered applause and bestowed the epithets reserved for deity upon the imperial form and voice' (Tacitus, *Annals* 14.15). Examples of these epithets are given in Dio Cassius, according to whom the Augustans, during a performance in AD 59, led the applause and initiated the following exclamations: 'Glorious Caesar! Our Apollo, our Augustus, another Pythian! By thyself we swear, O Caesar, none surpasses thee' (*Roman History* 61.20.4-5). Similar exclamations occur on Nero's return from Greece in AD 68, when the city of Rome shouts in chorus:

> Hail, Olympian Victor! Hail, Pythian Victor! Augustus! Augustus! Hail to Nero, our Hercules! Hail to Nero, our Apollo! The only Victor of the Grand Tour, the only one from the beginning of time! Augustus! Augustus! O, Divine Voice! (63.20.4-5).

This reverence for Nero's divine voice was such a cult that Thrasea, a Stoic senator who refused to participate in it (Dio Cassius, *Roman History* 61.20.4), was condemned under Nero in AD 66 for, among other offences, never having 'offered a sacrifice for the welfare of the emperor or for his celestial voice' (Tacitus, *Annals* 16.21-22).[44] The Neo-Pythagorean philosopher and holy man Apollonius of Tyana and his pupils were, according to Philostratus, similarly accused of 'violating Nero's majesty and of being enemies of his divine voice' (Philostratus, *The Life of Apollonius of Tyana* 4.39). Consequently, Apollonius was summoned 'to defend himself from the charge of impiety against Nero' (4.44).[45] In similar vein, the daughter of a senator, charged with the performance of magic rites, declared that she never mentioned the emperor except as deity (Tacitus, *Annals* 16.31). All these examples show that Nero indeed claimed to be divine. This is also apparent from the acclamation of Nero as god by Tiridates, who was granted

---

[44] 'In behalf of Nero's preservation and the continuance of his power,' as the proclamation of AD 60 puts it, Nero also 'instituted some quadrennial games, which he called Neronia' (Dio Cassius, *Roman History* 61.21.1).

[45] Philostratus also gives as his opinion that Nero ordered 'the Eleans to put the Olympic festival off until his own visit, in order that they might sacrifice to him rather than to Zeus' (*The Life of Apollonius of Tyana* 5.7). According to Philostratus, Nero also accused the Greeks in the following way: 'You have not offered a sacrifice in behalf of his voice nor prayed that it may be more splendid than ever at the Pythian festival' (5.7).

the kingship of Armenia when he visited Nero in Rome in AD 66. Tiridates did obeisance to Nero in the following words: 'Master, (...) I have come to thee, my god, to worship thee as I do Mithras. The destiny thou spinnest for me shall be mine; for thou art my Fortune and my Fate' (Dio Cassius, *Roman History* 63.5.2). This happened in front of the Rostra on the Forum Romanum, where a construction had been built with curtains which, in the centre, showed 'an embroidered figure of Nero driving a chariot, with golden stars gleaming all about him'—a clear suggestion of Nero's identity with the Sun (Dio Cassius, *Roman History* 63.4.3-6.2).[46]

There are instances, however, in which Nero seems to show some moderation in his claim. After the suppression of the Pisonian conspiracy, the proposal was made in the Roman senate 'that a temple should be built to Nero the Divine, as early as possible and out of public funds', Tacitus relates. Nero, however, vetoed this proposal. Yet the reason for this was not so much that Nero disagreed with regard to his divine status, but rather

> because by other interpreters it might be wrested into an omen of, and aspiration for, his decease; for the honour of divinity is not paid to the emperor until he has ceased to live and move among men (Tacitus, *Annals* 15.74).

Modesty is only at issue at the very beginning of Nero's reign when, contrary to the resolution of the Senate 'that the new year should begin in December, the month which had given Nero to the world' (his date of birth being 15 December 37), Nero 'retained as the opening day of the calendar the first of January with its old religious associations' (Tacitus, *Annals* 13.10). Yet, the years to come showed that Nero did not refrain from considering himself a god. This feature too accords with the picture of the opponent which arises from 2 Thess 2, where this figure is said to claim to be God.

The authors of book 5 of the *Sibylline Oracles*, in their portrayal of Nero Rediturus, also highlight this feature. According to them, Nero 'will return declaring himself equal to God. But he will prove that he is not' (5.33-34). He is also called 'a godlike man from Italy'; 'Him, they say, Zeus himself begot and Lady Hera' (5.138-140). Whereas Antiochus IV Epiphanes, in the Book of Daniel, does not explicitly claim

---

[46] On Nero and the Sun-god, see Smith 2000 (review article of Bergmann 1998).

to be a god but is only guilty of rebelling against God, the authors of 2 Thess and book 5 of the *Sibylline Oracles* depict the threatening figure as someone who clearly claims divinity for himself. If they had Nero in mind, as the Sibylline authors, at least, certainly did, this depiction accords wholly with the way the classical picture of Nero is drawn.

2.4. *Powerful omens, portents, and signs in heaven*

Finally, the author of 2 Thess also expects that the appearance of the threatening figure will be accompanied by powerful signs (σημεῖα) and marvels (τέρατα; 2.9). Both words can also be translated in the sense of 'signs of the future', 'signs from the gods', 'omens' or 'portents' (Liddell & Scott, 1593 s.v. σημεῖον), and 'signs', and 'portents', especially of the 'signs in heaven' (1776 s.v. τέρας).

For the present, I shall translate σημεῖα and τέρατα with 'omens and portents'. In this mantic, astrological sense, these terms occur in the reports of the ancient historians on Nero's life. According to Dio Cassius,

> The following signs (σημεῖα) had occurred indicating that Nero should one day be sovereign. At his birth just before dawn rays not cast by any visible beam of the sun enveloped him. And a certain astrologer, from this fact and from the motion of the stars at that time and their relation to one another, prophesied two things at once concerning him—that he should rule and that he should murder his mother (*Roman History* 61.2.1).[47]

Just as signs (σημεῖα) at his birth referred to his future rule, so other vicissitudes of his life were also indicated by portents (τέρατα), as Dio Cassius tells in another passage: 'When some portents (τέρατα) took place at this time, the seers declared that they meant destruction for him and they advised him to divert the evil upon others' (61.18.2).

These are just a few examples of the various omens and portents, both positive and negative, which, according to the ancient sources, occurred at the different stages of Nero's life and which were also related to the major incidents which took place. The emperor's entire life seems to have been interpreted in this way. Nero's birth, his adoption by the emperor Claudius, and the assumption of the *toga virilis*; his enthronement; the victories of the Roman army in the Parthian war; his performance in the theatre of Naples, which collapsed after

---

[47] On the topic of Nero and the stars, see Martin 1983 and Grzybek 1999.

Nero and the audience had left; the murders of Britannicus, son of
Claudius, and of Agrippina, Nero's mother; the fire of Rome; the
Gallic and Spanish revolts against Nero by Vindex and Galba; and,
finally, the end of Nero's reign and his death, predicted by a comet
and by other omens—all these events and stages of his life were, in
the view of the ancient historians, engulfed with the appearance of
comets, earthquakes, lightning, and portents from dreams, auspices
and all kinds of omens.[48]

Admittedly, these omens, portents, and signs in heaven relate to
Nero's career until his death or supposed flight in AD 68 and do not
offer full parallels for the omens and portents which are associated
with *the return* of Nero in 2 Thess. Yet, the important passage from
Suetonius on the future of Nero in the East is relevant in this respect,
too. According to Suetonius, not only '(had) some of the astrologers
(...) promised Nero the rule of the East, when he was cast off, a few
expressly naming the sovereignty of Jerusalem', but, moreover, several of them had also promised him 'the restitution of all his former
fortunes' (*Nero* 40.2). This clearly implies that they, being astrologers,
had based their expectation of Nero's return to the West on astrological observations. In that respect, the author of 2 Thess is not too far
out of line with these astrologers if he believes Nero's return to be
accompanied by powerful omens, portents, and signs in heaven. He
is also in tune with the general picture drawn of Nero before AD 68,
and in particular with the many people who, at Nero's birth, according to Suetonius (*Nero* 6.1), 'made many direful predictions from his
horoscope'. This makes the expectation of the author of 2 Thess all

---

[48] Circumstances and predictions at Nero's birth: Dio Cassius, *Roman History* 61.2.1-4; Suetonius, *Nero* 6.1-2. Adoption by emperor Claudius and the assumption of the *toga virilis*: Dio Cassius, *Roman History* 60.33.2. Nero's enthronement: Suetonius, *Nero* 8. The victories of the Roman army in the Parthian war: Tacitus, *Annals* 13.41. Nero's performance in the theatre of Naples: Tacitus, *Annals* 15.34. The murders of Britannicus: Tacitus, *Annals* 13.17 and 13.24, and of Agrippina: Dio Cassius, *Roman History* 61.16.4-5; cf. Philostratus, *The Life of Apollonius of Tyana* 4.43-44; and Tacitus, *Annals* 14.12. The fire of Rome: Tacitus, *Annals* 15.41; Suetonius, *Nero* 39.1. The Gallic and Spanish revolts against Nero by Vindex and Galba; Vindex: Tacitus, *Annals* 15.74; Dio Cassius, *Roman History* 63.26.5-27.1; and Suetonius, *Nero* 41.2; Galba: Dio Cassius, *Roman History* 63.28.1-29.3; Vindex and Galba: Suetonius, *Nero* 46.1. The end of Nero's reign and his death, predicted by a comet: Suetonius, *Nero* 36.1 and Tacitus, *Annals* 14.22 and 15.47, and by other omens: Tacitus, *Annals* 15.22; Suetonius, *Nero* 48.2 and 56; Dio Cassius, *Roman History* 63.29.3. On Nero and magic, see Rochette 2003.

the more understandable. He did not deny nor play down the mantic and astrological world-view which the ancient world exhibited and which is also reflected in the ancient historians.

2.5. *The restraining force, and the restraining figure*

While all characteristics of the threatening figure in 2 Thess now seem to fit the historical Nero, there is one last item which needs discussion. In 2 Thess, this figure is contrasted with a restraining force and a restraining figure which are thought to operate in the present, at the first stage of the author's eschatology (cf. p. 186 above), before the threatening figure will (re-)appear at his appointed time (2.6-7). As the dating of 2 Thess is already implied in the discussion above, it might be possible to seek some opportunity to identify this mysterious force and person.[49]

If the threatening figure is indeed Nero Rediturus, the earliest possible date for the composition of 2 Thess must be 9 June 68, when Nero supposedly disappeared from Rome and escaped to the East (Suetonius, *Nero* 40.2). The fact that he is expected to take his seat in the temple of Jerusalem, gives us August AD 70 as a date ante quem, because until that date the temple was still standing. Perhaps the date ante quem should be advanced to July 69, because Vespasian, who had been sent by Nero to put down the Judean revolt, was himself proclaimed emperor by the troops of Egypt and Judaea between 1 and 11 July 69.[50] At that stage, it would have been awkward to suppose that Nero would still take up residence in Jerusalem. Although one should allow for sufficient time for news to travel from one place to another in the ancient world, this state of affairs leaves us an approximate date between June 68 and July 69 (or somewhat later), roughly in the first year of Nero's disappearance (cf. the timetable in appendix A; see

---

[49] I do not agree with those who understand both the threatening figure and the restraining force as non-historical, apocalyptic designations, most vividly so Lietaert Peerbolte 1996, 82-3: 'The unspecified character of the restraining force has led to many speculations as to its identity. Although many have tried to settle the case by identifying the κατέχον/κατέχων as some institution or person contemporary to the author, this *zeitgeschichtliche* method has proven to be rather fruitless. (...) It is highly probable that even the author himself had no clear idea of what exactly was restraining the eschatological opponent from being revealed.'

[50] On Vespasian's proclamation, see Tacitus, *Histories* 2.79: 1 July 69 (Alexandria) and 3 July 69 (Judaea); and Suetonius, *Vespasian* 6.3: 1 July 69 (Egypt) and 11 July 69 (Judaea).

appendix B for the ensuing question of whether 2 Thess is authentic or pseudepigraphic).

If this dating is correct, and the author of 2 Thess is writing in the period immediately after Nero's disappearance in AD 68, it is not too difficult to imagine what he has in mind when he refers to a restraining force in the present, which prohibits Nero's return (2.6-7). This must apply to the uprisings against Nero by Julius Vindex in Gaul and by Galba in Spain in AD 68. Suetonius and Tacitus credit Vindex with setting in motion the whole train of events which led to the fall of Nero.[51] According to Suetonius, 'After the world had put up with such a ruler (i.e. Nero) for nearly fourteen years, it at last cast him off, and the Gauls took the first step under the lead of Julius Vindex, who at that time governed their province as propraetor' (*Nero* 40.1; cf. Tacitus, *Annals* 15.74). Nero had already been warned of growing disaffection in the West and had been persuaded to return to Rome from his Greek Tour (Dio Cassius, *Roman History* 63.19). When he finally understood that Galba had been proclaimed emperor by the soldiers, he made plans to sail to Alexandria and took flight (63.27-29).

Against this background, the almost automatic transition in 2 Thess 2.6-7 from the neuter restraining force (2.6: τὸ κατέχον) to the personified singular masculine restraining figure (2.7: ὁ κατέχων) seems to reflect the combined, abstract force of Vindex and Galba, as well as the individual figure of Galba in particular, who actually puts Nero to flight. Given the expectation that Nero would eventually return, it also makes a great deal of sense to depict the pressure exerted by Vindex and Galba as 'restraining', and to call Galba 'the one who restrains', because—within the logic of the Nero Rediturus expectation—they are not the successors to Nero, but only a temporary force which will restrain Nero's reappearance for some time. They are 'restraining' in the sense that they restrain Nero from returning soon to the West.

In my reconstruction of the historical setting of 2 Thess, this logic also underlies the assumption of 2 Thess 2.6-7 that, as soon as the one who restrains is removed from the historical scene, Nero will be able to return and reveal himself openly again in the West. Though absent from Rome, he is already secretly active in the East, planning his return

---

[51] For a precise reconstruction of the revolt of Vindex and the fall of Nero, see Brunt 1959.

in due course. Nero's absence from Rome and secret activity in the East seem to be hinted at by the remark by the author of 2 Thess, that 'the *mystery* of lawlessness is already at work': τὸ γὰρ μυστήριον ἤδη ἐνεργεῖται τῆς ἀνομίας (2 Thess 2.7a). That this mystery of lawlessness is the mystery of a lawless *individual* is evident from the context (2.8: καὶ τότε ἀποκαλυφθήσεται ὁ ἄνομος), and the idea that Nero is even active in the East during his absence from the West is paralleled in book 5 of the *Sibylline Oracles*: 'But even when he (i.e. Nero) disappears he will be destructive. Then he will return' (5.33).[52] The inevitability of the sequence of Nero's tactical withdrawal to the East and his current plotting to return makes the author of 2 Thess speak of the secret mystery of Nero already being at work (2.7), although he is currently restrained in his actions by the rebellion against him.

It might also be that the author of 2 Thess is alluding explicitly to the revolt against Nero by Vindex and Galba. According to the author, the final day will not come before the ἀποστασία occurs in the first place (πρῶτον) and, in the second place (δεύτερον), as we may supply as the answering clause,[53] the man of lawlessness is revealed: ὅτι ἐὰν μὴ ἔλθῃ ἡ ἀποστασία πρῶτον καὶ ἀποκαλυφθῇ ὁ ἄνθρωπος τῆς ἀνομίας, ὁ υἱὸς τῆς ἀπωλείας (2.3). In this interpretation, the ἀποστασία and the appearance of the man of lawlessness are two distinct, successive phases. Even if 'in the second place' is not to be supplied explicitly as the answering clause, it need not follow that the ἀποστασία and the appearance of the lawless one occur at the same time, as one event. This means that the ἀποστασία does not necessarily coincide with the lawless one's appearance.

If read in this way, the ἀποστασία does not refer to the apostasy, the *religious* rebellion against God of the man of lawlessness (2.3-4), whose power will climax at the second and still future stage of the author's eschatology, but to the *political* rebellion which is well under way during the present first stage.[54] In that case the first part of the prophecy of 2.3, which deals with the necessity of the rebellion which

---

[52] Cf. 12.85: 'But he will be destructive to the Italians, even when he has disappeared.'

[53] See Liddell & Scott, 1534-5 s.v. πρότερος and πρῶτος B.III.3 at 1535: 'frequently as adverb in neut. sg. and pl., πρῶτον, πρῶτα, a. *first, in the first place*, πρῶτόν τε καὶ ὕστατον (vulg. ὕστερον) (...); πρῶτον μὲν ..., δεύτερον αὖ ... (...); sometimes the answering clause must be supplied (...): also πρῶτον μὲν ... δεύτερον μήν ...'.

[54] Both translations are possible, according to Liddell & Scott, 218 s.v. ἀποστασία

must occur before the end, is in fact a *vaticinium ex eventu*, a prophecy which is already turning into a historical event; still in the future, however, is the (re-)appearance of Nero, whose general characteristics were of course already known, but who was now thought to be moving to Jerusalem, from where he would make his (re-)appearance in due time. The passage on the ἀποστασία in 2.3 may be understood differently, not in terms of the political rebellion against Nero, but in terms of Nero's religious rebellion against God. It does not make any difference to the overall theory developed in this paper, but the interpretation of the ἀποστασία as referring to the political revolt against Nero would fit the historical circumstances remarkably well.

If the ἀποστασία is indeed the political rebellion led by Vindex and Galba against Nero, the author of 2 Thess does not only refer to the political revolt by Vindex and Galba in terms of 'restraining' Nero's reappearance (2.6-7), but also in terms of political 'revolt' against Nero (2.3). Ancient historians do call the revolt by Vindex and Galba ἀποστασία. According to Dio Cassius, Vindex, having called together the Gauls,

> delivered a long and detailed speech against Nero, saying that they ought to revolt from the emperor (λέγων δεῖν ἀποστῆναί τε αὐτοῦ ...), because (...) he has despoiled the whole Roman world, because he has destroyed all the flower of their senate, because he debauched and then killed his mother, and does not preserve even the semblance of sovereignty (*Roman History* 63.22.2-3).

And Plutarch calls their revolt explicitly 'the revolt against Nero', ἡ ἀπὸ Νέρωνος ἀποστασία (*Galba* 1.5).

Be this as it may, the power of Vindex and Galba is only regarded as a temporary counterforce against Nero, because the latter will return in due course. Yet, at that stage he will be quickly met by the Lord Jesus (2.8) who, uniquely for the Pauline literature, is called 'the Lord of Peace' (3.16: ὁ κύριος τῆς εἰρήνης), probably in deliberate contrast to the designation of the Roman emperors as 'Lords of *War* and Peace' (πολέμου καὶ εἰρήνης κύριοι).[55] Significantly, the author of

---

I.1: 'defection, revolt (...); esp. in religious sense, rebellion against God, apostasy'.

[55] This term is applied to Greek and Roman rulers, Roman emperors, and non-Roman rulers appointed by Rome. See Xenophon, *Hellenica* 2.2.18 about the rulers at Sparta, the ephors, who are 'masters of peace and war': ἀποκρίναιτο (...) ἐκείνους κυρίους εἶναι εἰρήνης καὶ πολέμου, whereas the Spartan general has no

2 Thess ends his letter, which he wrote amidst the political turmoil of the year AD 68/69, with the wish that 'the Lord of Peace himself may give you peace at all times and in all ways': Αὐτὸς δὲ ὁ κύριος τῆς εἰρήνης δῴη ὑμῖν τὴν εἰρήνην διὰ παντὸς ἐν παντὶ τρόπῳ (3.16).

3. *Conclusion and final observations*

In this paper, I have set out to demonstrate that book 5 of the *Sibylline Oracles* and 2 Thess have much in common. Both understand Nero Rediturus as a historical figure, whom they expect to return from the East. Although the Egyptian authors of book 5 of the *Sibylline Oracles* are primarily concerned with Egypt and reckon with Nero's final return to Egypt, they also have an open eye for the consequences of Nero's return in the broader world. Nero is expected to conquer the West first and, after that, to turn his attention to Egypt (5.93-110). There seems to be a slight inconsistency in the authors' expectation, however, inasmuch as they also express their conviction that Nero, on his return to Rome, will be subdued in Macedonia: 'Wrath will drip in the plains of Macedonia, an alliance [to the people] from the West, but destruction for the king [i.e. for Nero]' (5.361-396 at 373-374). Yet, following this short-lived peace, 'a wintry blast will blow throughout the land, and the plain will be filled again with evil war' (5.375-376) before final, lasting peace is achieved (5.377-385). This diversity of opinions may be caused by the fact that book 5 of the

---

authority in these matters (2.2.16-17); cf. the same distinction between the authority of generals, and the authority of political rulers in Dionysius of Halicarnassus, *Roman Antiquities* 8.35.1 about General Marcius: 'I am general of the army, but these men here are lords of war and peace': ἐγὼ στρατηγός εἰμι τῆς δυνάμεως, πολέμου δὲ καὶ εἰρήνης οὗτοι κύριοι. See further Strabo, *Geography* 17.3.25 about Augustus Caesar: 'he became established as lord for life of war and peace' (καὶ πολέμου καὶ εἰρήνης κατέστη κύριος διὰ βίου); Appian of Alexandria, *Roman History: The Punic Wars* 8.106 about the son of the Carthaginian ruler Masinissa, Gulussa, whom Scipio makes 'lord of peace and war' (πολέμου καὶ εἰρήνης κύριος); and Dio Cassius, *Roman History* 42.20.1 about Julius Caesar whom the foremost men 'appointed lord of war and peace with all mankind (...) without the obligation even of making any communication on the subject to the people or the senate': καὶ πολέμων καὶ εἰρήνης κύριον (...) πρὸς πάντας ἀνθρώπους ἀπέδειξαν αὐτόν, κἂν μηδὲν μήτε τῷ δήμῳ μήτε τῇ βουλῇ περὶ αὐτῶν κοινώσηται. For the importance of peace in the historical setting of the Thessalonians, see also Vom Brocke 2001, chap. 2.5, 167-85.

Sibylline Oracles is a composite writing which, in its constituent parts, reflects slightly varying outlooks.[56]

Given their remarks on Nero's return to the West and the specific mention of an ensuing war in Macedonia, it is very likely that the Sibylline authors assumed that this return would take place via the Egnatian Road in Macedonia, where West meets East. This heightens our awareness for the very genuine reasons for apocalyptic fears in Thessalonica, as expressed in 2 Thess. Re-reading this letter against the background of book 5 of the *Sibylline Oracles* and within the context of Greco-Roman reports about Nero, it seems that in the Christian community of Thessalonica Nero's prospective return to the West via Macedonia instilled in them the conviction that the end had begun. In his letter, however, the author of 2 Thess offers an alternative interpretation of the history of his day. He assumes that, at least for the imminent future, Galba will prevent Nero from returning from his Eastern residence in Jerusalem, to which Nero is now thought to be moving.

It seems that 2 Thess can be historically contextualized in the so-called 'year of the four emperors' following the death of Nero in June AD 68. Galba, Nero's immediate successor, was soon to be followed by Otho and Vitellius, before Vespasian was proclaimed emperor in July AD 69. As I have argued, 2 Thess was written during the first phase of the developments of AD 68/69.[57] The impact this year made on Christian apocalyptic thinking seems to be greatly underestimated. As I shall argue in another forthcoming publication, it seems that there are strong indications that the Book of Revelation was also written in this year, albeit during the later part of its developments, once Galba had already been succeeded by Otho and Vitellius, who consciously imitated Nero. Both seem to have been regarded by the author of the Book of Revelation as accomplices of Nero, foreshadowing his imminent return.

As we have seen, the Thessalonian community, still under Galba, waited anxiously to see whether Nero would return along the Egnatian Road. The author of 2 Thess, however, reassures his readers that Nero

---

[56] On book 5 of the *Sibylline Oracles* as a composite writing, see particularly Felder 2002, esp. 382-3 on the various versions of the prediction of Nero's demise.

[57] An extensive treatment of the year of the four emperors is offered by Wellesley 2000 and Morgan 2005.

would be decisively defeated by the arrival of the Lord Jesus, the Lord of Peace. That the author of 2 Thess cast his beliefs and reassurances in such veiled language might be explained by the secrecy which he had to maintain in the sphere of the political instability of his day. As Klauck states with regard to the Book of Revelation:

> One reason for this speaking in riddles is related to the status of apocalyptic writings as underground literature: The criticism is carefully veiled, and the veil should not too easily be pierced by outsiders. Otherwise, things might get dangerous for author and reader alike.[58]

This secrecy, however, is not just characteristic of Jewish and Christian apocalyptic literature such as Daniel, the Book of Revelation, and 2 Thess. According to Philostratus, when the Stoic philosopher Musonius Rufus 'lay confined in the dungeons of Nero', he and Apollonius of Tyana

> did not openly converse with one another, because Musonius declined to do so, in order that both their lives might not be endangered; but they carried on a correspondence through Menippus and Damis, who went to and fro the prison (*The Life of Apollonius of Tyana* 4.46).

This caution might also characterize the correspondence of 2 Thess and reflect the same atmosphere of unrest and turmoil.[59]

---

[58] Klauck 2001, 693.

[59] An earlier version of this paper was discussed in the Paul Seminar of the British New Testament Conference at Edinburgh in September 2004. I wish to thank all participants for their criticism and suggestions, in particular Prof. James Dunn, Prof. John Barclay, Dr Barry Matlock, Dr Eddie Adams, and Dr Simon Gathercole. I also gratefully acknowledge the comments of the members of the Ancient World Seminar at Groningen, notably Prof. Ruurd Nauta, Prof. Onno van Nijf, Prof. Jan Bremmer, and Ms M. Schipperheijn. As always, Dr Maria Sherwood-Smith (Leiden) was so kind as to correct the English. Last but not least, my fellow editor Dr Ton Hilhorst made valuable suggestions and corrections on what I mistakenly believed to be the last version.

APPENDIX A:

TIMETABLE CONCERNING 2 THESS

Summer AD 64	Fire of Rome and Nero's persecution of the Christians at Rome
September 66-Spring 68	Nero's Greek Tour: Nero, the first persecutor of Christians, is in Greece, alarming the Thessalonians (Alarm phase I). In the same period, the beginning of the Jewish Revolt against Rome and Nero's measures to put it down contribute to further apocalyptic fears (Alarm phase II)
March 68	Restraining power: Vindex
April 68	Restraining power: Galba
9 June 68	Nero is thought to have disappeared from Rome to the East and is expected to take up residence in Jerusalem. This starts off Alarm phase III, because it is anticipated that Nero will return from the East to the West, in all likelihood via the Egnatian Road which passes along the edge of Thessalonica. The increasing degrees of alarm cause some Thessalonians to become idle.
1 July 69	Vespasian proclaimed emperor by the Eastern troops in Egypt
3 or 11 July 69	Vespasian proclaimed emperor by the Eastern troops in Judaea
August 70	Destruction of the Jerusalem temple

APPENDIX B:

THE QUESTION OF 2 THESS'S AUTHENTICITY

Although I do not wish to rehearse the discussion about the authenticity of 2 Thess, as recently revived by Malherbe (Malherbe 2000, 349-75) and Nicholl (Nicholl 2004, 187-218), both of whom contend for its authenticity,—I will refrain from taking a stance in this highly complicated discussion—, I shall nevertheless address the matter briefly. The reason for this is that my dating of 2 Thess arouses curiosity about the letter's authorship. If 2 Thess is dated to the time immediately following Nero's alleged disappearance in AD 68, this dating leaves open the possibility that 2 Thess is authentic, i.e. written by Paul himself. Although Malherbe dates 2 Thess to AD 51, immediately after the writing of 1 Thess, my proposals for a dating of 2 Thess in AD 68/69 would not render the authenticity of its authorship impossible, even though it necessarily implies that it would have been written during Paul's Roman captivity at what was supposedly the end of his life.

The fact that it is not unthinkable that someone would remain so long in Nero's custody is demonstrated by the case of a particular Publius Celer in AD 57, who, like Paul, was awaiting trial by Nero himself. According to Tacitus, 'Publius Celer (...), indicted by the province of Asia, the Caesar [i.e. Nero] could not absolve: he therefore held the case in abeyance until the defendant died of old age' (*Annals* 13.33). This underlines the possibility that Paul could have been still alive in AD 68/69, despite his long custody.

Yet, the question put forward by the author of 2 Thess in 2.5: 'Do you not remember that I told you this while I was still with you?' (Οὐ μνημονεύετε ὅτι ἔτι ὢν πρὸς ὑμᾶς ταῦτα ἔλεγον ὑμῖν;) seems to impede the positive assessment that the letter is by Paul himself. If (a) ταῦτα in 2.5 refers back to the detailed information given in 2.3-4, including the expectation that Nero will enthrone himself in God's temple in Jerusalem (2.4), and (b) the latest possible occasion for Paul himself to have visited Thessalonica was in AD 56, on his way from Corinth via Macedonia (Acts 20.1-3; cf. Romans 15.25-26) to Jerusalem, it is clear that Paul can hardly be the author of 2 Thess. In AD 56, just two years after Nero's ascension to power and still during the so-called 'Quinquennium Neronis', Nero's first five years as a good emperor (AD 54-59; cf. Tacitus, *Annals* 15.67; Dio Cassius, *Roman History* 61.3.3-5.1), Paul had as yet no reason to be so negative about Nero's emperorship; this is confirmed by Paul's positive attitude towards the Roman state under Nero in Romans 13.1-7, written in AD 56. This all seems to point to the pseud-epigraphic nature of 2 Thess.

However, the matter will probably remain undecided because the author-ship of the letter is shared between Paul, Silvanus, and Timothy (1.1). The entire letter is written in the first person plural, except for two passages, which are written in the first person singular: (a) 2.5, the verse under discussion, and (b) 3.17, the final greeting, which is explicitly said to be in Paul's handwrit-ing. Apart from these exceptions, the entire letter is written from the shared perspective of Paul, Silvanus, and Timothy. This close cooperation between Paul, Silvanus, and Timothy is not only apparent from 1 Thess, which is also authored by all three of them (1.1), but also from 2 Cor, where Paul speaks about the Son of God being 'proclaimed by us, i.e. by me and Silvanus and Timothy': δι᾽ ἡμῶν κηρυχθείς, δι᾽ ἐμοῦ καὶ Σιλουανοῦ καὶ Τιμοθέου (1.19). Given the shared authorship of 2 Thess and its consistent use of the first person plural throughout the letter, it could be that the 'I (who) told you this while I was still with you (ἔτι ὢν πρὸς ὑμᾶς)' in 2.5 is either Paul, or Silvanus, or Timothy.

Of necessity, one of these three authors must have been meant, but which one was not specified. He could have been simply identified by adding his name. This occurs in 1 Thess 2.18, where the authors write that 'we made up our minds to visit you' and Paul suddenly breaks the first person plural perspective by adding that he, in contrast with the other two authors, did so more than once: 'So we made up our minds to visit you—I, Paul, more than once' (1 Thess 2.18: διότι ἠθελήσαμεν ἐλθεῖν πρὸς ὑμᾶς, ἐγὼ μὲν Παῦλος καὶ ἅπαξ καὶ δίς). Because of the fact that the entire letter of 1 Thess was authored by Paul, Silvanus and Timothy and, like 2 Thess, is written in the first person plural, Paul, breaking the common perspective here in 2.18 and later in the same passage (2.17-3.5) again in 3.5, needed to identify his 'I' by adding his name: ἐγὼ μὲν Παῦλος.

The same need arises at the end of 2 Thess, when, at the end of the letter, one of the (alleged) authors, Paul again, wishes to distinguish himself from the other (alleged) authors by stating that 'the greeting is in my hand-writing, that of Paul, which is a mark in every letter; in this way I write': Ὁ ἀσπασμὸς τῇ ἐμῇ χειρὶ Παύλου, ὅ ἐστιν σημεῖον ἐν πάσῃ ἐπιστολῇ· οὕτως γράφω (2 Thess 3.17). When the consistency of the first person plural perspective in a multi-authored letter is broken and changed for a first person singular perspective, it seems necessary to identify the newly adopted 'I' specifically.

My point is that, whereas this happens in 1 Thess 2.18 and 2 Thess 3.17, such a specification does not, however, occur in the case of 2 Thess 2.5. As I have already stated, the 'I' of this passage could be either Paul, Silvanus or Timothy. Although we might be inclined to take this 'I' as that of Paul, whether the authentic or the pseudepigraphic Paul, this is not compelling. On my understanding of the dating and further historical setting of 2 Thess, and if 2 Thess is authentic, this 'I' could not have been Paul's because Paul would have been in Nero's custody in Rome for many years at this stage.

This means that this 'I', who rhetorically asks the Thessalonians: 'Do you not remember that I told you this while I was still with you?' (2.5), must refer to either Silvanus or Timothy. Either of them could have visited Thessalonica prior to the writing of 2 Thess. And since the Thessalonian readers would have known the identity of this 'I' who had (recently) visited them alone, there was no need to specify for them in 2 Thess 2.5 which 'I' was meant. That the comment refers to an *individual* visit by either Silvanus or Timothy seems to be confirmed by the fact that when, later on in 2 Thess, the authors refer back to their *collective* visit to the Thessalonians in the past, they again choose the first person plural and write: 'When *we* were with you (ὅτε ἦμεν πρὸς ὑμᾶς) we laid down this rule ...' (3.10). This seems to corroborate my suggestion that the 'I' in 2 Thess 2.5 need not be Paul's.

If this interpretation is correct, the above-mentioned obstacle to Paul's involvement in the authorship of 2 Thess seems to have been removed. The letter could have been written by Paul, Silvanus and Timothy, whereas the 'I' who had visited them recently, when the dramatic developments concerning Nero were already in full swing, could have been either Silvanus or Timothy. Nevertheless, the historical contextualization and dating of 2 Thess undertaken in my paper are not affected by either its authenticity or inauthenticity.

Bibliography

Barclay, J.M.G. 1996. *Jews in the Mediterranean Diaspora from Alexander to Trajan (323 BCE—117 CE)*, Edinburgh.

Bell, A.A., Jr. 1979. 'The Date of John's Apocalypse: The Evidence of Some Roman Historians Reconsidered', *New Testament Studies* 25 (1979) 93-102.

Bergmann, M. 1998. *Die Strahlen der Herrscher: Theomorphes Herrscherbild und politische Symbolik im Hellenismus und in der römischen Kaiserzeit*, Mainz.

Bradley, K.R. 1978. *Suetonius' 'Life of Nero': An Historical Commentary* (Collection Latomus 157), Brussels.

Brunt, P.A. 1959. 'The Revolt of Vindex and the Fall of Nero', *Latomus: Revue d'études latines* 18 (1959) 531-59.

Cobet, J. 2002. 'Tyrannis, Tyrannos', in: *Der neue Pauly*, xii.1, 948-50.

Collins, J.J. 1974. *The Sibylline Oracles of Egyptian Judaism* (SBL Dissertation Series 13), Missoula, Montana.

Collins, J.J. 1983. 'Sibylline Oracles: A New Translation and Introduction', in: J.H. Charlesworth (ed.), *The Old Testament Pseudepigrapha*, New York, i, 317-472.

Felder, S. 2002. 'What is *The Fifth Sibylline Oracle*?', *Journal for the Study of Judaism* 33 (2002) 363-85.

Firpo, G. 1993. 'Le tradizioni giudaiche su Nerone e la profezia circa il "regnum Hierosolymorum"', in: M. Sordi (ed.), *La Profezia nel Mondo Antico* (Contributi dell'Istituto di Storia Antica 19; Scienze Storiche 53), Milan, 245-59.

Geffcken, J. 1902. *Die Oracula Sibyllina* (Die griechischen christlichen Schriftsteller der ersten drei Jahrhunderte), Leipzig.

Goodman, M. 1986. 'The Sibylline Oracles', in: E. Schürer, G. Vermes, F. Millar, and M. Goodman, *The History of the Jewish People in the Age of Jesus Christ (175 BC—AD 135)*, Edinburgh, iii.1, 618-54.

Goodman, M. 1989. 'Nerva, the *Fiscus Judaicus* and Jewish Identity', *The Journal of Roman Studies* 79 (1989) 40-4.

Grzybek, E. 1999. 'L'astrologie et son exploitation politique: Néron et les comètes', in: J.-M. Croisille, R. Martin and Y. Perrin (eds), *Neronia V. Néron: histoire et légende* (Collection Latomus 247), Brussels, 113-24.

Hilhorst, A. 1976. *Sémitismes et latinismes dans le Pasteur d'Hermas* (Graecitas Christianorum Primaeva 5), Nijmegen.

Jakob-Sonnabend, W. 1990. *Untersuchungen zum Nero-Bild der Spätantike* (Altertumswissenschaftliche Texte und Studien 18), Hildesheim.

Klauck, H.-J. 2001. 'Do They Never Come Back? *Nero Redivivus* and the Apocalypse of John', *Catholic Biblical Quarterly* 63 (2001) 683-98.

Lichtenberger, H. 1996. 'Jews and Christians in Rome in the Time of Nero: Josephus and Paul in Rome', in: W. Haase and H. Temporini (eds), *Aufstieg und Niedergang der römischen Welt*, Berlin/New York, vol. 2.26.3, 2142-76.

Lietaert Peerbolte, L.J. 1996. *The Antecedents of Antichrist: A Traditio-Historical Study of the Earliest Christian Views on Eschatological Opponents* (Supplements to the Journal for the Study of Judaism 49), Leiden.

Malherbe, A.J. 2000. *The Letters to the Thessalonians* (Anchor Bible 32B), New York.

Martin, J.P. 1983. 'Néron et le pouvoir des astres', *Pallas: Revue d'études antiques* 30 (1983) 63-74.

Mazzarino, S. 1973. *L'Impero Romano* (Universale Laterza 243-245), 3 vols, Rome/Bari.

Menken, M.J.J. 1994. *2 Thessalonians* (New Testament Readings), London/New York.

Molnar, M.R. 1998. 'Greek Astrology as a Source of the Messianic Portent', *The Ancient World* 29 (1998) 139-49.

Molnar, M.R. 1999. *The Star of Bethlehem: The Legacy of the Magi*, New Brunswick, New Jersey.

Molnar, M.R. 2003. 'The Evidence for Aries the Ram as the Astrological Sign of Judea', *Journal for the History of Astronomy* 34 (2003) 325-7.

Morgan, G. 2005. *69 AD: The Year of Four Emperors*, Oxford.

Müller, C.D.G. 1992. 'The Ascension of Isaiah', in: W. Schneemelcher and R.McL. Wilson (eds), *New Testament Apocrypha* (English translation edited by R.McL. Wilson), Cambridge ii, 603-20.

Nicholl, C.R. 2004. *From Hope to Despair in Thessalonica: Situating 1 and 2 Thessalonians* (Society for New Testament Studies Monograph Series 126), Cambridge.

Nikiprowetzky, V. 1987. 'Oracles sibyllins', in: A. Dupont-Sommer and M. Philonenko (eds), *La Bible: Écrits intertestamentaires* (Bibliothèque de la Pléiade 337), Paris, 1035-40.

Pease, A.S. and D.S. Potter. 1996. 'Sibyl', in: S. Hornblower and A. Spawforth (eds), *The Oxford Classical Dictionary* (Third Edition), Oxford, 1400-1.

Rathmann, M. 2002. 'Via Egnatia', in: *Der neue Pauly*, xii.2, 161-2.

Rochette, B. 2003. 'Néron et la magie', *Latomus: Revue d'études latines* 62 (2003) 835-43.

Roller, D.W. 1998. *The Building Program of Herod the Great*, Berkeley.

Smith, R.R.R. 2000. 'Nero and the Sun-god: Divine Accessories and Political Symbols in Roman Imperial Images', *Journal of Roman Archaeology* 13 (2000) 532-42.

Schumann, G. 1930. *Hellenistische und griechische Elemente in der Regierung Neros*, Leipzig.

Tresch, J. 1965. *Die Nerobücher in den Annalen des Tacitus: Tradition und Leistung* (Bibliothek der Klassischen Altertumswissenschaften), Heidelberg.

Trilling, W. 1987. 'Die beiden Briefe des Apostels Paulus an die Thessalonicher: Eine Forschungsübersicht', in: W. Haase and H. Temporini (eds), *Aufstieg und Niedergang der römischen Welt*, Berlin/New York, vol. 2.25.4, 3365-403.

Tuplin, Chr.J. 1989. 'The False Neros of the First Century AD', in: C. Deroux (ed.), *Studies in Latin Literature and Roman History* (Collection Latomus 206), Brussels, 364-404.

Van Henten, J.W. 2000. '*Nero Redivivus* Demolished: The Coherence of the Nero Traditions in the *Sibylline Oracles*', *Journal for the Study of the Pseudepigrapha* 21 (2000) 3-17.

Vom Brocke, C. 2001. *Thessaloniki—Stadt des Kassander und Gemeinde des Paulus: Eine frühe christliche Gemeinde in ihrer heidnischen Umwelt* (WUNT II.125), Tübingen.

Wellesley, K. 2000. *The Year of the Four Emperors* (Third Edition, with a new introduction by B. Levick), London.

Wilson, J.C. 1993. 'The Problem of the Domitianic Date of Revelation', *New Testament Studies* 39 (1993) 587-605.

LOOKING AT THE CONDEMNING HEART OF 1 JOHN 3.18-20 THROUGH THE EYES OF AN ANCIENT EGYPTIAN

Herman te Velde

The organ through which wisdom is received was considered by the Egyptians to be the heart.[1] Ancient Egyptian and ancient Israelite texts mention the heart on numerous occasions. When Jahweh tells the proverbially wise King Solomon that he may ask for whatever he wishes, he does not ask for a long life or riches or for the lives of his enemies but for a listening heart (1 Kings 3.9). This listening heart is not something discovered by Solomon or by the author of the biblical story, it is the centuries-old ideal of an Egyptian gentleman held by officials such as the famous sage Amenhotep son of Hapu,[2] who says that he is listening of heart. It seems that the word 'heart' in Egypt and Israel can be used to mean the same thing. Sometimes, however, that meaning can be very different. For example, the idiomatic expression 'to be hard of heart' has a positive sense in Egyptian texts but has acquired a negative connotation in the Bible.[3]

Unlike many other cultures, for example Greece, both Egypt and Israel can be considered to be cultures of the heart.[4] The Hebrew word for heart, לב or לבב, which appears over 850 times in the Old Testament, is not always translated with καρδία in the Septuagint; sometimes it is interpreted as διάνοια, ψυχή, φρένες, νοῦς, etc. The New Testament continues the descriptive use of language of the Septuagint. It is interesting that the Coptic translation of the Old Testament does not seem to have considered these Greek alternatives to be necessary and they have mainly disappeared again. The translation has returned to the single Egyptian-Coptic word ϩⲏⲧ.[5]

The Egyptian word for heart is written with a hieroglyph that

---

[1] Brunner 1957, 110.
[2] Helck 1958, 1817.8; Brunner 1988, 5.
[3] Shupak 1985.
[4] Assmann 1996, 144.
[5] Böhlig 1983.

depicts the heart of an animal. It can be read phonetically as *ib*. It is related etymologically to the Hebrew *leb*, because the 'l' is not written in Egyptian. Over the course of the history of the Egyptian language, a new word (*ḥȝty*) comes into use, and it is this word that survives alone in the later Coptic. For a long time the two words were used alongside each other. There have been many unsuccessful attempts to find differences between these two words. Without going into too much linguistic detail here, I would like to present a provisional hypothesis that has not yet appeared in the Egyptological literature. Just like *ib*, many other Egyptian words for parts of the body have a Semitic origin, for example ear (*idn*), hand (*id*) and eye (*'in*). These originally Egyptian words were replaced by a paraphrase of their function which can be translated: the ear (*msḏr*) is what one sleeps on, the hand (*ḏrt*) is the seizer, the eye (*irt*) is the doer.[6] I would like to suggest that the new word for heart is also a paraphrase of its function. The new word *ḥȝty* does not mean breast but rather the 'foremost one', 'the first'. This expresses the concept that the heart is the foremost of all the body parts. The heart was indeed regarded as the centre/core of every living being. The heart 'speaks', i.e. beats, in all parts of the body and when all is well it guides them. It should be mentioned that the Egyptians, like many ancient peoples, did not yet know of the principle of the circulation of the blood. They thought that the veins and arteries not only transported blood but also saliva, urine, etc. Nevertheless, the heart was regarded by them as the foremost (*ḥȝty*) of all the body parts of which a living being consists. The heart is not only the physical but also the spiritual leader of an individual.[7] The following text was recited to someone who would physically and spiritually rise from the dead: 'Look, your heart is guiding you and your limbs obey you.'[8] Many Egyptian texts[9] show that just as in Israel, the heart was regarded not only as the seat of feeling, but also of understanding and memory. Someone with no heart was a madman and not necessarily an insensitive person.[10]

When a body was mummified, the internal organs, stomach, lungs, liver, intestines and also the heart, were removed from the body and

---

[6] Te Velde 1977, 45.
[7] De Buck 1944.
[8] Sethe 1906, 519.14.
[9] Cf. Brunner 1977.
[10] Cf. Te Velde 1990, 83-101, esp. 93-4.

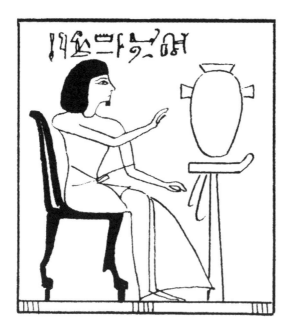

Fig. 1. The deceased seated with his heart on a standard. Vignette from the Book of the Dead of Nakhtamun, Spell 29B, after Naville 1886, pl. 41.

embalmed separately. Although the other parts were usually put into special pots, called canopic jars, the heart as the foremost, guiding body part had to be put back into the body itself: 'Your heart is given to you in your body so that you will remember what you have forgotten'[11] or the following was recited: 'My heart does not forget its place. It stays in its place. I know my name and will not forget it.'[12] To be absolutely sure, a sort of reserve heart was added to the mummy which could not decay, a stone heart in the form of a scarab or beetle. One has to do what one can to overcome dangers!

Thus an Egyptian had to have his heart in the right place, and his heart had to be resolute and strong (*rwd*) and not tired or weak (*wrd*). Osiris, the god of the dead, the first of those who have gone to the West (i.e. the realm of the dead), is never directly referred to as the deceased or dead god. After all, his life has no absolute end. He

---

[11] De Buck 1935, 256e-f.
[12] De Buck 1956, 176.

is called the one whose heart is weary. This is how the decline of a person is referred to; once the heart is in danger of losing its guiding and central function, it signals the collapse and disfunctioning of parts of the body, thus signalling death. In the *Instructions of Ptahhotep*, signs of age that precede the inevitable demise of a person are referred to as the weariness of the heart:[13]

> Elderliness has occurred, old age descended;
> woe is come and weakness is renewing itself;
> the heart passes the night in pain, every day;
> the eyes are shrunk, the ears made deaf;
> strength now perishes because of the heart's weariness;
> the mouth is silent and cannot speak;
> the heart has stopped and cannot recall yesterday;
> the bones hurt because of their length;
> good has become evil;
> all taste is gone.
> What age does to people
> Is evil in every aspect;
> The nose is blocked and cannot breathe,
> Because of the difficulty of standing and sitting.[14]

The increasing bodily and spiritual weariness also leads to what we call dementia. What we call a mental illness was an illness of the heart for the Egyptians. According to the *Wisdom of Amenemope*, 'he whose heart is injured is in a sorry state (hd-ib). His words are quicker than wind and rain'.[15] He is characterized by lack of control, deceitfulness and mendacity. He is quarrelsome and 'a beast of prey (wolf) in the fold'.[16] During life, too, the heart can in a manner of speaking temporarily leave a person, for example when he loses his senses through homesickness or as a result of falling in love.

It's a great deal more drastic, however, when the heart leaves a person during the dying process. In addition to the mummification process, when the heart is first removed and then returned to the body of the deceased, there is another moment when the separation of heart and individual threatens to be definitive. In the Egyptian Divine Tribunal,[17] the deceased has to answer to a divine court of

---

[13] Burkhard 1988.
[14] Parkinson 1997, 250.
[15] Cf. Brunner 1977, 1162.
[16] Te Velde 1990, 94.
[17] Seeber 1976.

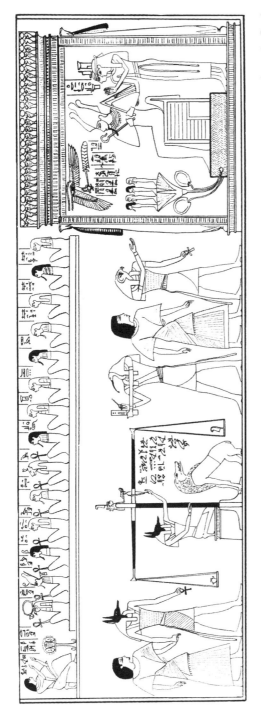

Fig. 2. The judgement of the dead. The heart of the deceased is weighed against the feather symbolizing world order. Vignette from the Book of the Dead of Hunefer, Spell 125, after Naville 1886, pl. 136.

law presided over by Osiris the god of the dead or the sun god Re. Various other gods also play a part: the divine scribe Thoth keeps a close record of events, Maat the goddess of truth and justice acts as hostess, Anubis, who as the god of mummification has opened the body and thus investigated or 'counted' the heart and innermost parts of the person, sometimes functions as the weigh-master together with Horus, the son of the mummified god Osiris, etc. The actual individual biography of the deceased hardly plays a significant role at all. The deceased recites a long list of possible transgressions, sometimes more than 80 of them, and emphatically declares that he has not committed any of them. There is a weighing scales set up in the scene. In one of the trays is the heart of the deceased, on the other tray is an ostrich feather, the symbol of the goddess Maat, the goddess of truth and justice. Whatever the mouth of a person avers must be confirmed by the heart. If the heart were to be heavier or lighter than the ostrich feather and the weighing scales thus not in balance or harmony, then the deceased would not be acquitted by Thoth but condemned. Heart and mouth must continue to be a unit and not fight against each other. Otherwise the person will suffer the dreaded second death, which is also mentioned in the Bible (Revelation 20.14-15). This can be the lake of fire mentioned in Book of the Dead, chapter 126, which consumes the condemned person, but in Book of the Dead, chapter 125 it is usually a hybrid monster-like being consisting of parts of a lion, a hippopotamus and a crocodile, or a sort of hound of hell, the so-called 'devourer' or 'devourer of the dead', who eats the deceased.

Several verses from the Book of the Dead were designed to be recited at this crucial moment, with the mouth of the person speaking in an aside to the heart in order to prevent the heart accusing the deceased:

> O my heart which I had from my mother, O my heart which I had upon earth, do not rise up against me as a witness in the presence of the Lord of Things; do not speak against me concerning what I have done, do not bring up anything against me in the presence of the Great God, Lord of the West.[18]

---

[18] BD 30A; Faulkner 1985, 55.

Clearly there is anxiety speaking here, resulting from experience with the conscience. The aim is to prevent the heart testifying as accuser in the hereafter, betraying what the deceased wants to keep quiet, and giving the lie to what he is declaring to the Divine Tribunal.[19]

BD 30B is also an invocation or plea to the heart to indemnify the deceased during the Divine Tribunal. It goes into more detail concerning the weighing scales, the judges and the cross-examination. Spell Book of the Dead 30B is not only found in Book of the Dead papyri but also as an inscription on so-called heart scarabs, which as said above were added to the mummy to function as a reserve heart. On no account should these reserve hearts accuse the deceased:

> O my heart which I had from my mother!
> O my heart which I had from my mother!
> O my heart of my different ages!
> Do not stand up as a witness against me,
> do not be opposed to me in the tribunal,
> do not be hostile to me in the presence of the Keeper of the Balance,
> for you you are my ka [soul] which was in my body,
> the protector who made my members hale.
> Go forth to the happy place whereto we speed;
> do not make my name stink to the Entourage who make men.
> Do not tell lies about me in the presence of the god;
> it is indeed well that you should hear!
> Thus says Thoth, judge of truth, to the Great Ennead
> which is in the presence of Osiris:
> Hear this word of very truth.
> I have judged the heart of the deceased,
> and his soul stands as a witness for him.
> His deeds are righteous in the great balance,
> and no sin has been found in him.[20]

This text continues with a description of the ideal situation, where the deceased's own heart does not accuse him.

The belief that one's own heart could act as an accuser is not limited to Ancient Egypt. Nor is this the first time that the condemning heart in the Bible text 1 John 3.18-21 has been linked to the accusing heart in the Egyptian Divine Tribunal.[21] The aim here is not to provide a thorough grammatical and exegetical explanation of this rather dif-

---

[19] See chap. 30B; De Buck 1944, 22.
[20] BD 30B; Faulkner 1985, 27-8.
[21] Kügler 1993.

ficult passage. For the sake of completeness, here is the translation of the passage from the Revised Standard Version:

> (18) … let us not love in word or speech but in deed and in truth. (19) By this we shall know that we are of the truth, and reassure our hearts before him (20) whenever our hearts condemn us; for God is greater than our hearts, and he knows everything. (21) Beloved, if our hearts do not condemn us, we have confidence before God.

When one reads this passage with Egyptian eyes, it is clear that the heart is being balanced against truth. However, this passage goes further than the Old Testament tradition, where God weighs the heart (Proverbs 21. 2). The most significant thing about this biblical passage is not that the heart is the place or the object of a divine investigation, but rather that it operates independently before the judge, although not just as one of the many random human witnesses. The heart in 1 John 3.20-21 is obviously considered to be able to condemn independently as a separate entity. This can indeed be called a trace of Egyptian anthropology.[22]

If Egypt and Israel can both be called 'cultures of the heart', all sorts of links and influences become immediately possible between Egyptian wisdom and biblical truth, so that it is no longer necessary to prove a direct historical link between the Egyptian Book of the Dead and 1 John 3.18-21. The Israelite tradition and the New Testament that builds on it, however, never went so far as to regard the human heart as a god, as in the Egyptian-humanist tradition:[23] 'The heart of a man is his own god. My heart is satisfied with what I have done. It is in my body, while I am a god. The gods are delighted to see me.'

Bibliography

Assmann, J. 1990. *Ma'at: Gerechtigkeit und Unsterblichkeit im Alten Ägypten*, Munich.

Assmann, J. 1996. 'Zur Geschichte des Herzens im Alten Ägypten', in: G. Berkemer and G. Rappe (eds), *Das Herz im Kulturvergleich*, Berlin, 143–72.

Böhlig, A. 1983. '"Herz" in der Übersetzung des koptischen Neuen Testaments', in: M. Görg (ed.), *Fontes atque Pontes: Eine Festgabe für H. Brunner* (Ägypten und Altes Testament 5), Wiesbaden, 47–62.

Brunner, H. 1957. *Altägyptische Erziehung*, Wiesbaden.

---

[22] Kügler 1993.
[23] Otto 1954, 38; Assmann 1990, 120.

Brunner, H. 1977. 'Herz', in: W. Helck and W. Westendorf, *Lexikon der Ägyptologie*, Wiesbaden, ii, 1158–68.

Brunner, H. 1988. *Das hörende Herz: Kleine Schriften zur Religions- und Geistesgeschichte Ägyptens*, Hrsg. von W. Röllig (Orbis Biblicus et Orientalis 80), Freiburg/Göttingen.

Burkhard, G. 1988. 'Ptahhotep und das Alter', *Zeitschrift für Ägyptische Sprache und Altertumskunde* 115 (1988) 19–30.

De Buck, A. 1935. *The Ancient Egyptian Coffin Texts*, i: *Text of Spells 1–75* (Oriental Institute Publications 34), Chicago.

De Buck, A. 1944. 'Een groep Dodenboekspreuken betreffende het hart', *Jaarbericht Ex Oriente Lux* 9 (1944) 9–24.

De Buck, A. 1956. *The Ancient Egyptian Coffin Texts*, vi: *Text of Spells 472—865* (Oriental Institute Publications 81), Chicago.

Faulkner, R.O. 1985. *The Ancient Egyptian Book of the Dead*, Translated by R.O. Faulkner and Edited by C. Andrews, London.

Helck, W. 1958. *Urkunden des aegyptischen Altertums*, iv: *Urkunden der 18. Dynastie*, Heft 21, Berlin.

Kügler, J. 1993. '"Wenn das Herz uns auch verurteilt …": Ägyptische Anthropologie in 1 Joh. 3,19–21?', *Biblische Notizen* 66 (1993) 10–14.

Naville, E. 1886. *Das aegyptische Todtenbuch der XVIII. bis XX. Dynastie*, i: *Text und Vignetten*, Berlin.

Otto, E. 1954. *Die biographischen Inschriften der ägyptischen Spätzeit: Ihre geistesgeschichtliche und literarische Bedeutung* (Probleme der Ägyptologie 2), Leiden.

Parkinson, R.B. 1997. *The Tale of Sinuhe and Other Ancient Egyptian Poems 1940–1640 BC: Translated with an Introduction and Notes*, Oxford/New York.

Seeber, C. 1976. *Untersuchungen zur Darstellung des Totengerichts im Alten Ägypten* (Münchner Ägyptologische Studien 35), Munich/Berlin.

Sethe, K. 1906. *Urkunden des aegyptischen Altertums*, iv: *Urkunden der 18. Dynastie*, Heft 7, Leipzig.

Shupak, N. 1985. 'Some Idioms Connected with the Concept of "Heart" in Egypt and the Bible', in: S. Israelit-Groll (ed.), *Pharaonic Egypt, the Bible and Christianity*, Jerusalem, 202–12.

Te Velde, H. 1977. *Seth, God of Confusion: A Study of his Role in Egyptian Mythology and Religion*, Reprint with some corrections (Probleme der Ägyptologie 7), Leiden.

Te Velde, H. 1990. 'Some Remarks on the Concept of "Person" in the Ancient Egyptian Culture', in: H.G. Kippenberg, Y.B. Kuiper, A.F. Sanders (eds), *Concepts of Person in Religion and Thought*, Berlin/New York, 83–101.

THE EGYPTIAN BACKGROUND OF
THE 'OINTMENT' PRAYER IN THE EUCHARISTIC
RITE OF THE *DIDACHE* (10.8)

HUUB VAN DE SANDT

The textual value of the *Didache* recension in the Manuscript of Jerusalem (H 54), discovered by Philotheos Bryennios in 1873, has been criticized by some because the manuscript stems from the eleventh century.[1] It is often assumed that a series of alterations, such as interpolations and harmonisations, were made to the manuscript between the time of the text's first emergence and its final reproduction. On the other hand, it has recently been established that the central part of the manuscript's text (including the version of the *Didache*) probably reflects a valuable source which dates from a much earlier age than was previously thought. The latter document may have contained a major part of the so-called Apostolic Fathers and probably should be assigned to the patristic period.[2]

The reliability of H 54 remains controversial as regards the Eucharistic prayers of *Didache* 9-10. The manuscript contains the thanksgiving prayers for the cup and bread, but omits the third thanksgiving prayer between 10.7 and 11.1 which is found in the editions of the *Didache* in Bihlmeyer and Wengst.[3] The alternative version in Bihlmeyer and Wengst is based on two sources. The first is a text in the Greek *Apostolic Constitutions* (= *AC*), a compilation which originated between 375 and 380 CE and covers the whole of the *Didache* in the main part of its seventh book (7.1.2-32.4). In *AC* 7.27.1-2, the third thanksgiving prayer reads as follows:

> Concerning the ointment, give thanks this way: O God, the Creator of all, we give you thanks both for the fragrance of the ointment and for

---

[1] Peterson 1959, 181; Audet 1958, 52-78; Wengst 1984, 6; for a summary and support of Wengst's alterations, see Dehandschutter 1995, 37-46.

[2] For a discussion, see Rordorf & Tuilier 1998, 102-10, and especially Van de Sandt & Flusser 2002, 16-24.

[3] Cf. Bihlmeyer 1956, p. XX; Wengst 1984, 57-9, 82; see also Peterson 1959, 157.

the age of immortality which you have made known to us through Jesus
your child, for yours is the glory and the power forever. Amen.

The second source is a papyrus covering *Did* 10.3b-12.2a, which
probably dates from the fifth century. The text, now preserved in
the British Museum (PLond Or. 9271), is written in Coptic but is
a translation of a Greek text. The prayer, occurring in the Coptic
fragment, closely corresponds to *AC* 7.27.1-2:

> But concerning the saying for the fragrance (ϭⲧⲓⲛⲟⲩϥⲓ), give thanks
> just as you say, 'We give thanks to you Father concerning the fragrance
> which you showed us, through Jesus your servant/son. Yours is the glory
> forever. Amen.'

The compiler of the *Apostolic Constitutions* and the writer of the Coptic
fragment found the third thanksgiving prayer in a copy of the Greek
Didache, where it was located immediately after the injunction to the
prophets. A crucial question addressed in this study concerns the
authenticity of the *Didache* version in the Jerusalem manuscript. Was
the third thanksgiving prayer found in the Coptic fragment of the
Didache and in *AC* 7 a genuine element of the *Didache* text that was
then suppressed by the Jerusalem Manuscript (or its source), or does
it represent a later addition? In the present study, attention will be
given to two aspects in particular.

First, the correct Greek text of the thanksgiving prayer—apart from
the possibility of its having been part of the *Didache* Eucharist—has to
be established (§1). Second, before moving on to the *Didache* itself, we
will deal at some length with the development of the Jewish prayers
underlying the *Didache* Eucharist. Most scholars nowadays agree that
the text in *Did* 10 evolved from the Birkat Ha-Mazon, that is, the
prayer that concludes the Jewish ritual meal. Nevertheless, *Did* 9-10
is not a reworking of the Hebrew but of *Greek* table prayers which
have been lost to us. Evidence of a meal prayer indicating a triadic
arrangement of cup, bread, and ointment is found in the first-century
Hellenistic story of *Joseph and Aseneth*. This shows that a Greek version
of fixed table prayers which included the third blessing in addition to
those over the cup and bread may have existed (§2).

These insights have important consequences for the evaluation of
the third thanksgiving prayer in the *Didache* Eucharist. In view of the
evidence in the Jewish Hellenistic apocryphon of *Joseph and Aseneth*,
which is likely to have originated in Egypt, we argue that the third
thanksgiving prayer does not belong to the oldest form of the *Didache*

Eucharist but was interpolated in the original materials within Jewish Christian circles in Hellenistic Egypt (§3).

1. *The text of the 'ointment' prayer in* Didache *10.8*

In order to establish the correct text of the third thanksgiving prayer the focus will be placed primarily on the terms 'fragrance' and 'ointment', as each of these terms may represent the authentic text. Once this problem is solved, attention will be paid to the genealogical relationship between the Greek ('ointment') and Coptic ('fragrance') versions of the third thanksgiving prayer.

For what was thanks being given in the original version of the third thanksgiving prayer? It is clear that the passage in *AC* refers to ointment (μύρον), whereas the Coptic text (cτιnoγϩι) is related to fragrance or incense (εὐωδία). Let us turn first to the Coptic text, which uses the term cτιnoγϩι (*stinoufi*). According to J. Ysebaert, the word *stinoufi* corresponds to the Greek εὐωδία, which in the context of *Did* 10.8 means the 'good smell of Jesus that Christians are to God.'[4] It cannot be proven, however, that this implied thought was common belief in the *Didache* community considering the primitive stage of Christology in the manual. Moreover, the Coptic *Didache* provides a thanksgiving prayer for something which, on the face of it, is concrete and comparable to the preceding 'cup' and 'fragment' (bread), whereas in Ysebaert's interpretation the prayer has become purely metaphorical. St. Gero also proposed εὐωδία as the most obvious Greek equivalent of *stinoufi*. In his view, however, the Coptic text refers to an archaic Christian liturgical practice of burning incense at the end of a solemn communal meal.[5] A prayer of blessing was spoken over incense, which was then burned. Indeed, the obligatory blessing over the incense which was burned at the meal is considered in *m.Ber* 6.6, although the form of the blessing is not given. The burning of incense during and after festive meals (*comissatio*) is also well attested in Greco-Roman antiquity.[6]

Nevertheless, it is doubtful whether a prayer over incense in the Coptic *Didache* would reflect an actual liturgical practice. First of all,

---

[4] See Ysebaert 2002, 10.
[5] Gero 1977, 70, 83-4.
[6] Klinghardt 1996, 472 and note 25.

there is no literary evidence for the use of incense in Jewish synagogue services in the first century CE.[7] Moreover, there is widespread
scholarly consensus that incense was not ritually burned in Christian
congregations until the fourth century. This view is based on statements by second- and third-century Christian writers who reject the
use of incense in the Christian rite as a sign of paganism.[8] Finally, the
third thanksgiving prayer—whether Coptic or not—obviously concerns
a saving gift made known by God to his own people 'through Jesus'.
It is hardly conceivable that a subject such as 'incense', or a 'good
smell' for that matter, would be consistent with the general drift of
the prayer.[9]

The evidence surveyed so far may be regarded sufficient to conclude
that it is not for εὐωδία ('fragrance', 'aroma', 'incense') that thanks is
being given in the third thanksgiving prayer in *AC* and the Coptic
fragment. On the contrary, the indications support the alternative
μύρον ('ointment') as being the direct object of the thanksgiving prayer.
Relevant biblical and ancient Jewish parallel material of a ritual within
the context of a single meal corroborating the μύρον reading is found
in Ps 22.5 (LXX),[10] 2 Esdras 3.7 (LXX),[11] Dan 10.3 (LXX),[12] and
b.Ber. 42a.[13] To be sure, the distinction between the different unctions
used for anointing such as μύρον, ἔλαιον, etc. was blurred in the first
centuries CE as these were often used interchangeably.[14]

---

[7] See Gero 1977, 82.

[8] See Fehrenbach 1922, 6-8; Lietzmann 1926, 86-7 (= Richardson 1979, 71-2);
Dix 1945, 425-7; Gero 1977, 74-8.

[9] Niederwimmer 1993, 209.

[10] 'You have prepared a table (τράπεζαν) before me in presence of them that
afflict me: you have thoroughly anointed my head with oil (ἐλίπανας ἐν ἐλαίῳ); and
your cup cheers me like the best wine.'

[11] 'And they gave ... meats and drinks, and oil (καὶ βρώματα καὶ ποτὰ καὶ
ἔλαιον) to the Sidonians and Tyrians, ...'

[12] 'I ate no pleasant bread, and no flesh or wine entered into my mouth, neither
did I anoint myself with oil (ἔλαιον οὐκ ἠλειψάμην), until three whole weeks were
accomplished.'

[13] 'If one is accustomed to [rub his hands with] oil (שמן) [after a meal], he can
wait for the oil.'

[14] 'Allerdings bleibt eine Verdichtung auf einen einzigen Begriff aus. Wir stossen
in unserem Bereich sehr wohl auf immer wiederkehrende Wortfelder—χρίειν κτλ.,
ἀλείφειν κτλ., ἔλαιον, μύρον, νάρδον καταχεῖν (oder andere Derivate von χεῖν),
lat. ung(u)ere etc.—, aber nicht auf eine herausragende Bevorzugung des uns besonders interessierenden χρίειν ...' (Karrer 1991, 191-2); 'In der Grunddi-
mension dienten sie (i.e., die Salbungen)—ausgedrückt mit den Verben χρίειν,
(ἀπ-)ἀλείφειν, καταχεῖν κτλ. (neben Öl auch mit anderer Salbe: "Myron"),

In addition to the evidence reflected in the gospels (Mark 14.3 par; John 12.3; Luke 7.36-50), which presupposes the use of 'ointment' throughout dinner, an important parallel is found in Isa 25.6-7a: 'And the Lord of hosts shall make a feast for all the nations on this mount. They shall drink gladness, they shall drink wine, they shall anoint themselves with ointment (πίονται οἶνον, χρίσονται μύρον).' Since the Eucharist of the *Didache* anticipates eternal life in *Did* 10.3, this quotation reflects a comparable eschatological orientation and might thus provide an appropriate framework for understanding *Did* 10.8.[15] Moreover, the 'ointment' variant is supported not only by literary evidence in the Septuagint, in Jewish sources, and in the Gospels, but also by various Hellenistic materials referring to unctions which took place after the meal proper.[16] Consider also the instance in *Joseph and Aseneth* 8.5 which refers to blessed bread, cup, and ointment being consumed in the course of what was probably a ritual meal.

The authentic text, like the Greek *Apostolic Constitutions*, probably read τὸ μύρον ('ointment') in the rubric and τῆς εὐωδίας τοῦ μύρου ('the fragrance of the ointment') in the body of the prayer.[17] This solution is plausible since the Coptic word *stinoufi* in some cases also refers to μύρον. Out of the 18 occurrences in the Septuagint and the 13 occurrences in the New Testament there are two cases (Luke 23.56 and Rev 18.13) where the Greek μύρον is rendered in the Coptic translation of the Bible as *sti/stoi* ('smell') and one case (Ezek 27.17) where μύρον is translated as *stinoufi* ('fragrance').[18]

A retranslation of the Coptic fragment into Greek compared with the passage in the *Apostolic Constitutions* (7.27.1-2) shows the two texts of the third thanksgiving prayer to have by and large the same wording and sequence:

---

ung(u)ere etc.—einer Reinigung, die als Befreiung von den bösen, ... eine volle oder erneute Kultteilnahme erst ermöglichte' (Id., 196). See also Groen 1991, 3.

[15] Kollmann 1990, 91.

[16] Klinghardt 1996, 471, 475. One anointed oneself not only during the *comissatio* after the meal but also at an earlier stage, during the first part of the meal or in between the first part and the second part (Mayer 1917, 32-5; Karrer 1991, 205).

[17] Cf. e.g. Schmidt 1925, 95; Wengst 1984, 82; Niederwimmer 1993, 209 note 134.

[18] See Ysebaert 2002, 4-5 and note 12. Interestingly, P.A. Mirecki in his English translation of the text renders the Coptic ⲥⲧⲓⲛⲟⲩϥⲓ twice as 'ointment' (see Jones & Mirecki 1995, 53). Was he influenced by the wording of the parallel passage in *AC* 7.27.1-2?

Coptic fragment	AC 7.27.1-2
περὶ δὲ τοῦ λόγου τοῦ	περὶ δὲ τοῦ
μύρου	μύρου
οὕτως εὐχαριστήσατε	οὕτως εὐχαριστήσατε·
λέγοντες·	--
Εὐχαριστοῦμέν σοι,	Εὐχαριστοῦμέν σοι,
πάτερ,	θεὲ δημιουργὲ τῶν ὅλων,
ὑπὲρ τῆς εὐωδίας τοῦ μύρου	καὶ ὑπὲρ τῆς εὐωδίας τοῦ μύρου
--	καὶ ὑπὲρ τοῦ ἀθανάτου αἰῶνος
οὗ ἐγνώρισας ἡμῖν διὰ Ἰησοῦ	οὗ ἐγνώρισας ἡμῖν διὰ Ἰησοῦ
τοῦ παιδός σου·	τοῦ παιδός σου·
σοὶ ἡ δόξα	ὅτι σοῦ ἐστιν ἡ δόξα
--	καὶ ἡ δύναμις
εἰς τοὺς αἰῶνας· ἀμήν.	εἰς τοὺς αἰῶνας· ἀμήν.[19]

If the Coptic text, despite its closeness to the *AC*, represents a separate thanksgiving prayer, one may ask which of the two versions represents the tradition's earlier form? Since the prayer preserved in the Coptic papyrus is slightly briefer than the one in the *AC*, we are inclined to consider the latter passage to be secondary. The simple address 'Father' (πάτερ) in the Coptic version has probably been replaced here by the address 'O God, the Creator of all' (θεὲ δημιουργὲ τῶν ὅλων). Moreover, the closing doxology 'yours is the glory' (σοὶ ἡ δόξα) may have been amplified in the wording 'for yours is the glory and the power' (ὅτι σοῦ ἐστιν ἡ δόξα καὶ ἡ δύναμις).

This does not mean that the Coptic version provides a more reliable preservation of the prayer in every respect. If the criterion of brevity is applied to the introductory rubric of this thanksgiving prayer, the additional phraseology of the Coptic fragment ('But concerning *the saying for* the fragrance, give thanks *just as you say*') seems to be secondary to the terminology in *AC* which simply reads 'Concerning the ointment, give thanks this way.' The wordings λόγου τοῦ and λέγοντες do not correspond to the linguistic usage of other *Didache* rubrics (8.2; 9.1, 3; 10.1). One clause not touched upon so far is the phrase 'and for the age of immortality' (καὶ ὑπὲρ τοῦ ἀθανάτου αἰῶνος) in the *AC*. It has no parallel in the Coptic version but cannot be explained as a straightforward development of the text form from the shorter recension reflected in the Coptic. It is dangerous to assume that this phrase

---

[19] For the Greek text, see Metzger 1987, 58.

is simply an elaboration or expansion of a later editor.[20] A literary dependence of the prayer in the *Apostolic Constitutions* on the predecessor of the Coptic fragment cannot be taken for granted; it is more likely that both the Greek source underlying the Coptic version and the passage in *AC* are connected in their dependence on a common ancestor.

2. *Did the 'ointment' prayer belong to a Hellenistic version of Jewish table prayers?*

In the last decades it came to be generally accepted that the ultimate roots of the Christian Eucharist in *Did* 9-10 lay in Jewish liturgical practice. The benedictions before the meal in *Didache* 9 evolved out of the synagogue service and the prayers after the meal in *Didache* 10 are probably a reworking of the Birkat Ha-Mazon, the Hebrew Grace that concludes the Jewish ritual meal.[21] Admittedly, there may have been a degree of variation and fluidity in the phraseology of the Hebrew prayers in the first century CE. On the other hand, the extant materials from Qumran of non-Qumranic origin confirm that the initial step in the formation of fixed prayers was taken already in the Second Temple period.[22]

2.1. *The Hellenistic version of the Jewish table prayers*

A proper appraisal of the Eucharistic prayer in the *Didache* can best be achieved by postulating various layers of composition. If *Did* 10 evolved from the Birkat Ha-Mazon, it is clear that the initial form of the Hebrew Grace after meals underwent a significant development as the tripartite structure of the Jewish Grace changed into a bipartite pattern. While the Birkat Ha-Mazon is divided into three strophes,[23]

---

[20] Gero 1977 considers the phrase to be a redactional explanation (p. 72). Further, see below, note 49.

[21] For references to further literature, see Van de Sandt & Flusser 2002, 312 note 122.

[22] More details and references can be found in Van de Sandt & Flusser, 271-2.

[23] '(1) Blessed art Thou, O Lord, our God, King of the Universe, Who feedest the whole world with goodness, with grace and with mercy. (2) We thank Thee, O Lord, our God, that Thou hast caused us to inherit a goodly and pleasant land, the covenant, the Torah, life and food. For all these things we thank Thee and praise Thy name forever and ever. (3) Have mercy, O Lord, our God, on Thy people

its structure has been adapted to a bipartite use in *Did* 10.[24] The bless-ing-thanksgiving-supplication pattern of the Birkat Ha-Mazon becomes a prayer of thanksgiving and supplication. The reorganization of the Grace after meals reflected in the *Didache* took place in a second stage when the Birkat Ha-Mazon was translated from Hebrew into Greek within Jewish Hellenistic circles.

At the same time the benedictions before the meal are likely to have been rearranged in line with the liturgical composition of the Greek version of the Birkat Ha-Mazon. The blessing over the cup and the bread before the meal reproduces to a certain extent the wording of the lengthy prayer of thanksgiving after the meal. The resemblance of phraseology and content between the prayers of *Did* 9 and 10 is clear. Later, in a third stage of the prayer's history, these benedictions were appropriated by one or more Jewish Christian *Didache* communities, which seem to have Christianized them superficially using specific phrases like διὰ Ἰησοῦ τοῦ παιδός σου ('through Jesus your servant' in 9.2, 3; 10.2, 3) or διὰ Ἰησοῦ Χριστοῦ ('through Jesus Christ' in 9.4). All this leads to the conclusion—as also will become clear below—that *Did* 9-10 is a reworking not of the Hebrew but of the Greek version of the Jewish table prayers.[25]

Since the ritual expresses the religious experience of Israel in its own particular Palestinian setting, it did not survive transplantation into the Hellenistic world without enduring profound transformations. When the prayers were transferred from their Hebrew background to the Hellenistic setting and translated into Greek, they received a new dimension. Admittedly, we do not know to what extent the Hellenis-tic Jewish model behind the *Didache* prayers had already expanded beyond the original Hebrew form as the Greek version of the Jewish table prayers has been lost to us. Nevertheless, a translator would have

---

Israel, and on Thy city Jerusalem, and on Thy Temple and Thy dwelling-place and on Zion Thy resting-place, and on the great and holy sanctuary over which Thy name was called, and the kingdom of the dynasty of David mayest Thou restore to its place in our days, and build Jerusalem soon.' (See Finkelstein 1928-29, 215-17. For the possibly earlier version of the third benediction, see Id., 233.)

[24] Cf. Middleton 1935, 263; Talley 1976, 125-9; and see, also for the following, Van de Sandt & Flusser 2002, 313-25.

[25] For *Did* 10, see Dibelius 1938, passim; Sandelin 1986, 212-18. Compare also Lietzmann 1926, 233-4 (= Richardson 1979, 190); Koester 1957, 193; Wengst 1984, 48-9, 53 note 177; Ledogar 1968, 127-8; Kollmann 1990, 80-9; Wehr 1987, 346-7.

had little occasion to use a word like 'immortality' or the juxtaposition 'knowledge and belief' in a triad such as 'knowledge and belief and immortality' (γνώσεως καὶ πίστεως καὶ ἀθανασίας) in *Did* 10.2.[26] The word 'immortality' returns in such Septuagintic writings as Wis 3.4; 4.1; 8.13, 17; 15.3 and 4 Macc 14.5; 16.13, books that were unknown in ancient Hebrew or Aramaic literature. The term seems to express a general aspiration of Hellenistic Judaism (cf. 2 Macc 7.9, 14, 36).[27] Similarly, relying on Philo, we ascertain that the word γνῶσις appears to have been a term which was also central to Hellenistic Jewish thought.[28]

A different idea about how eternal life may be acquired is found in the succeeding strophe of the prayer in *Did* 10.3. The 'life' that God had made known in 9.3 is probably understood here as immortality too. When this strophe speaks of the gift of 'spiritual food and drink and eternal life' (πνευματικὴν τροφὴν καὶ ποτὸν καὶ ζωὴν αἰώνιον), the language used unquestionably reveals that special significance was seen in the elements themselves.[29] But what was meant by spiritual food and drink? From the perspective of the Hellenistic Wisdom literature, the spiritual nourishment is the teaching that God gives through Wisdom (cf. Prov 9.5-6 LXX).[30] The prayer in *Did* 9.3-4 seems to rest upon a Jewish prayer tradition in which everyday food was regarded to be a heavenly endowment bestowing life and wisdom. The consuming of spiritual food in 10.3 is seen as causing the effect of eternal life. We ascertain a shift from a ritualized meal in which the divine presence is felt through the sharing of the communal table to a cultic event with divine food connotations assigned to Eucharistic elements.

---

[26] The terminology is reminiscent of John 6.69-70 and 17.8 (cf. also 3.36; 17.3) where γινώσκειν, πιστεύειν, and ζωὴ αἰώνιος are interconnected. As there are insufficient indications proving a relation of dependence between *Did* 9-10 and the Gospel of John, they may draw on common Jewish-Hellenistic tradition (cf. Kollmann 1990, 84-5).

[27] Cf. also Schnackenburg 1971, 228-342.

[28] For instances, see Bultmann 1933, 702.

[29] An early parallel is found in the statement of Paul in 1 Cor 10.3-4 which mentions that the generation of the desert ate 'the same spiritual food' (πνευματικὸν βρῶμα) and drank 'the same spiritual drink' (πνευματικὸν πόμα).

[30] See Dibelius 1938, 34, 37-8. The thanksgiving for the 'life and knowledge' in *Did* 9.3 is a traditional concept not only in Hellenistic Judaism, where the predicate 'life' as representing God's gift is identified with the Torah (Sirach 17.11; 45.4; Prov 8.35; cf. Acts 7.38), but also in rabbinic Judaism, where it is recognized as Wisdom (cf. Borgen 1965, 148; see also Klinghardt 1996, 440-1 and note 33).

2.2. Joseph and Aseneth *and a Hellenistic version of the Jewish table prayers*

A striking parallel with the ritual of the Eucharist in the Coptic fragment and *AC* 7.27.1-2 is found in the story of *Joseph and Aseneth*, as it contains blessings to be said over the bread, cup, and ointment. Participation in these blessings is the key to salvation, which is eternal life, immortality, and incorruption. Here, the idea of divine food has become so prominent that the meal has assumed sacred qualities. Since it is almost generally accepted that the story of *Joseph and Aseneth*—which was probably composed in Greek—is of Jewish provenance, our interest will centre on whether these bread-cup-ointment passages could be related to a Greek version of a more or less standardized Jewish table prayer.

Attention will be given first, however, to the legend of *Joseph and Aseneth*. Virtually all specialists have taken Egypt as its place of origin[31] and the period between 100 BCE and 115 CE as its date of composition.[32] The milieu from which *Joseph and Aseneth* emerged was one in which Jews lived in dynamic tension with gentiles, and the socio-historical context was the problem of mixed marriages.[33] Any sort of contact between Jews and gentiles, whether intermarriage or table fellowship, appears to have been forbidden on the grounds that it pollutes. In order to explain this, however, there is no need to presume a distinct sectarian milieu since a relatively 'mainstream' (if the term is appropriate) Hellenistic Jewish community may also be an appropriate setting for understanding and appreciating the peculiarities of the work.[34]

---

[31] Similarities between Aseneth and the goddesses Isis and Neith have been established; cf. Philonenko 1968, 61-79; see also Schürer 1986, 548; Chesnutt 1995, 76-81. M. de Goeij develops the idea suggested originally by Philonenko (1968, 83-9) that this is a Gnostic drama. In a second-century Valentinian Gnostic setting, the pagan Aseneth is summoned to come from her digression to the true gnosis (1981, 15-22). However, the disdain for matter, commonly shown by Gnostic thinkers, is lacking in the narrative.

[32] See Philonenko 1968, 108-9; Burchard 1985, 187-8; Burchard 1987, 104; Chesnutt 1995, 80-5; Docherty 2004, 31.

[33] Tromp 1999, 33.

[34] We follow the reconstructed Greek eclectic text, largely founded on *b* manuscripts, which has recently been edited in a critical edition by Burchard 2003.

2.2.1. *The ritual passages in* Joseph and Aseneth

The narrative about *Joseph and Aseneth* consists of two different though interconnected stories: the conversion of Aseneth (chaps. 1-21) and the envy of the Pharaoh's son (chaps. 22-29). Only the first tale is relevant to our subject. According to Gen 41.45, Joseph married a foreign woman, the daughter of an Egyptian priest. The problem of the wedding of the chaste and pious Joseph to the pagan Aseneth[35] is couched in terms of the fundamental antithesis between Jews and Egyptians. The contrast is clearly marked by Joseph's refusal to eat with the Egyptians and to kiss Aseneth. When she has fallen in love with him and is about to kiss him, Joseph says:

> It is not fitting that a pious man[36]
> who worships (εὐλογεῖ) with his mouth the living God
>   and eats (ἐσθίει) blessed bread of life (ἄρτον εὐλογημένον ζωῆς)
>   and drinks (πίνει) a blessed cup of immortality (ποτήριον εὐλογημένον ἀθανασίας)
>   and anoints himself (χρίεται) with blessed ointment of incorruption (χρίσματι εὐλογημένῳ ἀφθαρσίας), should kiss an alien woman,
>   who blesses with her mouth dead and dumb idols
>   and eats from their table bread of strangling,
>   drinks from their libations a cup of treachery
>   and anoints herself with the ointment of perdition (8.5).[37]

Joseph prays for her instead. Utterly shaken, Aseneth exchanges her royal robes for sackcloth, destroys her idols, and casts them and her rich foods out the window. She mourns, fasts, and repents for seven days. Aseneth definitively breaks with her ancestral religion and becomes a proselyte. On the morning of the eighth day, an unnamed chief messenger of God, a celestial visitor, appears, declares her reborn, and feeds her a piece of honeycomb. He interprets the honeycomb as the spirit of life, made by the bees of paradise from the roses of life:

---

[35] This is the spelling of the LXX and the Greek text of *Joseph and Aseneth*. In the MT of Gen 41.45, Joseph's wife's name is Asenath.

[36] The wording ἀνδρὶ θεοσεβεῖ in this context means 'observant Jew', and as such he will not eat with the Egyptians (7.1). In the same way, the prohibition of marriage to Gentiles is implied in Joseph's initial rejection of Aseneth (7.6).

[37] For the Greek text, see Burchard 2003, 116.

> And the man stretched out his right hand and broke a small portion
> off the comb,
> and he himself ate and what was left he put with his hand into Aseneth's
> mouth,
> and he said to her, 'Eat.' And she ate.
> And the man said to Aseneth, 'Behold,
>> you have eaten bread of life (ἄρτον ζωῆς),
>> and drunk a cup of immortality (ποτήριον ἀθανασίας),
>> and been anointed with ointment of incorruption (χρίσματι ἀφθαρσίας)
>> (16.15-16a).[38]

He promises her that Joseph will come to marry her. And so he does;
the wedding ceremony takes place, performed and presided over by
the Pharaoh himself.

2.2.2. *Do the ritual passages in* Joseph and Aseneth *refer to a Greek version of the Jewish table prayers?*

As shown above, the question of ritual arises in two types of passages
of the apocryphon. The first is the much-debated so-called 'meal
formula' (8.5), the formulaic reference to eating the blessed bread of
life, drinking the blessed cup of immortality, and anointing with the
blessed oil of incorruption. Such phrases return in 8.9; 15.5; 16.16;
19.5, and 21.21. The second passage concerns the mysterious honeycomb in chaps. 14-17.

The crucial question in the research of *Joseph and Aseneth* is whether
the somewhat stereotypical meal language refers to a ritual or cultic
meal in the author's community, or whether it is to be explained in
another way. A number of scholars have objected to the assumption
that the clauses mentioning bread, cup, and ointment refer to liturgical
usage, since the variations do not allow us to speak of a liturgically
fixed formula. The repeated expression is triadic in three occurrences
mentioning bread, cup, and ointment (8.5; 15.5, and 16.6) and dyadic
in another three occurrences referring to just bread and cup (8.9; 19.5,
and 21.21).[39] The distinct references are considered too divergent to
allow us to draw any conclusions in this respect, and it is assumed
that these passages relate to the entire Jewish way of life.[40]

The language employed may have functioned to describe the spe-

---

[38] For the Greek text, see Burchard 2003, 212.
[39] Cf. Sänger 1980, 169-70; Chesnutt 1995, 128-9.
[40] See especially Jeremias 1960, 27; Burchard 1965, 121-33; Burchard 1987,
113-17; Schnackenburg 1971, 335-40; Chesnutt 1995, 128-35.

cial prototypical nature of Aseneth's conversion from idolatry. In 8.5, the positive clauses are set within a prohibitive framework ('it is not fitting that a pious man [woman] …') which serves to highlight the fundamental difference between Jew and non-Jew. The contrast is such that there can be no intimacy, and certainly no intermarriage, between the worshipper of God and the idol worshipper. Aseneth must renounce the idols. The fourfold series of antitheses in relative clauses spells out the difference between the two classes of people, enforced by the antithetical use of meal terminology to characterize a lifestyle diametrically opposed to an existence marked by idolatry. Jews remain apart from non-Jews, with whom they may coexist but must not mingle: no table-fellowship with pagans and no physical intimacy with a pagan woman is permitted.

The rejection of the idea that the meal language refers to an ordinary Jewish meal ritual may also be explained by the unsuccessful attempts in the past to elucidate these clauses about the bread, cup, and ointment by analogies with a Jewish mystery cult, an archetypal Jewish meal, a Qumran meal, or the meal of the Therapeutae.[41] Especially the inclusion of the anointing was problematic as it was commonly felt that it had no exact parallel in ancient Judaism. Researchers were forced to posit a ritual where the benediction of the unction comes after the blessing of the bread and the wine.[42] The methodological problem involved is, of necessity, circular in that some hypothetical pre-existing ritual is required to interpret the text whereas it is impossible to demonstrate the correctness and reality of the ritual behind the text. The extant parallel in the alternative *Didache* version was unnoticed or not considered at all to check the reference in *Joseph and Aseneth*.[43]

Another objection to a ritual interpretation of the bread, wine, and ointment passages is found in chaps. 14-17. The privileges enjoyed by Jews over non-Jews are brought out clearly here in the report about the

---

[41] See e.g. Philonenko 1968, 89-98; Kilpatrick 1952, 6-8; Nauck 1957, 169-71; and Kuhn 1957, 76-7, respectively.

[42] At first sight, it might refer to a description of Levi's vision of his 'ordination' to the priesthood in *Testament of Levi* 8.4-17. In vv. 4-5, bread, wine, and anointing are mentioned, among other elements, in this second investiture of Levi, but this place is problematic as unction is mentioned before the consumption of the bread and the wine.

[43] The first, to my knowledge, to suggest the 'ointment' prayer in *Did* 10.8 as a parallel was B. Kollmann (Kollmann 1990, 90). He did not develop this idea, however.

heavenly visitor. In *Joseph and Aseneth* 16.14-16, the angel gives Aseneth a piece of honeycomb. She is told that in eating it she has eaten bread of life, drunk a cup of immortality, and been anointed with ointment of incorruption (16.16; 19.5). The eating of honey is equated with the triadic meal formula, and it seems that eating, drinking, and being anointed mean the same thing as eating the honeycomb. If the blessed bread, cup, and ointment were consumed in the course of a special religious rite, one would expect to find such a rite or rites mentioned in the narrative of *Joseph and Aseneth*. It is remarkable that Aseneth does not eat the bread and drink the cup and be anointed. There is little in the document itself, then, to suggest a Jewish ritual meal. On the contrary, the fact that she receives a heavenly honeycomb implies that the bread, cup, and ointment were not so consumed. As Randall D. Chesnutt states:

> It is an extremely important but often overlooked fact, that Aseneth never actually receives any bread, cup or ointment anywhere in the narrative. Instead she eats a piece of honeycomb ... This explicit equation of eating the honey with eating the bread, drinking the cup, and being anointed with the ointment makes it highly unlikely that allusion to a fixed ritual form is intended in either half of the equation.[44]

Therefore, the idea of a ritual meal is abandoned by many, suggesting that the formula refers to the entire Jewish way of life over against pagan standards of behaviour.

There are, however, good reasons to assume that the formulaic references under discussion in *Joseph and Aseneth* may be taken as allusions to some sort of ritual meal. Firstly, it cannot be said with certainty whether the honey and the honeycomb have replaced the bread, wine, and ointment. It is more likely that the honeycomb is merely used at the initiation of Aseneth since eating the honeycomb is linked to repentance and conversion[45] whereas the clause in 8.5 (and elsewhere) referring to the eating and drinking (and anointing) indicates everyday Jewish custom. The present tense of the verbs reflects the recurring ritual practice of those who worship God. Moreover, these formulas can hardly echo an initiation ritual, because it is Joseph, and not Aseneth, who is characterized in 8.5 as a pious man worshipping God.

---

[44] Chesnutt 1995, 131.
[45] Kollmann 1990, 88.

Secondly, the negative clauses about the bread, cup, and ointment in
8.5 indicate sacrificial meals normally held in a temple at a god's table.
They display an inescapable analogy with 1 Cor 10.18, 21: 'Consider
the people of Israel; are not those who eat the sacrifices partners in
the altar? ... You cannot drink the cup of the Lord and the cup of the
demons; you cannot partake of the table of the Lord and the table of
the demons.' For Paul, the table of the Lord represents a cultic meal
such as the Eucharist. No Jew could be a co-religionist of the pagans,
worshipping his God while also upholding the gods associated with
Roman society. Indeed, *Joseph and Aseneth* does not mention the table of
the Lord in 8.5, but, since the negative clauses about the bread, cup,
and ointment indicate sacrificial meals usually taking place in pagan
temples destined for the cult of idols, this contrast clearly suggests that
a ritual meal is involved.

Thirdly, the similarity between the passages shows that the expression 'to eat the blessed bread of life and to drink the blessed cup of
immortality (and to anoint oneself)' is a technical formula, especially
since the narrative itself does not require such an expression. The
wording of the bread-cup-ointment passages seems to confirm an
understanding that did not necessitate any further elaboration. The
formula is not a natural product of the events described in the story,
but is best explained as referring to an independent and established
ritual meal where bread, cup, and ointment are consumed together.

In sum, the similarity of the six references to ritual in shape and
language allow us to speak of a somewhat fixed form. The bread, cup,
and ointment are evidently linked, and often, in the frequent mention
of them in parallel constructions, they stand together. It is reasonable
to suppose, therefore, that these passages in *Joseph and Aseneth* attest to a
meal of some sort, and it is possible that they refer to a Greek version
of the Jewish table prayers used in Hellenistic Egypt. This suggestion
may be supported by the evidence that the alternative *Didache* version
gives a place to the blessing over ointment as well. Moreover, the
repeated use of the Greek benediction formula in the passive participle
in *Joseph and Aseneth* (εὐλογημένον) reflects the benediction found in the
Hebrew meal blessings (ברוך) as rendered, for example, in *m.Ber.* 6.1
and in Finkelstein's reconstruction of the Birkat Ha-Mazon.[46] If the
reading of the 'ointment' prayer is included, and if our understanding

---

[46] Finkelstein 1928-29, 215-17, 225-33.

of it is correct, then the alternative *Didache* form supports the contention that the bread, cup, and ointment are consumed in the course
of a religious meal framed within a Greek version of the Jewish table
prayers.

3. *Conclusion: The 'ointment' prayer as an Egyptian interpolation in the Didache*

Did the alternative Eucharist develop from an Egyptian version of the
Jewish table prayers? A positive answer to this question would imply
that the 'ointment' prayer is not a product of editorial expansion to
the *Didache* but was part of the *Didache* from the very beginning. The
suggestion is attractive but unlikely. The 'ointment' prayer appears
to represent a later interpolation for two reasons. Firstly, the prayer
gives thanks for the aroma of the 'ointment'. While the first two
thanksgiving prayers merely show appreciation of the spiritual gifts
of salvation ('the holy vine of David' and 'the life and knowledge')
which are represented by the material cup and bread, the 'fragrance
of the ointment' does not appear to imply a sacred endowment of
deliverance only.[47] Instead, the 'ointment' prayer also thanks for the
material gift, for 'the fragrance of the ointment' itself. There is a shift
in diction and connotation here because the thought of this verse is
loosely connected to the first two thanksgiving prayers, and, thus,
intrudes into the context.

Secondly, the position of the 'ointment' prayer at this specific location raises special difficulty. The Coptic papyrus and the Greek *Apostolic Constitutions* append the prayer to the very end of the Eucharistic
prayers in chaps. 9-10, where it follows the ruling in 10.7 allowing the
prophets freedom to give thanks to the extent they wish. The latter
instruction was apparently a transitional verse leading the reader to
the materials on church discipline which are disclosed in chaps. 11-
15. The present position of 10.8, therefore, leaves the clear impression that the liturgical passage was awkwardly inserted between the
non-liturgical injunction concluding the Eucharistic prayers and the
instructions on the reception of prophets and apostles in chap. 11.

Since there is clearly imitation of the table prayers in *Did* 9.1-2

---

[47] Vööbus 1968, 56-7; Niederwimmer 1993, 207-8.

and 9.3⁴⁸—cf. the emphasis on the thanksgiving in the rubric (περὶ ... οὕτως εὐχαριστήσατε) and in the prayer proper (Εὐχαριστοῦ-μέν σοι, πάτερ ἡμῶν, ὑπὲρ), and a continuing Christianization (διὰ Ἰησοῦ τοῦ παιδός σου· σοὶ ἡ δόξα εἰς τοὺς αἰῶνας)—there can be little doubt that the 'ointment' prayer is a Christian addition to the basic Eucharistic prayers of the *Didache*. In the formative stage of Christianity in first-century Egypt, Jewish 'converts' to Christian faith brought with them their rituals, worldview, and lifestyle, and, obviously, these Judeo-Christians continued to faithfully observe their religious customs. The original *Didache* text was modified, amended, and updated to fit the version of the table prayers with which the Jewish Christian community in Egypt was familiar. In this way, local diversity, for example in the form of an 'ointment' prayer, could easily have crept into the ritual.⁴⁹

Bibliography

Audet, J.-P. 1958. *La Didachè: Instructions des Apôtres* (Études Bibliques), Paris.

Bihlmeyer, K. 1956². *Die Apostolischen Väter: Neubearbeitung der Funkschen Ausgabe* (Sammlung ausgewählter Kirchen- und dogmengeschichtlicher Quellenschriften II.1.1), Tübingen.

Borgen, P. 1965. *Bread from Heaven: An Exegetical Study of the Concept of Manna in the Gospel of John and the Writings of Philo* (Supplements to Novum Testamentum 10), Leiden.

Bultmann, R. 1933. γινώσκω, γνῶσις, ἐπιγινώσκω, κτλ., in: G. Kittel (ed.), *Theological Dictionary of the New Testament* (English transl.: G.W. Bromiley), Grand Rapids, MI, i, 688-719.

Burchard, C. 1965. *Untersuchungen zu Joseph und Aseneth: Überlieferung—Ortsbestimmung* (Wissenschaftliche Untersuchungen zum Neuen Testament 8), Tübingen.

Burchard, C. 1985. 'Joseph and Aseneth (First Century BC—Second Century AD): A New Translation and Introduction', in: J.H. Charlesworth (ed.), *The Old Testament Pseudepigrapha*, London, ii, 177-247.

Burchard, C. 1987. 'The Importance of Joseph and Aseneth for the Study of the New Testament: A General Survey and a Fresh Look at the Lord's Supper', *New Testament Studies* 33 (1987) 102-34 (repr. in: Id., *Gesammelte Studien zu Joseph und Aseneth* [Studia in Veteris Testamenti Pseudepigrapha 13], Leiden 1996, 263-95).

Burchard, C. 2003. *Joseph und Aseneth* (Pseudepigrapha Veteris Testamenti Graece 5), Leiden.

---

⁴⁸ See Audet 1958, 69; Vööbus 1968, 57.

⁴⁹ A characteristic feature—though in a mitigated form—of the Hellenistic milieu from which the ointment prayer came is still perceptible in *AC* 7.27.1-2. The emphasis on the divine nature of blessed food suggested in *Joseph and Aseneth* is echoed here in the phrase 'for the immortal eon' (ὑπὲρ τοῦ ἀθανάτου αἰῶνος).

Chesnutt, R.D. 1995. *From Death to Life: Conversion in Joseph and Aseneth* (Journal for the Study of the Pseudepigrapha. Supplement Series 16), Sheffield.

Dehandschutter, B. 1995. 'The Text of the *Didache*: Some Comments on the Edition of Klaus Wengst', in: C.N. Jefford (ed.), *The Didache in Context: Essays on Its Text, History and Transmission* (Supplements to Novum Testamentum 77), Leiden, 37-46.

Dibelius, M. 1938. 'Die Mahl-Gebete der Didache', *Zeitschrift für die neutestamentliche Wissenschaft* 37 (1938) 32-41 (repr. in: H. Kraft and G. Bornkamm [eds], *Botschaft und Geschichte: Gesammelte Aufsätze*, ii, *Zum Urchristentum und zur hellenistischen Religionsgeschichte*, Tübingen 1956, 117-27).

Dix, G. 1945[2]. *The Shape of the Liturgy*, Westminster.

Docherty, S. 2004. 'Joseph and Aseneth: Rewritten Bible or Narrative Expansion?', *Journal for the Study of Judaism* 35 (2004) 27-48.

Fehrenbach, E. 1922, 'Encens', in: *Dictionnaire d'archéologie chrétienne et de liturgie*, Paris, v.1, 2-21.

Finkelstein, L. 1928-29. 'The Birkat Ha-Mazon', *Jewish Quarterly Review* 19 (1928/29), 211-62 (repr. in: Id., *Pharisaism in the Making: Selected Essays*, New York 1972, 333-84).

Gero, St. 1977. 'The so-called Ointment Prayer in the Coptic Version of the *Didache*: A Re-evaluation', *Harvard Theological Review* 70 (1977) 67-84.

Goeij, M. de, 1981. *Josef en Aseneth: Apokalyps van Baruch* (De Pseudepigrafen 2), Kampen.

Groen, B.J. 1990. *'Ter genezing van ziel en lichaam': De viering van het oliesel in de Grieks-Orthodoxe kerk* (Theologie & Empirie 11), Kampen/Weinheim.

Jeremias, J. 1960[3]. *Die Abendmahlsworte Jesu*, Göttingen (English transl. from the 2nd edn: *The Eucharistic Words of Jesus*, Oxford 1955).

Jones, F.S. and P.A. Mirecki 1995. 'Considerations on the Coptic Papyrus of the *Didache* (British Library Oriental Manuscript 9271)', in: C.N. Jefford (ed.), *The Didache in Context: Essays on Its Text, History and Transmission* (Supplements to Novum Testamentum 77), Leiden, 47-87.

Karrer, M. 1991. *Der Gesalbte: Die Grundlagen des Christustitels* (Forschungen zur Religion und Literatur des Alten und Neuen Testaments 151), Göttingen.

Kilpatrick, G.D. 1952. 'The Last Supper', *Expository Times* 64 (1952) 4-8.

Klinghardt, M. 1996. *Gemeinschaftsmahl und Mahlgemeinschaft: Soziologie und Liturgie frühchristlicher Mahlfeiern* (Texte und Arbeiten zum neutestamentlichen Zeitalter 13), Tübingen/Basel.

Koester, H. 1957. *Synoptische Überlieferung bei den apostolischen Vätern* (Texte und Untersuchungen 65), Berlin.

Kollmann, B. 1990. *Ursprung und Gestalten der frühchristlichen Mahlfeier* (Göttinger Theologische Arbeiten 43), Göttingen.

Kuhn, K.G. 1957. 'The Lord's Supper and the Communal Meal at Qumran', in: K. Stendahl (ed.), *The Scrolls and the New Testament*, New York, 65-93 and 259-65 (published previously as 'Über den ursprünglichen Sinn des Abendmahles und sein Verhältnis zu den Gemeinschaftsmahlen der Sektenschrift', *Evangelische Theologie* 10 [1950-51] 508-27).

Ledogar, R.J. 1968. *Acknowledgment: Praise-verbs in the Early Greek Anaphora*, Rome.

Lietzmann, H. 1926. *Messe und Herrenmahl: Eine Studie zur Geschichte der Liturgie* (Arbeiten zur Kirchengeschichte 8), Berlin (English transl.: *Mass and Lord's Supper: A Study in the History of the Liturgy. With Introduction and Further Inquiry by R.D. Richardson*, Leiden 1979).

Mayer, C. 1917. *Das Öl im Kultus der Griechen* (Diss.), Würzburg.

Metzger, M. 1987. *Les Constitutions Apostoliques*, iii, *Livres VII et VIII* (Sources Chré-
    tiennes 336), Paris.
Middleton, R.D. 1935. 'The Eucharistic Prayers of the *Didache*', *Journal of Theological
    Studies* 36 (1935) 259-67.
Nauck, W. 1957. *Die Tradition und der Charakter des ersten Johannesbriefes: Zugleich ein Beitrag
    zur Taufe im Urchristentum und in der alten Kirche* (Wissenschaftliche Untersuchungen
    zum Neuen Testament 3), Tübingen.
Niederwimmer, K. 1993². *Die Didache* (Kommentar zu den Apostolischen Vätern 1),
    Göttingen (English transl.: *The Didache* [Hermeneia], Minneapolis 1998).
Peterson, E. 1959. 'Über einige Probleme der Didache-Überlieferung', in: Id., *Frühkirche.
    Judentum und Gnosis: Studien und Untersuchungen*, Rome, 146-82 (published previously
    in *Rivista di archeologia cristiana* 27 [1951] 37-68).
Philonenko, M. 1968. *Joseph et Aséneth: Introduction, texte critique, traduction et notes*,
    Leiden.
Rordorf, W. and A. Tuilier. 1998². *La Doctrine des douze Apôtres (Didachè)* (Sources
    Chrétiennes 248bis), Paris.
Sandelin, K.G. 1986. *Wisdom as Nourisher: A Study of an Old Testament Theme, its Devel-
    opment within Early Judaism and its Impact on Early Christianity* (Acta Academiae
    Aboensis; Humaniora 64.3), Åbo.
Sänger, D. 1980. *Antikes Judentum und die Mysterien: Religionsgeschichtliche Untersuchungen
    zu Joseph und Aseneth* (Wissenschaftliche Untersuchungen zum Neuen Testament
    II.5), Tübingen.
Schmidt, C. 1925. 'Das koptische Didache-Fragment des British Museum', *Zeitschrift
    für die neutestamentliche Wissenschaft* 24 (1925) 81-99.
Schnackenburg, R. 1971. 'Das Brot des Lebens', in: G. Jeremias, H.-W. Kuhn, and
    H. Stegemann (eds), *Tradition und Glaube: Das frühe Christentum in seiner Umwelt* (FS
    K.G. Kuhn), Göttingen, 228-342.
Schürer, E. 1986. *The History of the Jewish People in the Age of Jesus Christ (175 BC-AD
    135)*, iii.1 (Rev. by G. Vermes, F. Millar and M. Goodman), Edinburgh.
Talley, T.J. 1976. 'From Berakah to Eucharistia: A Reopening Question', *Worship*
    50 (1976) 115-37.
Tromp, J. 1999. 'Response to Ross Kraemer: On the Jewish Origin of Joseph and
    Aseneth', in: A. Brenner and J.W. van Henten (eds), *Recycling Biblical Figures:
    Papers read at a NOSTER Colloquium in Amsterdam, 12-13 May 1997* (Studies in
    Theology and Religion 1), Leiden, 266-71.
Van de Sandt, H. and D. Flusser. 2002. *The Didache: Its Jewish Sources and its Place in
    Early Judaism and Christianity* (Compendia Rerum Iudaicarum ad Novum Testa-
    mentum 3/5), Assen/Minneapolis.
Vööbus, A. 1968. *Liturgical Traditions in the Didache* (Papers of Estonian Theological
    Society in Exile 16), Stockholm.
Ysebaert, J. 2002. 'The so-called Coptic Ointment Prayer of *Didache* 10,8 Once More,'
    Vigiliae Christianae 66 (2002) 1-10.
Wehr, L. 1987. *Arznei der Unsterblichkeit: Die Eucharistie bei Ignatius von Antiochien und im Johan-
    nesevangelium* (Neutestamentliche Abhandlungen; Neue Folge 18), Münster.
Wengst, K. 1984. *Didache (Apostellehre), Barnabasbrief, Zweiter Klemensbrief, Schrift an Diognet*
    (Schriften des Urchristentums 2), Darmstadt.

THE *LETTER OF BARNABAS* IN EARLY SECOND-CENTURY EGYPT

Janni Loman

The so-called *Letter of Barnabas*[1] was traditionally attributed to Barn-abas, probably the Barnabas mentioned in the New Testament, the co-worker of Paul (Acts 13.2). Few contemporary scholars accept this attribution. Since the text itself reveals no name of the author, it is correct to say that the author is anonymous, rather than pseudonymous. Seeing its popularity in the East and especially with the theologians Clement of Alexandria and Origen, the letter was probably written in Alexandria, near Egypt,[2] in the early second century. Although *Barnabas* shows almost no sign of the type of philosophical exegesis characteristic of the Alexandrian tradition (for instance the logos tra-dition), it is highly probable that the document was written within a Christian movement that took shape in a number of esoteric groups or 'schools' such as were to be found in early Alexandrian Christianity.[3] The letter includes historical allusions that seem to reflect the time and events of the early second century.[4] The complete text was delivered, together with the *Shepherd* of Hermas, in the fourth century Codex Sinaiticus, one of the most ancient manuscripts of the Bible. There is a Latin translation, which probably dates from the late second or the early third century.[5]

Barnabas is an important document of early Christianity. It was at least for some centuries on the verge of the canon. *Barnabas* is sometimes

---

[1] For editions of the text see Holmes 1999 and Wengst 1984.

[2] Alexandria (i.e. the *polis* of Alexandrian citizens) was officially called 'Alexandria *near* Egypt' (Alexandria *ad* Aegyptum), not 'Alexandria *in* Egypt', because the political fiction held that it was autonomous. Tcherikover 1957, 61.

[3] Cf. Klijn's words on *Barnabas*: 'If the Epistle of Barnabas was written in Egypt, it is a fine example of Egyptian Christianity with its "gnosis" (1.5) and its "Hinter dem Barnabasbrief stehenden Schulbetrieb" (Wengst, *Tradition und Theologie*, 119).' Klijn 1986, 173 note 71. See also Pearson who argues that *Barnabas* is almost certainly of Alexandrian origin. Pearson 1986, 151.

[4] For a reference both to the destruction of the temple in 70 CE and the promise of the rebuilding of a temple see 16.3-4.

[5] On the Latin translation see Heer 1908.

seen, together with Justin's *Dialogue with Trypho*, as the beginning of the *Adversus Iudaeos* literature.[6] *Barnabas* has a strong Jewish character but is at the same time known by its anti-Judaism. It is sometimes studied in the light of the relationship between Jews and Christians in the Roman Empire of the second century.[7]

In this essay, I will first discuss the high repute it had among Christians in Alexandria and Egypt in the second century and after. Second, I will deal with its interpretation of Scripture and its references to the Jews and the Jewish religion. *Barnabas* is first of all a treatise on early biblical interpretation with a marked anti-Judaic bias. The author maintains that he has the correct understanding of the tradition, while his opponents, the Jews, do not hold the proper view of it. Third, I will view *Barnabas* against the background of the origin of Christianity and Christianity's relation to Judaism in Alexandria.

1. Barnabas *in early Christianity*

It is from witnesses usually associated with Alexandria that we have direct references to *Barnabas*. It was a popular writing for the two ante-Nicene Alexandrian theologians Clement and Origen. Clement of Alexandria (born 140/150) is its earliest witness, and he did use *Barnabas* frequently in his writings. According to Clement the author of *Barnabas* was the apostle Barnabas, one of the seventy and a co-worker of Paul.[8] He treats *Barnabas* as a venerated text and probably saw it as part of his canon because in the now almost entirely lost *Hypotyposeis*, according to Eusebius,[9] he states that he presented summary expositions of the whole of Scripture, among which the *Epistle of Barnabas*. Clement found a good deal in the letter with which he could agree. Both Clement and the author of *Barnabas* take a high view of the laws of Moses, while attributing to it an essentially spiritual value. In one of his writings Clement comments that *Barnabas* shows a hint of 'Gnostic' tradition.[10] For both Clement and the author of

---

[6] For a broad general survey of the literary documents to which is usually referred as the *Adversus Iudaeos* literature see Schreckenberg 1995.

[7] According to R. Hvalvik, *Barnabas* was written in a situation where Judaism and Christianity were competitors. See Hvalvik 1996, 324-5.

[8] *Stromateis* 2.116.3.

[9] *Historia Ecclesiastica* 6.14.1.

[10] *Stromateis* 5.63.2.

Barnabas the idea of *gnosis* is inseparable from the interpretation of Scripture as both intend to give the true meaning of scriptural texts. But there is a difference. While in *Barnabas* the idea of *gnosis* is first of all concerned with knowing the requirements of the will of God which are to be found in Scripture, the idea of *gnosis* in Clement is much more complex. For Clement *gnosis* indicates, first of all, a deeper comprehension and knowledge of the Christian doctrines, which must be achieved by means of a particular interpretation or 'demonstration' of Scripture.[11] Clement and *Barnabas* are to be seen as products of the same Christian environment, in the context of the varied theological climate of Alexandria during the second century.[12]

Among the ante-Nicene writers of the Eastern Church, the greatest by far was Origen (c. 185-253), both as a theologian and a biblical scholar. His testimony concerning the books of the New Testament is important. Due to his travels he had the opportunity of observing the usage of books by the churches not only in Egypt and Palestine but also in Arabia, Asia Minor, Greece and Rome.[13] Unlike Clement, Origen does not mention *Barnabas* with any frequency. This is not exceptional, because Origen seldom cites authors outside the Bible.[14] He valued *Barnabas* highly and attributed its composition to Barnabas, presumably Barnabas, the companion and co-worker of Paul. He quotes from *Barnabas* as 'the catholic epistle of Barnabas' without comment, going directly on to cite Luke and 1 Timothy, and envisaging that Celsus might himself have known the letter.[15] Origen attributed an extraordinary value to a spiritual or allegorical reading of Scripture, particularly the laws of Moses.[16] Although he does not quote from the passages of the scriptural interpretation in *Barnabas* he might have felt attracted to it. He values *Barnabas* highly and also quotes from it in his other writings.[17]

Barnabas is also quoted in a treatise preserved in an unpublished

---

[11] For a discussion of the concept of *gnosis* in Clement see Lilla 1971, 142-89.

[12] Cf. Kraft's comment: 'There is a real sense in which Clement is still the best commentary on Barnabas. Not only does he quote from the epistle, but he breathes the same atmosphere of gnosis.' Kraft 1965, 45-6.

[13] Metzger 1989, 135-6.

[14] Trigg 1992, 44.

[15] *Contra Celsum* 1.63.

[16] On Origen's view of the Mosaic Law see De Lange 1976, 90-6.

[17] *De Principiis* 3.2.4, 3.2.7; *Homiliae in Lucam* 35.

fourth century papyrus codex[18] that has simply been referred to as the 'Coptic Book'. There has already been a pre-publication of certain pages.[19] The text was originally composed in Greek and is extant only in this one copy of the Coptic translation. Judging by the remains of the codex, it must have been a theological treatise that betrays highly speculative philosophical thinking on a great variety of topics, mainly problems that result from interpreting Scripture. *Barnabas* belongs to the texts that are quoted and interpreted in the codex as Scripture. All the evidence of the codex gathered thus far points to a world of thought in the vicinity of Alexandria. The text seems to give rather early testimony to some variety of Alexandrian Christian theology. Its main themes appear to be God's creation and God's wrath.[20]

The author of the Coptic Book quotes *Barnabas* several times. It is clearly quoted as belonging to Scripture. This is shown from the way he quotes not only what nowadays is normative Scripture, but also, on the same level of authority, what are now considered non-canonical texts.[21] In the context of creation the focus is on *Barnabas* 6.11-13a, which is quoted even twice. This passage of *Barnabas* is used in the context of the author's doctrine of creation that it is God alone who, with the help of the Logos, created man. *Barnabas* provides the main proof for the argument that God in speaking to his Son, speaks to himself. The author of the Coptic Book wants to exclude any false doctrine of creation that attributes a plurality of persons involved in the creation account in Gen 1.26.[22] In 6.11-13a the author of *Barnabas* wants to show that Gen 1.26 on the creation of man did not refer to Adam, but the verse should be interpreted allegorically referring to the new creation of man in and through Christ. The passage in Genesis actually refers to the Christians: 'For the Scripture speaks about us when he says to the Son: "Let us make man according to our image and likeness"' (6.12a). In 6.13a the author adds that the creation of man in Gen 1.26 refers to the eschatological recreation of the Christian: πάλιν σοι ἐπιδείξω, πῶς πρὸς ἡμᾶς λέγει κύριος. δευτέραν πλάσιν ἐπ᾽ ἐσχάτων ἐποίησεν ('Again, I will show you how

---

[18] Papyrus Berolinensis 20915.
[19] Schenke 1999, 53-75.
[20] See Schenke Robinson 2000, 240-1.
[21] Schenke Robinson 2000, 141.
[22] Schenke 1999, 75.

the Lord speaks to us. He made a second creation in the last days'). The last part of this verse is not quoted in the Coptic Book, but it is conjectured.[23]

A second quotation in the Coptic Book is from *Barnabas* 6.17-18 where the 'milk and honey' of the Promised Land refers to the nourishment of the Christian. In the preceding verses the author of *Barnabas* has explained that the Christians are the ones that were brought into the Promised Land through the new birth. The fact that *Barnabas* is quoted as Scripture in the Coptic book shows that the author had read it as belonging to the Bible (perhaps his Bible was the Codex Sinaiticus, which contained *Barnabas* among its writings). Such a valuation of *Barnabas* is only found elsewhere with Clement of Alexandria and with Origen.[24] *Barnabas* has not been attested in the Coptic language until now. The quotations in Papyrus 20915, however, should not be seen as evidence of the existence of a Coptic translation of *Barnabas*. We have to assume that the Greek quotations of *Barnabas* were translated together with the translation of the Coptic book from Greek.[25]

2. *Interpretation of Scripture*

Barnabas is a document of scriptural interpretation, together with an explanation of some post-biblical material. It covers a wide range of topics. The author has added to his exegesis of Scripture a second part to his letter (chapters 19-20), which is a piece of moral teachings of the Christian community, called the *Two Ways*, a tradition which is found in other early Jewish and Christian writings.[26] The author often uses traditional material, which he weaves together with his own comments to make his arguments clear. In the first chapter he states that it is the purpose of his letter to bring the Christians for whom he writes to a 'perfect knowledge' (τελεία γνῶσις). This knowledge is to be found in Scripture and has been revealed in advance to the Christians (3.6; 6.7; 7.1; 11.1). After a discussion on offerings and fasting in chapters 2 and 3 the author concludes in 3.6 with the statement that because God

---

[23] Schenke 1999, 64.
[24] Cf. Schenke 1999, 75.
[25] Cf. Schenke 1999, 74-5.
[26] *Didache*; *Doctrina Apostolorum*; *Apostolic Church Order*; 1QS 3.13-4.26.

foresaw that the people whom He had prepared would believe in all
purity, He revealed everything to the Christians in advance in order
that they should not shipwreck themselves by becoming 'proselytes to
their law'. Here the Christians are the ones who believe in all purity,
and not the Jews. It is the literal interpretation of the Jewish law that
the author rejects. Therefore he says that to become a proselyte to
the Jewish law is equivalent to being shipwrecked.

Whether or not the author had contemporary Jews in mind when
he wrote his letter, he considered literal law observance of the Jews as
a dangerous threat. Therefore he especially warns his readers against
those institutions like circumcision, particular food laws, and observance
of the Sabbath that identify the Jews as a religious people. In chapter
9 the physical circumcision is rejected as belonging to the sphere of
evil. The author attributes the physical circumcision to the deception
of 'an evil angel', and says that God has rejected it, because circumcision in its true sense was always meant to be spiritual and not literal
(9.4). In chapter 10 a literal understanding of the food laws is rejected.
Moses had a correct understanding of the food laws, which are to be
understood spiritually and not literally: 'It is not God's commandment that they should not eat; rather Moses spoke spiritually' (10.2).
The prohibition to eat swine should be understood as a prohibition
not to associate with men who are like swine (10.3). In chapter 15
the observance of the Jewish Sabbath is rejected. The true Sabbath
is the eschatological Sabbath at the end of times. In 16.7 we find a
veiled reference to the Jewish temple, the centre of its religious life, as
a house full of idolatry. The author compares the Jewish temple with
a heathen temple, and implies that God has rejected it, because it is
man-made (16.2). Here the Jewish temple is put on one line with its
heathen equivalent.[27] The true temple of God is the spiritual temple
that is to be found in the Christian community and in the divine
indwelling of the human heart (16.6-10).

2.1. *Methods of interpretation*

The author of *Barnabas* has primarily a spiritual/allegorical interpretation of Scripture, which often seeks to uncover its deeper meaning. His

---

[27] It is quite probable that in 16.3-4 the author refers to the foundation of the
Roman Jupiter-temple on the site of the destroyed Jewish temple in Jerusalem during
Hadrian's reign in 130.

rather intensive use of the allegorical method is seen in his exegesis of the circumcision of Abraham's 318 servants (Gen 14.14), which constitutes a mystical prophecy of Jesus' death on the cross (9.7-9). In *Barnabas* 9.8 an early form of the *nomen sacrum* IH ('Iησοῦς) is probably presupposed. The form IH occurs in the Egerton gospel, one of the Greek manuscripts discovered in Egypt that date to the second century. The use of *nomina sacra*[28] is a Christian invention but is obviously influenced by the Jewish reverence for the name of God. The *nomina sacra* occur in the earliest Christian manuscripts, and this scribal practice arose already in the first century in the church in Jerusalem.[29] The use of *nomina sacra* reflects a primitive Jewish Christian theology such as is found in early Alexandrian Christian literature. C.H. Roberts draws the conclusion from this that Jerusalem is the source of the earliest Egyptian Christianity, a Christianity that was essentially Jewish (see below, p. 261).[30]

The author of *Barnabas* also interprets episodes from the history of Israel typologically in a Christian context. All the events recorded in the Old Testament happened for the sole purpose of their being a prophetic act. The account of Israel's war with Amalek (Exodus 17) with Moses piling up one shield upon another in the midst of the battle and standing with his hands stretched out, did happen for the sole purpose of its being a symbol of the cross and of the one who was crucified on the cross (12.2). Here the Jews are warned that unless they place their hope in Jesus, war will be waged against them forever. The author's argument is supported in verse 3 by a quotation from Isaiah 65.2: 'All day long I have stretched out my hands to a disobedient people who oppose my righteous way', implying that it is Christ himself who is addressing these words from Isaiah to the Jews. The outstretched arms foreshadow, for the author, the crucifixion. In 12.8-9 Joshua, the son of Nun, is a type of Jesus who will cut off all the house of Amalek in the last days (cf. Exod 17.14). Moses actually gave him the name 'Jesus', for the sole purpose that the people might

---

[28] These *nomina sacra* consist of certain proper names and religious terms that are given special treatment in writing, usually by means of abbreviation with superlineation.

[29] For a discussion of the use of *nomina sacra* in early Christian manuscripts see Roberts 1979, 35-46. Cf. Pearson 1986, 133-4.

[30] Roberts 1979, 49-73.

hear that God revealed everything about his Son.[31] Here the whole
event of the story of Joshua fighting Amalek happened for the sole
reason of its being a type of Christ.

Although the author often accompanies passages connected with
the interpretation of Scripture with γνῶσις language (6.9; 9.8; 10.10;
13.7), the letter should not be connected in any way with Gnosticism. It
has sometimes been argued that the author's Christology is somewhat
'docetic' in character.[32] Although the letter falls short of later 'orthodox' standards in its treatment of the pre-existing Son of God who has
come in the flesh, there is no hint in *Barnabas* that Jesus only *seemed*
to come in the flesh, or only *seemed* to suffer. The consistent theme of
Barnabas 5-8 is that it was necessary for the Lord to be manifested and
to suffer and to endure in the flesh.[33] What the author is interested in
is the true Christian sense of the Scriptures as opposed to the Jewish
literal sense, particularly the ritual law, and for this he uses a variety
of methods, including γνῶσις language. The knowledge that the author
wants to communicate is, however, sometimes somewhat esoteric in
character. So he states in 17.2 that there are certain secrets, which
cannot be communicated to those he is addressing, suggesting that the
knowledge he wants to give to them cannot be understood by all.

2.2. *Christians and Jews*

Throughout chapters 2-16 the author is concerned with proving
that his form of Christianity is superior to that of Judaism, at least
the Judaism that he was acquainted with. He sees Christians and
Jews as 'us' and 'them' (2.7; 3.6; 8.7; 10.12; 13.1; 14.1, 4-5). By his
references to the Jews as 'they' (ἐκεῖνοι) and 'them' he expresses his
distance from them. His interpretation of Scripture is constantly set
in opposition to what he takes to be the false literal interpretation of
the Jews, which he rejects. Sometimes he distributes parts of Scripture
between 'us' and 'them'. He then applies the negative statement of a
part of Scripture to the Jews and the positive statement of a part to
the Christians. In chapter 2 he criticises the Jewish sacrificial system.

---

[31] Cf. *Numbers* 13.16 (LXX): καὶ ἐπωνόμασεν Μωυσῆς τὸν Αυση υἱὸν Ναυη Ἰησοῦν.
[32] See Walter Bauer's evaluation of *Barnabas* as essentially 'Gnostic' with a Christology that 'seems docetic'. Bauer 1971, 47-8.
[33] Cf. Kraft 1962, 407.

In 2.7-10 the Jews are commanded not to bear a grudge in their heart against their neighbours and not to love a false oath (Zechariah 8.17), while the Christians know that a sacrifice to God is a broken heart (Psalms 51.17 [LXX 50.19]). In an exposition of the Jewish fasts in chapter 3 the author uses the same device. He divides Isaiah 58.3-10 into two parts whereby verses 4-5 are applied to the Jews and verses 6-10 to the Christians. As in the discussion on sacrifices, the statements addressed to the Jews are in the negative, while the statements addressed to the Christians are in the affirmative (3.1-5). The author explains this method of distributing parts of Scripture between 'us' and 'them' in 5.2: 'For the Scripture concerning him relates partly to Israel and partly to us.' By this device the author wants to show that the Jews misunderstood the law when applying it in its literal sense. Fasting was never meant to be a practical institution. It should be interpreted in a spiritual way.

In an exposition of the ritual of the Jewish Day of Atonement, the author uses some extra-biblical material in 7.6-8, the details of which are to be found in *Mishnah Yoma*.[34] He stresses that the Jews did not understand the meaning of the ritual. The whole ritual refers to the death and second coming of Christ. The two goats of the Day of Atonement (Leviticus 16) who must resemble one another[35] are both types of Christ. In chapter 8 the author gives an exposition of the Jewish rite of the offering and slaughter of the red heifer (Numbers 19.17-22), adding some extra-biblical details. Again, the Jews are the ones who are unable to understand the meaning of the ritual. The whole rite was intended to be a type of Christ who was sacrificed (8.1-2). Thus the author concludes his expositions of these Jewish rituals in 8.7 with the statement: 'So, that these things happened for this reason is obvious to us, but to them they were quite obscure, because they did not listen to the voice of the Lord.' The inability of the Jews to understand the meaning of the Old Testament laws is also stressed in a discussion of the food laws, which the author interprets allegorically. So he states in 10.12: 'But how could those people grasp or understand these things? But we, however, having rightly understood the commandments, explain them as the Lord intended.'

---

[34] *Mishnah Yoma* 4.2; 6.1.

[35] That the two goats must resemble one another is recommended in *Mishnah Yoma* 6.1. It is also found in Justin, *Dialogue* 40.4-5 and Tertullian, *Adversus Iudaeos* 14.9-10.

Familiar concepts in *Barnabas* are the covenant and the law, especially the ritual law. The author has a theory of the one covenant,
which the Jews lost as a result of their idolatry with the golden calf.
The breaking of the tables of the law by Moses cancelled the covenant
with Israel at the moment of its reception (4.6b-8 and 14.2-4). From
then on the covenant is the possession of the Christians. The validity
of the covenant and the law (especially the ritual law) was an issue in
the conflict between Jews and Christians. Christians claimed that the
covenant had been abrogated at the very moment of its reception by
the adulterous act of the Israelites by making the golden calf. Polemical uses of the story of the golden calf are found in early Christian
texts. In these texts the story is used either to attack the Jews for their
idolatrous tendencies or general sinfulness, or to explain why the Jewish ceremonial laws had been given.

In order to understand *Barnabas* in this respect, it might be useful to
sketch the outline of comparable yet differing views in Justin, Irenaeus,
the *Apostolic Constitutions* and in the Gnostic Ptolemaeus. At the end of
Dialogue 18 Justin asks the Jew Trypho why the Christians should not
observe the Jewish rites such as the circumcision of the flesh, the Sab-
baths, and the festivals. In *Dialogue* 19 Justin answers that Christians do
not observe these rites, because they are not essential for all men, but
only for Jews, to mark them off for the suffering they deserve because
of their iniquities. God gave them his laws not because Israel is God's
chosen people, but because this people abandoned God continually.
After the people made a golden calf as an idol in the desert, God,
adapting His laws to that weak people, ordered them to offer sacrifices
to His name, in order to save them from idolatry. For Justin the laws
of the Jews are meant as a punishment, to force them to remember
Him. In *Dialogue* 20 Justin argues with Trypho about the Jewish food
laws. The reason that God gave the Jews these laws is that they would
keep Him before their eyes, for they were always disposed to forget
Him. Here the golden calf incident is not explicitly mentioned, but
it is in the background: 'The people ate and drank, and rose up to
play' (see Exod 32.6). In *Dialogue* 21 Justin quotes an extensive passage
from Ezekiel 20.19-26 confirming again that it is because of the sins of
the people that God imposed upon them the laws: 'Therefore I gave
them statutes that were not good, and judgements whereby they shall
not live' (cf. Ezek 20.25). It is clear that Ezek 20.25 functions here in
the context in which it is proved from the Old Testament that God

punishes his people with commandments.[36] The author of *Barnabas*, however, does not use Ezek 20.25 in his critique of the ritual laws. For the author of *Barnabas* all the laws are part of Scriptures, and they are good laws. Except they have to be interpreted in their original sense, which is spiritual and not literal.

Reference to the golden calf incident is also found in Irenaeus. Irenaeus makes a clear distinction between the Decalogue and the ceremonial law. In his *Adversus Haereses*[37] he writes that at first God warned mankind by *naturalia praecepta*, which he implanted in the hearts of men and which are written in the Decalogue. They are eternal and needing only to be fulfilled, that is developed, extended, enlarged by Christ. It was only after the sin with the golden calf, which was a spiritual return into Egypt (cf. Acts 7.39-40), that Israel received all the other commandments, which were meant to reduce them to slavery. These commandments were afterwards delivered through Moses and imposed upon the people as a punishment for their sins, as is proved by the quotations of Ezek 20.25 and a very long quote from Acts 7.38-43 (Stephen's speech).[38] They are the so-called second law. A more sophisticated theory of a second law is found in the early third-century *Didascalia apostolorum*.[39] The writer of the *Didascalia*[40] comes nearest in his treatment of the law to Irenaeus. Here the law consists of the Ten Words and the judgements which God spoke before the people made the golden calf and served idols. The second law was given to the people after the sin of the golden calf and was abolished with the coming of Christ. Here Ezek 20.25 is also used to show that the second law was given to the people because of their sins. Unless Irenaeus, however, the author of the *Didascalia* leaves no room for the second law as a factor in the spiritual education of the people.[41]

Another early attempt to solve the problem of the law is found in the *Letter to Flora*[42] by the Gnostic teacher Ptolemaeus, a disciple of the famous Valentinus. This early Christian text deals especially with the

---

[36] Cf. Van der Horst 1994, 134.

[37] *Adversus Haereses* 4.15.1.

[38] Cf. Van der Horst 1994, 135.

[39] Connolly 1929.

[40] On the Second Legislation in the *Didascalia* see chapters 1-2 and 26 (Connolly).

[41] For a discussion of the second law in the *Didascalia* see Van der Horst 1994, 135-8.

[42] For the text see Quispel 1966.

law of Moses dividing it into three parts, of which the first part, the law of God, in turn, is divided into three parts: the Decalogue, fulfilled by the Saviour; an imperfect part, abolished by the Saviour; and a third (cultic) part that must be interpreted 'spiritually', that is, allegorically (5.1-7.1). This text, of course, belongs to the Gnostic literature. In 7.2-7 Ptolemaeus reveals his Gnostic stance by identifying the 'God' who gave the law as the Demiurge, the Creator of the world, who is actually inferior to the perfect God, the Father. The *Letter to Flora* has the unique interest that it gives us at some length, and in the form of a complete document, the authentic words of a member of one of the great Gnostic sects.

In *Barnabas* we do not find a division between the Decalogue and the so-called second law. The author of *Barnabas* is familiar with the concept of a second law, but he differs from the treatment of it in Justin, Irenaeus and the *Didascalia*. In *Barnabas* the second law is as much part of Scripture as the Decalogue. The second law is identified with the legislation constantly misunderstood by the Jews, but from the beginning meant for Christians, and given to them alone together with the covenant. Although the author seeks the inward meaning of the ritual law, he refrains from scoffing at its institution as the Gnostics did. He does not say like Justin and Irenaeus that the ritual law was given to the Jews as a punishment for their sins. He says that the Jews did not understand the laws in their original sense. The laws should be interpreted spiritually, and not literally. The author of *Barnabas* has a high respect for the Jewish Scriptures, especially the law. This respect, however, takes the form of a Christian claim to the law and its associated covenant which is at the same time an exclusion of any Jewish claims whatever to the covenant and the law.[43] *Barnabas* is an early example of the allegorical timeless harmonisation of the testaments as can be seen in Origen and his successors in Alexandria, as opposed to the more historical harmonisations found in Justin and Irenaeus where the legislation is divided into moral and ceremonial laws, and where the latter were valid in their literal sense for a limited time, that is the time before Christ.[44]

Some scholars have argued for a similarity between the under-

---

[43] Cf. Horbury 1992, 331.
[44] Cf. Horbury 1992, 330.

standing of the ritual law in *Barnabas* and that entertained by Philo.[45] Especially in chapter 10 on an exposition of the Jewish food laws, the author of *Barnabas* comes close to the spiritualised/ethical readings of the food laws found in Philo[46] and in the *Letter of Aristeas to Philocrates*[47] (c. 150-100 BCE). It seems likely that in *Barnabas* 10 the author has borrowed from a quite common Jewish-Hellenistic tradition of inter-pretation and has given it an anti-Jewish colouring. The same sort of interpretation is to be found in Philo and *Aristeas*, where in an apologetic context, and through allegorical interpretation, the Jewish dietary laws are explained within a Greek ambience. The interpretation of the food laws in *Barnabas* differs, however, from that found in Philo and *Aristeas* in that in *Barnabas* Moses' legislation of the food laws was never meant to be interpreted in a literal sense, but always spiritually. While Philo interprets the food laws allegorically to give a rational defence for the prohibitions against the various animals, he criticises a group of Jews (allegorists) who neglect the letter of the law and derive from it only spiritual truths. They ignore the external observance of the feasts and circumcision.[48] Philo agrees with those allegorists concerning the 'inner meaning of things', but he also stresses to pay heed to the let-ter of the law.[49] In *Aristeas* the ethical interpretation of the food laws may be seen as an apology for the Jewish practice of separation from the Gentiles.[50] But *Aristeas* also presupposes that the Mosaic laws are observed according to their literal meaning. He values both the literal and symbolic meaning of sacrifices.[51] For the author of *Barnabas* the

---

[45] Carleton Paget 1994, 36-8, 150-1; and Hvalvik 1996, 121-2, 133-4.

[46] *De specialibus legibus* 4.100-118; *De agricultura* 131-145.

[47] *Aristeas* 128-171.

[48] *De migratione Abrahami* 89-94. 'Why, we shall be ignoring the sanctity of the Temple and a thousand other things, if we are going to pay heed to nothing except what is shown us by the inner meaning of things. Nay, we should look on all these outward observances as resembling the body, and their inner meaning as resembling the soul' (92-93; English trans. Colson).

[49] In *Questions and Answers on Genesis* Philo first explains the literal meaning of the words in Genesis, and then he goes on to explain its deeper meaning. See 2.18, 20 etc.

[50] 'An additional significance is that we are set apart from all men' (151; English trans. Hadas).

[51] 'Men must take these from the herds and flocks, and must sacrifice tame animals and nothing wild, so that those who offer sacrifices, bearing in mind the symbolic meaning of the legislator, might be conscious of no arrogance in themselves. For it is of the entire character of his own soul that he who brings a sacrifice makes offering' (170; English trans. Hadas).

food laws (including the other laws) should not be understood in their literal sense at all. They should be interpreted in an allegorical/ethical sense. There is no place for a literal understanding of these laws at all in *Barnabas*. The Mosaic laws were always meant to be spiritual and not literal. Moses understood this when he gave these laws to Israel (10.2).

Somehow the author of *Barnabas* is involved in opposition against Jews. Against A. von Harnack[52] who saw the Judaism in *Barnabas* as something entirely abstract, an entity no longer of relevance to the Christian community, recent research has shown that in *Barnabas'* time Judaism, far from coming to an end, had to be reckoned with as a real and active force, and often a rival and competitor of Christianity.[53] Many references in *Barnabas* support the view that the anti-Judaic bias in the letter reflects a split between Christians and Jews. We are told from the beginning not 'to go astray like they did' (2.9), not 'shipwreck ourselves by becoming proselytes to their law' (3.6), not to be like certain people who claim that 'the covenant is both theirs and ours' (4.6). Although the author presents his teaching as 'knowledge' in general, it often involves a criticism of Jews and the Jewish religion in particular. If we say that the author of *Barnabas* was opposed to Judaism, we should be aware, however, that early Judaism appears to have been rather diverse. It would be better then to speak of early Judaisms. As I hope to show elsewhere, it is quite probable that the author of *Barnabas* was not opposed to all Jews and every form of Judaism of the second century,[54] but was especially worried by nationalist Jews who regarded Palestine as their homeland, and who had a strict literal interpretation of the law.[55]

3. Barnabas *in Alexandria*

Barnabas is not often discussed against the background of the origin of Christianity, and Christianity's relation to Judaism in Alexandria. The

---

[52] Harnack 1893, 414.

[53] First published shortly after the Second World War, and now widely cited as the fundamental work in this area, is Marcel Simon's *Verus Israel*. Simon 1986.

[54] Against R. Hvalvik, who sees Judaism pictured in *Barnabas* as a real threat, even as a rival to Christianity. Hvalvik 1996, 326.

[55] From the time of the edict of Claudius in 41 CE a new form of Judaism, not that of *Aristeas* and Philo, arose in Alexandria. Unlike the Hellenised Jews, these nationalist Jews regarded not their *polis*, but Palestine as their homeland. See Tcherikover 1957, 74-93.

evidence for early Christianity and its relationship to Jews and Judaism in Alexandria is rather scanty. It was the absence of any clear reference to Christianity before the time of bishop Demetrius at the beginning of the third century that allowed Walter Bauer to construct his well-known thesis about the heretical origins of Egyptian Christianity.[56] In recent times this thesis has been challenged, particularly in the light of the work of C.H. Roberts, one of the most prominent papyrologists of our time. His study of early Christianity in Egypt called into question Bauer's theory that the earliest type of Christianity in Egypt was heretical and more specifically 'Gnostic'. Roberts maintains that Christianity in Egypt emerged out of a Jewish context (see above, p. 253). He argues that the complete absence of references to Christians in the first and early second century may have arisen from the fact that they were identified with the Jews.[57]

According to B.A. Pearson, in the large and well-established Jewish population that existed in first-century Alexandria, a considerable degree of religious and cultural diversity was found. He refers to the writings of Philo where we can obtain a good picture of the range of attitudes toward the law found among the Jews of Alexandria: 'From a strict literalist interpretation to an espousal of the kind of allegorical interpretation represented by Philo himself, from a total rejection of the Scriptures and their "myths" to a spiritual reading of the Scriptures leading to a rational abandonment of the observances of the ritual law.'[58] Philo himself was loyal to Judaism and its institutions. He was so strict in his emphasis on loyalty to the Jewish ethnic community and its cause, that he had advocated immediate execution of apostates without any formal trial: 'But if any members of the nation betray the honour due to the One they should suffer the utmost penalties ... And it is well that all who have a zeal for virtue should be permitted to exact the penalties offhand and with no delay, without bringing the offender before jury or council.'[59] The evidence from the papyri, inscriptions, and literary sources indicates forms of Judaism often independent and sometimes in conflict with each other.[60]

There were Jews who were involved in Greek philosophy and they

---

[56] Bauer 1934.
[57] Roberts 1979, 47-8.
[58] Pearson 1986, 148.
[59] *De specialibus legibus* 1.54-56 (cf. 1.315-318; English trans. Colson).
[60] MacLennan 1990, 39.

interpreted the Mosaic laws allegorically. Allegorical interpretation of the law must have led to divisions in Diaspora Judaism between conservative Jews who observed the letter of the law and Jews who regarded the letter of the law as peripheral.[61] We have seen that Philo himself testifies to such divisions. After Philo's death (c. 45 CE) the Jewish community in Alexandria went into decline. The Jews rebelled against the Roman protectors.[62] After the destruction of Jerusalem in 70 CE the Jewish population disrupted and disintegrated. The deterioration of the situation of the Jews, and the hatred against them, eventually led to the Jewish revolt (115-117) under Trajan (98-117). The revolt resulted into the almost total extermination of the Egyptian Jews. The main place where Jews are known to have survived is Alexandria.[63]

After the Jewish revolt under Trajan the cultural life of the Jewish communities had changed. Jews with their earlier inclination toward the Hellenistic culture now became more faithful to their national and ancient traditions. From the second century there was a steady correspondence and contact between the Palestinian Rabbis and the Egyptian Jews. Jewish Palestine began to exert a greater influence on the Jewish Diaspora, shaping the Jewish community according to new principles of Judaism, as laid down by the Talmudic authorities. The strivings of the Egyptian Jews towards Hellenism had vanished. Already Philo is the last Hellenistic Jewish author of importance in Alexandrian literature.[64] The lower strata of the Jewish population of Egypt had always been less in touch with the Greeks and more deeply devoted to the national tradition. The Egyptian Jews in the Ptolemaic age, and to a greater extent in the early Roman period, were already divided into two groups, one seeking close contact with Greeks, the other more influenced by Palestinian Jewry and strongly devoted to the ancient national creed and customs. The national trend achieved its final victory in the revolt of 115-117 CE, as a result of which the Egyptian Jews were virtually exterminated.[65]

The Jewish revolt did result in a final split between Jews and Chris-

---

[61] Pearson 1990, 12.
[62] As a consequence of the imposition of the poll-tax, known in Egypt as *laographia*, Alexandrian Jews had good reason of their own to hate Rome. Tcherikover 1957, 60.
[63] Tcherikover 1957, 92-3.
[64] See Tcherikover 1957, 106-7.
[65] Tcherikover 1957, 92.

tians. The earliest Christians of Alexandria are to be placed in the variegated Jewish context of the first century. They probably lived in the same areas of the city as the other Jews, and can be presumed to have participated in the life of the synagogues. They would also have worshipped in house churches.[66] It was not until the early second century that Christians emerged as a group that was distinct from the Jewish community.[67] *Barnabas* is evidence of at least one type of Christianity in Alexandria during the first part of the second century. There were other types of Christianity such as are to be found in other early Christian sources. It is quite probable that the author of *Barnabas* was a Christian convert from Judaism, who was opposed to a form of Judaism with a nationalist tendency and a strict literal interpretation of the law. Perhaps the author wanted to moderate fanatical feelings within and without his community for the hope of the rebuilding of the temple in Jerusalem. Even if for many Jews the Jewish religion had reached a spiritual level and there was no need for animal sacrifices and the rebuilding of a temple, this was not a universal view.[68] The author never mentions the Jews by name, but always refers to them as 'they' or 'them', indicating his distance from them. The author was not a follower of a writer or Christian group of which we still have evidence. Yet his letter was a popular writing in his time, and was read in the churches of Egypt in the second century and after.

Bibliography

Sources

The Apostolic Fathers: Greek Texts and English Translations, J.B. Lightfoot, J.R. Harmer, and M.W. Holmes (1891). Grand Rapids: Baker Books, 1999² (1891¹).
Aristeas to Philocrates (Letter of Aristeas), M. Hadas (Jewish Apocryphal Literature), New York 1951.
Clément d'Alexandrie: Stromate I. Introduction, Traduction et Notes, C. Mondésert and M. Caster (Sources chrétiennes 30), Paris 1951.
Clément d'Alexandrie: Stromate V. Tome I. Introduction, Texte Critique et Index, A. Le Boulluec and P. Voulet (Sources chrétiennes 278), Paris 1981.
Didache (Apostellehre), Barnabasbrief, Zweiter Klemensbrief, Schrift an Diognet, K. Wengst (Schriften des Urchristentums 2), Darmstadt 1984.
Didascalia Apostolorum: The Syriac Version Translated and Accompanied by the Verona Latin

---

[66] Pearson 1986, 150.
[67] Pearson 1986, 145.
[68] See Smallwood 1981, 346-7.

Fragments. With an Introduction and Notes, R.H. Connolly, Oxford 1929.
Eusèbe de Césarée: Histoire ecclésiastique V-VII. Texte Grec, Traduction et Annotation, G. Bardy (Sources chrétiennes 41), Paris 1955.
Eusebius: The History of the Church from Christ to Constantine, G.A. Williamson, New York 1965.
Irenaeus von Lyon: Adversus Haereses IV. Gegen die Häresien IV, N. Brox (Fontes Christiani 8.4), Freiburg 1995.
Iustini Martyris: Dialogus cum Tryphone, Miroslav Marcovich (Patristische Texte und Studien 47), Berlin/New York 1997.
Writings of Justin Martyr, T.B. Falls (The Fathers of the Church; A New Translation 6), Washington D.C. 1977³.
Midrash Rabbah, vol. ii, H. Freedman and M. Simon, London/Bournemouth 1951.
The Mishnah, H. Danby, London 1933/1954.
Origène: Traité des Principes. Tome II (Livres III et IV). Introduction, Texte Critique de la Philocalie et de la Version de Rufin, H. Crouzel and M. Simonetti (Sources chrétiennes 268), Paris 1980.
Origène: Contre Celse. Tome I (Livres I et II). Introduction, Texte Critique, Traduction et Notes, M. Borret (Sources chrétiennes 132), Paris 1967.
Origenes: In Lucam Homiliae. Homilien zum Lukasevangelium, H.-J. Sieben (Fontes Christiani 4.2), Freiburg 1992.
Philo: Works, 12 vols, F.H. Colson, G.H. Whitaker, and R. Marcus (The Loeb Classical Library), Cambridge, Mass./London 1929-53/1981-87.
Ptolémée: Lettre à Flora. Analyse, Texte critique, Traduction, Commentaire et Index Grec, G. Quispel (Sources chrétiennes; Série annexe de Textes non chrétiens 24 bis), Paris 1966².
Tertullianus: Adversus Iudaeos, H. Tränkle, Wiesbaden 1964.

Literature

Bauer, W. 1934. *Rechtgläubigkeit und Ketzerei im ältesten Christentum* (Beiträge zur historischen Theologie 10), Tübingen (1964²).
Bauer, W. 1971. *Orthodoxy and Heresy in Earliest Christianity* (Edited by R.A. Kraft and G. Krodel, Translated by P.J. Achtemeier et al., with Added Appendices by G. Strecker, Philadelphia.
Carleton Paget, J. 1994. *The Epistle of Barnabas: Outlook and Background* (WUNT 2.64), Tübingen.
Dahl, N.A. 1950. 'La terre où coulent le lait et le miel selon Barnabé 6.8-19', in: *Aux sources de la tradition chrétienne: Mélanges offerts à M. Maurice Goguel*, Neuchâtel/Paris, 62-70.
De Lange, N.R.M. 1976. *Origen and the Jews: Studies in Jewish-Christian Relations in Third-Century Palestine* (University of Cambridge Oriental Publications 25), Cambridge.
Harnack, A. 1893. *Geschichte der altchristlichen Literatur bis Eusebius*, i.1, *Die Überlieferung und der Bestand*, Leipzig (1958).
Heer, J.M. 1908. *Die Versio Latina des Barnabasbriefes und ihr Verhältnis zur altlateinischen Bibel*, Freiburg im Breisgau.
Horbury, W. 1992. 'Jewish-Christian Relations in Barnabas and Justin Martyr', in: J.D.G. Dunn (ed.), *Jews and Christians: The Parting of the Ways* AD *70 to 135* (WUNT 66), Tübingen, 315-45.
Hvalvik, R. 1996. *The Struggle for Scripture and Covenant: The Purpose of the Epistle of Barnabas and Jewish-Christian Competition in the Second Century* (WUNT 2.82), Tübingen.
Klijn, A.F.J. 1986. 'Jewish Christianity in Egypt', in: B.A. Pearson and J.E. Goehring

(eds), *The Roots of Egyptian Christianity* (Studies in Antiquity and Christianity), Philadelphia, 161-75.

Kraft, R.A. 1962. Review of 'P. Prigent, *Les Testimonia dans le christianisme primitif: L'Épître de Barnabé 1-XVI et ses Sources*', *Journal of Theological Studies* 13 (1962) 401-8.

Kraft, R.A. 1965. *Barnabas and the Didache* (The Apostolic Fathers; A New Translation and Commentary 3), New York.

Lilla, S.R.C. 1971. *Clement of Alexandria: A Study in Christian Platonism and Gnosticism* (Oxford Theological Monographs), London.

MacLennan, R.S. 1990. *Early Christian Texts on Jews and Judaism* (Brown Judaic Studies 194), Atlanta.

Metzger, B.M. 1989³. *The Canon of the New Testament: Its Origin, Development and Significance*, Oxford.

Pearson, B.A. 1986. 'Earliest Christianity in Egypt: Some Observations', in: B.A. Pearson and J.E. Goehring (eds), *The Roots of Egyptian Christianity* (Studies in Antiquity and Christianity) Philadelphia, 132-56.

Pearson, B.A. 1990. *Gnosticism, Judaism, and Egyptian Christianity* (Studies in Antiquity and Christianity), Philadelphia.

Roberts, C.H. 1979. *Manuscript, Society and Belief in Early Christian Egypt*, London.

Schenke, H.-M. 1999. 'Der Barnabasbrief im Berliner "Koptischen Buch" (P. Berol. 20915)', *Enchoria* 25 (1999) 53-75.

Schenke Robinson, G. 2000. 'Sethianism and the Doctrine of Creation in a Partially Restored Coptic Codex (Papyrus Berolinensis 20915)', *Le Muséon* 113 (2000) 239-57.

Schreckenberg, H. 1995³. *Die christlichen Adversus-Judaeos-Texte und ihr literarisches und historisches Umfeld (1-11. Jh.)* (Europäische Hochschulschriften 23/172), Frankfurt am Main.

Simon, M. 1964. *Verus Israel: A Study of Relations between Christians and Jews in the Roman Empire (135-425)*, London (1986).

Smallwood, E.M. 1981². *The Jews under Roman Rule from Pompey to Diocletian: A Study in Political Relations* (Studies in Judaism in Late Antiquity 20), Leiden.

Tcherikover, V.A. (ed.) 1957. *Corpus Papyrorum Judaicarum*, i, Cambridge, Mass.

Trigg, J.W. 1992. 'Origen', in: *The Anchor Bible Dictionary*, v, 42-8.

Van der Horst, P.W. 1994. *Hellenism-Judaism-Christianity: Essays on Their Interaction* (Contributions to Biblical Exegesis & Theology 8), Kampen.

PAUL'S RAPTURE TO PARADISE IN EARLY CHRISTIAN LITERATURE

Riemer Roukema

Our knowledge of early Christianity sometimes depends on fortuitous scraps of information. In 2 Corinthians 12.1-10 Paul commits several interesting confidences to paper, which would have remained unknown had he not been so terribly provoked by some itinerant evangelists who were active in the Corinthian church. Reluctantly, as it seems, he tells of visions and revelations (ὀπτασίαι καὶ ἀποκαλύψεις), since apparently his adversaries had boasted of their own ecstatic experiences and had accused Paul of being deficient in this respect. First, Paul tells about a man in Christ—i.e., Paul himself—who had been caught up (ἡρπάγη) to the third heaven and to paradise, where he had heard ineffable words (ἄρρητα ῥήματα) that man may not declare. He dates this experience fourteen years ago, which goes back to a fairly unknown period of his life, in the beginning of the forties of the first century CE. He professes not to know if he remained in his body in this experience, nor does he explain if his rapture to the third heaven is identical with his rapture to paradise, nor what exactly is his cosmology: did he assume that the third heaven was the highest one, or was it one of seven, or more? Was paradise in the third heaven or elsewhere? In spite of these and other questions that he leaves unanswered, Paul makes it clear to the Corinthian Christians that he is not wholly uninitiated into this type of mystical experiences. Next, he continues with another confidence that seems closely related to his rapture to heaven and to paradise.[1] He tells about a thorn in his flesh, an angel of Satan who harasses him, in order to save him from being too elated (2 Cor 12.7). Thirdly, he testifies to the Lord's answer to his threefold prayer that his tormentor leave him; the answer was, 'My grace is sufficient for you, for my power is made perfect in weakness' (2 Cor 12.9).

---

[1] Since it seems most likely that Paul speaks of one rapture and not of two, we will use the singular 'rapture' and not the plural.

It is true that in his other epistles Paul does sometimes refer to
visions and revelations, so that his confidences in 2 Corinthians 12.1-10
do not come as a bolt from the blue. He says that he has seen Jesus
and that Christ appeared to him (1 Cor 9.1; 15.8). He claims that
he did not receive the gospel from man, but through a revelation (δι'
ἀποκαλύψεως) of Jesus Christ (Gal 1.12). When after a long period he
went again to Jerusalem (coincidentally fourteen years after his former
visit), he went there according to a revelation (κατὰ ἀποκάλυψιν; Gal
2.1-2). Once he mentions in passing the possibility of being 'beside
ourselves' (εἴτε γὰρ ἐξέστημεν ...; 2 Cor 5.13), by which he most
likely alludes to his ecstatic experiences.[2]

Yet in these short references Paul neither informs us about his
rapture to the third heaven and to paradise nor about his struggle
with Satan's messenger and the Lord's answer to his prayer. We may
be grateful to Paul's adversaries for having provoked him to such an
extent that he threw off his usual reticence about the revelations he
received and that he raised a corner of the veil, for these confidences
give us a deeper insight into Paul's biography. Moreover, the book of
Acts confirms that Paul regularly had visions, but historically speaking
these testimonies are less reliable, since the author might have piously
attributed these experiences to his spiritual hero.[3]

The pericope of 2 Corinthians 12.1-10 has been studied from many
angles. To mention only some publications from the last decades: Alan
F. Segal and C.R.A. Morray-Jones associated Paul's rapture with Jew-
ish merkabah mysticism,[4] but Peter Schäfer denied this connection.[5]
James D. Tabor collected testimonies to similar journeys to heaven
from the Mesopotamian, Greek, Roman, and Jewish cultures, and
Bernard Heininger wrote an interesting book on 'Paul the Visionary'.[6]
Recently, J.R. Harrison analysed the two 'Apocalypses of Paul' that

---

[2] R.P. Martin, *2 Corinthians* (Word Biblical Commentary 40), Waco, Texas 1986,
126-7.

[3] Acts 9.3-6; 16.9; 18.9-10; 22.6-10; 22.17-21; 23.11; 26.12-18; 27.23.

[4] A.F. Segal, *Paul the Convert: The Apostolate and Apostasy of Saul the Pharisee*, New
Haven 1990, 34-71; C.R.A. Morray-Jones, 'Paradise Revisited (2 Cor 12.1-12): The
Jewish Mystical Background of Paul's Apostolate', *Harvard Theological Review* 86 (1993)
177-217, 265-92.

[5] P. Schäfer, 'New Testament and Hekhalot Literature: The Journey into Heaven
in Paul and in Merkavah Mysticism', *Journal of Jewish Studies* 35 (1984) 19-35.

[6] J.D. Tabor, *Things Unutterable: Paul's Ascent to Paradise in its Greco-Roman, Judaic,
and Early Christian Contexts*, Lanham, New York 1986; B. Heininger, *Paulus als Visionär:
Eine religionsgeschichtliche Studie* (Herders Biblische Studien 9), Freiburg 1996.

were inspired by Paul's remarks on his heavenly journey.[7]

The present paper pursues the investigation how Paul's notice on his rapture to heaven and to paradise was received and imitated in early Christianity, both 'Catholic' and 'Gnostic'. We will not only examine some literary references and comments, but we will also investigate if Paul's testimony to this tradition according to which one could be caught up to heaven has been used as proof of the legitimacy of similar experiences. Besides analysing these references to Paul's rapture, we will also briefly evaluate them and go into the hermeneutical question how far they can be considered faithful to Paul's intention to be reticent about his ecstatic or mystical experiences. This implies that, in our opinion, Paul's reluctance to share such experiences is sincere and not only a rhetorical device. As far as the dating of the sources and their authors can be established, they will be presented more or less in a chronological order.

The 'Gnostic' Apocalypse of Paul

The fifth Nag Hammadi Codex contains an *Apocalypse of Paul* that is apparently inspired by the apostle's confidences in 2 Corinthians 12.1-4, although it does not explicitly quote this text. The *Apocalypse* may have been written in the second century.[8] In the Coptic manuscript several lines and words are lacking, but in general the plot has been well preserved.

The *Apocalypse* tells that, when Paul stood on 'the mountain of Jericho', he met a little child, i.e. the risen Christ who is also the Holy Spirit, who exhorted him to let his mind awaken and to know the hidden things (ΝⲈⲦϨⲎⲠ) in those that are visible. He told Paul to go to Jerusalem, to his fellow apostles (cf. Gal 1.18; 2.1-10), who are called 'elect spirits'. Then Paul saw them greeting him (18.3-22; 19.10-20). Without any transition, we read that 'the Holy [Spirit] who was

---

[7] J.R. Harrison, 'In Quest of the Third Heaven: Paul & his Apocalyptic Imitators', *Vigiliae Christianae* 58 (2004) 24-55; see also H.J. Klauck, 'Die Himmelfahrt des Paulus (2 Kor 12,2-4) in der koptischen Paulusapokalypse aus Nag Hammadi (NHC V/2)', *Studien zum Neuen Testament und seiner Umwelt A* 10 (1985), 151-90.

[8] Nag Hammadi Codex V.2; edition and introduction by W.R. Murdock and G.W. MacRae, 'The Apocalypse of Paul', in: D.M. Parrott (ed.), *Nag Hammadi Codices V.2-5 and VI with Papyrus Berolinensis 8502, 1 and 4* (Nag Hammadi Studies 11), Leiden 1979, 47-63.

speaking with [him] caught him up ([ⲁϥ]ⲧⲱⲣⲡ̄ ⲙ̄ⲙⲟϥ) on high to the third heaven, and he passed beyond to the fourth [heaven]' (19.20-25).[9] Apart from the title, 'Apocalypse of Paul', this is in fact all that reminds us of the wording of 2 Corinthians 12.1-4.

Next, the Holy Spirit told Paul to look at his likeness upon the earth. This probably means that he was asked to look at his own body, for it is told that when Paul gazed down he saw those who were upon the earth and the twelve apostles at his right hand and at his left (19.26-20.4); this implies that he also saw himself, i.e. his body. The uncertainty of 2 Corinthians 12.2-3, 'whether in the body or out of the body I do not know', is thus subtly removed in this *Apocalypse*. Its implicit message is that Paul was caught up without his physical body.[10]

In the fourth heaven Paul saw angels whipping a soul. Because of its sins committed in the body it was cast down to another body (20.5-21.22). Invited by the Spirit and accompanied by the other apostles Paul went up to the fifth heaven, where he saw angels goading the souls on to judgment (21.22-22.10). Via the sixth heaven the Spirit led him up to the seventh heaven, where he met an old man sitting on a throne brighter than the sun. After a short dialogue about Paul's origin and destination he gave a password and a sign to the old man, who was thus forced to let Paul go up to the eighth heaven (22.11-24.1). There the twelve apostles greeted him. Finally, Paul went up to the ninth and the tenth heaven, where he greeted his fellow spirits (24.1-8).[11]

Compared with Paul's own words in 2 Corinthians 12.1-4, it is striking that neither paradise nor the ineffable words recur in this *Apocalypse*, let alone the thorn in the flesh and the angel of Satan mentioned in 2 Corinthians 12.7. Paul's original confidence about his rapture appears to be used as a pretext for writing an account of the heavenly journey of his soul or spirit, which should serve as a Gnostic model, either of a mystical experience during one's life, or of the vicissitudes of the soul or spirit after the death of the body.[12] Moreover, an important theme

---

[9] Translation Murdock and MacRae, 'Apocalypse', 53.

[10] Harrison, 'Quest', 28. Less likely is the initial interpretation of Klauck, 'Himmelfahrt', 169, who suggests that Paul's likeness upon the earth is 'wohl allgemein die Menschen'. Later on he identifies Paul's likeness with his body (p. 177).

[11] For a broader analysis and interpretation, see Klauck, 'Himmelfahrt', 159-90; Harrison, 'Quest', 28-32.

[12] Cf. the *First Apocalypse of James* (Nag Hammadi Codex V.3) 32.28-36.1. Other

of this *Apocalypse* appears to be that Paul is depicted on the same level as the twelve apostles.[13]

Patristic testimonies to Gnostic views

Several Church Fathers testify to Gnostics who related Paul's rapture with their own knowledge. Hippolytus of Rome's report on the Naassenes, 'who call themselves γνωστικοί',[14] informs us that their view of spiritual regeneration, resurrection, and divinization included that one should enter into heaven through a gate.[15] They said that this was the gate of which Paul wrote that 'he was caught up by an angel and had ascended to the second and third heaven, into paradise, and that he has beheld what he has beheld and has heard ineffable words that man may not declare'.[16] It is remarkable that the Naassenes added an angel, the second heaven, and visions to Paul's own testimony. Hippolytus does not clarify whether they located paradise in the third heaven. However that may be, according to his report the Naassenes identified the ineffable words that Paul heard with their own secret mysteries, of which Paul—as they understood it—also wrote in 1 Corinthians 2.13-14, 'which <also we declare> not in words taught by human wisdom, but in those taught by the Spirit, comparing spiritual things with spiritual. But the psychic man does not receive the things of the Spirit of God, for they are folly to him'.[17] We may conclude that the Naassenes' entrance through the heavenly gate should not be interpreted as an ascent of the soul or spirit after the death of the body, but as a mystical experience after which one was considered initiated into the secret knowledge.

---

testimonies of persons 'caught up' (ⲧⲱⲣⲡ) occur in the *Paraphrase of Sem* (Nag Hammadi Codex VII.1) 1.7-16; *Allogenes* (Nag Hammadi Codex XI.3) 58.28-37.

[13] If the author understood the description ὑπερλίαν ἀπόστολοι in 2 Cor 11.5 and 12.11 as a reference to the twelve apostles, which was a common interpretation among the Church Fathers of the fourth century (e.g. John Chrysostom, *Hom. in secundam epistulam ad Corinthios* 23.3; Patrologia Graeca 61, col. 556), then he also confirms Paul's remark in these verses that he was not inferior to these 'superlative apostles'.

[14] Hippolytus, *Refutatio Omnium Haeresium* 5.2; 5.11 (ed. M. Marcovich, Patristische Texte und Studien 25).

[15] *Refutatio* 5.8.18-24.

[16] *Refutatio* 5.8.25.

[17] *Refutatio* 5.8.26. In Marcovich' edition the words 'also we declare' (καὶ λαλοῦμεν) are added from 1 Cor 2.13.

In his report on Basilides of Alexandria Hippolytus quotes, with
a minor change, Paul's words, 'I heard (ἤκουσα) ineffable words that
man may not declare'.[18] This quotation figures in a detailed report of
Basilides' alleged teachings that we shall not fully discuss here.[19] Suffice
it to note that, according to Hippolytus, Basilides assumed that once
there was an absolute Nothing that could not even be called ineffable
(ἄρρητον), since it was 'above every name that is named' (Eph 1.21).[20]
After an elaborate exposé on the creation of the Ogdoad that is ineffable, and the Hebdomad that can be enunciated (is ῥητός), Hippolytus
relates the coming of the Light of the Gospel to the Hebdomad, which
is the planetary world to which the earth belongs.[21] In this context
the report refers to the revelation of 'the mystery that was not made
known to previous generations' (Eph 3.4-5), of which it is written, 'by
revelation the mystery was made known to me' (Eph 3.3), as well as
to the ineffable words that Paul heard.[22] It appears that Basilides, or
the Gnostics who appealed to him, pretended to know the contents
of these ineffable words and related them to their view of salvation
and illumination.

Epiphanius of Salamis confirms that Gnostic circles connected
their doctrines with Paul's testimony to his rapture. He informs us
that Cainites had fabricated a writing in the name of Paul, full of
ineffable deeds (ἀρρητουργίας ἔμπλεον), entitled the *Ascension of Paul*
(᾽Αναβατικὸν Παύλου), which allegedly contained the ineffable words
Paul heard in the third heaven.[23]

Irenaeus of Lyons

In Irenaeus' discussion of the Valentinians' beliefs he ridicules their
cosmology, according to which the Demiurge reigned over the seven

---

[18] *Refutatio* 7.26.7.
[19] See the analysis of *Refutatio* 7.20-27 by W.A. Löhr, *Basilides und seine Schule:
Eine Studie zur Theologie- und Kirchengeschichte des zweiten Jahrhunderts* (Wissenschaftliche
Untersuchungen zum Neuen Testament 83), Tübingen 1996, 284-323, who concludes that these teachings were attributed to Basilides, but did not originate from
him personally.
[20] *Refutatio* 7.20.1-3.
[21] *Refutatio* 7.25.4.
[22] *Refutatio* 7.26.7.
[23] Epiphanius, *Panarion Haeresium* 38.2.5 (Griechische Christliche Schriftsteller
31).

heavens of the Hebdomad, above which there should be the intermediate sphere of the Mother Achamoth and the Pleroma. For what
profit would Paul have had of his rapture to the third heaven and to
paradise, which were supposed to be under the power of the Demiurge, if in fact he should have beheld and heard the mysteries that,
according to the Valentinians, are above the Demiurge? But if Paul
had not ascended higher than the third heaven, Irenaeus concludes
that the Valentinians will not ascend above the seventh heaven, since
they are certainly not superior to the apostle.[24]

It has been contended that Irenaeus reacts here to a Valentinian
speculation on 2 Corinthians 12.2-4.[25] Yet a careful analysis of Irenaeus' account proves that actually he does not refer to explicit Gnostic
speculations on Paul's ascent, but constructs and refutes a hypothetical
Gnostic account of Paul's ascension.[26]

Irenaeus shares the common opinion that there are seven heavens.[27]
In his account of Paul's ascent he appears to equate the third heaven
and paradise. In his view, it was certainly possible that Paul's body
was included in the rapture.[28] He maintains that the ineffable words
that Paul heard did not come from a psychic Demiurge, but from the
Spirit of God.[29] Moreover, it is noteworthy that he shares the Platonic
idea that in spite of all the properties one may ascribe to God, God
is above all these and therefore ineffable (*inenarrabilis*).[30]

---

[24] Irenaeus, *Adversus Haereses* 2.30.7 (Sources Chrétiennes 294). See the analysis
by R. Noormann, *Irenäus als Paulusinterpret: Zur Rezeption und Wirkung der paulinischen
und deuteropaulinischen Briefe im Werk des Irenäus* (Wissenschaftliche Untersuchungen zum
Neuen Testament II.66), Tübingen 1994, 106-8.

[25] Murdock and MacRae, 'Apocalypse', 49.

[26] M. Kaler, L. Painchaud, M.P. Bussières, 'The Coptic Apocalypse of Paul, Irenaeus' Adversus Haereses 2.30.7, and the Second Century Battle for Paul's Legacy',
Journal of Early Christian Studies 12 (2004) 173-93.

[27] Irenaeus, *Demonstratio Apostolicae Praedicationis* 9 (Sources Chrétiennes 62).

[28] *Adversus Haereses* 2.30.7 (Sources Chrétiennes 294); see the commentary by A.
Rousseau and L. Doutreleau, Sources Chrétiennes 293, pp. 331-2. Cf. also *Adversus
Haereses* 5.5.1 (Sources Chrétiennes 153).

[29] *Adversus Haereses* 2.30.8 (Sources Chrétiennes 294). Rousseau and Doutreleau,
Sources Chrétiennes 293, p. 332, explain *Spiritus Dei* as an explicative genitive ('le
Dieu Esprit'), but since Irenaeus may allude to the Spirit's unutterable intercessions
of Rom 8.26 (τὸ πνεῦμα ὑπερεντυγχάνει στεναγμοῖς ἀλαλήτοις), it is preferable to
translate 'the Spirit of God'.

[30] *Adversus Haereses* 2.13.4 (Sources Chrétiennes 294); see E. Osborn, 'Irenaeus
on God—Argument and Parody', in: M.F. Wiles, E.J. Yarnold (eds.), *Studia Patristica*
36, Louvain 2001, 271-81 (p. 272).

Tertullian of Carthage

In comparison with Irenaeus, Tertullian reacts more explicitly to the claim of heretics that they knew what had been revealed to Paul when he was caught up. He stresses that it is impossible that what Paul heard in the third heaven and in paradise has changed his teaching, since these revelations were not to be communicated to any human being. He ironically argues that, if a heresy claims to know what these revelations were about, then either Paul had betrayed the secret, or someone else had been caught up to paradise and was permitted to declare what was forbidden to Paul.[31]

Clement of Alexandria

In a similar vein, Clement of Alexandria criticizes heretical Gnostics who pretended to know 'what no eye has known, nor has entered into the mind of man' (cf. 1 Cor 2.9); in Clement's view, the knowledge from face to face (1 Cor 13.12) will be granted us only after our departure from earthly life. He wonders how Gnostics can pretend to know 'what no ear has ever heard' (cf. 1 Cor 2.9), but he is willing to except the ear that was caught up to the third heaven. However, he awkwardly subjoins that this ear was commanded to keep silent.[32] Thus Clement excluded the possibility that the heretics knew the ineffable words heard by Paul. These remarks occur in his instruction of newly baptised Christians.

In his miscellaneous essays for advanced Christians Clement points to the consensus of Moses, Plato, and Orpheus, that God is invisible and ineffable.[33] In his view this is confirmed by Paul's testimony to his rapture to the third heaven and 'from there' (κἀκεῖθεν) to paradise. Clement concludes that one begins to designate the divinity by words only above the third heaven, and that it is the task of 'those up there' to initiate the elect souls.[34] By 'those up there' Clement

---

[31] Tertullian, *De Praescriptione Haereticorum* 24.5-6 (Corpus Christianorum Series Latina 1; Sources Chrétiennes 46). The same argument is used by Augustine, *Tractatus in Evangelium Ioannis* 98.8 (Corpus Christianorum, Series Latina 36).

[32] Clement, *Paedagogus* 1.36.6-37.1 (Sources Chrétiennes 70).

[33] Clement, *Stromateis* 5.78 (Sources Chrétiennes 278).

[34] *Stromateis* 5.79.1.

means the angels above the third heaven whose task it is to instruct the ascending souls.[35]

In his worldview there are seven heavenly spheres, above which there is the eighth sphere of the fixed stars and the intelligible world.[36] Because he includes 'from there' in his free quotation of 2 Corinthians 12.2-4, he apparently assumes that paradise is above the third heaven, but he does not locate it more specifically. He may have shared the Valentinian view that paradise was in the fourth heaven.[37]

Like Irenaeus, Clement agreed with the Platonic view that God himself is ineffable. Unlike the heretic Gnostics he did not pretend to know anything about the revelations granted to Paul.

Origen of Alexandria

Origen often refers and alludes to Paul's rapture and to the ineffable words he heard. Once he notes the question why Paul could not say whether his rapture took place in the body or out the body, but he does not go into it.[38] In those allusions that contain a location of the revelation imparted to Paul, Origen repeatedly mentions only the third heaven and omits paradise,[39] even though he says twice, like Clement, that the apostle 'was caught up to the third heaven and *from there* to paradise', where he heard the ineffable words.[40] However, we have this version only in Rufinus' translation (*et inde in paradisum*), which may not be completely trustworthy on such details. In his interpretation of 1 Thessalonians 4.17 Origen explains that Paul heard the ineffable words because he was caught up to the *third* heaven and not just to heaven.[41] In his book *On First Principles* he surmises that paradise is

---

[35] Thus A. Le Boulluec, Sources Chrétiennes 279, p. 259.

[36] *Stromateis* 4.159.2; 5.106.2-4; 7.57.5 (Sources Chrétiennes 463; 278; 428).

[37] Clement, *Excerpta e Theodoto* 51.1 (Sources Chrétiennes 23); cf. Irenaeus, *Adversus Haereses* 1.5.2 (Sources Chrétiennes 264).

[38] Origen, *Contra Celsum* 1.48 (Sources Chrétiennes 132).

[39] Origen, *De Oratione* 1 (Griechische Christliche Schriftsteller 3); *Hom. in Josue* 23.4 (Sources Chrétiennes 71); *Hom. in Psalmos* 38.1.8 (Sources Chrétiennes 411); *Contra Celsum* 1.48 (Sources Chrétiennes 132); *Philocalia* 15.19 (Sources Chrétiennes 302). Of these texts, *De Oratione*, *Contra Celsum*, and *Philocalia* have been preserved in Greek.

[40] Origen, *Comm. in Canticum* 1.5.6 (Sources Chrétiennes 375); *Comm. in Romanos* 10.43 (Aus der Geschichte der Lateinischen Bibel 34).

[41] Origen, *Comm. in Thessalonicenses* III; in Jerome, *Epistula* 119.10 (ed. Labourt VI, p. 117).

a place on the earth located in heaven, where the souls of deceased saints go after death, in order to receive instruction before they ascend to the higher heavenly spheres.[42] Elsewhere in this book he deals with 'some people' who referred to a book of Baruch that says (in a text unknown to us) that there are seven heavens. They assumed that the sphere of the fixed stars above the seven heavens is the heaven promised to God's people. For his own view Origen refers to his early *Commentary on Genesis* 1.1, but this is lost.[43] In his apology *Against Celsus* he notes that the Scriptures accepted in the churches of God do not declare that there are seven heavens or any other definite number of them, but only speak of 'heavens'.[44] It may be concluded that Origen does not attach much value to the question where exactly Paul heard the secret words.

In a fragment from Origen's *Commentary on Genesis* that has been preserved (on Gen 1.14), he says with regard to astrology that 'our wise men' are taught the unutterable things (τὰ ἀπόρρητα) by the Spirit of God. He then quotes Paul, 'I heard ineffable words that man may not declare', and explains that these sages knew about solstices, the alternation of the seasons, year cycles, and the positions of the stars.[45] It appears that in this early commentary Origen relates the ineffable words to cosmological knowledge. Although in later works Origen seems well aware that the ineffable words revealed to Paul might not be declared,[46] he says in a sermon on the promised land as mapped in the book of Joshua that Paul shared the secret knowledge revealed to him with his intimate collaborators like Timothy and Luke. He explains that the ineffable words might not be declared *to men* (*hominibus*) and interprets this as carnal men, referring to Paul's reproach, 'are you not men and do you not walk according to man?' (cf. 1 Cor 3.3-4). Origen even knows that the ineffable words deal with heavenly Jerusalem, Zion, Bethlehem, Hebron, and so on. In his view, Paul reminds Timothy of these ineffable words, saying 'remember the words

---

[42] Origen, *De Principiis* 2.11.6; cf. 2.3.6-7; 3.6.8 (ed. H. Görgemanns and H. Karpp). This interpretation was undoubtedly inspired by Luke 23.43, where Jesus says to the repentant criminal: 'today you will be with me in paradise'.

[43] *De Principiis* 2.3.6.

[44] Origen, *Contra Celsum* 6.21; 23 (Sources Chrétiennes 147).

[45] Origen, *Comm. in Genesin* III, in *Philocalia* 23.19 (Sources Chrétiennes 226)

[46] Origen, *De Oratione* 2.3 (Griechische Christliche Schriftsteller 3); *Hom. in Exodum* 4.2 (Sources Chrétiennes 321); *Hom. in Psalmos* 38.1.8 (Sources Chrétiennes 411); *Comm. in Johannem* 13.28-29; 34; 58; 316; 20.304; 32.351 (Sources Chrétiennes 222; 290; 385).

that you have heard from me, and entrust them to faithful men who are able to teach others also' (cf. 2 Tim 2.2, 8).[47] In his *Commentary on Canticles* Origen supposes that the secrets Paul heard were encouragements to make progress and to persevere, in order to be able to enter the King's chamber (Cant 1.4).[48] In general Origen assumes that there was a secret, unwritten knowledge, which the Scriptures do not explicitly teach even though they refer to it,[49] and which is known to advanced Christians.[50]

As for God's ineffability, Celsus pretended to uphold the Platonic view that God is ineffable (ἄρρητος) and unnameable (ἀκατονόμαστος), but Origen reacts that Plato said that God cannot be declared *to all*, which implies that Plato considered God ῥητός for a few. Origen basically agrees with Celsus that God is ineffable, and even adds that there are also other ineffable beings inferior to God, for which he points to Paul's plural ἄρρητα ῥήματα. Yet Origen also maintains that in spite of God's ineffability, he revealed himself in his incarnate Son and Word.[51]

As far as we know, Origen did not criticize any heretical interpretation of Paul's rapture. From a formal point of view, his opinion that Paul transmitted the ineffable words to his fellow workers, and his recognition of a secret, unwritten doctrine, are close to the Gnostic presumption to know Paul's secret teaching. However, Origen would not agree with the contents of the Gnostic knowledge.

Mani

So far, Hippolytus' account of the Naassenes was the only testimony in which Paul's rapture was referred to as an example to be imitated. The first book that first-hand defends the legitimacy of heavenly visions with reference to Paul's rapture is the *Mani Codex*. This tiny booklet

---

[47] Origen, *Hom. in Josue* 23.4 (Sources Chrétiennes 71).

[48] Origen, *Com. in Canticum* 1.5.6 (Sources Chrétiennes 375).

[49] Origen, *Com. in Johannem* 13.30; 34; 58; 316 (Sources Chrétiennes 222); *Contra Celsum* 6.6 (Sources Chrétiennes 147); *Philocalia* 15.19 (Sources Chrétiennes 302). Other texts that, in Origen's view, refer to unwritten secrets are, e.g., Ezek 2.9-3.2; Mark 4.34; 1 Cor 2.9; 4.6; 13.12; Rev 10.4; 10.9-10.

[50] Origen, *Fragmenta in Ephesios* 8 (ad Eph 1.13; ed. J.A.F. Gregg); cf. *De Principiis* 2.7.4 (ed. Görgemanns and Karpp).

[51] Origen, *Contra Celsum* 7.42-43 (Sources Chrétiennes 150); cf. Plato, *Timaeus* 28c.

has probably been translated from Aramaic into Greek in Egypt in the mid-fourth century CE, and contains most valuable information about Mani's life. It may originally have been compiled in the beginning of the fourth century, but it unmistakably contains older parts.[52] It testifies that Mani had experienced a rapture in which his personal angel (σύζυγος) 'revealed to me mysteries that are hidden to the world and that no man may either see or hear'.[53] In the damaged manuscript he is quoted thus: 'he revealed to me the truest and unutterable (ἀπορρήτους) [teachings]', and as speaking of 'height and depth, rest and punishment', which seems to be part of the contents of the revelation.[54] In order to justify Mani's rapture and revelations, the author of this part—probably Mani's disciple Baraies, from the third century—quotes the apocalypses of Adam, Seth, Enosh, Sem, and Enoch, all of which testify to the raptures and revelations granted to the respective patriarchs.[55] Finally he refers to Paul and quotes an abbreviated version of 2 Corinthians 12.1-5, from which he omits the third heaven (60.30-61.14). As a further proof that, like Mani, Paul too had received revelations, Galatians 1.11-12 is quoted freely, 'I show you, brothers, the Gospel that I preached to you, that I did not receive it from man, but through a revelation of Jesus Christ' (61.15-22). Then the author mentions Paul's rapture to the third heaven and to paradise; the damaged manuscript may originally have read that Paul was caught up [ὡς ἐκ]τὸς ἑ[αυτοῦ], which means that he was out of the body. The author affirms that the apostle wrote in riddles (αἰνιγματωδῶς, cf. 1 Cor 13.12) about his rapture and apostleship to those who were initiated with him into the secrets (ἀπόκρυφα) (61.22-62.9).

After these references to authoritative texts, a letter of Mani to his disciples in Edessa is quoted, in which he testifies to his divine vocation and to the ineffable things (ἀπόρρητα) revealed to him. These secrets dealt with the heavenly Father, Mani's pre-existence, and the foundation of good and evil works (64.8-65.18). According to a quotation from Mani's *Gospel* (εὐαγγέλιον) he wrote that he had hidden these secrets

---

[52] L. Koenen and C. Römer, *Der Kölner Mani-Codex: Über das Werden seines Leibes. Kritische Edition* (Papyrologica Coloniensia 14), Opladen 1988, p. xv.
[53] *Mani Codex* 43.4-7; other references to Mani's rapture in 46.4-5; 47.13-48.14; 63.13-15; 70.10-17.
[54] *Mani Codex* 35.21-36.2; 43.1-4.
[55] *Mani Codex* 48.16-60.12; again in 71.1-72.7.

from sects and pagans, but revealed them to his disciples.[56]

This Codex shows that Mani's first disciples appealed to Paul's rapture as a proof of the legitimacy of their master's experience of rapture and revelation. Most probably this appeal originates from Mani himself. It should be noted that neither the precise location of the third heaven or paradise is considered important, nor does Mani claim to know the ineffable words that were revealed to Paul. Furthermore, it seems that in Manicheism Mani's rapture remained an isolated phenomenon, since we do not know about similar experiences among his adherents. Apparently, it was considered sufficient that Mani had received a revelation about the new religion he was prompted to found.

The 'Catholic' Apocalypse of Paul

Apart from the Gnostic *Apocalypse of Paul* discovered in Nag Hammadi, there is another *Apocalypse of Paul* that was popular among Catholic Christians. It was originally written in Greek in Egypt,[57] and was translated into many languages. This *Apocalypse* is often dated to the first half of the third century, because Origen seems to allude to it and Gregory Barhebraeus affirms that Origen accepts it as canonical.[58] But since Origen's alleged allusion is no proof that he knew precisely this *Apocalypse*,[59] and Gregory Barhebraeus lived ten centuries after Origen so that his information about him might be untrustworthy, it

---

[56] *Mani Codex* 68.6-15. Moreover, in *Mani Codex* 126-134 Mani tells that he was lifted up to 'unutterable places' (εἰς ἀπορ[ρήτου]ς τόπους). Unfortunately the manuscript is severely damaged here, but it can be understood that he saw a beautiful landscape, where he met a man fully covered with hair and a king and his rulers to whom he proclaimed his message.

[57] L. Dudley, *The Egyptian Elements in the Legend of the Body and Soul*, Baltimore 1911, 16-17, 143; T. Silverstein and A. Hilhorst, *Apocalypse of Paul: A New Critical Edition of Three Long Latin Versions* (Cahiers d'Orientalisme 21), Genève 1997, 9.

[58] Gregory Barhebraeus, *Nomocanon* 7.9: Origen accepted 'the *Apocalypse of Paul* together with the other apocalypses' (ed. P. Bedjan, p. 105, l.1-2). The plural 'apocalypses' shows that Gregory's information is to be distrusted, since Origen did not accept any other apocalypse than the Apocalypse of John. See R. Roukema, 'La tradition apostolique et le canon du Nouveau Testament', in: A. Hilhorst (ed.), *The Apostolic Age in Patristic Thought* (Supplements to Vigiliae Christianae 70), Leiden 2004, 86-103 (101-2). I thank Dr Floris Sepmeijer for his help in interpreting Gregory's text.

[59] Origen, *Hom. in Psalmos* 36.5.7 (Sources Chrétiennes 411), is supposed to draw on *Apocalypsis Pauli* 13-16.

is not sure whether this dating of the *Apocalypse of Paul* is correct. At least for the origin of the versions that are now at our disposal a dating around 400 seems more appropriate.[60] We will use the long Latin version, since the Greek manuscripts available to us contain only an abridged text.[61] In the incomplete Coptic text Paul's heavenly journey is more elaborated,[62] whereas the Syriac version, as far as published, is less elaborated.[63]

The *Apocalypse* tells that Paul was bodily caught up to the third heaven, where the Lord ordered him to warn the Christians not to sin anymore.[64] Next, an angel leads him through 'heaven', where he sees the firmament, the powers that sojourn there, and the souls of the righteous and the sinners (11). Then the angel leads him again to the third heaven, where he enters paradise and meets Enoch and Elijah. The angel commands him not to reveal to anybody on earth the words that he is going to hear at that moment. Consistently, these words are only referred to and not included. However, the angel says that Paul must divulge the other things he will see. Together they descend through the second heaven to the firmament and travel over the gates of heaven. Here Paul sees the promised land, where the souls of the righteous remain temporarily (19-21). Of the detailed description of this lower part of heaven and of the city of Christ we only note the angel's announcement that David will sing psalms before Christ and the Father in the seventh heaven (29). After a journey out of heaven through the places of torment of the souls of wicked people (31-44), Paul is again led to paradise, where he meets the Virgin Mary and many Old Testament saints (45-51). In these sections there is no mention of the third heaven. Then the *Apocalypse* ends abruptly in the Latin and Greek versions. According to the Coptic manuscript Paul is finally led to the Mount of Olives, where he finds the apostles, who

---

[60] P. Piovanelli, 'Les origines de l'*Apocalypse de Paul* reconsidérées', *Apocrypha* 4 (1993) 25-64, dates it between 395 and 416 (p. 53).

[61] For the Latin versions (usually called *Visio Pauli*), see the edition of Silverstein and Hilhorst. The Greek text is available in the edition of K. von Tischendorf, *Apocalypses apocryphae*, Leipzig 1866 (Hildesheim 1966), 34-69; cf. Piovanelli, 'Origines', 26. See Silverstein and Hilhorst, *Apocalypse*, 47-58, for editions and translations.

[62] Edited by E.A.W. Budge, *Miscellaneous Coptic Texts in the Dialect of Upper Egypt*, London 1915, 534-74; translation pp. 1043-84.

[63] G. Ricciotti, *Apocalypsis Pauli Syriace iuxta codices Vaticanos cum versione Latina* (*Orientalia* N.S. 2, 1933), Rome 1932. See A. Desreumaux, 'Des symboles à la réalité: la préface à l'*Apocalypse de Paul* dans la tradition syriaque', *Apocrypha* 4 (1993) 65-82.

[64] *Apocalypsis Pauli* 3: *in [cor]pore*; cf. 46: *in corpore ..., in carne*.

command Mark and Timothy to write down all that Paul has seen. Then Christ appears and commands that this *Apocalypse* should be preached throughout the world.[65] The Syriac version tells that Paul wrote this book and hid it in Tarsus, where it was found again in the time of Theodosius.[66] The same story of the discovery of the *Apocalypse* figures in the beginning of one Latin and of the Greek manuscripts.

It would take us too far to go into the long descriptions of what Paul sees on the several levels in heaven and in the places of torment. It is clear that his short notice in 2 Corinthians 12.1-4 is used as a pretext to ascribe popular Catholic views of the hereafter to the authority of the apostle. The texts as we have them give the impression that the author hardly had a precise cosmology, but felt obliged to integrate Paul's reference to the third heaven in his ideas about the post-mortem abodes of the righteous and the wicked souls.[67] It may be observed that according to this *Apocalypse* Paul's rapture took place in his body, that paradise is located in the third heaven, and that the seventh heaven was considered the highest one. The apparent contradiction between Paul's own silence about the ineffable words and the abundant descriptions in this *Apocalypse* is solved by applying these words to a special message that remains secret.

Conclusions

We might pursue our investigation with Didymus of Alexandria's detailed comments on 2 Corinthians 12.1-5, with the interpretations of non-Egyptian authors like Methodius, who considered paradise a real place on earth and not in heaven, and with the frequent references to the ineffable words in apophatic theology, but this would take up too much room and will therefore have to wait for another occasion.[68] Our conclusions from the texts presented in this paper are as follows.

Only some authors solve Paul's ambiguity as to whether his rapture

---

[65] *Apocalypsis Pauli* ed. Budge, pp. clxxii-clxxiii, 572-4, 1082-4.

[66] *Apocalypsis Pauli* 50-53 (ed. Ricciotti).

[67] See the analysis by J.M. Rosenstiehl, 'L'itinéraire de Paul dans l'au-delà: Contribution à l'étude de l'Apocalypse de Paul', in: P. Nagel (ed.), *Carl-Schmidt-Kolloquium an der Martin-Luther-Universität 1988*, Halle 1990, 197-212.

[68] I intend to write a volume on the early Christian interpretation of 2 Corinthians in the new German series Novum Testamentum Patristicum.

took place in or out of the body. Irenaeus deemed it possible that Paul's body was part of the experience. The Gnostic *Apocalypse* suggests that the apostle ascended without his body, whereas its Catholic counterpart says that he was lifted up in his body. This difference corresponds with the more negative appreciation of man's physical body in Gnosticism and with the more positive view of the body as part of God's creation in Catholic Christianity. The *Mani Codex* also seems to read that Paul was caught up without his body. Origen only notes Paul's own ambiguity without explaining it. Probably he would have said that Paul was caught up in a spiritual body.

As for the location of the third heaven and of paradise, different views came to light. In the Gnostic *Apocalypse* paradise is left out, and the third heaven is one of ten. Irenaeus shares the traditional view that there are seven heavens, and appears to locate paradise in the third heaven. Clement's cosmology is similar to the Gnostic view that there are higher spheres above the seventh heaven; he locates paradise above the third heaven. Origen seems not much interested in this question. In his allusions to Paul's rapture he can easily omit paradise, sometimes he seems to distinguish between the third heaven and paradise, sometimes he locates it on the earth that is situated in heaven. The Catholic *Apocalypse* says that there are seven heavens and faithfully locates paradise in the third heaven, but Paul's second visit to paradise has no reference to the third heaven.

The ineffable words revealed to Paul do not surface in the Gnostic *Apocalypse*, whereas according to some Church Fathers Gnostic groups pretended that these words were included in their secret knowledge, which implies that Paul did not fully keep silent about them. Clement and Tertullian contest the Gnostic claim and emphasize that no human being can know these words. Like these Gnostics, however, Origen thinks that Paul shared these revelations with some of his fellow workers, and that these words contain the Church's unwritten teaching. In the fragmentary *Mani Codex* Mani does not pretend to know the words revealed to Paul. In the Catholic *Apocalypse of Paul* these words are limited to a special message Paul had to keep secret, but apart from this the apostle is instructed to make known on earth what he saw in heaven.

Finally we go into the hermeneutical question how far these respective texts and authors can be considered faithful to Paul's reservation about such experiences. It is telling that we did not find any relationship between Paul's rapture and his subsequent witness to the thorn in his flesh, the angel of Satan, and the power made perfect in weakness. We saw that the divulgence of his rapture to which he was challenged by his Corinthians opponents has sometimes been turned into proof that Paul had a secret knowledge that he shared with his intimate collaborators and that was still available to advanced, or Gnostic, Christians. Ignoring Paul's reluctance to speak about his rapture, Gnostics like the Naassenes taught how one could imitate Paul's ascent. The first Manicheans appealed to Paul's testimony as a proof that Mani's rapture too was legitimate, so that the revelations imparted to him were trustworthy. The irony of such appeals to Paul's rapture is that they may rather be associated with Paul's Corinthian opponents. It may have been more legitimate—if we may ever pass such a judgment—to connect Paul's reference to the ineffable words with the Platonic notion of God's ineffability, as Clement does. Origen, who claimed to have some knowledge of the ineffable words, also pointed dialectically both to God's ineffability and to his revelation in his incarnate Son and Word. Our suggestion is that, if Paul had known about the further dissemination of Christianity in the Hellenistic world, he might have appreciated this appeal to his brief and enigmatic testimony.

THE SPHINX: SCULPTURE AS A THEOLOGICAL SYMBOL IN PLUTARCH AND CLEMENT OF ALEXANDRIA

JOHN HERRMANN AND ANNEWIES VAN DEN HOEK

Introduction

One of the peculiarities of human nature is our identification with and even affection for savage beasts—when kept at a certain physical and/or imaginative distance. In the dangerous world of antiquity, it must have been the desire to stay at the top of the food chain that led to the frequent use of pitiless predators such as the lion or the eagle as personal and civic emblems. In real life, humans have always had a strong instinct to exterminate such nuisance creatures. In modern times a more sentimental spirit has led to a fondness for dangerous animals inadvertently blessed with plump, rotund proportions, such as the bear and the hippopotamus. Perhaps because of the shared Nilotic habitat of the hippo and the Nag Hammadi manuscripts, this creature has notoriously been a favorite of our honorand. We would like to explore another ferocious monster connected both with ancient Egypt and with Greco-Roman culture: the sphinx. This creature has the disadvantage of being imaginary as well as reputedly lethal, yet she too has had a durable popularity. While not rotund and cuddly, she is often soft and feminine. When you add to that her special mysterious charm, it is small wonder that she was a great favorite in times of classicism (fig. 1).[1] There is a further, more contemporary reason to propose the sphinx as a subject of meditation for our honorand; in spite of a number of recent admirable studies on the sphinx in ancient art and literature, this mysterious creature remains somewhat misunderstood. Moreover, a theologian from Egypt, Clement of Alexandria, unexpectedly provides considerable insight into her nature.

Two recent publications have brought together research on both texts

---

[1] On the sphinxes of Wertheim Park in Amsterdam, see the website of Amsterdam's Bureau of Monumenten en Archeologie, http://www.bmz.amsterdam.nl/adam/nl/meubilair/wertheim.html.

Fig. 1. Sphinxes on gateway to the Wertheim Park in Amsterdam. Carrara marble replacements by Hans 't Mannetje in 1982 for the zinc originals of 1898. Photo: authors.

and artistic monuments dealing with the sphinx. The eighth volume of the *Lexicon iconographicum mythologiae classicae* has an impressive entry on the sphinx in Greek, Etruscan and Roman art.[2] For our purposes, the most relevant of the group of authors responsible for this entry are Nota Kourou, the leader of the team on Greek art, and Stylianos Katakis, who reports on the Roman sphinx. In the catalogue of the recent exhibition on early Greek monsters organized at Princeton University, Despoina Tsiafakis has written another comprehensive study of the sphinx.[3] Drawing on a long tradition of interest in this monster, these studies reach a considerable degree of unanimity on

---

[2] N. Kourou, M. Komvou, S. Raftopoulou, I. Krauskopf, and S. Katakis, 'Sphinx,' in: *Lexicon iconographicum mythologiae classicae* 7 (1994) 1149-74.

[3] D. Tsiafakis, "ΠΕΛΩΡΑ": Fabulous Creatures and/or Demons of Death?,' in: M. Padgett (ed.), *The Centaur's Smile: The Human Animal in Early Greek Art*, Princeton/ New Haven 2003, 78-83.

the sphinx's pedigree and use. The composite creature originated in Old Kingdom Egypt, where it was a lion-bodied monster with the head of the pharaoh, identifiable by his *nemes* head cloth and often by inscriptions. Sphinxes could also have the heads of rams. By the Early Bronze Age the sphinx had migrated to Mesopotamia, where he acquired wings, and with these attributes he passed on to Late Bronze Age (Mycenaean) Greece. In Greece he had a sex change, becoming female. The rare male sphinxes of Greece and Italy probably reflect renewed influence from Egypt. In Greek, Etruscan and Roman contexts, the sphinx has other ambiguities: does she have the body of a dog or lion? Should she have the breasts of a woman or the udders of a female animal? Roman artists frequently resolved the latter anatomical problem by giving her both animal and human breasts.

The interpretative problem

Current scholarship has addressed the issue of the meaning or meanings this composite creature had (or did not have) for ancient culture: why does she appear in ancient art and literature? Answers to this question have become brief, restricting the sphinx to a relatively small number of clear-cut roles. In the most succinct formulation, Katakis has classified these roles under three headings. The sphinx appears in the Oedipus story, in the realm of death and the Underworld, and in decorative and apotropaic functions.[4]

The Oedipus story dominates both the ancient literary tradition and current studies of the sphinx. As Kourou tells it, citing numerous sources, the sphinx was sent by Hera (or various other gods) to Thebes to punish king Laios for his illicit love for Chrysippos. Every day the sphinx asked passing men of Thebes a riddle suggested by the Muses; what walks on four legs in the morning, two legs at midday, and three legs at night? The answer was a human being, going metaphorically from babyhood, through maturity, to old age. When a man of Thebes failed to answer correctly, the sphinx devoured him. After Laios' death, the regent Kreon offered the kingdom and the hand of the royal widow Jocasta to whoever could remove this affliction

---

[4] Katakis is speaking of the sphinx in Roman art, but his basic organization is seen in other writers as well: Katakis, 'Sphinx,' 1174.

from the city. Oedipus answered the riddle, and the sphinx committed suicide.[5] Although the sphinx is not directly involved, it is perhaps not without significance for the artistic usage of this monster that by his success Oedipus fulfilled a double prediction of the Delphic oracle. Although he had done his best to avoid fulfilling the prophecy, he had married his mother and killed his father. In this story, the sphinx is portrayed as a murderous monster that eventually reveals a self-destructive streak.[6] Clear-cut examples of the Oedipus story form a minority of the ancient representations of sphinxes.

Death and the Underworld represent a major realm for the sphinx, as the compilations in the *Lexicon iconographicum mythologiae classicae* show. The murderous Theban sphinx was said by Euripides to have been sent by Hades.[7] In Greek vase painting sphinxes flank scenes of battle as an allusion to the fatal outcome.[8] Sphinxes appear on countless funerary monuments, where they seem to function as tomb guardians. This benevolent role is articulated in a fifth-century BCE tombstone from Pagasai, Thessaly addressed to a sphinx: 'Sphinx, dog of Hades, whom do you…watch over, sitting over the dead?'[9] This role as funer-

---

[5] Kourou, 'Sphinx,' 1150.

[6] Oedipus is frequently involved in psychiatric discussions, but the sphinx seems to have displayed more severe emotional problems.

[7] Euripides, *Phoen.* 810-811, 1019-1020: 'and would that the Sphinx, that winged maid, monster from the hills, had never come as a grief to our land with her inharmonious songs, she that once drew near our walls and snatched the sons of Cadmus away in her taloned feet to the untrodden light of heaven, [810] sent by Hades from hell to plague the men of Thebes; once more unhappy strife is coming into bloom between the sons of Oedipus in home and city. For never can wrong be right, [815] nor can there be good in unlawful children, their mother's birth pangs, their father's pollution; she came to the bed of her son' ... 1019-1020: 'You came, you came, O winged creature, born of earth [1020] and hellish viper, to prey upon the sons of Cadmus, full of death, full of sorrow, half a maiden, a murderous monster, with roving wings [1025] and ravening claws; you once caught up youths from the haunts of Dirce, with discordant song, [1030] and you brought, you brought a murderous grief, a deadly curse to our native land. A deadly god he was who brought all this to pass. Mourning of mothers, mourning of maidens, [1035] filled the houses with groans; a lamenting cry, a lamenting song, one after another wailed out, in turn throughout the city. The roar of the groaning [1040] was like thunder, whenever the winged maiden bore a man out of sight from the city' (translated by E.P. Coleridge). Passage cited in Kourou, 'Sphinx,' 1150.

[8] Kourou, 'Sphinx,' 1161, cat. nos. 189-92, pl. 805; Tsiafakis, in: Padgett, *The Centaur's Smile*, 80-1, 100 note 66.

[9] σφίξ, ha͜ίδαο [κ]ύον, τίν' ἔ[χοσ']||ὄπιν [ἀὲ φυ]λάσεις
hε̄μέν[α hε̄]||ροφ [ίλο κᾱ]δο[s ἀπ]οφθιμ[ένο]; —
ξεῖ[νε — — — —
— — — — —].

ary guardian was shared with the Egyptian sphinx. Tsiafakis cites a funerary inscription from the Saite Dynasty (663-525 BCE) that echoes the words of an Egyptian sphinx: 'I protect the chapel of the tomb. I guard thy sepulchral chamber. I ward off the intruding stranger. I hurl thy foes to the ground.'[10] Analogous pharaonic texts of earlier date show that the sphinx had a long-established role as a protector of cemeteries.[11]

While these first two realms ('Theban' and 'funerary') are clear-cut and well documented, the third major category, defined by Kourou, Katakis, and Tsiafakis as 'decorative,'[12] is rather shapeless and ambiguous—especially from an interpretive point of view. The term 'decorative' implies something that is drained of meaning and used purely as ornament. This is surely a valid interpretation in some, if not many cases. A sphinx might simply be a conventional artistic subject or appreciated as a precious object. A case in point is Cicero's witticism about a certain Hortensius: Hortensius owned an ivory sphinx, but it did not give him the ability to solve riddles.[13] The object apparently signified little more than an attractive and valuable piece of craftsmanship.

Modern writers also suggest that the decorative use of the sphinx

---

W. Peek, *Griechische Vers-Inschriften*, Berlin 1955, no. 1831; P.E. Hansen, *Carmina Epigraphica Graeca*, Berlin 1983, I 66, no. 120; G. Richter, *The Archaic Gravestones of Attica*, London 1961, p. 6. For a mid-fifth century date, see L.H. Jeffery, *The Local Scripts of Archaic Greece* (rev. ed.), Oxford 1990, 97-8. D. Kurtz and J. Boardman, *Greek Burial Customs*, London 1971, 239; Müller 1978, 335; Kourou, 'Sphinx,' 1150; D. Tsiafakis, in: Padgett, *The Centaur's Smile*, 82. It is hard to find any sphinx on a tomb monument in the passage of Diogenes Laertius (1.89) cited by Tsiafakis, in: Padgett, *The Centaur's Smile*, 82.

[10] G. Hanfmann, 'Ionia, Leader or Follower?,' *Harvard Studies in Classical Philology* 16 (1953) 230; Tsiafakis, in: Padgett, *The Centaur's Smile*, 82.

[11] A. Dessenne, *Le sphinx: étude iconographique*, i, Paris 1957, 176.

[12] Tsiafakis, in: Padgett, *The Centaur's Smile*, 81-3; N. Kourou, 'Sphinx,' 1165; Katakis, 'Sphinx,' 1174.

[13] Plutarch, *Cicero*, 7, 8 (Ziegler): τοῦ δὲ ῥήτορος Ὁρτησίου τὴν μὲν εὐθεῖαν τῷ Βέρρῃ συνειπεῖν μὴ θελήσαντος, ἐν δὲ τῷ τιμήματι πεισθέντος παραγενέσθαι καὶ λαβόντος ἐλεφαντίνην Σφίγγα μισθόν, εἶπέ τι πλαγίως ὁ Κικέρων πρὸς αὐτόν· τοῦ δὲ φήσαντος αἰνιγμάτων λύσεως ἀπείρως ἔχειν, 'καὶ μὴν ἐπὶ τῆς οἰκίας', ἔφη, 'τὴν Σφίγγα ἔχεις', 'When the orator Hortensius did not wish to advocate the cause of Verres directly but was persuaded to stand by when the penalty was given and received an ivory sphinx as reward, Cicero spoke to him in a somewhat oblique way; when Hortensius said that he was unused to solving riddles, Cicero said 'but you have the sphinx at home.'

had an apotropaic function. That is, the sphinx would frighten off the 'evil eye' or other demons.[14] The decorative category encompasses a great range of objects, from votive sphinxes in temple precincts, through architectural decoration, furniture, attachments to vessels, personal emblems on ring stones, and civic emblems on coinage. At times sphinxes seem (loosely) associated with specific gods, such as Athena, Artemis, Hera, Dionysos, and Salus.[15] They may also evoke Egypt, the land of their first origin.[16]

This 'decorative' category is to some degree unsatisfying because of its intellectual looseness, its excessive reliance on primitive and unarticulated forms of belief applied to highly articulate societies, the great number of highly disparate objects that it brings together, and the absence of meaning imputed to them. An inclination to see no significance in works of art has long been a preference in archaeo-logical circles,[17] but this 'no-nonsense' approach may in some cases underestimate ancient observers. Not only is the category displeasing as presently defined, but some pronouncements of ancient authors make it clear that the sphinx was viewed as meaningful in ways not taken into consideration in current surveys.

A common shortcoming of current and past rounds of studies on the sphinx is to overemphasize the dominance of the Theban tale in the Greek literary tradition.[18] The murderous sphinx and her riddle were, indeed, the only true narrative she was involved in, and the tale was told in many works of art. Illustrations of this story, how-ever, form a minority of the preserved representations of sphinxes, and the brutal Theban sphinx was only one manifestation of this kind of monster. For the ancient imagination there was no difficulty in seeing her as a member of a larger group. Some ancient writers accepted sphinxes as a breed akin to Minotaurs, Pans, and Centaurs. Like the Minotaur and Pan, they might have started or have been represented by an individual case (the Cretan Minotaur, the god Pan, the Theban sphinx), but, like centaurs, they were also recognized as categories with multiple members. Dio Chrysostom explicitly called

---

[14] Formulated explicitly by Tsiafakis, in: Padgett, *The Centaur's Smile*, 82-3.

[15] Kourou, 'Sphinx,' 1165; Katakis, 'Sphinx,' 1174.

[16] Katakis, 'Sphinx,' 1174.

[17] For a repentant former adherent of this positivistic position, see H. Hoffmann, 'Rhyta and Kantharoi in Greek Ritual,' *Greek Vases in the J. Paul Getty Museum* 4 (1989) 131.

[18] Especially Kourou, 'Sphinx,' 1149-50.

them entirely imaginary artistic creations,[19] but Plutarch speculated
on the sexual relations between humans and animals that could have
produced them.[20] As a group, sphinxes were thought to have notable
talents. They were of an artistic temper. Already Euripides evokes
'sphinxes, carrying in their talons quarry won by song.'[21] Plutarch
could imply that the Theban sphinx herself had wisdom.[22]

Symbolic interpretations in ancient writers

Not only were there multiple sphinxes, but multiple and clear-cut
meanings can also be identified within the amorphous group of
'decorative' and 'apotropaic' sphinxes. Sphinxes came to be seen by
ancient writers as having symbolic significance. The symbolism was
in great part derived from aspects of the Oedipus story; the Theban
sphinx's riddle came to loom larger than her murders. The human
and animal components of the monster were also the basis for symbolic elaboration.

---

[19] Dio Chrysostom, *Discourses* 32.28 (von Arnim): ὥστε πάνυ ποικίλον τε καὶ δεινὸν
εἶναι θηρίον, οἷα ποιηταὶ καὶ δημιουργοὶ πλάττουσι Κενταύρους τε καὶ Σφίγγας
καὶ Χιμαίρας, ἐκ παντοδαπῶν φύσεων [εἰς] μίαν μορφὴν εἰδώλου ξυντιθέντες, 'so
that it (sc. democracy) is a very changeable and dreadful beast, just as those which
poets and sculptors create, Centaurs, Sphinxes, and Chimairas, put together from
all kinds of natural forms into one fantastic image.'

[20] Plutarch, *Do brute animals use brains?*, Mor. 991A (Hubert): καὶ γὰρ αἰγῶν
ἐπειράθησαν ἄνδρες καὶ ὑῶν καὶ ἵππων μιγνύμενοι καὶ γυναῖκες ἄρρεσι θηρίοις
ἐπεμάνησαν· ἐκ γὰρ τῶν τοιούτων γάμων ὑμῖν Μινώταυροι καὶ Αἰγίπανες, ὡς δ'
ἐγῷμαι καὶ Σφίγγες ἀναβλαστάνουσι καὶ Κένταυροι, 'For men tried to have intercourse with goats, pigs, and horses, and women went mad for male animals. From
such matings spring forth your Minotaurs and goat-footed Pans and, as seems to me,
also your Sphinxes and Centaurs.'

[21] Euripides, *Electra* 464-472 (Diggle): ἐν δὲ μέσωι κατέλαμπε σάκει φαέθων κύκλος
ἁλίοιο ἵπποις ἅμ πτεροέσσαις ἄστρων τ' αἰθέριοι χοροί, Πλειάδες Ὑάδες, Ἕκτορος
ὄμμασι τροπαῖοι· ἐπὶ δὲ χρυσοτύπωι κράνει Σφίγγες ὄνυξιν ἀοίδιμον ἄγραν φέρουσαι,
'In the middle of the shield the sun disk shone brightly upon winged horses, and
choirs of heavenly stars, the Pleiades and Hyades, were appalling to the eyes of
Hector; on his helmet wrought of gold were sphinxes carrying in their talons quarry
won by song.'

[22] Plutarch, *Do brute animals use brains?*, Mor. 988A (Hubert): καὶ τὴν Σφίγγα
ἐκείνην οὐκ ἂν ὤνησεν ἡ σοφία περὶ τὸ Φίκιον ἄνω καθεζομένην, αἰνίγματα καὶ
γρίφους πλέκουσαν, εἰ μὴ ῥώμη καὶ ἀνδρείᾳ πολὺ τῶν Καδμείων ἐπεκράτει, 'And
wisdom would not have benefited that sphinx seated high up on Mount Phikion
contriving puzzles and riddles, if she had not greatly prevailed over the Kadmeians
in strength and courage.'

A primary symbolic meaning of the sphinx was as an emblem of theological ambiguity and mystery. This interpretation appears in Plutarch:

> The (Egyptian) kings were appointed from the priests or from the military class, since the military class had eminence and honor because of valor, and the priests because of wisdom. But the king who was appointed from the military was at once made one of the priests and participated in their philosophy, which is mostly concealed in myths and words containing faint hints and glimpses of the truth, as they themselves (the Egyptians) actually indicate by their custom of placing sphinxes in front of their holy places, suggesting that their theology contains wisdom full of riddles.[23]

This symbolism is fleshed out more fully by Clement of Alexandria. Not only does the sphinx represent theological ambiguity, but she also stands for divine retribution.

> Therefore also the Egyptians place sphinxes in front of their temples to indicate that the discourse about god is enigmatic and obscure. Perhaps one should both love and fear the divine: love it as gentle and kind to the pious and fear it as implacably just to the impious. For the sphinx shows enigmatically at the same time the image of a wild beast and of a human being.[24]

Clement at no point appears to be quoting Plutarch; apparently there was an independent tradition of interpretation to which both writers referred. Only indirectly was the tradition pharaonic. In a native Egyptian context, as Jean Hani has pointed out, the sphinx was associated with the pharaoh and the sun god, and the image expressed

---

[23] Plutarch, *Isis and Osiris* 345bc (Sieveking): Οἱ δὲ βασιλεῖς ἀπεδείκνυντο μὲν ἐκ τῶν ἱερέων ἢ τῶν μαχίμων, τοῦ μὲν δι' ἀνδρείαν τοῦ δὲ διὰ σοφίαν γένους ἀξίωμα καὶ τιμὴν ἔχοντος. ὁ δ' ἐκ μαχίμων ἀποδεδειγμένος εὐθὺς ἐγίνετο τῶν ἱερέων καὶ μετεῖχε τῆς φιλοσοφίας ἐπικεκρυμμένης τὰ πολλὰ μύθοις καὶ λόγοις ἀμυδρὰς ἐμφάσεις τῆς ἀληθείας καὶ διαφάσεις ἔχουσιν, ὥσπερ ἀμέλει καὶ παραδηλουσιν αὐτοὶ πρὸ τῶν ἱερῶν τὰς σφίγγας ἐπιεικῶς ἱστάντες, ὡς αἰνιγματώδη σοφίαν τῆς θεολογίας αὐτῶν ἐχούσης. This passage was quoted centuries later by Joannes Stobaeus, *Anthologium*, IV 2, section 27.

[24] Clement, *Stromateis* 5.31.5 (Stählin): Διὰ τοῦτό τοι καὶ Αἰγύπτιοι πρὸ τῶν ἱερῶν τὰς σφίγγας ἱδρύονται, ὡς αἰνιγματώδους τοῦ περὶ θεοῦ λόγου καὶ ἀσαφοῦς ὄντος, τάχα δὲ καὶ ὅτι φιλεῖν τε δεῖν καὶ φοβεῖσθαι τὸ θεῖον, ἀγαπᾶν μὲν ὡς προσηνὲς καὶ εὐμενὲς τοῖς ὁσίοις, δεδιέναι δὲ ὡς ἀπαραιτήτως δίκαιον τοῖς ἀνοσίοις. θηρίου γὰρ ὁμοῦ καὶ ἀνθρώπου ἡ σφὶγξ αἰνίσσεται τὴν εἰκόνα. See also A. van den Hoek's translation, in: J. Herrmann, in: Padgett, *The Centaur's Smile*, 283.

their combined power to defend Egypt and destroy its enemies.[25] The sphinx thereby became a guardian of both temples and tombs, and rows of sphinxes were placed before temple entrances.[26] The three-kilometer avenue of sphinxes that originally linked the temples of Karnak and Luxor is the most conspicuous example. Nearer Alexandria at Memphis an avenue of sphinxes led up to the Serapeum.[27] In the late pharaonic period and in Ptolemaic and Roman times the sphinx took on a new meaning in Egypt as a manifestation of the protective divinity Tutu (in Greek, *Tithoes*).[28]

Riddles and ambiguity, however, were not the stock-in-trade of pharaohs or their emblematic monsters and probably not of the ferocious Tithoes either. As Hani rightly saw, the interpretation of the sphinx as theological ambiguity is much more at home in the Hellenic tradition.[29] The symbolism must have developed in Greece from speculation on the Theban story. The sphinx's riddle appeared comparable in some respects to puzzling theological doctrines and to mysterious religious rituals. She could therefore symbolize cryptic theology. The sphinx, moreover, was not a horror that afflicted Thebes arbitrarily, but she was the instrument through which a divinity exacted retribution for

---

[25] In pharaonic relief sculpture the sphinx was shown trampling foreign enemies. See, for example, the armrest of a wooden throne from the tomb of Thutmose IV, showing the king as a victorious sphinx trampling Asians: Museum of Fine Arts, Boston, 03.1131; Gift of Theodore M. Davis: J. Sliwa, 'Some Remarks concerning Victorious Ruler Representations in Egyptian Art,' *Fortschritt und Berichte* 16 (1974) 106, fig. 9; *Ägyptens Aufstieg zur Weltmacht*, Catalogue of Hildesheim, Exhibition, Aug. 3—Nov. 29, 1987 (Mainz am Rhein), 362-3, no. 314.

[26] J. Hani, *La religion égyptienne dans la pensée de Plutarque*, Paris 1976, 262.

[27] The avenue of Sphinxes at the Serapeion of Memphis had no less than 370 to 380 sphinxes of Egyptian type; they dated from the time of Nectanebo 1 (378-360 BCE) and Nectanebo II (359-341 BCE). The exedra in front of the temple had sphinxes of Greek type: J.P. Lauer and C. Picard, *Les statues ptolémaïques du Serapieion de Memphis*, Paris 1955, 3, 12, 15-21, 24-7, 210-15, pl. 1, figs. 2, 13-4, 113-16. Many of the sphinxes had been buried by wind-blown sand by the first century BCE: Strabo, *Geography* 17.1.32.

[28] Tutu was a lion-bodied, human-headed monster, which could have a tail in the form of a cobra. The cobra as well as the human head could wear divine crowns. See R. Bianchi, 'Pharaonic Egyptian Elements in the Decorative Arts of Alexandria during the Hellenistic and Roman Periods,' in: *Alexandria and Alexandrianism: Papers Delivered at a Symposium Organized by the J. Paul Getty Museum and the Getty Center for the History of Art and the Humanities and Held at the Museum, April 22-23, 1993*, Malibu, Calif. 1996, 197, 202 note 53, fig. 3; D. Frankfurter, *Religion in Roman Egypt: Assimilation and Resistance*, Princeton 1998, 115-16.

[29] Hani, *La religion égyptienne*, 262. The same observation was already made in the sixteenth century by H. Estienne, *Thesaurus graecae linguae*, s.v. σφίγξ, col. 1617C.

a crime committed by the Theban king Laios. She could therefore represent divine retribution in a more general sense.

Clement could well have learned not only of the Egyptian use of sphinxes in temples but also of their theological symbolism in his adopted city of Alexandria rather than elsewhere in Egypt. Large numbers of older sphinxes had been moved there from Ptolemaic times and onwards. Many stone sphinxes have recently been retrieved from the harbor,[30] and others have been excavated at the Serapeum (fig. 2)[31] and at other sites. Alexandria, however, was a city in which the Greek component was dominant, and its cults were usually Greek in origin or, as in the case of the cult of Serapis, highly interwoven with Hellenic elements.[32]

Greek sphinxes in religious settings

The sphinx's role as guardian of temples as well as tombs passed from Egypt to the Aegean at an early date—according to Jean Hani possibly as early as the Bronze Age.[33] In the Archaic period Greeks frequently set up marble and stone sphinxes in front of their temples. During the sixth and fifth centuries BCE, splendid sculptures, often mounted on columns, were erected in temple precincts at Delphi (fig. 3), Cyrene, Delos, Athens, and possibly on Aegina, Naxos, Paros, and Thasos. Most if not all of these monuments were gifts to the sanctuaries made by various individuals or communities in gratitude for perceived acts of divine favor. Commentators have long considered such votive monuments under the heading of 'decorative,'[34] but it

---

[30] Twenty-five from the waters around Fort Qait Bey, the site of the pharos: J.-Y. Empereur, photographs by S. Compoint/Sygma, *Alexandria Rediscovered* (translated by M. Maehler), New York 1998, 71-5.

[31] P.M. Frazer, *Ptolemaic Alexandria*, Oxford 1972, i, 27-8; ii, 83-92 notes 190-202; G. Grimm, 'City Planning?', in: *Alexandria and Alexandrianism*, 63-65, figs. 11-15; Empereur, *Alexandria Rediscovered*, 105, 108-9; G. Grimm and J.-Y. Empereur, *La gloire d'Alexandrie* (Exhibition catalogue, Musée du Petit Palais), Paris 1998, 94-5.

[32] Frazer, *Ptolemaic Alexandria*, i, 190, 246-61; Grimm, *La gloire d'Alexandrie*, 94. The cult of Serapis was redefined by a Graeco-Egyptian theological commission under the first Ptolemy. Isis and Demeter were also transformed in this process: J. Herrmann, 'Demeter-Isis or the Egyptian Demeter? A Graeco-Roman Sculpture from an Egyptian Workshop in Boston,' *Jahrbuch des Deutschen Archäologischen Instituts* 114 (1999) 65-123.

[33] Kourou, 'Sphinx,' 1153, cat. nos. 31-32, with bibliography.

[34] In addition to the recent studies, see, for example, F. Poulsen, *Delphi* (translated by G.C. Richards), London 1920, 97-100, figs. 29-30.

Fig. 2. Alexandria, Serapeum: sphinxes by the column of Diocletian. Photo: authors.

is highly likely that there was a fairly specific reason for choosing the sphinx as the subject for these sculptures in prominent public places. It is likely that they were set up to some degree in imitation of Egyptian sanctuaries—a decorative intention—, but it seems likely that articulate reasoning would also have been necessary to make these monsters appropriate in a sacred setting in Greece. The Theban tale, in which the sphinx was a serial killer, would not in itself have provided an adequate motivation for her prominent display. On the other hand, Greek travelers to Egypt would not only have observed the arrays of sphinxes before temples, but also they could easily have found out from Greek residents of Egypt—presumably in the Greek enclave of Naukratis—the meaning of the practice: namely, that the sphinxes served as emblems of divine protection. In all probability Greek artists and patrons took over not only this sculptural theme but also its protective content from Egypt.

A protective message would also have been embodied by sphinxes carved onto temples themselves. Pairs of reclining sphinxes confronting one another on either side of a diminutive Aeolic column were carved on the architrave of the temple of Athena on the acropolis of Assos in the Troad about 550-525 BCE (fig. 4).[35] Reconstructions place these pairs of sphinxes in a conspicuous position on the main axis of the temple (fig. 5).[36] Other Archaic temples had sphinxes carved beside doorways and used as acroteria or antefixes on their roofs.[37] Bonna Wescoat has pointed out that paired sphinxes took on a great importance in the architecture of the Ionian coastlands in the second half of the sixth century BCE, appearing on temples, accessory religious buildings, and altars.[38] Sphinxes were also shown flanking or carved

---

[35] J.T. Clarke, F.H. Bacon, and R. Koldewey, *Investigations at Assos*, London/ Cambridge, Mass. 1902, 147-53; M. Comstock and C. Vermeule, *Sculpture in Stone: The Greek, Etruscan, and Roman Collections of the Museum of Fine Arts, Boston*, Boston 1976, cat. no. 20; *Enciclopedia dell'arte antica classica ed orientale: Atlante dei complessi figurati e degli ordini architettonici*, Rome 1973, pls. 13, 15; U. Finster-Hotz, *Der Bauschmuck des Athenatempels von Assos*, Rome 1984, 90, 135, no. 8b, figs. 22-3; M. Hamiaux, *Les sculptures grecques*, in: *Des origines à la fin du IVe siècle avant J.-C.*, Paris 1992, cat. no. 67; B. Wescoat, *The Temple of Assos*, Oxford (forthcoming). Reliefs A1 and A2.

[36] Clarke, Bacon, and Koldewey, *Investigations at Assos*, 147, 153. Other pairs of sphinxes appeared in the temple's metopes.

[37] Kourou, 'Sphinx,' 1165, citing cat. nos. 26, 33, 41, and 49.

[38] Wescoat, *The Temple of Assos*. Reliefs A1 and A2. In addition to the temple of Assos, Wescoat observes that 'on Samos, fragments of sphinxes in relief have been

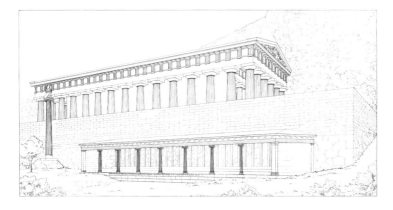

Fig. 3. Reconstruction of the monuments below the temple of Apollo, Delphi: at the left, the column and sphinx of the Naxians; at the right, the portico of the Athenians. Drawing by D. Laroche, courtesy of the École Française d'Athènes: from J.-F. Bommelaer and D. Laroche, *Guide de Delphes: Le site* (École Française d'Athènes 1991) fig. 57.

Fig. 4. Andesite sphinxes flanking an Aeolic colonnette, from the architrave of the temple of Athena, Assos, Troad, Turkey, Greek, ca. 550-525 BCE. Museum of Fine Arts, Boston, gift of the Archaeological Institute of America, 84.68. Photograph: Museum.

---

restored to the upper antae of the Rhoikos Altar (c. 550-540), the South Building (c. 530-520), and the Polykratean Heraion (c. 520-510). If the Roman archaistic altar at Samos mirrored its archaic predecessor, then the frieze on the Rhoikos Altar also included recumbent sphinxes set around a rosette upon which they rest the inner forepaw. Sphinxes decorate the inner and outer side walls of an altar from Miletos (end of the sixth century) and an altar (or building for a sacred spring) from Didyma (early fifth century), where they raise a paw heraldically onto a floral motif.' She further notes that the sphinx's 'repeated appearance on antae and built altars in Asia Minor, on antefixes and as akroteria (not to mention independent votive dedications) indicates a significance beyond the appropriate but essentially decorative.'

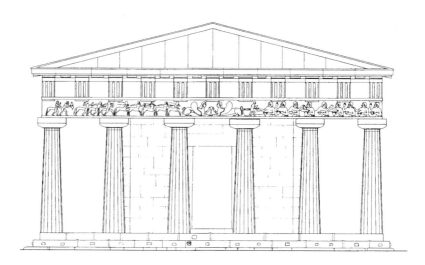

Fig. 5. East front of the temple of Athena, Assos, Turkey: the sphinxes are located on the main axis. Reconstruction by Bonna Wescoat.

on the thrones of divinities,[39] further reinforcing their role as divine protectors and perhaps as projections of divine power, wisdom, and inscrutability.

The sphinx soon came to symbolize protection of religious places in a more general sense. The monster was used to decorate religious gear in the private realm. During the Classical period, terracotta household altars in South Italy gained magical or metaphorical protection from sphinxes. On a fragmentary altar of 480-460 BCE in Boston (fig. 6),[40] the sphinx perches on a column, much as she did on the monument at Delphi (fig. 3). A tripod of the late seventh century BCE in New York is topped by three sphinxes and three horses' heads (fig. 7).[41] The tripod, which presumably was preserved in the tomb of a private individual,

---

[39] Kourou, 'Sphinx,' 1162, 1165; Katakis, 'Sphinx,' 1174.

[40] J. Herrmann, in: Padgett, *The Centaur's Smile*, cat. no. 67. For other South Italian altars with sphinxes, see H. van der Meijden, *Terrakotta-arulae aus Sizilien und Unteritalien*, Amsterdam 1993, 63-4, 282-9, pls. 49-50.

[41] C. Picon, in: *Metropolitan Museum of Art Bulletin*, Fall 1997, 10; C. Stibbe, *The Sons of Hephaistos: Aspects of the Archaic Greek Bronze Industry*, Rome 2000, 127-42, figs. 85, 88.

Fig. 6. Fragment of a terracotta altar with a sphinx seated on an Aeolic column. Greek, Calabria, Italy, ca. 480-460 BCE. Museum of Fine Arts, Boston, gift of Ariel Herrmann in memory of Lucia Torossi, 2001.851. Photograph: Museum.

would have carried a cauldron for burning sacrifices. Sphinxes return on basins and candelabra of Roman Imperial date.[42]

Early metaphorical interpretations of the sphinx: sphinx and sibyl

The question remains of when the sphinx came to take on the richly developed symbolic role outlined by Plutarch and Clement. When did she come to stand for or allude to theological obscurity? Hani saw

---

[42] Katakis, 'Sphinx,' 1170, cat. nos. 271-273, 329, pls. 811, 817.

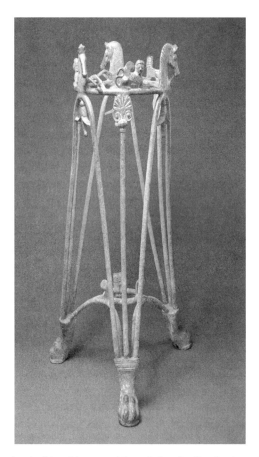

Fig. 7. Bronze tripod with sphinxes and horse's heads, Greek, about 600 BCE Metropolitan Museum of Art, New York, gift of Mr. and Mrs. Klaus G. Perls, 1997.145.1. Photograph: Museum.

this as a typically Hellenistic approach.[43] Metaphorical interpretation of the sphinx, however, clearly dates to even earlier times. In addition to her other roles, the sphinx had an association with sibyls, an association that had no apparent basis in mythology. As early as the late Classical period of the first half of the fourth century BCE, coins of Gergis in the Troad display on one side a sphinx and on the other a female head crowned with laurel leaves, who must be the

---

[43] Hani, *La religion Égyptienne*, 262.

Fig. 8. Bronze coin of Gergis, Troad, Turkey: obverse, head of the sibyl of Marpessos; reverse: sphinx. Greek, about 400-330 BCE. Private collection. Photograph: authors.

sibyl of Marpessos (fig. 8). She was known variably as the Gergithian, Trojan, Hellespontic, or Phrygian Sibyl, and her tomb lay near the temple of Apollo Gergithius.[44] Phlegon of Tralles, a writer of the second century CE provides this interpretation of the coins,[45] which has been accepted by a long line of modern commentators.[46] It has been suggested that a Greek ring of the late fifth century BCE showing the sphinx crouching on a tripod and facing a seated woman reflects the connection between sphinx and sibyl (fig. 9).[47] Should this be so,

---

[44] M. Caccamo Caltabiano, in: *Lexicon iconographicum mythologiae classicae* 7 (1994) 753, cat. no. 1. She dates the issue to early Hellenistic times. Alan Walker of Leu Numismatics assures us, however, that the issue belongs to the preceding period.

[45] *FGrH* 257 F 2: (Steph. Byz. s. Γέργις: πόλις Τροίας .....) Γεργιθία ἡ χρησμολόγος Σίβυλλα, ἥ τις καὶ ἐτετύπωτο ἐν τῶι νομίσματι τῶν Γεργιθίων αὐτή τε καὶ σφίγξ, ὡς Φλέγων ἐν Ὀλυμπιάδων <α>. ἐν δὲ τῶι ἱερῶι τοῦ Γεργιθίου Ἀπόλλωνος Σιβύλλης φασὶν εἶναι τάφον, 'Gergis, city of the Troad' ...) 'Gergithia, the divining sibyl, who is also stamped on the coin of the Gergithians, she and a sphinx, according to Phlegon in the first book of the Olympians. Reportedly there is a tomb of a sibyl in the temple of Apollo of Gergis.'

[46] For example, B. Head, *Historia Numorum: A Manual of Greek Numismatics*, Oxford 1911 (reprinted by S. Durst, 1983), 545-6; Caccamo Caltabiano, in: *Lexicon iconographicum mythologiae classicae* 7 (1994) 753.

[47] Paris, Musée du Louvre, Bj 1084. The interpretation originated with E. Coche de la Ferté, *Les bijoux antiques*, Paris 1956, 84, 120, pl. 39, 1. See also *Enciclopedia dell'arte antica classica ed orientale* 5, Rome 1963, 767, fig. 929; H. Hoffmann and P. Davidson, *Greek Gold: Jewelry from the Age of Alexander*, Boston/Richmond 1965, cat. no. 108; J.

Fig. 9. Gold ring with a sibyl facing a sphinx on a tripod. Greek, late fifth century BCE.
Paris, Musée du Louvre, Bj 1084. Photograph: Réunion des Musées Nationaux.

a metaphoric or symbolic interpretation of the sphinx would have
been current in the High Classical period. In such cases, the riddles
of the sphinx (or sphinxes) were clearly considered metaphors for the
obscure but divinely inspired pronouncements of sibyls. As Katakis
put it, sphinxes are emblems of sibyls because of their 'enigmatic
significance.'[48] The early sixth-century sphinx at Delphi may have
already alluded to a sibyl; in the time of Pausanias (2nd century CE)
the rock on which the Delphic sibyl sat was a tourist attraction near
the temple of Apollo, and the find spot of the marble sphinx was
not far away.[49]

Boardman, photographs by R. Wilkins, *Greek Gems and Finger Rings*, London 1970,
221, pl. 707; Kourou, 'Sphinx,' 1163, cat. no. 9.

[48] '...ihrer rätselhaften Bedeutung': Katakis, 'Sphinx,' 1174.

[49] Pausanias, *Description of Greece* 10.10.12. For rejection of an association between
sibyl and sphinx at Delphi, see F. Poulsen, *Delphi* (translated by G. C. Richards),
London 1920, 97-9.

Fig. 10. Silver denarius of T. Carisius: obverse, head of sibyl; reverse, sphinx. Mint of Rome, 46 BCE. Museum of Fine Arts, Boston, Catharine Page Perkins Fund, 95.165. Photograph: Museum.

Sphinxes were associated with sibyls in Roman contexts as well. A denarius of T. Carisius issued in 46 BCE displays a head of a sibyl on the obverse and a sphinx on the reverse (fig. 10). This pairing of images echoes and was perhaps inspired by the coins of Gergis (fig. 8).[50] Sphinxes had a special connection with Octavian/Augustus. Early in his career he used two identical gemstones with a sphinx inherited from his mother as his personal seal.[51] A sphinx appeared on the Augustan

---

[50] M. Crawford, *Roman Republican Coinage*, London/New York 1974, 464/1, pl. 54; Caccamo Caltabiano, in: *Lexicon iconographicum mythologiae classicae* 7 (1994) 755, cat. no. 9, pl. 548; Katakis, 'Sphinx,' cat. no. 316, pl. 815.

[51] Pliny the Elder, *Hist. nat.*, 37.4.10: *divus Augustus inter initia sphinge signavit. duas in matris anulis eas indiscretae similitudinis invenerat. altera per bella civilia absente ipso signavere amici epistulas et edicta quae ratio temporum nomine eius reddi postulabat, non inficeto lepore accipientium, aenigmata adferre eam sphingem. quippe etiam Maecenatis rana per collationes pecuniarum in magno terrore erat. Augustus postea ad devitanda convicia sphingis Alexandri Magni imagine signavit,* 'At the beginning the divinized Augustus used the sphinx as a seal. Among his mother's rings he had found these two that were of indistinguishable similarity. During the civil wars whenever he himself was absent counselors used one of them to seal letters and proclamations that the circumstances required to be issued in his name. The recipients made the not unwitty joke that the sphinx brought riddles. In fact the frog (signet) of Maecenas was also greatly feared because of its solicitations of money. Later Augustus used the image of Alexander the Great as seal to avoid insults about the sphinx.'

Suetonius, *Augustus* 50: *in diplomatibus libellisque et epistulis signandis initio sphinge usus est, mox imagine Magni Alexandri, novissime sua, Dioscuridis manu scalpta, qua signare insecuti quoque principes perseverarunt,* 'At first he used the sphinx to seal letters of recommendation, responses to petitions, and private letters, then the image of Alexander the Great, and finally his own, which was engraved by the hand of Dioscurides; also the succeeding emperors continued to use this as their seal.'

coinage of Pergamon, on the breastplate of the statue of Augustus
from Primaporta, and in other media of the time.[52] Paul Zanker has
pointed out how these Augustan sphinxes alluded to the sibyl and her
prophecies of a brighter future, which—along with other portents of
a new age—were widely believed to refer to Octavian even before
he achieved supreme power.[53] While Zanker's reconstruction must
capture the official thinking of the time, the symbolism was ambiguous
enough to become a source of unwanted humor. Augustus's sealed
dispatches were received as 'riddles' (*aenigmata*), leading (according to
Pliny and Suetonius) Augustus to replace the sphinx with an image of
Alexander the Great as his seal. In any case, it is again clear sphinxes
had been identified with mysterious pronouncements in general rather
than being tied specifically to the Theban tale.

Sphinxes after Clement

In spite of the attractive 'theological' interpretations offered by Plutarch and Clement, sphinxes in temple settings became rather rare in
Roman times—except in Alexandria and in connection with Serapis.
The sphinxes in Roman Imperial religious contexts, moreover, seem
usually to be reused Egyptian carvings of much earlier times.[54] A late
case of sphinxes in a possible religious context is offered by the two
granite sphinxes of pharaonic style and Egyptian manufacture in
Diocletian's palace at Split, Croatia. Not only are the sphinxes wing-
less, but also they originally had heads of pharaohs. One headless
sphinx is on the podium of the temple commonly identified as that
of Diocletian's favorite protector Zeus.[55] The other (with head) is

---

[52] P. Zanker, *The Power of Images in the Age of Augustus* (translated by A. Shapiro),
Ann Arbor 1988, 48-9, 192, 199, figs. 36, 38, 148, 155a; Katakis, 'Sphinx,' 1170,
1174, cat. No. 278-80, pls. 811-12.

[53] Zanker may, however, overemphasize the connection of the sphinx with Apollo:
Zanker, *The Power of Images in the Age of Augustus*, 48-9.

[54] Many Egyptian sphinxes were found in Hadrian's villa at Tivoli, where they
were intended to evoke Egypt; many were also found in the Iseum Campense: A.
Roullet, *The Egyptian and Egyptianizing monuments of Imperial Rome*, Leiden 1972, 23-35,
51, 132-40, cat. nos. 289-322, pls. 198-217. Another manifestation of the connection
with Serapis is a second or third century gold and lapis lazuli miniature shrine to
Serapis in the Louvre; the bust of the god is flanked by winged sphinxes: Louvre,
Bj 2095: *Spätantike und frühes Christentum*, Frankfurt am Main 1983, cat. 129.

[55] We owe this information and the following reference to Beat Brenk: J. Marasović

Fig. 11. Reused granite Egyptian sphinx, peristyle of palace of Diocletian, Split, Croatia, about 300 CE. Photograph by N. Gattin, from J. Marasović and T. Marasović, *Diocletian Palace* (Zagreb: Zora 1970) pl. 51.

and T. Marasović, photographs by N. Gattin, *Diocletian Palace*, Zagreb 1970, pl. 92. The sphinxes do not appear to be mentioned in the text.

on a pedestal flanking the grand staircase at the end of the peristyle (fig. 11).[56] Neither appears to be in its original position within the palace complex.[57] In a late antique imperial setting the symbolism could have been very rich, and the Clementine interpretation might have been part of it.[58] The sphinxes might also have underlined the universal significance of Zeus, equating him with the popular cult of (Zeus-)Serapis.

Interpreting a being with two natures

Clement offers another symbolic interpretation of the sphinx, and this too seems highly applicable to a great variety of artifacts in the private as well as public spheres. In this second passage, he interprets the sphinx as a symbol of protection and sagacity. He writes

> in addition, the lion is for them (sc. the Egyptians) a symbol of might and vigor, just as the ox is clearly a symbol of earth itself, of farming and food, the horse of courage and confidence, and the sphinx of protective strength with intelligence. Her entire body is that of a lion, but her face that of a human. Likewise hinting enigmatically at intelligence, memory, strength, and skill, a human is carved by them for their holy places.[59]

Some two centuries later Synesius of Cyrene (ca. 370-414) seems to reaffirm Clement's interpretation: 'as it seems also the sphinx is set up for them in the precincts of their temples as a sacred symbol of the coupling of virtues, animal with regard to strength, human being

---

[56] Marasović and Marasović, *Diocletian Palace*, pls. 45, 47, 51.

[57] S. Rinaldi Tufi, *Dalmazia* (Museo della Civiltà Romana, Le province dell'Impero 2), Rome 1989, 67-8, figs. 66-7. The sphinx on the temple podium is on a modern block designed for the damaged present condition of the sphinx. The pedestal in the peristyle fills in an intercolumniation in an awkward way, and from photographs there appears to be no trace of a symmetrical pedestal on the other side of the grand staircase. Reconstructions eliminate this pedestal: Marasović and Marasović, *Diocletian Palace*, fig. 32.

[58] 'a conferma della simpatia di Diocleziano per i simboli originari dell'antico Egitto (e per la tradizione, di derivazione faraonica, del sovrano divinizzato):' Rinaldi Tufi, *Dalmazia*, 67-8, figs. 66-7.

[59] Clement, *Stromateis* 5.42.3: πρὸς τοῖσδε ἀλκῆς μὲν καὶ ῥώμης σύμβολον αὐτοῖς ὁ λέων· ὥσπερ ἀμέλει γῆς τε αὐτῆς καὶ γεωργίας καὶ τροφῆς ὁ βοῦς, ἀνδρείας τε καὶ παρρησίας ὁ ἵππος, ἀλκῆς τε αὖ μετὰ συνέσεως ἡ σφίγξ, τὸ μὲν σῶμα πᾶν λέοντος, τὸ πρόσωπον δὲ ἀνθρώπου ἔχουσα. ὁμοίως τε τούτοις σύνεσιν καὶ μνήμην καὶ κράτος καὶ τέχνην ὁ ἄνθρωπος αἰνισσόμενος τοῖς ἱεροῖς πρὸς αὐτῶν ἐγγλύφεται.

with regard to wisdom.'[60] While the sphinx may at times have been used in primitive fashion as a magical protector against hostile magic (the evil eye), the protective function is here formulated in terms of a rather rational symbolism acceptable in more cultivated circles, where patrons capable of commissioning or buying attractive works of art are more likely to have been found. This rationalization of the sphinx in terms of the best qualities of her human and animal components could well have played a role in the popularity of the monster for many apparently 'decorative' roles, as personal emblems on intaglios or as civic emblems on coinage.

It is striking that Clement, a Christian writer of the late second and early third century, had no reservations about citing these uses of a mythological creature. Apparently the sphinx was worthy of inclusion in his *Stromateis*, first, because she was not an object of cult and, second, because her symbolism dignified theology in general. This was to some degree characteristic of Clement, who went as far as any ancient Christian theologian in incorporating aspects of the surrounding non-Christian world into his writing.

Conceptualized interpretations of the sphinx continued to develop in the literary tradition. Early Christian and Byzantine authors commented on sphinxes and other such creatures in discussions about the difference between 'image' and 'likeness.' They distinguished between an image of unsubstantiated form (εἴδωλον) and a likeness reflecting real substance (ὁμοίωμα). Sphinxes, Tritons and Centaurs belonged to the former, while sun, moon, stars, humans, animals and the like were part of the latter category.[61] Applying the anatomical dichotomy of the sphinx to the division of body and soul was another staple of later theological speculation. In this context the sphinx was viewed as nothing else than a human being composed of unequal parts, which reflected the human ties with both rational and irrational capabilities. The rational part was perceived as belonging to the realm of the mind

---

[60] Synesius of Cyrene, *On the kingdom* 7 (Terzaghi): ταῦτ' ἄρα καὶ ἡ Σφὶγξ αὐτοῖς ἐπὶ τῶν προτεμενισμάτων ἱδρύεται, τοῦ συνδυασμοῦ τῶν ἀρετῶν ἱερὸν σύμβολον, τὴν μὲν ἰσχὺν θηρίον, τὴν δὲ φρόνησιν ἄνθρωπος. See also *On providence*, 1, 11.

[61] See Theodoret of Cyrrhus (4th–5th cent. CE), *Quaestiones in Octateuchum*, p. 127 (N. Fernández Marcos and A. Sáenz-Badillos). The same thoughts resurface in Georgius Monachus (9th cent. CE), *Chronicon*, p. 65 (de Boor); Suda (10th cent. CE), *Lexicon*, epsilon iota, 45 (Adler); Georgius Cedrenus (11th–12th cent. CE), *Compendium Historiarum*, i, 570 (Bekker); *Etymologium Gudianum* (11c.), omicron, p. 482 (Sturz).

and the divine while the irrational part was viewed as drawing heavily on the material world. In this way the figure of the sphinx was adapted to an anthropological scheme of a largely Platonic tradition.[62]

Sculpted sphinxes in Christian contexts

In spite of the attractive symbolism developed for the sphinx through-out antiquity, the sphinx seems not to have been a popular subject in Early Christian or Early Medieval art. Not until the thirteenth century does anything like a 'Clementine' symbolic sphinx seem to have appeared. The Cosmati, a group of marble workers active in and around Rome revived Egyptian-style lions and sphinxes in their ecclesiastical decorations. Lions and sphinxes, which often wear *nemes* head cloths, provided visual protection for church furniture, including choir screens, paschal candlesticks, pulpits and sacristy doors.[63] The Cosmatesque pulpit in the church of S. Cesario provides a particu-larly resonant example; small sphinxes are carved under the bases of the pulpit's colonnettes (fig. 12).[64] As part of the setting for reading and interpreting holy scripture, the sphinxes are perfectly suited to represent the mysteries of thinking about God and the retribution that evil-doers should fear. Regrettably the symbolic interpretation of the monster seen in Plutarch, Clement, and Synesius seems to have left no trace in the Latin church fathers, and it remains impossible to prove that the inspiration for the Cosmatesque sphinxes at Rome was literary as well as artistic and decorative.

In summation then, current presentations of the sphinx fail to reflect the full range of meaning that the sphinx had for ancient writers. The roles for the sphinx in ancient art should be expanded beyond those of Theban killer, tomb guardian, and decorative motif. The sphinx also served as temple guardian, and she (or he) had a series of symbolic roles, representing prophetic utterance, theological ambiguity, divine mystery, divine retribution, and protection with intelligence. Drawing

---

[62] See, for example, Michael Psellus (11c.), *Opuscula logica, physica, allegorica, alia,* Opusculum 44, ll. 24-89 (Duffy).

[63] A. Roullet, *The Egyptian and Egyptianizing monuments of Imperial Rome,* 7-9, figs. 1-6.

[64] H. Decker, *Romanesque Art in Italy* (translated by J. Cleugh), S.l. 1958, 61, cat. no. 116.

Fig. 12. Marble pulpit of S. Cesario, Rome, about 1230. Below the twisted columns a zone with sphinxes, evangelist symbols, and grotesque figures. Photograph from H. Decker, *Romanesque Art in Italy* (translated by J. Cleugh), S.l. 1958, cat. no. 116.

on his Hellenized Egyptian environment, Clement of Alexandria gave the fullest formulations of these rich interpretations.[65]

---

[65] Our thanks go to Lawrence Berman, Beat Brenk, Mary Comstock, Eric Junod, Alan Walker, and Bonna Wescoat, who kindly provided information and assistance.

FOOLISH EGYPTIANS: APION AND ANOUBION IN THE *PSEUDO-CLEMENTINES*

Jan N. Bremmer

Although Egypt was renowned for its wisdom in antiquity,[1] there were of course foolish Egyptians too—at least from a Christian point of view. Good examples must have been Appion and Annoubion, since they were so 'foolish' as to follow Simon Magus in the *Pseudo-Clementines*.[2] The 'foolish duo' first appears in the *Pseudo-Clementines*, when the protagonist of the novel, Clement, arrived in Tyre together with his companions Aquila and Nicetas. It was their task to investigate what Simon Magus was saying in order to prepare Peter for a confrontation with him. However, their arrival was in vain, since

> in the morning, a friend of Bernice came and said that Simon had set sail for Sidon. From his pupils he had left behind him Appion Pleistonikes, a man of Alexandria, a grammarian by profession (whom I knew as being a friend of my father), Annoubion the Diospolitan, an astrologer, and Athenodorus the Athenian, who was a dedicated follower of the doctrine of Epicurus (H[omilies] 4.6).[3]

Both Appion and Annoubion are also known from other sources, and

---

[1] See the contribution of A. Hilhorst to this volume.

[2] For Simon Magus see most recently K. Rudolph, 'Simon – Magus oder Gnosticus', *Theol. Rundschau* 42 (1977) 279-359; M.J. Edwards, 'Simon Magus, the Bad Samaritan', in: M.J. Edwards and S. Swain (eds), *Portraits*, Oxford 1997, 69-91; F. Heintz, *Simon 'le Magicien'*, Paris 1997; R. Hanig, 'Simon Magus in der Petrusakten und die Theodotianer', *Studia Patristica* 31 (1997) 112-20; T. Adamik, 'The Image of Simon Magus in the Christian Tradition', in: J.N. Bremmer (ed.), *The Apocryphal Acts of Peter*, Leuven 1998, 52-64; A. Schneider and L. Cirillo, *Les Reconnaissances du pseudo Clément*, Turnhout 1999, 559-70; G. Theissen, 'Simon Magus – die Entwicklung seines Bildes vom Charismatiker zum gnostischen Erlöser: Ein Beitrag zur Frühgeschichte der Gnosis', in: A. von Dobbeler et al. (eds), *Religionsgeschichte des Neuen Testaments: Festschrift für Klaus Berger zum 60. Geburtstag*, Tübingen/Basel 2000, 407-32; J. Zangenberg, '*Dynamis tou theou*: Das religionsgeschichtliche Profil des Simon Magus', ibid., 519-40; A. Tuzlak, 'The Magician and the Heretic: The Case of Simon Magus', in: P. Mirecki and M. Meyer (eds), *Magic and Ritual in the Ancient World*, Leiden 2002, 416-26.

[3] The translations of the *Recognitions* and *Homilies* are adapted from those of the *Ante-Nicene Christian library*, vols 3 and 17, Edinburgh 1868 and 1870, respectively.

recent papyri have enriched our knowledge of them. In my contribution I will look at their pre-Clementine careers and briefly compare these with the representations of Anoubion and Apion in the *Pseudo-Clementines*. These are of course imaginative interpretations by an author who was well informed about them, but who did not strive for conscientious, historical portraits. I will start with their 'partner in crime' Athenodorus, who is the most obscure of this infamous triad.

1. *Athenodorus*

In the *Homilies* Athenodorus is regularly mentioned in company with Simon Magus, Appion or Annoubion,[4] but he does not have a life of his own. Nowhere do we receive any information about his ideas and he remains a mere puppet on the Pseudo-Clementine stage. Dirk Obbink persuasively notes that 'Athenodorus of Athens is otherwise unknown; perhaps his name was chosen for its geographical associations, adding Athens to Alexandria and Diospolis, and implying that Simon drew followers from a broad spectrum of centres of learning'.[5] However, as Appion and Annoubion were chosen for their backgrounds in historical Egyptian intellectuals, one may wonder whether Athenodorus was not in fact modelled on the philosopher Athenodorus from Cilician Tarsus, the teacher of Augustus.[6] Although we do not have sufficient information about him to explain that choice, we should not forget that the *Pseudo-Clementines* are fiction and do not necessarily aim at providing precise historical knowledge. In any case, labelling him as a Epicurean was surely meant to make Athenodorus immediately suspect in the eyes of the Christian (and Jewish!) reading public.[7]

---

[4] H 6.1; 7.9; 16.1; 20.13, 17, 21-22 = R[ecognitions] 10.55, 59, 63-64.

[5] D. Obbink, 'Anoubion, Elegiacs', in: *The Oxyrhynchus Papyri*, ed. N. Gonis et al., vol. LXVI, Oxford 1999, 57-109 at 61.

[6] For Athenodorus see C. Cichorius, *Römische Studien*, Leipzig and Berlin 1922, 279-82; B.L. Hijmans, 'Athenodorus on the Categories and a Pun on Athenodorus', in: J. Mansfeld and L.M. de Rijk (eds), *Kephalaion: Studies in Greek Philosophy and its Continuation offered to C. J. de Vogel*, Assen 1975, 104-14.

[7] For the Christian and Jewish rejection of Epicurus see W. Schmid, 'Epikur', in: *RAC* 5 (1962) 682-819 at 774-803 and F. Niewöhner, 'Epikureer sind Atheisten: Zur Geschichte des Wortes apikuros in der jüdischen Philosophie', in: Id. and O. Pluta (eds), *Atheismus in Mittelalter und in der Renaissance*, Wiesbaden 1999, 11-22, respectively.

2. *Annoubion*

Our first 'foolish' Egyptian is introduced as 'an astrologer' (τινὰ ἀστρολόγον) and an inhabitant of Diospolis, but later he is characterised as 'the best of the astrologers' (ἀστρολόγων ἄριστος) and 'inseparable' from Simon Magus (H 14.11). That is the sum total of what we are told about Annoubion. He is no longer an important figure in the *Pseudo-Clementines*, and his presence in the *Recognitions* (10.52, 56, 58-9, 62-3) is clearly due to the influence of the *Homilies*.[8] Yet his role must have been much more prominent in the elusive *Grundschrift* of the *Pseudo-Clementines*. Inspired by Heintze,[9] Schmidt has pointed out that the *Grundschrift* contained a disputation on the *genesis*, the moment of birth that determined man's life according to astrology.[10] This debate must have taken place at Laodicea and was abbreviated by the *Recognitions* (8.2.2). In the *Homilies* we read in the last book that Peter says: 'God arranges our affairs in a most satisfactory manner; for we have with us Annoubion the astrologer. When we arrive at Antioch, he will discuss the *genesis*, giving us his genuine opinions as a friend' (H 20.21). Yet, as in earlier passages (H 14.12, 20.11), the debate never materialises and the reader of the *Homilies* is left unsatisfied in this respect. Apparently, in the *Grundschrift* Annoubion was the opponent of Clemens in a debate about astrology, just as Athenodorus must have been the opponent in a debate about providence.

Sufficient material has survived to see that Annoubion was modelled on a well known Egyptian astrologer, Anoubion, who used to be located in the time of Nero.[11] The Pseudo-Clementine spelling

---

[8] C. Schmidt, *Studien zu den Pseudo-Clementinen*, Leipzig 1929, 70-1.

[9] W. Heintze, *Der Klemensroman und seine griechischen Quellen*, Leipzig 1914, 49.

[10] Schmidt, *Studien*, 210-13. For *genesis*: H 4.12 and *passim*; astrological authors, like Vettius Valens, O. Neugebauer and H.B. van Hoesen, *Greek Horoscopes*, Philadelphia 1959, *passim*; in inscriptions, L. Robert, *Opera minora selecta*, ii, Amsterdam 1968, 988-9; J. and L. Robert, *REG* 89 (1976) 502. The term was so normal in astrological literature that it was also used in Latin: Petronius, *Sat.* 39.8, cf. M.G. Cavalca, *I grecismi nel Satyricon di Petronio*, Bologna 2001, 91 (with thanks to Stelios Panagiotakis); Pliny, *NH* 36.19; Juvenal 6.579; 14.248; Augustine, *C. Faust.* 2.5.212; *Historia Apollonii Regis Tyri* 38 RA; *L'Année Épigraphique* 1903.377; 1905.25; 1916.7-8; 1968.455; *CIL* II² 5.50; *CIL* III.13529.

[11] E. Riess, 'Anubion', *RE* 1 (1894) 2321-2; W. Gundel and H.G. Gundel, *Astrologumena: Die astrologische Literatur in der Antike und ihre Geschichte*, Wiesbaden 1966, 155 (who even consider an earlier date possible), 380; D. Pingree, *Dorotheus Sidonius: Carmen Astrologicum*, Stuttgart 1976, 344: 'saeculo secundo vel tertio p.C.n. floruisse videtur'.

of his name with its doubling of the *n*, Anoubion/Annoubion, will have been invented by the author of the *Grundschrift*, as he also wrote Appion instead of Apion (§3 below) and Mattidia (H 13 etc.) instead of Matidia, the name of the daughter of Trajan's sister, whose own daughter Matidia was the sister-in-law of Hadrian.[12]

Unfortunately, we do not have much information about the historical Anoubion. He has a common Egyptian-Greek name,[13] which is formed from the root of Anubis,[14] the jackal-headed Egyptian divinity,[15] who has also given us the names Anoubarion, Anoubas, Anoubiaina and Anoubias.[16] The name of the god was already used for theophoric names in the Middle Kingdom and remained productive well into Coptic times.[17] I see therefore no reason to consider Anoubion a pseudonym, as has recently been suggested by Dirk Obbink.[18] Annoubion's origin from Diospolis fits the Egyptian background of his name, but Schmidt states that we do not know which of the three cities with the name Diospolis is meant.[19] However, we may firmly locate Annoubion in the old capital of Egypt, which the Greeks called Thebes,[20] since the city was well known for its temples and esoteric wisdom, and the autobiography of Thessalos, the magician, mentions Thebes as a place for necromancy.[21]

---

[12] *PIR*² M 367; H. Temporini, 'Matidia', in: *Der neue Pauly* 7 (1999) 1025.

[13] P.M. Fraser and E. Matthews, *A Lexicon of Greek Personal Names*, Oxford 1987ff., I.42; *SEG* 40.1568; *I.Kios* 22 and *passim* in the papyri.

[14] In later times, Anubis is also associated with astrology, cf. W. Gundel, *Neue astrologische Texte des Hermes Trismegistos*, Munich 1936, 307.

[15] For Anubis see B. Altenmüller, 'Anubis', in: W. Helck and E. Otto (eds), *Lexikon der Ägyptologie*, i, Wiesbaden 1975, 327–33.

[16] For Anoubiaina see *SEG* 40.1568, 36, 56; the other names can be found *passim* in the papyri.

[17] H. Ranke, *Die ägyptischen Personennamen*, i, Glückstadt 1935, 36-7 and ii (Glückstadt/New York, 1952), 112.

[18] Contra Obbink, 'Anoubion, Elegiacs', 58, 61, who ascribes the suggestion to Weinstock. However, S. Weinstock, 'A New Anubio Fragment', *Chron. d'Eg.* 27 (1952) 210-17 at 216-7 considered the possibility but rejected it on the basis of Anoubion being a normal Egyptian name.

[19] Schmidt, *Studien*, 297 note 1.

[20] Thebes as Diospolis: A. Geissen and M. Weber, 'Untersuchungen zu den ägyptischen Namenprägungen', *ZPE* 144 (2003) 277-300 at 292-3.

[21] Thessalus, 12, ed. H.-V. Friedrich, *Thessalos von Tralles*, Meisenheim 1968. For the autobiography see most recently A.-J. Festugière, *Hermétisme et mystique païenne*, Paris 1967, 141-80 (with French translation and commentary); J.Z. Smith, *Map is not Territory*, Leiden 1978, 172-89; G. Fowden, *The Egyptian Hermes*, Princeton 1993², 162-5; M.W. Dickie, *Magic and Magicians in the Greco-Roman World*, London/New York 2001, 216-7.

The only reason for Anoubion's traditional chronology is his occurrence in the *Pseudo-Clementines*, and it cannot be excluded that he lived somewhat earlier, like Apion (§3), or somewhat later. In any case, Obbink notes that it is unlikely that he is to be dated after the second century.[22] This argument can be strengthened by an observation of Hermann Usener (1834-1905) in 1900 that traces of Anoubion can be found most likely in Pseudo-Manetho's *Apotelesmatika*,[23] which has a firm *terminus post quem* of AD 80, as the author provides his own horoscope.[24]

Gradually the content of the work of the historical Anoubion has become clearer.[25] In 1887 it was noted that Anoubion was known to Firmicus Maternus in his *Mathesis* (III.11), and in 1900 Wilhelm Kroll (1869-1939) argued that in his Book VI Firmicus had used material of Anoubion, on the basis of correspondences between Firmicus and a prose paraphrase of material 'from Anoubion'.[26] In 1914 Werner Heintze (1889-1914?), one of the many scholarly victims of the First World War, compared four astrological schemata in the *Recognitions* with the meagre fragments of Anoubion published by A. Olivieri in the *Catalogus codicum astrologorum Graecorum* (= *CCAG*: II.202-3, 208).[27] 1921 saw the publication of an elegiac distich of Anoubion in the work of the early Byzantine astrologer Rhetorios (*CCAG* VIII.4, 208),[28]

---

[22] For the historiography of this paragraph I am indebted to Obbink, 'Anoubion, Elegiacs', 62.

[23] H. Usener, *Kleine Schriften*, iv, Leipzig/Berlin 1913, 329-30; see also A. Ludwich, 'Das elegische Lehrgedicht des Astrologen Anubion und die Manethoniana', *Philologus* NF 17 (1904) 129-30. For Pseudo-Manetho's borrowing of various sources see Weinstock, 'A New Anubio Fragment', 216 note 1.

[24] For Pseudo-Manetho see the editions by Didot (1851, 1858); *POxy*. XXXI.2546; P.J. Sijpesteijn, 'Manetho, Apotelesmatika IV 231-235', *ZPE* 21 (1976) 182; *The Apotelesmatika of Manetho*, ed. and transl. by R. Lopilato (Diss. Brown University, Providence, 1998). For Pseudo-Manetho's date of birth see R. Garnett, 'On the Date of the Ἀποτελεσματικὰ of Manetho', *J. of Philol.* 23 (1875) 238-40; Neugebauer and Van Hoesen, *Greek Horoscopes*, 92.

[25] For a survey of our knowledge in 1966 see Gundel and Gundel, *Astrologumena*, 155-7.

[26] A. Engelbrecht, *Hephästion von Theben und sein astrologisches Compendium: ein Beitrag zur Geschichte der griechischen Astrologie*, Vienna 1887, 36; W. Kroll, in *Catalogus codicum astrologorum Graecorum*, ii, Brussels 1900, 159-60, see now Dorotheus, frg. II 14-33 (pp. 345-67 Pingree).

[27] Heintze, *Der Klemensroman*, 109-10.

[28] For Rhetorios (ca. AD 620) see D. Pingree, 'Antiochus and Rhetorius', *Class. Philol.* 72 (1977) 203-23 at 220-2 and 'From Alexandria to Baghdād to Byzantium: The Transmission of Astrology', *Int. J. Class. Trad.* 8 (2001-2) 3-37.

and in 1952, on the basis of these publications, Stefan Weinstock
(1901-71) could connect the astrological elegiacs of *P. Schubart* 15 and
Firmicus VI.31.78-85, pointing to Anoubion as their author.[29] In 1991
Simonetta Feraboli identified a further number of passages in which
Anoubion and Firmicus VI coincided.[30] Finally, the publication in 1999
by Obbink of *POxy.* LXVI.4503-4505 from Anoubion's book III has
definitively demonstrated that Firmicus II.4.1-6 and VI.29-31 are an
almost word-for-word translation of Anoubion. In fact, Obbink has
now also noted that the predictions in *Recognitions* 10.9 are authenti-
cally Anoubionic, both in the content of the horoscopes and their
form: he has included them as fragments and has attempted a Greek
version in elegiacs in his forthcoming Teubner edition of Anoubion,
which the publisher K.G. Saur has recently announced.[31]

It should be clear by now that the author of the *Grundschrift*, when
looking for an astrologer as opponent of Clement, had chosen an
Egyptian astrologer whose work, a didactic poem in elegiacs of at least
four books,[32] must have been widely circulating in Late Antiquity. It
is not immediately clear, though, why the author of the *Grundschrift*
dedicated so much attention to astrology. Two possibilities come to
mind. First, astrology was so pervasive in Greco-Roman society that
it played a large role in many ancient novels. This was especially the
case in the original Greek version of the *Historia Apollonii Regis Tyri*,[33]
which recent research has now established as an important model for
the *Grundschrift*.[34] Consequently, the author of the latter may well have
thought it necessary to still pay attention to astrology but to approach
it now from a Christian point of view. Second, the *Grundschrift* was
probably written in Edessa.[35] Here the heterodox Christian philosopher

---

[29] Weinstock, 'A New Anubio Fragment'.

[30] S. Feraboli, 'Un utile confronto tra Anubio e Firmico', *Paideia* 46 (1991)
201-5.

[31] Personal communication (Email 19 November 2003), cf. Anubio, *Carmen astrologicum elegiacum*, ed. D. Obbink, Munich 2004.

[32] For the content of the work see now Obbink, 'Anoubion, Elegiacs', 58-9.

[33] For a persuasive argument in favour of a Greek background see now G.
Kortekaas, *The Story of Apollonius, King of Tyre*, Leiden 2004. Prominence of astrology:
G. Kortekaas, 'The Historia Apollonii Regis Tyri and Ancient Astrology', *ZPE* 85
(1991) 71-85.

[34] M. Vielberg, *Klemens in den Pseudoklementinischen Rekognitionen*, Berlin 2000, 139-
44.

[35] Bremmer, 'Achilles Tatius and Heliodorus in Christian East Syria', in: H.
Vanstiphout (ed.), *All Those Nations … Cultural Encounters within and with the Near East*,
Groningen 1999, 21-9 at 25-6.

Bardaisan had been much influenced by current astrological thinking, even though he partially rejected these thoughts as constraining human liberty too much.[36] The *Grundschrift*, which must have been written shortly after Bardaisan's death in AD 222,[37] was perhaps engaged in a polemic against the views of Bardaisan's followers, who continued for many centuries to propagate the master's ideas.[38] Unfortunately, the loss of the *Grundschrift* does not allow any certainty in this respect.[39]

3. *Appion*

The second 'foolish' Egyptian in the *Pseudo-Clementines* is Appion, whose name is clearly based on the Egyptian sacred bull at Memphis.[40] Its cult has given us such Greek names as Apia/os,[41] Ap(p)ianos, Apias and, of course, Apion, but theophoric names with the element 'Apis' can be found throughout Egyptian history, from the Old Kingdom onwards.[42] The spelling Appion is attested in both inscriptions (SB I 4549 [AD 226]; *I. Creta* IV.460 [AD 539]) and in about 10 mainly second-century papyri. In literature we find the spelling in some manuscripts of Pliny, *NH* 30.18 (r) and 35.88 (VRF); in variant readings of Tatian 27 and 38 (P);[43] in a variant reading of the critic Achilles Tatius, *Intr. Arat.*, p. 30 Maass (B); in the treatise traditionally known as Pseudo-Justin, *Cohortatio ad Graecos* (9.2);[44] in the preface of

---

[36] H.J.W. Drijvers, *Bardaisan of Edessa*, Assen 1966, 157-63; K. von Stuckrad, *Das Ringen um die Astrologie: Jüdische und christliche Beiträge zum antiken Zeitverständnis*, Berlin/New York 2000, 655-63.

[37] Bremmer, 'Achilles Tatius', 26-7.

[38] Drijvers, *Bardaisan*, 227-8.

[39] The possible connections between the *Grundschrift* and Bardaisan have been often discussed, although no consensus has been reached, see the survey by F.S. Jones, 'The Pseudo-Clementines: A History of Research', *The Second Century* 2 (1982) 1-33, 63-96, reprinted in E. Ferguson (ed.), *Studies in Early Christianity*, ii, New York/London 1993, 195-262 at 214-18.

[40] E. Otto, *Beiträge zur Geschichte der Stierkulte in Ägypten*, Leipzig 1938, 11–34; J. Vercoutter, 'Apis', in: Helck and Otto, *Lexikon der Ägyptologie*, i, 338-50.

[41] W. Swinnen, 'Problèmes d'anthroponymie ptolémaïque', *Chron. d'Eg.* 42 (1967) 156-71 at 157-8 (Apios); Fraser and Matthews, *A Lexicon of Greek Personal Names*, i, 50; iiiA, 48-9.

[42] H. Ranke, *Die ägyptischen Personennamen*, i, Glückstadt 1935, 236-8.

[43] The variants are not mentioned in the most recent edition by M. Whittaker, *Tatian, Oratio ad Graecos and Fragments*, Oxford 1982.

[44] In fact, C. Riedweg, *Ps.-Justin (Markell von Ankyra?) Ad Graecos de vera religione (bisher 'Cohortatio ad Graecos')*, 2 vols, Basel 1994, i, 167-82 makes a convincing case

Hesychius; in *Etymologicum Genuinum* s.v. ἄχος κλιτύς, ὅπλα[45] and in one of its manuscripts s.v. κολαφίζω καὶ κόλαφος (Laurentianus S. Marco 304); in *Etymologicum Gudianum* s.v. νήδυμος and in two of the manuscripts s.v. ὕνις (= p. 540, 30-33 Sturz: Borterius gr. I 70 and Paris. suppl. gr. 172); in *Etymologicum Magnum* and *Symeonis* s.v. Ἀθριβίς; in the Greek translation of Eutropius (6.11); in Photius (112-3, 90b), who clearly refers to the *Homilies*; in the scholia on Homer (*Il.* 5.403); in the Suda (s.v. Ἰώσηπος) and in Syncellus (120 Mosshammer, where it is wrongly corrected to Apion).

To explain the spelling Appion, Riedweg suggests an influence from the Latin Appius.[46] Yet that name was much more popular in the Greek world than in Palestine, where it occurs only once on an ostrakon (*O. Masada* 788), and in Egypt. Here the name is virtually limited to Appius Prostates, chairman of the town council of Panopolis (ca. AD 298) and Appius Sabinus, a Roman prefect of Egypt (ca. AD 250). Moreover, the spelling Appion for Apion is clearly a later development that is not yet visible in the contemporaries of Apion himself and of which the explanation is unclear. Consequently, the spelling Appion need not be connected with developments in Greek onomastics or in Greek spelling. Given the other names in the *Pseudo-Clementines* with a doubling of a consonant (Anoubion/Annoubion and Matidia/Mattidia: §2 above),[47] the doubling of the *p* seems to have been part of the stylistic repertory of the author of the *Grundschrift*.

Apion was born in Upper Egypt in the later second half of the first century BC. Traditionally, his place of birth is located in the oasis of El Khargeh (ancient Hibis), but more recently there seems to have developed a preference for the Dakhleh oasis.[48] Apion studied in Alexandria under Didymus Chalkenteros and later succeeded Theon as head of the Alexandrian school.[49] His enormous industry gained

---

for the authorship of Marcellus of Ancyra; note also the supporting arguments by P.W. van der Horst, *Mnemosyne* 50 (1997) 366-7.

[45] S. Neitzel, in: *Dionysius Thrax; Tyrannion Amisenus; Diocles Alexandrinus; Apion*, ed. K. Linke, W. Haas and S. Neitzel, Berlin 1977, corrects Appion into Apion in these cases (= Apion, frgs 27, 50 and 86) and does not mention the spelling Appion in Apion, frgs 79 and 132.

[46] Riedweg, *Ps.-Justin*, ii, 287.

[47] F.T. Gignac, *A Grammar of the Greek Papyri of the Roman and Byzantine Periods*, 2 vols, Milan 1976-81, i, 161-2 gives only a few examples of the doubling of consonants.

[48] G. Wagner, *Les Oasis d'Égypte*, Cairo 1987, 138.

[49] The prestige of Alexandria as a centre of Greek civilisation is also illustrated by the fact that Simon Magus received his education there (H 2.22).

him his nickname Μόχθος.[50] During the reigns of Claudius and Caligula he worked in Rome, and in AD 39 he acted as the leader of the Alexandrian delegation to Rome after the Greek pogrom that had cost the lives of so many Jews.[51] He died about the middle of the first century AD.[52]

It is of course impossible to discuss here the historical Apion in any depth, but it may be interesting to compare his occurrence and role in the *Pseudo-Clementines* in order to see in what ways Apion was remembered in the times after his death. As we have seen in our introduction, Appion was introduced together with Annoubion and Athenodorus as Ἀππίωνα τὸν Πλειστονίκην, ἄνδρα Ἀλεξανδρέα, γραμματικὸν τὴν ἐπιστήμην (H 4.6). He is also called Pleistonikes in two other passages (H 20.11; R 10.52).[53] The qualification must have immediately identified Appion's model for the educated readership of the *Pseudo-Clementines*, as Pliny the Elder, who followed his lectures, already mentions it, and Pleistonikes was clearly a standing epithet of Apion.[54] Jacobson has argued that in this case Pleistonikes does not have its usual meaning 'victor in many contests' but means 'quarrelsome'.[55] Yet the inscription Ἀπίων Πλειστονί[ικης] ἤκουσα τρίς on one of the two colossi of Memnon hardly favours this opinion.[56] The oldest datable inscription on the colossi is from AD 20 and the next from AD 65,[57] and the death of Apion (above) falls between these dates. As Van der Horst observes, 'it would be most remarkable if there were

---

[50] Apollonius Dyskolos, *Synt.* p. 124 Uhlig; Suda s.v. *Anterôs, Apiôn*; Scholion on Aristophanes, *Pax* 778.

[51] See now P.W. van der Horst, *Philo's Flaccus: The First Pogrom*, Leiden 2003.

[52] For a good survey of Apion's life and work see P.W. van der Horst, *Japhet in the Tents of Shem*, Leuven 2002, 207-21 ('Who was Apion?') = (Dutch) 'Apion, "cymbaal van de wereld"', *Lampas* 35 (2002) 228-42; K.R. Jones, 'The Figure of Apion in Josephus' *Contra Apionem*', *JSJ* 36 (2005: I warmly thank Kenneth Jones for showing me his informative study beforehand). L. Cohn, 'Apion', *RE* 1 (1894) 2803-6 remains useful.

[53] Note that Rehm, Paschke and Strecker, in their edition of the *Homilies*, capitalise Pleistonikes in the first case, but not in the second one.

[54] Pliny, *NH* 37.75; Josephus, *C. Ap.* 2.3; Gellius, *NA* 5.14.1; 7.8.1; Clement of Alexandria, *Str.* 1.21.3; Achilles Tatius, *Intr. Arat.* p. 30 Maass; Eusebius, *PE* 10.12.2; Suda s.v. *Apiôn* (who mistakenly makes Apion the son of Pleistonikes).

[55] H. Jacobson, 'Apion's Nickname', *Am. J. Philol.* 98 (1977) 413-5.

[56] A. and É. Bernand, *Les inscriptions grecques et latines du Colosse de Memnon*, Cairo 1960, 165.

[57] For the colossus and its inscriptions see now G.W. Bowersock, *Studies on the Eastern Roman Empire*, Goldbach 1994, 253-64.

to have been two Apions with a nickname that began with *Pleiston-*'.[58] Surely, a vain person like Apion would not have propagated a negative nickname,[59] and it is hardly in favour of Jacobson's argument that Apion's pupil Pliny also mentions the nickname.

Apion's Alexandrian origin is also confirmed by other sources. In his *Contra Apionem*, Josephus informs us that Apion congratulated Alexandria for having such a great man like himself as citizen.[60] And in a discussion of the games played by Penelope's suitors, Athenaeus mentions the opinion of 'Apion the Alexandrian'.[61] Given his Egyptian origin, Apion must have acquired Alexandrian citizenship by special grant. Such grants were liberally awarded to dramatic and athletic victors from the Greek world, but it was extremely rare that a native Egyptian acquired Alexandrian citizenship: only one other case is known.[62] This points to a very special occasion or service to the city, and it seems most likely to connect Apion's franchise with his leadership of the Alexandrian embassy to Rome in AD 39.

The third qualification, 'grammarian', is also well attested in both Greek and Latin literature and was already part of his reputation during his lifetime.[63] It is not exactly clear how Apion himself interpreted the qualification or how we should do so. The term γραμματικός means 'grammarian/scholar' but also 'cultured person'.[64] Apion was both,

---

[58] Van der Horst, *Japhet*, 209; similarly, L. Holford-Strevens, *Aulus Gellius: An Antonine Scholar and His Achievement*, Oxford 2003, 69: the objections against the identification are 'hypersceptical'.

[59] For Apion's vanity see Pliny, *NH Praef.* 25, which relates that Tiberius called him *cymbalum mundi*; Gellius 5.14.1; note also that Syncellus 120 (= 282) Mosshammer calls Apion 'the most pedantic of the grammarians'.

[60] Josephus, *C. Ap.* 2.29, 41 and 135, cf. H. Jacobson, 'Apion Ciceronianus', *Mnemosyne* IV 53 (2000) 592.

[61] Athenaeus 1.16F, quoted by Eustathius on *Od.* 17.401.

[62] D. Delia, *Alexandrian Citizenship during the Roman Principate*, Atlanta 1991, 56.

[63] Seneca, *Ep.* 88.40; Pliny, *NH Praef.* 25; 30.18; Josephus, *C. Ap.* 2.2, 12, 15; Tatian, *Or.* 38; Athenaeus 7. 294F; Clement of Alexandria, *Str.* 1.22; Eusebius, *HE* 3.9.4; *PE* 10.10.16; 10.11.14; 10.12.2; Cosmas Indicopleustes 12.4; Suda, s.v. *Apiôn, Pasês*.

[64] For the term see most recently A.D. Booth, 'Litterator', *Hermes* 91 (1981) 371-8; R.A. Kaster, *Guardians of Language*, Oxford 1988, 445-54 and *C. Suetonius Tranquillus, De Grammaticis et Rhetoribus*, Oxford 1993, 86-93; U. Schindel, 'Der Beruf des Grammaticus in der Spätantike', in: J. Dummer and M. Vielberg (eds), *Leitbild Wissenschaft?*, Stuttgart 2003, 173-90 (I owe a copy of this article to the kindness of the author). For prosopographies of *grammatici* see Kaster, *Guardians of Language*, 233-440; S. Agusta-Boularot, 'Les références épigraphiques aux grammatici et grammatikoi de l'Empire romain (I s. av. J.-C. – IV s. ap. J.-C.)', *Mél. Éc. Fr. Rome (Ant.)* 106 (1994) 653-764; R. Cribiore, *Writing, Teachers, and Students in Graeco-Roman Egypt*, Atlanta 1996, 167-9; add now *I. Smyrna* II.1, 652; *I. Hadrianoi* 173; *SEG* 44.1178-9, 1182A.

but his main fame derived from his historical and philological work, in which he was clearly not unsuccessful: Gellius (5.14.1) mentions his *libri non incelebres*. Apion's Homeric scholarship was his main claim to fame,[65] and his creativity and fertility with Homeric etymologies fitted the taste of his time.[66] Yet this side of his activities is not explicitly mentioned in the *Pseudo-Clementines*, although we may perhaps see a reference to it in a passage in which he praises and explains Homer:

> There was once a time when nothing existed but chaos and a confused mixture of orderless elements, which were as yet simply heaped together. This nature also testifies, and great men have been of opinion that it was so. Of these great men I shall bring forward to you as witness him who excelled them all in wisdom, Homer, where he says, with a reference to the original confused mass: 'But may you all become water and earth' (*Il.* VII.99), implying that from these all things had their origin, and that all things return to their first state, which is chaos, when the watery and earthy substances are separated (H 6.3).

It would be interesting to know to what extent this passage illustrates the Homeric teaching of the historical Apion, but there is too little left of his works for a proper evaluation.

The recent entry on Apion in *Der neue Pauly* states that it is 'sehr wahrscheinlich' that he also worked on other authors.[67] Unfortunately, it provides only one example and has missed the most recent one. In itself it is not so surprising that Apion's other work has escaped attention. As can be easily seen from recent studies of Apion, interest in this author is highly compartmentalised. Students of Judaism have focused on his anti-Semitic side, whereas Hellenists concentrated on his Homeric scholarship. As marginalia are regularly omitted in standard editions of ancient authors, one often has to go back to the original publications of the papyri in order to gain a better view of Apion's scholarship. The following is only a sampling, but it represents more

---

[65] S. Neitzel, in: *Dionysius Thrax; Tyrannion Amisenus; Diocles Alexandrinus; Apion*, 185-300; C. Theodoridis, 'Drei neue Fragmente des Grammatikers Apion', *Rhein. Mus.* 132 (1989) 345-50; M. Haslam, 'The Homer lexicon of Apollonius Sophista: I, Composition and constituents', *Class. Philol.* 89 (1994) 1-45. J. Dillery, 'Putting Him Back Together Again: Apion Historian, Apion Grammatikos', *Class. Philol.* 98 (2003) 383-90, connects Josephus' attack on Apion in particular with the latter's Homeric scholarship.

[66] R. Cribiore, *Gymnastics of the Mind: Greek Education in Hellenistic and Roman Egypt*, Princeton/Oxford 2001, 209-10.

[67] F. Montanari, 'Apion', in: *Der neue Pauly* 1 (1996) 845-7.

than can be found anywhere else. So far, it is clear that, in addition
to Homer, Apion has also worked on the following lyric poets:

1. Alcaeus

a) *POxy*. XXI.2295, frg. 4 col. ii (= Alcaeus F 143 Voigt: the papyrus
possibly mentions Apion, although this is not mentioned by Voigt)
b) *POxy*. XXI.2295, frg. 28 (= Alcaeus F 167 Voigt)
c) *POxy*. XXI.2295, frg. 40 col. ii (= Alcaeus F 179 Voigt: Apion
possibly mentioned)
d) Apollonius Dyskolos, *Synt.* p. 124 Uhlig (cf. Alcaeus F 308 Voigt)

2. Simonides

a) *POxy*. XXII.2327, frg. 2a col. i (= Simonides F 21 West[2]).
b) *POxy*. XXII.2327, frg. 19 col. ii (= Simonides F 46 West[2]).
c) *POxy*. XXII.2327, frg. 21 col. i (= Simonides F 21 West[2]).
d) *POxy*. XXII.2327, frg. 27 col. i (= Simonides F 11, 22 West[2]).[68]
e) *POxy*. XXII.2327, frg. 31 col. i (= Simonides F 31 West[2]).
f) *POxy*. LIX.3965, frg. 2 (= Simonides F 11, 32 West[2]).
g) *POxy*. LIX.3965, frg. 18 (= Simonides F 64 West[2]).

3. Other poets?[69]

Apion is probably also mentioned in *POxy*. XXI.2295, frgs 54 and
55, which are 'very doubtfully assigned' to Alcaeus by Edgar Lobel
(ad loc.). This means that we cannot be certain which author Apion
(if it is him) commented upon: it might have been even Homer.
The same abbreviation αμ that means ἀμ(φότεροι) in the scholia on
Alcaeus and Simonides, i.e. Apion and Nicanor, we also read in the
scholia on *POxy*. XXXII.2617, frg. 12 (= Stesichorus S30 Davies)
and frg. 22 (Stesichorus S34 Davies). However, lack of context
prevents us from knowing which critics are meant here.

Whereas Apion's philological activity was typical of the ancient
grammarian,[70] the *Pseudo-Clementines* mention at least two more aspects
of Appion, in addition to those that we already have discussed, that

---

[68] For the identification see D. Obbink, 'The Genre of Plataea', in: D. Boedeker
and D. Sider (eds), *The New Simonides*, New York 2001, 65-85 at 75 note 37.
[69] I am most grateful to Peter Parsons for advice on these cases.
[70] Cribiore, *Gymnastics of the Mind*, 185-219.

can be paralleled from other sources: his anti-Semitism and his interest in magic. Let us start with the first aspect. Before Clement visits Appion in Tyre, he first relates his previous experiences with him:

> And while I was confined to bed Appion came to Rome, and being my father's friend, he stayed with me. Hearing that I was in bed, he came to me, as being not unacquainted with medicine, and inquired the cause of my being in bed. But I, being well aware that the man exceedingly hated the Jews, as also that he had written many books against them, and that he had formed a friendship with this Simon, not through desire of learning, but because he knew that he was a Samaritan and a hater of the Jews, and that he had come forth against the Jews, therefore he had formed an alliance with him, that he might learn something from him against the Jews (H 5.2).

It is interesting to see that this episode is located in Rome, as Apion's Roman stay is also known from other sources.[71] Moreover, Clement directs the attention of his audience to Appion's anti-Semitic writings.[72] Unfortunately, there is little left from Apion's best known anti-Semitic work, the *Aigyptiaka* in five books, which is known mainly from Pliny, Gellius and Josephus' polemics in his *Contra Apionem*.[73] However, the passage in the *Homilies* suggests more than one title. In the English revision of Emil Schürer's history of the Jewish people, Martin Goodman flatly rejects the notice: 'this is of course not to be taken seriously'.[74] Admittedly, it is certainly possible that the author exaggerated the amount of Apion's anti-Semitic writings, but recent scepticism in this regard may have gone too far. In his *Stromata* (1.21.3), Clement of Alexandria mentions both Apion's *Aigyptiaka* and a 'book *Against the Jews* (*Kata Ioudaiôn*)'. He is quoted by his somewhat younger contemporary Julianus Africanus,[75] who in turn is quoted by pseudo-Justin (*Ad Graecos* 9). Felix Jacoby (ad *FGrH* 616 F 2) tried to harmonize the titles by suggesting that *Kata Ioudaiôn* was the fourth book of the *Aigyptiaka*. However, Goodman argues that 'the very fact that he (Josephus) is silent about it suggests that such a work never existed,

---

[71] Pliny, *NH* 30.18; Suda s.v. *Apiôn*.

[72] Note also H 5.27.

[73] For the fragments see Apion *FGrH* 616 F 1-21, cf. P. Schäfer, *Judeophobia*, Cambridge Mass. 1997, *passim*.

[74] E. Schürer, *The History of the Jewish People in the Age of Jesus Christ*, Edinburgh 1985, iii.1, 607, followed by Van der Horst, *Japhet*, 211.

[75] Africanus, *Chron.* 3, frg. 22 Routh = Eusebius, *PE.* 10.10.16 = (abbreviated) Syncellus 120 = 282 Mosshammer.

and it is clear that these Church writers had no direct knowledge of it'. The latter seems perfectly true, as Clement of Alexandria regularly presents second-hand knowledge in his *Stromata*. Yet, Clement's erudition and Alexandrian origin, the complete loss of Apion's writings and the notice of the evidently well informed *Pseudo-Clementines* should make us wary of rejecting the notice out of hand.[76]

The episode of our Clement's illness has another interesting aspect as well. When Appion asked Clement the reason of his illness, the latter answered that he was lovesick. Appion then told Clement that he had been in the same situation, but

> happened to meet an Egyptian who was exceedingly well versed in magic, and having become his friend, I disclosed to him my love. He not only assisted me in all that I wished, but, honouring me more bountifully, he even did not hesitate to teach me an incantation by means of which I obtained her. And as soon as I had obtained her, by means of that secret instruction, being persuaded by the liberality of my teacher, I was cured of love (H 5.3).

The passage is a nice illustration of that strange human habit of losing interest in something or someone at the moment that one has finally got possession of it. It was probably inspired by the well known episode of the Seleucid queen Stratonice and her stepson, the prince Antiochus, whose lovesickness was diagnosed by the famous physician Eresistratus.[77] The passage also illustrates the ubiquity of love magic in antiquity and the use of erotic charms, several of which have been found in Egypt.[78] Even Jewish magicians practised love magic, as is illustrated by the activities of the Jewish magician Atomus at the

---

[76] For a different view see Jones, 'The Figure of Apion', Appendix.

[77] As noted by W. Adler, 'Apion's "encomium of adultery": A Jewish satire of Greek paideia in the Pseudo-Clementine Homilies', *Hebr. Un. Coll. Ann.* 64 (1993) 15-49. For the fullest enumeration of the sources and the secondary literature see now J. Lightfoot, *Lucian, On the Syrian Goddess*, Oxford 2003, 373-9; add R. Falconi, 'Il motivo del malato d'amore in un argumentum di Seneca Padre', *Giorn. It. Filol.* 13 (1960) 327-35; I. Garofalo, 'Il principe e il medico', *Annali della Facoltà di Lettere dell'Università di Siena* 11 (1990) 291-9; B. Coers, 'Zitat, Paraphrase und Invention: Zur Funktion pompejanischer Wandmalerei im Historienbild am Beispiel von J.A.D. Ingres' "Antiochus und Stratonice" und Anselm Feuerbachs "Gastmahl des Plato"', in: M. Baumbach (ed.), *Tradita et Inventa: Beiträge zur Rezeption der Antike*, Heidelberg 2000, 367-88.

[78] E. Voutiras, Διονυσοφῶντος γάμοι: *Marital Life and Magic in Fourth Century Pella*, Amsterdam 1998; C. Faraone, *Ancient Greek Love Magic*, Cambridge, Mass./London 1999; M.W. Dickie, 'Who Practised Love-Magic in Classical Antiquity and in the Late Roman World?', *Class. Quart.* 50 (2000) 563-83.

court of Felix, the *procurator* of Judaea.[79] Erotic charms could range from quite simple ones, such as: 'Horion, son of Sarapous, make and force Nike, daughter of Apollonous, to fall in love with Paitous, whom Tmesios bore', to quite elaborate ones.[80] The historical Apion may well have dabbled in love magic too, since Pliny (*NH* 24.167) says that according to someone *celeber arte grammatica paulo ante*, clearly Apion, the touch of the plant called *anacampseros*, 'love's return', caused either the return of love or its rejection with hatred.

Finally, the passage is one more example of the enormous importance of Egypt as the country of magic *par excellence* in antiquity.[81] This importance is demonstrated more than once in evidence in the *Pseudo-Clementines*. Already at the beginning of the *Homilies* (1.5 = R 1.5) Clement decides to go to Egypt to solve the problem of the immortality of the soul:

> I shall go into Egypt, and I shall become friendly with the hierophants and prophets of the shrines. And I shall seek and find a magician, and persuade him with large sums of money to effect the calling up of a soul, which is called necromancy, as if I were going to inquire concerning some business.[82]

Simon Magus also stayed in Egypt to practise magic (H 2.24), and his miracles were compared to those of the Egyptian magicians with whom Moses had to compete (R 3.56).[83]

According to *Recognitions* (1.30.2-3), the Egyptians were even genea-

---

[79] Josephus, *Ant.* 20.142.

[80] R. Daniel and F. Maltomini, *Supplementum Magicum*, Opladen 1990, i, 115-213 (our example on pp. 115-7); see also the contribution of Pieter van der Horst to this volume.

[81] For Egypt as the country of magic *par excellence* see P. Achtemeier, 'Jesus and the Disciples as Miracle Workers in the Apocryphal New Testament', in: E. Schüssler Fiorenza (ed.), *Aspects of Religious Propaganda in Judaism and Early Christianity*, Notre Dame/London 1976, 149-86 at 155-6; F. Graf, 'How to Cope with a Difficult Life: A View of Ancient Magic' and D. Frankfurter, 'Ritual Expertise in Roman Egypt and the Problem of the Category "Magician"', in: H. Kippenberg and P. Schäfer (eds), *Envisioning Magic*, Leiden 1997, 93-114 at 94-5 and 115-35 at 119-21, respectively; Dickie, *Magic and Magicians*, 203-5, 215-17, 229-31.

[82] Apparently, Clement was prepared to pay heavily for the services of a magician, as was usual in antiquity, whereas in Christian fiction it is always stressed that the Christians, apostles or otherwise, performed their miracles 'for free', cf. J.N. Bremmer, 'Magic in the Apocryphal Acts of the Apostles', in: J.N. Bremmer and J.R. Veenstra (eds), *The Metamorphosis of Magic from Late Antiquity to the Early Modern Period*, Leuven 2002, 51-70 at 54-5.

[83] For the contest between Moses and the Egyptian magicians see most recently R.

logically connected with the inventor of magic. One of Noah's grand-sons is said to have been the inventor of magic, the altar for demons, and animal sacrifice. Later we learn that the inventor really was Noah's son Ham, who taught the art to his son Mestraim (R 4.27; H 8.3: Mestrem), the ancestor of the Egyptians, Babylonians and Persians. In the Old Testament Mesraim, 'Egypt', is the second son of Ham (Gen 10.6). Anyone who looks at the critical apparatus of the Göttingen Septuagint edition of *Genesis* ad loc., will be surprised how varied the spelling of the name actually is: we find Mesrem, Misraeim, Mesrai, Mesrain, Mestrem, Metraim, and Messaraeim—amongst many others. It may look strange to us that the *Pseudo-Clementines* spell the name in two different ways, but we find the same in, for example, *Jubilees*, where Ham's son is called both Mestrem (7.13) and Mesrem (9.1). Different scribes had perhaps different recollections of the name, depending on the individual manuscript of their text. In any case, the difference in spelling may imply that the author of the *Grundschrift* knew some Hebrew. This is perhaps not so surprising in the light of his possible Jewish connections (below).

According to *Recognitions* (4.27), his contemporaries called Mestraim Zoroaster, but the *Homilies* (H 8.4) are slightly more detailed:

> 'Of that family there was born in due time somebody who took up with magical practices, called Nebrod, who chose, giant-like, to devise things in opposition to God. Him the Greeks have called Zoroaster … He, after the deluge, being ambitious of sovereignty, and being a great magician, by magical arts compelled the world-guiding star of the wicked one who now rules' (H 8.4). The devil did not accept this competition and destroyed him. 'Therefore the magician Nebrod … for this circumstance had his name changed to Zoroaster, on account of the living (ζῶσαν) stream of the star (ῥοήν/ἀστέρος) being poured upon him' (H 8.5).

The passage is an interesting combination of later Jewish specula-tions on Nimrod and the attempts of the Greeks to make sense of

---

Bloch, 'Moses und die Scharlatane', in: F. Siegert and J.U. Kalms (eds), *Internationales Josephus-Kolloquium Bruxelles 1998*, Münster 1999, 142-57 and 'Au-delà d'un discourse apologétique: Flavius Josèphe et les magiciens', in: N. Belayche and S.C. Mimouni (eds), *Les communautés religieuses dans le monde gréco-romain*, Turnhout 2003, 243-58 at 249-51; T.C. Römer, 'Competing Magicians in Exodus 7-9: Interpreting Magic in the Priestly Theology', in: T. Klutz (ed.), *Magic in the Biblical World*, London/New York 2003, 12-22.

the name of Zarathustra, which is still not satisfactorily explained, to whom they ascribed the origin of *mageia*.[84]

The connection of Appion with magic is also reflected in our knowledge about the historical Apion.[85] Above we already saw Apion's interest in love magic and Pliny (*NH* 30.18) also relates that as a young man he had Apion heard saying that the *cynocephalia*, 'dog's head', was called in Egyptian *osiritis*. The plant was divine and afforded protection against all magic potions. Whoever uprooted it in one piece would die immediately! Apion even practised necromancy, as he had called up the soul of Homer to ask about his homeland and his parents.[86] Unfortunately, he did not dare to reveal the answer to these pressing questions. It is no wonder, then, that he was reputed to have written a book *On the Magus*, in which he explained the expression 'The half-obol of Pases'.[87] Pases was an effeminate magician,[88] a kind of modern illusionist, who could make expensive dinners and their serving staff appear and disappear, just as Simon Magus could let household equipment appear without seemingly anyone bringing it in (H 2.32). Evidently, Pases paid with a half-obol, which he subsequently could bring back into his possession. Apion, then, was apparently interested in a wide range of magic beliefs and practices.

---

[84] For the close association of Nimrod with Zoroaster see P.W. van der Horst, *Essays on the Jewish World of Early Christianity*, Fribourg/Göttingen 1990, 220-32 at 230. Origin of magic: Pseudo-Plato, *Alc.* 155A. For the name Zarathustra/Zoroaster see I. Gershevitch, 'Approaches to Zoroaster's Gathas', *Iran* 33 (1995) 19-24; R. Schmitt, 'Onomastica Iranica Platonica', in: C. Mueller-Goldingen and K. Sier (eds), *Lenaika: Festschrift für Carl Werner Müller*, Stuttgart/Leipzig 1996, 81-102 at 93-8 and 'Iranische Personennamen bei Aristoteles', in: S. Adhami (ed.), *Paitimāna: Essays in Iranian, Indo-European, and Indian Studies in Honor of Hanns-Peter Schmidt*, Costa Mesa 2003, 275-99 at 283-4.

[85] Dickie, *Magic and Magicians*, 214-6.

[86] For ancient necromancy see most recently Dickie, *Magic and Magicians*, 237-9; D. Ogden, *Greek Necromancy*, Princeton 2001; Bremmer, *The Rise and Fall of the Afterlife*, London/New York 2002, 71-86; C. Faraone, 'The Collapse of Celestial and Chthonic Realms in a Late Antique "Apollonian Invocation" (*PGM* 1 262-347)', in: R. Boustan and A.Y. Reed (eds), *Heavenly Realms and Earthly Realities in Late Antique Religions*, Cambridge 2004, 213-32; J. Dingel, 'Sextus Pompeius als Nekromant (Anth. Lat. 406 R)', *Philologus* 148 (2004) 116-25.

[87] Suda s.v. *Pasês*, quoted by Pseudo-Plutarch, *Prov.* 50, cf. Dickie, *Magic and Magicians*, 214-15.

[88] The fact that the Suda calls Pases μαλακός, 'effeminate', suggests a hostile source, cf. M. Gleason, *Making Men*, Princeton 1995.

4. Conclusion

With these observations on Apion's interest in magic we have come to
the end of the discussion of our two 'foolish' Egyptians. It is clear that
the author of the *Grundschrift* was well informed about both Anoubion
and Apion. Where and how did he obtain his knowledge about these
two 'foolish' Egyptians? The case of Anoubion is perhaps the easiest
one to answer. It is clear that Egyptian astrology was known in Edessa,
as Bardaisan was familiar with 'books of the Egyptians in which all
the different things that may befall people are described'.[89] The poem
of Anoubion, then, may well have circulated in Edessa.

The case of Apion is more difficult. Older source-critical studies
suggested that the section concerning Apion derives from a Jewish
'Disputationsbuch'.[90] In addition, Schmidt has reasonably argued that
the figure of Appion could hardly have been imagined before Josephus'
Contra Apionem (ca. AD 93), whereas the existence of comparable apologetic treatises is improbable after the Jewish uprising under Trajan and
the revolt of Bar Kokhba.[91] The lost source, then, should date from
the intervening years. The use of Jewish material is certainly possible,
as Stanley Jones has also identified a Jewish-Christian source in the
Grundschrift that has survived in the *Recognitions*.[92] Yet the existence of
(Alexandrian) Jewish apologetic at the time of Josephus' *Contra Apionem*
has become less certain,[93] and current ideas about Jewish apologetics
are clearly in need of a thorough revision.[94] Moreover, the derivation
of all material about Apion from just one book presupposes that the
author of the *Grundschrift* had no other knowledge about Apion available
to him. Such a presupposition cannot be substantiated, and we should

---

[89] Philippus (Bardaisan), *Book of the Laws of Countries*, 38-40, cf. Fowden, *Egyptian
Hermes*, 203-4; Von Stuckrad, *Das Ringen*, 661-2; Id., *Geschichte der Astrologie*, Munich
2003, 150-4.
[90] H. Waitz, *Die Pseudoklementinen Homilien und Rekognitionen*, Leipzig 1904, 251-6;
Heintze, *Der Klemensroman*, 160-239 at 196.
[91] Schmidt, *Studien*, 296-8.
[92] F.S. Jones, *An Ancient Jewish Christian Source on the History of Christianity: Pseudo-
Clementine Recognitions 1.27-71*, Atlanta 1995.
[93] M. Goodman, 'Josephus' Treatise *Against Apion*', in: M. Edwards et al. (eds),
Apologetics in the Roman Empire: Pagans, Jews, and Christians, Oxford 1999, 45-58 at
47-50.
[94] Note now the sensible observations of J. Barclay, 'Apologetics in the Jewish
Diaspora', in: J.R. Bartlett (ed.), *Jews in the Hellenistic and Roman Cities*, New York/
London 2002, 129-48.

perhaps be reticent in our attempts at reconstructing the *Grundschrift*'s sources, as previous attempts have not been particularly successful.[95] In any case, the continuation of our investigations into the complex sources of the *Pseudo-Clementines* would lead us too far away from the 'foolish' Egyptians and hardly be a token of wisdom![96]

---

[95] For the 'Disputationsbuch' and the Jewish background of the *Pseudo-Clementines*, both much debated, see the survey by Jones, 'The Pseudo-Clementines: A History of Research', in: Ferguson, *Studies in Early Christianity*, 221-5 and 250-62, respectively.

[96] I would like to thank Jaap van Dijk, Kathleen McNamee, Jacques van Ruiten, Eibert Tigchelaar and Klaas Worp for information. Ton Hilhorst, George van Kooten and Peter van Minnen read the whole manuscript and saved me from several mistakes, and Ken Dowden kindly corrected my English.

POTAMIAENA: SOME OBSERVATIONS ABOUT MARTYRDOM AND GENDER IN ANCIENT ALEXANDRIA

Henk Bakker

The ancient Christian church was not a monolithic unity—in studying the complexity of early Christian history my naive presuppositions were proven wrong. This, for a student in theology, was of course a happy and necessary lesson. Puzzled by the plurality of Christian opinion in the early church, I could not but profit from the scholarly insights of my 'Doktorvater' Gerard Luttikhuizen.

Among the many forms of Christian patterns of thought, one of the most enigmatic and bizarre seems to me to be the eagerness of some Christians for martyrdom. Bishop Ignatius of Antioch, for example, was transported to Rome for execution and wrote his letters to impress upon the churches that he died 'freely for God' (*Rom* 4.1).[1] He in fact longed for the wild beasts, even yearned for death (*Rom* 5.2; 7.2). Christians were often voluntary victims, and after Ignatius we read about more examples of this kind of martyrdom in early Christian literature.[2] Voluntary deaths might have cost more Christian lives than involuntary.[3] The motives for such morbid desires were, however, divers, and are not of our concern here.[4]

---

[1] On Ignatius' martyrology, see H.A. Bakker, *Exemplar Domini: Ignatius of Antioch and His Martyrological Self-Concept* (Ph.D. thesis University of Groningen, 2003).

[2] Cf. Agathonice (circa AD 165; *Martyrium Carpi* 44); a group of Christians (AD 185; Tertullian, *Ad Scapulam* 5); Pionius and others (middle of the third century; *Passio Pionii* 18.2); Apollonia (middle of the third century; Eusebius, *HE* 6.41.7); Anthimus and the circle around him (at the end of the third century; *HE* 8.6.6); Euplus (29th of April, AD 304; *Acta Eupli* 1). Not all details of these *acta* are historically reliable.

[3] A.J. Droge and J.D. Tabor, *A Noble Death: Suicide and Martyrdom Among Christians and Jews in Antiquity*, San Francisco 1992, 140, 154, 156.

[4] These motives might briefly be described as follows: (1) To inspire others to confess their faith, see: *Passio Sanctorum Mariani et Iacobi* 3.5 and 9.2-4; Lucius (between AD 150 and 160) in *Martyrium Ptolemaei* 11-20 (Justin Martyr, *Apologia sec.* 2.1-20); *Acta Cypriani* 5.1 (14 September, AD 258); Eusebius, *HE* 8.9.5 (at the beginning of the fourth century), cf. Eusebius, *De martyribus Palaestinae* 3.2-4. (2) Penitential reasons: Eusebius, *HE* 7.12.1. (3) To take care of the imprisoned confessors, see: Vettius Epagathus in the *Martyrium Lugdunensium* (AD 177), in Eusebius, *HE* 5.1.9-10; Alexander, in Eusebius, *HE* 5.1.49-50; Saturus in the *Passio Perpetua* 4.5 (AD 203); *Passio Phileae* (*recensio Latina*)

Somewhere at the beginning of the third century AD a young Egyptian woman named Potamiaena was killed by her executioners. The
details are gruesome. She too displayed no resistance to her trial and
ordeal and her fame spread all over the country. The story about the
martyrdom of Potamiaena has until now been largely ignored. Only
a few references in articles or monographs reflect some awareness of
this episode, but they do not hide the neglect of this woman in the
field of early Christian martyrology. In this article I will first take a
historical-critical approach to the narrative (§1), next offer some struc-
tural-analytical observations (§2), then close with a short discussion of
the androcentrism evident in the Potamiaena tradition (§3).

1. *The history of Potamiaena*

Eusebius and Palladius

Only two sources provide any information about the martyrdom
of Potamiaena, Eusebius, *Historia ecclesiastica* (*HE*) 6.5 and Palladius,
Historia Lausiaca 3. The only useful source for the *Martyrium Potamiaenae* is the *Ecclesiastical History* of Eusebius.[5] The sixth book of this
work (written or finished around AD 313) deals particularly with
Alexandrian Christianity in the first half of the third century and
lists the celebrated martyrs from the school of the famous Origen.
Among the martyrs mentioned here is one Basilides, a soldier who
was converted to Christianity when Potamiaena, it is said, appeared
to him after her death. The story does revolve around Basilides, but
it is, however, focused on Potamiaena. It can, in fact, be doubted if
Basilides' martyrdom has any Origenian roots in it (see next section).
Von Harnack describes this story as dependent on a 'zeitgenössische
Quelle' of Eusebius,[6] probably because there are no known pre-
Eusebian traditions regarding Potamiaena. Eusebius used some of

---

7.1-3 (cf. Eusebius, *HE* 8.9.7). Cf. R. Lane Fox, *Pagans and Christians in the Mediterranean
World From the Second Century AD to the Conversion of Constantine*, London 1986, 441-5.
   [5] Quotations are taken mainly from J.E.L. Oulton, *Eusebius: The Ecclesiastical History*,
ii, (Loeb), Cambridge/London 1932, and H. Musurillo, *Acts of the Christian Martyrs:
Introduction, Texts and Translations*, Oxford 1972.
   [6] A. von Harnack, *Die Mission und Ausbreitung des Christentums in den ersten drei
Jahrhunderten*, Wiesbaden 1924[4], 377. Cf. W.H.C. Frend, 'A Severan Persecution?
Evidence of the *Historia Augusta*', in: *Forma Futuri: Studi in onore del Cardinale Michele
Pellegrino*, Torino 1975, 471-80 at 480.

MARTYRDOM AND GENDER IN ANCIENT ALEXANDRIA 333

his letters and oral information by friends who were still alive, and apparently had at his disposal much more information than he could use at that moment (*HE* 6.2.1).

Palladius, bishop of Helenopolis at the beginning of the fifth century, dates the story in his *Historia Lausiaca* to the time of persecutions under Diocletian (and Maximian) in the early fourth century (AD 303-311).[7] The ultimate source of this account was the holy desert father Antony (AD 251-356), who spent most of his life in the eastern regions of Egypt and was close to the Alexandrian Christian tradition. Palladius makes no mention of either the soldier Basilides or Potamiaena's mother Marcella, both of whom are present in Eusebius' version, and one may therefore wonder if both stories deal with the same woman. Palladius' clear description of the facts of the matter differs strikingly from Eusebius' manifest silence with regard to any of the circumstances leading up to the trial. Eusebius relates only that Potamiaena was severely tortured and that she, because of her bodily purity and virginity, 'struggled much against her lovers' (*HE* 6.5.1). Yet, it seems precisely this detail that is made into the main theme of Palladius' version: the girl was the servant of an intemperate and lecherous lord who failed in his attempts to beguile her and subsequently denounced her as a Christian to the local prefect. Moreover, a large sum of money was promised to the judge if he would succeed in persuading her to consent to her master's desires. The Christian woman refused to do so and was consequently ordered to be subjected to heinous instruments of torture. Even then, Potamiaena did not succumb to the will of her oppressors. Thereupon the judge commanded a large cauldron to be filled with hot pitch into which the tormented girl, stripped of her clothes, was lowered inch by inch. It took three hours before she gave up her spirit, when the pitch reached up to her neck, and here Palladius' tradition about Potamiaena ends.

At this point, however, another parallel to Eusebius' story comes in. Eusebius writes of 'boiling pitch being poured out slowly and drop by drop over different parts of her body from head to toe' (*HE* 6.5.4). The mention of hot pitch—Eusebius is the first reference to pitch in early Christian martyr stories—undoubtedly connects both stories together. One and the same Potamiaena acts and dies in two rather different but somehow related accounts that are separated by a gap of almost

---

[7] Palladius, *Historia Lausiaca* 3.

three generations. We may infer that Eusebius, who lived during the
reign of Maximian (AD 286-310), would have known if the martyrdom
of Potamiaena had been wrongly dated to the early years of the third
century and should have redated it to his own era. He would also
have known that the judge 'Aquila' he refers to (*HE* 6.5.2) was in fact
Subatianus Aquila, Prefect of Egypt from AD 205/6 to 210.[8]

Palladius, in his turn, took his story from Isidore, who heard it from
the holy Antony. Now Antony was a contemporary of the emperor
Maximian while Palladius was not. I take the view that Palladius independently and mistakenly fixed the wrong date to the legend, reasoning
that the only emperor who could have possibly persecuted the Christian
Church and reigned over Egypt somewhere in the second half of the
third and the beginning of the fourth century was Maximian.[9]

The Life of Origen

Eusebius found the source for his praise of Potamiaena in a version
of a *Life of Origen*.[10] Fragments of this *Life* were inserted throughout
the sixth book of the *Historia ecclesiastica*. The list of seven martyrs
issuing from the Origenian school closes with Basilides, whose fame
is meant to be enhanced by the fame of Potamiaena. For Eusebius
it was important to show that neither Origen nor his students ever
denounced the fate of martyrdom, for rigoristic opponents had accused
the teacher of avoidance of martyrdom and spiritual laxity.[11] Eusebius
wrote in defence of the hero, and he attempts to demonstrate by both
example and argument that his accusers were altogether wrong. The
Life of Origen is an apology in panegyrical style[12] and is intended to

---

[8] Cf. Musurillo, *Acts of the Christian Martyrs*, xxvii: 'Eusebius would hardly have been
so misled if the martyrdom were as recent as Maximian's reign'. See also the revision
of the article 'Praefectus Aegypti' s.v. 'Subatianus Aquila' of O.W. Reinmuth, in:
Pauly-Wissowa, *Real-Encyclopädie der classischen Altertumswissenschaft*, Suppl. VIII (Stuttgart,
1956), 530-1. Subatianus Aquila was Prefect of Egypt from at least 205/206 to 210.
His brother Subatianus Proculus was *legatus* of Numidia (AD 208-210).

[9] Cf. K.S. Frank, *Lehrbuch der Geschichte der alten Kirche*, Paderborn 2002³, 91-3.

[10] For the *Vita Origenis* in his *Church History*, Eusebius used the sources which
Pamphilus collected about Origen (*HE* 6.36.2-4); cf. R.M. Grant, 'Eusebius and His
Lives of Origen', in: *Forma Futuri: Studi in onore del Cardinale Michele Pellegrino*, 649.

[11] According to Harnack and Loofs, Origen was influenced by Gnostic notions,
cf. A. Harnack, *Lehrbuch der Dogmengeschichte*, i, Freiburg/Leipzig 1894³, 605, 613; F.
Loofs, *Leitfaden zum Studium der Dogmengeschichte*, Tübingen 1968⁷, 158. Gnostics were
suspected of easily renouncing their faith.

[12] See Eusebius, *HE* 6.23.4; 6.33.4; 6.36.4. The panegyric genre (also called

move the reader to admiration and imitation of the virtues Eusebius found in Origen.[13] His selection and presentation of material reflects values which ought to be associated with Christian rhetoric rather than with the conventions of secular historians.[14] According to Eusebius, Origen longed after martyrdom from his youth, and it was due to his mother, who hid his clothes, that the boy did not early succeed in this (*HE* 6.2.3-5). He also wrote his father, Leonides, who was imprisoned due to Severus' repressive measures, and urged him to stay firm and face martyrdom (6.2.6).

So far we have observed that the *Martyrium Potamiaenae* in Eusebius reaches back to Origen-oriented sources and is also somehow subservient to the death of Basilides. But the testimony concerning this soldier contains no references whatsoever to Origen. Plutarch, Serenus, Heraclides, Hero, a second Serenus and Herais were pupils of Origen because they were catechumens, students in his Alexandrian school of faith (*HE* 6.4.1-3). Not so Basilides. The text reports neither that he was a catechumen, educated in the school of Origen, nor that he was baptised (whereas the baptisms of Hero and Herais are mentioned). Only after Potamiaena visited him posthumously, Basilides declared swearing to be forbidden and openly acknowledged that he was a Christian (and consequently was imprisoned). We simply do not know for sure whether he had been a Christian before this event. Probably not, because it was only in prison that the 'seal in the Lord' (meaning baptism)[15] was imparted to him by some Christian brethren (*HE* 6.5.6); further, being a Christian and a soldier at the same time was definitely a very controversial issue in the second half of the second century.[16] Consequently the short story provided here about Basilides differs substantially from those concerning the other six.

Yet somehow the martyr Basilides came to be associated with and

---

epideictic, demonstrative, encomiastic, or academic) is characterized by the method of praise (*amplificare*) and blame (*minuere*). Cf. H. Lausberg, *Handbuch der literarischen Rhetorik: Eine Grundlegung der Literaturwissenschaft*, Stuttgart 1990³, §61.3 and 239-54.

[13] Cf. R.M. Grant, 'Eusebius', 635.

[14] G.A. Kennedy, *Greek Rhetoric Under Christian Emperors*, New Jersey 1983, 186-97 at 187.

[15] Musurillo, *Acts of the Christian Martyrs*, 135 note 3, interprets 'the seal' as the Eucharist. But see J. Ysebaert, *Greek Baptismal Terminology: Its Origins and Early Development* (Graecitas Christianorum Primaeva 1), Nijmegen 1962, 382-5, 395-9.

[16] Cf. Tertullian, *De corona militis* 1-2 and 11-13. Christians should decline public offices according to Origen, see *Contra Celsum* 8.75.

brought into the traditions about Origen. The visiting 'brethren' who baptized the converted soldier are, as a matter of course, identified as Origenists. That is probably why the dramatic event was enlisted by Eusebius' plea for Origen, even though the latter may not have been acquainted with Basilides at all. If the association of Basilides with Origen raises questions, the historical circumstances provided concerning Potamiaena are even more puzzling. The text does not say why she and her mother were singled out to be brought before the prefect. We hear of no allegations against her and the report we have focuses attention merely on her bodily beauty and sufferings. Whereas the other martyrs were described as Christians or martyrs, no such information is found in the account regarding Potamiaena. For example: Basilides confessed being a Christian, and the first martyr on the list, Plutarch, was likewise blessed with a 'divine martyrdom' (*HE* 6.3.2). Both Serenus and Heraclides earned the title 'martyr', and Hero is described as 'lately baptized'. The other Serenus was honoured with the words 'champion of piety', while Herais, finally, was 'baptized by fire'. Had Potamiaena not replied 'something pro-fane' to the judge (τι ... ἀσεβές, which probably included something impious for Roman ears [6.5.2]) and promised to pray for Basilides to 'her Lord' (6.5.3), we would not have known that she died the death of a Christian martyr.

Septimius Severus

In order to understand why Christians like Potamiaena and Basilides were persecuted, we need to explore the character of the Severan persecutions. The persecutions referred to in *HE* 6.1 and 6.2.3 were instigated by Septimius Severus during the second half of his reign. The imperial family, however, was characterized by its virtue of relative open-mindedness concerning religious pluriformity (*liberali-tas*). The Roman court became transformed into a religious melting pot. The emperor's wife Julia Domna, daughter of the high priest of Baal in Emesa, her sister Julia Maesa and daughter Julia Mamea all favoured religious syncretism and in so doing ushered in a new era.[17] Julia Mamea even invited Origen to explain his theories to her (*HE* 6.21.3-4). The emperor himself, so Tertullian asserts, 'was graciously

---

[17] Frank, *Lehrbuch*, 84.

mindful of the Christians.'[18] The question then arises, why a tolerant emperor of such a noble stature would initiate a campaign against the Christians.

The circumstances giving rise to this apparent inconsistency have been the focus of much discussion.[19] Was there a kind of a Severan edict and was the intolerance against the Christian Church somehow connected to Severus' admiration of the cult of Serapis? Central to these issues is the search for authenticity and historical accuracy in the relevant texts in the *Historia Augusta*, a collection of biographies of Roman emperors probably compiled in the late third and early fourth century. Aelius Spartianus writes in his chronicle about Severus:

> After this [reaching Antioch, HB], having first raised his soldiers' pay, he [Severus, HB] turned his steps toward Alexandria, and while on his way thither, he conferred numerous rights upon the communities of Palestine. He forbade conversion to Judaism under heavy penalties and enacted a similar law in regard to the Christians. He then gave the Alexandrians the privilege of a local senate, for they were still without any public council, just as they had been under their own kings, and were obliged to be content with the single governor appointed by Caesar. Besides this, he changed many of their laws. In after years Severus himself continually avowed that he found this journey very enjoyable, because he had taken part in the worship of the god Serapis, had learned something of antiquity, and had seen unfamiliar animals and strange places. For he visited Memphis, Memnon, the Pyramids, and the Labyrinth, and examined them all with great care (*Historia Augusta*: *Severus* 17.1-4).[20]

Although some scholars consider the words 'and enacted a similar law in regard to the Christians' (*idem etiam de Christianis sanxit*, 17.1) to be a biased, late fourth-century forgery,[21] I believe the passage in dispute to be genuine.

---

[18] Tertullian, *Ad Scapulam* 4.5 (*Ipse etiam Severus, pater Antonini, Christianorum memor fuit*; possibly AD 212).

[19] See J.G. Davies, 'Was the Devotion of Septimius Severus to Serapis the Cause of the Persecutions of 202-3?', *Journal of Theological Studies* 5 (1954) 73-6; K.H. Schwarte, 'Das angebliche Christengesetz des Septimius Severus', *Historia* 12 (1963) 185-208; Frend, 'A Severan Persecution?', 471-80.

[20] D. Magie, *Scriptores Historiae Augustae* (Loeb), i, Cambridge/London 1921, 409, 411.

[21] Cf. Frank, *Lehrbuch*, 81, and Schwarte, 'Das angebliche Christengesetz', 207-8. J.E. Salisbury, *Perpetua's Passion: The Death and Memory of a Young Roman Woman*, New York/London 1997, 22. Salisbury accepts the edict as a matter of fact.

Serapis worship

Severus' visit to Egypt in AD 201[22] seems indeed to have turned the emperor's mind in the direction of the Alexandrian worship of Serapis. Severus was an African by birth, from Leptis Magna (contracted to Labdah; nowadays Al Khums, Libya) and would likely have felt attracted to African religion from his youth. He was not converted to the Serapis cult, but had had plenty of opportunity to deepen his knowledge and experience of this cult during his stay in Egypt[23] and became deeply interested in Egyptian beliefs. Dio Cassius confirms that Severus toured almost the whole country of Upper Egypt and 'inquired into everything, including things that were carefully hidden … Accordingly he took away from practically all sanctuaries all the books that he could find containing any secret lore' (76.13.2). In addition, he accentuated his admiration for Serapis by a change of coiffure.[24] From AD 202 onward, Severus is portrayed in the style of Serapis, with curly hair on the forehead, and a forked beard. The emperor, who by then was the undisputed master of the empire, identified himself with the popular god, portraying himself as his associate.[25]

Serapis was not a traditional Egyptian god, as were Isis and Osiris. Ptolemy I introduced the anthropomorphic god, intending to unify Greek and Egyptian religious legacies. Serapis (Asar-Hap, from Osiris and Apis [a bull])[26] had his cultic centre in Alexandria, but his cult, in which he was worshipped as an almost unique and monotheistic god, quickly spread throughout the country. Indeed, we observe a general drift of religion into monotheism, especially from the first century onwards, which is particularly evident in the cult of Serapis.[27] A series

---

[22] Or in 200, see T. Franke, 'Imp. Caesar L. Septimius Severus Pertinax Augustus', in: H. Cancik and H. Schneider (eds), *Der neue Pauly: Enzyklopädie der Antike*, Stuttgart/Weimar 2001, xi, 431-5 at 433-4.

[23] Cf. Davies, 'The Devotion', 75.

[24] Davies, 'The Devotion', 74-5; Salisbury, *Perpetua's Passion*, 20-2, 27-8. Cf. *Historia Augusta*: *Severus* 19.9 (*promissa barba, cano capite et crispo* ['long beard, grey and curly hair']).

[25] Cf. S.A. Takacs, 'Serapis', in: *Der neue Pauly*, xi, 445-8 at 446-7; Salisbury, *Perpetua's Passion*, 21.

[26] Egyptian images show Serapis as a human with the head of a bull, crowned with the sun and two horn-like plumes. In the disc of the sun figures a cobra. The Greek images show him with long hair and beard, seated on a throne with Cerberus at his feet, and frequently wearing the *modius*, a small pot, on his head, indicating fertility.

[27] Cf. Lane Fox, *Pagans and Christians*, 34-5.

of cults and titles were merged, a trend that coalesced into a definite syncretism in the course of the third century. Serapis is addressed as 'one Serapis', or 'Helioserapis', or 'Zeus Helios Serapis'. Such epitheta increased the attraction of the cult which gained even more worshippers. They undoubtedly became conscious of honouring a mighty divinity to whom the lesser divine powers were subordinate. Worship of lesser gods, however, was not excluded and real monotheism was never within reach. The exclamation 'one Serapis' only meant that, for the worshipper, Serapis was 'the one' at this particular moment.

Severus' intolerant 'open-mindedness' and personal identification with the supreme god Serapis excluded any kind of making proselytes or converts on the part of Jews or Christians. He himself 'was regarded as a god by the Africans' (*Historia Augusta*: *Severus* 13.8; cf. 21.9), and the striking progress Christianity, a threatening competitor, was making in Upper Africa was deeply resented by the local pagans.[28] Judaism retained its status as a *religio licita*, yet had to be confined within strict limitations. Severus' prescript (the edict) forbade the making of any converts; only those who were born Jews were allowed to be circumcised and subscribe to the Mosaic code of law. It is entirely credible that Christianity, because it was associated with Judaism and attracted converts, was also officially prohibited to engage in proselytism. We read about young converts in the early third century who were persecuted, whereas their spiritual leaders remained apparently undisturbed.[29] Vibia Perpetua and her slave-girl Felicitas were both catechumens who were executed for their beliefs in Carthage at the dawn of the third century.[30] Eusebius' list, moreover, consists mainly of recently initiated Christian converts. As Tertullian said: *Fiunt, non nascuntur Christiani* (*Apologeticum* 18.4). New converts had to be made and were obliged to attend a catechetical school for several years before they were baptized.

So far, we can conclude that Subatianus Aquila, the Prefect of Egypt, backed the harassment of Christian converts in particular. Local devo-

---

[28] See Eusebius, *HE* 6.3.6-7; cf. Tertullian, *Apologeticum* 1.7 (*Obsessam vociferantur civitatem; in agris, in castellis, in insulis Christianos; omnem sexum, aetatem, condicionem, etiam dignitatem transgredi ad hoc nomen quasi detrimento maerent*), 37.4 (*Hesterni sumus, et orbem iam et vestra omnia implevimus, urbes, insulas, castella, municipia, conciliabula, castra ipsa, tribus, decurias, palatium, senatum, forum; sola vobis reliquimus templa*), and 37.8 (*... paene omnium civitatum paene omnes cives Christianos habendo*).

[29] Frend, 'A Severan Persecution?', 477-9.

[30] *Passio Perpetuae* 2.

tees of the emperor and Serapis were encouraged to bring in charges
against Christian initiates. Although there are only a few indications
to this effect, we can safely assume Basilides and Potamiaena to have
been counted among this group.

2. *The story of Potamiaena*

A carmen Potamiaenae?

In the first quarter of the fourth century, Eusebius still witnessed to
Potamiaena's popularity, claiming that 'the praise of this woman is to
this day loudly sung by her fellow-countrymen' (*HE* 6.5.1).[31] A better
translation would be that, up to Eusebius' time, Potamiaena was held
'much in honour among her own people'.[32] After more than a century
she was still remembered, and Eusebius almost repeats himself in the
fifth paragraph when he once again underscores her fame (6.5.5).
The assumption that the memory of Potamiaena may have been kept
alive by singing songs about her may be worth the test. Though the
genre of poetic martyr-literature only really began to flourish with
Prudentius in the fourth century, this genre may reach back to broad
and old traditions. Poetic treatment of martyrdom was not wholly
without precedent, and Prudentius was particularly influenced by the
works of Tertullian and Cyprian.[33]

It is Tertullian, who, in an antidote against Gnostic poison, almost
incidentally reports that 'the death of martyrs is also praised in song'
(*cantatur enim et exitus martyrum*, *Scorpiace* 7.2). He wrote this while at
Carthage in AD 211 or 212, only a few years after Potamiaena (at the
end of the first decennium) was executed at Alexandria. We cannot
say if Tertullian knew about the death of this martyr, but Potamiaena's
victorious contest must have been proverbial in the North-African third
century Church. It is quite possible that our text in Eusebius contains
bits and phrases from just such a martyr-song, and the structure of
the chapter would show this to be plausible.[34] The story as it is told

---

[31] Oulton's translation, 25.
[32] Musurillo, *Acts of the Christian Martyrs*, 133.
[33] Cf. A. Coşkun, 'Die Programmgedichte des Prudentius: *praefatio* und *epilogus*', *Zeitschrift für antikes Christentum* 7 (2003) 212-36 at 213 note 3; A.-M. Palmer, *Prudentius on the Martyrs*, Oxford 1989, 32-56 at 53, 227-54 at 233.
[34] Ancient ordinary speech was both prosaic and poetic in style. The differ-

begins in the second paragraph ('It is said', 6.5.2 [φασί γέ]). The first paragraph may hold some reminiscences of a song; immediately after ᾄδεται we read: μυρία μέν ..., μυρία δέ. The structure of the sentence is balanced by three participles:

a. μυρία μὲν
    b. ὑπὲρ τῆς τοῦ σώματος ἁγνείας
        c. τε καὶ παρθενίας,
            d. (ἐν ᾗ διέπρεψεν),
e. πρὸς ἐραστὰς ἀγωνισαμένης
(καὶ γὰρ οὖν αὐτῇ ἀκμαῖον πρὸς τῇ ψυχῇ καὶ τὸ τοῦ σώματος ὡραῖον ἐπήνθει),
a. μυρία δὲ
    b. ἀνατλάσης
        c. καὶ τέλος μετὰ ... βασάνους
            d. (δεινὰς καὶ φρικτὰς εἰπεῖν)
e. ἅμα μητρὶ Μαρκέλλῃ διὰ πυρὸς τελειωθείσης (6.5.1).

I have put between parenthesis the clauses which, by way of explanation, may have been added to the original lines of the song. If we leave these explanatory phrases out, the bare strophe reads like this:

μυρία μὲν ὑπὲρ τῆς τοῦ σώματος ἁγνείας τε καὶ παρθενίας πρὸς ἐραστὰς ἀγωνισαμένης,
μυρία δὲ ἀνατλάσης καὶ τέλος μετὰ βασάνους ἅμα μητρὶ Μαρκέλλῃ διὰ πυρὸς τελειωθείσης.

She struggled much with lovers on behalf of the purity and virginity of her body,
She endured much and, after tortures in the end, was together with her mother Marcella perfected by fire.

The focus of the author is partly drawn to Potamiaena's bodily beauty and perfection. In parenthesis he argues: 'for sure, her soul and body were in the full bloom of its beauty' (or: 'Yes, in top form, besides her soul, also her bodily beauty flourished'). Bodily perfection is a very common panegyrical and hagiographic topos in funerary discourses celebrating the virtues the orator wishes his audience to keep in mind and imitate.[35] Inserted into Eusebius' apology for Origen, the eulogy

---

ence between 'Kunstprosa' and lyrics was not always clear; cf. E. Norden, *Die antike Kunstprosa vom VI. Jahrhundert vor Christus bis in die Zeit der Renaissance*, ii, Leipzig/Berlin 1923, 626-31.

[35] See Aristotle, *Ars Rhetorica* 1.3.4; 3.14.11, and *Rhetorica ad Herennium* (wrongly circulating by Cicero's name) 1.5.8; 2.30.47; 3.6.11.

aims at recalling the excellence of the teacher's life and school. The martyrdom of Potamiaena pushes his fame to splendid heights, and merited a song. Potamiaena, like Origen, was capable of physical self-control in extreme and dire circumstances. Origen for many years disciplined himself to perform heavy labour during the day while studying the holy Scriptures during the night. He slept on the floor, wore no shoes, persevered in cold and nakedness, and was inclined to extreme fasting (*HE* 6.3.9-12). In an attempt to silence all slander concerning his contact with female catechumens, Origen even castrated himself (*HE* 6.8.1-2). His sincerity and blameless reputation are beyond any suspicion.

The passio Potamiaenae

Paragraphs 2-4 form a separate unit, beginning with 'it is said' and ending with 'such was the contest waged by this maiden celebrated in song'. Typical of this section is the repetition (three times) of the word 'body' (twice in the first paragraph) and the term 'insult(ers)'. The story opens with the infliction of 'severe tortures upon her entire body', and closes with a similar picture: 'boiling pitch being poured out slowly and little by little over different parts of her body from head to toe'. The cruel and sadistic tortures brought on her complete body receive full emphasis here. The insults hurled at Potamiaena formed a further and constant threat to her fidelity. After the first series of torments, Aquila threatened to hand her over for bodily insult and abuse by gladiators. After a short period of reflection Potamiaena's reply was 'something profane' (impious). Unexpectedly, we are informed neither about what decision Aquila required of her, nor about the kind of profanation she committed. Precisely at this decisive moment the tradition and Eusebius leave us ignorant. Instead, all attention is drawn to here immediate removal, and to the insults hurled at her from the crowd. Subsequently, Potamiaena endured a final series of torments, and died.

The flow of thought in paragraphs 2-4 displays a chiastic structure as follows:

a. The torturing of Potamiaena's complete body (κατὰ παντὸς τοῦ σώματος).

b. Aquila threatens with bodily insult (ὕβρει τοῦ σώματος).

c. Potamiaena's decision (she replied something 'profane', τι ἀσεβές).

b´. Basilides restrained the insulters (ἐνυβρίζειν ... τοὺς ἐνυβρίζον-
τας).

a´. Destruction of Potamiaena's complete body (κατὰ διάφορα μέρη
τοῦ σώματος ἀπ᾽ ἄκρων ποδῶν καὶ μέχρι κορυφῆς).

So far the initial story of the passion of Potamiaena.

The story of Basilides

Paragraphs 5-7, which deal with the imprisonment and martyrdom of
Basilides, may easily represent a separate tradition. A first indication
is that the word 'body' is not mentioned at all, nor do we read of
any insults, ignominies, or gory details of the execution of Basilides.
Here, however, we are informed about the charges held against the
accused. After Basilides protected Potamiaena from the raging crowd,
she promised to pray, after her death, that he be rewarded. Not long
afterwards this sensitive soldier refused to swear an oath in front of
his fellow-soldiers, who then reported the incident to their superiors.
Basilides explained that he was indeed a Christian, and courageously
affirmed the Christian confession in presence of the judge. In prison
some delegates from the school of Origen questioned Basilides' sudden
decision. The astonishing answer is that Potamiaena, three days after
her execution, appeared to Basilides by night, conferred him with
a crown, and assured him that 'before long she would take him to
herself' (*HE* 6.5.6). The brethren subsequently baptized him, and on
the following day the convict was beheaded.

    The story of the martyrdom of Basilides is very soberly outlined in
a manner quite different from the account of Potamiaena's maniacal
slaughter. It may be that both, as separate traditions, were intertwined
for edificational reasons. Remember that Basilides had no role in Palladius' version of the martyrdom of Potamiaena. The way Eusebius
redactionally inserts paragraphs 2-4 into the list of Origen's heroes
of faith changes the original perspective of the drama, and enhances
the glory of her male counterpart. Potamiaena's fame and history is
used to the advantage of Basilides'. She was famous (περιβόητος, 6.5.1),
noble (γενναῖος, 6.5.4), and a strong contestant (6.5.5), although none
of these terms were used in reference to Basilides.

    Since Basilides' gentle demeanour was in no way what we could
expect from a third-century Roman soldier escorting a convicted
woman to the scaffold, and since this is the first recorded incident
involving a rebellious soldier swayed by his sympathy for a Christian,
the person of Basilides actually arouses suspicion, especially if we point

at some striking parallels with the *Passio Perpetuae*. Only a couple of years before Potamiaena's death in Alexandria, the distinguished Christian woman Perpetua was killed in the Carthaginian amphitheatre (March, AD 203). A few days before execution she and other prisoners were transferred from the civil prison to the military prison. There the *morituri* met the prison director, Pudens, who kindly gave permission to receive visitors because the strength of the Christians impressed him (*Passio Perpetuae* 9.1). In the following days Pudens was converted to Christianity (16.4) and quickly acquired great fame on the occasion of the death of Perpetua's spiritual associate Saturus. When Saturus was thrown to the cats in the amphitheatre and badly mauled by a leopard, Pudens was standing nearby at the gate. Saturus bade him goodbye and urged him to remember him and the faith (21.4). He asked for the ring on Pudens' finger, dipped it in his wound and gave it back to Pudens 'as a pledge and as a record of his bloodshed' (21.5).

   Just like Pudens, Basilides was a soldier who had become a Christian in the process of guarding believers. Both were also eye-witnesses of the execution of celebrated Christians and had the privilege of receiving a pledge: Basilides an oral promise from Potamiaena, Pudens a tangible gesture from Saturus, whose actions were in every respect approved by Perpetua for whom Saturus was a spiritual guide. These striking similarities may tempt us to call into question the authenticity of the connection of Potamiaena and Basilides as it is presented here. For her part, the maiden Potamiaena made a deep impact on Egyptian Christianity. She was indisputably remembered and praised, and her story was even reported by Antony the Great, although doubts remain about her deep involvement with Christianity. That Potamiaena and Basilides never met at all is a definite possibility.

3. *The woman Potamiaena*

Bodily integrity

If Potamiaena was prosecuted for her religious conviction, this certainly played no significant role in the tradition as it was handed down to Eusebius and to Palladius. Clearly she was troubled by obtrusive 'lovers' who could not cope with rejection and were searching for revenge, and the immediate circumstance of the show trial lies here. The real cause, however, may have been her alleged belief. Potamiaena's incessant refusal to return the intimacies of some men unfortunately had fatal consequences for her. She died a horrific death because she would not sacrifice her bodily integrity and act against her own rights and principles.

The notion of corporality in the accounts of Potamiaena's suffering is so dominant that its focus shifted from faithfulness towards God to personal integrity and loyalty to one's own conscience. Potamiaena chose rather to be offended and brutalized and to take all responsibility for her own life than to be reduced to only a body. It was her honour to bear the consequences of her decision and to remain free to relate to a man for whom she felt some sympathy. Basilides moved her, she 'accepted his concern for her' (*HE* 6.5.3) and it is he whom she wanted to welcome in her life. Moreover, she requested from the Lord that she could 'take him to herself' for eternity (παραλήψεσθαι, *HE* 6.5.6). Potamiaena crowned him and honoured him for his gracious deed. For his part, Basilides acted as if he was her husband and strove to protect her from shameful violation. She was undefiled and, right from the start, in a position of spiritual authority over Basilides.[36] She bade God to bring about his martyrdom and, as God's delegate, she crowned him in anticipation of this event. Their union seems to bring the story to a dénouement every reader would wish to happen. In the end Potamiaena and Basilides were united in what we could call a spiritual matrimony, a syneisactic love in which both partners are equal.

Androcentrism

Equality of sexes is almost absent and generally unknown in antiquity. Understandably, then, the *Martyrium Potamiaenae* shows traces of this dominant male thinking, and its androcentrism is masked in a very subtle way. On the one hand Potamiaena is portrayed as a chaste and honest lady who claims her bodily freedom, but on the other hand she is forced into the stereotyped images men have of women. She is pictured as a very attractive virgin who upsets lecherous men—almost as if she hooks them and dumps them before any untoward behaviour be suspected. Suspicious and slanderous people may have started to think: if so many 'lovers' were competing for her, it seems inexpli-

---

[36] Cf. F.C. Klawiter, 'The Role of Martyrdom and Persecution in Developing the Priestly Authority of Women in Early Christianity: A Case Study of Montanism', *Church History* 49 (1980) 252-61 at 254, 257-8, 260-1.

cable to suppose that she herself, after all, was not to be blamed for provocative behaviour; didn't she love the attention, the gazes and whistles of the boys?

It was a persistent cliché that women are more inclined to promiscuity because they are the weaker sex. The dominant prejudice concerning women was that they could not resist sexual temptation and for this reason had to be kept in chastity. Men may feed their sexual desires unrestrained, and cannot help it if they knuckle under. So women are mostly to be blamed when men lose control sexually.

This sad accusation has contributed to a general atmosphere of androcentrism (sometimes bordering on misogyny) that has clung to antiquity. The most important difference between men and women in ancient Mediterranean life was the necessity of women to maintain a sense of shame.[37] This quality was tied to modesty, restraint and discretion. If a man felt dishonoured by a woman of lower standard, he risked irreparable social damage if he did not disgrace her and subject her to public humiliation.[38] For men, honour is to be kept and restored, but women should restrict themselves to the paralysing uncertainties of shame. In cases of social conflict they would bear the brunt of any guilt and would be held culpable simply because they were inferior to men. Every woman was by definition in need of the patronizing help of a man, without whom she had no safe future.

Convicted women by definition not only lost their rights, possessions and social identity, but also their female identity. A female criminal, sentenced to be executed, was no longer considered a woman. She was exposed to male-treatment inasmuch a 'masculine' punishment awaited her and brought her on a level with her male counterpart.[39] In fact, women especially were shown no mercy in punishment for they were held in no esteem at all. In his *Metamorphoses*, Apuleius tells

---

[37] J.M. Arlandson, *Women, Class, and Society in Early Christianity: Models From Luke-Acts*, Peabody 1997, 155-6.

[38] Cf. concerning the Mediterranean mind: B.J. Malina, *The Social World of Jesus and the Gospels*, London/New York 1996; Id., 'Understanding New Testament Persons', in: R. Rohrbauch (ed.), *The Social Sciences and New Testament Interpretation*, Peabody 1996; W. Meeks, *The First Urban Christians: The Social World of the Apostle Paul*, New Haven/London 1983[2]; G. Theissen, *Social Reality and the Early Christians*, Edinburgh 1992.

[39] C. Jones, 'Women, Death, and the Law', in: D. Wood (ed.), *Martyrs and Martyrologies* (SCH 30), Oxford 1993, 23-34 at 34, and S.G. Hall, 'Women among the Early Martyrs', ibid., 1-21 at 21.

a story about a man who was turned into an ass and experienced all kinds of frightening adventures. In Corinth the donkey was forced to copulate in public with a woman who was convicted *ad bestias* for murder. Even the animal felt ashamed to have intercourse with the 'stained bitch' and ran off (10.34). The executions of female criminals in Roman amphitheatres often took on a sexual dimension, and deteriorated regularly into violent sexual torture.[40]

And here the misogyny comes in—this kind of sexual martyrdom makes the woman into a man. The female dimension of the woman had to be destroyed. After all, women were a kind of failed males or mutilated men. A woman who stood the test of severe torture was indeed reckoned a man. Her womanhood was never to be recognized. On the contrary, we notice that pre-eminently her female private parts were considered free for exposure. Even Christian reports of martyrdom suffer from this eroticising tendency. Take for example the young Thecla of Iconium, who in all probability was a contemporary of the apostle Paul and endured several trials.[41] Thecla was stripped and brought to be burnt at the stake. She had been engaged but after hearing Paul speak she lost interest in marriage. Paul was expelled from the city whereas Thecla was condemned to the stake (*Acta Pauli et Theclae* 13-14, 21-22). After her release—the fire was extinguished by sudden rain and hail—she cut her hair and travelled along with Paul dressed like a boy (25, 40). One may wonder if this initiative was freely of her own; it would seem that she was forced to dress like a boy, in order to be safe and to keep men like Alexander at a distance.[42]

In Pisidian Antioch, however, Thecla was once again convicted. A Syrian man, Alexander, had fallen in love with Thecla, and because he was rich and influential, the fellow dared embracing her in public. Very annoyed, she tore up his mantle, snatched the wreath from his head, and started to mock him. Alexander had her condemned for

---

[40] See K.M. Coleman, 'Fatal Charades: Roman Executions Staged as Mythological Enactments', *The Journal of Roman Studies* 80 (1990) 44-73 at 46, 59, 61, 64.

[41] See J.N. Bremmer, 'Magic, Martyrdom and Women's Liberation in the Acts of Paul and Thecla', in: J.N. Bremmer (ed.), *The Apocryphal Acts of Paul and Thecla* (Studies on the Apocryphal Acts of the Apostles 2), Kampen 1996, 36-59 at 48-9, 50-5. Cf. A. Jensen, *Thekla: die Apostolin; ein apokrypher Text neu entdeckt*, Gütersloh 1999.

[42] Still, it is true that 'men are not depicted as opposed to Thecla all the time'. The main purpose of the *Acts of Paul and Thecla* is not 'to show the equality of the sexes or advocate the liberation of women', E.Y.L. Ng, '*Acts of Paul and Thecla*: Women's Stories and Precedent?', *The Journal of Theological Studies* 55 (2004) 1-29 at 28 and 29.

defamation (here we notice a slight correspondence with Palladius' story about Potamiaena), and Thecla was ordered to fight the animals. Immediately after the verdict she requested the favour of maintaining her virginity until the fight (26-27). On the day before the contest Thecla was tied to a lion in procession, but the lion did not harm her—instead he licked her feet (28).[43] The next day Thecla was stripped again, and pushed into the stadium, carrying only a towel round her waist. There she jumped into a pit full of water, with a cloud of fire covering her nudity. Because the animals did not touch her on this occasion, she was tied with her feet to two bulls in order that she be trampled but again she was spared (33-35). Following these events, Thecla was finally dressed (38) because Tryphaena, a relative of the emperor and Thecla's confidant,[44] had fainted close to the arena. Afraid that Tryphaena might die because of her sorrow concerning Thecla, the authorities quickly released the Christian maiden (36).

In general the animals selected for the female victims were carefully chosen. Being thrown to a bull indicated sexual humiliation. Bulls were a symbol of male superiority. Stripping a woman naked, or to a bare covering, in an encounter with a male animal stigmatized her as an adulteress. Perpetua and Felicitas did not have to face a bull but a mad cow; this implied utter shame and rejection, as if the two were not even female enough to be able to commit adultery.[45] The unknown reporter writes: 'This was an unusual animal, but it was chosen that their sex might be matched with that of the beast' (*Passio Perpetuae* 20.1). The previous day Perpetua received a vision (the fourth vision reported in her own prison diary) in which she had to fight vehemently with a vicious Egyptian. In it her clothes were suddenly stripped off and she appeared to be transformed into a man (*et expoliata sum et facta sum masculus*, 10.7). Only as a man could she stand

---

[43] This is a familiar Christian motif in martyr stories. Cf. the *Passion of Maxima, Donatilla and Secunda*, where a ferocious bear licked Donatilla's feet. M.A. Tilley, *Donatist Martyr Stories: The Church in Conflict in Roman North Africa* (Translated Texts for Historians 24), Liverpool 1996, 24.

[44] See M. Misset-Van de Weg, 'A Wealthy Woman Named Tryphaena: Patroness of Thecla of Iconium', in: Bremmer, *The Apocryphal Acts*, 16-35 at 27-31.

[45] For a discussion of Perpetua's fourth vision and her final contest, see: Jan N. Bremmer, 'Perpetua and Her Diary: Authenticity, Family and Visions', in: W. Ameling (ed.), *Märtyrer und Märtyrerakten* (Interdisziplinäre Studien zur Antike und zu ihrem Nachleben 6), Stuttgart 2002, 77-120 at 112-19.

the test. Thus she proclaimed her own revelatory dream.[46] Perpetua consequently experienced the confrontation with the mad heifer in the mode of a spiritual male existence. She was not robbed of her womanhood by her oppressors—God took it gently from her.[47]

In utter nakedness Perpetua and Felicitas were crammed into nets and thrown to the wild cow. But the sight of the two women shocked the crowd. Felicitas was a gorgeous young maiden, and Perpetua a young mother whose breasts were dripping with milk. The two were removed and brought back in unbelted tunics (20.2-3). After being tossed around by the heifer, Perpetua sat up and pulled down the tunic to cover her thighs. Then she asked for a pin to tidy her hair, got up and helped Felicitas, who had been crushed to the ground. Both stood side by side, in absolute solidarity, though Felicitas was merely a slave. With 'manly' vigour the female friends endured sordid maltreatment and extreme fear. Their sexual integrity was assaulted, though not sadistically violated. One wonders, however, why redactors of the Christian tradition did not erase the sexualising details of the story. I assume that even the Church leaders were not able to see through and correct the androcentric biases of their time.[48]

A sad conclusion

Thecla, Perpetua and other female *confessores* were forced to undergo brutal ordeals but the suffering of Potamiaena seems to outstrip them all. The sexual sadism inflicted on her is more than disgusting, and more than a storyteller could bear. Twice her entire body (stripped, we suppose) was tortured and defiled. She was threatened by rape at the hands of the gladiators, insulted and finally destroyed inch by inch. All her persecutor's anger was directed against her body, for this they could destroy and do away with. For her assailants Potamiaena was reduced to mere body, an object, a lump of flesh. They were

---

[46] Cf. Bremmer, 'Perpetua and Her Diary', 116: 'The significance of this motif is not immediately clear, but it may well have had something to do with her sense of chastity.' I think this is true, but that it does not explain enough.

[47] Cf. A. Pettersen, 'Perpetua: Prisoner of Conscience', *Vigiliae Christianae* 41 (1987) 139-53 at 148-9 ('Perpetua, the martyr, became an *alter Christus*').

[48] Cf. Sarah Barnett, 'Death and the Maidens: Women Martyrs and Their Sexual Identity in the Early Christian Period', at *Culture@home* (www.anglicanmedia.com.au/old/cul/DeathandtheMaidens.htm).

angry with her, because they failed in their bid to possess and master her body. So now the object of love was turned into an object of hate, and had to be pulverized. The urge is obsessive, and borders on liminal behaviour, such as sexual abuse and fetishism.[49] She was loved, yet killed. Her assassins in effect displayed the attitude: 'If I can't have her, she can't live'. One is again left wondering why no Christian redactor interfered and took the side of Potamiaena over against the androcentric exhibitionism of his own tradition. It seems that Church leaders, and even Christian female martyrs themselves, generally were hopelessly locked into androcentric, gender-stereotyped ways of thinking, fabricated by culture and society.[50] A gender analysis of the martyrdom of Potamiaena yields to such an assessment.[51]

---

[49] See Iki Freud, *Mannen en moeders: De levenslange worsteling van zonen met hun moeders*, Amsterdam 2002, and *Electra versus Oedipus: Het drama van de moeder-dochterrelatie*, Amsterdam 2002. Freud, a psychotherapist in Amsterdam, argues for a paradigm shift in psychiatric theory from the well-known Oedipus-complex to a balanced Electra-complex. Her insights are innovative.

[50] The 'dynamic involvement' of women in the construction of religious traditions presupposes more freedom of movement and thinking than women actually had; pace J.M. Lieu, 'The "Attraction of Women" into Early Judaism and Christianity: Gender and the Politics of Conversion', *Journal of the Study of the New Testament* 72 (1998) 5-22.

[51] I thank my colleague Arie Zwiep for reading the first draft of this manuscript and Ton Hilhorst and Jan Bremmer for their complementary corrections and comments. I am also very grateful to Peter Crossman for his corrections on the English text.

'MULIER EST INSTRUMENTUM DIABOLI': WOMEN AND THE DESERT FATHERS

Monika Pesthy

Introduction

In his paper 'The Creation of Man and Woman in *The Secret Book of John*'[1] G.P. Luttikhuizen examined the role of Eve as the archetype of every woman in this Gnostic writing and showed that she possessed a positive as well as a negative side. Positive: because she comes from the spiritual world and is a bringer of help to Adam; negative: because sexuality appeared with her in the world. And, as Luttikhuizen notes: 'The negative view of the creation of woman is connected with (if not derivative of) the utterly negative evaluation of sexuality in this and many other late classical (Gnostic and non-Gnostic) texts.'[2]

I would like to align myself with these ideas, so the present paper will focus on the attitude toward women within other ascetic circles in early Christian Egypt: the Desert Fathers. It has been often remarked that the Gnostic and the monastic ascetic practice exhibited certain similarities[3] and the rigorous rejection of sexuality was common to both. Nevertheless, their attitude toward women is quite different.

In many Gnostic writings (as in the *Secret Book of John*), the Fall is connected with the appearance of sexuality, which often means the seduction or defilement of Eve by the archons or the chief-archon. Consequently, later on she 'teaches' Adam sexuality, and in this way becomes the originator of all the earthly troubles of mankind.[4] Notwithstanding, she is never depicted as a wanton temptress or a Satanic

---

[1] G.P. Luttikhuizen, 'The Creation of Man and Woman in *The Secret Book of John*', in: Id. (ed.), *The Creation of Man and Woman: Interpretations of the Biblical Narratives in Jewish and Christian Traditions* (Themes in Biblical Narrative 3), Leiden 2000, 140-55.

[2] Luttikhuizen, 'The Creation of Man and Woman', 155 note 57.

[3] Cf. G.G. Stroumsa, 'Ascèse et gnose: aux origines de la spiritualité monastique', in: Id., *Savoir et salut* (Patrimoines: Gnosticisme), Paris 1992, 145-9.

[4] Cf. G. Sfameni Gasparro, *Enkrateia e antropologia: Le motivazioni protologiche della continenza e delle verginità nel cristianesimo dei primi secoli e nello gnosticismo* (Studia Ephemeridis Augustinianum 20), Rome 1984, 115-65.

being, instead, she is considered rather (along with Adam) as a victim of the evil powers.

As against this, in early Egyptian monastic literature the woman is considered a constant danger to the virtue of the monk, an instrument of Satan, almost identical with Satan himself. Monks do not permit women to visit them, not even their own mother or sister, because 'it is through women that the Enemy fights against the saints'.[5]

I shall try to examine the reasons and roots of this misogyny: how it came about that woman, the 'Mother of all living beings', turned into a Satanic being, aiming expressly at the destruction of pious men. Another question which can be raised is why the appreciation of women in monastic circles was so much more negative than in Gnostic circles. Both were ascetic currents that existed not very far away from one another in space and time, and were based more or less on the same traditions. Nonetheless, the more rigorously encratic Gnostic thinking could entertain a much more favourable idea of woman than the orthodox monastic tradition.

1. *Women as Satanic beings? The views of the Desert Fathers*

The great theologian of the desert, Evagrius Ponticus (AD 346-399), established the list of the eight evil thoughts suggested by the demons: gluttony, fornication, greed, anger, sadness, carelessness [acedia], vanity, pride. This list has become a classic and has survived under the form of the seven deadly sins.[6] As we can see, fornication occupies the second place, which means that it appears at the beginning of spiritual evolution and therefore must be considered as not highly dangerous. However, in popular monastic literature it is depicted so often and with such vivacity that it tends to eclipse all the other evil thoughts.[7]

A favourite topic of this literature is the disguising of Satan in the form of a beautiful and lascivious woman in order to seduce the pious

---

[5] An *apophthegm* quoted in E. Giannarelli, 'Women and Satan in Christian Biography and Monastic Literature (IVth–Vth Centuries)', in: *Studia Patristica* 30 (ed. E.A. Livingstone), Louvain 1997, 197 note 6.

[6] Concerning the processes through which the list of the eight passions changed and received its definite form see A. Guillaumont (ed.), *Évagre le Pontique: Traité pratique 1* (SC 170), Paris 1971, 65-7.

[7] 'Among the trials the ascetic has to face, sexual temptations have a particular place', see Giannarelli, 'Women and Satan', 196.

monk. The results are varying: Antony resists firmly,[8] the vainglori-
ous monk of the *Historia Monachorum* falls to her/him.[9] But not only
Satan appears in the form of a woman: real women act just in the
same way. The best description of this womanly-Satanic seduction is
found exactly by the great theorician of the ascetic life, Evagrios:

> Avoid the encounter with women, if you want to live in abstinence, and
> never let them speak confidently to you. At the beginning they show or
> feign respect, but later on they dare shamelessly everything. At the first
> encounter they look downwards, talk modestly, shed tears compassionately,
> their behaviour is grave, they moan bitterly, ask about chastity and listen
> attentively to you. You see them the second time: they raise their eyes a
> little bit; the third time: they watch you without shame; you smile, they
> began to laugh without restraint. Later on they adorn themselves and
> parade openly before you, they cast you glances which promise passion,
> raise their eyebrows, roll their eye-balls, denude their neck, they try to
> seduce you with their whole body, they pronounce words which make
> passion sweet and utter sounds which charm the ears, until they besiege
> your soul from every side. All this is for you the hook which leads you to
> death with its bait, and a close-woven net which pulls you into destruc-
> tion. Don't let their modest talk lead you astray: the evil poison of the
> beasts is hidden within them (fem.).[10]

In this text, women really appear as Satanic beings and Satan in the
Historia Monachorum applies exactly the same methods of seduction.
We can now ask ourselves how matters stand concerning the ascetic
women (we know very well that there were such): we could very well
imagine that they were tortured by the demon of fornication in the
same way as their masculine counterparts and that Satan tried to
seduce them disguised in the form of a beautiful young man. This is,
however, not the case: we find no such descriptions. On the contrary:
in the stories about ascetic women, it is again they that are depicted
as presenting a constant danger to men (without willing it, naturally); they even consider themselves as such and punish themselves
accordingly. The *Historia Lausiaca* tells us about a woman who lived
in a tomb for ten years without letting anyone see her, because the

---

[8] Athanasius, *The Life of Antony* 5. This is probably the first instance that this
motif appears.
[9] Chapter 4. The story in Rufinus' Latin translation is much more colourful
than in the original Greek version, cf. ed. E. Schulz-Flügel (Patristische Texte und
Untersuchungen 34), 1990, 262-4.
[10] *De octo spiritibus malitiae* 4 (Patrologia Graeca 79.1149).

mind of a man was once disturbed because of her.[11] E. Wipszycka mentions the case of a virgin, related by John Moschos, who put out her own eyes because a young man had fallen in love with her and she blamed her eyes for having caused this passion.[12] This story is fictitious, as Wipszycka remarks, but therefore it is only the more valuable for us, because we are interested in the mentality behind it. E. Giannarelli sees very well that the temptations of male and female ascetics are described in quite a different way and remarks that 'no text presents Satan disguised as a handsome boy in order to provoke a girl who has devoted herself to God.'[13] However, she explains this difference by the fact that the ancient writers, who were men, were reluctant to speak about the sexual problems of women and female ascetics were often considered as 'virile women'.[14] I, on my part, would look for other reasons. The authors of these stories (whether about male or female ascetics) were men, tortured by their own desires, but instead of admitting it and trying to subdue it, it was easier and more comfortable to exteriorize their weakness and to put the blame on other, and quite real, human beings. Behind the story of the virgin who put out her own eyes we can divine the hatred with which the author would destroy all feminine beauty just because it attracts him so much. The fact that ascetic women are considered as men is rather the consequence than the reason of this mentality.

2. *The background*

This attitude towards women has a long history of which we can only give an outline here. The Old Testament does not consider women a danger to the chastity of man. In the sapiential books, there are several passages containing warnings against women (never against women in general, but only against the 'bad' ones) because of practical reasons: illicit relations could endanger the well-being or even the life of men.[15] In the New Testament, the apostle Paul has no great

---

[11] Cf. chap. 5.

[12] E. Wipszycka, 'Le monachisme égyptien et les villes', in: Id., *Études sur le christianisme dans l'Egypte de l'Antiquité tardive* (Studia Ephemeridis Augustinianum 52), Rome 1996, 289-90 note 14.

[13] Giannarelli, 'Women and Satan', 201.

[14] Ibid.

[15] For example Prov 2.16-19; 6.20-7.27.

esteem for women, but never considers them as Satanic or dangerous. The only passage in the Bible where a woman really appears
as a temptress is the story of Joseph and the wife of Potiphar (Gen
39.7-20). What is involved is female seduction but no devilish temptation: the woman acts only in order to satisfy her own desire (there
is no evil power at work which wants to destroy the virtue of Joseph
and nobody wants to put it to the proof, either) and Joseph resists
because he respects his master and the law of God, but not because
of any concern for his chastity.

Intertestamental literature reinterprets the story of Joseph. The
Book of Jubilees, dating from the second century BC, paraphrases the
biblical narrative without adding much. At the same time, however,
Joseph's motives undergo a certain change: he resists because

> he remembered the Lord and what his father Jacob would read to him
> from the words of Abraham—that no one is to commit adultery with
> a woman who has a husband; that there is a death penalty which has
> been ordained for him in heaven before the most High Lord. The sin
> will be entered regarding him in the eternal books forever before the
> Lord (39.6).[16]

That is to say, he acts not out of loyalty to his master, but in view of
the salvation of his soul. The *Testaments of the Twelve Patriarchs*, written in the first century BC, embellishes the adventure with many new
details. The wife of Potiphar deploys all the manoeuvres of seduction: feminine charms, flattery, threatening suicide, feigned sickness
and equally feigned interest in Joseph's religion, she even makes use
of a love-potion (*Testament of Joseph* 3-8). Her assaults constitute one
of the ten tests Joseph has to pass. He, on his part, affirms that the
spirit of Beliar acts in her (cf. *Testament of Joseph* 7.4). Women have
thus become an instrument of Satan and womanly seduction turned
out to be Satanic temptation.

The *Testaments of the Twelve Patriarchs* are characterised in general
by a fear (or hatred) of women, but it appears nowhere with such
vehemence as in the *Testament of Reuben*. For him, all women are evil
(cf. 5.1) and since they cannot win men by force, they all make use
of the ways of prostitutes (cf. 5.4).[17] We know that the *Testaments*
were written, or at least used, by Essenes, famous for their misogyny.

---

[16] Trans. by J.C. VanderKam (CSCO 511), Louvain 1989, 257.
[17] One of the manuscripts even adds: βλέμμασι σατανικοῖς; cf. M. de Jonge (ed.),
The Testaments of the Twelve Patriarchs, Leiden 1978, 10.

Its most brutal expression is found in the treatise entitled 'The Wiles of the Wicked Woman' (4Q184)[18] which gives evidence of such an extreme hatred of women that most of its interpreters take it for an allegory directed against Rome, or other Jewish groups, or Simon Maccabee or idolatry in general.[19] Perhaps A. Dupont-Sommer is the only one who advocates a literal interpretation: '…si l'auteur a dépeint la femme sous les traits d'une courtisane, d'une prostituée, c'est parce que toute femme lui apparaît telle; pour lui, toute femme est une prostituée, une débauchée, et représente le danger constant …'[20] and 'L'auteur voit bien en la femme une créature de malice, un être méchant et diabolique'.[21] I completely agree with this opinion and think that it perfectly harmonises very well with the statement of Josephus Flavius concerning the Essenes: '… they guard themselves from the licentiousness of women and are convinced that no woman remains faithful to a man' (*The Jewish War* 2.121).

After all that, it is by no means surprising that intertestamental literature makes women responsible for all the evil in the world.[22] These writings know of two different traditions concerning the Fall: one based on Gen 3, and the other one on Gen 6.1-4. In the first case, it was very easy to put the blame on Eve (cf. *Sirach* 25.24; *ApocMos* 7.1; 14.2),[23] but in the second, 'the daughters of men' played a rather passive role. Nevertheless, the *Testament of Reuben* sees temptresses in them: 'They seduced in this way the Watchers …' (5.6).

From the combination of the two traditions (Eve led astray by Satan and the daughters of men seduced by the Watchers) a new variant was born: Eve seduced sexually by Satan. Besides the Gnostic writ-

---

[18] The English title itself is misleading: the original text has no title and the first word is missing, only the feminine ending can be seen. To assume that it concerns only 'wicked women' or prostitutes is already an interpretation, not fully justified by the text. For the Hebrew text with English translation see: F. García Martínez and E.J.C. Tigchelaar (eds), *The Dead Sea Scrolls: Study Edition*, i, Leiden 1997, 376-7.

[19] Cf. R. D. Moore, 'Personification of the Seduction of Evil: "The Wiles of the Wicked Woman"', *Revue de Qumran* 10/4 (1981) 505-19.

[20] A. Dupont-Sommer and M. Philonenko (eds), *La Bible: Écrits intertestamentaires* (Bibliothèque de la Pléiade), Paris 1987, 448 note 1.

[21] Op. cit., 448 note 2.

[22] Cf. N. Forsyth, *The Old Enemy: Satan and the Combat Myth*, Princeton, N.J. 1987, 212-18.

[23] This mentality found its way into the New Testament, too; cf. 1 Tim 2.11-15.

ings, we find this motif especially in the targums,[24] but it is present in *1 Enoch* and perhaps also in the New Testament.[25] The forbidden fruit is then identified with sexuality or with desire.[26] Therefore, the opposite extreme, encratism aims at destroying sexuality in order to annihilate the consequences of the Fall. On this line of the tradition we shall not insist, because, on the one hand, it was very thoroughly dealt with by Sfameni Gasparro, and on the other, it is not really connected with our topic. That is to say, encratism is not the equivalent of misogyny. On the contrary, in the definitely encratic apocryphal acts of the apostles, women play a very important and positive role.

The Jewish literature discussed so far showed ascetic as well as misogynous tendencies. Women, however, were not treated much better by Philo, the Hellenised Alexandrian Jew. Summarising Philo's opinion about women, A. van den Hoek writes:

> As Dorothy Sly has shown,[27] women are the hallmark for Philo of everything undesirable: pleasure, wickedness, defilement, corruption, unsteadiness, multiplicity, irrationality, lack of understanding and good sense, inferiority, passivity, weakness and mortality.

(Man naturally personifies all the opposing virtues.)[28] Van den Hoek has proved that Philo, interpreting Gen 3, finally identifies women with the senses, or sense perception which caused the fall of man-intellect.[29]

---

[24] The *Targum Pseudo-Jonathan* to Gen 4.1 reads: 'Adam knew his wife Eve who had conceived from Sammael, the angel of the Lord', or it could be translated: 'Adam knew that his wife...' Since Gen 5.3 states that Seth was in the likeness and image of Adam and of Cain this is not said, the conclusion was drawn that he was not Adam's son; cf. M. Maher (trans.), *Targum Pseudo-Jonathan, Genesis*, Edinburgh 1992, 31 and note 2

[25] Cf. John 8.44.

[26] For the first time probably in the *Life of Adam and Eve* 19.3.

[27] *Philo's Perception of Women* (Brown Judaic Studies 209), Atlanta 1990, 216. Unfortunately, I was not able to consult this work.

[28] This opinion, as it seems, survived within the Alexandrian Jewry. In the fourth century CE (just the period we are interested in) the Jewish physician Adamantius writes: βελτίω δὲ τὰ ἄρρενα τῶν θηλειῶν· ὡς γὰρ ἐπὶ πλεῖστον τὸ μὲν ἄρρεν γενναῖον, ἄδολον, δίκαιον, θυμοειδές, φιλότιμον, ἄκακον· τὸ δὲ θῆλυ ἀγεννές, πικρόν, δολερόν, κουφόνουν, ἄδικον, φιλόνεικον, θρασύδειλον (*Physiogn.* II.2; cf. A. van den Hoek, 'Endowed with reason or glued to the senses: Philo's thoughts on Adam and Eve', in: Luttikhuizen, *The Creation of Man and Woman*, 75 note 34).

[29] Cf. Van den Hoek, 'Endowed with reason', 63-75.

Let us now see how pleasure approaches and seduces the intellect through the senses:

> 165 Pleasure does not venture to bring her wiles and deceptions to bear on the man, but on the woman, and by her means on him. This is a telling and well-made point: for in us mind corresponds to man, the senses to woman; and pleasure encounters and holds parley with senses first, and through them cheats with her quackeries the sovereign mind itself (καὶ τὸν ἡγεμόνα νοῦν φενακίζει): for when each sense has been subjugated to her sorceries (τοῖς φίλτροις αὐτῆς ὑπαχθῇ) delighting in what she proffers, (...) then all of them receive the gifts and offer them like handmaids to the Reason (τῷ λογισμῷ) as to a master, bringing with them Persuasion to plead that it reject nothing whatever. Reason is forthwith ensnared (δελεασθεὶς) and becomes a subject instead of a ruler, a slave instead of a master, an alien instead of a citizen, and a mortal instead of an immortal. 166 In a word we must never lose sight of the fact that Pleasure, being a courtesan and a wanton, eagerly desires to meet with a lover, and searches for panders, by whose means she shall get one on her hook. It is the senses that act as panders for her and procure the lover. When she has ensnared these she easily brings the Mind under her control (*De opificio mundi* 165-166).[30]

At the end, perception and pleasure are practically identified[31] and allegory ceases to be allegory: women have really become seducers. We can verify the truth of this statement by looking at a passage of the *Hypothetica (Apologia pro Iudaeis)* where Philo writes the following about the Essenes:

> For no Essene takes a wife, because a wife is a selfish creature, excessively jealous and an adept at beguiling the morals of her husband and seducing him by her continued impostures (καὶ συνεχέσι γοητείαις ὑπάγεσθαι). For by the fawning talk which she practises and the other ways in which she plays her part like an actress on the stage she first ensnares the sight and hearing, and when these subjects as it were have been duped she cajoles the sovereign mind (τὸν ἡγεμόνα νοῦν φενακίζει). (...) For he who is either fast bound in the love lures of his wife (γυναικὸς φίλτροις ἐνδεθεὶς) or under the stress of nature makes his children his first care ceases to be the same to others and unconsciously

---

[30] Trans. by F.H. Colson and G.H. Whitaker, *Philo* (The Loeb Classical Library), i, London/Cambridge, Mass. 1962, 131.

[31] 'The allegory concentrates on the hapless senses which woman exploits and also embodies and which are virtually identical with sensuality and wrongly directed sexuality'; Van den Hoek, 'Endowed with reason', 73.

has become a different man and has passed from freedom into slavery (*Hypothetica* 11.14-15, 17).[32]

Concerning real women he uses here in a literal sense the same expressions he used allegorically in the former text. That is, allegory and reality are fused—women are the reason for evil: in general, allegorically as well as actually.

All the motifs treated in the preceding passages can be equally found with the Greeks. For example, Phaedra wants to seduce her stepson, Pandora, the goddess who 'gives everything', becomes the source of all trouble,[33] Hesiod's warnings against women[34] are very similar to what we find in biblical wisdom literature, while Aristotle sees in women an inferior being, 'a deformed male'.[35]

Let us now summarise the factors which constitute this extremely negative view of women presented above: the woman as a temptress (the Joseph-tradition, Phaedra); the woman as an inferior being (Aristotle); the woman as a constant danger to man (Hesiod, sapiential books, the Essenes, Philo); the woman as the cause of the Fall of men (Eve, the 'daughters of men', Pandora). These traits combined can easily make up a Satanic being.

The Christian literature of the first three centuries, however, does not show such an extremely negative attitude towards women. Even Tertullian, who has no great esteem for them (see the beginning chapters of *De cultu feminarum*), does not consider them either as Satanic beings, or as temptresses: when he warns them against all forms of feminine embellishments, he is first of all concerned with their own virtue.

During this period early Christianity had to affirm itself in a hostile pagan world, amidst persecution, and to define itself in the face of heresies, that is to say, it had enough enemies to contend with, so there was no need to look for any within its own circles. Satan

---

[32] Trans. by F.H. Colson, *Philo* (The Loeb Classical Library), ix, London/Cambridge, Mass. 1967, 443.

[33] Concerning the similarities of the Eve- and Pandora-traditions see J.N. Bremmer, 'Pandora or the Creation of a Greek Eve', in: Luttikhuizen, *The Creation of Man and Woman*, 19-33.

[34] Women are doing nothing good, only evil and they are the source of all the troubles (*Theogony* 601-602); the gods filled Pandora's bosom with treachery, flattering words and an inclination to theft (*Works and Days* 77-78); the woman lures man with her swaying hips and flattering words because of his wealth (373-374).

[35] Aristotle, *De generatione animalium* 737a.

appeared in the form of the persecutors and the heretics, not in the form of beautiful women.

3. *Conclusions*

With the coming of peace for the Church, the situation changes: the ideal of the martyr is replaced by the ascetic ideal. *Imitatio Christi* does not mean physical death for Christ, but mortification of the passions. As the martyr defeated Satan the very moment he perished, the ascetic defeats Satan by cutting off all the passions of his soul. Clement of Alexandria affirms that a soul living in purity in the knowledge of God and observing the commandments is also a martyr, i.e. a witness.[36] He describes the struggle against passions as an athletic competition,[37] the same way as Tertullian described martyrdom.[38] A pseudo-Chrysostomian homily about Thecla places in a close parallel the sufferings of the martyr and those of the virgin:

> All this made the virginity of the blessed virgin into a great martyr-dom:[39] she fought against lusts as against wild beasts; she wrestled with thoughts as the martyr with pains; she suffered from lascivious images as the martyr under the torture of the executioner.[40]

Struggling with his own passion, the monk struggles with Satan, and it was not very difficult to identify the object of the passions, the woman, with Satan. Naturally, we can ask ourselves why it happened only in the case of *porneia* and not in the case of the other seven passions, but the answer is probably quite easy: in the other cases (such as carelessness, vain glory, etc.) it was not possible to exteriorize the passion (it makes no sense to struggle against silver instead of struggling against one's own cupidity). For the same reason it is no wonder that scenes where Satan tries to seduce the monk in the

---

[36] Cf. *Stromateis* 4.4.15.3.

[37] Cf. *Stromateis* 7.3.20.3-5.

[38] Cf. *Ad martyras* 3.3.

[39] According to the tradition Thecla did not die a martyr's death. Instead, she finished her life peacefully in an old age. The homily tries to prove that her sufferings were just as bad as those of the martyr and, therefore, she can be considered as such.

[40] Patrologia Graeca 50.746. The English translation is from my article: 'Thecla Among the Church Fathers', in: J.N. Bremmer (ed.), *The Apocryphal Acts of Paul and Thecla* (Studies on the Apocryphal Acts of the Apostles 2), Kampen 1996, 172-3.

form of a woman are represented by painters with great predilection: they are probably easier to depict than the assaults of vainglory, for example. And, as I have tried to show in the foregoing lines, early Jewish and Greek misogynous tradition made it very easy to see in women inferior and malicious beings.

At the beginning of the paper, we posed the question why monastic tradition represents women as Satanic temptresses, whereas the encratic Gnostic writings never see them as such. G. Stroumsa argues that even if the ascetic practice of the two groups do show similarities, the underlying ideas are radically different: whereas Gnostics hate the world and consider themselves as totally strange to it, monks never hate it, because it was created by God and they need sustained ascetic efforts to detach themselves from it.[41] Probably the same is true in the case of sexuality: Gnostics loathe it as something belonging to the material (i.e. evil) world, whereas on the monks it exercises a very strong attraction against which they have to struggle very hard. To demonstrate this, let us finish this paper by a text written by a Church Father for whom this struggle must have been especially hard: Jerome. Although he was not one of the Egyptian Desert Fathers, the feelings expressed in his text are probably shared by many other monks. In his *Life of Saint Paul* he describes the tortures Decius and Valerian used against Christians (chap. 3): one of the martyrs was smeared with honey and then exposed to the sunshine, another one, a young man, was led in a beautiful garden with flowers, spring and gentle breeze, and tied up with flowery tendrils on a soft bed. When he was left alone

> a most beautiful prostitute came to him and began to embrace his neck with her tender arms and (it is a crime even to speak about it) to touch his virile parts in order to excite him to lust and to mount him victoriously in an indecent way. What to do and where to turn—the soldier of Christ did not know. Pleasure began to subdue him who was not defeated by the torments. But on divine inspiration he bite off his own tongue, spit it in the face of the wanton woman who was kissing him and the enormity of pain extinguished the desire of lust in him.[42]

Naturally, we must realise that there is no historical reality behind this description. All the motifs appearing in it are *topoi* taken from other writings: the torture mentioned at the beginning appears in Apuleius,[43]

---

[41] Cf. Stroumsa, 'Ascèse et gnose', 159.
[42] Patrologia Latina 23.20.
[43] Cf. *Metamorphoses* 8.22.

the scene itself is taken from Petronius,[44] the final solution can be
found in Tertullian.[45] The whole is a result of Jerome's imagination
and it reveals to us what sexuality meant for him (and probably for
many other monks, if not in such an exaggerated manner): sweet
delight (so desirable!) and cruel torture.

---

[44] Cf. *Satyrica* 131-132; M. Fuhrmann, 'Die Mönchsgeschichten des Hieronymus:
Formexperimente in erzählender Literatur', in: A. Cameron et al. (eds), *Christianisme et
formes littéraires de l'Antiquité tardive en occident* (Entretiens Fondation Hardt 23), Geneva
1977, 41-99, esp. 71-2.
[45] *Ad martyras* 4.7.

PART THREE

GNOSTICISM & EGYPT

LE GNOSTICISME ALEXANDRIN AUX PREMIERS TEMPS DU CHRISTIANISME

ATTILA JAKAB

Suivant l'opinion longtemps dominante du théologien allemand Walter Bauer, formulée encore en 1934, «le premier christianisme alexandrin aurait été hétérodoxe, et plus exactement gnostique. (...) C'est pourquoi, après le triomphe de l'orthodoxie au tournant du IIe siècle, ...[il] aurait été rétrospectivement condamné à l'oubli».[1] Cette représentation, qui suppose l'antériorité de l'«hérésie» par rapport à l'«orthodoxie», est en relation étroite avec l'absence des sources qui caractérise la période précédant l'époque de Pantène, de Clément et d'Origène. Pour le premier siècle, par exemple, nous n'avons pratiquement pas d'informations: ni persécution, ni martyr, ni conflit. Paul n'est jamais allé à Alexandrie, qui est quasiment absente des écrits du Nouveau Testament.

Au cours des décennies, la vision simplificatrice, supposant l'homogénéité du phénomène chrétien dans l'Antiquité, a beaucoup évolué. Les érudits sont arrivés à la conclusion que les écrivains chrétiens bataillaient en réalité contre les disciples, ou les disciples des disciples (qui furent essentiellement leurs contemporains) de grands maîtres «gnostiques», dont les idées et les enseignements propres sont habituellement enfouis dans des interprétations ou des polémiques. Dès lors, il est devenu de plus en plus évident qu'il faut procéder par périodisation dans l'analyse. D'autant plus qu'à leur époque, ce qui est tout à fait remarquable, ces maîtres «gnostiques»—selon l'état actuel de nos connaissances—furent peu, ou pas du tout, inquiétés pour leur enseignement. C'était le cas notamment de Basilide à Alexandrie ou de Valentin à Rome. Nous pouvons donc déduire qu'il y a eu un temps de «cohabitation pacifique» entre les chrétiens gnostiques (ou gnosticisants) et les non-gnostiques au sein même des diverses communautés chrétiennes des premiers temps. Il me paraît d'ailleurs peu probable (au moins au second siècle) que le monde environnant ait

---

[1] Mélèze-Modrzejewski 1997, 306.

jamais fait la distinction entre les diverses sensibilités présentes dans le christianisme.[2]

Alexandrie—jusqu'au premières décennies du troisième siècle—est indéniablement un témoin privilégié de cette intégration des gnostiques dans la communauté chrétienne de la cité. Cela s'explique aussi par le fait que la société multiculturelle y s'est avérée un terrain propice pour ce «courant» d'idées du christianisme ancien. Ce n'est certainement pas un hasard si «les deux seuls chrétiens alexandrins que nous pouvons *nommer* avant le milieu du second siècle, sont d'une façon significative les deux plus importants chefs d'écoles chrétiennes gnostiques, Basilide et Valentin».[3]

D'après Clément (*Strom.* VII.106.4), Basilide—d'origine syrienne, dont la vie nous est inconnue—enseignait à Alexandrie sous les règnes des empereurs Hadrien (117-138) et Antonin le Pieux (138-161). Fondateur d'une école gnostique il aurait été le disciple de Glaucias, dont les basilidiens ont fait un interprète de Pierre. Irénée de Lyon (*Adv. Haer.* I.24.1), en revanche, nous informe que—pareillement à Saturnin («originaire d'Antioche près de Daphné»)—le point de départ de son enseignement a été la doctrine de Simon le magicien et celle de son successeur, Ménandre. Dans la liste des hérétiques d'Epiphane (*Panarion* XXIV.1), il est également le second successeur de Ménandre, immédiatement après Saturnin; tandis que l'auteur de l'*Elenchos* (VII. 20.1) rattache Basilide à l'apôtre Matthias.[4]

En ce qui concerne le début de son activité, Eusèbe, qui dans son *Histoire Ecclésiastique* suit la notice d'Irénée,[5] dans sa *Chronique* donne l'an 132, ce qui recoupe le témoignage de Clément.

Si Basilide est réputé être un auteur fécond, de ses travaux littéraires il nous restent seulement des fragments qui sont largement insuffisants pour nous faire une idée exacte de son système doctrinal «singulière-

---

[2] Voir Eusèbe, *Hist. Eccl.* IV.7.2 & 10-11; Irénée, *Adv. Haer.* I.25.3.

[3] Ritter 1987, 162.

[4] «Selon Basilide et Isidore, Matthias leur avait dit des paroles secrètes qu'il avait entendues du Sauveur lorsqu'il recevait son enseignement en particulier» (A. Le Boulluec [Sources Chrétiennes 428], Paris 1997, 322 n. 5).

[5] «De Ménandre donc, que nous avons dit plus haut avoir été le successeur de Simon, sortit, semblable à un serpent à deux gueules et à deux têtes, une puissance qui produisit les chefs de deux hérésies différentes: Saturnin, originaire d'Antioche, et Basilide d'Alexandrie. De ces hérétiques, l'un installa en Syrie, l'autre en Égypte, les écoles d'hérésies ennemies de Dieu.» Eusèbe, *Hist. Eccl.* IV.7.3 (Sources Chrétiennes 31, Paris 1986, 167).

ment original».[6] En ce qui concerne sa personne, en revanche, E. de Faye pense que Basilide fut «un esprit profondément religieux», un homme préoccupé par le problème du mal et de la souffrance qui prêchait une morale élevée, très en contraste avec celle de ses successeurs. Ayant soif de rédemption, «comme tant d'hommes de son temps», il pensait la trouver dans le christianisme.[7] N'empêche que le portrait et la biographie de Basilide nous restent toujours inaccessibles. Car, en dépit du résumé d'Irénée (*Adv. Haer.* I.24.3-4) et de l'analyse rapide d'Eusèbe (*Hist. Eccl.* IV.7.6-8) de la «réfutation très puissante ... due à Agrippa Castor», l'absence de nos renseignements sur l'école et l'enseignement de Basilide subsiste toujours.

Pour ce qui est de son œuvre, nous savons, par le témoignage de Clément (*Strom.* IV.81.1) et d'Eusèbe (*Hist. Eccl.* IV.7.7), qu'il avait écrit un commentaire de l'Évangile[8]—les *Exegetica*—, en vingt-quatre livres, qui le place surtout parmi les exégètes. Clément, dans le IVe livre des *Stromates* (81.1—88.5), donne plusieurs passages du vingt-troisième livre de cet ouvrage, où son auteur traitait du problème de la souffrance. En outre, Basilide composa aussi des psaumes ou *Odes* qui nous sont signalés par le fragment de Muratori (83-85) et que nous devons considérer comme perdus. A en croire B.A. Pearson, Basilide aurait utilisé plusieurs écrits, devenus «canoniques» par la suite—comme les *Épîtres de Paul*, l'*Évangile de Matthieu* ou l'*Évangile de Marc*—, pour l'élaboration de ses œuvres; ce qui témoignerait de leur présence à Alexandrie vers le milieu du IIe siècle ap. J.-C.[9]

L'enseignement de Basilide—où D. Vigne discerne trois éléments: grec, chrétien et juif[10]—fut perpétué[11] (au moins jusqu'au IVe siècle[12]) et sans doute altéré par ses disciples, parmi lesquels son fils, Isidore. Mais au sujet de ce dernier nous sommes encore plus mal renseignés que sur le père. Si Irénée de Lyon (*Adv. Haer.* I.24.5-7) parle de la

---

[6] Grant 1979, 202.

[7] De Faye 1913, 38.

[8] D'après le témoignage d'Origène (*Hom. sur Luc* I.2), Basilide aurait même eu «l'audace d'écrire un évangile et de lui donner pour titre son propre nom». Pierre Nautin, en revanche, a montré que Basilide n'a pas écrit d'évangile. Nautin 1975-76, 311-12.

[9] Pearson 1990, 204: «Gnosticism in Early Egyptian Christianity».

[10] Vigne 1992, 293.

[11] Voir le témoignage de Clément (*Strom.* I.146.1) au sujet de la commémoration du baptême de Jésus par les basilidiens.

[12] L'hérésie des basilidiens est encore «florissante» à l'époque d'Epiphane (*Panarion* 24.1.1).

doctrine des basilidiens—pour qui «les juifs, disent-ils, n'existent plus et les chrétiens n'existent pas encore»—il garde en revanche le silence sur Isidore.

Le peu d'information que nous avons sur lui concerne, pour l'essentiel, quelques-uns de ses écrits—*De l'âme adventice*,[13] *Commentaires du prophète Parchor*,[14] *Ethica*[15]—, connus par le seul témoignage de Clément d'Alexandrie.

Contemporain de Saturnin et de Basilide (Eusèbe, *Hist. Eccl.* IV.7.9), Carpocrate est le second maître «gnostique» rattaché habituellement à Alexandrie, suivant les témoignages hésitants de Clément (*Strom.* III.5.2; 10.1). Ce dernier fut confronté aux disciples de ce maître—dont l'œuvre est perdu—et à ceux de son fils, Epiphane, pour des questions avant tout d'ordre moral (mise en commun des femmes).[16]

Au sujet d'Epiphane—dont la mère, Alexandreia, était originaire de Céphallénie—Clément nous laisse tout d'abord entendre qu'il fut un véritable enfant de génie. Éduqué par son père—ce qui présente un bien curieux parallèle avec la vie d'Origène—Epiphane écrit plusieurs ouvrages, connus par Clément, avant de mourir à l'âge de 17 ans. Honoré comme un dieu, après sa mort, à Samé—la patrie de sa mère—, il fut, à en croire Clément (*Strom.* III.5.2-3), le véritable fondateur de l'hérésie des carpocratiens. Ce fait pourrait expliquer, au moins en partie, l'absence des œuvres de Carpocrate, à moins que ce dernier ne fut un maître donnant un enseignement essentiellement oral, comme le fera Pantène ou Ammonius Saccas plus tard.

L'absence des renseignements plus précis s'explique sans doute aussi par le fait que le groupe des carpocratiens semble avoir eu une durée très limité dans le temps à Alexandrie. Clément déjà les connaît plutôt mal, et Origène (*Contre Celse* V.62) déclare n'en avoir jamais rencontré d'adeptes.

Mais, au-delà de Basilide et de Carpocrate, le maître qui a probablement le plus contribué à accréditer la thèse d'un christianisme alexandrin gnostique, ou au moins dominé par le gnosticisme à ses origines, fut Valentin (100-175). Fondateur de la plus importante école gnostique, il était, selon E. de Faye, «l'un des hommes les plus remarquables du IIe siècle»,[17] même si nous connaissons à peine sa vie.

---

[13] Cf. Clément, *Strom.* II.113.3 & 113.4–114.2.
[14] Cf. ibid., VI.53.2 & 3-5.
[15] Cf. ibid., III.2.2 & 2.2–3.2.
[16] Cf. ibid., III.5.1.
[17] De Faye 1913, 40.

D'après Irénée (*Adv. Haer.* III.4.3), il «vint en effet à Rome sous Hygin [137-140]; il atteignit son apogée sous Pie [140-154] et se maintint jusqu'à Anicet [154-166]». Eusèbe (*Hist. Eccl.* IV.11.1-3), à son tour, reprend ce bref témoignage d'Irénée sur la personne de Valentin sans rien y ajouter, si ce n'est qu'Irénée «met à nu la méchanceté cachée et sournoise» de ce dernier, «pareille à celle d'un serpent qui se tapit dans un trou».

«Le premier à nous apprendre que Valentin naquit en Égypte, reçut son instruction à Alexandrie, et répandit sa doctrine en Égypte avant de se rendre à Rome»[18] est l'hérésiologue Epiphane de Salamine. Dès lors, son rattachement traditionnel à Alexandrie—au moins en ce qui concerne le début de sa «carrière»—fut acquis.

Des informations plus précises sur Valentin, et plus particulièrement sur cette période alexandrine de sa vie, auraient été d'un très grand intérêt afin de mieux connaître (et de comprendre) le début du christianisme dans la ville, et vérifier la véracité de son caractère gnostique. Mais le témoignage très tardif d'Epiphane doit plutôt nous inciter à la prudence. S'il n'est pas question de mettre en doute son éventuelle présence (ou passage?) dans cette grande métropole méditerranéenne, nous pouvons toutefois douter de l'importance de cette période et tout particulièrement sur l'activité qu'il y a éventuellement déployé. D'autant plus que, contrairement à l'école occidentale (Héracléon et Ptolémée) ou orientale (Théodote), la pensée valentinienne ne disposera pratiquement jamais de représentant de marque à Alexandrie.

Ce que nous pouvons constater après ce passage en revue des personnages qualifiés généralement comme «gnostiques», et en rapport avec la cité méditerranéenne, c'est que le caractère considéré par la suite comme initialement «hétérodoxe» de son christianisme est loin de s'imposer. Ce qui ressort avant tout c'est essentiellement le fait que ces hommes, qui ont vécu et enseigné plus ou moins en même temps et dans la même ville (sinon dans un même milieu)—sans nous fournir pour autant la moindre information sur un quelconque contact entre eux—, n'ont jamais été excommuniés, ni même inquiétés, par l'éventuelle Église «orthodoxe» du lieu (c'est-à-dire d'Alexandrie). Dès lors, tout en admettant la diversité des groupes que formeront leurs disciples (basilidiens, carpocratiens, valentiniens), je considère néanmoins qu'ils s'insèrent—au moins dans un premier temps—dans un

---

[18] Quasten, I, 1955, 296.

ensemble plus vaste, dynamique et encore en perpétuel mouvement qu'est la communauté chrétienne avant son «institutionnalisation».

En conséquence, le système valentinien, qui différencie les *hylikoi* (= non-chrétiens) les *psychikoi* (= chrétiens non-gnostiques) et les *pneumatikoi* (= gnostiques)—tel que Clément d'Alexandrie (*Extraits de Théodote* 56.2) nous le rapporte—, témoignerait de cette insertion, mais aussi de l'abîme qui sépare les deux principaux «courants» (gnostique et non-gnostique) au sein du christianisme, quitte à provoquer malaise, tension et finalement rupture, dont nous pouvons nous apercevoir dans l'histoire de la communauté chrétienne de la grande métropole méditerranéenne.[19]

Si l'importance du gnosticisme (ou plus précisément du «courant» chrétien gnosticisant) a toujours été mise en avant pour l'histoire du christianisme au second siècle ap. J.-C. à Alexandrie, elle s'est encore largement accrue à la suite de la découverte d'écrits (en majorité) gnostiques de Nag Hammadi, vers la fin de l'année 1945.[20] C'est ainsi qu'en 1968 J.E. Ménard, dans un article sur *Les origines de la gnose*,[21] pouvait écrire (presque en guise de conclusion) que «les gnoses du IIe siècle et les originaux vraisemblablement grecs des textes gnostiques coptes de Nag Hamadi [*sic*] sont nés dans un milieu alexandrin». Pour lui, «les deux grandes cultures»—hellénistique et judaïque—de ce milieu «semblent avoir le plus marqué les écrits gnostiques du IIe siècle».

Depuis ces propos, le regard des chercheurs sur les textes de Nag Hammadi a considérablement évolué. Avec la publication des facsimilés (en 12 volumes, entre 1972 et 1984) et les projets de leur édition et traduction, la complexité des problèmes à résoudre n'a pas tardé à émerger.[22] Outre les difficultés au sujet de la datation et de la localisation de ces écrits (essentiellement en ce qui concerne les originaux), parfois le caractère même de quelques-uns ne cesse de partager les spécialistes. Dès lors, il n'est nullement surprenant que les écrits de Nag Hammadi sont loin de confirmer le caractère largement gnostique du christianisme alexandrin des premiers temps.

En réalité, parmi les écrits dont la rédaction peut être situé à Alexandrie (*L'Authentikos Logos* [NH VI.3], *Les Leçons de Silvanos* [NH

---

[19] Cf. Jakab 2004.
[20] Voir Poirier 1986.
[21] Ménard 1968.
[22] Voir à ce sujet les actes du colloque tenu à Québec du 15 au 19 septembre 1993: Painchaud & Pasquier 1995.

VII.4], *L'Hypostase des Archontes* [NH II.4], *Les Sentences de Sextus* [NH XII.1]) il n'y a que *L'Exégèse de l'Âme* (NH II.6) qui soit clairement reconnu comme écrit gnostique et chrétien par ses éditeurs (M. Scopello et J.-M. Sevrin), en dépit de leurs opinions divergentes sur la datation. Mais, cette reconnaissance de principe est aussitôt nuancée par les auteurs. Si J.-M. Sevrin parle d'un gnosticisme «bien primitif, saisi à l'état naissant», qui «n'implique pas a priori qu'il soit chronologiquement antérieur à Valentin, sauf s'il vient d'un milieu où les doctrines valentiniennes auraient aussi été répandues»,[23] M. Scopello en revanche définit le texte «comme un écrit gnostique à caractère fortement judaïsant», dont le «genre littéraire en fait un document de nature ésotérique, coloré parfois de syncrétisme, [et] marqué par une volonté de diffusion du message de la Gnose».[24]

Pour J.-M. Sevrin, il s'agit d'un texte religieux et de surcroît chrétien, d'un «sous-produit scolaire», sans «étape judaïsante antérieure» et relevant «d'une seule rédaction». «L'auteur lui-même—dit-il—se donne pour chrétien, puisqu'il s'assimile au groupe de ses auditeurs par l'emploi, dans l'exhortation, de la 1ère personne du pluriel.» Toutefois ce christianisme n'est que «très apparent» et «très superficiel»; «la doctrine non seulement ne procède pas de la foi chrétienne, mais n'en est même que fort peu affectée». D'après J.-M. Sevrin, *L'Exégèse de l'Âme* serait donc «une œuvre syncrétiste dans laquelle une religion gnostique, à peine dégagée de ses racines platonisantes, intègre, sans peine et sans profondeur, le christianisme et ses Écritures, ne se souciant ni d'intégrer vraiment le contenu du christianisme, ni de christianiser réellement sa propre pensée». Si «une telle synthèse suppose que, dans le milieu où le texte est écrit, le christianisme existe déjà de façon relativement organisée, puisqu'il y a un corpus d'Écritures» il «ne saurait [cependant] représenter la seule forme du christianisme là où» il fut produit.[25]

M. Scopello reconnaît également la part que cet écrit doit à «une culture d'école»[26], mais elle considère—contrairement à J.-M. Sevrin, qui nous suggère plutôt «un texte gnostique prévalentinien»[27]—que ce document «romanesque de nature exotérique» est marqué, avant

---

[23] Sevrin 1983, 59.
[24] Scopello 1985, 100.
[25] Sevrin 1983, 56–58.
[26] Scopello 1985, 97.
[27] Sevrin 1983, 58.

tout, «par la volonté de l'auteur de simplifier les données difficiles de
la pensée de la Gnose», afin de «favoriser la compréhension de l'écrit
par un public de formation culturelle variée». D'après elle, *L'Exégèse
de l'Âme* a aussi «emprunté des traditions et des modes de pensée au
judaïsme», tout en les relisant et les réinterprétant «à la lumière d'une
idéologie nouvelle, celle de la Gnose, en les pliant à l'illustration du
mythe gnostique de l'âme».[28]

Que les deux éditeurs se divisent au sujet de la datation de ce texte,
cela va de soi. D'après M. Scopello, la rédaction grecque se situe «entre
la fin du IIe et le début du IIIe siècle, en Égypte, peut-être même à
Alexandrie».[29] J.-M. Sevrin en revanche propose «une datation haute»
et une rédaction plus évidente à Alexandrie:

> Pour la date, il existe un repère relatif sûr: la citation de Jean, qui sup-
> pose que cet Évangile soit non seulement rédigé, mais encore diffusé
> et reçu à côté des autres. Cela permet bien—le Papyrus Rylands 457
> et le commentaire d'Héracléon nous y autorisent—de remonter assez
> haut dans le IIe siècle, mais il serait téméraire d'aller jusqu'au début du
> siècle: l'an 120 constitue un *terminus post quem* raisonnable.

Quant au *terminus ante quem*, il propose «le départ de Valentin pour
Rome, vers 135». D'après lui,

> écrit dans un milieu pénétré de thèmes philosophiques, imbu de con-
> naissances et de procédés scolaires, marqué par une religiosité gnostique
> naissante, notre traité [c'est-à-dire *L'Exégèse de l'Âme*] adressé à des chré-
> tiens, selon toute vraisemblance à Alexandrie dans le deuxième quart
> du IIe siècle, apporterait un précieux éclairage à la question des origines
> du gnosticisme comme à celle des commencements du christianisme
> alexandrin.[30]

En prenant en considération la disparition brutale du judaïsme en
Égypte et à Alexandrie, au début du IIe siècle (suite à la révolte sous
Trajan), et la diffusion tardive (dès le second quart du IIIe siècle) du
christianisme dans la *chôra*, je partage plutôt l'opinion de J.-M. Sevrin
que celle de M. Scopello. D'autant plus qu'à la lumière de *L'Exégèse de
l'Âme*, la conjoncture dans laquelle les maîtres «gnostiques» d'Alexandrie
(Basilide, Carpocrate, Valentin ainsi qu'Isidore et Epiphane) ont vécu
et enseigné peut être mieux précisé. Mis en rapport avec la *Prédica-*

---

[28] Scopello 1985, 100.
[29] Ibid.
[30] Sevrin 1983, 59–60.

tion de Pierre,[31] nous avons, par ce fait même, un petit aperçu de ce qu'a pu être la communauté chrétienne naissante à Alexandrie avec ses diverses tendances, dont celle gnosticisante n'était pas, et de loin, *la* déterminante pour son évolution. Assurément faible du point de vue numérique, la communauté chrétienne de la métropole méditerranéenne du second siècle ne peut être nullement considérée comme gnostique, même si ce courant y est bien attesté à cette époque.

Le gnosticisme a sans doute réussi à se maintenir longtemps à Alexandrie, mais d'une manière peu visible, et surtout sans être en mesure de s'organiser et, qui plus est encore, de faire émerger par la suite des représentants de la taille des maîtres de la première moitié du second siècle. Nous pouvons donc considérer ce courant du christianisme alexandrin comme une sorte de source d'idées qui, tel une rivière souterraine, a abondamment arrosé la pensée des auteurs de la «Grande Église»: Clément et Origène. Il n'est sans doute pas un hasard, que le véritable titre de l'un des œuvres de Clément, dont un des sujets principaux est l'articulation de la gnose et de la foi, est *Stromates de notes gnostiques selon la véritable philosophie*. Dans le sixième livre (*Strom.* VI.71-114) l'auteur—qui fut obligé de justifier ses activités d'écrivain—dresse même le portrait du «vrai gnostique», qu'il oppose à la fois aux «hérétiques» et aux «simpliciores», ces gens qui s'estimaient si bien doués qu'ils prétendaient ne pas toucher ni à la philosophie ni à la dialectique, ni aux sciences naturelles, et qui ne demandaient que la foi nue (*Strom.* I.43.1). Il n'est d'ailleurs pas sans intérêt que Clément exigeait des presbytres qu'ils soient parfaits comme les «vrais gnostiques»:

> il est donc possible—écrit-il—, aujourd'hui encore, à ceux qui s'exercent dans les commandements du Seigneur et qui vivent de manière parfaite et gnostique selon l'Évangile, d'être ajoutés à la liste des Apôtres. Un homme est réellement πρεσβύτερος τῆς ἐκκλησίας et διάκονος véritable de la volonté de Dieu s'il fait et enseigne ce que dit le Seigneur. Il n'est pas choisi par un vote humain (ὑπ' ἀνθρώπων χειροτονούμενος) ni considéré comme juste parce qu'il est πρεσβύτερος, mais il est inscrit au presbyterium (ἐν πρεσβυτερίῳ καταλεγόμενος) parce qu'il est juste. Même si, sur cette terre, il ne reçoit pas l'honneur d'être au premier rang (πρωτοκαθεδρία), il siégera sur l'un des vingt-quatre trônes pour juger le peuple, comme le dit Jean dans l'Apocalypse. (...) Les rangs progressifs d'évêques, de presbytres et de diacres (προκοπαὶ ἐπισκόπων, πρεσβυτέρων, διακόνων) qui existent ici-bas dans l'Église reproduisent,

---

[31] Cf. Cambe 2003.

d'après moi, la gloire des anges et ce régime attendu, d'après les Écritures, par ceux qui ont vécu en marchant sur les pas des Apôtres, avec une justice parfaite selon l'Évangile. Lorsqu'ils auront été emportés sur les nuées, écrit l'Apôtre, ils commenceront d'abord par la diaconie (διακονήσειν μὲν τὰ πρῶτα), puis ils seront admis dans le presbyterium par un progrès en gloire—car il y a gloire et gloire—jusqu'à ce qu'ils parviennent à l'homme parfait.[32]

Ainsi, d'après Clément, ce qui importe le plus ce ne sont pas les honneurs reçus dans la communauté ecclésiastiques, mais plutôt la disposition personnelle de l'individu, la progression dans la perfection pour arriver finalement au stade de la conduite parfaite du «vrai gnostique». Dès lors, celui qui se conduit de la sorte est un vrai presbytre ou un vrai diacre même s'il ne fait pas partie de ceux qui sont réellement honorés. Plus encore, il peut être même considéré comme un «Apôtre» (car ajouté «à la liste des Apôtres»), distinction bien plus significative que les fonctions ecclésiastiques proprement dites.

A quelques années de distance par rapport a Clément, Origène entre également en contact avec un représentant de la gnose ou du christianisme gnosticisant à Alexandrie. Après le martyre de son père et se trouvant «dans le besoin des choses nécessaires à la vie», Origène, de par la grâce de la Providence, écrit Eusèbe:

trouva l'accueil en même temps que la tranquillité auprès d'une femme très riche des biens nécessaires pour vivre et pour le reste très remarquable, mais qui entourait de considération un homme célèbre parmi les hérétiques qui vivaient alors à Alexandrie: celui-ci était antiochien de naissance et cette femme l'avait avec elle comme un fils adoptif qu'elle entourait entièrement de ses soins.

Mais,

alors qu'une foule immense s'assemblait auprès de Paul (tel était le nom de cet homme), parce qu'il paraissait disert—c'étaient non seulement des hérétiques, nais encore des nôtres—, Origène ne consentit jamais à s'unir à lui pour la prière, conservant dès son enfance la règle de l'Église et éprouvant de l'horreur, comme il le dit lui-même en propres termes, pour les doctrines hérétiques.[33]

---

[32] Clément, *Strom.* VI.106.1-2 & 107.2-3 (Traduction de P. Descourtieux légèrement modifiée [Sources Chrétiennes 446], Paris 1999, 273-5).
[33] Eusèbe, *Hist. Eccl.* VI.2.13-14 (Traduction de G. Bardy [Sources Chrétiennes 41], Paris 1994, 85-6).

Cet épisode, rapporté par Eusèbe, montre qu'au début du troisième siècle la «cohabitation (relativement) pacifique» des diverses sensibilités (ou tendances) du christianisme au sein d'une même communauté fonctionnait encore à Alexandrie, mais que la différenciation se profilait déjà à l'horizon. Plus tard on a sans doute reproché à Origène son séjour dans cette maison, ce qui explique le ton justificatif de l'historien.

Qui était exactement ce Paul, et qu'est-il advenu de son auditoire? Nous ne le savons guère, tout comme il nous est impossible de mesurer si Paul a joué un rôle dans le devenir de l'Origène; et à quel point? Mais, à en croire P. Nautin, «il est rare, en effet, qu'un adolescent reste complètement insensible au prestige et aux arguments d'un adulte brillant»,[34] tel que Paul se présente à nos yeux.

Quoi qu'il en soit, Origène ne pouvait pas échapper à la confrontation intellectuelle avec le gnosticisme. C'est effectivement de cela que témoigne sa rencontre avec le valentinien Ambroise, un notable fortuné d'Alexandrie. Son absence du *Traité des Principes* suggère que la rencontre s'est probablement produite après la rédaction de ce dernier.

D'après E. Junod,

> Ambroise (homme fort riche et sans doute cultivé) aimait Jésus. Mais il ne se contentait pas d'une foi irréfléchie et inepte (*pistis alogos kai idiôtikê*). C'est pourquoi, en l'absence de défenseurs du bien, c'est-à-dire de la saine doctrine, il a mis sa confiance dans les enseignements (*logoi*) des gnostiques. C'est donc en vertu d'une exigence rationnelle, d'une ambition intellectuelle qu'Ambroise, dans son amour pour Jésus, s'est tourné vers la gnose plutôt que vers l'Église.[35]

La rencontre quasi «providentielle» des deux hommes, vers la fin des années 220,[36] peut être considéré comme déterminante pour l'évolution de leurs vies. Ambroise «fut convaincu par la vérité» que lui proposa Origène et ce fut «avec une intelligence comme resplendissante de lumière qu'il passa à la doctrine de l'orthodoxie ecclésiastique (τῷ τῆς ἐκκλησιαστικῆς ὀρθοδοξίας)».[37] Dès lors, Ambroise—ce «saint frère,

---

[34] Nautin 1977, 415.
[35] Junod 1989, 158.
[36] Eusèbe, *Hist. Eccl.* VI.23.3.
[37] Eusèbe, *Hist. Eccl.* VI.18.1.

formé selon l'Évangile»,[38] et «homme de Dieu»,[39] «tout animé d'amour
de Dieu et de piété»[40] et véritable «contremaître de Dieu»[41]—stimulait
Origène «non seulement par mille exhortations et encouragements
en paroles» pour écrire «ses *Commentaires* sur les Écritures divines»,
celui *sur l'Évangile de Jean* avant tout (contre l'œuvre du gnostique
Héracléon), «mais encore en lui procurant très largement les secours
dont il avait besoin».[42]

> Plus de sept tachygraphes en effet étaient près de lui quand il dictait—dit
> Eusèbe—, se relayant les uns les autres aux temps fixés; il n'avait pas
> moins de copistes, ainsi que des jeunes filles exercées à la calligraphie.
> Ambroise fournissait abondamment ce qui était nécessaire à la subsis-
> tance de tous; bien plus, il apportait encore à l'étude et au zèle pour
> les oracles divins une indicible ardeur, grâce à quoi surtout il excitait
> Origène à la composition des commentaires.[43]

Les activités d'auteur et d'enseignant d'Origène ont fini par lui créer
des problèmes—comme ce fut déjà le cas avec Clément. Et les respon-
sables ecclésiastiques de la cité (les évêques Démétrios et Héraclas)
trouvèrent finalement les moyens pour l'éloigner définitivement. Après
le départ d'Origène les problèmes majeurs de l'église d'Alexandrie,
notamment sous l'épiscopat de Denys, sont devenus plus institution-
nels que doctrinaux. Ce qui signifie aussi que le courant gnosticisant
s'est considérablement rétrécie, pour devenir presque invisible, sinon
disparaître de la communauté.

Les lacunes de nos sources empêchent toute reconstitution qui nous
permettrait de suivre plus à la ligne cette histoire. Mais, en analysant
le développement du christianisme, nous pouvons aisément constater
que la gnose, comme source fécondante de la pensée, n'a jamais
disparu réellement. Et dès que les premières traces d'une présence
chrétienne deviennent perceptibles dans la *chôra* égyptienne, rien de
plus normal à ce que des écrits gnostiques ou gnosticisants apparaissent
également. C'est ainsi que nous pouvons interpréter le texte intitulé *La*

---

[38] Origène, *Comm. sur Jean* II.1. Voir aussi *Contre Celse* Préface 1; III.1; IV.1;
V.1; VI.1; VII.1 et VIII.76 qui constituent autant de témoignages sur les liens très
privilégiés entre les deux hommes.
[39] Origène, *Comm. sur Jean* XXXII.2.
[40] Ibid., XIII.1.
[41] Ibid., V.I (Préambule). D'après la *Philocalie* 5.
[42] Eusèbe, *Hist. Eccl.* VI.23.1.
[43] Ibid., VI.23.2 (Sources Chrétiennes 41; Paris 1994, 123).

Sagesse de Jésus-Christ,[44] et trouvé parmi les documents de Nag Hammadi. Même si leurs opinions divergent sur d'autres questions, ses éditeurs—M. Tardieu et C. Barry—s'accordent en effet pour situer son élaboration au milieu du IIIe siècle et en Égypte.[45] Cela semble d'autant plus vrai, que C. Barry considère ce texte comme une œuvre à part entière («un traité autonome»);[46] même si pour M. Tardieu il s'agit plutôt d'un plagiat, d'une simple réécriture christianisée du traité *Eugnoste le Bienheureux* (NH III.3 et V.1).[47] Ce dernier—«une lettre philosophico-religieuse, sans grande référence chrétienne explicite, d'un maître à ses disciples»[48]—serait l'œuvre d'un auteur «familier du platonisme pythagorisant» et sa composition se placerait «vers 175, probablement à Alexandrie».[49]

Si C. Barry sépare et M. Tardieu met en dépendance *La Sagesse* et l'*Eugnoste*, R. Kuntzmann et J.-D. Dubois en revanche leurs proposent «un original commun».[50] Mais quel que soit la relation de ces écrits, ce qui de notre point de vue semble être essentiel, c'est la dépendance du christianisme de la vallée du Nil de celui d'Alexandrie, y compris en ce qui concerne le courant gnostique (ou gnosticisant). De cette manière on peut sans doute dire, que le gnosticisme fut une sorte de force motrice intellectuelle du développement doctrinal du christianisme, et même si par la suite la Grande Église n'a jamais ménagé ses forces pour le gommer de son histoire, elle n'a toutefois pas réussi à le faire disparaître entièrement. Ce à quoi la découverte de Nag Hammadi a aussi contribué, c'est de prendre conscience à quel point il est incontournable dans la compréhension des premiers siècles chrétiens. Il n'est sans doute pas un hasard que c'est dans un même milieu intellectuel et spirituel, celui d'Alexandrie, que deux personnages de marque, Valentin et Origène, à un siècle d'intervalle, ont acquis leur formation. Et ce qu'ils ont tenté de faire était aussi comparable: répondre aux questions et aux angoisses existentielles de leurs contemporains. Ce que les théologies et les philosophies n'ont d'ailleurs jamais cessé de faire—avant et après eux.

---

[44] Barry 1993.
[45] Ibid., p. 36; Tardieu 1984, 60-2.
[46] Barry 1993, 21-2.
[47] Tardieu 1984, 59-60.
[48] Kuntzmann & Dubois 1987, 78.
[49] Tardieu 1984, 66.
[50] Kuntzmann & Dubois 1987, 78.

Des questions comme «Qui étions-nous? Que sommes-nous devenus? Où étions-nous? Où avons-nous été jetés? Vers quel but nous hâtons-nous? D'où sommes-nous rachetés? Qu'est-ce que la génération? Et la régénération?»[51] à divers degrés, certes, mais ont toujours hanté l'espèce humain, qui ne cesse de chercher le sens de la vie, à la fois individuellement et collectivement.

Bibliographie

Barry, C. 1993. *La Sagesse de Jésus-Christ (BG 3; NH III, 4)* (Bibliothèque Copte de Nag Hammadi; Section «Textes» 20), Québec.

Cambe, M. (éd.) 2003. *Kerygma Petri* (Corpus Christianorum; Series Apocryphorum 15), Turnhout.

De Faye, E. 1913. *Gnostiques et gnosticisme: Étude critique des documents du gnosticisme chrétien aux IIe et IIIe siècles* (Bibliothèque de l'École des Hautes Études; Sciences Religieuses 27), Paris.

Grant, R.M. 1979. «Place de Basilide dans la théologie chrétienne ancienne», *Revue des Études Augustiniennes* 25 (1979) 201-216.

Jakab, A. 2004. *Ecclesia alexandrina: Évolution sociale et institutionnelle du christianisme alexandrin (IIe et IIIe siècles)* (Christianismes anciens 1), Bern, 2e édition corrigée.

Junod, E. 1989. «Des apologètes à Origène», *Revue de Théologie et de Philosophie* 121 (1989) 149-164.

Kuntzmann, R. & J.-D. Dubois. 1987. *Nag Hammadi. Évangile selon Thomas: Textes gnostiques aux origines du christianisme* (Supplément au Cahier Évangile 58), Paris.

Mélèze-Modrzejewski, J. 1997. *Les Juifs d'Égypte de Ramsès II à Hadrien* (Quadrige 247), Paris, 2e édition revue et corrigée.

Ménard, J.E. 1968. «Les origines de la gnose», *Revue des Sciences Religieuses* 42 (1968) 24-38.

Nautin, P. 1975-76. «Patristique et histoire des dogmes I: L'«Évangile selon Basilide», *Annuaire de l'École Pratique des Hautes Études: Ve Section—Sciences Religieuses* 84 (1975-76) 311-312.

Nautin, P. 1977. *Origène: Sa vie et son œuvre* (Christianisme Antique 1), Paris.

Painchaud, L. & A. Pasquier (éds.). 1995. *Les textes de Nag Hammadi et le problème de leur classification* (Bibliothèque Copte de Nag Hammadi; Section «Études» 3), Québec, Louvain, Paris.

Pearson, B.A. 1990. *Gnosticism, Judaism, and Egyptian Christianity* (Studies in Antiquity and Christianity), Minneapolis.

Poirier, P.-H. 1986. «La bibliothèque copte de Nag Hammadi: sa nature et son importance», *Studies in Religion / Sciences Religieuses* 15 (1986) 303-316.

Quasten, J. 1955. *Initiation aux Pères de l'Église*, T. I, Paris.

Ritter, A.M. 1987. «De Polycarpe à Clément: aux origines d'Alexandrie chrétienne», dans H.M.J.S. de Lubac et al. (éds.), *Alexandrina: Hellénisme, judaïsme et christianisme à Alexandrie: Mélanges offerts au P. Claude Mondésert*, Paris, 151-72.

Scopello, M. (éd.) 1985. *L'Exégèse de l'Âme (NHC II, 6)* (Nag Hammadi Studies 25), Leiden.

---

[51] Clément, *Extr. de Théod.* 78.2 (Sources Chrétiennes 23; Paris 1970, 203).

Sevrin, J.-M. (éd.) 1983. *L'Exégèse de l'Âme (NH II, 6)* (Bibliothèque Copte de Nag Hammadi; Section «Textes» 9), Québec.

Tardieu, M. 1984. *Écrits gnostiques: Codex de Berlin* (Sources Gnostiques et Manichéennes 1), Paris.

Vigne, D. 1992. «Enquête sur Basilide», dans A. Dupleix (éd.), *Recherches et Tradition: Mélanges Patristiques offerts à Henri Crouzel* (Théologie Historique 88), Paris, 285-313.

THE *GOSPEL OF THOMAS* AND THE HISTORICAL JESUS: THE CASE OF ESCHATOLOGY

ALBERT L.A. HOGETERP

The potential relevance of the *Gospel According to Thomas* for Historical Jesus research has been a subject of scholarly debate for decades, since the initial facsimile edition of the complete Coptic text from the Nag Hammadi Library of Egypt was published in 1956.[1] For my interest in *Thomas* I am much indebted to Prof. G.P. Luttikhuizen. He taught me and other students Coptic grammar, and he has directed my attention to the pluriformity of earliest Christianity, taking into account possibly early Jesus-traditions in extra-canonical New Testament writings. This study will explore the question whether or not *Thomas* comprises authentic Jesus-traditions from the angle of eschatology.

1. *Methodical considerations about the genre of Thomas*

The fact that *Thomas* can be viewed as a Sayings Gospel goes almost without saying. The date of composition of the original text of *Thomas* ranges between the mid-first and mid-second century CE according to scholarly estimations.[2] The 'terminus ante quem' is based on the evidence of the Greek fragments of *P.Oxy. 1, 654* and *655*, which are generally considered to represent an older version than the Coptic text.[3] These fragments have been dated shortly after 200 CE, to the

---

[1] Pahor Labib, *Coptic Gnostic Papyri in the Coptic Museum at Old Cairo*, vol. 1, Cairo 1956. In my references to the Coptic *Gospel According to Thomas*, I will base myself on the more recent edition by B. Layton (ed.), *Nag Hammadi Codex II,2-7 together with XIII,2*, Brit. Lib. Or.4926(1), and P. Oxy. 1, 654, 655, i, Gospel According to Thomas, Gospel According to Philip, Hypostasis of the Archons, and Indexes* (Nag Hammadi Studies 20), Leiden 1989, 38-128 and 264-89.

[2] R. Uro, 'Introduction. Thomas at the crossroads: new perspectives on a debated gospel', in: Id. (ed.), *Thomas at the Crossroads: Essays on the Gospel of Thomas* (Studies of the New Testament and Its World), Edinburgh 1998, 1-7 at 1.

[3] Cf. Layton, 'Editorial Method', in: Id. (ed.), *Nag Hammadi Codex II,2-7*, 28, and H.W. Attridge, 'The Greek Fragments: Introduction', in: Layton (ed.), *Nag Hammadi Codex II,2-7*, 96-109 at 99: 'it is virtually certain that the Coptic was translated from a Greek form of the text', possibly 'based on one of the P.Oxy. texts'.

mid-third century, and between 200 and 250 CE respectively.[4] Apart
from this evidence, scholars differ about a more precise dating due to
their divergent interpretations of the 'social, political, and theological
setting' of *Thomas*.[5] With regard to the socio-historical setting, scholars
have proposed different views with regard to the identity of *Thomas* as,
for instance, an early independent Gospel,[6] an early Gospel dependent on the canonical Gospels,[7] a Gnostic Gospel,[8] and an 'encratite'
(strictly ascetic) gospel[9] respectively.

Thomas is excluded as a significant text for Historical Jesus research,
if it is seen as a late, Gnostic text. It is, however, included, if the text
is assigned a place among the earliest stages of the development of
Gnosticism, allowing for 'free (that is, independent) Jesus-tradition'
well into the beginning of the second century CE.[10] The debate partly
depends on the definition of Gnosticism, as A. Marjanen has pointed
out. Marjanen distinguishes between a minimalist and an maximalist
definition. The minimalist definition only characterises a text as Gnostic, when it presupposes a dualism between an earthly demiurge and
a heavenly divinity. According to the maximalist definition, a text is
Gnostic when we can discern a tension between the idea of the good
as opposed to a cosmos which is perceived as evil. According to the
maximalist interpretation, *Thomas* could be termed a Gnostic text, but

---

[4] Attridge, 'Greek Fragments: Introduction', 97-8.

[5] Cf. F.T. Fallon and R. Cameron, 'The Gospel of Thomas: A Forschungsbericht
and Analysis', in: W. Haase (ed.), *Aufstieg und Niedergang der römischen Welt* II.25.6, Berlin
1988, 4196-251 at 4224-30.

[6] Among proponents of this idea are, for example, H. Koester, *Ancient Christian
Gospels: Their History and Development*, London 1990, and S.J. Patterson, *The Gospel of
Thomas and Jesus*, Sonoma, Calif. 1993.

[7] See e.g. K.R. Snodgrass, 'The Gospel of Thomas. A secondary Gospel', *Second
Century* 7 (1989) 19-30, reprinted in: C.A. Evans (ed.), *The Historical Jesus: Critical
Concepts in Religious Studies*, iv, *Lives of Jesus and Jesus Outside the Bible*, London 2004,
291-308.

[8] See e.g. A. Marjanen, 'Is *Thomas* a Gnostic gospel?', in: Uro (ed.), *Thomas at
the Crossroads*, 107-39.

[9] See discussion of this scholarly position in R. Uro, 'Is *Thomas* an Encratite
Gospel?', in: Id. (ed.), *Thomas at the Crossroads*, 140-62; cf. R. Valantasis, 'The Gospel
of Thomas and Asceticism', in: Id., *The Gospel of Thomas* (New Testament Readings),
London 1997, 21-4.

[10] This supposition may not be too far-fetched, when we compare the possibility
of authentic Jesus-tradition in *Thomas* to that in John, which is often dated by scholars
between 100 and 110 CE.

according to the minimalist interpretation it does not correspond with developed forms of Gnosticism.[11]

The following objections may be raised against the maximalist interpretation. First, the Greek notion of cosmos (κόσμος; loanword ΠΚΟСΜΟС in the Coptic text) already comprises different connotations in the Septuagint, standing for the world, the universe, the earth, or mankind.[12] The pejorative sense of κόσμος as opposed to a heavenly divinity also occurs in early Christian writings which are not qualified as gnostic writings.[13] A juxtaposition between the κόσμος and the idea of the good may therefore by itself not be sufficient evidence of a Gnostic type of thinking. Second, the evidence from Jewish and the earliest Christian writings also comprises a notion of the cosmos as an entity in opposition to God,[14] without thereby fitting the description of Gnosticism.

The evidence of Greek and Coptic versions of *Thomas* may at least provide us insights in the early stages of the development of the text which are important for the transmission history of Jesus-traditions. I propose to read *Thomas* as a proto-Gnostic Gospel text, keeping the possibility that *Thomas* may comprise elements of authentic Jesus-tradition open for debate.

2. *Eschatology in the Synoptic Gospels*

Before turning to the specific case for our discussion, eschatology in *Thomas* and its relation to the historical Jesus, I will present a brief survey of eschatology in the Synoptic tradition. The Synoptic Gospels

---

[11] See Marjanen, 'Is *Thomas* a Gnostic gospel?', 107-39.

[12] J. Lust, E. Eynikel, and K. Hauspie, *Greek-English Lexicon of the Septuagint* (Revised Edition), Stuttgart 2003, 352.

[13] Á.P. Orbán, *Les dénominations du monde chez les premiers auteurs chrétiens* (Graecitas Christianorum Primaeva 4), Nijmegen 1970, 1-88 discusses several cases of a pejorative sense of κόσμος: in Paul's Letters (26-37), John (37-44), the Letters of Ignatius (53), the Epistle to Diognetus (64), Justin's *Dialogus* (74), and Clement of Alexandria (eleven instances, p. 86 note 2). Orbán leaves the possibility open that cosmic dualism could originate from a pluriform, syncretist background, taking into account Jewish apocalypticism, Iranian dualism (in the case of the Qumran community), and pre-Christian gnosis (17-26).

[14] W. Bauer, F.W. Danker, W.F. Arndt, and F.W. Gingrich, *A Greek-English Lexicon of the New Testament and other Early Christian Literature*, Chicago 2000[3], (lemma κόσμος) 562 no. 7 b refer to, among other passages, *1 Enoch* 48.7, *Testament of Issachar* 4.6, and 1 Corinthians 3.19; 5.10a; 7.31b.

provide the most relevant frame of reference for comparison, as much sayings material in *Thomas* runs parallel to the Synoptic tradition.[15] A brief survey of some main aspects of Synoptic eschatology may clarify the traditional starting point of New Testament scholarship on eschatology.[16]

2.1. *Markan eschatology*

Scholarship on Markan eschatology has been largely determined by two main issues: the imminent kingdom of God[17] and the 'eschatological discourse' in Mark 13 par.[18] In his recent commentary on Mark, J. Marcus has further pointed to the 'apocalyptic outlook' of the entire narrative of Mark, as reflected by the narrative 'context of the approaching end of the world' and the eschatological interpretation of Scripture.[19] It is a debated question how this Markan eschatology may be related to the historical Jesus. The Markan portrayal of Jesus as an apocalyptic prophet who actually prophesied the destruction of the Temple is accepted by certain scholars as an accurate description of the historical Jesus.[20] Even if one could concur with this scholarly

---

[15] See H. Koester, 'Introduction', in: Layton (ed.), *Nag Hammadi Codex II, 2-7*, 38-49 at 46-8 for an impressive list of 'Synoptic parallels to the Gospel According to Thomas'.

[16] See A.Y. Collins, 'The Eschatological Discourse of Mark 13', in: F. Van Segbroeck et al. (eds), *The Four Gospels 1992* (Festschrift F. Neirynck; Bibliotheca Ephemeridum Theologicarum Lovaniensium 100), Louvain 1992, 1125-40 at 1125 about the nineteenth- and early twentieth century scholarly idea that 'eschatology was central to the teaching and activity of the Synoptic Jesus'; cf. the survey by B.D. Ehrman, *The New Testament: A Historical Introduction to the Early Christian Writings*, Oxford 2000[2], 229-51 which assigns a prominent place to the Synoptic Gospels as 'our earliest sources' for the portrayal of Jesus as an 'apocalypticist'.

[17] D.E. Aune, 'Eschatology (Early Christian)', in: D.N. Freedman (ed.), *The Anchor Bible Dictionary*, 2, New York 1992, 603 notes that the term 'kingdom of God' 'occurs 14 times in Mark (1.15; 4.11, 26, 30; 9.1, 47; 10.14, 15, 23, 24, 25; 12.34; 14.25; 15.43), while the kingdom of David is mentioned just once (11.10)'.

[18] See e.g. Collins, 'The eschatological discourse of Mark 13', and J. Verheyden, 'Persecution and Eschatology: Mk 13,9-13', in: Van Segbroeck et al. (eds), *The Four Gospels 1992*, 1125-40 and 1141-59.

[19] J. Marcus, 'Mark's Apocalyptic Eschatology', in: Id., *Mark 1-8: A New Translation with Introduction and Commentary* (The Anchor Bible 27), New York 2000, 71-2.

[20] See e.g. C.A. Evans, 'Predictions of the Destruction of the Herodian Temple in the Pseudepigrapha, Qumran Scrolls, and Related Texts', *Journal for the Study of the Pseudepigrapha* 10 (1992) 89-147, and K. Paesler, *Das Tempelwort Jesu: Die Traditionen von Tempelzerstörung und Tempelerneuerung im Neuen Testament* (Forschungen zur Religion und Literatur des Alten und Neuen Testaments 184), Göttingen 1999.

position,[21] the communal experiences of persecution supposedly voiced in Mark 10.30 and 13 still lead to a dating of Mark 'in the shadow of [the] destruction [of the Temple]'.[22] Nevertheless, the Jesus-traditions about the kingdom in Mark may provide an important vantage point for studying the historical Jesus.

2.2. *Eschatology and the study of Q*

The other main part of the Synoptic tradition, the supposed sayings source Q shared by Matthew and Luke, also contains eschatological material. However, scholarly reconstructions of the compositional history of Q, in particular that by Kloppenborg,[23] have led to a debate whether or not apocalyptic eschatology was part of the earliest stage of Jesus-tradition. The influential supposition that the earliest recension of Q would have sapiential rather than prophetic characteristics has also been based on the reading of *Thomas* as a Sayings Gospel.[24]

D.C. Allison Jr. has in my view convincingly refuted this position with his own critical reconstruction of the compositional history of Q, suggesting that Q represents a mixed genre with both sapiential and eschatological elements in it.[25] Apart from the discussion about *Thomas* as evidence for or against the analysis of Q as a primitive Wisdom

---

[21] In my view, the idea of an early Jewish context of prophecies of destruction, as applied to the Second Temple, is too readily supposed. Josephus tried to explain perceived signs of its imminent destruction, writing his works *after the event*. Pseud-epigraphical texts may not provide entirely solid evidence for pre-70 CE prophecies either, since they have come down to us through Christian transmission. Cf. J.W. van Henten & B. Schaller, 'Christianization of Ancient Jewish Writings', and R.A. Kraft, 'Setting the Stage and Framing Some Central Questions', *Journal for the Study of Judaism* 32 (2001) 369-70 and 372-95; M. de Jonge, 'The "Pseudepigrapha of the Old Testament" and Early Christianity: Some General Questions', in: Id., *Pseude-pigrapha of the Old Testament as Part of Christian Literature: The Case of the Testaments of the Twelve Patriarchs and the Greek Life of Adam and Eve* (Studia in Veteris Testamenti Pseudepigrapha 18), Leiden 2003, 9-68.

[22] Marcus, 'Date', in: Id., *Mark 1-8*, 37-9 at 39.

[23] J.S. Kloppenborg, *The Formation of Q: Trajectories in Ancient Christian Wisdom Collections* (Studies in Antiquity and Christianity), Philadelphia 1987.

[24] D.C. Allison, Jr., 'An Early Sapiential Recension of Q?', in: Id., *The Jesus Tradition in Q*, Harrisburg, Pa. 1997, 3-8 at 8 n. 36, referring to C.M. Tuckett, 'Q and Thomas: Evidence of a Primitive 'Wisdom Gospel'? A Response to H. Koester', *Ephemerides Theologicae Lovanienses* 67 (1991) 346-60.

[25] D.C. Allison Jr., 'The Compositional History of Q', in: Id., *The Jesus Tradition in Q*, 1-66; cf. Id., 'The Eschatology of Jesus', in: J.J. Collins (ed.), *The Encyclopedia of Apocalypticism*, i, *The Origins of Apocalypticism in Judaism and Christianity*, New York 1998, 267-302.

Gospel, the evidence of eschatology in *Thomas* has received relatively little scholarly attention in its own right.[26] It is to this evidence that we will now turn.

3. *Eschatology in Thomas*

3.1. *The Greek evidence*

a. *The kingdom of God*

The Greek version of logion 3, preserved in lines 9-21 of *P.Oxy. 654*, relates of the kingdom of God, ἡ βασ[ιλεία τοῦ θεοῦ] (line 15).[27] D. Lührmann has observed that the expression 'kingdom of God' is characteristic only of the Greek evidence, not of the Coptic evidence.[28] The logion does not refer explicitly to the addressees of Jesus' words, but they are forewarned against 'those who mislead us', οἱ ἕλκοντες ἡμᾶς (line 10).[29] With regard to those who preach the kingdom as a completely external reality, Jesus emphasises that 'the kingdom of God is inside of you[, and it is outside of you]', ἐντὸς ὑμῶν [ἐσ]τι [κἀκτός] (lines 15-16).[30] The subsequent lines 16b-19 stress that the addressees should know themselves as 'children of the living Father'. This implies that the kingdom of God is not out of reach for human beings but a present reality among them.

The Greek text of logion 3 has been compared with Luke 17.20-21, which comprises Jesus' words about the kingdom of God in response to

---

[26] T. Zöckler, *Jesu Lehren im Thomasevangelium* (Nag Hammadi and Manichaean Studies 47), Leiden 1999, who appears to support Kloppenborg's thesis of an early sapiential recension of Q (96-7), only devotes a few pages in his monograph to the question of 'realized eschatology' in *Thomas* (178-80).

[27] Reconstruction by Attridge, 'The Greek Fragments', 114. Cf. *P.Oxy. 1* 7-8 (ἡ βασιλεία τοῦ θ(εο)ῦ).

[28] D. Lührmann, '"Das Reich Gottes ist ausgebreitet auf der Erde": Die griechische Überlieferung des Thomasevangeliums', in: Id., *Die apokryph gewordenen Evangelien: Studien zu neuen Texten und zu neuen Fragen* (Supplements to Novum Testamentum 112), Leiden 2004, 144-81 at 153-5 further refers to the evidence from the speech of Macarius/Simeon (35,5), as edited by H. Berthold, *Makarios/Simeon, Reden und Briefe*, vol. II: *Die Logoi B 30-64* (Die griechischen christlichen Schriftsteller der ersten Jahrhunderte), Berlin 1973, 43, as a parallel to the expression ἡ βασιλεία τοῦ θ(εο)ῦ.

[29] ἕλκω literally means to 'draw'. I here follow the translation offered by Bauer, Danker, Arndt and Gingrich, *A Greek-English Lexicon of the New Testament*, 318 no. 1 (lemma ἕλκω) against that by Attridge, 'Greek Fragments', 126 ('those who lead you'). Cf. Lührmann, 'Das Reich Gottes', 153 n. 52 on ἕλκω in Acts 21.30.

[30] Text and translation from Attridge, 'Greek Fragments', 114 and 126.

the question of the Pharisees 'when the kingdom of God was coming' (RSV).[31] Luke 17.21b, ἡ βασιλεία τοῦ θεοῦ ἐντὸς ὑμῶν ἐστιν, may be translated as 'the kingdom of God is *in the midst of* you' or '*within* you'. The idea of the kingdom of God as a reality among and/or within human beings is in my view not opposed to eschatology *per se*,[32] but it only indicates that the realisation of God's kingdom takes already place among human beings.

b. *Resurrection*

The Greek version of logion 5, preserved in lines 27-31 of *P.Oxy. 654*, appears to point out that the knowledge of both hidden and visible things is interrelated to the one who knows 'that which is ahead of your sight', [τὸ ὃν ἔμπροσ]θεν τῆς ὄψεώς σου, that is, that which goes beyond outward appearance.[33] The Greek version ends the logion with the assurance that 'there is nothing buried that will not be raised' (καὶ τεθαμμένον ὃ ο[ὺκ ἐγερθήσεται] (*P.Oxy. 654* 31).[34] This part is omitted in the Coptic version. The idea of the resurrection is related to the end of days in early Jewish and Christian traditions.[35] Furthermore, Gnostic texts from the Nag Hammadi Library of Egypt also appear to presuppose a future-eschatological dimension to the resurrection of the dead.[36] We may therefore conclude that this Greek logion has an eschatological dimension.

---

[31] Lührmann, 'Das Reich Gottes', 153-5; Zöckler, ἐντὸς ὑμῶν, in: Id., *Jesu Lehren im Thomasevangelium*, 166-73.

[32] Pace Zöckler, *Jesu Lehren im Thomasevangelium*, 173 who calls Luke 17.20-21 'anti-eschatological'.

[33] Greek text from Attridge, 'Greek Fragments', 115. On ἔμπροσθεν and ὄψις, see Bauer, Danker, Arndt & Gingrich, *A Greek-English Lexicon of the New Testament*, 325 and 746-7.

[34] Greek text from Attridge, 'Greek Fragments', 115. The reconstruction ἐγερθήσεται, which is the logical counterpart to τεθαμμένον, is also followed by R. Valantasis, *The Gospel of Thomas* (New Testament Readings), London 1997, 35-6 who speaks about a 'performative theology of revelation and resurrection' (36), and it may be preferred above different reconstructions by Grenfell and Hunt (οὐκ ἐγερθήσεται *or* γνωσθήσεται), by Bartlet (οὐκ ἐξορύξεται), and by Hofius (οὐκ ἀποκαλυφθήσεται; a redundant repetition of the verb in line 29) as mentioned in the critical apparatus of Attridge, 'Greek Fragments', 115.

[35] See e.g. the *Ascensio Isaiae*, 1 Corinthians 15, Luke 20.35, John 11.24, *m. Sanhedrin* 10.1.

[36] The Gnostic *Dialogue of the Saviour* 84-85, for instance, refers to the future afterlife in symbolical terms of being clothed with different 'garments'. The *Treatise on the Resurrection* refers to resurrection and salvation in the future tense, and to the destruction of evil and the revelation of the elect.

3.2. The Coptic Evidence

a. Eternal life

A recurring promise in the Coptic logia concerns eternal life or immortality in terms of 'not experiencing death'. The first logion sets the stage with the message that 'whoever finds the interpretation of these sayings will not taste death', ϥⲛⲁϫⲓⲧⲡⲉ ⲁⲛ ⲙ̄ⲡⲉⲙⲟⲩ.[37] The phrase recurs at the end of the Coptic logia 18, 19, and 85,[38] while logion 111 presents the variation of 'not seeing death', ϥⲛⲁⲛⲁⲩ ⲁⲛ ⲉⲙⲟⲩ.[39] In the case of logion 1, we can actually compare the Coptic and the Greek versions, as *P.Oxy. 654* 3b-5 has preserved an analogous text.[40] This link between Coptic and Greek versions attests to the fact that the phrase 'not to taste death', θανάτου οὐ μὴ γεύσηται in Greek, was already part of an early version of the text of *Thomas*. It is not specifically (proto-)Gnostic terminology, since we also have evidence from the Synoptic Gospels for this phrase in the plural: οὐ μὴ γεύσωνται θανάτου. In Mark 9.1, Jesus' saying addresses those who 'see that the kingdom of God has come with power'; in Matthew 16.28 those who 'see the Son of man coming in his kingdom', and in Luke 9.27 those who 'see the kingdom of God' (translations from the Revised Standard Version).

John 8.52 further comprises the following saying of Jesus: 'If any one keeps my word, he will never taste death', οὐ μὴ γεύσωνται θανάτου εἰς τὸν αἰῶνα. None of these canonical Gospel traditions comes close to the 'interpretation of these sayings' in logion 1 of *Thomas* as a precondition for 'not experiencing death'. Nevertheless, the Coptic text of *Thomas* includes a large number of sayings about or explicitly related to the kingdom (logia 3, 20, 22, 46, 54, 57, 76, 82, 96, 97, 98, 107, 109, 113, 114). The interpretation of many sayings therefore concerns the heavenly kingdom (see subsequent section), in which case *Thomas* may partly correspond to the Synoptic tradition.

---

[37] Text from B. Layton, 'The Gospel According to Thomas', in: Id., *Nag Hammadi Codex II,2-7*, 52.

[38] Logion 85 comprises a counter-to-fact statement about Adam, who did experience death.

[39] Text from Layton, 'The Gospel According to Thomas', 111.

[40] Attridge, 'Greek fragments', 113 presents the following reconstruction: [ὃς ἂν τὴν ἑρμηνεί]αν τῶν λόγων τούτ[ων εὕρῃ, θανάτου] οὐ μὴ γεύσηται. Thanks to this Greek evidence we can avoid the hypothetical and hazardous project of '*Rück-übersetzung*' from the Coptic to the Greek of a supposed *Vorlage*, as Lührmann, 'Das Reich Gottes', 155 n. 62 has called it.

Logion 19 still merits separate attention in this connection. The phrase 'not to taste death' in the future tense is preconditioned by acquaintance with five trees in Paradise (ΠΑΡΑΛΙⲤΟⲤ) in this logion. Since Paradise is clearly presented as a promise for Jesus' disciples,[41] not as a purely biblical phenomenon from the narrative of Genesis, the promise of eternal life is given a more explicitly eschatological direction.[42]

b. *The kingdom*

We have already noted that the kingdom is a prominent issue in *Thomas*. In the Coptic text, Jesus refers to the 'kingdom', ΤΜⲚⲦⲈΡΟ (logia 3, 22, 46, 82, 107, 109, 113), the 'kingdom of heaven', ΤΜⲚⲦⲈΡΟ ⲚⲚⲠⲎⲨⲈ (logia 20, 54, 114), and the 'kingdom of the Father', ΤΜⲚⲦⲈΡΟ ⲘⲠⲈⲒⲰⲦ (logia 57, 76, 96, 97, 98, 113) respectively.

Leaving aside the parables about the kingdom (logia 20, 57, 76, 96, 97, 98, 107, 109) which do not provide clear-cut arguments for or against eschatology in Jesus' message, we have a number of cases in which Jesus' sayings about the kingdom may somehow be more easily related to a vision of time. The Coptic logion 3, like the Greek version (see 3.1a above), stresses the presence of the kingdom among human beings who know themselves as children of the living Father. This does not necessarily imply a 'realized eschatology', since the evidence of other logia refers to the kingdom in the future tense. That is, logia 22, 46, and 114 imply a future perspective on the kingdom. The Beatitude in logion 54, 'Blessed are the poor, for yours is the kingdom of heaven',[43] does not provide evidence for realized eschatology either, since it only foretells the poor that a share in the kingdom of heaven is theirs.

Logion 113 provides a particularly interesting case in which Jesus responds to the eschatologically oriented question of his disciples when the kingdom will come in the following way:

---

[41] In Luke 23.43 Jesus' words also convey the idea that Paradise is the place of the righteous in the afterlife.

[42] On the connection between 'Resurrection and Paradise (as the future place of rest for the righteous)' in the Old Testament Pseudepigrapha, see J.H. Charlesworth (ed.), *The Old Testament Pseudepigrapha*, i, *Apocalyptic Literature and Testaments*, New York 1983, xxxiii.

[43] Translation from T.O. Lambdin, 'The Gospel According to Thomas', in: Layton (ed.), *Nag Hammadi Codex II,2-7*, 73. Coptic *Thomas* 54 corresponds partly with Luke 6.20b and Matt 5.3.

> It will not come by waiting for it. It will not be a matter of saying 'Here it is' or 'There it is'. Rather, the kingdom of the father is spread out upon the earth, and men do not see it.[44]

Jesus' response begins with the Coptic verb ⲛⲏⲩ which expresses the imminent future[45] and ends with the present tense. Although the end of the saying implies that the kingdom is a present, earthly reality, there is also a future aspect to it, as the future tense of ⲉⲩⲛⲁⲭⲟⲟⲥ ⲁⲛ ('it will not be a matter of saying') indicates.

c. *Apocalyptic transformation*

Logion 11 of the Coptic text of *Thomas* starts with an apocalyptic saying of Jesus in the future tense which may well be a symbolical description of the end of days:

> This heaven will pass away, and the one above it will pass away. The dead are not alive, and the living will not die. In the days when you consumed what is dead, you made it what is alive.[46]

The distinction between 'this heaven' and the 'one above it' implies a first and a second heaven, so that the subsequent phrase of the logion, 'when you come to dwell in the light', could be located in the third heaven,[47] which is also the traditional location of Paradise.[48] Paradise is the location of the righteous in the afterlife (see note 40 above), and the phrase 'when you come to dwell in the light' may thus have an eschatological connotation, denoting the new apocalyptic reality in the final age.

The apocalyptic transformation at the end of days appears to find yet another expression in logion 111, where Jesus says: 'The heavens and the earth will be rolled up in your presence. And the one who lives from the living one will not see death'.[49]

---

[44] Translation from Lambdin, 'The Gospel According to Thomas', 93.

[45] See W.E. Crum, *A Coptic Dictionary*, Oxford 1939, ⲛⲏⲩ under lemma ⲛⲟⲩ.

[46] Translation from Lambdin, 'The Gospel According to Thomas', 57.

[47] On the implication of a third heaven which will not pass away, I agree with M. Meyer, *The Gospel of Thomas: The Hidden Sayings of Jesus*, New York 1992, 73 against Valantasis, *The Gospel of Thomas*, 71, who, in my view unconvincingly, argues that 'this heaven' and 'the one above it' stands for the 'well-known binary construction of heaven and earth'.

[48] See e.g. *Testament of Levi* 2.7-10; 2 Corinthians 12.2-4; *Apocalypse of Paul* 20-21.

[49] Translation from Lambdin, 'The Gospel According to Thomas', 93.

d. *The end*

Logion 18 of the Coptic text of *Thomas* starts with the following
question of the disciples to Jesus: 'tell us how our end will be',
ⲭⲟⲟⲥ ⲉⲣⲟⲛ ⲭⲉ ⲧⲛ̄ϩⲁⲏ ⲉⲥⲛⲁϣⲱⲡⲉ ⲛ̄ⲁϣ ⲛ̄ϩⲉ.[50] Jesus' reaction illu-
minates the interrelation between the beginning and the end for the
one who has revelatory knowledge and who will not taste death. The
question is how the term ⲧⲛ̄ϩⲁⲏ, 'our end', should be interpreted.
Does it stand for the personal end in the sense of the disciples' fate or
for the collective ultimate fate of humanity? R. Valantasis has related
the disciples' question to the issue of 'immortality of the people in
this community'.[51] Since Jesus' answer refers to the end in general,
we may infer that the question of the disciples implicates humanity at
large and addresses Jesus as the one who has divine revelations about
humanity's ultimate fate. In this respect, the discussion between the
disciples and Jesus in logion 18 concerns the issue of eschatology.

e. *Revelation and resurrection*

Logion 37 of the Coptic text, for which we again have parallel Greek
evidence (*P.Oxy. 655* column i. 17-column ii. 1), centres on a question
of the disciples to Jesus about the time frame for his revelation to
them. The question, posed in the future tense, obviously does not deal
with an ordinary visibility, but a revelation of a divine nature. The
Coptic verb ⲟⲩⲱⲛϩ ⲉⲃⲟⲗ as well as the Greek word ἐμφανής (*P.Oxy.
655* column i. 19-20) denote the idea of appearance or revelation.
The two instances in the canonical New Testament for the occurrence
of the term ἐμφανής (Romans 10.20; Acts 10.40) concern revelation
through a divine cause.

Jesus' answer appears cryptic at first glance. I will cite here the
translation of the full Coptic text, for only part of which the Greek
version is a textual witness:

> When you disrobe without being ashamed and take up your garments and
> place them under your feet like little children and tread on them, then
> [will you see] the son of the living one, and you will not be afraid.[52]

---

[50] Text and translation from Layton, 'The Gospel According to Thomas', 60,
and Lambdin, 'The Gospel According to Thomas', 61.

[51] Valantasis, *The Gospel of Thomas*, 85.

[52] Translation from Lambdin, 'The Gospel According to Thomas', 69. The corresponding part of the preserved Greek text, from Attridge, 'Greek Fragments', 122,
reads: ὅταν ἐκδύσησθε καὶ μὴ αἰσχυνθῆτε [..] [οὐδὲ φοβη]θ[ήσεσθε].

This cryptic answer, which probably should be read in a symbolical way, has been interpreted by Valantasis as the rejection of the old person and the acceptance of a new identity.[53] However, there may be yet another symbolical dimension to this passage. The expression 'your garments', ⲛ̄ⲛⲉⲧⲛ̄ϣⲧⲏⲛ, in the Coptic text, as well as the comparison of the disciples with little children are two elements which also occur in the Egyptian Gnostic text *Dialogue of the Saviour* 84-85. For the sake of comparison, I cite the relevant text below:

> Judas said to Matthew, 'We [w]ish to understand the sort of garments in which we shall be clothed [when] we leave the corruption of the [fle]sh'. The Lord said, 'The archons [and] the governors possess garments which have been given them for a [ti]me and which do not last. [But] you, as children of truth, are not to clothe yourselves with these transient garments. Rather, I tell you that you will become bles[se]d when you strip your[selv]es!'[54]

The text which I have just cited is sometimes considered potentially relevant for Historical Jesus research, since it may comprise separate early sayings of Jesus.[55] The context in which 'garments' figure in this text evokes the idea that 'garments' are a metaphor for the body, the perishable body and the body of resurrection respectively. It should be noted that the metaphorical description of the afterlife in terms of clothing is not uniquely Gnostic. Paul also uses the imagery of clothing, when he discusses the transition from mortality to immortality (2 Corinthians 5.1-5), thereby attesting to its pre-70 CE usage.

If we read Coptic *Thomas* 37 in the light of this metaphorical understanding of the body as a garment, the question of the disciples and Jesus' answer could be related to revelations about resurrection. When the perishable body as a garment has been laid down, 'then [will you see] the son of the living one, and you will not be afraid'. It could be that logion 37 presupposes the delay of the Parousia, the second coming of Christ, thereby transferring it to the future Day of Resurrection, that is, the end of days.

---

[53] Valantasis, *The Gospel of Thomas*, 112-13.

[54] Translation from E. Thomassen, 'The Dialogue of the Saviour', in: W. Schneemelcher (ed.), *New Testament Apocrypha*, i, *Gospels and Related Writings* (Revised Edition, English translation edited by R.McL. Wilson), Cambridge 1991, 310.

[55] The text is ranged among Gnostic 'Dialogue Gospels' by Koester, *Ancient Christian Gospels*, 173-200; cf. G. Theißen and A. Merz, *Der historische Jesus: Ein Lehrbuch*, Göttingen 1996, 55-6.

f. *The repose of the dead and the new world*

The last item for our discussion of eschatology in the Coptic text of *Thomas* may be found in logion 51. This logion may present a clear-cut example of 'realized eschatology', for the text reads as follows:

> His disciples said to him, 'When will the repose of the dead come about, and when will the new world come?' He said to them, 'What you look forward to has already come, but you do not recognize it.'[56]

Thus Jesus counters the apparent future-eschatological expectation of the disciples with his answer which refers to the repose of the dead and the new world as a present reality. The 'repose of the dead', ⲦⲀⲚⲀⲠⲀⲨⲤⲓⲤ Ⲛ̄ⲚⲈⲦⲘⲞⲞⲨⲦ, may however denote an intermediate stage[57] preceding the end of days which is characterised by the Resurrection. The new world, apparently analogous with the kingdom, is already a reality among human beings. Jesus' words in this logion therefore make clear that certain conditions are already fulfilled in the present (realized eschatology), but this does not necessarily contradict a future dimension to the end of days (future eschatology). For one thing, the logion does not state that the Resurrection has already taken place or is a present reality.

4. *Conclusion*

Having discussed the Greek as well as the Coptic evidence for traces of eschatology in *Thomas*, the question remains what kind of eschatology *Thomas* reflects. As we have seen, certain scholars have denied a place to eschatology in *Thomas* altogether.[58] It may be time to move beyond an artificial dichotomy between sapiential and prophetic stages of Jesus-tradition. Wisdom and apocalyptic eschatology need not be considered mutually exclusive, but they may rather be complementary aspects, as we may analogically also infer from the study of other early Jewish and Christian texts and textual traditions.[59] The hypothesis of a dichotomy can in any case not be built on the basis

---

[56] Translation from Lambdin, 'The Gospel According to Thomas', 73.

[57] Cf. e.g. Josephus, *Jewish War* 2.155 about Greek and allegedly Essene beliefs about the afterlife as a place of *rest* for the (righteous) dead.

[58] See section 2.2 and note 21 above.

[59] Allison, *The Jesus Tradition in Q*, 4 and note 21 mentions 'ancient Jewish [and early Christian] literature which freely mix apocalyptic and wisdom materials', refer-

of the evidence from *Thomas*, as I hope to have demonstrated with regard to the case of eschatology.

I have argued that we may discern certain notions of eschatology in *Thomas*, not only with regard to the expectations of Jesus' disciples but also with regard to Jesus' sayings. Even though the lack of a narrative framework complicates the task of finding traces of eschatology, the interpretation of the internal logic in the sayings material and of symbolical references have given me the impression that *Thomas* does comprise eschatological Jesus-traditions.

Logia 51 and 113 of the Coptic text present aspects of a realized eschatology. Even though logion 113 refers to the kingdom of the Father as a present reality, which could convey a timeless situation, the perfect tense of ⲀⲤⲈⲒ ('has already come') in logion 51 appears to correspond to a dimension in time of 'now already' rather than a timeless dimension of 'already always'.[60] As we have already noted, logion 113 also implies a future aspect in Jesus' answer, so that we cannot infer a completely timeless dimension from this logion either. The future tenses in the other logia which we have discussed further corroborate the idea that *Thomas* is not devoid of a vision of time. *Thomas* appears to subscribe to the biblical linear vision of time, starting with the creation, as the chronological markers '*from* (Ⲭⲓⲛ) Adam *until* (ⲱⲁ) John the Baptist' in the Coptic logion 46 may indicate.

How do the notions of eschatology in *Thomas* relate to each other? There appears to be a tension between the idea of the kingdom which is 'already' present on earth on the one hand, and the future aspects of eschatologically oriented logia, such as resurrection, apocalyptic transformation, and future revelation of Jesus, which have 'not yet' been realised on the other. This tension has also been the subject of scholarly discussion about eschatology in the canonical New Testament.[61]

---

ring to the *Testaments of the Twelve Patriarchs*, *4 Ezra*, Tobit, the Wisdom of Solomon, Matthew and the *Didache*, and further bibliography. See also the recent scholarly attention for eschatological dimensions to wisdom texts among the Dead Sea Scrolls in F. García Martínez (ed.), *Wisdom and Apocalypticism in the Dead Sea Scrolls and in the Biblical Tradition* (BETL 168), Louvain 2003.

[60] Pace Zöckler, 'Realisierte Eschatologie?', in: Id., *Jesu Lehren im Thomasevangelium*, 178-80 who concludes that there is no dimension of 'Schon-jetzt' (realized eschatology), but rather a timeless dimension of 'Jetzt und schon immer' in *Thomas*.

[61] See e.g. J.D.G. Dunn, 'Until he comes' and 'The eschatological tension', in: Id., *The Theology of Paul the Apostle*, London 1998, 294-315 and 461-98 at 294 and 461 with further bibliography; T.D. Still, 'Eschatology in Colossians: How Realized is It?', *New Testament Studies* 50 (2004) 125-38; K. Niederwimmer, 'Zur Eschatologie im

Thomas may not be as far removed from the eschatological concerns of Christian communities in the first century CE as has sometimes been supposed.

How should we relate Thomasene eschatology to the historical Jesus? The milieu of the historical Jesus, his earliest followers and disciples who transmitted his teachings, was full of eschatological expectations, as both the canonical New Testament writings and *Thomas* (logia 18, 37, 51, 113) attest. It is beyond the scope of this article to undertake a redaction-critical study of the composition history of *Thomas*.[62] Nevertheless, we did find evidence that certain eschatological aspects to Jesus-traditions in *Thomas* (cf. e.g. logia 1, 37) are not peculiar to the Coptic text, but also already occur in some form in the Greek fragments. Apart from the Coptic text, the Greek version in addition refers to the Resurrection (Greek logion 5). The wording of Jesus-traditions in the Greek fragments, in particular in the case of logion 3, may sometimes reflect Hellenistic culture,[63] but this cultural context also plays a part in the historical-critical study of the canonical Gospels. There seems to be no reason to suppose a thoroughly reworked version of Jesus' eschatology through an Egyptian Gnostic lens in the cases which we have discussed. This is not to deny the existence of different stages of redaction, of which the differences between the Coptic text and the Greek fragments[64] as well as certain text-internal clues[65] testify.

In all its complexity, including the ambivalence between present-eschatological and future-eschatological aspects, Thomasene eschatology parallels Synoptic eschatologies in some ways, but it also provides new viewpoints from which the subject of the historical Jesus may

---

Corpus Johanneum', *Novum Testamentum* 39 (1997) 105-16; O.D. Vena, *The Parousia and Its Rereadings: The Development of the Eschatological Consciousness in the Writings of the New Testament* (Studies in Biblical Literature 27), New York 2001.

[62] The application of redaction criticism has as yet not yielded a consensus about *Thomas* and Historical Jesus research; cf. the reconsideration of the hypothesis of 'oral gospel tradition' as part of the redaction-critical approach to *Thomas* by R. Uro, '*Thomas* and oral gospel tradition', in: Id. (ed.), *Thomas at the Crossroads*, 8-32.

[63] The Greek proverb γνῶθι σεαυτόν may play in the background, but the Greek logion 3 reflects not just an instruction to the addressees to know themselves, but to know themselves as children of the living Father.

[64] See Attridge, 'Relationships among the Greek and Coptic Witnesses', in: Id., 'Greek Fragments', 99-101.

[65] See, for instance, the phrase 'Does not Jesus say' (translation from Lambdin, 'The Gospel According to Thomas', 93) in the Coptic logion 111, which appears to be redactional.

be approached. Some examples of new viewpoints may suffice here. *Thomas* puts more emphasis on God's kingdom as a present dimension than the Synoptic Gospels, which focus on the imminence of the kingdom, do. The idea that the Thomasene Jesus has an actualised understanding of the kingdom and the end of days brings out what may be implicit in some other Gospel traditions about Jesus (cf. e.g. Luke 4.21, 17.20-21). The fact that the Thomasene Jesus reacts to the disciples' question about the end by relating the understanding of the end to the beginning (logion 18) may be understood in the historical framework of Jesus' Jewish environment. As the 'beginning' stands for the creation in a biblical context, it also relates to the fall of man in the garden of Eden and human responsibility for the knowledge of good and evil since then. In early Jewish tradition Paradise, often described as a garden with fruitful trees, is the place for the righteous in the afterlife (cf. e.g. *1 Enoch* 32; *2 Enoch* 8-9; *y. Sanh.* 27c, 32-38). In fact, logion 19 refers to Paradise and to five trees in it, as we have seen (bottom of section 3.2 a). The five trees of Paradise also occur in fragments of a *Dialogue between John and Jesus*, where they are said to have been explained in an 'intelligible allegory'. It has been suggested that the five trees are part of terminology and ideas which 'point clearly to the realm of Gnosis'.[66] However, trees also have a symbolical function in early Jewish texts (e.g. *1 Enoch* 32) and in canonical Gospel traditions (cf. Matt 3.10/Luke 3.9, Matt 7.15-20, Luke 6.43-45), so that this Thomasene tradition may be understood in relation to the historical Jesus, even if its interpretation became Gnosticised in a later context.[67]

---

[66] H.-C. Puech & B. Blatz, 'Other Gnostic Gospels and Related Literature', in: Schneemelcher (ed.), *New Testament Apocrypha*, vol. 1, 388.

[67] I would like to thank Dr G.H. van Kooten and Dr A. Hilhorst for their helpful editorial comments.

BASILIDES OF ALEXANDRIA: MATTHIAS (MATTHEW) AND ARISTOTLE AS THE SOURCES OF INSPIRATION FOR HIS GNOSTIC THEOLOGY IN HIPPOLYTUS' *REFUTATIO*

Abraham P. Bos

In book 7 of his *Refutation of all heresies* the church father Hippolytus of Rome (c. 170-235 CE) also discusses the doctrine of the Gnostic Basilides of Alexandria,[1] who lived c. 125 CE. Hippolytus describes him as a follower of the Greek philosopher Aristotle. But he also notes that Basilides acquired his wisdom in Egypt.[2] In his introduction Hippolytus mentions Basilides in the same breath as his legitimate son Isidorus.[3]

Brief summary of Basilides' system according to Hippolytus[4]

The origin of all things for Basilides is a purely transcendent God, who is even beyond being and is the Cause of everything that is knowable via the senses or the intellect or thanks to enlightenment. This God was unknown throughout the ages, and beyond the comprehension of all the beings living in the cosmos, including the cosmic powers. Knowledge of this God was not present in the religions of the pagans,

---

[1] On the development of Christianity in this city, see G.P. Luttikhuizen, 'Veronderstellingen over het vroegste christendom in Alexandrië', in: J. Delobel et al. (eds), *Vroegchristelijke gemeenten tussen ideaal en werkelijkheid*, Kampen 2001, 207-22. On Basilides, see pp. 219-20. See also G.P. Luttikhuizen, *De veelvormigheid van het vroegste christendom*, Delft 2002, 98-111, esp. 115-17.

[2] Hippolytus, *Refutatio omnium haeresium* 7.27.13. For the Greek text, see P. Wendland (ed.), *Hippolytus: Werke*, vol. 3 (Griechische Christliche Schriftsteller 26), Leipzig 1916 (repr. Hildesheim 1977); M. Marcovich (ed.), *Hippolytus: Refutatio omnium haeresium*, Berlin/New York 1986. W.A. Löhr, *Basilides und seine Schule: Eine Studie zur Theologie- und Kirchengeschichte des zweiten Jahrhunderts*, Tübingen 1996, 29, includes this text as testimony 8.

[3] Hippolytus, *Refutatio omnium haeresium* 7.20.1. Cf. also Clement of Alexandria, *Stromateis* 6.53.2-5 = Basilides, frg. 15 (Löhr, *Basilides und seine Schule*).

[4] Cf. A.P. Bos, 'Basilides as an Aristotelianizing Gnostic', *Vigiliae Christianae* 54 (2000) 44-60, esp. 50-3.

nor in that of the Jewish people. It was only revealed through the
arrival of the Gospel in the cosmos from hypercosmic reality.

This transcendent God initiated a process of generation by means
of a World Seed. This process of generation occurs without his active
intervention, but does take place according to his plan. World history
is a goal-orientated process without external direction (comparable
with the growth process of a fertilized egg-cell from the moment of
conception). This World Seed turns out to be the original principle of
the entire cosmos, but—more importantly—it also contains the image
of the transcendent God, his 'Sonship'. As a result, the World Seed
is not just the original principle of the cosmos but also the principle
of theogony, because it produces divine beings.

Basilides represented the cosmos as flowing from the principles of
(a) the World Seed and (b) the Sonship. The cosmogony takes place in
the development of life on three distinct levels: the ethereal, the level of
air, and the earthly level. On each of these levels we find reproduction
and the birth of Sons. But under the influence of Light, deriving from
the Sonship, which acts on these sons, a decisive contact is achieved
between the divine Sonship and those cosmic beings who possess the
ability to unite with the Sonship.

Basilides interpreted the non-existent God as a purely spiritual
principle. He identified the non-existent World Seed with the divine
Logos in the prologue to the Gospel according to John[5] and explained
this text in the sense that the vital principles and the Light that they
contain proceeded from God and became active in the Formlessness (*Amorphia*) of non-divine reality. The divine Logos, in the World
Seed, contains the principles of all forms of life and brings about the
gradual development of these forms of life from their earliest stage
to their completion. As Logos of God, however, he also contains the
Sonship. As pure spiritual reality this cannot remain connected with
the Formlessness of material reality.

The first phase of theo-cosmogony is therefore the ascent of the
subtle Sonship out of the World Seed to the transcendent God. The
second phase centres on the vicissitudes of the less subtle Sonship,
which can only ascend thanks to the help of the holy *Pneuma*. This

---

[5] For this theme, cf. also G.P. Luttikhuizen, 'Johannine Vocabulary and the Thought
Structure of Gnostic Mythological Texts', in: H. Preißler et al. (eds), *Gnosisforschung
und Religionsgeschichte: Festschrift für Kurt Rudolph*, Marburg 1994, 175-81.

holy *Pneuma*, after the Second Sonship has separated from it, forms the Firmament, the boundary between transcendent reality and cosmic reality. The third phase is the complicated process of the ascent of the third Sonship, which 'needs purification'. This requires a process which takes place in all three parts of the cosmos.

The sphere directly bordering on the holy *Pneuma* is the domain of the Great Archon, the highest cosmic ruler. He produces and begets a Son, of higher quality than he himself, and thus, without realizing it, carries out the divine counsel. This Son is the leading and ruling principle for him. The sphere under the Ether contains the domain of the Lower Archon, the ruler of the Air. He, too, produces a Son who is of higher quality than he himself. Finally, there is the sphere of transient living creatures, burdened with metabolism and earthly bodies of different sexes. They include some who participate in the third Sonship.

Once the development of the cosmos has progressed far enough, the moment dawns which all the ages of world history have awaited, the moment of the great Enlightenment. Basilides represented this as the process which makes known the Gospel, the *gnosis* concerning the Unknown God and the Sonship which is of the same essence. Then, in the first place, the Son of the Great Archon becomes enlightened and, thanks to him, the entire ethereal sphere of the cosmos. In the second place the Son of the Lower Archon becomes enlightened and, thanks to him, the entire sphere of the air. Finally, Jesus of Nazareth becomes enlightened and, thanks to him, all the people who participate in the third Sonship and have opened themselves up to the effect of the *Pneuma*.

First the Son of the Great Archon unites with the hypercosmic Sonship (and separates from the ethereal sphere); secondly the Son of the Lower Archon unites with the hypercosmic Sonship (and separates from the sphere of the air); thirdly the Sons of God in the sublunary sphere, as the result of Jesus of Nazareth's preaching, unite with the Sonship (and separate from gross-material and fine-material reality).

Then the cosmos remains in utter Ignorance and world history has been completed, because the divine has united with itself.

Basilides as exegete of Matthias' 'secret words'

Hippolytus presents Basilides and Isidorus as people who did not
speak for themselves but saw themselves as interpreters of a doctrine
which had been passed down to them. This supposedly involved 'secret
words' (*logoi*) which Matthias, supposedly identifiable with the Matthias
of Acts (see below), had spoken to them and which he himself had
heard from the Saviour during private instruction.[6]

What can this refer to? We have various testimonies on writings
by Basilides, but they are all rather vague and difficult to place. W.A.
Löhr has discussed this information as 'Testimonia' in his study devoted
to Basilides.

In the first place Löhr reports that Eusebius mentions a certain
Agrippa Castor, who provided a 'Refutation' of Basilides' teachings
and revealed his 'mysteries'.[7] Agrippa also mentioned that Basilides
wrote twenty-four (!) books of commentary 'on the gospel'. But we
know nothing about the date of this Agrippa Castor. Löhr thinks
that he may have depended on the church father Irenaeus. As for
Basilides' commentary, it seems likely that it commented on an existing text. But we cannot infer from Eusebius' report whether this was
a work independent of Basilides or that Basilides had first composed
his 'own' gospel text.

Clement of Alexandria in his *Stromateis* reports that Basilides claimed
to base himself on Glaukias, who knew the words of the apostle Peter
and had passed them on.[8]

But more important for our purposes is Clement's mention further

---

[6] Hippolytus, *Refutatio omnium haeresium* 7.20.1: φασὶν εἰρηκέναι Ματθίαν αὐτοῖς
λόγους ἀποκρύφους, οὓς ἤκουσε παρὰ τοῦ σωτῆρος κατ' ἰδίαν διδαχθείς and 20.5.
Cf. Löhr, *Basilides und seine Schule*, 24-9. J.H. MacMahon, *Hippolytus: The Refutation of all
heresies* (ANCL 6.1), Edinburgh 1868, 273, notes that E. Miller, *Origenis Philosophumena
sive Omnium haeresium refutatio* (Oxford 1851), 'erroneously reads "Matthew"'. On the
theme of the 'secret words', cf. also G.P. Luttikhuizen, 'Vroege traditie over Jezus
in een niet-canonieke bron: het evangelie van Thomas', *Tijdschrift voor Theologie* 38
(1998) 120-43.

[7] Löhr, *Basilides und seine Schule*, 5-14, testimony 1 = Agrippa Castor, in Eusebius,
Historia Ecclesiastica 4.7.5-8.

[8] Löhr, *Basilides und seine Schule*, 19-23, testimony 5 = Clement, *Stromateis* 7.106.4-
107.1. This report is noteworthy because Papias of Hierapolis had mentioned that
Marcus had constructed his gospel on the basis of knowledge received from the apostle
Peter. F. Legge, *Hippolytus Philosophumena*, ii, London 1921, 66 note 1 suggests: 'Is
Matthias a corruption of Glaukias?'

on in the *Stromateis* that Valentinus, Marcion, and Basilides founded heretical movements, 'even though they appeal to the teachings of Matthias'.[9] And Clement adds that this fact cannot justify naming Basilides' sect after Matthias, for: 'Just as the teachings of all the apostles are one, so, too, the (later) tradition (of these teachings).'[10] For Clement, apparently, an appeal by sectarians like Basilides to Matthias is invalid because all the apostles were united in their preaching. Clement dismisses the idea of 'pluriformity of Christianity in its earliest days'.

Clement is also acquainted with a work entitled *Paradoseis* ('Traditions') attributed to Matthias and quotes from it a few times.[11] (But he does not make any link with Basilides.[12])

Finally, it is significant that Origen, the great third-century scholar, mentions a 'Gospel according to Basilides', but also a 'Gospel according to Matthias'.[13] But it is doubtful whether Origen's information amounts to more than his acquaintance with a work referred to as a 'Gospel according to Matthias'. It is uncertain whether he himself saw a text of it. A recently discovered text by Didymus the Blind contains the striking statement that Levi the publican, who has often been identified with Matthew the evangelist, should not be equated with Matthew but with Matthias.[14]

---

[9] Löhr, *Basilides und seine Schule*, 24, testimony 6 = Clement, *Stromateis* 7.108.1: κἂν τὴν Ματθίου αὐχῶσι προσάγεσθαι δόξαν. See also W. Schneemelcher, *Neutestamentliche Apokryphen in deutscher Übersetzung*, 2 vols, Tübingen 1987[5], i, 306-9.

[10] Löhr, *Basilides und seine Schule*, 24, testimony 6: μία γὰρ ἡ πάντων γέγονε τῶν ἀποστόλων ὥσπερ διδασκαλία, οὕτως δὲ καὶ ἡ παράδοσις.

[11] Clement, *Stromateis* 2.45.4; 3.26.3; 4.35.2; 7.82.1. But in the last passage A. Le Boulluec translates: 'On rapporte dans les *Traditions* que l'apôtre Matthias disait ...' On this reading the place contains no indication of the authorship of the *Paradoseis*.

[12] Cf. Löhr, *Basilides und seine Schule*, 25, 27.

[13] Cf. Löhr, *Basilides und seine Schule*, testimony 10 = Origen, *Homilia in Lucam* (Rauer 4-5). *The Book of Thomas the Contender* (Nag Hammadi II.7) also mentions a certain Matthaias as the one who recorded the 'secret words' which Jesus spoke to Judas Thomas. In his Introduction to the translation of this work in *The Nag Hammadi Library*, Leiden 1988, 199, J.D. Turner wonders whether this refers to 'the apostle Matthew'.

[14] S.P. Brock, 'A New Testimony to the "Gospel According to the Hebrews"', *New Testament Studies* 18 (1971/72) 220-2. The text in question is a *Commentary on the Psalms* (ed. M. Gronewald, Bonn 1969), 184.9-10: τὸν Ματθαῖον δοκεῖ ἐν τῷ κατὰ Λουκᾶν Λευὶν ὀνομάζειν. οὐκ ἔστιν δὲ αὐτός, ἀλλὰ ὁ κατασταθεὶς ἀντὶ τοῦ Ἰούδα ὁ Ματθίας καὶ ὁ Λευὶς εἰς διώνυμοί εἰσιν. ἐν τῷ καθ᾽ Ἑβραίους εὐαγγελίῳ τοῦτο φαίνεται.—'(Scripture) seems to name Matthew "Levi" in Luke's Gospel, but they are not the same person; rather Matthias, who replaced Judas, and Levi are one and the same person with a double

What conclusion can we draw from this information? Not much more than that an extensive work (24 books) regarded as a gospel commentary was attributed to Basilides. And that there was a relation between Basilides' teachings and the apostle Matthias.

The reference must be to the person who shortly after Jesus' ascension, as Luke tells us,[15] was chosen by the congregation in Jerusalem led by the eleven remaining disciples as the successor of Judas, the disciple who had not handed over the gospel but his master and had then taken his own life.[16] Matthias was qualified inasmuch as he had seen all Jesus' public actions from his baptism by John[17] to his ascension and could bear witness to them. Compared with the apostle Paul, he even had the advantage of having heard Jesus preach on earth.[18]

We must conclude, however, that the most precise information about Matthias' influence on Basilides is supplied by Hippolytus. We should also note that the fifteen pages of Greek text on Basilides in Hippolytus contain many references or allusions to biblical texts or gospel texts, but no recognizable trace of secret words of Matthias.[19]

---

name. This is apparent in the Gospel according to the Hebrews.' Brock notes on p. 222 that the *Gospel according to the Hebrews* was almost certainly written in a Semitic language, and that the difference in spelling between Matthias and Matthew is very small in these languages.

[15] Acts of the Apostles 1.21-26. The writer Luke is the only New Testament author to mention this person. This leads Löhr, *Basilides und seine Schule*, 26, 31-4, to suspect a preference for the Lucan tradition in Basilides. See also pp. 45 and 48.

[16] Acts 1.23-26. Cf. Clement, *Stromateis* 6.105.2.

[17] The feast of Jesus' baptism by John was the main ecclesiastical festival for the Basilidians. Cf. Clement, *Stromateis* 1.145.6-146 = frg. 2 (W.A. Löhr).

[18] A Matthias is also mentioned in the *Acts of Andrew and Matthias*, which have often been linked to the *Acta Andreae*. Cf. W. Schneemelcher, *Neutestamentliche Apokryphen*, Tübingen 1989[5], ii, 99; 399-402; 414-15, and, now much more precisely, F.L. Roig Lanzillotta, *The Apocryphal Acts of Andrew: A New Approach to the Character, Thought and Meaning of the Primitive Text* (diss. Groningen 2004). See also D.R. MacDonald, 'The *Acts of Andrew and Matthias* and the *Acts of Andrew*', in: D.R. MacDonald, *The Apocryphal Acts of Apostles* (SBL), Decatur, GA 1986, 9-26, with a response by J. Prieur and a reply (pp. 27-39).

[19] A possible objection here is that, according to Hippolytus, *Refutatio omnium haeresium* 7.20, Basilides emphatically linked his language theology of the 'names' and their inappropriateness to the hypercosmic reality of the highest, non-existent God to Matthias' 'secret words'. But this theory seems primarily developed on the basis of Basilides' explanation of Ephesians 1.21, which Hippolytus quotes in 7.20.3, and perhaps of 1 Corinthians 2.13, where the apostle talks about 'words (*logoi*) not taught by human wisdom but by the *Pneuma*', a text which is quoted in Hippolytus, *Refutatio omnium haeresium* 7.26.3.

For the sake of completeness I note that the name of the author of the 'secret words' occurs three times in Hippolytus, twice in *Refutatio omnium haeresium* 7.20.1 and once in 20.5. A complication is that the one manuscript which we possess of Hippolytus' text reads Ματθίαν the first time in 20.1 but Ματθαίου the second time. Obviously one of the two passages must be adapted to the other. In such cases it is good practice to opt for the less well-known name 'Matthias', on the principle that the *lectio difficilior* ('the more difficult reading') is more likely to drop out than the easier reading.

Secret words of Matthias or Matthew?

However, although Hippolytus' text probably mentioned Matthias only, it makes sense also to consider the possibility of a relation between Basilides and the Gospel according to Matthew. The motif of God as a 'sower' of seed, a motif central to Basilides' theology, is amply attested in the Gospel according to Matthew. Moreover, it is the evangelist Matthew who states that Jesus often instructed his disciples 'separately'.[20] This may have led to the conjecture that Matthew presented Jesus' true teachings as an esoteric doctrine which was not imparted to the crowds.

An argument for a special relation between the Gospel according to Matthew and Basilides is particularly found in chapter 13 of that gospel. In 13.34-35 Matthew says: 'All this Jesus said to the crowds in parables[21] and he said nothing to them without parables. This was to fulfil the words of the prophet, when he said: I will open my mouth in parables, I will proclaim what has been hidden since the καταβολή (RSV: foundation).'[22]

---

[20] Cf. Matt 13.10, 16-17, 34-35, 36; 17.19; 20.17; 24.3. Although Mark and Luke have important parallels there seems to be a closer relation with the Gospel of Matthew.

[21] Cf. *Apocryphon of James* 7: 'At first I spoke to you in parables and you did not understand; now I speak to you openly, and you (still) do not perceive.'

[22] Matt 13.35: ἐρεύξομαι κεκρυμμένα ἀπὸ καταβολῆς [κόσμου]. The prophet quoted here is the psalmist of Ps 78 (77 LXX), but in the second half of verse 2 he has: φθέγξομαι προβλήματα ἀπ' ἀρχῆς—'I will utter problems from of old'; see A. Pietersma, *The Psalms: A New English Translation of the Septuagint and the Other Greek Translations Traditionally Included Under that Title*, Oxford/New York 2000. Only Matthew makes this connection with Psalm 78, and there is an important textual tradition which has ἀπὸ καταβολῆς without κόσμου.

Here we have three central themes of Basilides in a few verses of
Matthew: the (apparent) reference to an 'esoteric doctrine' of Jesus;
the concealment of central matters from 'the beginning' or from the
καταβολή; and the notion of 'depositing', which Basilides explains as
'the depositing/the putting-in-the-ground of the *seed* of the world'.

These verses are followed in Matt 13.36-43 by an explanation for
the disciples of the parable of the wheat and the weeds. In this explanation Jesus says: 'He who sows the good seed is the Son of man; the
field is the world, and the good seed means the sons of the kingdom;
the weeds are the sons of the evil one, and the enemy who sowed is
the devil; the harvest is the close of the age [τοῦ αἰῶνος].' The end
of the teaching reads: 'Then the righteous will shine like the sun in
the kingdom of their Father.'

At the very least Basilides seems strongly influenced by the passage
from the Gospel according to Matthew. Perhaps Basilides even pro-
fessed to give the 'hidden, deeper meaning' of Matthew's text, in which
Matthew, in Basilides' view, claimed to record an esoteric doctrine
of Jesus. Basilides may have suggested that, for the first time, he was
explaining Matthew's public text 'spiritually', pneumatically.

If we follow this hypothesis, we might consider linking the words in
Hippolytus 7.19.9 that Basilides 'transposes the view of Aristotle on
the text of the gospel which is our salvation',[23] to the Gospel according to Matthew in particular. It is impossible that Hippolytus could
talk about 'the gospel which is our salvation' with reference to an
apocryphal Gospel according to Matthias, so that it seems as if he
had the Gospel of Matthew in mind.

Note, too, that chapter 13 of the Gospel according to Matthew
contains the parable of the sower (13.1-9); the parable of the mustard
seed (13.31-32); the parable of the treasure hidden in the field (13.44),
and the motif of the householder who brings out of his treasure new
and old things (13.52). Matthew also observes in 13.17 that the disciples
are blessed because they see what 'many prophets and righteous men

---

[23] Hippolytus, *Refutatio omnium haeresium* 7.19.9: Ἐὰν ὁ Βασιλείδης εὑρεθῇ ...
τὰ τοῦ Ἀριστοτέλους δόγματα εἰς τὸν εὐαγγελικὸν καὶ σωτήριον ἡμῶν λόγον
μεθαρμοζόμενος, ... Hippolytus accuses Marcion of dealing with the Gospel according to Mark in a comparable way, i.e. reading Greek philosophy (Empedocles) into
it. Cf. 7.30.1: ὃν συλαγωγῶν μέχρι νῦν λανθάνειν ὑπελάμβανε τὴν διαταγὴν πάσης
τῆς κατ᾽ αὐτὸν αἱρέσεως ἀπὸ τῆς Σικελίας εἰς τοὺς εὐαγγελικοὺς λόγους μεταφέρων
αὐταῖς λέξεσι.

longed to see ... and they did not see it.' And in 13.11: 'To you it has been given to know (γνῶναι) the mysteries (τὰ μυστήρια) of the kingdom of heaven.'[24] Basilides also explicitly based himself on the story of the wise men from the East in the Gospel according to Matthew.[25] I also think it is possible that Basilides' term παχυμερές, which he uses to characterize the second Sonship,[26] should be understood against the background of Matthew 13.15 (a verse from Isaiah not included in Mark and Luke): 'The heart of this people has grown dull and their ears have become hard of hearing.'[27] It is also conceivable that he borrowed his important concept of the 'separation' (φυλοκρίνησις) of different levels of reality from Matthew 19.28. And he bases himself on several gospels for the description of Jesus.[28]

So while it seems likely that Hippolytus took from his source text the name of Matthias as the inspirator of Basilides, we should perhaps consider that Basilides himself actually took the Gospel according to Matthew as his starting-point.

There is, however, an argument against admitting even the name of Matthias in Hippolytus' text, an argument which I believe is powerful but which no one has yet considered. I derive this argument from Hippolytus' exhortation in 7.20.1: 'Let us then see how Basilides together with Isidorus and their entire band clearly not only tell lies about Matthias but, what is worse, about the Saviour himself.' This exhortation makes no sense if it presupposes an esoteric work attributed to Matthias. On the basis of Hippolytus' exposition orthodox Christians would well be able to observe that Basilides' teachings clashed with those of Jesus as they knew them. But they could not possibly check whether Basilides also told lies about Matthias. However,

---

[24] There seems to be an allusion to this text in *Pistis Sophia* 1.42: 'Hear, Philip ... for thou and Thomas and Matthew are those to whom was given, through the First *Mystery*, to write all the words which I will say ...'; see also 1.43, where these three are called 'the three witnesses' (with reference to Matt 18.16 [and Deut 19.15]). Cf. *Pistis Sophia*, text ed. by C. Schmidt; trans. and notes by V. McDermot (Leiden 1978).

[25] Cf. Hippolytus, *Refutatio omnium haeresium* 7.27.5. See Matt 2.1-12.

[26] Hippolytus, *Refutatio omnium haeresium* 7.22.[7], 9, 10; 10.14.4. J.H. MacMahon translates παχυμερές as 'gross'. It is not used in the New Testament.

[27] Matt 13.15: ἐπαχύνθη γὰρ ἡ καρδία τοῦ λαοῦ τούτου, καὶ τοῖς ὠσὶν βαρέως ἤκουσαν. Matthew is the only witness among the evangelists to this quotation from Isaiah 6.9-10. Paul quotes it in Acts 28.27, after some Jews in Rome have joined the faith and others have remained unbelieving!

[28] Hippolytus, *Refutatio omnium haeresium* 7.27.8. On this theme, see below.

if Hippolytus' text mentioned Matthew, the remark makes sense. For around 225 CE (the time in which Hippolytus wrote his *Refutatio*) every Christian would be familiar with the Gospel according to Matthew, and Hippolytus could readily assume that the reader of this gospel would realize that Basilides' doctrine could not possibly be interpreted as agreeing with Matthew's proclamation.

Everything considered, it would not seem impossible that Hippolytus actually referred three times to Matthew and not to Matthias.

The final revelation of the cosmic mystery and of the 'Sons of God'

In the rest of my contribution I want to throw light on some themes in Basilides' discussions which have not received sufficient attention so far, and which are related to his view of the end of world history.

At the end of the cosmic development the 'third Sonship' must finally be revealed. For this theme Basilides seems to have linked up with an important chapter in Paul's Letter to the Romans on 'life in the spirit'.

Paul talks there about us 'who walk not according to the flesh but according to the Spirit', and he says to his readers: 'You are not in the flesh but in the Spirit, if the Spirit of God really dwells in you.' And further on the apostle says: 'For all who are led by the Spirit of God are sons of God.' And he continues with words which seem to have been very important for Basilides: 'For you did not receive the spirit of slavery to fall back into fear, but you have received the Spirit of Sonship, by which we cry Abba, Father. This Spirit bears witness with our spirit that we are children of God.'[29]

But while the apostle states this with great certainty, he also knows that the concrete situation of the Roman congregation (and his own) does not yet seem to agree with the high dignity of the faithful and their claim to the glory of Christ. He explains this in the next section by declaring that 'the sons of God' have yet to be revealed: 'For the creation waits with eager longing for the revealing of the sons of God'[30]

---

[29] Rom 8.15-16: οὐ γὰρ ἐλάβετε πνεῦμα δουλείας πάλιν εἰς φόβον, ἀλλὰ ἐλάβετε πνεῦμα υἱοθεσίας, ἐν ᾧ κράζομεν, Ἀββὰ ὁ πατήρ· αὐτὸ τὸ πνεῦμα συμμαρτυρεῖ τῷ πνεύματι ἡμῶν ὅτι ἐσμὲν τέκνα θεοῦ.

[30] Rom 8.19: ἡ γὰρ ἀποκαραδοκία τῆς κτίσεως τὴν ἀποκάλυψιν τῶν υἱῶν τοῦ θεοῦ ἀπεκδέχεται.

and: 'For we know that the whole creation has been groaning in travail together until now. And not only the creation, but we ourselves, who have received the Spirit as the first gift, groan inwardly as we await the sonship: the redemption of our bodies.'[31]

It seems likely that Basilides' theme of the '(threefold) Sonship' is rooted in Paul's repeated statements about 'the sonship (through adoption)'.[32] In particular for the situation of the 'third Sonship' he repeatedly refers to the passage in the Romans letter.[33]

But it is also useful to see how Basilides quotes this letter. In 7.25.1 he uses the words of Paul's text, merely adding to 'the revealing of the sons of God' his own words 'and are sorted out to their predestined position.'[34] In 7.25.5 he says that 'the children of God must be revealed', and presents the revelation of 'the mystery' by Jesus' preaching as its beginning.

In 7.27.1 Basilides (or Hippolytus) is freer in his quotation of Paul's words. He says there: 'For now it groans and is subject to torture' and 'it awaits the revealing of the sons of God.'[35] The metaphor of 'being in labour' has been replaced there by the concept of 'being tortured'.

It may be that Basilides' rewording constitutes a significant change. For Paul's text in Romans 8.23 continues with 'the redemption of our

---

[31] Rom 8.22-23: οἴδαμεν γὰρ ὅτι πᾶσα ἡ κτίσις συστενάζει καὶ συνωδίνει ἄχρι τοῦ νῦν· οὐ μόνον δέ, ἀλλὰ καὶ αὐτοὶ τὴν ἀπαρχὴν τοῦ πνεύματος ἔχοντες ἡμεῖς καὶ αὐτοὶ ἐν ἑαυτοῖς στενάζομεν υἱοθεσίαν ἀπεκδεχόμενοι, τὴν ἀπολύτρωσιν τοῦ σώματος ἡμῶν.

[32] It is important to note that Paul here uses the term υἱοθεσία twice in Rom 8.15 and 8.23 (as he also does in Gal 4.5 and Eph 1.5), which term does not occur in Basilides as reproduced by Hippolytus. The term υἱότης which Basilides uses does not occur in Paul.

[33] Hippolytus, *Refutatio omnium haeresium* 7.25.1; 25.5, and 27.1.

[34] Hippolytus, *Refutatio omnium haeresium* 7.25.1: ἀποκαλυφθῆναι καὶ ἀποκατασταθῆναι. On the meaning of ἀποκατάστασις, see below.

[35] Hippolytus, *Refutatio omnium haeresium* 7.27.1: «στένει γὰρ μέχρι τοῦ νῦν καὶ βασανίζεται», καὶ «μένει τὴν ἀποκάλυψιν τῶν υἱῶν τοῦ θεοῦ». Paul has: συστενάζει and ἄχρι τοῦ νῦν and συνωδίνει, and instead of μένει he has ἀπεκδέχεται. The verb βασανίζεσθαι is used again in 27.2, where the torture of the souls is said to end when the 'great ignorance' has come upon them! J.H. MacMahon translated 'is tormented' in 27.1 and 'wrung with torture' in 27.2. Hippolytus, *Refutatio omnium haeresium* 5.26.20, in the description of Justin's heresy, mentions that 'the *pneuma* of Elohim' present in people 'is tortured', because it is separated from Elohim himself and undergoes many torments. In his description of Marcion, whom he associates with Empedocles, Hippolytus likewise describes the fate of souls as 'tortured' and tormented by the Demiurge (*Refutatio omnium haeresium* 7.29.20-21, 24).

body'. While Paul must have meant this in the sense of 'buying the freedom of our body' from subservience to sin, it is almost certain that Basilides interpreted it in a strongly dualistic way as 'liberation from the earthly, gross-material body'. In my view, his statements about the unliberated pneumatics in terms of 'being tortured' can be linked to a famous text of Aristotle, who described mortal existence as a torture for the soul, comparable with the torment to which Etruscan robbers subject their living prisoners by tying them to the body of dead soldiers and abandoning them to their gruesome fate.[36] For in Aristotle this text describes the unnatural situation which the soul suffers during its earthly existence in a gross-material body, which Aristotle represented as a corpse.[37] In the context of Aristotle's lost work there seems to be reference to the malevolent nature of the Titans, who gained control over the body of Dionysus and devoured it. In the context of Gnostic mythology we should think of the Archons of the cosmos as the powers who entice the spiritual principles into their sphere of influence and who cause reproduction, and thus imprisonment of the spiritual principles, in human beings.[38]

Basilides, as we said, seems to interpret the end of the (revelatory) labour of the children of God as the *revelation of the mystery* of the hypercosmic God *to* the cosmos and to mankind.[39] For this purpose the Gospel has gone out through all the spheres up to earthly reality. Once again Basilides here uses the words of Ephesians 1.21, but in a different context: the Gospel 'passed through "every rule and authority <and power> and dominion and every name that is named"'. In typical Gnostic fashion, however, Basilides emphasizes that there was no question of an 'incorporation' or 'incarnation' on the part of hypercosmic reality (25.6). No descent of transcendent entities from

---

[36] Cf. Aristotle, *Protrepticus* 10b (Ross), 73 (Gigon), and A.P. Bos, *The Soul and Its Instrumental Body: A Reinterpretation of Aristotle's Philosophy of Living Nature*, Leiden 2003, 315-37 and Id., 'Aristotle on the Etruscan robbers: a core text of "Aristotelian dualism"', *Journal of the History of Philosophy* 41 (2003) 289-306. See now also Roig Lanzillotta, *The Apocryphal Acts of Andrew*, 301-5.

[37] Cf. J. Pépin, 'La légende orphique du supplice tyrrhénien', in: A. Cazenave and J.F. Lyotard (eds), *L'art des confins: Mélanges offerts à M. de Gandillac*, Paris 1985, 387-406.

[38] The same verb 'to torture', 'to torment' is used in Matthew 8.29 in the story of the two demoniacs in the country of the Gadarenes, where the evil spirits, on recognizing Jesus, ask him: 'Have you come here to torment us before the time?' (ἦλθες ὧδε πρὸ καιροῦ βασανίσαι ἡμᾶς;)

[39] Hippolytus, *Refutatio omnium haeresium* 7.26.7.

above to below took place, and there was no withdrawal of God or the Sonship from their own glory. God does bring about the great revolution or completion of the cosmic development, but as unmoved mover!

The final phase of cosmic generation: the great ignorance

We are confirmed in our conjecture of a salient Aristotelian feature in a text about Basilides' doctrine by the notion of the 'great ignorance' which, according to Basilides, is finally disseminated through the entire cosmos as a manifestation of God's compassion on the creation (of the Great Archon).[40] This theme, too, can be traced back to the great mythical narrative in Aristotle's *Eudemus*,[41] as I hope to show below.

This last phase of the great process of cosmic development is astonishing.[42] Once the 'third Sonship' has also ascended, compassion will be shown to the creation. God will bring a great ignorance upon the entire cosmos![43]—There will be absolute separation between the sphere of beings with perfect *gnosis*, i.e. the hypercosmic sphere, and the sphere of *agnoia*: the entire cosmos. For the travail of the cosmos will only end when the great process of separation has been completed and everything has got its own place and follows its own nature (27.2). This calls to mind the statement in 7.22.13 that fish perish if they are exposed to pure and dry air.

In my view, we should read this remarkable conclusion as correcting the description of the end of cosmic time in, for instance, the Gospel according to Matthew. There the harvest time, in which the good seed and the weeds will be separated, is identified with the 'close of the age'. Then the weeds will be gathered and thrown into the fire.[44]

---

[40] See Hippolytus, *Refutatio omnium haeresium* 7.27.1.

[41] In this connection I would also suggest that the Gnostic term αἰχμάλωτος in Hippolytus, *Refutatio omnium haeresium* 5.6.7 and *Gospel of Philip* 9 and 125 is drawn from this Aristotelian text.

[42] H. Staehelin, *Die gnostischen Quellen Hippolyts*, Leipzig 1890, 31, talks about a 'verblüffendes Nachspiel' and on p. 80 of 'ein überflüssiges Anhängsel'.

[43] This 'active intervention' by the non-existent God can also be understood as the ultimate phase in the realization of God's pre-ordained counsel, which takes place without any incidental interference by God himself.

[44] Matt 13.39-40: ὁ δὲ θερισμὸς συντέλεια αἰῶνός ἐστιν ... . ὥσπερ οὖν συλλέγεται τὰ ζιζάνια καὶ πυρὶ [κατα]καίεται, οὕτως ἔσται ἐν τῇ συντελείᾳ τοῦ αἰῶνος.

There is also talk of the 'furnace of fire' and 'wailing and gnashing of teeth'.[45] Basilides will have corrected this eschatological perspective as being insufficiently 'spiritual'. Basilides may have been convinced that his view was entirely consistent with the statement in the prologue to the Gospel according to John: 'the cosmos was made through him, but the cosmos did not know him.'[46]

But did Basilides perhaps follow another source of inspiration as well? The only parallel, to my knowledge, is that in 'the revelation of Silenus' to King Midas in Aristotle's lost dialogue the *Eudemus*. Silenus says there that, for beings unable to achieve the highest, it is better to possess no knowledge of it.[47] For 'hylic' beings like Midas, the 'Goldfinger' of primeval time, it is better not to find out what the highest good for people is. And this special turn in Basilides' cosmogony can only be explained by a connection with Aristotelian philosophy: the souls with rational powers are prompted by the effect of the transcendent Intellect to intellectual activity and so achieve a level of being that is entirely free (χωριστός) of any somatic, cosmic reality.

W.A. Löhr believes that this passage is 'in gewisser Spannung zum Vorhergehenden', because the Great Archon and the Lower Archon, too, will be overcome by ignorance.[48] But we could also argue that it is a consistent conclusion to Basilides' (Aristotelian) line of thought. Just as, in Hippolytus' account, Aristotle taught that in due course the soul dissolves into the ethereal sphere, after the intellect has been actualized and has abandoned the soul-body,[49] and just as Basilides asserts that the Sonship leaves behind all cosmic reality, including the holy *Pneuma*, when it unites with the transcendent God, so the 'enlightenment' of the Son of the Great Archon and of the Son of the Second Archon also means that their potential for intellectuality is realized *and* that they therefore become one with the 'first Sonship' and 'second Sonship' respectively. This must mean that they cast off all ties with the soul-body and their duality of 'entelechy with instrumental body' is transformed into the total unity of their intellect. It is therefore crucial

---

[45] Matt 13.42, 48-50.

[46] John 1.10: ὁ κόσμος δι' αὐτοῦ ἐγένετο, καὶ ὁ κόσμος αὐτὸν οὐκ ἔγνω.

[47] Aristotle, *Eudemus*, frg. 6 (Ross), 65 (Gigon): μετ' ἀγνοίας γὰρ τῶν οἰκείων κακῶν ἀλυπότατος ὁ βίος.

[48] Löhr, *Basilides und seine Schule*, 291, 299-300; earlier Staehelin, *Die gnostischen Quellen Hippolyts*, 31.

[49] Hippolytus, *Refutatio omnium haeresium* 1.20.4, 6.

to observe that, in Hippolytus' work, the Archon of the Hebdomad and the Archon of the Ogdoad are said to be overcome by *agnoia*,[50] but that the same is not said of the Sons of the Archons! As we saw, W.A. Löhr detects a certain tension between the statement that the Archons are overcome by ignorance and the statement in 7.26.2, where the Archons are said to have received instruction from their Sons.[51] But he has failed to see that this ignorance is *not* attributed to the Sons of the Archons. This is an essential point, and entirely consistent with Hippolytus' report that the Sons relate to their Fathers as the 'entelechy' relates to 'the instrumental body' in the duality of the soul according to Aristotle's formula.[52] In fact this crucial point from the eschatology of this text of Basilides or his school can only be explained as resulting from acceptance of notions from Greek philosophy, and therefore as an aspect of the 'Hellenization' of the theology that developed in the sphere of the Christian church.

On the basis of this and other information, W.A. Löhr has concluded that an original text in Hippolytus' account of Basilides underwent a later redaction. But this thesis must be rejected as unsound, because Löhr has disregarded the philosophical reasons underlying certain details of Hippolytus' report. If, on the other hand, we can reject his hypothesis of a later redaction of Hippolytus' information, this information can be viewed more positively than Löhr has done.

The 'apokatastasis' of all things

Basilides presented the phases of the Great Ignorance which comes upon the cosmos and all its parts as the '*apokatastasis* of all things'.[53] Again he uses terms which were current in contemporary philosophy and also occur in the New Testament. In Acts 3 Peter mentioned the 'time of the re-establishment of all things'.[54] Peter has in mind here the restoration of God's kingship over Israel and the world.[55] The

---

[50] Hippolytus, *Refutatio omnium haeresium* 7.27.3-4.

[51] Löhr, *Basilides und seine Schule*, 291.

[52] Hippolytus, *Refutatio omnium haeresium* 7.24.1-2.

[53] Hippolytus, *Refutatio omnium haeresium* 7.27.4: καὶ οὕτως ἡ ἀποκατάστασις ἔσται τῶν πάντων.

[54] Acts 3.21: ἄχρι χρόνων ἀποκαταστάσεως πάντων.

[55] Cf. Acts 1.6: ἐν τῷ χρόνῳ τούτῳ ἀποκαθιστάνεις τὴν βασιλείαν τῷ Ἰσραήλ;

Gnostic Basilides formed a different, more spiritual idea of the new kingdom, and does not talk about the 'apokatastasis' as the 'restoration' of an old, original situation. His starting-point in the World Seed makes this utterly impossible. A. Méhat has rightly noted that this view follows not from a cyclical but a linear conception of time, in combination with the notion of a 'broken time'.[56] The completion of all things means for Basilides that all things present in the World Seed have been brought to their 'destination' and their divinely pre-ordained location. And for some parts of the World Seed this ultimate location is very different from their original position. 'Completion' involves 'sorting out' and 'separation', segregation and discrimination. Thanks to the 'apokatastasis', the 'third Sonship' will receive its due place in the hypercosmos, to which it was entitled by virtue of its essential identity with the highest God, but which it had not yet occupied throughout world history.

Jesus as 'the first fruits of the separation'

A remarkable aspect of Hippolytus' discussion on Basilides is his presentation of Jesus as 'the first fruits of the separation (φυλοκρίνησις) of what was unseparated together'.[57] This text contains, first of all, the term 'first fruits', which has a typically Jewish and Christian colouring. 1 Corinthians 15.20 declares that Christ was raised from the dead as 'the first fruits of those who have fallen asleep'. And 1 Corinthians 15.23 uses the same term in a proclamation of the end of the world. But in Basilides Jesus is said to be 'the first fruits of the separation' of 'what was unseparated together'. In Hippolytus' discourse this clearly refers to what Hippolytus has said about the Aristotelian doctrine of *ousia*. Hippolytus there designates the species 'man' as being separated from the other species of living creatures,

---

[56] A. Méhat, '*Apokatastasis* chez Basilide', in: *Mélanges d'Histoire des Religions, offerts à Henri-Charles Puech*, sous le patronage et avec le concours du Collège de France et de la Section des Sciences Religieuses de l'École des Hautes Études, Paris 1974, 365-73 at 366 with reference to Id., '"Apocatastase": Origène, Clément d'Alexandrie, Actes 3,21', *Vigiliae Christianae* 10 (1956) 196-214. Méhat derive la notion d'un 'temps brisé' from an article by his teacher H.-C. Puech, 'La Gnose et le temps', *Eranos-Jahrbuch* 20 (1957) 57-113, esp. 87 and 60.

[57] Hippolytus, *Refutatio omnium haeresium* 7.27.8: γέγονε δὲ ταῦτα, φησίν, ἵνα ἀπαρχὴ τῆς φυλοκρινήσεως γένηται τῶν συγκεχυμένων ὁ Ἰησοῦς.

but otherwise 'unseparated together' and not yet formed into the shape of a truly existent being.[58]

On two successive pages in 7.27 Hippolytus says six more times that, according to Basilides, world history ends in a 'separation' of what was 'unseparated together'. In the first place Hippolytus says that, because the cosmos is divided into three levels, everything that was 'unseparated together' had to be separated by the separation which Jesus underwent.[59] This process results in the long-awaited purification of the third Sonship. Apparently purification of the Sonship means: separation of that hypercosmic reality from its pollution by cosmic parts.[60] Hippolytus goes on to emphasize that the entire doctrine of Basilides and Isidorus hinges on this 'being unseparated together' as of a totality of seeds, and on the separation of all that was 'unseparated together' and the restitution to their own places. And Jesus became the first fruits of this separation. His suffering served no other purpose than 'the separation' of what was 'unseparated together'.[61] Hippolytus continues by stating that 'the entire Sonship, which was left behind in formlessness ..., had to be "separated", just as Jesus was "separated"'.[62] For the sake of completeness, I mention here that the *Summary* of 10.14 says that the Power of the Gospel passed through the cosmos 'in order to enlighten and separate and purify the Sonship which had been left behind'.[63]

This rather striking term was apparently a central concept for Basilides.[64] In fact Hippolytus uses the term only in his account of

---

[58] Hippolytus, *Refutatio omnium haeresium* 7.18.1: τὸν δὲ ἄνθρωπον εἶδος, τῶν πολλῶν ζῴων ἤδη κεχωρισμένον, [ἔτι] συγκεχυμένον δὲ ὅμως ἔτι.

[59] Hippolytus, *Refutatio omnium haeresium* 7.27.9: ἀναγκαῖον ἦν τὰ συγκεχυμένα φυλοκρι<νη>θῆναι διὰ τῆς τοῦ Ἰησοῦ διαιρέσεως (Marcovich).

[60] We will therefore have to assume that the Son of the Great Archon and the Son of the Lower Archon each contained a part of this third Sonship that 'required purification' and that this part also 'separated' through Enlightenment.

[61] Hippolytus, *Refutatio omnium haeresium* 7.27.11: Ὅλη δὲ αὐτῶν ἡ ὑπόθεσις σύγχυσις οἱονεὶ πανσπερμίας καὶ φυλοκρίνησις καὶ ἀποκατάστασις τῶν συγκεχυμένων εἰς τὰ οἰκεῖα. τῆς οὖν φυλοκρινήσεως ἀπαρχὴ γέγονεν ὁ Ἰησοῦς, καὶ τὸ πάθος οὐκ ἄλλου τινὸς χάριν γέγονεν <ἀλλ' ἢ> ὑπὲρ τοῦ φυλοκρινηθῆναι τὰ συγκεχυμένα.

[62] Hippolytus, *Refutatio omnium haeresium* 7.27.12: φησὶν ὅλην τὴν υἱότητα, τὴν καταλελειμμένην ἐν τῇ ἀμορφίᾳ ... δεῖν φυλοκρι<νη>θῆναι, ᾧ τρόπῳ καὶ ὁ Ἰησοῦς πεφυλοκρίνηται.

[63] Hippolytus, *Refutatio omnium haeresium* 10.14.9: ἐπὶ τῷ φωτίσαι καὶ φυλοκρινῆσαι καὶ καθαρίσαι τὴν καταλελειμμένην υἱότητα.

[64] Méhat, '*Apokatastasis* chez Basilide', 369 note 2 also calls it a 'mot technique de la doctrine basilidienne, sans nul doute'.

Basilides. Basilides seems to have used the term in a conception in which the separation at issue in the doctrine of the gospel is an onto-logical separation, and not a separation of differences in direction or orientation.[65] This is a central point in the controversy between Christian proclamation and Greek philosophy (plus Gnosticism). Where the gospel presents a decisive choice for orientation to and service of God, the Origin, (in which God's spirit constantly directs man to the Creator) and rejection of the desires of 'the flesh' (as an orientation to the world and all that goes with it), Greek philosophy plus Gnosticism puts the emphasis on an ontological extraction of 'the truly divine' in mortal man and separation of it from the cosmic elements which together form the one concrete human being.

It is quite important in this connection that Clement of Alexandria uses the same term twice, and not coincidentally when talking about Basilides! Clement mentions that Basilides' explanation of the biblical text 'The fear of the Lord is the beginning of wisdom'[66] states that the Archon was dismayed when he heard the ministering *Pneuma* utter these words, and that he discerned the gospel through what he heard and saw. And his dismay was called 'fear' and it became the beginning of the wisdom which brought about 'separation' and discrimination and completion and restitution.[67] In 38.2 Clement makes it again clear that, for Basilides, 'fear' was the beginning of the 'separation' of the elect from cosmic reality.[68] Much more could be said about this passage

---

[65] On this distinction, cf. A.M. Wolters, *Creation Regained: Biblical Basics For a Reformational Worldview*, Grand Rapids, MI 1985, 49-56 and chap. 5: 'Discerning structure and direction', 72-95.

[66] See Clement, *Stromateis* 2.8.36.1, with reference to the biblical text in Prov 1.7, which he has quoted in 35.5, following on from a quotation of the *Letter of Barnabas*.

[67] Clement, *Stromateis* 2.8.36.1: Ἐνταῦθα οἱ ἀμφὶ τὸν Βασιλείδην τοῦτο ἐξηγούμενοι τὸ ῥητὸν αὐτόν φασιν Ἄρχοντα ἐπακούσαντα τὴν φάσιν τοῦ διακονουμένου πνεύματος ἐκπλαγῆναι τῷ τε ἀκούσματι καὶ τῷ θεάματι παρ' ἐλπίδας εὐηγγελισμένον, καὶ τὴν ἔκπληξιν αὐτοῦ φόβον κληθῆναι ἀρχὴν γενόμενον σοφίας φυλοκρινητικῆς τε καὶ διακριτικῆς καὶ τελεωτικῆς καὶ ἀποκαταστατικῆς. Löhr, *Basilides und seine Schule*, 61, translates: 'der Anfang einer auswählenden ... Weisheit', but adds in note 2 that 'able to distinguish', as G.W.H. Lampe, *A Patristic Greek Lexicon*, proposes, is also pos-sible. Cf. also p. 71. Méhat, '*Apokatastasis* chez Basilide', 368 translates φάσιν here as 'manifestation'.

[68] Clement, *Stromateis* 2.8.38.2: οὐδ' ἂν ἀρχὴν σοφίας ἐκ τοῦ φόβου ἔλαβεν εἰς τὴν φυλοκρίνησιν τῆς τε ἐκλογῆς τῶν τε κοσμικῶν. Méhat, '*Apokatastasis* chez Basilide', 369 note 2 observes that the terms φυλοκρινητική and φυλοκριτική are *hapax legomena* in Clement.

and the texts in Hippolytus' account. It seems natural to assume that Clement is going back to the same source here as Hippolytus.[69]

But it is more important to ask why Basilides, for the process of 'separation', which might also have been described by terms like διάκρισις or χωρισμός, apparently chooses a word which is rare in classical Greek and usually has the sense of 'to be registered with a tribe'.[70]

This striking terminological preference should make us consider that Basilides may have used this term to link up with a biblical eschatological theme, the judgement of the tribes of Israel. In Matt 19 the Saviour promises to his disciples: 'In the new world, when the Son of man shall sit on his glorious throne, you will also sit on twelve thrones, *in order to judge the* twelve *tribes* of Israel.'[71] We find a parallel statement in Luke.[72]

This conjecture is supported by Hippolytus, who refers to this gospel passage in describing the doctrine of the Naassenes and explains the refusal of many listeners to accept the gospel by the following remark: 'For what is contrary to nature for them is what is not according to their tribe.'[73] In Saturnilus we find the expression 'to ascend to what is of the same tribe'.[74]

If this conjecture is right, it confirms the existence of a remarkable relation between Basilides' theology and the text of the Gospel of Matthew.

---

[69] Cf. Méhat, '*Apokatastasis* chez Basilide', 369.

[70] It is striking that the verb φυλοκρινέω occurs in Aristotle, *Atheniensium Respublica* 21.2.

[71] Matt 19.28: ἐν τῇ παλιγγενεσίᾳ ... καθήσεσθε καὶ ὑμεῖς ἐπὶ δώδεκα θρόνους κρίνοντες τὰς δώδεκα φυλὰς τοῦ Ἰσραήλ. This text is quoted in *Pistis Sophia* 1.50.

[72] Luke 22.30: καθήσεσθε ἐπὶ θρόνων τὰς δώδεκα φυλὰς κρίνοντες τοῦ Ἰσραήλ. This hypothesis was proposed by Méhat, '*Apokatastasis* chez Basilide', 369 note 2. Löhr, *Basilides und seine Schule*, 71 note 41 rejects it for no good reason.

[73] Hippolytus, *Refutatio omnium haeresium* 5.8.12: ἔστι γὰρ αὐτοῖς παρὰ φύσιν τὰ μὴ κατὰ φυλήν.

[74] Hippolytus, *Refutatio omnium haeresium* 7.28.4: ἀνατρέχειν πρὸς τὰ ὁμόφυλα λέγει.

Conclusions and further considerations regarding Hippolytus' description of the doctrine of Basilides

The claim by J. Frickel[75] that Hippolytus made the connection between Basilides' doctrine and the philosophy of the pagan philosopher Aristotle, but that Basilides himself did not explicitly refer to Aristotle, should be accepted. This is not to say, however, that Aristotle's thought had no influence on Basilides. On the contrary. Some crucial features of Basilides' doctrine can only be adequately explained against the background of Aristotle's theology, noology, and psychology.[76]

Examples of crucial parts of Basilides which show the influence of Aristotle's philosophy are:

1. His theology. Basilides' highest, non-existent God is completely transcendent, 'exalted above every name'; he does not in any way form part of the cosmos; he is purely final goal; he is, however, the entity which contrives and controls all things; all other reality, in a way appropriate to it, has a desire (ὄρεξις) for this highest God; this God is not an efficient cause in the sense that Plato's Demiurge seems to be; he is, however, the Begetter of all things, through the production of a World Seed; he does not make a cosmos 'most like' (ὅμοιος) to himself,[77] but begets a Sonship that is 'of the same essence' (ὁμοούσιος).

This God is the source of Life and Power and of the Light that eventually severs the bonds of cosmic existence.

2. His psychology. The soul is understood to be cosmic and bound up with materiality; as such it is the principle of motion and production. On the cosmic level the Archons stand for psychic beings, the efficient cause of all generation; they do not possess the all-embracing Knowledge regarding the highest God, but a limited knowledge, though, without knowing it, they do carry out the counsel of the highest God.

On the microcosmic level the soul is the principle of vegetative, animal, and rational life.

---

[75] Cf. J. Frickel, *Die 'Apophasis Megale' in Hippolyt's Refutatio (VI 9-18): Eine Paraphrase zur Apophasis Simons*, Rome 1968.

[76] Cf. G.P. Luttikhuizen, 'Traces of Aristotelian Thought in the *Apocryphon of John*', in: H.-G. Bethge et al. (eds), *For the Children, Perfect Instruction: Studies in honour of Hans-Martin Schenke*, Leiden 2002, 181-202.

[77] Cf. Plato, *Timaeus* 29E3.

An essential element here is that this psychic human being sometimes possesses a capacity for higher knowledge as a potentiality of
this soul. But actualization of this potentiality, as in Aristotle's theory
of the soul's capacity for intellectuality, leads to separation of this
spiritual principle from the soul of which the spiritual principle was
a potentiality!

Basilides' theory on how the second Sonship leaves behind the
'holy *Pneuma*' is entirely parallel with Aristotle's theory on how the
intellect which has achieved actualization separates from the soul and
the soul-body of which it was a potentiality.

3. The concept of world history as a process in which increasingly
higher and more perfect potentialities develop from a first principle
regarded as the World Seed.

4. The theme of the Great Ignorance as the final condition of all
cosmic reality and the total separation of hypercosmic reality in relation to cosmic reality.

5. The notion that supralunary reality is governed providentially
and rationally, and sublunary reality is not.

6. More comprehensively, we should consider that Basilides' doctrine
of the tripartite Sonship, like all theories about a bipartite or tripartite *Anthrôpos* myth, are transformations, in Jewish and early Christian
contexts, of the myth of Dionysus which Aristotle elaborated in his
lost dialogue *Eudemus or On the Soul* and which had a distinctly Orphic
character.

In his well-known 1962 book *Der Gott 'Mensch'*, H.-M. Schenke
strongly disputed the theory of R. Reitzenstein and others about a
primal myth of a God 'Man', which was supposedly passed down in
various Gnostic variants.[78] His alternative was to see this Gnostic myth,
both in its pre-Christian version of the *Poimandres* and in its Christian-
izing forms, as deriving from the allegorizing exegesis of Genesis 1.27.
For Schenke, this meant support for the school of interpretation which
viewed these Jewish beliefs as a central factor in the development of
Gnosticism. But perhaps we should go even further back and investigate
whether the origin of Gnostic theology in fact lies in Greek philosophy,
in particular in the myth of the alienation of Dionysus, the young
son of God, from his father, through his entrance into the sphere of

---

[78] H.-M. Schenke, *Der Gott 'Mensch' in der Gnosis: Ein religionsgeschichtlicher Beitrag zur
Diskussion über die paulinische Anschauung von der Kirche als Leib Christi*, Göttingen 1962.

the cosmic Titans and, next, his descent into the sublunary sphere of nature and mortality. Such a myth with a strong Orphic colouring was presented at length in Aristotle's dialogue *Eudemus*. Traces of it have been found by J. Pépin in the work of Philo of Alexandria.[79]

Basilides seems to have given himself room for an adaptation of this myth by positing, like Philo of Alexandria,[80] that just as man is an image of the divine Logos, so the cosmos writ large must likewise be such an image. In this way he replaced the biblical view on man by a Greek philosophical anthropogony in connection with a cosmogony.[81]

---

[79] Cf. Pépin, 'La légende orphique', 391 note 10, with reference to Philo of Alexandria, *Legum allegoriae* 3.69-74; 1.33, 108; *De Gigantibus* 3, 15; *De agricultura* 5, 25; *De migratione Abrahami* 5, 21; *Quis heres* 12, 58, 61, 309 (cf. M. Harl, Introduction, 44 note 2); *De somniis* 2.36, 237; *Quaestiones in Genesim* 1.93.

[80] Philo, *De opificio mundi* 25.

[81] I would like to thank J.L. de Jong, M.A., in Papendrecht and my brother, Dr C.A. Bos in Zwolle, for their valuable contributions to the realization of this article.

EARLY CHRISTIAN APOCRYPHA AND THE SECRET BOOKS OF ANCIENT EGYPT

Jacobus van Dijk

In his recent book on the multiplicity of the earliest forms of Christianity, Gerard Luttikhuizen has reminded us again that the original meaning of the word 'apocryphal' is not so much 'uncanonical', but rather 'hidden', 'secret', referring to the secret or esoteric character of the composition to which this term is applied.[1] Thus the opening lines of *The Apocryphon of John* state that this book contains 'the teachings and the sayings of the Saviour' which he revealed to John 'as a mystery (μυστήριον) which is hidden in silence (ⲛⲉⲧϩⲏⲡ ϩⲛ ⲟⲩⲙⲛⲧ-ⲕⲁⲣⲱϥ)'.[2] These full and definitive teachings of the risen Jesus[3] are only to be passed on 'secretly' (ϩⲛ ⲟⲩϩⲱⲡ) to John's fellow believers,[4] and at the end of the text there is a strict prohibition on divulging this μυστήριον to the uninitiated: 'Cursed is anyone who will give it away for a present or for food or drink or clothing or any other such thing',[5] a prohibition also found in *The Book of the Great Mysterious Logos* in the Codex Brucianus, where Jesus says:

> These mysteries which I will reveal to you, safeguard them and do not give them away to anybody unless they are worthy of them. Do not give them away to father or mother, brother or sister or (any other) relatives, not for food or drink, nor for the sake of a woman, nor for gold or silver, or for anything at all in the world.[6]

In the *Apocryphal Epistle of James* the author speaks of a 'secret text' (ἀπόκρυφον) written in Hebrew script which the recipient of the letter is urged not to divulge to the masses since the Saviour himself did not

---

[1] Luttikhuizen 2002, 34-7. On the various meanings of the word 'apocryphal' see e.g. Frey 1928, 355; Schneemelcher 1991, 13-15.

[2] Krause and Labib 1962, 109 (Nag Hammadi Codex II) and 201 (Codex IV).

[3] As opposed to the incomplete and provisional teaching before his death and resurrection, see Luttikhuizen 1988, 161-2.

[4] Krause and Labib 1962, 198.

[5] Krause and Labib 1962, 198-9 (Codex II); Till 1955, 193 (Codex Berolinensis).

[6] Schmidt 1892, 100 (text), 194 (translation).

even reveal it to all of his disciples, but only to John and Peter.[7] The two books ascribed to Thomas are both said to contain 'the hidden (ⲉⲑⲏⲡ) sayings which the living Jesus (var. the Saviour) spoke'; the *Gospel of Thomas* even assures the reader that 'whosoever will find the explanation (ἑρμηνεία) of these sayings will not taste death.'[8]

In early Christian literature this type of statement appears to be limited to documents found in Egypt written in either Greek[9] or Coptic. Gnostic texts in particular appear in this respect to continue the tradition of Egyptian Hellenistic 'secret' books, the most famous of which is the *Corpus Hermeticum*,[10] and the Greek magical papyri.[11] The tradition of secret religious texts in Egypt is much older than Hellenistic times, however, and goes back as far as the age of the pyramid builders. It is to these Ancient Egyptian 'apocrypha' that the following brief remarks are devoted, in the hope that they will please the learned dedicatee of this volume.

The Egyptian equivalent of the Coptic word ϩⲱⲡ 'be hidden', 'hide'[12] used in some of the texts quoted above is *ḥȝp*. In a religious context this word is often used to describe the mummification and burial of Osiris who is hidden in the mysterious abode (*štȝw*) of the underworld. The ritual texts which are meant to revivify him are also 'hidden'; thus *The Book of Breathing* 'made by Isis for her brother Osiris in order to revivify his body and rejuvenate all his limbs', the oldest manuscripts of which date from the third century BC, addresses its owner: 'Keep it secret! Keep it secret! (*ḥȝp ḥȝp*) Do not let anybody else read it! It is effective for a man in the netherworld so that he will live again. Proven truly efficacious a million times.'[13] Far more common in religious texts than *ḥȝp*, however, are the adjective *štȝ* 'secret', 'mysterious', 'hidden', the verb *sštȝ* 'hide', 'conceal', and the noun *(s)štȝ(w)* 'secret', 'mystery'. This word has become obsolete in Coptic, where it survives only in the name for the planet Jupiter (ϩ(ⲁ)ⲣ-ϣⲱⲧ), *ḥrw-*

---

[7] Rouleau 1987, 32-3.

[8] Nag Hammadi Codex II, 32 and 138, resp.; cf. Meyer 1986, 32 and 41.

[9] Cf. Luttikhuizen 2002, 161 note 98.

[10] See Cumont 1937, 151-63, esp. 153 note 2, 154 note 1 and 155 note 2.

[11] Leipoldt and Morenz 1953, 92; Betz 1995. On the problem of survivals from Ancient Egypt in Coptic texts in general see the excellent survey in Behlmer 1996.

[12] Crum 1939, 695a; Černý 1976, 290.

[13] Coenen and Quaegebeur 1995, 72-3. A copy of this book (Pap. Joseph Smith I) became the fanciful *Book of Abraham* of the Mormons.

p3-št3 'Horus the Mysterious One') and in some other etymologically related words;[14] indeed, in Coptic texts the meaning of *št3(w)* appears to be covered by the Greek μυστήριον and by various derivations of the verb (ἀπο)κρύπτειν.[15] This is not the place to examine the wide range of meanings of the word *št3* and its derivations in detail, however; references to the relevant pages of the *Wörterbuch der aegyptischen Sprache*[16] and to the lemma 'Geheimnis' in the *Lexikon der Ägyptologie*[17] will suffice to give the interested reader an idea.

Secrecy is a phenomenon found in many religions,[18] and Ancient Egypt is no exception. The main purpose of the official cult in the state temples, in which the divine king plays a central role, is the maintenance of the cosmic order (*m3't*) which had been established at the beginning of time by the creator god by means of a perpetual cycle of daily rituals. These rites are a secret affair and the temples in which they are performed are accessible only to the king and the initiated priests who replace him, not to the ordinary Egyptians. Not only these rites are *št3*, 'secret', but so are the gods themselves, their images, shapes and forms, their names and their nature. The rituals perpetually re-enact the daily cycle of death and rebirth of the sun-god on his journey along the heavens and through the underworld, and this journey as well as the roads, portals and localities which he passes are all frequently called 'mysterious' or 'secret'. It is not surprising, therefore, to find that the ritual texts recited in the temple cult and the hymns sung for the gods as well as the papyrus rolls and writing boards on which they have been inscribed are also called secret. Thus the walls of the temple of Hibis, which dates from the time of Darius I, record 'the great secret hymns to Amun which are on the writing boards of *nebes* wood' and 'the great and secret hymn to Amun-Re spoken by the Eight Primaeval Gods'.[19] In Edfu, specialized priests were in charge of 'the secret spells of your majesty (i.e. the god Horus)';[20] when the rituals in the roof kiosk were performed they recited 'the

---

[14] Westendorf 1965-77, 328–30; Černý 1976, 254-5.

[15] Cf. Rudolph 1995, 271.

[16] *Wb.* IV, 296-300 (*sšt3*) and 551-5 (*sšt3(w)*).

[17] Altenmüller 1977. See also Schott 1990, 514 s.v. *sšt3* and 521 s.v. *št3*.

[18] See for the ancient Mediterranean world the essays collected in Kippenberg and Stroumsa 1995 and for the role of secret books in these cultures Leipoldt and Morenz 1953, 88-114.

[19] Davies 1953, pls. 31-32. On 'secret' hymns see Assmann 1995.

[20] Rochemonteix and Chassinat 1897, 568 [112].

secret spells for ascending the roof of the temple'[21] and the rites of 'overthrowing the enemies' were also performed according to 'the secret book of rituals'.[22]

Actual copies of such books of overthrowing the enemies have survived in several papyri dating from about the fourth century BC. They almost certainly originally belonged to a temple library, but they derive from tombs and must at some stage have been appropriated by private individuals for their use in the hereafter. One of these compositions, written in the classical Middle Egyptian language which even at this late time was still used for sacred texts, is accompanied in one copy by a 'translation' or 'explanation' in Late Egyptian. This book is entitled 'The Explanation of *The Secrets of the Ritual of Repulsing the Evil One* which is performed for the Temple of Osiris, Foremost of the West, the Great God, Lord of Abydos, in order to repulse Seth in his rage, in order to keep Seth away from Osiris'.[23] A similar composition, one of several texts preserved in the Bremner-Rhind Papyrus, is *The Secret Book of Overthrowing Apophis*, the primaeval archenemy of the sun-god Re. This book also explains the reason why it is secret: it deals with the mystery of the daily rebirth of the sun-god and his creation which Apophis is trying in vain to prevent: 'It is beneficial for a man when he knows this nature of Re and his transformations;[24] he will triumph over his enemies. It is a secret book of the House of Life (the temple scriptorium) which no eye is allowed to see, the Secret Book of Overthrowing Apophis.'[25]

This connection between secrecy and the mystery of creation and the renewal of life is made even more explicit in another famous papyrus from the same period, Papyrus Salt 825. The daily rebirth of the sun-god is the result of his mysterious unification with the body of the god Osiris which he encounters during his nocturnal voyage through the underworld. The mutual embrace of the two gods results in the resurrection of Osiris in the form of his son Horus and in the rebirth

---

[21] Rochemonteix and Chassinat 1897, 567-8 [101-102].

[22] Rochemonteix and Chassinat 1897, 557 [53].

[23] Schott 1929, 61.10-13; see also Schott 1954, especially 38-53 ('Die Übersetzung als Deutung').

[24] The *Book of Caverns*, inscribed on the walls of the royal tombs of the New Kingdom, which describes the nocturnal journey of the sun-god through the underworld, is called 'The Secret Book of Transformations', Piankoff 1944, pl. 60.III.

[25] Faulkner 1933, 73.15-74.2; Faulkner 1938, 42; Gardiner 1938, 169 (36).

of the sun-god, who emerges from the underworld in the morning as Re-Horakhty, 'Re-Horus-of-the-Horizon'. This one might call the central dogma of Egyptian religion on which the continued existence of the universe and of all human life depends, a matter of life and death. One of the compositions contained in Papyrus Salt 825 is a book with the somewhat obscure title *The End of the Work*. It begins as follows:

> The magical book *The End of the Work*. First month of the inundation season, day 20. The day on which books are received and books are sent and on which life and death emerge. One prepares the book *The End of the Work* on it, the secret book of counteracting magic, of tying knots and fastening knots, and of casting fear among the entire universe. Life is in it and death is in it. Do not reveal it, for whoever will reveal it will die a sudden death through being assassinated at once. You must keep well and truly away from it, for life and death are in it.[26]

Further on, the papyrus states that 'the mysteries of the writings of *The End of the Work*' are designed 'to rescue him' (the god and/or the user of the text) from his enemy,[27] and at the end of the text it is said that 'he who will reveal it will die by being assassinated, for it is a great mystery, it is Re, it is Osiris'.[28]

With these temple rituals reused for funerary purposes we enter the vast repertoire of Ancient Egyptian funerary literature. The texts from which we have just quoted were able to be reused by private individuals because the deceased constantly identifies himself with both Re and Osiris: Re's rebirth is his own rebirth, Osiris's resurrection is his resurrection and the gods' enemies are his enemies who threaten to prevent the perpetual renewal of his life after death. The funerary spells found in collections like *The Book of Leaving (the Underworld) by Day*, commonly known as the Book of the Dead, are frequently called 'secret'. Even during the Old Kingdom, when identification of the deceased with Re or Osiris appears to have been restricted to the divine king, we hear of 'the lector-priest who will perform for me the rites through which the blessed spirit is glorified according to that secret writing of the art of the lector-priest',[29] and 'the lector-priest who will read (litt.

---

[26] pSalt 825, V.9-VI.3; Derchain 1965, 139.
[27] pSalt 825, XIV.8-9; Derchain 1965, 142.
[28] pSalt 825, XVIII.1-2; Derchain 1965, 144.
[29] Sethe 1933, 186.14-15; cf. Junker 1947, 119. Similarly in the tomb of Ankhma-hor at Saqqara, Sethe 1933, 202.15-16. Cf. Weber 1969, 113-14.

"see") the secret words of the divine writings'.[30] In the tomb of the
lector-priest Khentika Ikhekhi he says: 'I was initiated into every secret
of the House of the Sacred Books of the *snw*[*t*-shrine]' as well as 'into
every secret of the work of the embalmer.'[31] A colophon added to
an obscure spell from the Middle Kingdom Coffin Texts also refers
to these secret rituals: 'This spell is to be written inside (the coffin?),
for the benefit of (??) the Hidden One (*sšt3*, i.e. the deceased), being a
secret (*št3*) of the senior lector-priest.'[32]

The deceased for whom the lector-priest recites his secret spells
becomes an *3ḫ*, a 'blessed spirit' who is 'well-equipped' ('*pr*) with religious knowledge and 'able' (*iḳr*) to act on behalf of those who live on
earth.[33] The summary version of the *Book of the Hidden Room* (Amduat),
the illustrated description of the journey of the sun-god through the
underworld inscribed inside the royal tombs of the New Kingdom,
is called

> The exclusive guide, the secret book of the underworld, which no-one
> knows except the happy few. This image is made accordingly in the con-
> cealment of the underworld, not to be seen, not to be beheld. He who
> knows these secret images is a well-equipped spirit. He is able to leave
> the underworld and come back to it and to speak to the living.[34]

Spell 148 in the Book of the Dead of Queen Nodjmet is also called
'A Book of Secrets of What is in the Underworld (and of) making the
blessed spirit able in the heart of Re'. On earth ordinary human beings
had no access to the gods in the temples, which were the exclusive
domain of king and priests, but in the hereafter the undivided world
which existed at the beginning of creation is restored and the deceased
is united with the gods. The spells in the Book of the Dead are meant
to initiate the deceased into this 'secret' world, just as priests on earth
had to be initiated before they could serve the gods in their temples.
Thus Spell 15B is called a 'secret spell of the Underworld, a secret
initiation in the god's domain, seeing the sun-disk when he sets (in
life) in the West and when he is being adored by the gods and the
blessed spirits of the Underworld, making the blessed deceased able

---

[30] Junker 1944, 233; cf. a similar text on p. 235.
[31] James 1953, pl. V, A9 and B11-12, resp.
[32] De Buck 1956, 194h-j (rubric of Spell 578); the spell is inscribed on the bottom
of the coffin.
[33] See on these notions Demarée 1983, 189-278.
[34] Hornung 1967, 26, 35.

in the heart of Re'. One manuscript replaces the beginning of this title with 'a spell for leaving (the underworld) by day', the title often given to the whole of the Book of the Dead.

The exclusive, restricted nature of this initiation is stressed in several spells. Spell 101 is 'a book for understanding the words (of the House of Life) ... to be hung around the neck of this blessed deceased without letting the word go round, not letting the mob know it, not letting an eye see it or an ear hear it'. The colophon of Spell 137A warns: 'Be very careful not to use it (i.e. the spell) for anyone except yourself, not even for your father or your son,[35] for it is a great secret of the West, a mystery of the underworld', it is 'to be used in the concealment of the underworld', being 'a secret of the underworld, a secret initiation in the god's domain'.[36] An appendix to Spell 148 which also occurs as a separate spell (Spell 190) further specifies the people who are not allowed to know or use these secret texts:

> Use it without letting anybody see (read) it except your truly trusted friend and the lector-priest who is with you, without letting any other person see it, let alone the servant who comes from outside (*iyi.w m rwty*), for it is a truly secret book which is not to be known to the mob of all people for ever.

A Ptolemaic addition to Spell 161 also says that 'he who is from outside (*nty m rwty*) is not allowed to know (this spell), for it is a secret, which the mob is not to know. Do not use it for anybody else, not even your father or your mother, except yourself. It is a real secret, nobody is allowed to know it.'[37] The mob (*h3w-mr*) are the great unwashed, the uninitiated rank and file of the populace, but 'he who is from outside' is even more sinister: this term refers to the enemies of the god and of the deceased, who belong to the chaotic world outside the created universe and who constantly threaten to upset the order of creation.[38]

---

[35] In the Book of the Dead of Any these words are inserted in the colophon to Spell 133.

[36] Cf. also Spell 144: 'use this book without letting anyone see it'; Spell 147: 'Do not use (it) for anyone (else)! Be very careful!'; Spell 156: 'Do not let anybody else see (= read) it, for there is nothing like it'. Similar statements can also be found in magical texts for use on earth, e.g. Pap. Chester Beatty VIII vs. 7.7 ('take good care of this book ... do not let someone else peruse it') or Mag. Pap. Harris VI.10 ('do not reveal it to other people, for it is a secret of the House of Life'), but they are not nearly as common as one might expect, perhaps because such restrictions are not very practical in spells against snakes, scorpions or crocodiles.

[37] Allen 1960, 284, pl. 49, col. clvi.9–12.

[38] Heerma van Voss 1973.

426 JACOBUS VAN DIJK

These phrases are echoed in the passage in the Codex Brucianus from which we quoted at the beginning of this article, where it is said that it is forbidden to reveal the mysteries even to one's father or mother, brother or sister, and which then continues: 'do not reveal it ... to any human being who is an adherent of the belief (πίστις) in the seventy-two archontes or to those who serve them, and do not reveal it to those who serve the Eighth Power (δύναμις) of the Great Archon', who claim that they possess the true knowledge and revere the true god, but whose god is evil.[39]

Revealing the mysteries to the enemies of creation would threaten its very existence and safeguarding these secrets is therefore essential. Another Ptolemaic addition to the Book of the Dead, this time to Spell 162, says: 'This is a book great of secrets. Do not let anyone see it, for that is taboo. He who knows it and keeps it secret (ḥȝp sy) will live again.'[40] The deceased who follows these directions 'shall not perish forever, his Ba shall live on for ever' (BD 137A), he 'shall exist there (i.e. in the hereafter) as Lord of Eternity in one body with Osiris' (BD Spell 147). These passages again refer to the mystery of the nocturnal unification of Re and Osiris, and the privileged knowledge of this great secret enables the deceased to gain eternal life, or, as the Gospel of Thomas says, 'he who knows its explanation will not taste death'.

Bibliography

Allen, T.G. 1960. *The Egyptian Book of the Dead Documents in the Oriental Institute Museum at the University of Chicago* (Oriental Institute Publications 82), Chicago.

Altenmüller, H. 1977. 'Geheimnis', in: W. Helck and W. Westendorf, *Lexikon der Ägyptologie*, Wiesbaden, ii, 510-13.

Assmann, J. 1995. 'Unio liturgica. Die kultische Einstimmung in götterweltlichen Lobpreis als Grundmotiv "esoterischer" Überlieferung im alten Ägypten', in: Kippenberg & Stroumsa 1995, 37-60.

Behlmer, H. 1996. 'Ancient Egyptian Survivals in Coptic Literature: an Overview', in: A. Loprieno (ed.), *Ancient Egyptian Literature: History and Forms* (Probleme der Ägyptologie 10), Leiden, 567-90.

Betz, H.D. 1995. 'Secrecy in the Greek Magical Papyri', in: Kippenberg & Stroumsa 1995, 153-75.

Černý, J. 1976. *Coptic Etymological Dictionary*, Cambridge.

Coenen, M. and J. Quaegebeur. 1995. *De Papyrus Denon in het Museum Meermanno-Westreenianum, Den Haag, of Het Boek van het Ademen van Isis* (Monografieën van het Museum van het Boek 5), Louvain.

---

[39] Cf. note 6 above.
[40] Allen 1960, 285, pl. 49, col. clvii.38-39.

Crum, W.E. 1939. *A Coptic Dictionary*, Oxford.

Cumont, F. 1937. *L'Égypte des astrologues*, Brussels.

Davies, N. de Garis 1953. *The Temple of Hibis in el Khargeh Oasis*, iii, *The Decoration* (Egyptian Expedition 17), New York.

De Buck, A. 1956. *The Ancient Egyptian Coffin Texts*, vi (Oriental Institute Publications 81), Chicago.

Demarée, R.J. 1983. *The ꜣḫ ỉḳr n Rꜥ-stelae: On Ancestor Worship in Ancient Egypt* (Egyptologische Uitgaven 3), Leiden.

Derchain, P. 1965. *Le papyrus Salt 825 (B.M. 10051), rituel pour la conservation de la vie en Égypte* (Académie Royale de Belgique, Classe des Lettres, Mémoires, Deuxième série: 58.1), Brussels.

Faulkner, R.O. 1933. *The Papyrus Bremner-Rhind (British Museum No. 10188)* (Bibliotheca Aegyptiaca 3), Brussels.

Faulkner, R.O. 1938. 'The Bremner-Rhind Papyrus – IV', *Journal of Egyptian Archaeology* 24 (1938) 41-53.

Frey, J.B. 1928. 'Apocryphes de l'Ancien Testament: Généralités sur le sens du mot apocryphe et sur les apocryphes', in: *Dictionnaire de la Bible, Supplément 1*, Paris, 354-7.

Gardiner, A.H. 1938. 'The House of Life', *Journal of Egyptian Archaeology* 24 (1938) 157-79.

Heerma van Voss, M. 1973. 'Wie buiten is', *Phœnix* 19 (1973) 282-4.

Hornung, E. 1967. *Das Amduat, die Schrift des Verborgenen Raumes*, iii, *Die Kurzfassung: Nachträge* (Ägyptologische Abhandlungen 13), Wiesbaden.

James, T.G.H. 1953. *The Mastaba of Khentika called Ikhekhi* (Archaeological Survey of Egypt 30), London.

Junker, H. 1944. *Bericht über die Grabungen ... auf dem Friedhof des Alten Reiches bei den Pyramiden von Gîza*, vii (Akademie der Wissenschaften in Wien, Phil.-hist. Klasse, Denkschriften 72.3), Vienna.

Junker, H. 1947. *Bericht über die Grabungen ... auf dem Friedhof des Alten Reiches bei den Pyramiden von Gîza*, viii (Akademie der Wissenschaften in Wien, Phil.-hist. Klasse, Denkschriften 73.1), Vienna.

Kippenberg, H.G. and G.G. Stroumsa (eds) 1995. *Secrecy and Concealment: Studies in the History of Mediterranean and Near Eastern Religions* (Studies in the History of Religions; Numen Book Series 65), Leiden.

Krause, M. and P. Labib 1962. *Die drei Versionen des Apokryphon des Johannes im Koptischen Museum zu Alt-Kairo* (Archäologische Veröffentlichungen des Deutschen Archäologischen Instituts Abteilung Kairo, Koptische Reihe 1), Wiesbaden.

Leipoldt, J. and S. Morenz 1953. *Heilige Schriften: Betrachtungen zur Religionsgeschichte der antiken Mittelmeerwelt*, Leipzig.

Luttikhuizen, G.P. 1988. 'The Evaluation of the Teaching of Jesus in Christian Gnostic Revelation Dialogues', *Novum Testamentum* 30 (1988) 158-68.

Luttikhuizen, G.P. 2002. *De veelvormigheid van het vroegste christendom*, Delft.

Meyer, M.W. 1986. *The Secret Teachings of Jesus: Four Gnostic Gospels*, New York.

Piankoff, A. 1944. 'Le Livre des Quererets [II]', *Bulletin de l'Institut Français d'Archéologie Orientale* 42 (1944) 1-62.

Rochemonteix, Marquis de and É. Chassinat 1897. *Le temple d'Edfou*, i (Mémoires publiés par les membres de la Mission archéologique française au Caire 10), Paris.

Rouleau, D. 1987. *L'Épître apocryphe de Jacques (NH I, 2)* (Bibliothèque copte de Nag Hammadi, Section 'Textes' 18), Quebec.

Rudolph, K. 1995. 'Geheimnis und Geheimhaltung in der antiken Gnosis und im Manichäismus', in: Kippenberg & Stroumsa 1995, 265-87.

Schneemelcher, W. 1991. 'The concepts: canon, testament, apocrypha', in: E. Hennecke and W. Schneemelcher (eds), *New Testament Apocrypha*, i, Cambridge/Louisville (Second, revised edition), 10-15.

Schmidt, C. 1892. *Gnostische Schriften in koptischer Sprache aus dem Codex Brucianus* (Texte und Untersuchungen zur Geschichte der altchristlichen Literatur 8), Berlin.

Schott, S. 1929. *Urkunden mythologischen Inhalts*, i, *Bücher und Sprüche gegen den Gott Seth* (Urkunden des aegyptischen Altertums 6), Leipzig.

Schott, S. 1954. *Die Deutung der Geheimnisse des Rituals für die Abwehr des Bösen: Eine altägyptische Übersetzung* (Akademie der Wissenschaften und der Literatur in Mainz, Abhandlungen der geistes- und sozialwissenschaftlichen Klasse, Jahrgang 1954; 5), Mainz/Wiesbaden.

Schott, E. 1990. *Bücher und Bibliotheken im Alten Ägypten: Verzeichnis der Buch- und Spruchtitel und der termini technici*, Wiesbaden.

Till, W.C. 1955. *Die gnostischen Schriften des koptischen Papyrus Berolinensis 8502* (Texte und Untersuchungen zur Geschichte der altchristlichen Literatur 60), Berlin.

Weber, M. 1969. *Beiträge zur Kenntnis des Schrift- und Buchwesens der alten Ägypter*, Diss. University Cologne.

Westendorf, W. 1965-77. *Koptisches Handwörterbuch*, Heidelberg.

BARAIES ON MANI'S RAPTURE, PAUL, AND THE ANTEDILUVIAN APOSTLES

EIBERT TIGCHELAAR

For Gerard Luttikhuizen, the so-called Cologne Mani Codex (here-after *CMC*) requires no lengthy introduction.[1] The text stands at the crossroads of his two main scholarly interests: Egyptian Gnostic texts and the Gnostic use of biblical and Early Christian traditions on the one hand, and Christian-Jewish sects on the other. However, although *CMC* describes the early life of the most successful Gnostic teacher ever, and in spite of the Egyptian connection of the manuscript,[2] Gerard mainly focused on the Elchasaite connection in *CMC* 72-99.[3]

---

[1] *Editio princeps*: A. Henrichs and L. Koenen, 'Der Kölner Mani-Kodex (P.Colon.inv.nr.4780) ΠΕΡΙ ΤΗΣ ΓΕΝΝΗΣ ΤΟΥ ΣΩΜΑΤΟΣ ΑΥΤΟΥ', *Zeitschrift für Papyrologie und Epigraphik* 19 (1975) 1-85; 32 (1978) 87-199; 44 (1981) 201-318; 48 (1982) 1-59. Hereafter references to the *editio princeps* are to the first part, *Zeitschrift für Papyrologie und Epigraphik* 19 (1975) 1-85. All citations from the text are from the *editio minor*: L. Koenen and C. Römer, *Der Kölner Mani-Kodex: Über das Werden seines Leibes*. Kritische Edition aufgrund der von A. Henrichs und L. Koenen besorgten Erstedition (Papyrologica Coloniensia 14), Opladen 1988. *Facsimile edition*: L. Koenen and C. Römer, *Der Kölner Mani-Kodex: Abbildungen und diplomatischer Text* (Papyrologische Texte und Abhandlungen 35), Bonn 1985. A recent English translation, by Judith and Samuel Lieu, is included in I. Gardner and S.N.C. Lieu (eds), *Manichaean Texts from the Roman Empire*, Cambridge 2004. Quotations are from that translation. For general discussions of *CMC*, see, e.g., S.N.C. Lieu, *Manichaeism in Mesopotamia and the Roman East* (Religions in the Graeco-Roman World 118), Leiden 1994, 78-87; I.M.F. Gardner and S.N.C. Lieu, 'From Narmouthis (Medinet Madi) to Kellis (Ismant el-Kharab): Manichaean Documents from Roman Egypt', *The Journal of Roman Studies* 86 (1996) 146-69, esp. 154-61.

[2] In the editio princeps, the editors surmised that the codex might stem from Oxyrhynchus, but later A. Henrichs, 'The Cologne Mani Codex Reconsidered', *Harvard Studies in Classical Philology* 83 (1979) 339-67, stated that '[r]umor has it that the remains of the codex were located several decades ago in Luxor, and it is a reasonable guess that they were found in the vicinity of ancient Lykopolis, a stronghold of Manichaeism in Upper Egypt' (at 349). The text is believed to have been written in Mesopotamia, but to have been translated into Greek in Egypt. Cf. A. Henrichs and L. Koenen, 'Ein griechischer Mani-Codex (P.Colon.inv.nr.4780; J. Kroll gewidmet)', *Zeitschrift für Papyrologie und Epigraphik* 5 (1970) 97–216 at 104-5, and Lieu, *Manichaeism in Mesopotamia and the Roman East*, 81.

[3] Cf. Gerard's own studies of this section in G.P. Luttikhuizen, *The Revelation of Elchasai: Investigations into the Evidence for a Mesopotamian Jewish Apocalypse of the Second*

My own interests in *CMC* arose from the passages that quote apocalypses attributed to the antediluvian patriarchs Adam, Sethel, Enosh,
Shem and Enoch (*CMC* 48.16-60.12). In the case of the apocalypse
attributed to Enoch (58.6-60.12), it has been argued that it demonstrates a dependence on *1 Enoch*, including the *Book of Parables*.[4] Mani's
knowledge of ancient Jewish texts has in fact been demonstrated by the
correspondence between Mani's own *Book of Giants*, and the fragments
of a *Book of Giants* found at Qumran.[5] Yet, apart from this section
from *CMC*, there is no other evidence of the existence of apocalypses
of Seth, Enosh or Shem, whereas the quotations from the apocalypses
of Adam and Enoch do not correspond to the preserved apocalypses
of these patriarchs. The scholarly discussion has moved from a positive
judgment of the Jewish origin of these apocalypses,[6] to the view that
they are on the whole Manichaean fabrications, be it with adaptations
of traditional lore.[7] This latter assessment of the authenticity of the

---

Century and its Reception by Judeo-Christian Propagandists (Texte und Studien zum antiken
Judentum 8), Tübingen 1985; 'Waren Mani's Täufer Elchasaiten?', in: J. Tubach
(ed.), *Die Inkulturation des Christentums im vorislamischen Persien* (forthcoming).

[4] B.A. Pearson, 'Enoch in Egypt', in: R.A. Argall, B.A. Bow, and R.A. Werline
(eds), *For a Later Generation: The Transformation of Tradition in Israel, Early Judaism and Early
Christianity*, Harrisburg, Pennsylvania 2000, 216-31 at 217 and 222. Pearson depends
on J.C. Reeves, *Heralds of That Good Realm: Syro-Mesopotamian Gnosis and Jewish Traditions*
(Nag Hammadi and Manichaean Studies 41), Leiden 1996, 192-4, 198.

[5] Cf. J.C. Reeves, *Jewish Lore in Manichaean Cosmogony: Studies in the Book of Giants
Traditions* (Hebrew Union College Monographs 14), Cincinnati 1991; W. Sunder-
mann, 'Mani's "Book of the Giants" and the Jewish Books of Enoch: A Case of
Terminological Differences and What It Implies', in: S. Shaked and A. Netzer (eds),
Irano-Judaica: Studies Relating to Jewish Contacts with Persian Culture throughout the Ages,
iii, Jerusalem 1994, 40-8; L.T. Stuckenbruck, *The Book of Giants from Qumran: Texts,
Translation, and Commentary* (Texte und Studien zum antiken Judentum 63), Tübingen
1997; É. Puech, 'Livre des Géants', in: *Discoveries in the Judaean Desert*, xxxi: *Qumrân
Grotte 4 XXII. Textes Araméens Première Partie 4Q529-549*, Oxford 2001, 9-115.

[6] A. Henrichs, 'Literary Criticism of the Cologne Mani Codex', in: B. Layton
(ed.), *The Rediscovery of Gnosticism*, ii, *Sethian Gnosticism*, Leiden 1981, 724-33 at 725
note 7: 'new texts of Jewish origin'; G. Quispel, 'Transformation through Vision
in Jewish Gnosticism and the Cologne Mani Codex', *Vigiliae Christianae* 49 (1995)
189-91 at 189: 'not the slightest reason to suppose that the Apocalypse of Seth did
not exist at that time [...], that it was not used by the Jewish Christians and was
not Jewish in origin'.

[7] J.C. Reeves, *Heralds of That Good Realm: Syro-Mesopotamian Gnosis and Jewish Traditions* (Nag Hammadi and Manichaean Studies 41), Leiden 1996, 210, concludes
that they are 'almost certainly not authentic products of [...] Jewish scribal circles
[...] rather, they are creative adaptations of the traditional lore which had gathered
around these primeval ancestors'. D. Frankfurter, 'Apocalypses Real and Alleged in
the Mani Codex', *Numen* 44 (1997) 60-73 at 68-9, does not deny the possibility that

alleged excerpts from apocalypses is based on a comparison of the contents and phraseology of these quotations with those of Early Jewish, Syriac, Manichaean and Mandaic sources. In this contribution, I will discuss the function of these excerpts within their literary context, that is within *CMC* as a whole, and, in particular, within the subsection in which they appear, Baraies' first homily.[8]

Baraies' first homily (CMC 45.1-72.7)

CMC is an anthology of testimonies and homilies of first generation Manichaeans concerning Mani's early life. The testimonies mention the witness, followed by words spoken by Mani, or by a description of events from his life. The variety of the materials and the witnesses suggests that a compiler arranged sections from written sources and perhaps also from oral testimonies of Mani's first disciples, in a chronological sequence.[9] Each section may reflect up to three stages of redaction: Mani's own narratives, the reproduction of his statements by his disciples, and the editor's arrangement and editing of the sources.[10] Only in the case of the materials attributed to Baraies the Teacher, one may discern a 'recognizable literary identity'.[11]

This Baraies was most probably an early disciple of Mani who held the highest function in Manichaeism, that of Teacher.[12] Compared

---

the cited texts existed within Mani's own literary milieu, but warns 'against viewing the list uncritically as a major witness to the use of apocalypses in antiquity'.

[8] Reeves, *Heralds of That Good Realm*, disregards the literary context altogether, whereas Frankfurter, 'Apocalypses Real and Alleged', considers the function of the excerpts within Manichaean theology as such, and to a lesser extent within Baraies' homily.

[9] Cf., e.g., R. Merkelbach, 'Wann wurde die Mani-Biographie abgefaßt, und welches waren ihre Quellen?', in: G. Wießner and H.-J. Klimkeit (eds), *Studia Manichaica*. II. Internationaler Kongreß zum Manichäismus 6.-10. August 1989 St. Augustin/Bonn (Studies in Oriental Religions 23), Wiesbaden 1992, 159-66, who argues that the homilies were available in a written form, but that the other testimonies are based on oral traditions. In view of the Manichaean criticism of the multiplicity of Christian gospels, this Mani-biography may have been intended to be the one and authoritative biography.

[10] Cf., more in detail, Henrichs, 'Literary Criticism'.

[11] Henrichs, 'Literary Criticism', 727: 'excerpts ascribed to him are more ambitious, more intelligent, and demonstrably more authentic than the others'.

[12] If Βαραίης is the Greek rendering of Syriac *Bar Ḥayyē*, 'Son of Life', then it may have been an epithet, rather than his proper name. Cf. J. Tubach, 'Die Namen von Manis Jüngern und ihre Herkunft', in: L. Cirillo and A. Van Tongerloo (eds), *Atti del*

to the other witnesses, with the possible exception of Timotheos, Baraies stands apart as an apologetic theologian, who not only gives testimony of what he heard from Mani, but also reflects on Mani's mission, and defends the authenticity of his revelation.[13] Within the anthology of *CMC*, the sections attributed to Baraies share a series of stylistic, literary, idiomatic and theological characteristics.[14]

CMC contains four sections attributed to Baraies: *CMC* 14.3-26.5; 45.1-72.7; 72.8-74.5; and 79.13-93.23.[15] The first and last conform to the prevailing type of testimonies, consisting of sayings of Mani introduced by ἔλεγεν ὁ κ(ύριό)ς μου οὕτως (14.4) and ἔφη ὁ κ(ύριό)ς μου (79.14). The second and third sections, however, are homilies addressed to the brothers (ὦ ἀδελφοί; 45.1; 63.17; 72.9-10).[16] The first of these homilies (45.1-72.7) has a complex structure, since it comprises citations from the apocalypses, from the writings of Paul, as well as from Mani's own *Living Gospel* and his *Letter to Edessa*. The structure of the homily may be presented schematically as follows:

Address of brothers (γνῶτε τοίνυν, ὦ ἀδελφοί, καὶ σύνετε; 45.1-10 ?)
Introduction about Rapture and Revelation of Mani (46.1-47.1 ?)
Reference to Forefathers (47.2-48.15)
Excerpts from Writings of the Forefathers (48.16-62.9)
    Excerpt from apocalypse of Adam (48.16-50.7)
    Excerpt from apocalypse of Sethel (50.8-52.7)
    Excerpt from apocalypse of Enosh (52.8-55.9)
    Excerpt from apocalypse of Shem (55.10-58.5)
    Excerpt from apocalypse of Enoch (58.6-60.12)
    Quotations from Paul [Gal 1.1; 2 Cor 12.1-5; Gal 1.11-12] (60.13-62.9)
Summary about Forefathers (62.10-63.1)

Terzo Congresso Internazionale Di Studi 'Manicheismo e Oriente Cristiano Antico'. Arcavacata di Rende, Amantea 31 agosto—5 settembre 1993 (Manichaean Studies 3), Louvain 1997, 375-93 at 382-3. Lieu, *Manichaeism in Mesopotamia and the Roman East*, 266, suggests Baraies 'may well have been the same person as Baḥrâjâ mentioned in the *Fihrist*'. This would presuppose metathesis of the second and third consonant.

[13] J. Ries, 'Baraiès le Didascale dans le Codex Mani. Nature, structure et valeur de son témoignage sur Mani et sa doctrine', in: Cirillo & Van Tongerloo, *Atti del Terzo Congresso Internazionale Di Studi 'Manicheismo e Oriente Cristiano Antico'*, 305-11 at 311.

[14] Cf. the *editio princeps*, p. 80 note 80.

[15] *CMC* 14.3 Βαρ<α>ίης ὁ διδάσκαλος; 72.8 and 79.13 Βαραίης ὁ διδάσκαλος. The *editio princeps* and the transcription of the *facsimile edition* read at the top of page 45 [του] σωμ[ατος αυτου], which was corrected in the *editio minor* to [Βα]ραί[ης ὁ διδάσκαλος]. Cf. the discussion in L. Koenen and C. Römer, 'Neue Lesungen im *Kölner Mani-Kodex*', *Zeitschrift für Papyrologie und Epigraphik* 66 (1986) 265-8 at 267-8.

[16] Cf. Ries, 'Baraiès le Didascale', does not distinguish between *CMC* 45.1-72.7 and 72.8-74.5.

First Conclusion about Rapture and Revelation of Mani (63.1-16)
Address of brothers (ἐπιστάμεθα γάρ, ὦ ἀδελφοί) introducing sections from
    Mani's writings (63.16-64.6)
Excerpts from Mani's Writings (64.7-70.9)
    Excerpt from Mani's *Letter to Edessa* (64.7-65.22)
    Excerpt from Mani's *Living Gospel* (65.23-68.4)
    Excerpt from a writing of Mani, possibly the *Living Gospel* (68.5-69.8)
    Excerpt from a writing of Mani, possibly the *Living Gospel* (69.9-70.9)
Second Conclusion about Rapture and Revelation of Mani (70.10-72.7)

The excerpts from the apocalypses are characterized by a recurrent
pattern, consisting of the following elements: epiphany of an angel (in
the case of Enoch seven angels), translation of the patriarch to another
place, revelation of secrets to the patriarch, reference (command,
description) to the writing down of the revelation by the patriarch.
These elements also occur in the quotations from Paul, although in
Paul there is no angel. Instead, an epiphany of Jesus Christ is implied.
The writing down of secrets is not part of the quotations from Paul,
but is described by Baraies in the homily. Both the quotation of these
specific patriarchs and Paul, as well as the contents of the quotations, serve to support Mani's own revelations in several respects.[17]
The Adamite patriarchs are, according to Manichaean doctrine, the
first in the series of incarnations of the apostle.[18] The emphasis on
the writing down reflects the Manichaean appreciation of religious
texts, which they gathered and included in their own works.[19] In that
sense, Baraies' homily has been qualified as essentially 'a catena of
citations' that 'collectively bear witness to the apostolic credibility of
Mani as a "teacher of truth"'.[20] This kind of general remark over-

---

[17] Cf., e.g., Henrichs, 'Literary Criticism', 731; Frankfurter, 'Apocalypses Real
and Alleged'.

[18] Cf., e.g., *Kephalaia* 12.9-12: 'The advent of the apostle has occurred at the occasion [… a]s I have told you: from Sethel [the first] born son of Adam up to Enosh,
together with [Enoch]; fr[om] Enoch u[p] to Sem [the] son of [Noah'. Note that this
section also mentions Buddha, Aurentes, Zarathustra, up to the advent of Jesus.

[19] Cf. explicitly *Kephalaia* 154: 'The writings and the wisdom and the apocalypses
and the parables and the psalms of all earlier [religions] were gathered everywhere
and came to my [religion] and were added to the wisdom which I revealed.' Coptic
text in C. Schmidt and H.J. Polotsky, 'Ein Mani-Fund in Ägypten. Originalschriften
des Mani und seiner Schüler', *Sitzungsberichte der preussischen Akademie der Wissenschaften*
1933, 4-90 at 86 (cf. also 31); English translation quoted from Frankfurter, 'Apocalypses Real and Alleged', 68.

[20] Reeves, *Heralds of That Good Realm*, 211. Frankfurter, 'Apocalypses Real and
Alleged', 60, mistakenly claims that 'Baraies quoted Mani explicitly invoking "apoca-

looks, however, the homiletic structure and focus of Baraies' text, to which we will now turn.

The homiletic focus of Baraies' homily

The first pages of the text are rather damaged, which makes it impossible to exactly ascertain the author's introduction. Yet, the text that has been preserved, suggests that the basic theme of the homily is the refutation of the real or fictitious charge that Mani's followers 'wrote about the rapture of their teacher in order to boast' (46.4-7 ὅτι οὗτοι μόνοι γεγράφασιν ἁρπαγὴν τοῦ διδασκάλου αὐτῶν πρὸς καύχησιν). Baraies shows, by quoting ancient apocalypses and Paul, that all earlier apostles wrote down themselves what had been revealed to them, whilst their disciples became the seal of their sending (71.21-72.7 ὁπηνίκα γὰρ ἕκα[στος αὐ]τῶν ἡρπάζετο [ἃ ἐθεώ]ρει καὶ ἤκουε [ταῦτα πάντα ἔ]γραφεν καὶ ὑπεδεί[κ]νυεν καὶ αὐτὸς αὐτοῦ [τ]ῆς ἀποκαλύψεως μάρτυς ἐγένετο· οἱ δὲ μαθηταὶ αὐτοῦ ἐγίγνοντο σφραγὶς αὐτοῦ τῆς ἀποστολῆς). These two quotations from the work may be seen as the framework of the homily proper: the first (46.4-7), in the initial part of the composition, sets forth the accusation; the last (71.21-72.7), at the very end of the homily, summarizes the refutation.

Baraies counters the charge that Mani's followers wrote down the revelation of their teacher, by presenting the cases of the five apocalypses and Paul. These examples serve to demonstrate that these apostles themselves wrote down what they saw and heard.[21] In all the quoted texts the apostle narrates in first person speech what he had seen. In the second part of the homily, Baraies proceeds to quote Mani himself, who, like the forefathers and Paul, tells in first person style what he had experienced, and that he had received divine revelation and had been sent. Those quotations from Mani's writings, as well as other similar statements in the books of 'our father', 'make

---

lypses" of Adam, Sethel, Enosh, Shem, and Enoch'. Not Mani himself, but Baraies refers to these apocalypses.

[21] In Manichaeism, Adam, Sethel, Enosh, Shem, and Enoch (usually in that order!) are regarded as the first incarnations of the apostle. In the case of Adam (49.5-10), Enosh (54.12-17), and Shem (58.2-5), angels order the visionaries to write down the revelations. *CMC* also tells that Enoch (60.10-12) and Paul (62.4-9) wrote down what they were told. Only in the case of Sethel this notice is missing, but such a command may have been included in one of the missing lines. In any case, 52.2 does refer to 'his writings'.

known his revelation and the rapture of his mission' (70.10-17). Of course, this kind of circular and internal evidence aims to strengthen the convictions of the believers, but may fail to persuade outsiders.

From a text-pragmatic point of view, Baraies' text is a homily that is not directed against opponents, but aims to boost the disciples' relation to Mani, and hence to the Manichaean community. Baraies achieves this by using second as well as first person plural forms in a rhetorical manner. In the introduction of the homily he addresses the brothers (45.1), uses imperatives (45.1-2; 47.2-3), and contrasts those who having changed their minds (46.3-4 μεταβληθεὶς εἴπη) question Mani's rapture, to those who are willing to listen (47.1-3 ὁ γάρ τοι βουλόμενος ἀκουέτω καὶ προσεχέτω).[22] In the second part of the homily, Baraies again addresses the brothers (63.17), but from now on he uses first person plural forms. The exhortation to listen changes into a communal confession (63.16-17 ἐπιστάμεθα γάρ, ὦ ἀδελφοί ... 63.23 ἣν [συ]νγιν[ώσκομεν]). In this second part, Mani is not referred to any more in terms used by the renegades ('their teacher'), but here is called 'our father' (70.14; 71.17), whereas those who question the truth are referred to as 'those who have clothed themselves with unbelief' (71.13-14). Ultimately, the homily is concerned with the question of discipleship, and this exactly is the issue that is raised in the framework: against the charge that Mani's followers bragged about Mani's rapture and fabricated reports, the homily ends with stating what disciples really should be: 'the seal of his sending'.

This last phrase is a clear allusion to 1 Cor 9.2 where Paul states that 'you are the seal of my sending'.[23] Within the homily, the allusions to and quotations of Paul are of central importance. Apart from the quotations from Galatians and 2 Corinthians in *CMC* 60.13-62.9, there is the charge against the Manichaeans (46.4-7) about the boasting about the rapture, which directly alludes to 2 Cor 12.1-5. More specifically, most of the central terms of the homily also occur in the Pauline quotations. This goes for the three key words 'revelation' (ἀποκάλυψις), 'rapture' (ἁρπαγή), and 'sending' (ἀποστολή).[24] 'Sending'[25]

---

[22] The preceding word of 47.1 is ἁμαρτάνει, and the *editio minor* tentatively reconstructs the missing words as follows: '[Wer aber das nicht glaubt, der] geht in die Irre'.

[23] Or, with NRSV and other translations: 'the seal of my apostleship'.

[24] In many cases in *CMC* ἁρπαγή is used in combination with ἀποκάλυψις or ἀποστολή. Cf. e.g. 55.3-4 περὶ τῆς αὐτοῦ ἁρπαγῆς καὶ ἀποκαλύψεως; 62.6-7 περί τε τῆς ἁρπαγῆς αὐτοῦ καὶ ἀποστολῆς; 63.14-16 ὡς ἂν γνωσθῇ αὐτοῖς ἥ τε ἁρπαγὴ αὐτοῦ

and 'revelation' are part and parcel of Manichaean theology, but the emphasis on 'rapture' is rather idiosyncratic in Manichaean texts, and one may wonder whether its use was influenced by 2 Cor 12.1-5.

Baraies on the rapture of Mani

The element of 'rapture' (or 'being brought up') recurs time and again in Baraies' description of the apostles. The term (either the verb ἁρπάζω or the noun ἁρπαγή) is employed with regard to Mani (46.5; 63.15; 70.16), apostles in general (47.14; 48.14-15; 71.9-10, 22), Sethel (52.3), Enosh (53.1, 14-15; 55.3-4), Shem (55.17), Paul (60.13-14; 62.1, 6-7), as well as in the quotation from 2 Cor 12.1-5 (61.7-8). The section on the apocalypse of Adam is very damaged, and the term may have been used there too. Only in the case of Enoch, Baraies uses a different expression to refer to his being brought up (59.21 ἀνήνεγκαν). In all these cases, the apostle is brought up from one place to another (to the top of a mountain; to another world; to paradise; to the third heaven), but Baraies does not tell where Mani was brought to. In the excerpts from Mani's books in the homily, Mani refers in different terms to his sending,[26] and repeatedly to revelations. However, he does not mention his being brought up to a different place, even though this was the issue which Baraies tried to demonstrate. The 'apocalyptic' parallels which Baraies adduces, concern the snatching away of apostles by angels, visions of mysteries, and the subsequent command to write down the revelations

---

καὶ ἀποκάλυψις; 70.14-17 αἳ δεικνύουσι τήν τε ἀποκάλυψιν αὐτοῦ καὶ ἁρπαγὴν τῆς αὐτοῦ ἀποστολῆς; 71.7-11 ἐδευτερώσαμεν ἀπὸ τῶν προγόνων ἡμῶ[ν] πατέρων τήν τε ἁρπαγὴν αὐτῶν καὶ ἀποκάλυψιν ἑνὸς ἑκάστου. One may observe that the three quotations from Paul centre on these three issues: Gal 1.1 on apostleship; 2 Cor 12.1-5 on revelation, in particular rapture; Gal 1.11-12 on revelation.

[25] Koenen and Römer, as well as Lieu and Lieu, render ἀποστολή, by 'Sendung', 'sending', 'mission', and, on the whole, avoid the terms 'apostleship' or 'apostolate' (but cf. Lieu and Lieu in 41.10). For a discussion of the *CMC* concept of apostleship see, most recently, J. van Oort, 'The Paraclete Mani as the Apostle of Jesus Christ and the Origins of a New Church', in: A. Hilhorst (ed.), *The Apostolic Age in Patristic Thought* (Supplements to Vigiliae Christianae 70), Leiden/Boston 2004, 139-57.

[26] The heading of the section from Mani's Gospel (66.4-7 ἐγὼ Μαννιχαῖος Ἰη(σο)ῦ Χρ(ιστο)ῦ ἀπόστολος διὰ θελήματος Θεοῦ Π(ατ)ρ(ὸ)ς τῆς ἀληθείας) is an intentional parallel to Gal 1.1 which is quoted in 60.17-20 (Παῦλος ἀπόστολος οὐκ ἀπ' ἀνθρώπων οὐδὲ δι' ἀνθρώπου ἀλλὰ διὰ Ἰησοῦ Χριστοῦ καὶ Θεοῦ Πατρὸς). Also, the χειροθεσίαν τὴν ἐκ τοῦ πατρὸς τοῦ ἐμοῦ (70.3-4) is a reference to his mission.

and bequeath them. Yet, in Mani's writings this apocalyptic mode of revelation is much less clear. The traditional view on Mani, expressed explicitly in the fourth quotation from Mani's writings (69.9-70.9), is not that Mani was snatched away, but that his twin (his Syzygos, the Paraclete of truth) came to him instead, and revealed to him the truth and all the mysteries.[27] How, then, did Baraies envisage Mani's rapture? And why did he emphasize this particular issue? One may consider several possibilities.

First, the 'rapture' does not refer to a physical translation of Mani, but to one of his psychic religious experiences, consisting of the epiphany of his Syzygos or Twin. In another context, such a metaphorical use would be understandable, but in Baraies' homily, which consistently refers to real physical raptures to other locations, this would be highly inconsistent and improbable.

Second, within Baraies' homily, the quotation from Mani's *Letter to Edessa* may perhaps imply the idea of a translation of Mani. The text states that the Blessed Father took Mani away (65.4-5 ἀπέσπασε) from the council of the multitude, disclosed to him his secrets, and revealed how they existed before the creation of the world. A similar use of the expression 'draw me away' is found in the fourth excerpt, possibly from the *Living Gospel*, which states that 'He (i.e. the Syzygos) came and chose me in preference to others and set me aside, drawing me away from the midst of those of that rule in which I was brought up'. In this quotation, the 'drawing away' (ἐπισπασάμενος) may seem to refer primarily to the psychic separation of Mani from the 'baptists', not necessarily to a physical separation from this world. However, this very section from Mani's writing is also quoted by Baraies in 19.7-20.17 in the description of Mani's enlightenment at the age of twenty-four. Here the text is somewhat more explicit: 'He released me and separated me and drew me away from the midst of that rule in which I was brought up. In this way he called me and chose me and drew me and separated me from their midst. He drew (me away to one) side' (20.8-17). The text, which is rather broken, enumerates the mysteries which the Syzygos showed Mani concerning his origin, but 'he also revealed to me, in addition, the measureless heights and

---

[27] Cf., e.g., also the first Kephalaion of the *Kephalaia of the Teacher*. Cf. the translation by I. Gardner, *The Kephalaia of the Teacher: The Edited Coptic Manichaean Texts in Translation with Commentary* (Nag Hammadi and Manichaean Studies 37), Leiden 1995.

unsearchable depths' (23.11-14). There is no explicit reference to any translation of Mani, and the 'revelation' (ἔφηνε) may have been either verbal, by means of a vision, or by means of a translation.

Third, in the other parts of *CMC*, the motif of a physical translation is attested explicitly in the two aerial journeys of Mani which are described in 126.2-129.17 and 130.1-135.6. Within the framework of a description of Mani's missionary journeys, the text describes that Mani's Twin raised him into the air (126.4 μετεωρίσας [με]) and brought him to secret places. These journeys may have been visions of the otherworld and of the future, which Mani described to Pattikios, his father and companion, in 135.6-136.16.[28] The first journey brings Mani to a paradisiacal place, where he encounters on the highest mountain 'a (man) who had growing on his body hair which was eighteen inches long, thick and (hanging down) in full curls'. From a historico-literary perspective, the man has Adamic features, but in the present context of the description of Mani's missionary journeys, this hairy anchorite may represent Christian ascetics. Mani instructs the man, who then is snatched away ([ἡρ]πάγη) from before Mani, in order to herald Mani's religion among the other people in that far-away region. In other words: this episode would demonstrate the superiority of Mani's instruction above that of Christian asceticism![29]

These otherworldly journeys may have been composed during the final process of compiling the Mani biography.[30] It is not known when the biography was assembled, though scholars allow for an early date.[31] Also, there is no means of determining the existence of the stories of Mani's aerial journeys prior to their incorporation in the biography. In short, one cannot exclude the possibility that Baraies knew these accounts of Mani's journeys. One may even go one step further: if the episode of the longhaired man was meant to elevate Mani's

---

[28] C.E. Römer, *Manis frühe Missionsreisen nach der Kölner Manibiographie: Textkritischer Kommentar und Erläuterungen zu p. 121-p. 129 des Kölner Mani-Kodex* (Papyrologica Coloniensia 24), Opladen 1994, 38-40.

[29] Cf. the long discussion in Römer, *Manis frühe Missionsreisen*, 46-63, who partly corrects her earlier article 'Manis Reise durch die Luft', in: L. Cirillo (ed.), *Codex Manichaicus Coloniensis: Atti del Secondo Simposio Internazionale (Cosenza 27-28 maggio 1988)*, Cosenza 1990, 77-91.

[30] Römer, *Manis frühe Missionsreisen*, 39.

[31] Henrichs, 'Literary Criticism', 353: 'Very likely it [sc. the compilation] was made soon after Mani's death in 276 from sources written during his lifetime.' Baraies' homily should be dated after Mani's death.

teaching above that of Christians, then Christians may have rightly interpreted this episode as a later Manichaean boastful fabrication. In short, the real or alleged accusation by the opponents which was referred to in *CMC* 46.4-7 may have been entirely justified.

Fourth, the lack of specificity on how the rapture should be envisaged, may be intentional. In view of the quoted accusation, namely that Mani's disciples boasted about his rapture, Baraies may have decided not to digress on details. Instead, the excerpts from the apocalypses suggest how Mani might have been raptured, whereas Paul's reticence would have legitimated Baraies' restraint to give details. This fourth possibility does not exclude the second (or even the third) possibility mentioned above. On the contrary: if the lack of specificity was intentional, it would suggest to the reader that the revelation by the Syzygos was accompanied by some form of rapture.

But why the rapture?

The question remains why Baraies put such an emphasis on Mani's rapture, as opposed to the disregard of such rapture in other Manichaean texts. From the point of view of Manichaean theology (or rather: apostolology), Mani's rapture should have been beyond dispute. Mani modelled himself on the previous apostles, in particular Jesus Christ and Paul.[32] What these apostles experienced, Mani did too. This goes, for example, for the suffering and endurance of the apostles (and their disciples) in the *Psalm Book*.[33] Baraies' homily focuses on the correspondence between Paul and Mani. The self-introduction of Mani in his *Living Gospel* is modelled on Paul's heading in his Letter to the Galatians.[34] Baraies underlines this correspondence by quoting both of these introductions (from Galatians and from the *Living Gospel*) in his homily. The framework with its allusions to 2 Cor 12.1-5 and 1 Cor 9.2, once again points towards the correspondence between Paul

---

[32] Cf. Van Oort, 'The Paraclete Mani', and M. Franzmann, *Jesus in the Manichaean Writings*, London/New York 2003, 15-26.

[33] *Psalm Book 2*, 143.15-18: 'All the godly that there have been, male, female, all have suffered; / down to the glorious one, the apostle Mani the living. / Our lord Manichaios himself also was made to drink the cup: / he received the likeness of them all, he fulfilled all their signs.' Cf. translation in Gardner & Lieu, *Manichaean Texts from the Roman Empire*, 243.

[34] Cf., in more detail, Van Oort, 'The Paraclete Mani', 149-50.

and Mani: since Paul had been raptured, one should also assume that Mani had been raptured.

However, it is unlikely that Baraies' emphasis on the rapture merely stems from the wish to model Mani in all respects on Paul. The apologetic tone of the homily indicates that the concern with the rapture evolved from a context of disputes or accusations. Presumably, the opponents of the early Manichaeans, who may have been originally followers themselves, valued 'apocalyptic' visionary experiences and journeys as a source of revelation or as a token of having been sent. Since Mani himself did not unequivocally refer to raptures or heavenly journeys, such critics would have thought his mission to be less authentic than that of those who encountered angels, were seized, and brought to paradise. By contrast, the lack of concern for Mani's rapture in other Manichaean texts would reflect different cultural contexts, in which Gnostic modes of revelation, instead of apocalyptic visionary journeys, were more readily accepted.

This indicates that Baraies' theology should not be regarded as a standard Manichaean view. In other respects, too, his homily departs from common Manichaean ideas. Baraies argues that all apostles wrote down what was revealed to them, in order to counter charges against Mani's disciples. Other Manichaean texts, though, emphasize that Mani alone wrote down his teachings, whereas the other apostles, in particular Jesus, only preached to their followers. In short, Baraies' homily can not be taken to reflect a uniform Manichaean theology (if there is one at all).

Conclusions

Even though the apocalypses in *CMC* may be alleged, Baraies had knowledge of both Jewish-Christian apocalyptic lore, and of Paul's letters. If the charge that Mani's followers wrote about the rapture of their teacher in order to boast (46.4-7, alluding to 2 Cor 12.1-5) was real, then Baraies' opponents were Christians who accepted Paul as an apostle. It therefore is not surprising that in his homily Baraies repeatedly refers and alludes to Paul, and that his quotations are quite literal.[35] This indicates a context in which Paul's letters were important.

---

[35] On the character of the quotations, cf. Henrichs & Koenen, 'Ein griechischer Mani-Codex', 114-16 ('Genauigkeit der Zitierweise').

On the other hand, the excerpts from the alleged apocalypses are not literal quotations, but assemblages of existing, and in some cases perhaps also new materials. This strongly indicates that apocalyptic texts did not have the same standing as the letters of Paul. These assemblages were meant to exemplify the basic pattern of epiphany, rapture, translation, visions, and command to write. In short: the interest is not in these apocalypses per se, but in the apostolic figures on the one hand, and in the paradigm of rapture, revelation and mission on the other.

The list of apostolic figures includes the five antediluvian heroes and Paul, but not specifically Jewish figures who also had been translated such as Abraham or Moses, nor Zoroaster, or Buddha, who are regarded as apostles in Manichaean traditions.[36] This points to a Christian background of Baraies and his Manichaean brothers, but also of their opponents, who may have kept these antediluvian apostles in honour, without being really interested in what they wrote.[37] For Baraies, Paul was the important apostolic example, whereas the ancient apocalypses of the antediluvian apostles merely served to illustrate and underline the apostolic pattern.[38]

---

[36] Cf. Frankfurter, 'Apocalypses Real and Alleged', for a lengthy discussion of the idea of a chain of True Prophets.

[37] This would be quite analogous to the Islamic attitude towards earlier prophets. Cf. Van Oort, 'The Paraclete Mani', 152 notes 61 and 62.

[38] I wish to thank Ton Hilhorst, George van Kooten, and Ronit Nikolsky for their critical questions and comments.

DEVOLUTION AND RECOLLECTION, DEFICIENCY AND PERFECTION: HUMAN DEGRADATION AND THE RECOVERY OF THE PRIMAL CONDITION ACCORDING TO SOME EARLY CHRISTIAN TEXTS

F. Lautaro Roig Lanzillotta

> Siglos y siglos de idealismo no han dejado de influir
> en la realidad
> (J.L. Borges, *Tlön, Uqbar, Orbis Tertius*).

Introduction

Can any of us, unhappy about the current situation, truly say that they have never felt that they are no longer what they used to be; that youth, strength, beauty or intelligence have abandoned them for ever? Or, pondering on an ideal past time, have never felt that ancient times were better and that the times we live in are a sort of second-class version of more magnificent periods, when women were more beautiful or more refined, men braver, gentler, or more educated? This morbid malice against ourselves, which in the words of D. Hume a person may extend even to 'his present fortune, and carry it so far as designedly to seek affliction, and increase his pains and sorrows' is the theme I have chosen to honour Professor G.P. Luttikhuizen on the occasion of his retirement.

It goes without saying that the view that present times are a degradation of glorious past times is a topos of Western literature. Hesiod immortalised it in his *Works and Days* by graphically comparing momentous past generations to noble metals such as gold, silver or bronze and his own to iron.[1] Interesting though it might be, however, I shall not focus on the myth of the ages of man but on a more radical variation on the theme: the view in which man's environment, body and life in the sublunary world is a pale reflection of 'real life' in the supramundane.

---

[1] Hesiod, *Op.* 11-285, on which see the excellent paper by J.P. Vernant, 'Le mythe hésiodique des races: Essai d'analyse structurale', *Revue de l'Histoire des Religions* 157 (1960) 21-54.

It is well known that in the first centuries of the Christian era this impression became almost an obsession and was to a certain extent radicalised.[2] Combined with the Orphic view that regarded the human body as a prison and the old Pythagorean idea that it was a tomb,[3] devolution was no longer seen as a historical but as an ontological matter. If the intellect or the soul was the real being, the material body could be nothing but a degraded accretion, the result of a devolutionary process at the end of which man had become what he currently was: a prisoner in the world of nature, an alien in the tangible reality.

People of that period were not as pessimist as they are sometimes supposed to be, however. In spite of depicting their current condition in such dark hues, they did not resignedly accept their sad destiny. This is why, in order to recover their lost condition, and alongside the complicated explanations of how and why man fell from the heights of transcendence to the lowest abode, they also developed equally complicated ways that were intended to overcome a degraded state which, in their view, was alien to their true nature.

Early Christianity was not immune to these developments. Several early Christian texts explain the appearance of the physical world, or at any rate the appearance of humans, by means of the myth of devolution. At the same time, they encourage people to distance themselves from their false existence and attempt to recover their original transcendent condition. The *Acts of Andrew* (*AA*)[4] includes interesting versions both of the process of devolution and of that of recollection,

---

[2] E.R. Dodds, *Pagan and Christian in an Age of Anxiety: From Marcus Aurelius to Constantine*, Cambridge 1965.

[3] For the Orphic view, see frg. D-K 1 B 3 and J. Mansfeld, 'Bad World and Demiurge: A "Gnostic" Motif from Parmenides and Empedocles to Lucretius and Philo', in: R. van den Broek and M.J. Vermaseren (eds), *Studies in Gnosticism and Hellenistic Religions presented to G. Quispel on the Occasion of His 65th Birthday*, Leiden 1981, 261-314 at 292. Plato, *Phd* 62b-e; for the Pythagorean conception, see Philolaus, D-K 44 B 14, on which C.A. Huffman, *Philolaus of Croton, Pythagorean and Presocratic: A Commentary on the Fragments and Testimonia with Interpretive Essays*, Cambridge 1993, 402-6, who includes it among the spurious or doubtful fragments. For the difference between the Orphic and Pythagorean views see Mansfeld, 'Bad World', 292-3.

[4] On the basis of the conclusions of our exhaustive study of the *Acts of Andrew* (*The Apocryphal Acts of Andrew: A New Approach to the Character, Thought and Meaning of the Primitive Text*, Diss. University of Groningen, 2004), we exclusively focus on the text provided by *AA*'s fragment in codex Vaticanus graecus 808, ff. 507ʳ-512ᵛ. We quote our edition of the text (Vʳ), ibid., 139-59, but we will also provide the numbering in Bonnet's edition (Vᵇ). For the peculiarities of this fragment and its material framework, see our 'Vaticanus Graecus 808 Revisited: A Re-evaluation of the Oldest Fragment of *Acta Andreae*', *Scriptorium* 56 (2001) 126-40.

which show interesting similarities with the Valentinian myth as presented by the *Tripartite Tractate*, the *Gospel of Truth* and the report by Irenaeus.[5] The purpose of the present article is to examine this version and its numerous Gnostic parallels in order to show that the Gnostic affiliation of *AA* is more important than scholars are normally inclined to accept. Within this scope, the first section will analyse the anthropological views underlying *AA*'s conception and the second will focus on the myth of devolution proper. The third section will examine the counterpart to the devolution, namely the recollection that must achieve the reunion of what was dispersed through degradation.

1. *The anthropological background*

The anthropology current in the first centuries of the Christian era is mainly dualistic, since within the same individual it tends to distinguish between a visible and physical being engaged in sense-perception and an invisible, incorporeal one that just glances at the intelligible world. Most of the texts documenting this view appear to contain Plato's conception that identifies the true and essential being with the soul or its higher part endowed with reason.[6] The *Corpus Hermeticum*, for instance, widely echoes this view: according to *The Secret Sermon on the Mountain*, man's nature is clearly dual as it distinguishes between the physical body, which can be dissolved and is mortal, and the 'essential generation', which is indissoluble and immortal.[7] This is also the case in the *Asclepius*, which explicitly states that only man has a double nature, namely a simple and divine nature, which is called essential (οὐσιώδης), and another material one (ὑλικός), which is formed out of the four elements.[8] The same can be said of certain Nag Hammadi

---

[5] Irenaeus, 1.2.3 and 1.2.4.

[6] For Plato's conception, see *Phdr.* 247b 7, where in spite of the apparent trichotomy intellect, soul, body, the νοῦς is the guiding principle of the soul. On the issue, A.P. Bos, 'The Distinction between "Platonic" and "Aristotelian" Dualism Illustrated from Plutarch's Myth in *de facie in orbe lunae*', in: A. Pérez Jiménez and F. Casadesús (eds), *Estudios sobre Plutarco: Misticismo y religiones mistéricas en la obra de Plutarco*, Madrid and Málaga 2001, 57-70 at 61.

[7] *C.H.* 13.14 (206.12-14 N-F), τὸ αἰσθητὸν τῆς φύσεως σῶμα πόρρωθέν ἐστι τῆς οὐσιωδοῦς γενέσεως· τὸ μὲν γάρ ἐστι διαλυτόν, τὸ δὲ ἀδιάλυτον, καὶ τὸ μὲν θνητόν, τὸ δὲ ἀθάνατον.

[8] Man's duality in *Asclep.* 7 (304.2-6 N-F); 8 (305.15-306.2 N-F); 11 (309.5-6 N-F); 22 (323.25 N-F; 324.18 N-F); see *Asclep.* 10 (309.3 N-F); 22 (324.18 N-F); see also *C.H.* 9.5 (98.13-17 N-F).

texts, which explicitly preserve the opposition exterior-interior or vis-
ible-not visible and contrast the inner and true man with the external
and material, sensible being. Thus, for instance, *The Interpretation of
Knowledge*, where the body is associated with the rulers and authorities
and described as a prison for the 'man within'.[9] This is also the case
of *The Letter of Peter to Philip*, in which, however, the interest focuses
on the 'inner man' who ascends to heaven where the archons fight
with him.[10]

However, there are several important texts in which the basic
dichotomy that opposes a true to an untrue nature is combined with
a trichotomic conception of man. These texts tend to apply the Aristotelian scheme that elevated the status of the intellect above that of
the soul and the body[11] and which we already find in some Middle
Platonists.[12] As we have already shown elsewhere, *AA* belongs to this
group of texts, for it combines a dualistic anthropology with a clear
triadic conception of man consisting of body, soul and intellect.[13] Even

---

[9] *InterprKnow* (NHC XI.1) 6.30-35. For a similar but more general opposition see
SentSextus (NHC XII.1) 34.16-20; *GosPhil* (NHC II.3) 123, 82.30-83.9.

[10] *EpPetPhil* (NHC VIII.2) 137.20-23. For the trichotomic conception of man
and for the 'inner man' as man's spiritual part, see M.W. Meyer, *The Letter of Peter
to Philip*, Michigan 1981, 142. See also H.G. Bethge, *Der Brief des Petrus an Philippus*,
Berlin 1997, 110-11.

[11] E. Barbotin, *La théorie aristotélicienne de l'intellect d'après Théophraste*, Louvain
1954, 220; A.H. Armstrong, 'Aristotle in Plotinus: The Continuity and Discontinu-
ity of Psyche and Nous', in: H. Blumenthal and H. Robinson (eds), *Aristotle and the
Later Tradition*, Oxford 1991, 117-27 at 117-18. This differentiation is also stressed
by Atticus, frg. 7 Des Places (apud Eusebius, *PE* 15.9.14). See P. Merlan, 'Greek
Philosophy from Plato to Plotinus', in: A.H. Armstrong (ed.), *The Cambridge History of
Later Greek and Early Medieval Philosophy*, Cambridge 1967, 11-132 at 73-4; A.P. Bos,
'"Aristotelian" and "Platonic" Dualism in Hellenistic and Early Christian Philosophy
and in Gnosticism', *VChr* 56 (2002) 273-91 at 277 note 16 and Id., *The Soul and Its
Instrumental Body: A Reinterpretation of Aristotle's Philosophy of Living Nature*, Leiden/Boston
2003, 216-29; G.P. Luttikhuizen, 'Traces of Aristotelian Thought in the Apocryphon
of John', in: H.G. Bethge et al. (eds), *For the Children, Perfect Instruction*, Leiden/Boston
2002, 181-202 at 190.

[12] So, for example, Plutarch, *De facie* 28, 943a: νοῦς γὰρ ψυχῆς, ὅσῳ ψυχὴ
σώματος, ἄμεινόν ἐστι καὶ θειότερον. See H. Dörrie, 'Zum Ursprung der neupla-
tonischen Hypostasenlehre', *Hermes* 82 (1954) 331-42 (= *Platonica Minora*, 286-96),
passim; in particular Bos, 'Distinction', 57-70; see also Alcinous, *Didask.* 164.18-19: ἐπεὶ
δὲ ψυχῆς νοῦς ἄμεινων; in general our 'Bridging the Gulf between Transcendence
and Immanence in Late Antiquity', in: A.A. MacDonald, M.W. Twomey and G.J.
Reinink (eds), *Learned Antiquity: Scholarship and Society in the Near-East, the Greco-Roman
World and the Early Medieval West*, Louvain 2003, 37-51 at 40-4 and Roig Lanzillotta,
Apocryphal Acts, 285-91.

[13] See Roig Lanzillotta, *Apocryphal Acts*, 279-91.

though continuously opposing the external and material being to the immaterial and true nature, *AA* significantly refrains from using the metaphor of the 'inner man', either in its Platonic (ὁ ἔντος ἄνθρωπος)[14] or in its Pauline variant (ὁ ἔσω ἄνθρωπος).[15] Instead, it speaks of the 'own' or 'true nature' (ἰδία, ἀληθὴς φύσις),[16] of 'essence' (οὐσία)[17] or, on occasion, simply uses the term 'man' (ἄνθρωπος).[18] This is more than a simple terminological difference. As we will immediately see, in line with certain Hermetic tractates,[19] with Middle Platonic[20] and Gnostic sources, *AA* equates the essential man not with the soul but with the 'intellect'.[21]

This same tripartition and the same equation of the essential man with man's intellect can be found in *The Thought of Norea*. According to this text, the essential man called Adamas allows Norea to see the pleroma and not to be deficient,[22] and it is through him that she is

---

[14] Plato, *Rep.* 588-589, on which C. Markschies, 'Die platonische Metapher vom "Inneren Menschen": Eine Brücke zwischen antiker Philosophie und altchristlicher Theologie', *Zeitschrift für Kirchengeschichte* 105 (1994) 1-17 and Id., 'Innerer Mensch', *Reallexikon für Antike und Christentum* 18 (1998) 266-312.

[15] 2 Cor 4.16; Eph 3.16. See also Origen, *C. Cels.* 6.63. On the Pauline use, see, in general, T.K. Heckel, *Der innere Mensch: Die paulinische Verarbeitung eines platonischen Motivs*, Tübingen 1993, and, more recently, W. Burkert, 'Verso Platone e Paolo: l'essere umano "interno"', in his *Antichità classica e cristianesimo antico*, Cosenza 2000, 117-50; see also H.D. Betz, 'The Concept of the "Inner Human Being" (ὁ ἔσω ἄνθρωπος) in the Anthropology of Paul', *NTS* 46 (2000) 315-41.

[16] Vʳ 134-35, 217 (Vᵇ 42.3-4, 44.16).

[17] Vʳ 96-97 (Vᵇ 41.3-4).

[18] Vʳ 85-90 (Vᵇ 40.26-31).

[19] See *C.H.* 1.15 (11.18-22, 11.20-12.1 N-F); 10.6 (115.14-19 N-F).

[20] See above, note 12.

[21] Plato's conception of an internal dichotomy in man opposing his soul to his body is redefined by Aristotle when he opposes the νοῦς or 'intellect' to the ψυχή or 'soul'; see above, note 11. Aristotle not only denies immortality to the human soul, but repeatedly states that the intellect is man's most divine and only eternal element. See Aristotle, *EN* 1177b 26-1178a 2: the intellect as divine element in man by which he achieves complete happiness and partakes in the divine. See his conclusion in *EN* 1178a 2-7, that the intellect is man's true self; *EN* 1179a 22-32, the man who lives according to his intellect—that is, the man who pursues intellectual activity—cultivates his intellect and keeps it in the best condition is the most beloved of the Gods; *EE* 1248a 24-29, where the intellect is said to be man's highest element and to be connected with God; *De an.* 430a 23-25; *Metaph.* Λ, 1072b 23-26; *PA* 656a 8; 10; 686a 27-28; *GA* 736b 28; 737a 8-11; *Protr.* frg. 108 Düring. See P. Moraux, *Der Aristotelismus bei den Griechen*, i, Berlin/New York 1973, 230 and additional bibliography in note 24.

[22] *Norea* (NHC IX.2) 28.24-29.5. On the νοῦς in the present passage, which characterises both the Gnostic soul and God, see B.A. Pearson and S. Giversen,

able to 'inherit the first mind which <she> had received'.[23] As for the *Treatise on Resurrection*, its conception of the intellect also shows clear Aristotelian traces.[24] This triadic conception of man further appears in the *Paraphrasis of Shem*, in the *Gospel of Mary*, and the *Teachings of Silvanus* (see below). In line with *AA*, not only do all these texts consider the intellect to be man's highest aspect and clearly differentiated from the soul and the body, they also assert that the intellect or 'essential man' is a portion of the divine intellect that dwells in man.

1.1. *The intellect: Divine element in man*

It is interesting that *AA* does not seem to place special importance on the human soul, which although certainly of higher rank than the physical body can nevertheless be considered part of man's inferior being. Admittedly, *AA* repeatedly mentions the human soul and the term ψυχή may refer either to this intermediary part between intellect and body or to the whole person.[25] However, when *AA* describes or refers to the divine element in humans that transcends physical existence and can be liberated from the constrictions of the realm of movement, our text exclusively refers to the intellect and considers both soul and body as obstacles to this liberation.[26]

The emphasis on the intellect as the only divine and immortal element in man also appears in the *Treatise on Resurrection*, which states that neither the minds of those who have known the Son of Man nor their thoughts shall perish.[27] The same holds true for the *Paraphrasis of Shem*, where the pneumatic race is exalted by their partaking in the mind of the light[28] and in which salvation is achieved by those 'who possess the mind and the mind of the light of the spirit'.[29]

The *Gospel of Mary* is even more explicit in describing the role and

---

'The Thought of Norea', in: B.A. Pearson (ed.), *Nag Hammadi Codices IX and X*, Leiden 1981, *ad* 28.18-19 and 28.30-29.2.

[23] *Norea* (NHC IX.2) 28.3-5.

[24] *TreatRes* (NHC I.4) 46.22-24, on which, see above, note 23.

[25] V^r 85, 128-29, respectively (V^b 40.25, 41.34-35).

[26] V^r 83-101 (V^b 40.23-41.7).

[27] *TreatRes* (NHC I.4) 46.22-24. On the issue M.L. Peel, *The Epistle to Rheginos: A Valentinian Letter of the Resurrection: Introduction, Translation, Analysis and Exposition*, Philadelphia 1969, 114 note 25 and 'Treatise on Resurrection', 173; Layton, *Treatise*, 71-2. Both scholars suggest conspicuous similarities between the conception of the intellect in our treatise and in Aristotle.

[28] *ParaphShem* (NHC VII.1) 24.15-30.

[29] *ParaphShem* (NHC VII.1) 35.1-5.

character of man's intellect. Mary relates to the Saviour that she has seen a vision of him and he says to her 'Blessed are you, that you did not waver at the sight of me. For where the mind is, there is the treasure'.[30] Mary does not seem to understand, because she asks whether he who sees a vision sees it through the soul or through the spirit. Jesus' answer, however, clears up her doubts: 'He does not see through the soul nor through the spirit, but the mind which [is] between the two—that is [what] sees the vision.'[31] The same ideas pervade the *Teachings of Silvanus*, which presents a triadic conception of man formed out of a physical body, a soul and a 'divine mind which has come into being in conformity with the image of God. The divine mind has the substance of God.'[32]

The resolute assertions of the previous testimonies contrast with other sources of the period, which, though affirming that the divine dwells in man, significantly hesitate concerning the precise nature of this divine element. This hesitation is stressed (ridiculed?) by Celsus when in his *Alethes logos* he mentions

> those who hope that they will posses their *soul or mind* eternally with God, whether they wish to call this mind spiritual, or holy and blessed intellectual spirit, or a living soul, or a supercelestial and indestructible offspring of a divine and incorporeal nature, or whatever nature they care to give it.[33]

This hesitation is also evident in the heresiologists' interpretation of the nature of the Gnostic ψυχαῖος σπινθήρ or 'scintilla animae', namely the 'divine spark' or portion of the intelligible light in man.[34] Whereas according to some testimonies this Gnostic metaphor referred either to the soul or to the πνεῦμα or 'spirit',[35] according to others this spark is clearly identified with the νοῦς or 'intellect'.[36]

---

[30] *GosMary* (BG I) 10.14-16, which, incidentally, appears to be an echo of Matt 6.21 and Luke 12.34.

[31] *GosMary* (BG I) 10.20-23.

[32] *TeachSilv* (NHC VII.4) 92.23-26, the trichotomic conception in 92.10-32.

[33] Celsus, *ap.* Origen, *C. Cels.* 8.49, translation H. Chadwick (my italics).

[34] On the issue, M. Tardieu, 'ΨΥΧΑΙΟΣ ΣΠΙΝΘΗΡ: Histoire d'une métaphore dans la tradition platonicienne jusqu'à Eckhart', *Revue des études Augustiniennes* (1975) 225-55.

[35] See Irenaeus, *Adv. haer.* 1.13.3; Satornilus apud Epiphanius, *Pan.* 37.4.1-3; Clement of Alexandria, *Exc. Theod.* 1.3; 3.1 generally refers to the spark and identifies it in 53.5 as ἡ λογικὴ οὐράνια ψυχὴ or 'rational soul'.

[36] Hippolytus, *Ref.* 5.19.13-17; 10.11.7-10 at 10.11.10, where the σπινθήρ is explicitly explained with νοῦς.

2. Man's devolution and the appearance of the lower aspects of his being

It is obvious that if we assert that there is something divine in man, we also have to explain how and why the divine intellect has been degraded to its present condition and how the allegedly inferior parts of his being have developed. Devolution is indeed a possible explanation.

The idea of a devolution that brings the intellect (or the soul) to the lower abode of physical reality was so widespread in Late Antiquity that Iamblichus, the pupil of Porphyry, drew up a list including the numerous variants of this view. Festugière, who collected and systematised these examples,[37] has distinguished two main groups. On the one hand, we have the so-called 'optimistic' explanation, which is based on Plato's *Timaeus* and considers the fall of the soul or intellect as due to the will of God.[38] On the other hand, there is the so-called 'pessimistic' view, which includes two subcategories. According to the first one ('fault before the fall'), degradation is the result of the punishment inflicted for the soul's curiosity, audacity, or disobedience.[39] According to the second subcategory ('fault due to the fall'), devolution arises from the urge to create,[40] or from the contact with the demiurgical sphere, or, finally, from the union with physis.[41]

According to *AA*, however, things went differently. To begin with, our text significantly explains the intellect's degradation without recurring to external factors such as the influence of affections or of matter. The devolution that affects the intellect and that will finally cause it to be constrained by externals arises from its own deficiency, which is conceived of as a dispersal or division. The motif of dispersal of the primal unity is rather widespread in Gnosticism[42] and, as the

---

[37] Festugière, *La Révélation*, iii, 73-7; J. Dillon, *The Middle Platonists*, London 1977, 245-6.

[38] Alcinous, *Didask.* 178.30; Plotinus, *Enn.* 4.8.1.41; Iamblichus, 378.25 Wachsm.; *TriTrac* (NHC I.5) 76.23-77.11. On the latter passage see L. Painchaud and E. Thomassen, *Le Traité Tripartite* (NHC I.5), Quebec 1989, 333-4; see also *AuthTeach* (NHC VI.3) 26.6-20 and on the issue R. van den Broek, 'The Authentikos Logos', *VChr* 33 (1979) 260-86.

[39] For example in *Kore Kosmou* 21-24 (IV, 7.6-8.6 N-F), see Festugière, *La Révélation*, iii, 83-5.

[40] *C.H.* 1.11-13 (10.5-11.5 N-F); Gnostics of Plotinus (*Enn.* 2.9.11.21).

[41] Numenius, frg. 11.16-20 Des Places, on which Festugière, *La Révélation*, iii, 91-2; Gnostics of Plotinus (*Enn.* 2.9.10.19ff.).

[42] In general, H. Jonas, *Gnosis und spätantiker Geist*, i, *Von der Mythologie zur mystischen*

heresiologists more precisely affirm, played an important role in the Valentinian system.[43] As a matter of fact, it appears in the *Gospel of Truth*, where the return to the primal unity intends to restore the value lost in the dispersal, and in the *Tripartite Tractate* (see below).

Although *AA* is silent about the cause of this primal dispersion, it does explicitly refer to the intellect's split (καταχθείς)[44] and to its alienation (ἀπολισθήσας)[45] as the reason for its suffering. The intellect's dispersion results in ignorance and ignorance is the cause of a second stage of degradation because it initiates a series of affections: first of all insecurity and doubt, then fear and, finally, a desire to know, since knowledge can remove all previous affections. *AA* describes these affections by referring to the 'suffering' of both the intellect and of Eve.[46] It is noteworthy that the aforementioned *Gospel of Truth* presents a very similar exposition, since it puts the main focus on the appearance and development of affections and on how they generate the psychic and hylic levels of reality. Anguish and fear appear as direct consequences of ignorance, and as anguish grows solid like a fog, it provides the suitable context for error to appear, which 'became powerful' and 'worked on its own matter foolishly [or, in a void]'.[47]

The question of whether *AA* conceived matter as a substantialisation of the very affections, as the *Gospel of Truth* implies and Irenaeus reports of the Valentinian system,[48] is difficult to answer conclusively, given the

---

Philosophie, Göttingen 1954, 104-5; 139-40; A. Orbe, *Cristología Gnóstica: Introducción a la soteriología de los siglos II y III*, Madrid 1976, 293-8; G.P. Luttikhuizen, 'Gnostic Hermeneutics', in: R. Kessler and P. Vandermeersch (eds), *God, Biblical Stories and Psychoanalytic Understanding*, Frankfurt am Main 2001, 171-85 at 173-4.

[43] Heracleon, frg. 18 (apud Origen, *In Joh.* 13.11); Irenaeus, *Adv. haer* 1.14.5; 2.12.3; Clement of Alexandria, *Exc. Theod.* 36.2.

[44] We understand καταχθείς as passive aorist participle of κατάγνυμι 'break in pieces, shatter' or 'weaken, enervate' (LSJM, s.v.) and not as proceeding from κατάγω 'bring down' (act.). See Roig Lanzillotta, *Apocryphal Acts*, 147 note 58.

[45] V^r 75-77 (V^b 40.15-17). This dispersion seems also to be implied by Andrew's statement that he corrects Adam's (and the intellect's) imperfection by taking refuge in God (V^r 78-79 [V^b 40.18-19]) and by his description of the transcendent intellect as 'having recollected yourself (*scil.* the ἄνθρωπος) in your true condition' (V^r 95-97 [V^b 41.2-3]).

[46] See V^r 74-77 (V^b 40.14-17) and Roig Lanzillotta, *Apocryphal Acts*, chap. 4, §3.2.4.

[47] *GosTruth* (NHC I.3) 17.10-17.

[48] Irenaeus, *Adv. haer.* 1.2.3; see also Pseudo-Tertullian, *Adversus omnes haereses* 4.4 (CCSL 2, 1406.24-1407.4), on which C. Markschies, *Valentinus Gnosticus?*, Tübingen 1992, 408-9. H. Jonas, *Gnostic Religion*, Boston 1970 (1958), 183-4.

fragmentary condition of our text. The hypothesis, however, is plausible. Be that as it may, the final stage of devolution is the alienation of the intellect and of the soul in the realm of physis.[49] The original ignorance remains unaltered and is perpetuated by oblivion and by the deficiency of the body's cognitive means. Sensorial perception not only does not help man to achieve knowledge, it also prolongs his ignorance since it delivers him to the delusion of externals.[50]

How and why this devolution takes place and which are its immediate consequences is the subject matter of the two following subsections.

2.1. *The dispersion of the intellect*

As far as the dispersion of the intellect in *AA* is concerned, its alienation must be explained as a result of the appearance of a discrepancy between subject and object in the intellect's act of knowing.[51] As soon as the object of the intellect's acts of knowing is not the intellect itself, it loses its self-centred activity and, consequently, its unity. As a result, knowledge is no longer a direct and immediate matter and ignorance appears.

However, *AA* is not explicit about the first cause of this discrepancy within the intellect. This silence might simply be due to the fragmentary nature of our text, but it is also plausible that *AA* was more interested in the effects than in the cause of this primal dispersal. As a matter of fact, this is also the case in the *Gospel of Truth*. This text, which as we have seen presents many similarities with *AA*'s conceptual background, begins its narration about the fall of the Totality[52] simply by referring to the appearance of ignorance, without explaining how this ignorance originated.[53] According to this text 'oblivion did not come into existence

---

[49] V^r 213-14 (V^b 44.12-14), on which Roig Lanzillotta, *Apocryphal Acts*, chap. 4, §3.4.2.1.

[50] V^r 208-09 (V^b 44.7-8) with Roig Lanzillotta, *Apocryphal Acts*, chap. 4, §3.4 *passim*.

[51] See above, note 44 and Roig Lanzillotta, *Apocryphal Acts*, chap. 4, §5.1.1.

[52] On the question of whether we should see a reference to the totality of spiritual beings in the term 'Totality' as in other Valentinian texts, such as Irenaeus, *Adv. haer.* 1.14.1 or Clement of Alexandria, *Exc. Theod.* 30.2, or a reference to the totality of all creatures, see H.W. Attridge and G.W. MacRae, 'The Gospel of Truth', in: H.W. Attridge, *Nag Hammadi Codices I. Notes*, 39-135 at 42-3.

[53] *GosTruth* (NHC I.3) 17.10ff. See on the issue H.W. Attridge and G.W. MacRae, 'The Gospel of Truth', in: Attridge, *Nag Hammadi Codices I. Texts*, Leiden 1985, 55-122 at 77.

from the Father, although it did come into existence because of him.' It might be that in *AA*, as the *Gospel of Truth* and the *Tripartite Tractate* also seem to imply, ignorance, even though not directly produced by God, is necessarily implied by his transcendence.[54]

Despite the fact that the *Tripartite Tractate* is as silent about the primary cause of the intellect's dispersal as *AA* and the *Gospel of Truth*, this text may help us in understanding at least its implications. The *Tripartite Tractate* includes a particular version of the Valentinian process of devolution, since unlike the versions of Irenaeus[55] and the *Gospel of Truth* where the suffering is experienced by Sophia and by the Totality, respectively, in the *Tripartite Tractate* it is the Logos that experiences affections. Obviating now the fact that according to its writer the fall of the Logos has been planned by God,[56] it is interesting to note that, due to the Logos' inability to grasp the ungraspable and to bear the intensity of the light, it 'doubts' and 'looks down to the abyss'.[57] As a result, a 'division' and a 'turning away' take place and these in turn produce the appearance of ignorance and oblivion.[58] Similarly, the *Gospel of Truth* hints at the same wandering when it asserts that when the Totality '*went about* searching for the one from whom they had come forth (...), ignorance of the Father brought about anguish and terror'.[59]

2.2. *Man's ignorance and deficiency as a result of dispersion*

In any case, *AA* clearly refers not only to the division and alienation of the intellect, but also to its imperfection (τὸ ἀτελές).[60] Since Andrew states that he restores the imperfection of the intellect/Adam by taking refuge in God, it seems obvious that the intellect's original imperfection

---

[54] *Gos Truth* (NHC I.3) 18.1-3; 18.35-36, on which see Attridge & MacRae, 'Gospel of Truth. Notes', 47. They follow J.-É. Ménard, *L'Évangile selon Thomas*, Leiden 1975, 86 in relating our section to Irenaeus, *Adv. haer* 2.17.10 (*magnitudinem enim et virtutem Patris causas ignorantiae dicitis*) and link it with *TriTrac* (NHC I.5) 62.12ff., 71.7ff., 121.7-8, where ignorance of the Father arises indirectly from his withholding his essence in virtue of his transcendence.

[55] Irenaeus, *Adv. haer* 1.2.3; 1.4.1.

[56] *TriTrac* (NHC I.5) 76.23-77.11. See R. Kasser et al., *Tractatus Tripartitus Pars I: De supernis*, Bern 1973, 340 and Painchaud & Thomassen, *Traité Tripartite*, 333ff.

[57] *TriTrac* (NHC I.5) 77.15-20.

[58] *TriTrac* (NHC I.5) 77.21-25.

[59] *GosTruth* (NHC I.3) 17.4-11.

[60] V^r 77-78 (V^b 40.17), τὸ ἐνδεές; 78-79 (V^b 40.18), τὸ ἀτελές.

was its inability to focus its activity on God, as a result of which it was distracted or deviated from its source and origin.[61] This internal discrepancy of the intellect corresponds to the duality between the subject who thinks and the objects of thought and therefore presents a clear parallel to Plotinus' first hypostasis, which, as it presents the duality ἓν πολλά, occupies a lower rank of perfection than the One or absolute unity beyond thought.[62] Consequently, the imperfection and deficiency of the first couple, which Andrew and Maximilla restore through their behaviour, consists in their ignorance of the Father.

As we have already seen, this also appears to be the case in the *Tripartite Tractate*.[63] Division or dispersion is also a clear sign of deficiency in the *Gospel of Truth*: 'For the place where there is envy and strife is deficient, but the place where (there is) unity is perfect.'[64] According to this text, too, the first consequence of the dispersion is ignorance: 'since deficiency came into being because the Father was not known, therefore, when the Father is known, from that moment on the deficiency will no longer exist'. The *Gospel of Truth* repeatedly affirms that dispersion implies ignorance and ignorance deficiency: 'For he who is ignorant is in need, and what he lacks is great, since he lacks that which will make him perfect.'[65] In contrast, the unity of the Father is his perfection, which he 'retains within himself (...) granting it to them as a return to him and a perfect and unitary knowledge.'[66]

Consequently, as in Valentinianism, ignorance in *AA* is the cause of all steps of devolution: first, it is the origin of the degradation of the intellect to the level of the soul, and then that of the soul to the level of physical reality. We can therefore affirm that in *AA* the fall does not result from the punishment of sins such as curiosity, audacity or disobedience,[67] nor from the intellect's will to create[68] nor from its

---

[61] So already Orbe, *Cristología*, 162.

[62] Plotinus, *Enn.* 5.1.5; 2.4.5; 5.3.11; 6.7.15; see Dörrie, 'Zum Ursprung', 286-7 and notes 7 and 8.

[63] See above, note 56.

[64] *GosTruth* (NHC I.3) 24.25-29. Compare Irenaeus, *Adv. haer.* 1.16.2; 1.21.4. For the underlying Valentinian technical use of κένωμα or ὑστέρημα, see R. Haardt, 'Zur Struktur des Plane-Mythos im Ev. Veritatis des Cod. Jung', *WZKM* 58 (1962) 33. See also Clement of Alexandria, *Strom.* 4.13.90.1 (= Valentinus, frg. 5). Further, Ménard, *L'Évangile*, 120 and Attridge & MacRae, 'Gospel of Truth. Notes', *ad* 24.21.

[65] *GosTruth* (NHC I.3) 21.14-18; cf. 18.35, 19.9; see also Clement of Alexandria, *Exc. Theod.* 78.2.

[66] *GosTruth* (NHC I.3) 19.4-7.

[67] See above, note 39.

[68] See above, note 40.

union with the realm of φύσις.[69] *AA*'s conception of ignorance not only as the first motor of the process of devolution but also as the cause of each of the successive steps in degradation clearly exonerates the intellect of responsibility in its current degraded condition.

3. *Recollection as a return to unity and perfection through knowledge*

Obviating now the effects of the intellect's devolution,[70] man's current degraded condition can be thus explained from a purely epistemological perspective. The downward movement, which is equated with deficiency and imperfection, actually depicts the progressive dispersion of discursive thinking in its search to supersede lack of knowledge. As this movement begins in ignorance it is unavoidably conducive to error, then to wandering in the realm of phenomena and finally ends up in oblivion.[71]

But if dispersion was the origin of ignorance and ignorance in its turn the origin of deficiency, knowledge should be the starting point of the recovery of unity and perfection. Thus, it seems obvious that the upward movement, which is equated with perfection and completion, can also be seen from an epistemological perspective. In point of fact, *AA* does describe the inversion of the (discursive) cognitive process, by means of which what was dispersed is gradually recollected in order to recover the primal unity preceding ignorance.[72] However, things are not that simple. Before the intellect can engage itself in the liberation of its present constrictions, it must be woken from its state of lethargy.

Even though lacking the spark metaphor, *AA* conceives of man's intellect as a portion of divine light.[73] However, as is frequently the case in Gnostic texts, this godly spark appears to be powerless under

---

[69] See above, note 41.

[70] For which see above, §2.2, and Roig Lanzillotta, *Apocryphal Acts*, 233-5.

[71] *AA*'s fragment in V and its abundant vocabulary regarding ignorance and knowledge allow us to reconstruct the following sequence: ignorance (ἀγνοέω) → dispersion (κατάγνυμι, ἀπολισθάνω) → error (σφάλλω, πταῖσμα) → wandering (πλάνη) → oblivion (λήθη). See Roig Lanzillotta, *Apocryphal Acts*, 317.

[72] As in the case of the devolution, recollection and its epistemological steps can be reconstructed as follows: remembrance (ὑπομιμνήσκω, ὁράω) → return (μετανοέω, ἐπιστρέφω) → correction (διορθόω, κατορθόω, ἐπανορθόω) → recollection (συλλαμβάνω, ἀπολαμβάνω) → knowledge (ἐπίσταμαι, οἶδα, καταμανθάνω).

[73] V^r 91-93 (V^b 40.31-41.1) and above, §1.1.

the influence of the body and externals on the one hand and, on the other, of the soul and its affections.[74] This conception of the intellect as a potentiality explains why the ἄνθρωπος or essential man is simultaneously the highest part of immanent man as well as the intellect transcending all the constrictions of its physical imprisonment. As God is conceived of as light, by means of the light of logos he sets the human intellect aflame,[75] which until this moment existed in man as a simple potentiality. By exercising his intellective potential, man can gradually develop his intellect until in a last moment he achieves its full immanent actuality.

However, the essential man only regains his original condition by superseding all bodily hampering and recovering his true separated nature.[76] The starting point for this inversion of his current situation is the external, divine intervention that facilitates the remembrance and subsequent understanding that allows the change of mind (μετάνοια), which in turn generates the ἐπιστροφή, i.e. the 'turn around' of the intellect toward its proper objects.[77] At this point the first error is corrected and this provides direct knowledge and understanding. Once so far, the next step is intelligising, and this direct and immediate act of knowledge is no longer described in cognitive terms but simply as 'to see, to look at'.[78] Consequently, by recollecting what was dispersed in the world of nature, man supersedes his deficient condition and regains his original perfection.

Like the motif of a dispersal of the primal unity, that of gathering or recollection is also frequent in Gnostic texts. If the *Gospel of Truth* affirms that deficiency originates in ignorance, it also maintains that it will vanish with the knowledge of the Father. At that moment everything will be restored to its original unity:

> So from that moment on the form is not apparent, but it will vanish in the fusion of Unity, for now their works lie scattered. In time Unity will perfect the spaces. It is within Unity that each one will attain himself; within knowledge he will purify himself from multiplicity into Unity,

---

[74] See Roig Lanzillotta, *Apocryphal Acts*, chap. 4, §§3.4.2, 3.3.2 and 3.3.3, respectively.

[75] V^r 253-54 (45.14-16).

[76] V^r 83-101 (V^b 40.23-41.7) For a similar Aristotelian influence on the soteriology of the Gnostic *Apocryphon of John*, see Luttikhuizen, 'Traces of Aristotelian Thought', 194-5.

[77] V^r 130-38 (V^b 41.36-42.6).

[78] V^r 91-101 (V^b 40.31-41.7).

consuming matter within himself like fire, and darkness by light, death by life.[79]

Also, the *Tripartite Tractate* is clear about the need to restore 'that which used to be a unity'.[80] Those who live among the multiplicity of forms, inequality and change are restored to this unity when they confess 'the kingdom which is in Christ'.[81] The restoration of what is dispersed is also due to the knowledge received by the perfect man 'so as to return in haste to his unitary state'.[82]

The motif of dispersal and gathering also appears in a fragment of the Gnostic *Gospel of Eve* preserved by Epiphanius: 'I am thou and thou art I, and wheresoever thou art, there am I; and I am sown in all things. And from wheresoever thou wilt gatherest thou me, but in gathering me, thou gatherest thyself.'[83] According to H.M. Schenke, this fragment transmits the Gnostic idea that the 'Urmensch' is scattered among humans. Whereas the revealer is the 'Urmensch' in its original state, he who receives the revelation is the scattered anthropos. By recollecting the anthropos, man recollects himself, that is, he knows himself and restores the dispersal originated by ignorance.[84]

A fragment of the Gnostic *Gospel of Philip*, also preserved by Epiphanius, stresses both the notion of dispersal and its counterpart, viz. the recollection achieved by means of self-knowledge:

> 'I have recognized myself', it saith, 'and gathered myself from every quarter, and have sown no children for the archon. But I have pulled up his roots, and gathered my scattered members, and I know who thou art. For I', it saith, 'am of those on high'.[85]

The same notions also appear in Porphyry's *Letter to Marcella*, where

---

[79] *GosTruth* (NHC I.3) 25.3-19, trans. H.W. Attridge and G.W. MacRae.

[80] *TriTrac* (NHC I.5) 133.7.

[81] *TriTrac* (NHC I.5) 132.17-18.

[82] *TriTrac* (NHC I.5) 123.6f. For the motif of dispersal and gathering in other Nag Hammadi texts, see *StelesSeth* (NHC VII.5) 121.9-11; *TrimProt* (NHC XIII.1) 49.36ff.; *Thunder* (NHC VI.2) 16.19-20; 19.11-14.

[83] Epiphanius, *Pan.* 26.3.1, trans. F. Williams. See also *TriTrac* (NHC I.5) 66.24-25; *ManichKeph.* 228.1-13; *ManPs.* 175.19.

[84] H.-M. Schenke, *Der Gott 'Mensch' in der Gnosis: Ein religionsgeschichtlicher Beitrag zur Diskussion über die paulinische Anschauung über die Kirche als Leib Christi*, Göttingen 1962, 102-3.

[85] Epiphanius, *Pan* 26.13.2, trans. F. Williams. On this passage, see M. Tardieu, *Trois mythes gnostiques: Adam, Éros et Les animaux d'Égypte dans un écrit de Nag Hammadi (II,5)*, Paris 1974, 111 and note 176; Orbe, *Cristología*, 295-6. Note the parallelism with *AA*'s passage in V^r 75-77 (V^b 40.15-16).

he presents the Neoplatonic inner ascent from multiplicity to unity as the reunion of what was dispersed and scattered.[86] This ascent has an ethical character in a first stage, but afterwards becomes theoretical and finally contemplative.[87] We should not forget that Porphyry was Plotinus' pupil and that the motif of dispersal and gathering plays a central and mystical role in the system of the latter.[88]

Conclusions

The above survey has clearly show that *AA* presents a peculiar combination of elements, which appear dispersed through various philosophical and religious milieus, so as to provide a purely cognitive explanation of the devolution as well as of the way to restore the value lost in the downward movement. At a general level, the closest parallels to *AA*'s conception are to be found both in Hermetic and Gnostic sources, where ignorance is indeed the origin of disgrace and degradation, and knowledge that of redemption.[89] At a particular level, however, it is in the Gnostic milieu that we find the best parallels for *AA*'s views. As we have already seen, the discrepancy between subject and object in the act of knowledge as the origin of primal ignorance can be found in different Nag Hammadi texts.[90] These very same texts tend to consider that the result of this ignorance is dispersion, but that knowledge restores the unity of what was dispersed.

The heresiologists indeed reported that these notions were current among Gnostics. As stated above, the ideas of dispersal and ignorance and that of the restoration of unity through knowledge appear in the fragments of the Gnostic *Gospel of Eve* and *Gospel of Philip* preserved

---

[86] Porphyry, *Ad Marc.* 10; See Jonas, *Gnosis*, i, 140; Orbe, *Cristologia*, 296-7.

[87] Jonas, *Gnostic Religion*, 61.

[88] For the relevance of the motif in Augustine (plausibly through the mediation of Porphyry's writings, see Jonas, *Gnostic Religion*, 61-2), see *Confes.* 10.29.40: 'By continency verily are we bound up and brought back into One, whence we were dissipated into many'; *De trinit.* 4.11; cf. *Ord.* 1.3.

[89] The seventh Hermetic tractate (*C.H.* 7.2 [81.18-19 N-F]), for instance, states that lack of knowledge is the origin of evil and urges people to take off the 'cloth of ignorance' (τὸ τῆς ἀγνωσίας ὕφασμα) and similar instances can also be found both in *The Key* and in the eleventh tractate (*C.H.* 10.8 [117.4 N-F]; 11.21 [156.9-10]). See also *C.H.* 13.8 [204.3-6 N-F]. At the same time, knowledge is the only means to put an end to evil and to restore man's true nature to where it belongs (*C.H.* 10.15 [120.7-12 N-F]; 13.8 [204.3-6 N-F]; 13.18 [208.3-13 N-F]).

[90] See above, note 53.

by Epiphanius. Most interesting is that, according to the testimony of Irenaeus, these notions played a central role in the Valentinian system. If ignorance is the origin of deficiency, knowledge resolves lack of knowledge and imperfection.[91] Also, the notions of sleep or slumber that originate in ignorance as well as that of awakening seem to have played an important role in this system.[92] Most significant, however, is that we also see exactly the same combination of ideas among Valentinians: μετάνοια and ἐπιστροφή,[93] correction[94] and recollection of dispersal follow one another on the way to the recovery of the primal knowledge and the unity of perfection.[95]

Both the parallel between *AA*'s views and the ideas preserved by the heresiologist reports on the Valentinian system and the frequent contacts with Nag Hammadi texts with a Valentinian background suggest a close proximity between *AA*'s thought and this Gnostic group.

---

[91] For ignorance as deficiency, see Irenaeus, *Adv. haer.* 1.21.4; cf. 1.16.2; 1.186.10; Epiphanius, *Pan.* 34.20.9-12. See Valentinus, frg. 5 (= Clement of Alexandria, *Strom.* 4.13.90.1). For knowledge as restoration, see Irenaeus, *Adv. haer.* 1.16.2; 1.161.11-13.

[92] For the former, see Jonas, *Gnosis*, i, 113ff.; Painchaud & Thomassen, *Traité*, 342. *GosTruth* (NHC I.3) 17.10ff.; *TriTrac* (NHC I.5) 77.22-25 and Clement of Alexandria, *Exc. Theod.* 3.1-2

[93] See Roig Lanzillotta, *Apocryphal Acts*, 332-7.

[94] See Plotinus, *Enn.* 2.9.15.21ff., on which Orbe, *Cristología*, 163.

[95] See the version of this provided by the *Gospel of Truth*; Roig Lanzillotta, *Apocryphal Acts*, chap. 5, §5.3.2 and note 792.

REISEWEGE DER APOSTEL IN DEN *ACTA PETRI* AUS NAG HAMMADI

JÜRGEN TUBACH

Die Petrusakten aus Nag Hammadi und andere pseudepigraphische
Apostelgeschichten

Unter den Texten aus Nag Hammadi gibt es in Kodex VI (= NHC
VI.1) eine kleine Schrift, die analog zur neutestamentlichen Apostelgeschichte den Titel „Taten des Petrus und der Zwölf Apostel" (niPraksis
[< πράξεις] ĕnte Petros mĕn niMĕntsĕnows ĕnApostolos) trägt.[1] Sie
weist kaum gnostische Spuren auf und wird in der altkirchlichen
Literatur nie erwähnt. Der Buchtitel wird erst am Ende genannt (p.
12,20-22) und umschreibt den Inhalt so gut oder so schlecht wie die
Bezeichnung πράξεις (τῶν) ἀποστόλων, die seit Irenäus von Lyon und
Clemens Alexandrinus für die neutestamentliche Schrift gebräuchlich
ist.[2] Von der Form her reiht sich das Werk aus Nag Hammadi in die
Gruppe der älteren *Acta* ein, die den Namen eines Apostels tragen
(Johannes, Petrus, Andreas, Thomas, sowie Paulus) und Ende des
2./Anfang des 3. Jh. entstanden.[3] Mit den gerade genannten Petrus-
Akten[4] hat der Text nichts zu tun.[5] Diese fünf Apostelgeschichten
gehören gewissermaßen der biblisch inspirierten Unterhaltungsliteratur
an und weisen mehr Gemeinsamkeiten mit dem antiken Roman[6] auf
als mit der kanonischen Apostelgeschichte.

---

[1] Robinson 1972; Krause & Labib 1971, 36-41, 107-21 [Text/Übers.]; Wilson &
Parrott 1979, 204-29 [Text/Übers.]; Schenke 1973, 15-19, Schenke 1989, 374-80
und Schenke 2003, 443-53; Parrott & Wilson 1977, 289-94; Molinari 2000ᵃ, xiii-
xxv. Molinaris Datierung der Schrift in die Zeit von Kaiser Decius (249-251) musste
unberücksichtigt bleiben.
[2] Kümmel 1967[15], 100/1983[21], 127.
[3] Vgl. Plümacher 1978.
[4] Dazu jetzt Baldwin 2004.
[5] Plümacher 1978, 20; Schenke 1973, 15 und Schenke 1989, 370-1, anders
Krause 1972, 56-8.
[6] Hägg 1987, 190-203; Söder 1932, 181-87 u.ö. Die erhaltenen Texte und Textfrag-
mente aus der Antike sind in einer deutschen Ausgabe zugänglich: Kytzler 1983.

Die Reise von Petrus und den Zwölf Aposteln

Inhaltlich lässt sich die Nag Hammadi-Schrift nach ihren Schauplätzen im wesentlichen in drei oder vier größere Abschnitte unterteilen: die Stadt am Meer, die kleine Stadt auf einer Insel mitten im Meer, die Heimatstadt des Kaufmanns und Arztes Lithargoēl und die Rückkehr in die kleine Stadt auf der Insel. Die Hauptpersonen der Handlung sind Petrus, der gelegentlich in der 1. Person berichtet, und Lithargoēl. Am Ende kommen auch die Apostel in Wir-Form zu Wort, als hätte der anonyme Autor Tagebuchnotizen von Petrus und den Aposteln verwertet. Diesem Umstand ist es wohl zu verdanken, dass die Schrift *Acta Petri/Apostolorum* genannt wird. Einmal ergreift gegen Ende des Textes noch Johannes das Wort. Lithargoēl gibt sich Petrus in einer Szene, die in Lithargoēls Stadt spielt, als der Herr persönlich zu erkennen, was Petrus völlig entgangen war.

Während die beiden ersten Szenen den innerweltlichen Rahmen nicht sprengen, handelt es sich bei Lithargoēls Stadt um das himmlische Jerusalem, obwohl dieser Name nicht fällt und die Stadtbeschreibung nichts mit dem himmlischen Jerusalem der Johannesapokalypse gemein hat. Die Stadt, die Johannes (1,9) in einer visionären Schau aus dem Himmel herabkommen sieht (21,10), hat 12 Tore (mit den eingravierten Namen der 12 Stämme, cf. 21,12f) und eine kubische Form,[7] Lithargoēls Stadt besitzt dagegen nur 9, weshalb sie im Text quasi den Namen „Gotteslob in Neun-Toren" (p. 6,23-25)[8] trägt. Sonst gibt es keine Besonderheiten, die aus dem Rahmen fallen (z.B. Stadtmauer aus Jaspis, Innenstadt aus Gold durchsichtig wie Glas[9]). Nichts erinnert daran, dass die Reise der Apostel die Schwelle der Immanenz zur Transzendenz überschreitet außer der Bemerkung, dass der Weg zu dieser Stadt beschwerlich und mit großen Gefahren verbunden sei.

Die Quintessenz von Lithargoēls Botschaft spezifiziert gewissermaßen

---

[7] Sim 1996, 97-106.

[8] Da Ortsnamen eigentlich nicht mit dem unbestimmten Artikel versehen werden, ist es besser an dieser Stelle *hen* im Sinne von *hēn-* „in" zu verstehen und zum folgenden Satzteil zu ziehen (Schenke 1973, 17 und Schenke 1989, 371-2, 377, anders Wilson & Parrott 1979, 217; Parrott & Wilson 1977, 291). Im Saʿidischen wird die Präposition allerdings nie mit Vollvokal geschrieben. Die Passage müsste dann folgenden Wortlaut haben: „Das ist der Name meiner Stadt: in neun Toren lasst uns Gott preisen, wobei wir bedenken, dass das zehnte Tor das Haupt ist."

[9] Apk 21,18.21: Sim 1996, 106ff.

den Missionsbefehl aus Mt 28,16-20 unter Rückgriff auf Logia oder
Geschichten, die irdischen Reichtum als ein Hindernis für den Eingang
in das himmlische Reich anprangern,[10] und auf neutestamentliche
Krankenheilungen, in denen der Glaube an Jesu als unmittelbares
Resultat der vorangegangenen Heilung geschildert wird. Christus-
Lithargoēl ermahnt seine Jünger, sich von den Reichen fernzuhalten
und sich stattdessen, den Armen zuzuwenden, da nur sie die evange-
lische Botschaft mit offenem Herzen annehmen würden. Gleichzeitig
ernennt er die Jünger zu Spezialisten einer ganzheitlichen Medizin,
die sowohl den Leib als auch die Seele heilt, während die Ärzte dieser
Welt allenfalls dazu in der Lage sind, physische, nicht aber psychische
Gebrechen zu kurieren.

In der Eingangsszene—leider sind die ersten Zeilen dieser Passage
stark zerstört—scheint vorausgesetzt zu sein, dass die 11 Apostel (p.
9,21) sich versammelt und feierlich den Entschluß gefaßt haben, den
Missionsbefehl gemeinsam in die Tat umzusetzen (vgl. p. 5,12-14). Die
Kooptierung von Matthias per Losentscheid (Apg 1,15-26)[11] ließ der
anonyme Verfasser unberücksichtigt. Daraus könnte man den Schluß
ziehen, dass die Schiffsreise der Apostel, wie sie in den *Acta* (NHC)
geschildert wird, noch vor der Himmelfahrt (Apg 1,1-14) oder vor der
Wahl des Matthias stattfand. Die ganze Szenerie erinnert an das erste
Kapitel der Thomasakten.[12] Hier sitzen die Apostel zusammen und
bestimmen per Losverfahren das jeweilige Missionsgebiet.[13] Bekanntlich
wird Thomas als Missionsland Indien zugewiesen. Weder in den *Acta
Petri* (NHC) noch in den Thomasakten wird der Ort, an dem sich die
Apostel versammelt haben, näher spezifiziert. Theoretisch müsste es
in beiden Fällen Jerusalem sein. Der Fortgang der Handlung schließt
eine solche Annahme im Prinzip aus. Das Aposteltreffen findet in den
Thomasakten in einer Hafenstadt statt, da Thomas unmittelbar darauf
von Christus höchstpersönlich an den Kaufmann Ḥabbān (griech.
Abbanēs) verkauft wird, der für den „indischen" König Gondophares
einen Architekten sucht. Nach Unterzeichnung des Verkaufskontraktes
begeben sich Thomas und Ḥabbān auf ein im Hafen vor Anker lie-
gendes Schiff und segeln nach Indien. In den *Acta Petri* (NHC) gehen

---

[10] Z.B. das Bildwort Mk 10,25 (vgl. dazu Jeremias 1962, 194).
[11] Vgl. dazu Zwiep 2004.
[12] Syr. T.: Wright 1871, i, 171-333; Bedjan 1892, iii, 3-175; griech. T.: Bonnet
1903, 99-288, sowie Klijn 1962, Bornkamm 1964, Drijvers 1989.
[13] Vgl. Kaestli 1981.

die Apostel nach ihrer Zusammenkunft ans Meer und besteigen ein
Schiff, das dort ankert. Von den Seeleuten werden sie sehr freundlich
aufgenommen (p. 1,14ff). Vorausgesetzt ist offenbar, dass sich die Apostel in einer Stadt getroffen haben, deren Hafen sich in unmittelbarer
Nähe befand. Nach einer Schiffsreise, die einen Tag und eine Nacht
dauert, gelangen sie bei günstigem Wind[14] „zu einer kleinen Stadt
mitten im Meer" (p. 1,24-29). Petrus erkundigt sich an der Anlegestelle
des Schiffes nach dem Namen der Stadt. Einer der Hafenarbeiter
erklärt ihm, dass die Stadt „Siedlung" oder „Gründung" (kjōrĕkj)
hieße (p. 2,3) und fügt noch als Erklärung hinzu, dass der Name
„Festigkeit" (taro) und „Standhaftigkeit" ([hy]po[m]onē < ὑπομονή)
bedeute. Nachdem das Gepäck der 11 Reisenden ausgeladen worden war, begibt sich Petrus in die Stadt, um nach einer Herberge,
quasi einem Hotel, Ausschau zu halten. Seine Mitapostel bleiben mit
dem Gepäck im Hafen zurück. Zu den unverzichtbaren Utensilien
gehören u.a. Bücher, was aus einer Notiz von Petrus hervorgeht, wo
explizit gesagt wird, dass er eine kleine Handbibliothek mitgenommen
habe (p. 2,26f). In der Stadt trifft er einen Perlenhändler, der durch
die Straßen geht und mit lautem Ruf „Perlen, Perlen" (p. 2,32 u. p.
3,13) seine kostbare Ware anpreist. In seiner linken Hand hält er ein
Buchfutteral, das dem von Petrus gleicht (p. 2,26f), und in der linken
einen Wanderstab aus Amberholz.[15] Das letztere ist ein feinsinniger
Hinweis auf die Profession des Arztes, die der Fremde ausübt, wie der
Leser später noch erfährt. Das Balsam des orientalischen Amberbaumes
in Form von rohem oder flüssigem Storax wird zur Behandlung von
Krätze und Katarrh verwandt. Petrus fühlt sich auf geheimnisvolle
Weise zu dem Fremden, der als Mann von schöner Gestalt beschrieben
wird (p. 2,17-19), hingezogen. Da er ihn für einen Einheimischen hält,
fragt er ihn höflich nach einem Raum in einer Herberge der Stadt (p.
2,34ff). Doch der Fremde bekennt, dass er ebenfalls fremd in der Stadt
sei. Die Offerte des Fremden verhallt im Nichts. Als die Reichen der
Stadt den Ruf „Perlen" hören, kommen zwar einige auf die Straße,
andere beobachten den fahrenden Händler aus den Fenstern der
Obergeschosse, lassen sich aber die angebotene Ware nicht zeigen.
Sie glauben, dass der Fremde sie zum Narren halten will, da er keinen

---

[14] P. 1,26f: „Danach wehte ein Wind hinter dem Schiff" (vgl. Wilson & Parrott
1979, 205, anders Schenke 1973, 16 und Schenke 1989, 375: ... erhob sich ein
Sturm"). Weder *tēw* (Wind, Luft, Atem) noch das Verbum *nife* legen nahe, dass ein
Sturm aufzog.
    [15] „Ein Stab aus Styrax-Holz."

„Reisesack (pēra < πήρα) über seiner Schulter" trägt und auch keinen „Beutel (mit Perlen) in seinem Gewand" verborgen hat. Ferner hat er sich noch ein Schweißtuch (sudarion < σουδάριον < lat. sudarium) umgelegt, als wäre er ein Arbeiter und müsste sich ständig bei seiner Tätigkeit den Schweiß abwischen. Stattdessen kehren die Reichen dem vermeintlichen Perlenhändler den Rücken und verschwinden in ihren Häusern (3,29-31). Nur die Armen der Stadt strömen, als sie den Ruf des Fremden hören, herbei und sind neugierig (p. 3,32ff). Sie möchten die Perle nur ein einziges Mal sehen, damit sie ihren Freunden sagen können, „wir haben eine (echte) Perle mit (unseren eigenen) Augen gesehen" (vgl. p. 4,10.24-27). Die anwesenden Armen sind völlig verblüfft, als ihnen der Fremde das überraschende Angebot unterbreitet, er würde ihnen die Perle sogar schenken, wenn sie zu ihm in seine Stadt kämen (p. 4,11ff). Den Einwand der Armen, niemand würde einem Bettler eine Perle schenken, höchstens Brot oder Geld, lässt der Fremde nicht gelten und wiederholt seine Offerte. Dieser nochmaligen Bekräftigung des Angebots schenken die Armen und Bettler Glauben und freuen sich (p. 4,35). Seine wertvolle Perle zeigt der Perlenhändler nicht. Er besitzt nämlich nur eine einzige, mit der es natürlich eine besondere Bewandtnis hat.

Aus den folgenden Zeilen ergibt sich, dass Petrus den Weg in die Stadt irgendwie kennt, trotzdem läßt er sich nochmals von dem Fremden, „der diese Perle verkauft", den Reiseweg erklären. Er bekennt u.a., dass er und seine Mitbrüder treue „Diener (od. Sklaven)[16] Gottes" seien, denen aufgetragen sei, „das Gotteswort übereinstimmend in jeder Stadt zu verkünden" (p. 5,10-14). Gleichzeitig erkundigt er sich nach dem Namen des Fremden, der ihm bereitwillig Auskunft gibt und auch eine „Etymologie" liefert (p. 5,17f). Er heiße Lithargoēl, was „der Gazellenstein, der leicht ist" bedeute, womit auf die verhältnismäßig großen hellen Augen der Gazelle als Synonym für eine besonders kostbare Perle angespielt sein dürfte.[17] Lithargoēl ist ein typischer Engelname, wie aus der Endung –ēl (< hebr. 'ēl, Gott) ersichtlich

---

[16] Hier wird statt des häufigen hĕmhal „Diener, Sklave" der gebrochene Plural von bōk benutzt, das eigentlich nur im Bohairischen und Fayyumischen vorkommt. Die Bedeutung ist dieselbe, d.h. es wird nicht zwischen „Diener" und „Sklave" differenziert.

[17] Vgl. Wilson & Parrott 1979, 215 Anm, ähnlich Schenke 1989, 376 Anm. 6. Der vermutete Zusammenhang des griechischen δορκάς (= kopt. kjahse) mit δέρκομαι (sehen, Augen haben, strahlen) ist nur scheinbar und beruht auf Volksetymologie (Pokorny 1959, Frisk 1973).

ist. Fast alle Engelnamen enden auf –ēl. Während ein Großteil der
Engel Namen trägt, die dem Hebräischen oder Aramäischen entlehnt
sind,[18] sofern es sich nicht um Phantasienamen handelt, ist Lithargoēls
Name eine Zusammensetzung aus zwei griechischen Wörtern, nämlich lithos (λίθος), „Stein" und argos (ἀργός) „glänzend, schimmernd,
weiß". Der „weiß glänzende Gottesstein", wie das griechisch-hebrä-
ische Kompositum wiedergegeben werden müsste, ist für eine Perle
ein durchaus passender Name. Daß jeweils eine Anspielung auf die
Perle in Name und Deutung vorliegt, ergibt sich erst aus dem Fortgang der Handlung.[19]

Nur wer auf die Güter dieser Welt verzichtet und beständig fastet,
wird auf diesem Weg das Ziel nicht verfehlen und darf schließlich
Lithargoēls Stadt betreten. Wer aber dem Verzicht und dem Fasten
nichts abgewinnen kann, fällt unter die Räuber und wilden Tiere, die
am Wegesrand lauern und Tod und Verderben bringen. Als überflüs-
sigen Luxus gelten schöne Kleider und die übertriebene Sorge um das
tägliche Brot. Konkret wird folgendes genannt: Wer sich in schönen
Kleidern auf diesen Weg macht und meint auf diese Weise die Stadt
Lithargoēls zu erreichen, täuscht sich. Die am Wegesrand lauernden
Räuber rauben ihn aus und bringen ihn um. Wer Brot mitnimmt, wird
von den schwarzen Hunden getötet. Nach Wasser als Wegzehrung
lechzen die Wölfe. Bei Fleisch und Gemüse als Nahrungsvorrat, kann
man sicher sein, dass der Löwe und der Stier kommen, von denen
der eine vegetarisch lebt, der andere nicht (p. 5,21-6,8 und 7,26-34).
Angesichts dieser Gefahren seufzt Petrus und gedenkt des Beistandes
Christi. Lithargoēl versichert ihm, dass Jesus ihm helfe, wenn er fest an
ihn glaube. Auf die Frage, wie die Stadt heiße, erhält Petrus die bereits
erwähnte Antwort „Gotteslob in neun Toren". Nach dem Abschied
von Lithargoēl ist Petrus im Begriff zu seinen Mitaposteln zu gehen,
als er plötzlich eine Stadt sieht, die von Wasser und hohen Mauern
umgeben ist. Es ist jedoch nicht die kleine Stadt mitten im Meer,
sondern anscheinend die Stadt Lithargoēls, in der diejenigen wohnen,
wie ihm ein alter Mann erklärt, die das Joch des Glaubens auf sich
genommen haben. Petrus holt seine Gefährten. Da sie dem beständigen
Fasten verpflichtet sind und auch keine kostbaren Gewänder tragen,
kommen sie wohlbehalten in jener Stadt als ihrem Ziel an. Als sie vor
dem Stadttor (pylē [< πύλη]) stehen und sich noch über die glücklich

---

[18] Vgl. die Liste bei Michl 1962, 200-39.
[19] Vgl. auch den Beitrag von István Czachesz in diesem Band, § 2.

überstandenen Gefahren unterhalten, kommt ihnen Lithargoēl als Arzt gekleidet entgegen. Unter dem Arm trägt er ein Heilmittel aus Narde (nartos [< νάρδος] ĕmpahre) und sein Famulus, der hinter ihn hergeht, bringt den Arzneikasten „voll mit Heilmitteln".

Ähnlich wie die Jünger von Emmaus (Lk 24,16) oder Maria aus Magdala (Joh 20,11-18) erkennen die Apostel nicht, wer der Arzt eigentlich ist, der ihnen entgegen kam (p. 8,20). Petrus bittet den Arzt, sie zum Haus von Lithargoēl zu führen, ehe es Abend wird (vgl. Lk 20,29). Der Arzt ist erstaunt, dass Petrus und die Seinen mit Lithargoēl Bekanntschaft geschlossen haben, der sich nicht jedem offenbare, da er „der Sohn eines großen Königs" sei. Im folgenden enthüllt der Arzt seine wahre Identität. Als Lithargoēl-Christus gibt er sich seinen Jüngern zu erkennen. Die Geschichte ist nach Vorbild von Joh 20,11-18 gestaltet, wo Maria aus Magdala dem Auferstandenen am Grab begegnet, ihn aber nicht sofort erkennt. Den Abschluß des Textes bildet die Mahnung, die Reichen bei der Mission zu meiden, womit offenbar gemeint ist, dass die Apostel nicht in den Häusern der Wohlhabenden einkehren und sich fürstlich bewirten lassen sollen.

Eine fiktive Reise nach realen Vorbildern?

Bei der Textlektüre stellt sich unweigerlich die Frage, ob die Komposition des Textes frei der Phantasie entsprungen ist oder ob der Autor bei der Stadtbeschreibung und der Reiseroute sich an einem realen Vorbild orientierte. Biblische Vorbilder als Inspirationsquelle scheiden aus, da die himmlische Stadt ganz unneutestamentlich beschrieben wird. Die Reise zu einer Stadt mitten im Meer, die als größere Handelsstadt vorgestellt ist, fehlt ebenfalls im Neuen Testament. Der exegetischen Verarbeitung in einem narrativen Kontext entstammt die Warnung vor den Reichen verbunden mit der gleichzeitige Hochschätzung der Armen. Die Enthüllung der Identität des Arztes als Lithargoēl bzw. Jesus folgt biblischen Vorbildern. Daß Lithargoēl ein Perlenhändler ist, der aber nur eine einzige Perle im Angebot hat, geht auf eine allegorische Interpretation des Gleichnisses von der Perle (Mt 13,45) zurück, die im Thomas-Evangelium (Log. 76)[20] in einer älteren Form überliefert

---

[20] Guillaumont 1959, 42; Leipoldt 1967; Koester 1989; Meyer 1992; Fieger 1991.

ist.[21] Im Grunde ist es eine Fortsetzungsgeschichte des Gleichnisses, die beschreibt, was geschieht, nachdem der Kaufmann die eine Perle, ein Sinnbild des wahren Glaubens, erworben hat.

Wie oben erwähnt, besitzt die Eingangsszene eine gewisse Ähnlichkeit mit dem Eröffnungskapitel der Thomasakten. Die Reise beginnt jeweils an dem Ort, an dem die Zusammenkunft der Apostel stattfand. In den Akten ist es explizit eine Hafenstadt. In den *Acta Petri* (NHC) ist der Hafen in unmittelbarer Nähe der Stadt. Zwischen dem anvisierten Zielort und dem Ausgangspunkt liegt in beiden Fällen ein Aufenthalt in einer Hafenstadt. In den Thomasakten segelt Thomas mit dem Kaufmann Ḥabbān bei günstigem Wind bis nach Andrapolis (oder Androapolis, in der syrischen Version aber Snṭrwyq, wohl Sanaṭrūq),[22] wo sie am Hochzeitsfest der Königstochter teilnehmen, das von der ganzen Stadt feierlich begangen wird (3-16). Petrus und die Apostel segeln ebenfalls mit einem günstigen Wind und erreichen eine Stadt. In der nächsten Szene beider Texte ist das Ziel erreicht. Thomas gelangt in die Städte Indiens bzw. ins Reich von Gondophares und Petrus betritt die Stadt Lithargoēls. Daß es mit dieser Stadt eine besondere Bewandtnis hat, lässt sich nur aus der Identität Lithargoēls mit Christus schließen und, wie wir noch sehen werden, aus den Gefahren des Weges.

In den *Acta Petri* (NHC) ist auffällig, dass den Aposteln quasi der Umgang mit den Reichen verboten wird. Sie sollen sich den Armen zuwenden und sich unter allen Umständen von den Wohlhabenden fernhalten. Kein Reicher betritt daher die Bühne des Geschehens. Sie sind stumme Randfiguren der Erzählung. Vergleicht man diesen Zug der Geschichte mit den Thomasakten, kann man sich des Eindrucks nicht erwehren, dass der anonyme Autor gegen einen bestimmten Typus von Schriften polemisiert, die seinem Armutsideal zuwiderlaufen. Die enkratisch geprägten Thomasakten warnen zwar wiederholt vor den Gefahren des Reichtums, lassen aber den Apostel stets in den Kreisen des Hochadels verkehren. Das gewöhnliche Volk besitzt nur eine Statistenrolle. Thomas sucht im Verlauf der Handlung nie die Behausungen der Armen auf. Stets übernachtet er in den Häusern seiner adligen Gönner. Ähnliches gilt von der Doctrina Addai, der Legende von der Christianisierung Edessas.[23] Addai wohnt bei einem

---

[21] Jeremias 1962, 198; [TB], 132.
[22] Vgl. Delauny 1974, 12, bes. Anm. 2, anders Waldmann 1996, 48-9.
[23] Phillips 1876; Howard 1981; Desreumaux 1993; González Nuñez 1995.

reichen Kaufmann und hält sich am liebsten am Hof von Abgar, dem Schwarzen, auf (= V. Ukkāmā, 4 v. Chr.-7 n. Chr. und 13-50 n. Chr.). Offenbar wird in den *Acta Petri* (NHC) die allzu große Nähe der christlichen Sendboten zur Oberschicht einer kritischen Würdigung unterzogen, zumal im Neuen Testament sich Jesus mit dieser sozialen Schicht in der Regel nicht abgibt. Daß die Missionare den engen Kontakt zu den herrschenden Schichten suchten, kommt in erster Linie in den Regionen jenseits des Euphrats vor, im Reich der Arsakiden und Sasaniden und in den kulturell von ihnen beeinflussten Gebieten. Das nördliche Mesopotamien gehörte zwar seit 165 n. Chr. zum römischen Reich, vollzog aber erst allmählich einen Paradigmenwechsel. Der edessenische Adel und das Königtum sind auch in der römischen Zeit östlichen Vorbildern verpflichtet. In Armenien gehörte der Katholikos, zumindest in der Sasanidenzeit, dem Hochadel an.

Die Reiseroute in den Thomasakten und den *Acta Petri* (NHC) besitzt eine gewisse formale Ähnlichkeit. Es handelt sich jeweils um Abfahrt von einem Hafen, Zwischenaufenthalt in einer anderen Hafenstadt und die Ankunft am Zielort. Liegt tatsächlich eine Polemik gegen das Verhalten der Missionare im Perserreich und den Nachbargebieten vor, ließe sich erwägen, ob die Reiseroute abgesehen vom Zielort mehr oder weniger identisch ist und obendrein einem realen Vorbild nachempfunden ist. Wenn die Thomasakten in Edessa oder Umgebung Anfang des 3. Jh. entstanden sind, stellte sich ein Leser die Indienfahrt des Apostels mit Sicherheit als Reise durch das Erythräische Meer vor, aber nicht durch das heutige Rote Meer, sondern durch den Persischen Golf. Segelten Kaufleute aus Mesopotamien nach Indien, begaben sie sich in die Hauptstadt der Mesene,[24] nach Spasinou Charax[25] oder nach Forat und bestiegen ein Schiff, das Kurs auf Indien nahm. Spasinou Charax war ein internationaler Umschlagplatz für Waren aus dem Osten wie dem Westen und in der parthischen Zeit einer der wichtigsten Seehäfen des Erythräischen Meeres. Man konnte von hier aus nicht nur nach Indien segeln,[26] sondern bei Bedarf auch weiter nach Südostasien und China. Da Thomas ins Reich des Gondophares im östlichen iranischen Hochland (Afghanistan, Pakistan) reist und offensichtlich bis ins Indus-Delta segelt, kommt eine Reise durch das

---

[24] Vgl. Schuol 2000; Nodelman 1959/60.
[25] Zur Lokalisierung vgl. Hansman 1967, 1984, 1992.
[26] Vgl. Schuol 2000, 427ff.

Rote Meer nicht in Frage.[27] Der Monsunwind hätte das Schiff eher
nach Mittel- oder Südindien getrieben als an den Indus. Daher ist
anzunehmen, dass die Protagonisten der beiden Akten eine (fiktive)
Reise durch den Persischen Golf machen. Meistens weht hier das
ganze Jahr über ein Nordostwind,[28] der eine Fahrt in Richtung Indien
begünstigt. Daher wird sowohl in den Thomasakten als auch den *Acta*
(NHC VI,1) betont, dass ein günstiger Wind aufkam. Den Spuren des
Apostels Thomas folgt später Mani und unternimmt eine Indienreise.
Er segelt von Forat nach Deb im Indus-Delta mit einer Zwischenstation
in einem Hafen der Golfküste, eventuell auf der Insel Baḥrayn.[29] An
eine ähnliche Route dachte offenbar der Autor der Thomasakten, der
den Apostel nur in einer nicht näher lokalisierbaren Stadt einen Zwischenaufenthalt einlegen lässt, ehe er indischen Boden betritt. Petrus
und die Apostel beginnen ihre Seereise offenbar in Spasinou Charax
und steuern eine Hafenstadt an, die eine Tagesreise (oder mehr) entfernt ist. Das könnte die Insel Ḥarg sein, die in der spätparthischen
und sasanidischen Zeit auf der Fahrt nach Indien angesteuert wurde,
um die Wasservorräte der Seefahrer aufzufrischen.[30] Ein weiterer Ort,
der auf der Route nach Indien von Schiffen angelaufen wurde, ist die
bereits erwähnte Insel Baḥrayn,[31] das Dilmun der altorientalischen
Zeit, das bereits den alten Babyloniern nicht nur als Handelsplatz
bekannt war, sondern auch als paradiesischer Ort, an den Ziusudra,
der babylonische Noah, entrückt wird.[32] Für eine Begegnung mit einem
Sendboten der himmlischen Welt wäre das natürlich eine geeignete
Lokalität.[33] Statt mit dem Schiff weiter nach Osten zu reisen, begeben

---

[27] Anders Waldmann 1996, 48-9 u.ö.
[28] Schuol 2000, 407.
[29] Vgl. Tubach 1995, 165-9.
[30] Schuol 2000, 407.
[31] Schuol 2000, 209-211, 402-3.
[32] Edzard 1965, 129, 138; Ringgren 1979, 85.
[33] Der substantivierte koptische Infinitiv kjōrĕkj „Gründung, Siedlung" erweckt
Klangassoziationen an den Namen der mesenischen Hauptstadt Spasinou Charax/aram.
Karak ʾAspasinā, später meist Karak(ā di) Mayšān (syr. Karḵā dMayšān) genannt, die
mehrmals durch Überschwemmungen zerstört wurde. Das griechische charax (Pfahl,
Pfahlwerk, Verschanzung) lehnt sich teilweise an das aramäische karak „befestigte
Stadt" an, bezieht sich aber in erster Linie auf die Befestigung des Untergrundes durch
Pfähle. Charax lag nicht direkt am Zusammenfluß von Euphrat und Tigris, sondern
etwas davon entfernt. Der Eulaios floß in einer Schleife an der Stadt vorbei. Hier lag
auch der Hafen. Stadtgelände und die Schiffsanlegestellen waren räumlich getrennt (vgl.
dazu Hansman 1967, 1984, 1992, vgl. auch Tubach 1993). Im Frühjahr, wenn Euphrat
und Tigris Hochwasser führten, verwandelte sich die Umgebung von Charax in einen

sich Petrus und die Apostel an das Tor der himmlischen Stadt und werden zur Mission an den alten Ort zurückgeschickt, jedoch mit einem modifizierten Missionsauftrag.

Der Seelenaufstieg als Himmelsreise

Daß der Text tatsächlich eine engere Beziehung zum südlichen Mesopotamien hat, ergibt sich aus einer weiteren Beobachtung. Die geschilderten Gefahren, die mit dem Reiseweg zu Lithargoēls Stadt verbunden sind, besitzen eine enge Parallele zum Seelenaufstieg in der mandäischen Religion, der auch den Manichäern nicht unbekannt war.[34] In den *Acta Petri* (NHC) handelt es sich um die Prolepsis des Seelenaufstiegs, eine Himmelsreise der Seele, wofür es in der Ginza ebenfalls eine Analogie gibt. Die Mandäer sind in religiöser Hinsicht die letzten Ausläufer der antiken Gnosis und konnten dank der Sumpflandschaft des südlichen Babylonien bis in die Gegenwart überleben. Stirbt ein Mandäer, durchwandert seine Seele die 7 Planetensphären nebst der Fixsternsphäre,[35] bis sie, sofern sie zu Lebzeiten dem Ruf des Lebens folgte, in die Lichtwelt eingeht, was gewissermaßen der letzte Himmel, also der neunte, ist, der mit der Transzendenz identisch ist. Lithargoēls Stadt hat daher 9 Tore als einem Sinnbild der einzelnen Sphären, die man überwinden muß, um in die transzendente Welt zu gelangen. Da sich die Tore nicht sinnvoll auf eine quadratische Stadtanlage wie dem himmlischen Jerusalem im Neuen Testament verteilen lassen, muß der Anonymus an eine orientalische Rundstadt gedacht haben, wie man sie häufig in Mesopotamien und Persien findet. Das 10. Tor, das im Text erwähnt wird,[36] ist der Zugang zum Palast des

---

See, aus dem nur Charax herausragte. Dann wandelte sich Charax gewissermaßen zu einer Stadt im Meer, wie es in den *Acta Petri* beschrieben wird. Bei den beiden irdischen Orten der Akten ist jedes Mal vorausgesetzt, dass es zwischen Hafen und Stadt eine räumliche Trennung gibt. Sofern man die im Text gegebene Deutung des Stadtnamen nicht allegorisch auffasst, kann man sie auf die Bemühungen der Baumeister beziehen, der Stadt einen festen Grund als Schutz vor Hochwasser zu verleihen. Vermutlich muß man zwischen Reiseroute und Stadtbeschreibung einen Unterschied machen, da der Autor die Städte immer ähnlich beschreibt.

[34] Vgl. Richter 1997.

[35] Brandt 1889, 74-5; Rudolph 1970, i, 123.

[36] Schenke 1973, 14, dachte an die Tore des herodianischen Tempels, was aber nur auf das Innenheiligtum zutrifft, sofern man das „Große Tor" als zehntes zählt und den eigentlichen Tempelbau und den Außenhof mit seiner Mauer und ihren 12 Toren unberücksichtigt lässt (Busink 1980, 1063ff., 1178ff, Abb. 242, 253). Nach der

himmlischen Großkönigs und seines Sohnes Lithargoēl-Christus.

Menschen, die nicht nach den Geboten der Religion leben, ereilt
nach mandäischer Vorstellung im Diesseits wie Jenseits ein schlimmes
Schicksal. Ihnen lauern „räuberische Wölfe" und „verderbliche Löwen"
auf.[37] Besonders gefahrvoll ist die *massiqtā*. Jeder Planetenherrscher
verfügt über eine Unzahl an furchterregender Gehilfen, die den Seelen beim Aufstieg durch die Himmelssphären zusetzen, ehe sie in die
Lichtwelt gelangen. Wer sich bestimmter Vergehen schuldig gemacht
hat, wird an einer der Wachtstationen (maṭṭarāṭā) festgehalten und
seinen Peinigern ausgeliefert. Nur wer sich an den Wachtstationen der
einzelnen Sphären durch gute Taten ausweisen kann–man braucht
u.a. einen Reisepaß (pruḏkā), eine Art Transitvisum–darf seine Reise
fortsetzen. Beschreibungen des Seelenaufstieges sind in der Ginza
an drei Stellen erhalten. Im „linken Ginza" (ginzā smālā) handelt
es sich um eine relativ lange Passage,[38] im „rechten Ginza" (ginzā
yammīnā) wird einmal die postmortale Reise der Seele[39] geschildert
und einmal eine Himmelsreise, die den *Acta Petri* (NHC) gleicht d.h.
der Hauptakteur kehrt mit einem Missionsauftrag auf die Erde, die
Tībīl (hebr., aram., syr. tēbēl/tēḇēl, „Erde" < akk. tābālu, „trockenes
Land") zurück.[40] Dem Aufstieg der Seele in die Lichtwelt widmet sich
ferner der Diwān ʾAḇāṭūr.[41] Das dritte Stück des fünften Buches der
„rechten Ginza" ist als Ich-Erzählung der Seele gestaltet, die an verschiedenen Wachtstationen vorbei zur Lichtwelt emporsteigt. An der
ersten maṭṭartā begegnet die Seele „gierigen, tollwütigen Hunden", die
ihr großen Schrecken einjagen, obgleich sie blind und taub sind.[42] Bei
jeder Wachstation, die die Seele passiert, erkundigt sie sich, wer dort

---

Johannesapokalypse kann das himmlische Jerusalem wegen der dauernden Präsenz
Gottes eines Tempels entbehren (21,22).

[37] Lidzbarski 1925, 183.

[38] Lidzbarski 1925, 443-52.

[39] Lidzbarski 1925, 183-90.

[40] Lidzbarski 1925, 205-12, volkstümliche Tradition: Drower 1937, 300-8.

[41] Drower, 1950.

[42] Lidzbarski 1925, 183, vgl. die „Hunde des Feuers" in den manichäischen Psal-
men des Herakleides (Richter 1997, 153 Anm. 6, 161, 164). In den „Chaldäischen
Orakeln" kommen die chthonischen Hunde aus der Erde hervor und hindern die
Seelen am Aufstieg zu Gott (Lewy 1978, 545; Loth 1994, 796; Richter 1997, 153
Anm. 6). Der Hund ist in der Spätzeit das heilige Tier des Gottes Nergal (-Herakles),
der mit Ereschkigal, der Herrin der Unterwelt verheiratet ist. Nergal wurde bis in
die sasanidische bzw. römische Zeit in Mesopotamien und teilweise in Syrien ver-
ehrt. Im RAC-Artikel von Loth wird der Hund als Begleiter und heiliges Tier von
Nergal-Herakles nicht behandelt.

seine verdiente Strafe verbüßen muß. Da ihr keine Verfehlungen zur Last gelegt werden, kann sie unbehelligt weiterziehen. Sie erfährt, was mit den Mördern, Ehebrechern, Dieben und Meineidigen geschieht.[43] An der nächsten Station erfährt die Seele, dass hier Richter und Adlige inhaftiert sind nebst den Frauen, die ihre eigenen Kindern umkommen ließen, während sie bei den Reichen als Ammen ihren Dienst verrichteten.[44] Im übernächsten Wachthaus begegnet die aufsteigende Seele dem Hochadel, den Großen, die die Armen ausplündern, die Bedürftigen von ihren Haustüren vertreiben und keine Almosen geben.[45] Nachdem die Seele, „der Mann von erprobter Gerechtigkeit", auch die achte Wachtstation unbemerkt passiert hat, erreicht sie das Lichtreich jenseits der sichtbaren Welt, wo das „Leben" (ḥayyē), der Höchste der Lichtwelt, in der Transzendenz thront. Die Passage aus der „linken Ginza" enthält eine Stelle, die vor falschem Fasten warnt,[46] überschneidet sich aber mit der zuvor erwähnten nur an wenigen Stellen. Wesentlich interessanter ist das sechste Buch des rechten Teils der Ginza, das eine Parallele zur Himmelsreise der Apostel und ihrer anschließenden Rückkehr bietet. Der Held der Ich-Erzählung, die aber nicht konsequent durchgehalten wird, ist Dīnānūkt (< pers. Dēnānūḫt, „derjenige, der der Religion gemäß redet"), „der weise Schriftgelehrte, das Tintenbuch der Götter",[47] dessen Seele eine Reise in die Lichtwelt antritt, zum „großen Leben (ḥayyē rabbē), dem ersten Vater ('ābā qadmāyā)".[48] Dīn-Mlīk-'Uṭrā, der fortan als Psychopomp fungiert, lässt Dīnānūkts Seele aus dem Körper treten. Winde tragen sie empor zu den einzelnen Wachthäusern, vor deren Herren sich Dīnānūkt verneigen will, aber stets von Dīn-Mlīk-'Uṭrā abgehalten wird, da eine Proskynese nur dem „ersten Vater" gebührt. Nachdem die beiden die letzte maṭṭartā passiert haben, die hier 'Abāṭūr gehört,[49] gelangen sie an die Schwelle des Lichtreiches. Dīnānūkts Psychopomp fordert den bibliophilen Dīnānūkt auf, dass er all seine Bücher verbrenne und auf Erden den Ruf des Lebens verkünde. Zum Entsetzen von seiner Frau Nūrāitā („die Feuerige") wirft Dīnānūkt seine Bücher ins Feuer,

---

[43] Vgl. die entsprechenden Gebote des Dekalogs (Ex 20,13.14.15.16). Die Reihenfolge ist dieselbe wie in der Ginza (Lidzbarski 1925, 185).
[44] Lidzbarski 1925, 186.
[45] Lidzbarski 1925, 188; vgl. „linker Ginza" 448, 451.
[46] Lidzbarski 1925, 456.
[47] Lidzbarski 1925, 205-7.
[48] Lidzbarski 1925, 208-9.
[49] Lidzbarski 1925, 210, vgl. „linker Ginza" 451.

zieht in die Welt hinaus, verkündigt den Ruf des Lebens und sammelt
Jünger um sich. Nach seinem Tode wird seine Seele „zum Tor des
Hauses des Lebens" geführt. Man öffnet ihm das Tor und zieht den
„großen Vorhang der Sicherheit in die Höhe", d.h. Dīnānūkt erhält das
Privileg, unmittelbar vor den Thron des Lichtkönigs treten zu dürfen,
was an rabbinische Vorstellungen erinnert, nach denen der göttliche
Thron durch einen Vorhang verhüllt ist. Bei Audienzen thronte der
sasanidische Herrscher ebenfalls hinter einem Vorhang.[50]

Die in den *Acta Petri* (NHC) geschilderten Gefahren auf dem Weg in
die himmlische Stadt sind nicht bis ins Detail mit den Beschreibungen
des Seelenaufstiegs in der Ginza bzw. den Gefährdungen des Lebens-
weges identisch. Es kommen als Tiere Hunde, Löwen und Wölfe vor.
Der Stier taucht nur in Form des Engelnamens Taurēl („Gottesstier")
auf. Taurēl, wohl ein mandäischer Nachfahre des Himmelsstiers[51] in
der babylonischen Mythologie, zählt unter die verschiedenen Namen,
die ʾAbātūr, dem Herrn über das oberste Wachthaus unterhalb der
Lichtwelt, beigelegt werden.[52] Identisch ist die Warnung vor dem
Reichtum. Das Fasten spielt an den Ginza-Stellen nur eine unter-
geordnete Rolle. In den *Acta Petri* (NHC) treten auf der Reise in die
himmlische Welt nur 5 Gefährdungen auf. Im Prinzip müssten es 7
bzw. 8 sein. Bei den Mandäern besitzen Sonne und Mond unter den
sieben Planeten eine Sonderstellung. Da sie aufgrund ihres Lichtes der
oberen Welt näher stehen als dem Reich der Finsternis, gelten sie nicht
als generell böse. Häufig werden daher nur die „Fünf" genannt unter
Ausschluß von Sonne und Mond.[53] Damit lässt sich die Fünfzahl der
Gefährdungen in den *Acta Petri* (NHC) erklären.

Dīnānūkts Himmelsreise gleicht von der äußeren Struktur her der
letzten Episode der *Acta Petri* (NHC). Die Seelen der Apostel, obwohl
nicht explizit erwähnt, erfahren gewissermaßen einen Aufstieg zu
den Pforten der Lichtwelt d.h. der Stadt Lithargoēls, die sie aber so
wenig wie Dīnānūkt betreten dürfen, da sie noch am Leben sind. Das
letzte Tor, hinter dem sich das Throngemach des Lebens bzw. von
Christus-Lithargoēl befindet, öffnet sich erst nach dem Tod, wenn
die Seele zu ihrer endgültigen Ruhestätte in die Lichtwelt heimge-
kehrt ist. An der Schwelle zur Welt des Lichts kehren die Helden der

---

[50] Abkaʿi-Khavari 2000, 75, 78.
[51] Edzard 1965, 79.
[52] Rudolph 1965, 123.
[53] Rudolph, 1960, i, 147 Anm. 2; Ders. 1970, 419.

beiden Erzählungen auf die Erde zurück. Sie nehmen den gleichen Auftrag in unterschiedlicher Ausprägung wahr. Die Apostel begeben sich wieder in die Inselstadt und kommen dem Missionsbefehl aus Mt 28 nach. Dīnānū<u>k</u>ts Seele kehrt in ihren Körper zurück. Wieder zum Leben erwacht, missioniert Dīnānū<u>k</u>t in der Tibil, d.h. auf Erden. Wie Dīnānū<u>k</u>t ist Petrus, aber auch Christus-Lithargoēl, bibliophil veranlagt. Bei Mani steigert sich die Liebe zum Buch noch beträchtlich. Der Manichäismus ist daher die einzige Religion, die das Prädikat „Buchreligion" voll und ganz verdient.[54] Ohne die heiligen Schriften zogen Manis Sendboten nicht aus, um zu missionieren.

In der ostsyrischen Tradition erhält Christus häufig das Epitheton „Arzt" (ʾāsyā).[55] Selbst im *Oriens extremus*, im Uighuren-Reich Qočo (östlich der Turfan-Oase), ist Christus ein Arzt.[56] In der Sasanidenzeit vertrauten die Großkönige auf die Geschicklichkeit ihrer nestorianischen Ärzte. Das gleiche taten später die Kalifen in Bagdad. Unter ihrem medizinischen Personal findet man auffallend viele Ärzte, die zur Alten Kirche des Ostens gehörten.[57] Häufig sind auch Theologen medizinisch geschult oder besitzen medizinische Kenntnisse. In dem aus der Turfan-Oase stammenden syrischen Fragment[58] der Baršabbā-Erzählung, die über die Anfänge des Christentums in der mittelasiatischen Oasenstadt Merw berichtet, wird zwischen psychischen und physischen Krankheiten unterschieden. Baršabbā beantwortet die Frage, ob er Šīr, die Gemahlin Šāpūrs, heilen könne, nicht mit einem eindeutigen Ja. Er schränkt vielmehr seine Antwort ein und differenziert scharf zwischen zwei Kategorien von Krankheiten: Es gibt Krankheiten, die eine körperliche (physische) Ursache haben und solche, die einen seelischen (psychischen) Ursprung haben. Nur die letzteren könne er heilen, da er kein Arzt im landläufigen Sinne sei.[59] In der arabischen Kurzversion wird diese Differenzierung später aufgegeben.[60]

Als „Arzt" gilt Jesus bereits in *Acta Thomae*. Einmal fordert der Apostel seine Zuhörer auf, an diesen Arzt zu glauben (Kap. 143).[61]

---

[54] Vgl. Tubach 2000, 622-38.
[55] Widengren 1975, 54.
[56] Vgl. Tubach 2002, 323-346.
[57] Whipple 1936, 1967.
[58] Müller 1934, 559-564 (= *Ergebnisse*, 365-70).
[59] Müller 1934, 559-560 (= *Ergebnisse*, 365-6).
[60] Kawerau 1976, i, 24-28; ii, 81-90, vgl. dazu Sachau 1918.
[61] Bornkamm 1964, 363; Drijvers 1989, 358.

An einer anderen Stelle wird zwischen einem Seelenarzt und einem gewöhnlichen Arzt unterschieden (Kap. 95).[62] Mygdonia, die Frau von Charisios, ließ sich von Thomas für die neue Religion gewinnen, was ihrem Mann missfällt, da er von der Enkrateia nichts wissen will. Von Charisios zur Rede gestellt, wo sie denn gewesen sei, antwortet sie, dass sie einen Arzt aufgesucht habe. Charisios vermutet nämlich, dass sie quasi in der „Sprechstunde" des Apostels gewesen ist, und frägt, ob der Fremde ein Arzt sei. Mygdonia bejaht das und erklärt, dass der Apostel ein Seelenarzt sei. Der Unterschied zwischen einem Arzt, der psychische Krankheiten heilt, und einem, der auf physische spezialisiert ist, ist im Fall des Apostels nur eine theoretische Differenzierung, da der Apostel als Doppelgänger Christi–Thomas (= aram. Zwilling) ist der Zwillingsbruder Christi–selbstverständlich beides vermag, obwohl seine Spezialität Erkrankungen der Psyche sind. In den *Acta Petri* (NHC) wird Petrus und den übrigen Jüngern die Gabe der Krankenheilung von dem Arzt Christus-Lithargoēl verliehen, indem er ihnen den Arzneikasten überreicht und sie förmlich dazu auffordert. Den Einwand des Johannes, dass ihnen ein Medizin-Studium fehle, lässt Christus nicht gelten. Sie sollen die Krankheiten des Körpers und der Seele heilen.

Die Herkunft der Acta Petri *(NHC)*

Aus den vorgegangenen Zeilen könnte man den Schluß ziehen, dass die *Acta Petri* (NHC) in Babylonien[63] in einem gnostisch-baptistischen Umfeld entstanden sind und ursprünglich auf Aramäisch verfasst waren, ehe sie auf dem Umweg über eine griechische Version ins Koptische gelangten. Gegen eine solche Annahme spricht der griechische Engelname. Für eine Schrift, die im syro-mesopotamischen Raum verfasst wurde, würde man eher annehmen, dass die Vertreter der himmlischen Welt in erster Linie hebräische oder aramäische Namen tragen, sofern es sich bei Lithargoēl nicht um eine Umsetzung eines semitischen Wortes ins griechische handelt. Eine mit Lithargoēl verknüpfte Tradition gab es nur in der koptischen Kirche,

---

[62] Bornkamm 1964, 345; Drijvers 1989, 339.
[63] Schenke 1989, 370, dachte wegen der asketischen Grundstimmung des Texts ganz vage an Syrien.

doch nicht in Form einer Art Engelchristologie[64] wie in den *Acta Petri* (NHC). Im „Buch von der Einsetzung des Erzengels Gabriel" (7. Jh.) erscheinen 25 Engelfürsten den Aposteln, die in Gruppen zu je fünf Engeln vor sie treten. Litharkūēl nimmt den fünften Rang der letzten Fünfergruppe ein und steht als 25. Engelfürst somit in der Hierarchie der himmlischen Welt ziemlich weit unten.[65] Ähnlich wie in den *Acta Petri* (NHC) tritt er mit einem Salbgefäß (nardiks < νάρθηξ) auf, gefüllt mit der Lebenssalbe, mit der er die Seelen salbt. In der Kathedrale von Pachoras (Faras), der einstigen Hauptstadt von Nobatien und dem Sitz des Eparchen nach der Vereinigung mit Makurien, gab es ein Fresko des Engels, das aber schlecht erhalten ist. Das Bittgebet neben dem Gewandsaum[66] beginnt mit einer Anrufung von Christus und Litharkūēl ([... Κύρι]ε Ἰ[ησο]ῦ Χ[ριστο]ῦ Λιταρκουῆλ ...).[67] Streicht man das in der Übersetzung hinzugefügte „und", läge eine Identifikation mit Christus vor.

Da Alexandreia eine kosmopolitisch geprägte Stadt war, wäre es ohne weiteres denkbar, dass ein Kaufmann oder ein Student aus der Mesene oder den angrenzenden Regionen in Alexandreia unter Verwendung heimischer Traditionen, die er seit seiner Jugend kannte, eine Erzählung wie die *Acta Petri und der Zwölf Apostel* niederschrieb, indem er sie gleichzeitig ihrer häretischen oder aus dem großkirchlichen Rahmen fallenden Elemente beraubte. Daß Alexandreia auch Studenten aus der Golfregion anlockte, zeigt eine Notiz im Chronicon anonymum (de ultimis regibus Persarum), wo berichtet wird, dass ein Philosophiestudent aus Qatar namens Petrus, dem anrückenden persischen Heer 612 den entscheidenden Tipp zur schnellen Einnahme von Alexandreia gegeben haben soll.[68]

---

[64] Vgl. dazu Barbel 1941; Michl 1962, 148-9.

[65] Müller 1959, 230; Müller 1962, 71,3-5 und 86 [Text/Übers.]. Da der Name dem koptischen Phoneminventar angepasst ist, das ein γ nur in Lehnwörtern kennt, kann man davon ausgehen, dass der Engel längst in Ägypten heimisch geworden ist.

[66] Michałowski 1974, 250-3, Nr. 55, Abb. 55.

[67] Jakobielski 1974, 311, Nr. 31; statt des Buchstabens ξ ist vermutlich ein ρ zu lesen (vgl. Schenke 1989, 374 Anm. 8). Vgl. ferner Kubińska 1976; Scholz 2001, 199, 209-11 und Scholz 1987/88, 582ff.

[68] Guidi 1903, 25,22-26,8, bes. 25,26-28 und 22 [T./Übs.]; Nöldeke 1893, 25. Auch in späterer Zeit konnte zwischen dem Studien- und Heimatort eine erhebliche Distanz bestehen. Nach al-Fārābī studierte ein gewisser Ibrāhīm aus dem mittelasiatischen Merw in Antiochien am Orontes Philosophie (Meyerhof 1930, 19=405).

Zusammenfassung

Die Parallele in der Ginza berechtigt zu dem Schluß, daß es einen engen traditionsgeschichtlichen Zusammenhang gibt. Das bedeutet jedoch nicht, daß der pseudepigraphe Text in Babylonien oder gar in der Mesene selbst entstand. Für die Abfassung des Textes der *Acta Petri* (NHC) genügt die Annahme, daß der anonyme Autor seine Jugend in dieser Region verbrachte und deshalb mit den religiösen Überlieferungen hemero-baptistischer Gruppen vertraut war. Keineswegs ausgeschlossen ist, daß der Anonymus nur mittelbar mit diesem Traditionsgut vertraut war und alles nur aus zweiter Hand kannte. Die ursprünglich vorhandenen heterodoxen Elemente sind weitgehend getilgt. Eine zentrale Botschaft des Textes, die Hinwendung zu den Armen, ist implizit mit einer Kritik an den aus dem edessenischen Raum stammenden Schriften verbunden, die ihre apostolischen Helden am liebsten an Fürstenhöfen missionieren lassen.

Bibliographie

Abka i-Khavari, M. 2000. *Das Bild des Königs in der Sasanidenzeit. Schriftliche Überlieferung im Vergleich mit Antiquaria* (Texte und Studien zur Orientalistik 13), Hildesheim/Zürich/New York.

Baldwin, M.C. 2004. *Whose Acts of Peter? Text and Historical Context of the Actus Vercellenses* (Wissenschaftliche Untersuchungen zum Neuen Testament, 2.Reihe), Tübingen.

Barbel, J. 1941. *Christos Angelos. Die Anschauung von Christus als Bote und Engel in der gelehrten und volkstümlichen Literatur des christlichen Altertums, zugleich ein Beitrag zur Geschichte des Ursprungs und der Fortdauer des Arianismus* (Fotomechanischer Nachdruck [der Ausgabe von 1941] mit einem Anhang) (Theophaneia: Beiträge zur Religions- und Kirchengeschichte des Altertums 3), Bonn 1964.

Bedjan, P. [Pôlōs Bēǧān] 1892. *Acta Martyrum et Sanctorum* [syriace edidit], iii, Leipzig-Paris (Repr. Hildesheim 1968).

Bonnet, M. 1903. *Acta Apostolorum Apocrypha* post Constantinum Tischendorf denuo ediderunt Ricardus Adelbertus Lipsius et Maximilianus Bonnet II 2. *Acta Philippi et Acta Thomae accedunt Acta Barnabae* edidit Maximilianus Bonnet, Leipzig (Repr. Darmstadt 1959; Hildesheim 1972).

Bornkamm, G. 1964. Thomasakten, in: E. Hennecke, *Neutestamentliche Apokryphen in deutscher Übersetzung* herausgegeben von Wilhelm Schneemelcher II. *Apostolisches. Apokalypsen und Verwandtes*, Tübingen 1964³ = 1971⁴, 297-372 (> *New Testament Apocrypha* edited by W. Schneemelcher. English Translation edited by R.McL. Wilson II. *Writings relating to the Apostles: Apocalypses and related subjects*, London 1965/Louisville, Kentucky 1966).

Brandt, A.J.H.W. 1889. *Die mandäische Religion, ihre Entwicklung und geschichtliche Bedeutung, erforscht, dargestellt und beleuchtet* (Proefschr., Rijks-Univ. Utrecht), Utrecht (= A.J.H.W. Brandt, *Die mandäische Religion. Ihre Entwickelung und geschichtliche Bedeutung erforscht, dargestellt und beleuchtet*, Leipzig 1889 = W. Brandt, *Die Mandäische Religion.*

Eine Erforschung der Religion der Mandäer, in theologischer, religiöser, philosophischer und kultureller Hinsicht dargestellt; mit kritischen Anmerkungen und Nachweisen und dreizehn Beilagen, Amsterdam 1973).

Busink, Th.A. 1980. *Der Tempel von Jerusalem von Salomo bis Herodes. Eine archäologisch-historische Studie unter Berücksichtigung des westsemitischen Tempelbaus* II. *Von Ezechiel bis Middot* (Studia Francisci Scholten memoriae dicata 3), Leiden.

Delaunay, J.A. 1974. Rite et symbolique en *Acta Thomae vers. syr. 1,2 a et ss.*, in: *Mémorial [Pierre] Jean [André Moise] de Menasce* édité par Ph. Gignoux et A. Tafazzoli (Fondation culturelle iranienne 185), Louvain, 11-34.

Desreumaux, A. 1993. *Histoire du roi Abgar et de Jésus. Présentation et traduction du texte syriaque intégral de La Doctrine d'Addaï* et en appendices, Traduction d'une version grecque par A. Palmer, Traduction d'une version éthiopienne par R. Beylot (Apocryphes), Turnhout.

Drijvers, H.J.W. 1989. Thomasakten, in: *Neutestamentliche Apokryphen in deutscher Übersetzung* herausgegeben von Wilhelm Schneemelcher. 5. Auflage der von Edgar Hennecke begründeten Sammlung II. Apostolisches, Apokalypsen und Verwandtes, Tübingen 1989[5] = 1997[6] = 1999), 289-367.

Drower, E.S. 1937. *The Mandaeans of Iraq and Iran: Their Cults, Customs, Magic, Legends, and Folklore*, Oxford (Repr. Leiden 1962).

Drower, E.S. 1950. *Diwan Abatur or, Progress through the purgatories: Text with Translation, Notes and Appendices* (Studi e testi 151), Città del Vaticano (Repr. Piscataway, NJ 2002).

Edzard, D.O. 1965. Mesopotamien. Die Mythologie der Sumerer und Akkader, in: *Wörterbuch der Mythologie*. Erste Abteilung: *Die alten Kulturvölker* I. *Götter und Mythen im Vorderen Orient* herausgegeben von H.W. Haussig, Stuttgart (Repr. o.J. [1983 und 1990]), 17-139.

Fieger, M. 1991. *Das Thomasevangelium. Einleitung, Kommentar und Systematik* (Neutestamentliche Abhandlungen, NF, 22), Münster, Westfalen.

Frisk, H. 1973. *Griechisches etymologisches Wörterbuch* I. *A-Ko* (Indogermanische Bibliothek. Reihe 2, Wörterbücher), Heidelberg 1960, 1973[2].

Ginza Rba (The Great Treasure). 1998. Edited by Majid Fandi Al-Mubaraki, Rbai Haithim Mahdi Saaed, Brian Mubaraki, Sydney.

Ginza Rba. English transliteration. 1998. Based on the World's first complete typed Mandaic Ginza Rba edition [by] Majid Fandi Al-Mubaraki, Brian Mubaraki, Sydney.

Gonzalez Nuñez, J. 1995. *La leyenda del rey Abgar y Jésus: orígenes del cristianismo en Edesa; introducción, traducción y notas del texto siríaco de „La Enseñanza del apóstol Addai"* (Apócrifos cristianos 1), Madrid.

Guidi, I. 1903. *Chronica minora* I. *edidit / interpretatus est* (Corpus scriptorum Christianorum orientalium. Scriptores Syri. Textus/Versio Series tertia 4), Paris/Leipzig 1903 (= dsgl., Corpus scriptorum Christianorum Orientalium 1.2/Scriptores Syri 1.2, Louvain 1955, 1961).

Guillaumont, A., H.-C. Puech, G. Quispel, W.C. Till und Yassah Abd al Masáh. 1959. *Evangelium nach Thomas. Koptischer Text*, Leiden (Repr. 1976; = *Gospel according to Thomas*, Leiden 1959; Repr. 1976, 1998; = *L'Évangile selon Thomas*, Paris 1959).

Hägg, T. 1987. *Eros und Tyche. Der Roman in der antiken Welt* [Übers. von Kai Brodersen] (Kulturgeschichte der antiken Welt 36), Mainz am Rhein (< *Den antika romanen*, Stockholm 1980; > *The Novel in Antiquity*, Oxford/Berkeley, Calif. 1983; Repr. 1991).

Hansman, J. 1967. Charax and the Karkheh, in: *Mélanges [Roman] Ghirshman* (Iranica Antiqua 7), Leiden, ii, 21-58.

Hansman, J. 1984. The Land of Meshan, in: *Iran. Journal of the British Institute of Persian Studies* 22 (1984) 161-6.

Hansman, J. 1992. Characene and Charax, in: *Encyclopaedia Iranica*, v, 363-5.

Howard, G. 1981. *The Teaching of Addai translated* (Texts and Translations 16; Early Christian Literature Series 4), Chico, Calif.

Kytzler, B. 1983. *Im Reiche des Eros. Sämtliche Liebes- und Abenteuerromane der Antike* I.II (Winkler Weltliteratur Dünndruckausgabe), München (= Repr. Gütersloh, Düsseldorf 2001).

Jakobielski, S. 1974. Inschriften, in: Michałowski 1974, 287-323.

Jeremias, J. 1962. *Die Gleichnisse Jesu*, Göttingen [1947] 1962⁶. 1998¹¹ (> dsgl., Kurzausgabe, München/Hamburg 1965; Göttingen/Zürich 1996¹¹).

Kaestli, J.-D. 1981. Les scènes d'attribution des champs de mission et de départ de l'apôtre dans les Actes apocryphes, in: *Les Actes apocryphes des Apôtres. Christianisme et monde païen* ed. par F. Bovon, M. Van Esbroeck, R. Goulet et al. (Publications de la Faculté de Théologie de l'Université de Genève 4), Genf, 249-64.

Kawerau, P. 1976. *Christlich-arabische Chrestomathie aus historischen Schriftstellern des Mittelalters* I.1 *Texte*, II. *Übersetzung mit philologischem Kommentar* (Corpus Scriptorum Christianorum Orientalium 370, 385; Subsidia 46, 53), Louvain 1976, 24-8; 1977, 81-90 [= II]).

Klijn, A.F.J. 1962. *The Acts of Thomas. Introduction—Text—Commentary* (Supplements to Novum Testamentum 5), Leiden (> A.F.J. Klijn, *The Acts of Thomas. Introduction, Text and Commentary* [Supplements to Novum Testamentum 108], Leiden 2003²).

Koester, H., B. Layton, T.O. Lambdin, H.W. Attridge. 1989. Tractate 2: *The Gospel according to Thomas*, in: *Nag Hammadi Codex II.2-7 together with XIII.2*, Brit.Lib.Or. 4926(1), and P.Oxy.1, 654, 655 with contributions by many scholars edited by B. Layton, i: Gospel According to Thomas, Gospel According to Philip, Hypostasis to the Archons, and Indexes* (Nag Hammadi Studies 20), Leiden, 38-128.

Krause, M. und P. Labib. 1971. *Gnostische und hermetische Schriften aus Codex II und Codex VI* (Abhandlungen des Deutschen Archäologischen Instituts Kairo; Koptische Reihe 2), Glückstadt.

Krause, M. 1972. Die Petrusakten in Codex VI von Nag Hammadi, in: *Essays on the Nag Hammadi Texts in Honour of Alexander Böhlig* edited by M. Krause (Nag Hammadi Studies 3), Leiden, 36-58.

Kubińska, J. 1976. L'ange Litakskuel en Nubie, in: *Le Muséon. Revue d'études orientales* 89 (1976) 451-5.

Kümmel, W.G. 1967. *Einleitung in das Neue Testament*. Begründet von P. Feine und J. Behm, völlig neu bearbeitet, Heidelberg 1967¹⁵ (> *Einleitung in das Neue Testament*, dsgl., 1983²¹; Repr. Berlin 1989).

Leipoldt, J. 1967. *Das Evangelium nach Thomas. Koptisch und Deutsch* (Texte und Untersuchungen zur Geschichte der altchristlichen Literatur 101), Berlin.

Lewy, H. 1978. *Chaldæan Oracles and Theurgy. Mysticism, Magic and Platonism in the later Roman Empire*. Nouvelle édition par M. Tardieu, Paris (dsgl., Publications de l'Institut français d'archéologie orientale; Recherches d'archéologie, de philologie et d'historie 13, Le Caire 1956).

Lidzbarski, M. 1925. *Ginzā. Der Schatz oder das Große Buch der Mandäer übersetzt und erklärt* (Quellen der Religionsgeschichte. Gruppe 4: Gnostizismus einschließlich mandäische Religion 13), Göttingen/Leipzig (Repr. Göttingen 1978).

Loth, H.-J. 1994. Hund, in: *Reallexikon für Antike und Christentum. Sachwörterbuch zur Auseinandersetzung des Christentums mit der antiken Welt*, xvi, 773-828.

Meyer, M. 1992. *The Gospel of Thomas. The Hidden Sayings of Jesus. Translation, with Introduction, Critical Edition of the Coptic Text and Notes*. With an interpretation by H. Bloom, San Francisco (Repr. 1998¹⁰, 2004).

Meyerhof, M. 1930. Von Alexandrien nach Bagdad. Ein Beitrag zur Geschichte des philosophischen und medizinischen Unterrichts bei den Arabern, in: *Sitzungsberichte der Preussischen Akademie der Wissenschaften. Philosophisch-historische Klasse*, Berlin, Abh. XXII, 389-429 [= 1-43] (= dsgl., in: *Galen in the Arabic tradition. Texts and studies* III. Collected and reprinted by Fuat Sezgin in collaboration with Mazen Amawi [Publications of the Institute for the History of Arabic-Islamic Science Islamic Medicine 20], Frankfurt am Main 1996, 223-63).

Michałowski, K. 1974. *Faras. Die Wandbilder in den Sammlungen des Nationalmuseums zu Warschau.* Die Inschriften bearbeitete S. Jakobielski, Warszawa/Dresden (< *Faras. Malowidsa ycienne w zbiorach Muzeum Narodowego w Warszawie.* Inskrypcje opracowas S. Jakobielski, Warszawa 1974; > *Faras. Wall Paintings in the Collection of the National Museum in Warsaw,* with Chapter on Inscriptions by S. Jakobielski, Warsaw 1974).

Michl, J. 1962, Engel IV (christlich) / Engel V (Engelnamen), in: *Reallexikon für Antike und Christentum. Sachwörterbuch zur Auseinandersetzung des Christentums mit der antiken Welt,* v, 109-200/200-39.

Molinari, A.L. 2000[a]. *The Acts of Peter and the Twelve Apostles (NHC 6.1). Allegory, Ascent, and Ministry in the Wake of the Decian Persecution* (Society of Biblical Literature; Dissertation series 174), Atlanta, Georgia.

Molinari, A.L. 2000[b]. *„I never knew the man." The Coptic Act of Peter (Papyrus Berolinensis 8502.4): Its Independence from the Apocryphal Acts of Peter, Genre and Legendary Origins* (Bibliothèque copte de Nag Hammadi; Section 'Etudes' 5), Quebec.

Müller, C.D.G. 1959. *Die Engellehre der koptischen Kirche. Untersuchungen zur Geschichte der christlichen Frömmigkeit in Ägypten,* Wiesbaden.

Müller, C.D.G. 1962. *Die Bücher der Einsetzung der Erzengel Michael und Gabriel herausgegeben/ übersetzt* (Corpus Scriptorum Christianorum Orientalium 225-226; Scriptores coptici 31-32), Louvain.

Müller, F.W.K. 1934. Soghdische Texte II. Aus dem Nachlaß herausgegeben von W. Lentz, in: Sitzungsberichte der preußischen Akademie der Wissenschaften, Philosophisch-historische Klasse, Jg. 1934, Nr. 21, Berlin, 504-607 (= *Sprachwissenschaftliche Ergebnisse der deutschen Turfan-Forschung. Text-Editionen und Interpretationen* von F.W.K. Müller, A.A. von Le Coq, K. Foy, G. Rašid Rachmati. Gesammelte Berliner Akademieschriften 1904-1932 Bd. III [Opuscula. Sammelausgaben seltener und bisher nicht selbständig erschienener wissenschaftlicher Abhandlungen 3.3], Leipzig 1985, 310-413 [syr. Text nach H.J. Polotsky]).

Nodelman, S.A. 1959/60. A Preliminary History of Characene, in: *Berytus. Archeological Studies* 13 (1959/60) 83-121 (> Maisan, in: *al-Ustad* 12 [Bagdad 1963/64] 432-63 [= arab. Übs. von F. Gamil]).

Nöldeke, Th. 1893, *Die von Guidi herausgegebene syrische Chronik* (Sitzungsberichte der Akademie der Wissenschaften in Wien, Philosophisch-historische Klasse; 128, 9. Abh.), Wien.

Parrott, D.M./D.M. Parrott, R.McL. Wilson. 1977. The Acts of Peter and the Twelve Apostles (VI,1). Introduced/translated, in: J.M. Robinson (ed.), *The Nag Hammadi Library in English* translated and introduced by members of the Coptic Gnostic Library Project of the Institute for Antiquity and Christianity, Claremont, California. With an afterword by Richard Smith, Leiden [1977], 1996[4], 286-94.

Phillips, G. 1876. *The Doctrine of Addai, the Apostle. Now first edited in a complete form in the original Syriac, with an English Translation and Notes,* London.

Plümacher, E. 1978. Apokryphe Apostelakten, in: *Paulys Realencyclopädie der classischen Altertumswissenschaft. Supplement-Band* XV (1978), 12-70 (= *Apokryphe Apostelakten,* München 1978).

Pokorny, J. 1959. *Indogermanisches etymologisches Wörterbuch* I.II, Bern/München 1959. 1969, Tübingen 2002⁴.

Richter, S.G. 1997. *Die Aufstiegspsalmen des Herakleides. Untersuchungen zum Seelenaufstieg und zur Seelenmesse bei den Manichäern* (Sprachen und Kulturen des christlichen Orients 1), Wiesbaden.

Ringgren, H. 1979. *Die Religionen des Alten Orients* (Grundrisse zum Alten Testament. Das Alte Testament Deutsch. Ergänzungsreihe. Sonderband), Göttingen (Repr. Berlin 1987; < *Främre orientens religioner i gammal tid*, Stockholm 1967; > *Religions of the Ancient Near East*, London/Philadelphia 1973; = dsgl., London 1976).

Robinson, J.M. 1972. *The facsimile edition of the Nag Hammadi codices, Codex VI*. Published under the auspices of the Department of Antiquities of the Arab Republic of Egypt. In conjunction with the United Nations Educational, Scientific and Cultural Organization, Leiden.

Rudolph, K. 1960-61. *Die Mandäer* I. *Prolegomena: Das Mandäerproblem* (Forschungen zur Religion und Literatur des Alten und Neuen Testaments 74 [= NF 56]), Göttingen 1960, II. *Der Kult* (ebd. 75 [= 57]) ebd. 1961.

Rudolph, K. 1965. *Theogonie, Kosmogonie und Anthropogonie in den mandäischen Schriften. Eine literarische und traditionsgeschichtliche Untersuchung* (Forschungen zur Religion und Literatur des Alten und Neuen Testaments 88), Göttingen.

Rudolph, K. 1970. Die Religion der Mandäer, in: *Die Religionen Altsyriens, Altarabiens und der Mandäer* von H. Gese, M. Höfner, K. Rudolph (Die Religionen der Menschheit 10.2), Stuttgart, 403-62.

Sachau, E. 1918. Die Christianisierungs-Legende von Merw, in: *Abhandlungen zur semitischen Religionskunde und Sprachwissenschaft Wolf Wilhelm Grafen von Baudissin zum 26.September 1917* überreicht von Freunden und Schülern und in ihrem Auftrag und mit Unterstützung der Straßburger Cunitz-Stiftung herausgegeben von W. Frankenberg und F. Küchler (BZAW 33), Giessen, 399-409.

Schenke, H.-M. 1973. „Die Taten des Petrus und der zwölf Apostel". Die erste Schrift aus Nag-Hammadi-Codex VI eingeleitet und übersetzt vom Berliner Arbeitskreis für koptisch-gnostische Schriften, in: *Theologische Literaturzeitung. Monatsschrift für das gesamte Gebiet der Theologie und Religionswissenschaft* 98 (1973) 13-19.

Schenke, H.-M. 1989. Die Taten des Petrus und der zwölf Apostel, in: *Neutestamentliche Apokryphen in deutscher Übersetzung* herausgegeben von W. Schneemelcher. 5.Auflage der von E. Hennecke begründeten Sammlung II. Apostolisches, Apokalypsen und Verwandtes, Tübingen 1989⁵ = 1997⁶ = 1999, 368-80.

Schenke, H.-M. 2003. Die Taten des Petrus und der zwölf Apostel (NHC VI,1), in: Nag Hammadi Deutsch II. NHC V,2–XIII,1, BG 1 und 4. Eingeleitet und übersetzt von Mitgliedern des Berliner Arbeitskreises für Koptisch-Gnostische Schriften. Herausgegeben von H.-M. Schenke, H.-G. Bethge und U.U. Kaiser (Die Griechischen Christlichen Schriftsteller der ersten Jahrhunderte [GCS], N.F., 12; Koptisch-Gnostische Schriften 3), Berlin/New York, 443-53.

Scholz, P.O. 2001. Das nubische Christentum und seine Wandmalereien, in: *Dongola-Studien. 35 Jahre polnischer Forschungen im Zentrum des makuritischen Reiches* herausgegeben von S. Jakobielski & P.O. Scholz (Bibliotheca nubica et æthiopica [vormals Bibliotheca nubica] 7), Warszawa, 177-251.

Scholz, P.O. 1987/88. Gnostische Elemente in nubischen Wandmalereien: das Christusbild, in: *Nubica* 1/2 (1987-1988, ersch. 1990) 565-84.

Schuol, M. 2000. *Die Charakene. Ein mesopotamisches Königreich in hellenistisch-parthischer Zeit* (Oriens et Occidens 1), Stuttgart.

Sim, U. 1996. *Das himmlische Jerusalem in Apk 21,1-22,5 im Kontext biblisch-jüdischer Tradition und antiken Städtebaus* (Bochumer Altertumswissenschaftliches Colloquium 25), Trier.

Söder, R. 1932. *Die apokryphen Apostelgeschichten und die romanhafte Literatur der Antike* (Würzburger Studien zur Altertumswissenschaft 3), Stuttgart (Repr. Stuttgart 1969; Repr. Darmstadt 1969).

Tubach, J. 1993. Der Weg des Prinzen im Perlenlied, *Orientalia Lovaniensia Periodica* 24 (1993) 87-111.

Tubach, J. 1995. Mani und der palmyrenische Kaufmann aus Forat, *Zeitschrift für Papyrologie und Epigraphik* 106 (1995) 165-9.

Tubach, J. 2000. Mani, der bibliophile Religionsstifter, in: Studia Manichaica. IV. Internationaler Kongreß zum Manichäismus, Berlin, 14.-18. Juli 1997. Herausgegeben von R.E. Emmerick, W. Sundermann und P. Zieme (Berlin-Brandenburgische Akademie der Wissenschaften. Berichte und Abhandlungen. Sonderband 4), Berlin, 622-38.

Tubach, J. 2002. Der Besuch der drei Weisen aus dem Morgenland [bei Herodes Khan] in einer Erzählung aus der Turfan-Oase, in: W. Beltz und J. Tubach (Hrsg.), *Regionale Systeme koexistierender Religionsgemeinschaften. Leucorea-Kolloquium 2001* (Hallesche Beiträge zur Orientwissenschaft 34), 2002, 323-46. *Hallesche Beiträge zur Orientwissenschaft* 34 (2002) 323-46.

Waldmann, H. 1996. *Der Königsweg der Apostel in Edessa, Indien und Rom* (Tübinger Gesellschaft. Wissenschaftliche Reihe 5), Tübingen [1996]. 1997².

Widengren, G. 1975. „Synkretismus" in der syrischen Christenheit, in: *Synkretismus im syrisch-persischen Kulturgebiet. Bericht über ein Symposion in Reinhausen bei Göttingen in der Zeit vom 4. bis 8. Oktober 1971.* Herausgegeben von A. Dietrich (Abhandlungen der Akademie der Wissenschaften in Göttingen. Phil.-hist. Klasse. 3. Folge, Nr. 96), Göttingen 38-64.

Whipple, A.O. 1936. The Role of the Nestorians as the connecting link between Greek and Arabic medicine, in: *Annals of Medical History, New Ser.*, 8 (1936) 313-23.

Whipple, A.O. 1967. *The Role of the Nestorians and Muslims in the History of Medicine*, Princeton.

Wilson, R.McL. und D.M. Parrott. 1979. The Acts of Peter and the Twelve Apostles, in: D.M. Parrott (ed.), *The Coptic Gnostic Library. Nag Hammadi Codices V, 2-5 and VI, with Papyrus Berolinensis 8502, 1 and 4* (Nag Hammadi Studies 11), Leiden, 197-229.

Wright, W. 1871. *Apocryphal Acts of the Apostles, edited from Syriac Manuscripts in the British Museum and other Libraries* I. *The Syriac Texts*, London/Edinburgh 1871 (Repr. Amsterdam 1968. Repr. 1990).

Zwiep, A.W. 2004. *Judas and the Choice of Matthias. A Study on Context and Concern of Acts 1:15-26* (Wissenschaftliche Untersuchungen zum Neuen Testament II.187), Tübingen.

THE IDENTITY OF LITHARGOEL IN THE *ACTS OF PETER AND THE TWELVE*

István Czachesz

The *Acts of Peter and the Twelve*, the first writing in Nag Hammadi Codex VI, is very different from the other apostolic Acts transmitted in the Early Church.[1] Instead of reporting the teachings and miracles of an apostle, it contains narratives about the deeds of the twelve apostles preceding their ministry. The late Hans-Martin Schenke situated the book in the milieu of wandering monasticism in the second century CE.[2] In his recent monograph, A.L. Molinari suggested that the writing addressed the crisis of the Church immediately following the Decian persecutions (249-251).[3] Elsewhere I have argued that the book is an allegorical tale about engaging in monastic life, and its final redaction took place in a Pachomian monastery in Upper Egypt between 347 and 367.[4] This article proposes a new interpretation of the enigmatic character Lithargoel, who appears in different forms at various points of the narrative, and is ultimately identified as Jesus Christ.

1. *Lithargoel's appearances in the Acts of Peter and the Twelve*

Following some scattered words at the badly damaged beginning of the text,[5] we read about the apostles' readiness to fulfil their ministry.

---

[1] NHC VI.1. I adapt the translation by D.M. Parrott and R.McL. Wilson in J.M. Robinson (ed.), *The Nag Hammadi Library in English*, Leiden/New York 1996[4], 289-94.

[2] H.-M. Schenke, 'The Acts of Peter and the Twelve Apostles', in: W. Schneemelcher and R.McL. Wilson (eds), *New Testament Apocrypha*, ii, Cambridge/Louisville 1992, 412-25 at 414. Cf. D.M. Parrott, 'The Acts of Peter and the Twelve Apostles: Introduction', in: Id. (ed.), *Nag Hammadi Codices V.2-5 and VI*, Leiden 1979, 287-9 at 289.

[3] A.L. Molinari, *The Acts of Peter and the Twelve Apostles (NHC 6.1): Allegory, Ascent, and Ministry in the Wake of the Decian Persecution*, Atlanta 2000, 235.

[4] I. Czachesz, *Apostolic Commission Narratives in the Canonical and Apocryphal Acts of the Apostles* (Diss. Groningen), Groningen 2002, 155-71 and Id., *Commission Narratives: A Comparative Study of the Canonical and Apocryphal Acts*, Louvain, forthcoming.

[5] The upper parts of the first eight pages (of a total of twelve) are damaged, thus the beginning of the narrative is also unclear.

When the opportune moment comes from the Lord, they go down to the sea and find there a ship. After sailing for a day and a night, a wind comes that takes them to a small city called Habitation (ϭⲱⲣϭ) in the midst of the sea.

Lithargoel appears here for the first time. A man comes out of the city, 'beautiful in his form and stature', whose appearance is described in detail:

> A man came out wearing a cloth bound around his waist, and a gold belt girded [it]. Also a napkin was tied over [his] chest, extending over his shoulders and covering his head and his hands.
> I was staring at the man, because he was beautiful in his form and stature. There were four parts of his body that I saw: the soles of his feet and a part of his chest and the palms of his hands and his visage. These things I was able to see. A book cover like (those of) my books was in his left hand. A staff of styrax wood was in his right hand. His voice was resounding as he slowly spoke, crying out in the city, 'Pearls! Pearls!' (2.10-32).

Peter greets the man, who identifies himself as a fellow stranger. He cries again, 'Pearls, pearls!'—but the rich men of the city do not even recognise him because of their disdain. The poor, however, ask him to show them the pearls. The merchant invites them to his city where he will not only show them pearls but will also give pearls to them for free.[6] Peter asks the name of the merchant:

> 'I want to know your name and the hardships of the way to your city because we are strangers and servants of God. It is necessary for us to spread the word of God in every city harmoniously.' He answered and said, 'If you seek my name, Lithargoel is my name, the interpretation of which is, the light, gazelle-like stone' (5.8-18).

Then Lithargoel describes the road to his city: 'No man is able to go on that road, except one who has forsaken everything that he has and has fasted daily from stage to stage.'[7] On the road, there are black dogs which kill people for their bread; robbers who kill them for their garments; wolves which kill them for water; lions which eat them for the meat in their possession; and bulls which devour them

---

[6] There is a doublet in the dialogue (4.4-15/4.21-34), on which more will be said below.

[7] *Acts of Peter and the Twelve* 5.21-5. 'Fasting daily from stage to stage' ⲣ̄ⲛⲏⲥⲧⲉⲩⲉ ⲙ̄ⲙⲏⲛⲉ ⲭⲓⲛ ⲙⲟⲛⲏ ϣⲁ ⲙⲟⲛⲏ) may designate a spiritual journey (of preparation) or an actual manner of travelling from monastery (μονή) to monastery; cf. section 4 below.

for the vegetables that they carry. Finally, he tells the name of the city: 'Nine Gates'. The apostles forsake everything and set out for Lithargoel's city. They do not take garments with them, nor water, meat, or vegetables. Thus, they evade the robbers, wolves, lions, and bulls, and successfully arrive at the city.[8]

As they sit down in front of the gate and talk, Lithargoel appears for the second time in the narrative, now as a physician:

> As we discussed the robbers on the road, whom we evaded, behold Lithargoel, having changed, came out to us. He had the appearance of a physician, since an unguent box was under his arm, and a young disciple was following him carrying a pouch full of medicine (8.16-19).

The apostles do not recognise Lithargoel in the physician until he calls Peter by name:

> 'How do you know me, for you called my name?' Lithargoel answered, 'I want to ask you who gave the name Peter to you?' He said to him, 'It was Jesus Christ, the son of the living God. He gave this name to me.' He answered and said, 'It is I! Recognize me, Peter' (9.6-15).

At this point Lithargoel gives the apostles the unguent box and the pouch, and commands them,

> Go into the city from which you came, which is called Habitation. Continue in endurance as you teach all those who have believed in my name, because I have endured in hardships of the faith. I will give you your reward. To the poor of that city give what they need in order to live until I give them what is better, which I told you that I will give you for nothing (10.1-13).

When Peter doubts whether they can provide for the needs of the poor, the Lord answers that his name and the wisdom of God surpasses gold, silver and precious stones. He gives them the pouch (this is a repetition in the narrative, cf. above) and adds, 'Heal all the sick of the city who believe in my name' (10.34-11.1). The disciples ask, 'We have not been taught to be physicians. How then will we know how to heal bodies as you have told us?' (11.3-13).

The Lord answers,

> [T]he physicians of this world heal what belongs to the world. The physicians of souls, however, heal the heart. Heal the bodies, therefore, so that through the real powers of healing for their bodies, without

---

[8] The 'black dogs' appear on the list of dangers but are missing from the description of the journey; cf. Czachesz, *Apostolic Commission*, 163.

medicine of this world, they may believe in you, that you have power
to heal the illnesses of the heart also [...] (11.16-26).

Finally, the Lord warns the apostles against the partiality for the rich
in many churches, and orders them not to dine in the houses of the
rich, nor make friends with them, rather 'judge them in uprightness'
(12.8-9).

2. *The name Lithargoel and its implications*

The name Lithargoel is introduced in *Acts of Peter and the Twelve* 5.16-
9. 'If you seek my name, Lithargoel is my name, the interpretation
of which is, the light, gazelle-like stone.'[9] Scholars have unanimously
suggested that the name Lithargoel is a composite of three elements.
Two components are Greek: λίθος ('stone') and ἀργός ('light' or 'quick');
the third is Hebrew: *'el* ('God' or 'divine being').[10] There is less unanimity as to how the name should be translated and interpreted.
Krause translated it as 'Gott der Perle', Schenke as 'the angel of the
light bright stone(s)'; Molinari turns the possessive structure around
and suggests 'the shining stone of God'.

The usual explanation of Lithargoel's name basically follows the
redactional gloss, 'the interpretation of which is, the light, gazelle-like
stone'. This explanation has gone so far unchallenged; it seems, however, rather questionable. Did the first part of the name Lithargoel
originally mean 'shining stone'? Is it really a composite of λίθος and
ἀργός? A closer look reveals that the gloss probably contains a folk
etymology. The supposed Greek composite 'lithargos' meaning 'shining
stone' is grammatically problematic. There are, indeed, compounds
in classical Greek where an adjective modifies the meaning of a substantive, such as ἀκρόπολις (upper city). The majority of such compound words are adjectives themselves: ἀργυρότοξος (having a silver
bow), μακρόχειρ (long-armed), χρυσοκόμος (having golden hair). In
all compounds belonging to these two types, however, the adjective
precedes the substantive, never the other way around.[11] Therefore,

---

[9] *Acts of Peter and the Twelve* 5.16-9. ⲡⲱⲛⲉ ⲛ̄ⲃⲁϩⲥⲉ ⲉⲧⲁⲥⲓⲱⲟⲩ, 'a gazelle-like
stone that is light.'

[10] Wilson & Parrot, 'Acts of Peter and the Twelve', 214-15; Molinari, *Acts of
Peter and the Twelve*, 135.

[11] Cf. E. Schwyzer, *Griechische Grammatik*, i, Munich 1968, 452-5.

'shining stone' or 'having a shining stone' would be 'argolithos' rather than 'lithargos'.

The theophoric element *'el* is widespread in ancient Hebrew names.[12] Various instances suggest that *'el* remained in use for creating proper names in the second temple period. The *Book of Watchers* (*1 Enoch* 1-36), written originally in Aramaic,[13] contains two *onomastica* of rebelling angels and archangels, respectively. Sixteen of the nineteen names of rebelling angels in *1 Enoch* 6.7, and all seven names of the archangels in 20.1-8 are compounds with *'el*. Many of the rebels' names, as G. Nickelsburg suggests, may 'present imitations of the old morphology with no specific translation in mind, or one might read *'el* to refer to the angel, i.e., "the angel in charge of x".'[14] Similar names appear in the writings from the Nag Hammadi codices, such as Samael, Gamaliel, Yoel, Youel, Telmael, Telmachel, Harmozel, Poimael, Oroiael, Yobel, Gabriel, Nebruel, Balbel, Achiel, Iabel, Michael, Uriel.[15] Some of these names are known from Hebrew and Aramaic sources; others may simply imitate the traditional pattern.

Although our list is only exemplary, some trends can be observed which may be helpful in deciphering Lithargoel's name. (1) Most names ending with *'el* in Jewish-Aramaic texts and a great many in Nag Hammadi literature can be reasonably explained from Hebrew or Aramaic roots (which may or may not coincide with the etymology given in the texts themselves).[16] (2) Among the names in Nag Hammadi texts, there

---

[12] H. Haber, 'Theophoric Names in the Bible', *Jewish Bible Quarterly* 29 (2001) 56-9. J.D. Fowler, *Theophoric Personal Names in Ancient Hebrew: A Comparative Study*, Sheffield 1988, 38-44 and passim.

[13] G.W.E. Nickelsburg, *1 Enoch: A Commentary on the Book of 1 Enoch*, Minneapolis, MN 2001, 1; for dating the original form to the early third century BCE, see ibid., 169-70.

[14] Nickelsburg, *1 Enoch*, 179.

[15] Samael: *The Hypostasis of the Archons* (NHC II.4) 87.3; Samael and Armozel: *Trimorphic Protennoia* (NHC XIII.1); Gamaliel, Yo(u)el, Telmael, Telmachel, Harmozel, Poimael, Oroiael, Yobel, Gabriel, Nebruel: *Gospel of the Egyptians* (NHC III.2 and IV.2); Yo(u)el: *Zostrianos* (NHC VIII.1) 57.15, 125.14; Balbel and the rest: *Apocryphon of John* (NHC II.1 etc.) 16-17, cf. M. Waldstein and F. Wisse, *The Apocryphon of John*, Leiden 1995, 101-5. If 'Balbel' is the Palpel of Aramaic *bal* ('spoil'), it does not belong in this list.

[16] B.A. Pearson, 'Jewish Sources in Gnostic Literature', in: M.E. Stone (ed.), *Jewish Writings of the Second Temple Period*, Assen/Philadelphia 1984, 443-81 at 453-5, argues for a strong influence of *1 Enoch* on the *Apocryphon of John*, and proposes that *The Hypostasis of the Archons* was based on 'Jewish Gnostic' material, as were probably the *Trimorphic Protennoia* and the *Gospel of the Egyptians* (469). Samael is the chief antagonist

are Hebrew/Aramaic compounds, haphazard combinations, as well
as names probably based on Greek roots, such as Harmozel (ἁρμόζω)
and Poimael (ποιμήν). Telmael might be explained from both Aramaic
(טלם, 'deceive') and Greek (τέλμα, 'swamp') roots. (3) The ending *'el*
is never preceded by compound words (either Hebrew/Aramaic or
Greek).

With these observations in mind, we suggest that Lithargoel was
created from the Greek adjective λήθαργος. This was an equivalent
of the more archaic ἐπιλήσμων,[17] both meaning 'forgetful'. In Syriac,
lîth'argô(s) was used as a Greek loanword.[18] The name could originally designate an angel or mythological character that was 'forgetful
about God', or simply 'forgetful'. Below we will argue that there was a
semantic link between the meaning of the name and its original narrative context. As the narrative context changed during subsequent
phases of redaction, the name was also given a new interpretation.[19]

3. *Lithargoel in the sources of the* Acts of Peter and the Twelve

Right from the start, inconsistencies in the narrative (particularly
the repeated shifts of voice) have led scholars to distinguish different
sources and redactional layers in the text. Lithargoel's repeated metamorphoses (merchant, physician, Jesus Christ) supported additional
arguments for the source-critical approach. The different solutions
are neatly summed up by Molinari,[20] so there is no need to rehearse
the history of research here.

One piece of the text stands out due to its stylistic and logical
unity: the story of the pearl merchant in the first part of book (2.10-
5.1). This passage has a consistent narrative voice in the first person
singular; it focuses on a central theme: who receives a share of the

---

of God in Talmudic and post-Talmudic literature, cf. 'Samael' in: I. Singer (ed.),
The Jewish Encyclopedia, New York/London 1905, x, 665-6 and *Encyclopaedia Judaica*,
Jerusalem 1971, xiv, 719-22.

[17] Phrynichus, *Ecloga* 391.

[18] R. Payne Smith, *Thesaurus Syriacus*, Oxford 1879-1901, 1945 s.v. ܠܝܬܐܪܓܘ.

[19] An alternative possibility is that Lithargoel was composed by prefixing the name
Raguel (Hebrew רעואל) with the Aramaic negative copula לית. The meaning of the
name would be either 'No Friend of God' or 'No Shepherd of God'; cf. Nickelsburg,
1 Enoch, 311; J.A. Fitzmyer, *Tobit*, Berlin 2003, 94.

[20] Molinari, *Acts of Peter and the Twelve*, 20-31.

pearls?; finally, it has a clear story-line from the appearance of the merchant to the invitation of the poor to his city. Various elements of the merchant episode reappear in later parts of the book: the journey to the merchant's city, the giving of the pearl for free, and the preference for the poor over the rich. Scholars have recognised in the merchant story a possible source of the *Acts of Peter and the Twelve*; they do not agree, however, on when and how the subsequent passages (the explanation of the hardships and the apostles' journey) were connected to this episode.

On one hand, Krause and Schenke regarded Lithargoel's description of the hardships of the road as an original part of the merchant episode; they assigned the journey of the apostles to a separate source. Patterson and Molinari, on the other hand, reject this division. In Patterson's opinion, the story of the merchant (3.11-5.5) was inserted into the larger Peter narrative (1.1-8.9), which contained both Lithargoel's account of the hardships and the report about the apostles' journey. Molinari goes even further, assigning the first part of the book, including the merchant episode, the explanation of the road, and the apostles' journey, to one source called *The Story of the Pearl Merchant* (1.1-9.1).[21] He identifies various redactional elements within this unit, however.[22]

In Molinari's view, the original story of the merchant contained an elaborate Gnostic mythological apparatus.[23] The source included a journey to the heavenly spheres and explanations of both the journey process and other important details about how earthly conduct affects heavenly existence. Molinari hypothesises further details of the original narrative, such as fantastic heavenly creatures, the heavenly court room, the blissful lifestyle of the saved, and the sufferings of the damned.[24] Those details were eliminated by the redactor, and replaced by the dialogue about the hardships of the road.

During this redactional procedure, Molinari suggests, the name Lithargoel was introduced to associate the pearl with Jesus. The actual reinterpretation of the pearl as Jesus, according to Molinari, occurs during Lithargoel's second appearance outside the city, which he identifies as another source called *The Resurrection Appearance* (9.1-

---

[21] Molinari, *Acts of Peter and the Twelve*, 31.
[22] Molinari, *Acts of Peter and the Twelve*, 131-8.
[23] Molinari, *Acts of Peter and the Twelve*, 93-130.
[24] Molinari, *Acts of Peter and the Twelve*, 132 note 1.

9.29). Into this material, the redactor inserted the explanation: 'Do you not understand that my name, which you teach, surpasses all riches, and the wisdom of God surpasses gold and silver and precious stones?' (10.25-30).

In order to strengthen the link between Lithargoel and Jesus, the redactor inserted the physician material into both above-mentioned sources. The redactor took a special interest in the healing of bodies and souls.[25] Both the pearl merchant and Jesus Christ (in the dialogue before the city gates) are characterised as physicians. The former is equipped with a book cover and a staff of styrax wood, which, according to Molinari, may have had medical significance.

Molinari's source hypothesis has its advantages over the earlier theories. One of its merits is that it preserves the pearl narrative as one unit, including the journey to the Nine Gates. Molinari also shows how the theme of healing of souls and bodies, an important theological point of the redactor, was used to establish unity between the three sources. He is able to show that the pearl merchant story could serve as the core of the narrative, onto which the traditional Christian materials, the post-resurrection epiphany and the exhortatory discourse (*The Author/Redactor's Theology*, 9.30-12.19) could be systematically added.

At some points, however, we have to disagree with Molinari. His suggestion that Lithargoel's name was added to the text in order to identify the pearl with Jesus' name relies on weak arguments. If we take a closer look at the dialogue on which Molinari builds his theory, we have to dismiss this proposal. Indeed, Lithargoel/Christ claims his name (ⲡⲁⲣⲁⲛ) surpasses 'all riches' (10.26-27). In the subsequent lines, it is God's wisdom that 'surpasses gold and silver and precious stones' (10.28-30). The disciples will give those two things to the poor, Christ's name and God's wisdom. From the preceding part of the dialogue it becomes clear that neither is identical with the pearls. Christ instructs the disciples, 'To the poor of that city give what they need in order to live *until I give them what is better, which I told you that I will give for nothing*' (10.8-13). That is, the pearls will be given to the poor not by the disciples, but rather by Christ himself. Moreover, in the previous dialogue with the pearl merchant 'the name' is explicitly identified as 'Jesus', not 'Lithargoel': 'Why do you sigh, if you, indeed, know this name "Jesus" and believe in him?' (6.14-16). To sum up, the assumed

---

[25] Molinari, *Acts of Peter and the Twelve*, 51, 138-9.

redactional addition about giving Christ's name to the poor hardly establishes a link between Jesus and the pearls, as Molinari suggests.

If Molinari's theory of the redactor's identification of the pearls with Jesus' name does not hold water, can we still maintain that Lithargoel was added to the story by the final redactor? It seems a rather complicated redactional manoeuvre to introduce a third character (Lithargoel) to connect two others (merchant and Christ). Why did the redactor not simply identify the merchant as Christ in the resurrection dialogue (before the city gates)? Another problem, which has already been mentioned in the previous section, concerns the explanation of the name Lithargoel. If the redactor construed the name Lithargoel to suggest that Jesus is the pearl of God,[26] it is unlikely that he added an explanation omitting the theophoric element. To sum up, it is very probable that the final redactor did not invent the name Lithargoel, but that it was in one of his sources.

An alternative interpretation of the merchant story may resolve several difficulties in the earlier source theories. The reader of the merchant story is reminded of another famous passage about a pearl in one of the Apocryphal Acts, i.e. the Hymn of the Pearl in the *Acts of Thomas* 108-113. In both texts, people are sent or invited, respectively, to fetch a precious pearl from a distant city. As we will see below, the explanation of the hardships of the road and the apostles' journey also fit excellently into the plot known from the Hymn of the Pearl. It seems that the Hymn of the Pearl and the pearl merchant story are variants of the same *sujet*. We suggest that the major source of the *Acts of Peter and the Twelve* was centred around a Pearl Narrative.

Molinari's source theory requires him to hypothesise an elaborate Gnostic mythological apparatus in the original text. This becomes unnecessary if we compare the merchant story with the fully preserved Hymn of the Pearl. The latter was also interpreted as a Gnostic myth; recent scholarship, however, suggests that this was overinterpretation.[27] Gnostic claims about creation, the origin of evil, and the person and mission of Jesus Christ are missing from both texts. When identifying the source of the animal figures in the story, Molinari himself comes up with a non-Gnostic parallel, i.e. the famous vision of daemons in

---

[26] Molinari, *Acts of Peter and the Twelve*, 138.

[27] G.P. Luttikhuizen, 'The Hymn of Jude Thomas, the Apostle, in the Country of the Indians (ATh 108-113)', in: J.N. Bremmer (ed.), *The Apocryphal Acts of Thomas*, Louvain 2001, 101-14.

the *Life of Antony*.[28] The animal figures may indicate an ascetic, rather than Gnostic, theological setting.

How does the figure of Lithargoel fit into the Pearl Narrative? A closer examination of the text shows that the name Lithargoel does not appear at all in the merchant episode (2.10-5.1) or the final exhortatory dialogue (9.31-12.22). It occurs first in the explanation of the hardships of the journey, accompanied by the explanatory gloss analysed above (5.2-6.22). The description of the disciples' journey and arrival follows the discussion of the hardships logically, without mentioning Lithargoel's name again (6.23-8.11). Lithargoel reappears before the city gates as a physician (8.14-35). At the end of the episode, he abruptly leaves the disciples and then comes back in a hurry. When he arrives back, he identifies himself as Jesus to the disciples (9.1-30).

Is Lithargoel just a name that can be removed from the text without changing anything else? Do any of the above-mentioned episodes create an identity for Lithargoel which is distinct from other characters in the book? A closer look reveals that this actually happens at his appearance before the city gates (8.14-35). In this context we read that Lithargoel is a 'good man' (ⲁⲅⲁⲑⲟⲥ ⲡ̄ⲣⲱⲙⲉ), 'the son of a great king' (ⲡϣⲏⲣⲉ ⲛ̄ⲟⲩⲛⲟϭ ⲛ̄ⲣ̄ⲣⲟ), who 'does not reveal himself to every man' (ⲉⲛⲁϥⲟⲩⲟⲛ︦ϩ︦ⲁ̄ⲛ̄ⲧⲟϥ ⲉⲣⲱⲙⲉ ⲛⲓⲙ). This is a profile of Lithargoel as a literary character that can be clearly distinguished from both the pearl merchant in the previous parts of the book and Jesus Christ in the subsequent part.

In the Hymn of the Pearl, the hero is also the first son of 'the king of kings'.[29] During his stay in Egypt, the prince also hides his identity.[30] This raises the possibility that Lithargoel originally played a similar role in the pearl story as the prince in the Hymn of the Pearl. His name would also make perfect sense in that context. The forgetfulness of the hero is an essential part of the plot of the Hymn of the Pearl: 'I forgot that I was a son of kings / and served their king; / and I forgot the pearl, / for which my parents had sent me, / and because of the burden of their oppressions, / I lay in a deep sleep.'[31]

---

[28] *Life of Antony* 9. Cf. Molinari, *Acts of Peter and the Twelve*, 122; Czachesz, *Apostolic Commission*, 163.

[29] *Acts of Thomas* 110.

[30] *Acts of Thomas* 109.

[31] Trans. A.F.J. Klijn, *The* Acts of Thomas: *Introduction, Text, and Commentary*, Leiden 2003², 183. In the *Apocryphon of John* 56.2, forgetfulness and sleep symbolise

Interestingly, the 'shining stone' etymology also makes sense in the context of the Pearl Narrative. The Hymn of the Pearl makes repeated mention of the richness of the royal family; the parents have a robe made for the prince which is woven with gold and decorated with precious stones (διάλιθος). After his return from Egypt, the prince is solemnly invested with the robe, which is now said to be adorned with precious stones (λίθοι τίμιοι) and pearls, and filled with the image of the king of kings. In this attire, he is supposed to appear before the king. These motifs in the narrative might have inspired the redactor to add the naïve etymology to the name Lithargoel.

In this scenario, the merchant must have been the character who reminded the 'forgetful' protagonist of his original mission. He could also explain the difficulties of collecting the pearl. The prince in the Hymn of the Pearl has to snatch the pearl from the 'loud-breathing serpent':

> I remembered the pearl, / for which I was sent to Egypt, / and I began to charm him, / the terrible loud-breathing serpent. / I hushed him to sleep and lulled him into slumber, / for my father's name I named over him, / and the name of our second (in power), / and my mother, the queen of the East; / and I snatched away the pearl, / and turned to go back to my father's house.[32]

Since the Hymn of the Pearl was probably written in Christian East Syria in the second or third century CE,[33] it is likely that the Pearl Narrative originated in the same context. The presence of *lîth'argôs* as a loanword in Syriac (see above) makes it plausible that Lithargoel's name was also created in that context. Moreover, the symbol of the 'pearl' has been widely used in Christian Syrian tradition.[34]

If Lithargoel was the original hero of the Pearl Narrative, this also

---

the fallen state of Adam: 'This is the tomb of the form of the body with which the robbers clothed the man, the fetter of forgetfulness (ⲁⲏⲑⲏ).' (Waldstein and Wisse, *Apocryphon of John*, 122.)

[32] Transl. Klijn, *Acts of Thomas*, 185.

[33] H.J.W. Drijvers, in: W. Schneemelcher and R.McL. Wilson (eds), *New Testament Apocrypha*, Cambridge/Louisville, Kentucky 1992, ii, 332.

[34] 'Pearl' can stand metaphorically, among other things, for Eucharistic bread, a relic, virginity, and faith; cf. Payne Smith, *Thesaurus*, 2215-16 s.v. ‎ܡܪܓܢܝܬܐ. A. Guillaumont, 'De nouveaux actes apocryphes: les Actes de Pierre et de Douze Apôtres', *Revue de l'histoire des religions* 4 (1979) 141-52 at 145, argues for a Syrian origin of the *Acts of Peter and the Twelve* because of the important role of the pearls in the narrative. See also the Appendix below.

provides a motivation for his secondary identification as the Saviour. According to one of the usual interpretations of the Hymn of the Pearl, the Saviour was sent from the divine world in order to rescue the soul (the pearl) from its imprisonment by demonic powers.[35] Scholars who follow this interpretation also subscribe to the Gnostic understanding of the Hymn. However, it is not necessary to connect the two: the theme of Jesus' descent to the world and his subsequent return to heaven has inspired texts belonging to various genres, without implying Gnostic mythology.[36] The identification of Lithargoel as the Saviour happened prior to the final redaction. To this purpose, the post-resurrection scene of 9.1-30 was added to the original Pearl Narrative.

To sum up, we propose that Lithargoel was the protagonist of one of the sources of the present *Acts of Peter and the Twelve*. In this source, which we call the Pearl Narrative, the protagonist collected a precious pearl from a distant city, a plot that is similar to that of the Hymn of the Pearl. The hero was named Lithargoel, because he 'forgot about God'. The story was (later) interpreted as the descent of Jesus to the world and the post-resurrection episode was added, where the true identity of the hero was revealed.

4. *Lithargoel and the redaction of the* Acts of Peter and the Twelve

The final redaction of the *Acts of Peter and the Twelve*, Molinari suggests, took place in the years immediately following the Decian persecutions (249-251), probably in Alexandria.[37] Molinari bases his hypothesis mainly on the particular interest of the text in two subjects: rejection of the rich and concern about physical and spiritual healing.[38] The rejection of the rich, in his view, fits into the situation after the persecutions, because the rich denied their faith in greater numbers than the poor.[39]

Molinari's analysis of the Decian persecution and its consequences

---

[35] This interpretation has been suggested by E. Preuschen, G. Bornkamm, and W. Foerster; cf. Luttikhuizen, 'Hymn of Judas Thomas', 105. Luttikhuizen, following Klijn and Drijvers, offers a non-Gnostic reading of the text.

[36] Two early sources are, for example, *Philippians* 2.6-11 and *Ascensio Isaiae* 10-11.

[37] Molinari, *Acts of Peter and the Twelve*, 235-6.

[38] Molinari, *Acts of Peter and the Twelve*, 201-36.

[39] Molinari, *Acts of Peter and the Twelve*, 205-14.

does not provide sufficient arguments for his theory about the date and provenance of the text. First, if we accept that the *Acts of Peter and the Twelve* was written as a reaction to persecution against Christians, we can choose from many alternatives in the first to the third centuries. It goes without saying that Early Christian literature is replete with the discussion of persecution and martyrdom.[40] It is not necessary to discuss Molinari's arguments about the exceptionally harsh rejection of the rich in this writing, because his main concern is the connection of richness with apostasy. At this point, however, the text offers little: the dwellers of Habitation endure 'in the midst of the apostasies and the difficulties of the storms' (7.13-14). Apostasies do not play a role in the denunciation of the rich in the text. One can base such an argument only on 'veiled reference', as Molinari puts it.[41] As a consequence, Molinari has to make concessions that seriously weaken his theory of date and provenance:

> [T]he specific community that produced our text, with its strict policy of 'renunciation' of the world, probably did not have wealthy members. This would explain the rather vague reference to apostasies. The community is commenting upon the apostasies they have witnessed (probably from some distance) in the less ascetical, more worldly churches. [...] In my judgement the redactor has witnessed the persecution from afar [...].

The themes of bodily and spiritual healing and Jesus' presentation as a physician were also widespread in early Christian literature.[42] This does not mean, of course, that the redactor could not see these themes as highly relevant for his particular situation. Yet we face major problems when basing the theory of redaction on the arguments provided by Molinari. Let us imagine that our redactor has knowledge of the Decian persecutions, wants to criticise the lapses of the rich, and finds healing highly relevant to that situation. Why would he then pick sources which do *not* deal with his problems, invent a physician

---

[40] See for example A. Bernet, *Les chrétiens dans l'Empire romain: des persécutions à la conversion Ier-IVer siècle*, Paris 2003; P. Barceló, 'Christenverfolgungen: Urchristentum und Alte Kirche', in: H.D. Betz et al. (eds), *Die Religion in Geschichte und Gegenwart* (1999⁴), ii, 246-8; W.H.C. Frend, *Martyrdom and Persecution in the Early Church: A Study of a Conflict from the Maccabees to Donatus*, Oxford 1965. The rhetoric of endurance (10.1-7) also imitates well-known patterns: e.g., Matthew 11.28-30; 16.24; Revelation 3.21.

[41] Molinari, *Acts of Peter and the Twelve*, 190.

[42] Ignatius, *Epistle to the Ephesians* 7.2, already cites a hymn of Christ the Physician. For an overview, see M.E. Honecker, 'Christus medicus', *Kerygma und Dogma* 30 (1984) 307-23.

figure himself, and add all his theological interests as an appendix, as it were, to the sources?[43] Is it not more reasonable to hypothesise that a redactor selected sources that themselves contained material and ideas that were relevant to the redactor's purposes?

Since this article concentrates on Lithargoel, it would fall beyond its scope to fully resolve the redaction problems. We will focus instead on the question of how the Pearl Narrative and its protagonist Lithargoel fit into the concept of a redactor working in a Pachomian monastery. A monastic community, indeed, is implicitly suggested by Molinari himself: 'The redactor may well have been a member of a more rigorist sect of Christianity, loyal yet desirous of a greater expression of their faith, that had withdrawn to a location outside a major city.'[44] Whereas the existence of a monastic community shortly after 250 is rather improbable, it is easy to find such a formation a century later.

The constraints of this article make it impossible to rehearse the arguments for a Pachomian *Sitz im Leben*; for the sake of convenience, we will summarise the major points here.[45] (1) After their arrival at the Nine Gates, the disciples are not talking about that which is 'distraction of this world'; rather, they *continue* in contemplation (ⲙⲉⲗⲉⲧⲏ, exercise) of faith. The whole journey is thereby interpreted in the text itself as a spiritual exercise. (2) The hardships of the road receive substance when compared with the *Rules* of Pachomius. Various commands about clothing, bread, water, meat, vegetables can be compared with the 'hardships of the road'. (3) The disciples' arrival, waiting, and reception at the gates parallels the novice's experience as described in the *Rules*. The novice waits at the gate for a few days; he tells his story and demonstrates readiness to renounce his family and possessions; he is stripped of his clothes and garbed in a monastic habit; finally, he is handed over to the porter who brings him before the brothers at the time of prayer. (4) Monasteries were competing for patronage, and a great number of failed monks went begging in the cities.[46] As a consequence, 'partiality for the rich' was a recurring issue in monastic literature. (5) Pachomius taught about the connection between physical and spiritual healing in similar terms as the *Acts of Peter and the Twelve*:

---

[43] Cf. Molinari, *Acts of Peter and the Twelve*, 133-4 and passim.

[44] Molinari, *Acts of Peter and the Twelve*, 191.

[45] For a detailed discussion, see Czachesz, *Apostolic Commission*, 158-66.

[46] The mention of 'beggars' (ϣⲁⲁⲧⲛ̄ⲙⲛ̄ⲧⲛⲁⲉ) in 4.4-5.1 may refer to this group.

'Do not think that bodily healings are healings; but the real healings are the spiritual healings of the soul.' (6) Finally, the larger theory of the production and use of the Nag Hammadi Codices in a Pachomian monastery supports the hypothesis of a similar *Sitz im Leben* for the final redaction of the *Acts of Peter and the Twelve*.

The Pearl Narrative, as argued above, was an ancient layer of the text which probably originated in the same Syrian context as the Hymn of the Pearl. The interpretation of the text as a narrative of the Saviour's descent to the world was later made explicit by adding the post-resurrection episode. The physician material was introduced into the final part of the Pearl Narrative at the same time; it might have been part of the revelation material used by the redactor, or was derived from tradition. In this context, Lithargoel's attributes as a physician (8.15-19), as well as references to him as 'good man' and 'son of a great king' who 'does not reveal himself to every man' (8.35-37), anticipated his identification as Christ.

Just as the Hymn of the Pearl became part of the *Acts of Thomas*, the Pearl Narrative could have been integrated into a story of the apostles' commission, or even into a longer *Acts of Peter and the Twelve*, comparable to the 'major' Acts.[47] The doublet in 4.4-34 seems to support this idea. This passage contains the dialogue between the pearl merchant and the poor of the city (Habitation):

4.4-15	4.21-34
'Please take the trouble to show us the pearl so that we may then see it with our own eyes. For we are poor. And we do not have this price to pay for it. But show us that we might say to our friends that we saw a pearl with our own eyes.' He answered, saying to them: 'If it is possible, come to my city, so that I may not only show it before your very eyes but give it to you for nothing.'	'Now then, the kindness which we want to receive from you is that you show us the pearl before our eyes. And we will say before our friends proudly that we saw a pearl with our own eyes—because it is not found among the poor, especially such beggars as these.' He answered and said to them: 'If it is possible, you yourselves come to my city, so that I may not only show you it but give it to you for nothing.'

Since the two versions of this doublet do not literally agree, it cannot be a simple copying error. The most natural explanation is that it was

---

[47] Pace Schenke, 'Acts of Peter and the Twelve', 415.

produced as the redactor excerpted a larger narrative. The original
text had a repetitive structure, with two invitation episodes rather
than only one. Our hypothesis of the Pearl Narrative integrated in a
larger *Acts of Peter and the Twelve* would explain the repetition: the pearl
merchant first directed Lithargoel/Christ to the city; for the second
time, the apostles, imitating his example, were instructed similarly. The
doublet in 4.4-34, the shifts of narrative voice, and other inconsistencies in the first part of the text could result from the combination of
two travel narratives into a single one.

The monastic redactor could have found this source interesting
for several reasons. (1) He saw metaphorical potential in the journey
narrative to use it as an image of the difficulties of joining a monastic
community and living up to the rules of monastic life. (2) His attention was grabbed by the city where the pearl was hidden, and to
which the hero was directed by the pearl merchant. The city could
be understood as a symbol of the monastery. (3) The figure of the
pearl merchant inviting the hero to his city raised the possibility of
interpreting him as Pachomius, who invited hermits and others willing to denounce the world to his monasteries. In the Bohairic *Life of
Pachomius*, St Antony says, 'Then the path of the apostles was revealed
on earth. This is the work our able Apa Pachomius undertook. He
became the refuge for everyone in danger from the one who has done
evil from the beginning.'[48]

These points of interest determined the way the redactor changed
the Pearl Narrative, and added his own material to it. First, he had
one character too many in the story. In his understanding of the narrative, as Lithargoel/Christ invites the disciples to the heavenly city,
so Pachomius invites the monks to the monastery. Lithargoel's journey
to the city is not reported any more, and his figure almost completely
coalesces with the pearl merchant.

The pearl merchant received the attributes of a physician, and
identified himself as Lithargoel in the dialogue. The naïve etymology
of 'shining stone' was created by the redactor, because 'forgetful about
God' or 'forgetful angel' did not make sense in the new context. Second,
the dangers of the road, which might have been symbolised only by
animals originally (cf. the serpent in the Pearl of the Hymn and the

---

[48] Bohairic *Life of Pachomius* 127, trans. A. Veilleux, *Pachomian Koinonia*, Kalamazoo,
Michigan 1980, vol. i.

animals in St Antony's dream), became identified with various monastic precepts about clothing, bread, water, and so forth. Subsequently, the exhortation was added to the narrative, or alternatively, adopted from another source, or possibly from another part of a longer *Acts of Peter and the Twelve*. The theme of 'partiality for the rich', a major issue in the monastic world, was added to it, and possibly also the explanations about healing bodies and souls.

The authority of Pachomius in the monastic community cannot be overestimated. The *Lausiac History* claims that Pachomius received the *Rules* from an angel on a bronze tablet.[49] Obedience to the Pachomian rules was a matter of salvation: 'Whoever transgresses any of these commands shall, for his negligence and his contempt, do penance publicly without any delay so that he may be able to possess the kingdom of heaven.'[50] Pachomius had visions and regarded himself as a salient figure of salvation history. Tradition made him the successor of prophets and apostles.[51] His figure was especially idealised when Theodore assumed leadership of the community after an interim period of disturbances.[52] Having the superhuman image of Pachomius in mind, the redactor could easily understand his activity of establishing monasteries and calling monks to join his communities as an imitation of Jesus' calling and commissioning his disciples.

5. *Conclusion*

Lithargoel has received a new identity in this article. First, we have suggested a new etymology for his name. Deriving Lithargoel from the Greek λήθαργος is preferable to previous suggestions both from grammatical and semantic points of views. With the help of the Hymn of the Pearl in the *Acts of Thomas*, we have hypothesised a Pearl Narrative which served as a source for the book. In *Acts of Peter and the Twelve* 8.14-35, we have found passages which characterise Lithargoel in a way that fits excellently into the plot of the Pearl Narrative. We have also outlined subsequent levels of redaction before the Pearl Nar-

---

[49] Palladius, *Lausiac History* 32.3.
[50] *Rules* 144. Text in A. Boon, *Pachomiana Latina*, Louvain 1932.
[51] P. Rousseau, *Pachomius: The Making of a Community in Fourth-Century Egypt*, Berkeley, CA 1985, 57-63.
[52] Rousseau, *Pachomius*, 178-83.

rative reached the final redactor. Textual clues have been found which can be used to reconstruct the outline of a longer *Acts of Peter and the Twelve*. Finally, we have highlighted various aspects of the text that could be relevant for a redactor in a Pachomian monastery, as well as modifications that this particular *Sitz im Leben* probably motivated.

APPENDIX

The legend of Mār Awgen (St Eugene of Clysma) perhaps contains a trace of the pearl merchant motif. Awgen's legend, attested from the seventh century,[53] reports that the saint was a pearl diver before he joined a Pachomian monastery and later founded Syrian monasticism. He sold the pearls, and 'distributed [them? their price?] among the churches, the people, the poor, the needy, the orphans, and the widows.'[54] The legend may witness that the merchant story was known in the Syrian Church and confirm the Syrian origins of the Pearl Narrative. However, since Awgen's legend is not attested before the seventh century, the possibility that it was inspired by the *Acts of Peter and the Twelve* cannot be ruled out. Further, Awgen is presented as Pachomius's follower, which may indicate that his story originated in a Pachomian context. In that case, the legend may provide indirect evidence of the Pachomian *Sitz im Leben* of the *Acts of Peter and the Twelve*.

---

[53] N. Sims-Williams, 'Eugenius', in: *Encyclopedia Iranica* (Columbia University; http://www.iranica.com); M.G. Bianco, 'Eugenius', in: A. Di Berardino et al. (eds), *Encyclopedia of the Early Church*, i, Cambridge 1992, 296; N. Sims-Williams, 'Dādišoʿ Qatrāyāʾs Commentary on the *Paradise of the Fathers*', *Analecta Bollandiana* 112 (1994) 33-64, esp. 47 note 38.

[54] *Life of Awgen*, edited by P. Bedjan, *Acta Martyrum et Sanctorum Syriace*, ii, Paris 1892, 376-480 at 378, lines 11-13. For an English summary, see E.A. Wallis Budge, *The Book of Governors*, i, London 1893, pp. cxxv-cxxxi at cxxv. Cf. Awgen's legend in the *Chronicle of Seert*, text and translation in Addai Scher, *Histoire nestorienne inédite* (Patrologia orientalis 4.4), Paris 1908, 234-6.

GNŌSIS, MAGEIA, AND *THE HOLY BOOK OF THE GREAT INVISIBLE SPIRIT*

MARVIN MEYER

This essay, written in honor of a colleague whose career has focused upon the study of Gnostic texts, particularly texts from the Nag Hammadi library, examines features of *gnōsis* and *mageia* in one such text, *The Holy Book of the Great Invisible Spirit*, or *The Egyptian Gospel*. The present examination seeks to explore the adequacy of these two terms—*gnōsis* and *mageia*, along with related terms—that may be used to define and describe ancient texts and traditions, and then it attempts to apply these terms to *The Holy Book of the Great Invisible Spirit*, in order to raise issues of definition and taxonomy. Is *The Holy Book of the Great Invisible Spirit* a Gnostic text? Is it a magical text? Is it both? Is it neither?

Gnōsis

Gnōsis and *mageia*, or 'Gnosticism' and 'magic,' remain two of the most elusive of categories in our current scholarly repertoire. Both sets of terms are vigorously debated, both are commonly addressed in the scholarly literature.

Two recent monographs have suggested that 'Gnosticism' and related terms may no longer be viable for scholarly discussion. In the first of these books, *Rethinking 'Gnosticism': An Argument for Dismantling a Dubious Category*, Michael A. Williams proposes that the 'dubious category' to be dismantled is 'Gnosticism' itself.[1] Williams surveys a variety of efforts on the part of scholars to define and describe 'Gnosticism,' and he remains dissatisfied with them all. He states, 'The term "Gnosticism" has indeed ultimately brought more confusion than clarification.'[2] Some scholars have described 'Gnosticism' as

---

[1] M.A. Williams, *Rethinking 'Gnosticism': An Argument for Dismantling a Dubious Category*, Princeton 1996.
[2] Williams, *Rethinking 'Gnosticism'*, 263.

an anticosmic protest movement, others as a syncretistic religion that adapts various traditions, or a spiritual religion of people who hate the body, or a movement of ethical radicalism that may encourage either an ascetic or a bohemian lifestyle, and so on. The reason for this variation in scholarly definition and description, Williams maintains, is this: what is dubbed 'Gnosticism' is actually a widely diverse collection of religious expressions. As he puts it, 'What is today usually called ancient "Gnosticism" includes a variegated assortment of religious movements that are attested in the Roman Empire at least as early as the second century CE.'[3]

In the light of such scholarly obfuscation, Williams concludes, it is time for a new category to replace 'Gnosticism,' and the category Williams proposes is 'biblical demiurgical traditions.' He writes,

> I would suggest the category 'biblical demiurgical traditions' as one useful alternative. By 'demiurgical' traditions I mean all those that ascribe the creation and management of the cosmos to some lower entity or entities, distinct from the highest God. This would include most of ancient Platonism, of course. But if we add the adjective 'biblical,' to denote 'demiurgical' traditions that also incorporate or adapt traditions from Jewish or Christian Scripture, the category is narrowed significantly. In fact, the category 'biblical demiurgical' would include a large percentage of the sources that today are usually called 'Gnostic,' since the distinction between the creator(s) of the cosmos and the true God is normally identified as a common feature of Gnosticism.[4]

In *What Is Gnosticism?*, the second monograph to address the use of the term 'Gnosticism,' Karen L. King provides a more fundamental indictment of the term 'Gnosticism.'[5] With postmodern sensitivities, King points out that definitions in general 'tend to produce static and reified entities and hide the rhetorical and ideological interests of their fabricators,'[6] and that problem is compounded in the case of *gnōsis* and related terms (e.g., *gnōstikos*), since these terms have been used from the days of the heresiologists to the present to designate 'the other' and to classify it as heresy. As King sums up her analysis,

> By perceiving how thoroughly the study of Gnosticism is tied to defining normative Christianity, we have been able to analyze where and how

[3] Williams, *Rethinking 'Gnosticism'*, 3.
[4] Williams, *Rethinking 'Gnosticism'*, 51-2.
[5] K.L. King, *What Is Gnosticism?*, Cambridge, Massachusetts 2003.
[6] King, *What Is Gnosticism?*, 15.

the academic study of Gnosticism in the twentieth century reinscribes and reproduces the ancient discourse of orthodoxy and heresy.[7]

The basic problem with the term 'Gnosticism,' according to Karen King, is that it constitutes 'the reification of a rhetorical entity (heresy) into an actual phenomenon in its own right (Gnosticism).'[8] Actually, 'Gnosticism' never really was anything but a rhetorical construct. As a result, in the modern—or postmodern—world of the twenty-first century, a world that is postcolonial and pluralistic, King foresees new historiographical enterprises that abandon anti-Catholic, anti-Jewish, colonialist, and evolutionary approaches, along with preoccupations with origins, and rather embrace diversity and 'continuity in differ-ence.' As she describes such discourse,

> These twenty-first-century historical practices would without doubt result in more than one possible, legitimate narrative of Christianity, based as they would be not only in the different perspectives of scholars and the communities to which they are accountable, but also in different ethical orientations. Discussions of Christian identity, theology, spirituality, and practice would constructively and critically engage this enriched and complexified set of historical portraits.[9]

These significant books by Michael Williams and Karen King make important contributions to the ongoing discussion of *gnōsis* and 'Gnosti-cism,' and they remind us that polemical perspectives and heresiologi-cal biases play a large role in the study of 'Gnosticism' in particular and religion in general. Nevertheless, I remain convinced that we may continue to use the terms *gnōsis*, 'Gnostic,' and 'Gnosticism' in a meaningful way in our scholarly discussions, and I employ these terms in the present essay.[10] After all, the word *gnōsis* is commonly

---

[7] King, *What Is Gnosticism?*, 218.

[8] King, *What Is Gnosticism?*, 189.

[9] King, *What Is Gnosticism?*, 236.

[10] For a fuller discussion of how we might define and make use of the terms *gnōsis*, 'Gnostic,' and 'Gnosticism,' see M. Meyer, 'Gnosticism, Gnostics, and *The Gnostic Bible*,' in: W. Barnstone and M. Meyer (eds), *The Gnostic Bible: Gnostic Texts of Mystical Wisdom from the Ancient and Medieval Worlds—Pagan, Jewish, Christian, Mandaean, Manichaean, Islamic, and Cathar*, Boston/London 2003, 1-19; M. Meyer, *The Gnostic Gospels of Jesus: Mystical Gospels and Secret Books about Jesus of Nazareth*, San Francisco 2005; B. Layton, *The Gnostic Scriptures: A New Translation with Annotations and Introduc-tions*, Garden City, New York 1987; B. Layton, 'Prolegomena to the Study of Ancient Gnosticism,' in: L.M. White and O.L. Yarbrough (eds), *The Social World of the First Christians: Essays in Honor of Wayne A. Meeks*, Minneapolis Press 1995, 334-50; B.A.

attested in Gnostic and heresiological texts, and Irenaeus of Lyon's use of the phrase 'falsely so-called knowledge' makes it clear that a battle was being waged over whose *gnōsis* is true *gnōsis*. (Compare the language of 1 Timothy 6.20.) Irenaeus also seems to admit in his work *Adversus haereses* that some of his opponents referred to themselves as Gnostics, and among those opponents were followers of a teacher named Marcellina, and others who usually are identified as Sethians or Barbelognostics. And one of the primary texts of these Sethians who called themselves Gnostics is *The Holy Book of the Great Invisible Spirit*, which is being considered here.

Mageia

Like *gnōsis* and related terms, the category *mageia* has also generated a great deal of discussion. It is generally conceded by scholars that the term 'magic,' like the terms linked to the word *gnōsis*, is loaded down with polemical baggage, so that 'magic' is often considered to be primitive, evil, illegal, or frivolous. Like 'Gnosticism,' 'magic' too may designate 'the other,' so that it may be suggested that 'we' do miracles, practice religion, and engage in medicine and science, while 'they' resort to magic.

Unlike *gnōsis* and related terms, however, *mageia* seems not to have been typically employed by practitioners of ritual power as a term of self-reference. Other words, like the Egyptian word *heka*, could be used more positively, as we shall see.

The Greek term *mageia* (compare the Latin *magia*) derives from an Iranian word *magus*, which identified a person from an ancient Medo-Persian tribe with priestly functions. The Greek word *magos*, Fritz Graf observes, is known by the end of the sixth century BCE and occurs more frequently during the classical period.[11] Graf notes that Herodotus describes the *magoi* as those who constitute a tribe or secret society whose members perform religious rituals, Xenophon calls them divine

Pearson, *Gnosticism and Christianity in Roman and Coptic Egypt* (Studies in Antiquity and Christianity), New York/London 2004.

[11] F. Graf, 'Excluding the Charming: The Development of the Greek Concept of Magic,' in: M. Meyer and P. Mirecki (eds), *Ancient Magic and Ritual Power* (Religions in the Graeco-Roman World 129), Leiden 1995, 29-42. Also see F. Graf, *Magic in the Ancient World*, translated by F. Philip (Revealing Antiquity 10), Cambridge, Massachusetts 1997.

technicians, and Plato claims that the teaching of the *magoi* comes from the Persian sage Zoroaster. From the fifth century on, the *magoi* and their *mageia* came to be marginalized in Greek thought, and the *magos* was linked to the *goēs*, or 'sorcerer,' and *mageia* was compared to *goēteia*, or 'sorcery.' Thus, 'magic' in Greek thought was considered to be rooted in the foreign practices of the Persians, and it was increasingly thought that 'magic' violated the proper relationship between the human and the divine.

Further, the emergence of philosophical theology and scientific medicine, Graf suggests, ran counter to the ideas and practice of 'magic,' and this contributed to the strongly polemical meaning and connotation attached to the word 'magic.' Graf concludes,

> two intellectual developments in the Greek world caused magic to become a proper domain inside religion, a domain attributed to specialists, *magoi*, *goētes*, *agurtai*: the rise of philosophical theology as a radicalization and purification of traditional, civic theology, and the rise of scientific medicine, based on the conception of nature as a homogeneous and closed system. Both of these developments have a similar result: they stress the separation between the world of nature (humans included) and the divine realm. Philosophers and physicians become the enemies of the sorcerers, and *magos*, in this debate, becomes a term of polemic and denigration.[12]

In the Roman and early Christian world these tendencies only increase, and 'magic' becomes a strongly negative expression for 'the other.' Romans accused early Christians of practicing magic, early Christians turned the same accusation back on the Romans, and later Protestants brought the same accusation against Roman Catholics.

Meanwhile, in ancient Egypt, 'magic' (if we may even use such a term derived from Iranian, Greek, and Latin sources) originally was considered to be nothing short of a gift from the divine. Robert K. Ritner explains that in the beginning the creator conceived 'magical power,' *heka*, which became personified as Heka, the embodiment of the divine energy that empowered the performance of public and private rituals.[13] Ritner cites the aretalogical self-predication in Coffin Text Spell 261 as an example of an address of Heka to the gods:

---

[12] Graf, 'Excluding the Charming,' 40.

[13] R.K. Ritner, 'The Religious, Social, and Legal Parameters of Traditional Egyptian Magic,' in: Meyer and Mirecki, *Ancient Magic and Ritual Power*, 43-60.

I am he whom the Unique Lord made before duality had yet come
into being . . . I am the son of Him who gave birth to the universe . . .
I am the protection of that which the Unique Lord has ordained . . .
I am he who gave life to the Ennead of gods . . . I have come to take
my position that I might receive my dignity, for to me belonged the
universe before you gods had come into being. Down, you who have
come afterward. I am Heka.[14]

In ancient Egypt, *heka* was considered to be neither an illegal activity
nor social deviance, not even hostile magic—so-called 'black' magic.
Ritner observes,

> Unlike traditional Western concepts, Egyptian magic was amoral, not
> immoral. No term distinguished hostile from good magic, 'black' vs.
> 'white.' There was no devil for one, and god for another. The same
> principle was invoked; all was *heka*. Only when this weapon was directed
> against King Ramses III in a harem conspiracy (12th century BCE) do
> we have what has been called a 'trial for sorcery,' but this was not a trial
> against sorcery *per se*, but a trial for treason.[15]

This attitude toward 'magic' in Egypt changed, however, with the
Roman conquest of Egypt and the subsequent emergence of Christianity. Rome was suspicious of foreign religions, that is, religions of
'the other,' and Christians judged pagan religions to be simply 'magic.'
As Robert Ritner concludes,

> With the abandonment of its native religion, Egypt might maintain its
> religious vocabulary, but not its religious perspective. The cultural gulf
> which separates *heka* from *hik* is paralleled by that which divides Egyptian
> *'Imnt.t*, the abode of Osiris and the blessed dead, from Coptic *amente*,
> the devil's hell. Stripped of its ancient theological significance, Coptic
> *hik* was now reduced to a designation for *alien and demonic* religion, at
> once illegal, unorthodox, and socially deviant.[16]

Such circumstances in Coptic Egypt can produce peculiar but pre-
dictable results. *The Magical Book of Mary and the Angels* (P. Heid. Inv.
Kopt. 685) is a tenth-century parchment codex (a palimpsest) that
contains a variety of magical spells and recipes, two of which domi-

---

[14] In: Ritner, 'The Religious, Social, and Legal Parameters of Traditional Egyptian Magic,' 49.
[15] Ritner, 'The Religious, Social, and Legal Parameters of Traditional Egyptian
Magic,' 54. Here and below the quotation is slightly modified in the presentation
of the Egyptian terms.
[16] Ritner, 'The Religious, Social, and Legal Parameters of Traditional Egyptian
Magic,' 59.

nate the codex: the prayer of Mary (2.6-8.29) and the adjuration of nine guardian angels (12.1-16.7).[17] In the prayer of Mary, a prayer with clear 'magical' features in a codex that is obviously 'magical' in character, a 'magical' invocation is included in order to banish 'magic' from the person making use of the spell:

> Atōnai Cherem Atōma
> Chialas Babōth Stieph
> Ba Satha Chithi Tha Sabaōth,
> God, listen to me today,
> you who are seated upon your exalted throne,
> before whom there tremble all spirits,
> those of heaven
> and those of the earth
> and those who are under the earth
> and those who are in the air,
> who are troubled before your great, holy name,
> which is Yaō Sabaōth Atōnai Elōi,
> you who destroy everything in which there is malice,
> all acts of magic (*magia*) and sorcery (*pharmagia*)
> (that) happen through wicked and meddlesome people,
> whether blindness
> or lameness
> or speechlessness
> or headache,
> or attack of the demons,
> whether having a fever
> or being troubled
> or depressed
> or hemorrhaging
> or having pain from the demons,
> or oil or fruit <or> (?) a potion in a jar (?) (3.12-4.15).

Later in the text, in a Solomonic spell for exorcism and protection, another 'magical' invocation eradicates 'magic':

> I beg and I invoke you today, Nassklēn,
> who guards and protects the body of King Solomon,
> all the days (of) his life.
> I adjure you today,

---

[17] Cf. M. Meyer, *The Magical Book of Mary and the Angels (P. Heid. Inv. Kopt. 685): Text, Translation, and Commentary* (Veröffentlichungen aus der Heidelberger Papyrussammlung, N.F., 9), Heidelberg 1996. The translations below are from this edition.

> (by) your powers and your names and your figure(s),
> that at the moment that NN wears your figure,
> you must begin guarding him
> all the days (of) his life,
> from all evil spirits
> and unclean spirits
> and all powers of the devil
> and all temptations
> and attacks
> and all magic (*hik*)
> and all sorcery (*pharmagia*) {and} of the devil.
> Drive them from NN,
> Yea, yea, at once!
> It is done (10.1-18).

'Magic' is a slippery category, and *heka*, *mageia*, and *magia* are not one and the same thing. The English word 'magic' comes from the Greek and Latin terms, and the English word is encumbered with many of the negative connotations of the Greek and Latin words, particularly in Christian usage. As a result, some of us prefer to use the designation 'ritual power' rather than 'magic' to describe this phenomenon. We suggest that the real world of magic is the world of religious ritual, and these magical texts are essentially ritual texts. Richard Smith and I state in *Ancient Christian Magic*, 'They direct the user to engage in activities that are marked off from normal activity by framing behavior through rules, repetitions, and other formalities. Ritual instructions pervade these texts.'[18] The point of these ritual texts is empowerment, that is to say, the acquisition and manipulation of power in order to accomplish what one wishes. Hence, the category of 'ritual power' may free us from the unpleasant connotations of the term 'magic' and communicate what is significant about this important religious practice.

So we turn to *The Holy Book of the Great Invisible Spirit*, a text with outstanding features of ritual power.

---

[18] M. Meyer and R. Smith (eds), *Ancient Christian Magic: Coptic Texts of Ritual Power* (Mythos), Princeton 1999, 4.

The Holy Book of the Great Invisible Spirit

The Holy Book of the Great Invisible Spirit is a Nag Hammadi text preserved in two Coptic versions, as Nag Hammadi Codex III.2 and Nag Hammadi Codex IV.2.[19] The primary title of the document, *The Holy Book of the Great Invisible Spirit*, is given as a titular subscript to the Codex III version; the end of the Codex IV version no longer survives. The secondary title, *The Egyptian Gospel*, is found in the copyist's note at the very end of the Codex III version of the text, and the primary title is also included in the note:

> The Egyptian Gospel, a holy secret book, written by God. Grace, intelligence, perception, and understanding be with the copyist, Eugnostos the beloved in the spirit—my worldly name is Gongessos [Latin, Concessus]—and my fellow luminaries in incorruptibility. Jesus Christ, son of God, savior, ICHTHYS! The Holy Book of the Great Invisible Spirit is written by God. Amen (69).

The earlier title attributed by scholars to the text, *The Gospel of the Egyptians*, was based upon an erroneous understanding and interpretation of the Coptic of the incipits of the two versions of the text. In their edition of the text, *Nag Hammadi Codices III.2 and IV.2: The Gospel of the Egyptians*, Alexander Böhlig and Frederik Wisse translate the incipit of the Codex III version as 'The [holy] book [of the Egyptians] about the great invisible [Spirit] . . . ,' and the incipit of the Codex IV version, similarly but with different restorations, '[The] holy [book] of the [Egyptians about the] great [invisible Spirit] . . . .'[20] The Coptic of the Codex III version reads *pjōōme*

---

[19] On *The Holy Book of the Great Invisible Spirit*, see A. Böhlig and F. Wisse (eds), in cooperation with P. Labib, *Nag Hammadi Codices III.2 and IV.2: The Gospel of the Egyptians (The Holy Book of the Great Invisible Spirit)* (Nag Hammadi Studies 4), Leiden/Grand Rapids, Michigan 1975; R. Charron, *Concordance des textes de Nag Hammadi: Le Codex III* (Bibliothèque copte de Nag Hammadi, Section 'Concordances' 3), Quebec/Louvain 1995; Layton, *The Gnostic Scriptures*, 101-20; Meyer, *The Gnostic Gospels of Jesus*; U.-K. Plisch, 'Das heilige Buch des großen unsichtbaren Geistes (NHC III.2; IV.2) ("Das ägyptische Evangelium"),' in: H.-M. Schenke, H.-G. Bethge, and U.U. Kaiser (eds), *Nag Hammadi Deutsch*, 2 vols (Die Griechischen Christlichen Schriftsteller der ersten Jahrhunderte, Neue Folge, 8, 12), Berlin/New York 2001, 2003, 1.293-321. On Gnostic ritual in *The Holy Book of the Great Invisible Spirit*, see Pearson, *Gnosticism and Christianity in Roman and Coptic Egypt*, 231-36. The translations of *The Holy Book of the Great Invisible Spirit* in this essay are taken from *The Gnostic Gospels of Jesus*.

[20] Cf. Böhlig and Wisse, *The Gospel of the Egyptians*, 52-3. For some of the observations in this paragraph I wish to acknowledge the comments of W.-P. Funk, P.-H. Poirier, J.M. Robinson, and J.D. Turner at Laval University in July and August 2004.

ᵉnth[ie]r[a . . .] ᵉnte pinoc natnau er[of ᵉmpna], and this must be translated
'The book of the [holy] . . . of the great invisible [spirit].' Böhlig and
Wisse can approximate their translation only by assuming that the
t in *th[ie]r[a]* is extraneous, hence *{t}h[ie]r[a]*. The Coptic of Codex
IV reads somewhat differently: *[pjōōme etoua]ab ᵉnte ni. . . pinoc ᵉnna[tnau
erof ᵉmpna]*, '[The holy book] of the (pl.) . . . great [invisible spirit].'
In the copyist's note the reference to 'the Egyptian Gospel' is certain:
peuangelion ᵉnᵉmᵉnkēme. Again, Böhlig and Wisse can translate the Coptic
as 'The gospel of <the> Egyptians' only after emending the Coptic
to read *peuangelion <ᵉn>ᵉnᵉmᵉnkēme*. In no case is there an attestation
of the title 'the Gospel of the Egyptians.'

After the discovery of the Nag Hammadi library, then, the title
'Gospel of the Egyptians' should still be used only to refer to the
text—challenging as that text remains—that is cited, in fragments,
by Clement of Alexandria and other church fathers.[21]

In the context of the earlier discussion in this essay, *The Holy Book
of the Great Invisible Spirit* may safely be described as a Gnostic text with
a Sethian character. The word *gnōsis* itself is used once in the text, at
Codex IV.72, where it is said of the Sethians appearing through Edokla
that everyone will endure 'through knowledge' (*gnōs[is]*; Codex III.60,
which is parallel to Codex IV.72, also reads 'through knowledge,' but
it has the Coptic word *sooun*). The Sethian features are clear, though,
according to Régine Charron, there may also be Hermetic influences
upon the text, as may be intimated by the name Poimael, reminiscent
of the name Poimandres of Hermetic lore, at III.66 (the parallel in
IV.78 reads Pimael).[22] With regard to mythic names (with primacy
of place given to the great invisible spirit), technical terminology, and
overall themes, *The Holy Book of the Great Invisible Spirit* recalls other
Sethian texts, including the classic of Sethian spirituality, *The Secret
Book* (or, *Apocryphon*) *of John* (Nag Hammadi Codex II.1; III.1; IV.1;
Berlin Gnostic Codex 8502.2; cf. also Irenaeus of Lyon, *Adversus hae-
reses* 1.29), along with *Zostrianos* (Nag Hammadi Codex VIII.1), *The
Foreigner* (or, *Allogenes*, Nag Hammadi Codex XI.3), and *Three Forms of
First Thought* (or, *Trimorphic Protennoia*, Nag Hammadi Codex XIII.1).

---

[21] Cf. W. Schneemelcher, 'The Gospel of the Egyptians,' in: Id. (ed.), *New Testament
Apocrypha*, English translation edited by R. McL. Wilson, 2 vols, Cambridge/Louisville
1991-92, 1.209-15.
[22] Cf. R. Charron, *Le Livre sacré du Grand Esprit invisible* (Bibliothèque copte de
Nag Hammadi, Section 'Textes'), Quebec/Louvain, forthcoming.

As in *The Secret Book of John* and elsewhere, here in *The Holy Book of the Great Invisible Spirit* heavenly Seth is the hero of the Gnostic story, and his descendants, the seed of Seth, the incorruptible immovable generation, will come to salvation. Unlike *The Secret Book of John*, which is only lightly Christianized, *The Holy Book of the Great Invisible Spirit* is thoroughly Christian in perspective. In *The Holy Book* Jesus is explicitly said to be the incarnation of Seth:

> Through forethought Seth has instituted the holy baptism that surpasses heaven, by means of the incorruptible one, conceived by the word (*logogenēs*), the living Jesus, with whom great Seth has been clothed. He has nailed down the powers of the thirteen realms (III.63-64).

Christian references abound in *The Holy Book*, and even the reference to Yesseus or Yesseus Mazareus Yessedekeus may be based upon the name Jesus, even Jesus of Nazareth or Jesus the Nazarene (*nazōraios*), and perhaps Jesus the righteous (*ho dikaios*).

The genre of *The Holy Book of the Great Invisible Spirit* has proved to be elusive, but I propose to identify the text as a Sethian baptismal handbook that features materials from a baptismal ritual, including a baptismal hymn, all of which is introduced by an account of the origin of the universe, described in Sethian cosmological terms.[23] The account of the origin of the universe in *The Holy Book* is presented in a complex way, with an emphasis upon triads of divine beings and three advents (or descents) of Seth, at the time of the great flood, the conflagration of Sodom and Gomorrah, and the final judgment. The third advent of Seth results in the establishment of baptism through Jesus. The cosmogonic account in *The Holy Book of the Great Invisible Spirit* may be organized in such a way as to correspond with the baptismal ritual materials that dominate the last part of the text. Following the description of the Sethian origin of baptism (III.63-64) and a list of the exalted beings who participate in the baptismal liturgy (III.64-66), a baptismal hymn gives poetic and ritual expression to the power of baptism (III.66-68).

Throughout Sethian literature there is an emphasis upon baptism, often said to be baptism with five seals, but precisely what this baptism entails remains a bit of an enigma. After examining *The Holy Book of the Great Invisible Spirit* and *Three Forms of First Thought* (*Trimorphic Pro-*

---

[23] Cf. also Layton, *The Gnostic Scriptures*, 101-4.

tennoia), John D. Turner observes, in *Sethian Gnosticism and the Platonic Tradition*,

> in both these treatises, there are a series of references to certain gestures and verbal performances capable of ritual enactment: renunciation, stripping, invocation and naming of holy powers, doxological prayer to the living water, anointing, enthronement, investiture, baptismal immersion, and certain other manual gestures, such as extending the arms in a circle. Whether any of these acts, and if so, which ones, comprise the Five Seals is difficult to tell; certainly all these were frequently part of the baptismal rite in the wider church as well.[24]

Indeed, there may have been a Sethian ceremony in which living water was applied and various liturgical acts were mandated. On the other hand, the baptismal ceremony reflected in *The Holy Book of the Great Invisible Spirit* is said to take place in the presence of exalted heavenly beings, and thus it may be understood in a more spiritual sense.[25]

Particularly within the portions of *The Holy Book of the Great Invisible Spirit* that deal directly with baptism, there are obvious features of 'magic,' or, better, ritual power. Many of these features are well known from other texts of ritual power, and only a few will be highlighted here, in the order of their appearance in *The Holy Book*.

According to *The Holy Book of the Great Invisible Spirit*, one of the powers presiding over the baptismal liturgy is Sesengenbarpharangēs (IV.75; III.64 reads Sesengenpharangēn). Sesengenbarpharangēs is a commonly attested name or word of power in texts of ritual power, with numerous variations in spelling. Most likely the word derives from or imitates Aramaic (S. son of [*bar*-] P.?). In *Curse Tablets and Binding Spells from the Ancient World*, John G. Gager refers to a passage in Josephus and suggests the possibility of some kind of connection with a drug from a fig tree in 'the Baaras ravine' (in Greek [genitive], *pharangos*).[26]

A few lines later (III.65, and elsewhere) in *The Holy Book of the Great Invisible Spirit*, there is an occurrence of the name Abrasax, an exceed-

---

[24] J.D. Turner, *Sethian Gnosticism and the Platonic Tradition* (Bibliothèque copte de Nag Hammadi, Section 'Études' 6), Quebec/Louvain 2001, 105.

[25] Cf. also Layton, *The Gnostic Scriptures*, 19-20; J.-M. Sevrin, *Le dossier baptismal séthien: Études sur la sacramentaire gnostique* (Bibliothèque copte de Nag Hammadi, Section 'Études' 2), Quebec 1986.

[26] Cf. J.G. Gager (ed.), *Curse Tablets and Binding Spells from the Ancient World*, New York/Oxford 1992, 269; Meyer and Smith, *Ancient Christian Magic*, 392.

ingly common name in 'magical' contexts. Abrasax (again, with variations in spelling) is the name of a cosmic power. The numerical value of
the name Abrasax, via gematria, is 365, and thus the name corresponds
to the number of days in the solar year. The name probably comes
from Hebrew, possibly *Abra* (for *Arba*, 'four' in Hebrew?) *Sabaoth*, that
is, 'Four (= YHWH, the tetragrammaton) Sabaoth ("of hosts," here
shortened).' One text of ritual power, the invocation that opens the
Great Magical Papyrus of Paris (1-25), preserved in Old Coptic, reads,
in part, 'Hail, gods, Achnoui Acham Abra Abra Sabaoth.'[27]

Voces magicae abound in the baptismal hymn, as in the 'magical'
papyri. Many of these words and utterances of power consist of (Greek)
vowels in a series, e.g. *AEEĒĒĒIIIIIYYYYYŌŌŌŌŌŌŌŌŌ* (III.66, missing
in Codex IV; five omicrons are expected after the iotas, and the vowels
may be arranged in a pyramid form), or *A* and *Ō* (given once as *ĒI
AAAA ŌŌŌŌ*, possibly reflecting the Greek for 'you are *AAAA ŌŌŌŌ*').
Some of the *voces magicae* may be glossolalia, but some may also be
translated. At III.66 the Coptic text reads, *uaei eisaei eioei eiosei*, which
seems to be Greek (*u, aei eis aei, ei ho ei, ei hos ei*) and may be translated
as follows: 'U, forever and ever, you are what you are, you are who
you are.' The U may be a shortened form of *huie*, 'O son.'[28]

Just after this statement there is an apparent liturgical rubric in the
text, comparable to the liturgical rubrics found in other ritual texts,
including texts of ritual power.[29] Here the rubric may indicate that
the next portion of the baptismal hymn is to be chanted or uttered
in a different voice:

> Who can comprehend you?
> In another voice:
> Having known you
> I have now mingled with your constancy (III.66-67).

This entire section of *The Holy Book of the Great Invisible Spirit*, of course,
is ritualistic, and the point of it is ritual power: baptismal power,
Gnostic power, the power of true life. As the prayer concludes,

> So the sweet smell of life is within me.
> I have mixed it with water as a model for all the rulers,
> that I may live with you in the peace of the saints,

---

[27] Cf. Meyer and Smith, *Ancient Christian Magic*, 22-3, 389.
[28] Cf. Böhlig and Wisse, *The Gospel of the Egyptians*, 201.
[29] Cf. U.-K. Plisch, 'Das heilige Buch des großen unsichtbaren Geistes,' 318.

you who exist forever,
in truth truly (III.67-68).

Conclusion

Two sets of embattled terms, *gnōsis* and *mageia* and related terms,
meet as expressions of definition and description in *The Holy Book
of the Great Invisible Spirit.* On the basis of the preceding, I conclude
that *The Holy Book of the Great Invisible Spirit* may legitimately be called
a Gnostic text—a Sethian Gnostic text, perhaps with some further
qualification (e.g., a Christian Sethian Gnostic text with Hermetic influences). *The Holy Book of the Great Invisible Spirit* may also be described, I
would suggest, as a text with significant 'magical' elements, or, more
appropriately, elements of ritual power. Boundaries are crossed, tax-
onomies are up for grabs, as *gnōsis* and *mageia* meet in *The Holy Book
of the Great Invisible Spirit*, a text which is both a Gnostic text and a
text of ritual power. Further issues of definition and taxonomy also
emerge in the text, since the copyist named the text 'the Egyptian
Gospel' and applied the term *euangelion* to the text. For the copyist,
and perhaps for us, the term 'gospel' as a designation of genre may
need to be expanded beyond the synoptic and Johannine 'good news'
of the New Testament. *The Egyptian Gospel* is not a narrative gospel,
not a gospel of the cross, not a sayings gospel, but it is, according to
the ancient copyist, a gospel, showing another way that a Christian
message could be articulated and Jesus could be understood.[30]

   Gnōsis and *mageia* come together in fascinating ways in *The Holy
Book of the Great Invisible Spirit*, or *The Egyptian Gospel*. Ultimately, this is
not too surprising. A similar coalescence of the concerns of *gnōsis* and
mageia may be seen, among Gnostic texts, in *The Books of Jeu*, *The Three
Steles of Seth*, and *Zostrianos*,[31] and the heresiologists claim that the same
interests may be evident in Simon Magus, Marcus the Valentinian, and
others. And in magical texts, texts of ritual power, Gnostic names and
themes are evident in the roles of Sophia, Yaldabaoth, and the four
luminaries in such texts as Coptic Museum Papyrus 4958, London
Oriental Manuscript 5987, and a Coptic codex from the Macquarie

---

   [30] Cf. my discussion in *The Gnostic Gospels of Jesus*.
   [31] See the chapter 'Ritual Power in Coptic Gnostic Texts,' in: Meyer and Smith,
Ancient Christian Magic, 59-76.

University collection.[32] Finally, the world of *gnōsis* and *mageia* begins to look even more interesting as the concerns intersect and the inevitable questions of definition and taxonomy are acknowledged.

---

[32] Cf. M. Meyer, 'Mary Dissolving Chains in Coptic Museum Papyrus 4958 and Elsewhere,' in: M. Immerzeel and J. van der Vliet (eds), *Coptic Studies on the Threshold of a New Millennium: Proceedings of the Seventh International Congress of Coptic Studies, Leiden, 27 August-2 September 2000*, 2 vols (Orientalia Lovaniensia Analecta 133), Louvain/Paris 2004, 1.369-76; Meyer and Smith, *Ancient Christian Magic*, 129-33. At the time of the preparation of this essay, the Macquarie codex remains unpublished.

FATE, MAGIC AND ASTROLOGY IN *PISTIS SOPHIA*, CHAPS 15-21

JACQUES VAN DER VLIET

Recent scholarship shows a growing sensitivity to the links between Gnosticism and magic. Both religious phenomena, however they are defined, share certain forms of literary and ritual expression. Much of this shared idiom is found in one of the showpieces of Christian Gnostic literature, the *Apocryphon of John*, a work that has for many years occupied a central place in the research and publications of Gerard Luttikhuizen to whom these pages are a tribute.[1] The present paper will examine the relationship between magic and Gnostic Christianity from a different angle. It will study the views on magic and astrology of the third- or fourth-century Egyptian author[2] of the encyclopaedic work known as the *Pistis Sophia*. As it will become clear, his discussion of the subject is exceptional in its combination of mythical discourse with real technical knowledge. The following pages first consider the literary context of the discussion and then look at some of the central cosmological and soteriological concepts that underlie it. Finally, the ancient author's attitude towards magic and astrology is assessed.

The neglect of the *Pistis Sophia* is one of the riddles of modern Gnostic studies.[3] W.C. van Unnik's authoritative opinion that in the *Pistis Sophia* 'nicht nur Wahnsinn vorliegt, wie es beim oberflächlichen Lesen den Anschein hat' and that rather 'man durch sorgfältige Einzelexegese

---

[1] See his bibliography in the present volume. On magic in the *Apocryphon*, see K.L. King, 'Approaching the variants of the Apocryphon of John', in: J.D. Turner and A. McGuire (eds), *The Nag Hammadi Library after Fifty Years: Proceedings of the 1995 Society of Biblical Literature Commemoration*, Leiden 1997, 105-37 at 112-13; J. van der Vliet, 'The Coptic Gnostic texts as Christian apocryphal literature', in: S. Emmel et al. (eds), *Ägypten und Nubien in spätantiker und christlicher Zeit: Akten des 6. Internationalen Koptologenkongresses, Münster, 20.-26. Juli 1996*, ii, Wiesbaden 1999, 553-62 at 554-7.

[2] The word is used here in a strictly conventional sense; all questions of editorial history are left aside.

[3] For an excellent general introduction and bibliography, see M. Tardieu and J.-D. Dubois, *Introduction à la littérature gnostique*, Paris 1986, i, 65-82.

Einblicke bekommt in die Bildung gnostischer Systeme'[4] has hardly
met with any response. Nevertheless, this compendious volume of
Christian Gnostic teaching is a treasure-trove of ideas on soteriology,
cosmology, eschatology and biblical exegesis. It has been known since
the 18th century and has since been translated into several modern
languages. Its single extant manuscript is written in a clear and classic
Sahidic Coptic, which is a pleasure to read. It has profited from an
excellent edition by Carl Schmidt, the final version of which dates to
1925.[5] Yet it has hardly ever been noticed that in the very beginning
of the first of the work's four voluminous books a prominent place is
accorded to a unique discussion of magic and astrology.[6]

In a garment of light

The *Pistis Sophia* (henceforth abbreviated *PS*), similar to many other
Christian apocryphal writings, takes the form of a dialogue between
the risen Jesus and his disciples on the Mount of Olives.[7] Basically,
the work evolves as a play of question and answer, the disciples asking
questions and Jesus providing answers. In addition, an important role
is played by narrative and biblical exegesis. The dialogue is contained
within a narrative framework that not only inspires the dialogue but
also situates it historically and calendrically. Even within the ques-
tion-answer structure, however, narrative takes an important place:

---

[4] W.C. van Unnik, 'Die "Zahl der vollkommenen Seelen" in der *Pistis Sophia*',
in: *Sparsa Collecta*, iii, Leiden 1983, 214-23 at 222.

[5] C. Schmidt, *Pistis Sophia*, Copenhagen 1925; this remains the standard edition. It
has been reprinted, Leiden 1978, facing an English translation by V. MacDermot. All
translations below are my own; references are to the chapters of Schmidt's German
translation in *Koptisch-gnostische Schriften*, vol. i, Berlin 1905 (1981[4]), and to the page
and line numbers of his 1925 edition, all retained by MacDermot.

[6] A recent study of Jewish and Christian attitudes towards astrology, K. von
Stuckrad, *Das Ringen um die Astrologie: Jüdische und christliche Beiträge zum antiken Zeitverständnis*, Berlin/New York 2000, entirely ignores it. A notable exception is H.J. Hodges,
'Gnostic liberation from astronomical determinism: Hipparchan "trepidation" and
the breaking of fate', *Vigiliae Christianae* 51 (1997) 359-73; also, very briefly, H.O.
Schröder, 'Fatum (Heimarmene)', *Reallexikon für Antike und Christentum* 7 (1969) 524-636
at 628-9. Most discussions of magic and astrology in *PS* deal with the conceptions
of the fourth book, which are left out of the discussion here; see the references in
Tardieu, Dubois, *Introduction*, 79-80.

[7] On this genre: J. Hartenstein, *Die zweite Lehre: Erscheinungen des Auferstandenen als
Rahmenerzählungen frühchristlicher Dialoge*, Berlin 2000 (*PS* is hardly mentioned).

Jesus' answers do not only explain known facts and events, they also relate unknown facts and events. Both may then be interpreted as the fulfilment of Holy Scripture through an idiosyncratic exegesis of biblical passages (including the *Odes of Solomon*). The many digressions offer room for a variety of traditional materials that are sometimes quite heterogeneous.

All of these literary elements occur in chapters 15-21 that form part of a long narrative, punctuated by the questions of the disciples, in which Jesus relates the heavenly journey from which he has just returned.[8] His report, in turn, provides the framework for a long series of revelations aimed at documenting the relationship between man and the supernal powers as well as man's place within a complicated cosmology and soteriology. The opening scene of the work situates Jesus' journey at the very end of his activity on earth, after eleven years of teaching following Easter. He is reunited with the 'garment of light' that he had to leave behind in the world of light before entering the lower world. This garment now restores him to his full luminous (divine) nature and permits him to ascend through the various spheres of the supra-terrestrial world up to the thirteenth eon. The garment is, in a way, a magical device, for it is inscribed with an encoded message that invites Jesus to return to his transcendent home and, as will be seen, forces the celestial powers into submission. The inscription is described as a 'mystery' (μυστήριον) and it is verbally quoted in the text as a series of *voces magicae*, with long strokes over them that mark them as powerful (16.18).[9] Thus, the text on Jesus' garment may be seen as an example of the overlapping modes of discourse signalled at the very beginning of this paper.[10]

Once he is back on earth after a cosmic perturbation that lasts over a day, Jesus relates his ascension in a way that shows the strong influence of the *Ascension of Isaiah*, chap. 11. First, he comes to 'the

---

[8] For the motif of the 'heavenly journey', see M. Himmelfarb, *Ascent to Heaven in Jewish and Christian Apocalypses*, New York/Oxford 1993 (for its interest in cosmology, 72-94); in Gnostic sources: von Stuckrad, *Ringen*, 636-43 (with references to earlier literature).

[9] Their 'translation' takes up several pages (16.19-20.11). Such inscribed garments were not mere fictional constructs, see J. van der Vliet, '"In a robe of gold": Status, magic and politics on inscribed Christian textiles from Egypt', forthcoming in the proceedings of the conference *Textile Botschaften* (Berlin, January 2003).

[10] For magical names in *PS*, see the important articles by M. Tardieu, quoted in Tardieu, Dubois, *Introduction*, 79-80.

firmament' (στερέωμα) (chap. 11). This is characterized by 'gates' (πύλη), that open upon Jesus' arrival, and is inhabited by apparently personified elements that are called 'archons, authorities' (ἄρχων), 'powers' (ἐξουσία) and 'angels' (ἄγγελος), who are 'bound' (ⲙⲟⲩⲣ, ⲙⲏⲣ) to a certain 'rank' (τάξις). These are terrified when they view the 'garment of light' and the words written upon it. A great disorder then follows as their 'bonds' (ⲙⲣⲣⲉ) dissolve and they give up their 'ranks'. Finally, they all worship Jesus and let him pass.

The next stop is the first σφαῖρα (chap. 12). It is also characterized by 'gates' that open upon Jesus' arrival and through which he penetrates its 'houses' (οἶκος). This first sphere, too, is inhabited by 'archons' and they react in the same way as the powers of the firmament. Their 'bonds', 'places' (τόπος) and 'ranks' dissolve and they leave their fixed order. Jesus passes them and arrives at 'the gate of the second sphere, that which is Fate (ⲑⲓⲙⲁⲣⲙⲉⲛⲏ: εἱμαρμένη)'. Subsequently, this second sphere is often simply called 'Fate'. The events repeat and again authorities, bonds, places, ranks and houses are mentioned (chap. 13).

During Jesus' passage through each of these three supra-terrestrial zones, the events follow identical patterns: there is disturbance (ϣⲧⲟⲣⲧⲣ) and panic among both the physical (gates, houses, bonds, ranks) and the moral elements (archons, etc.) that make up these spheres. The latter, through the garment of light with its inscriptions, recognize Jesus as 'the Lord of the universe' in rhetorical questions that are almost literal quotes from the *Ascension of Isaiah*, 11.24 and 26. Their recognition is indirect, however, because Jesus emphasizes: 'They did not see me, but they saw only the light' (21.8-9). They then leave their 'ranks' to adore him and sing hymns of praise. Jesus' appearance as a superior power of light, therefore, entails disorder and fear as well as recognition and praise.

The situation changes when Jesus arrives at a more superior zone, that of the 'great eons of the archons' (chap. 14). These eons, which are twelve in number plus a thirteenth one on top of them, are more complex unities. They have not only 'veils' (καταπέτασμα) and 'gates', but show an intricate spatial organization comprising eons, spheres, heavens, 'arrangements' (κόσμησις) and 'places'. They are, moreover, inhabited by an extensive hierarchy of angels, archangels, gods, lords, tyrants, etc. (23.13-19). These angelic entities once again react to Jesus with fear. The disturbance even reaches their hierarchical heads, the Great Invisible Forefather and the Three Great Thrice-powerful (τριδύναμος) who, struck by panic, run around in their 'places' without being able to shut them (23.23-24.8). Thus far, the events may seem to copy that of Jesus' passage through the lower spheres in a more circumstantial way. Instead of submission, however, the powers of the twelve eons, unable to understand 'the mystery that happened' (24.25-25.1), show hostility: 'Adamas, the great tyrant, and all the tyrants that are in all the eons began to wage war, in vain, against the light' (25.1-3). Adamas (ⲡⲁⲗⲁⲙⲁⲥ: 'The-steel-one') is the head over all the archons of the twelve eons. Although mentioned only twice here, Adamas is one of the principal black characters of *PS*. In chapter 66 ff., he figures as one of the fiercest persecutors of Pistis-Sophia, whose sad adventures make up the core of the work named after her. He appears, here too, as the natural enemy of the light, which he and his fellow tyrants combat without even knowing its real, divine nature (24.19-25.5). The tyrants, of course, are chanceless against Jesus' light, which is simply beyond their reach: their vain combat 'exhausts' them one after another and they fall down into the eons to become 'like dead terrestrials in whom no breath is (anymore)' (25.8-9). Initially, Jesus remains passive under the attacks of the tyrants and he intervenes only following their defeat. This intervention, its modalities and immediate practical consequences are the subject of a long digression that takes up chapters 15-21. A further digression, in chapters 22-27, explains the long-term soteriological meaning of Jesus' intervention.

In chapter 15 (with a summary in chapter 16), Jesus relates how, after the fall of the tyrants, he undertakes a double action: first, he robs all the archons of a third part of their power (ϭⲟⲙ); secondly, he reverses the course of the first sphere and Fate, which are both ruled by the archons of the twelve eons (25.16-17), so that, during six months, both spheres are turned to the left and, during another six months, to the right. Whereas originally they were always effectuating their influences (ἀποτέλεσμα) and their actions (πρᾶξις) looking towards the left, they are now alternately facing left and facing right. This double action and its aims are explained and commented upon in both chapters 15-16 and in Jesus' replies to the ensuing questions and remarks of his disciples (chaps 17-21).

First, by taking away a third part of the archons' power, Jesus works against magic and magicians. He explains this right away in chap. 15:

In order that when the humans in the world invoke (ἐπικαλέω) them (i.e. the archons) in their mysteries (μυστήριον), which have been brought down by the angels who trespassed, that is their magic (μαγεία, plur.) in order then that when they invoke them in their evil practices, they will not be able to execute them (25.11-16; cf. 27.4-10; 29.10-17).

Jesus' weakening of the archons renders the power of magic and magicians ineffective.

Second, by reversing the course of the first sphere and the sphere of Fate, Jesus works against the art of the astrologers (ⲣⲉϥⲕⲁ ⲟⲩⲏⲟⲩ) and diviners (ⲣⲉϥϣⲓⲛⲉ) 'and those who inform the humans in the world about everything that is going to happen, in order that from that moment onwards, they are unable to inform them about anything that will happen' (27.11-13). A technical explanation is provided as well (in chap. 21; cf. chap. 27): 'When they (scil. the astrologers) happen to find Fate or the sphere turned to the right, they will not say anything reliable, for I turned around their influences (ἀποτέλεσμα) and their quadrangles and their triangles and their eight-figure'[11] (30.11-15). Likewise, the diviners, who are treated here as a related though different class of experts, when they invoke the names of the archons and their decans while these are turned to the right, will not be heard by them, since they are oriented in a way that differs from their original arrangement (31.3-7).

> For, Jesus explains, their names when they are turned to the left are different from their names when they are turned to the right, and when they (scil. the diviners) invoke them while they (scil. the archons and their decans) are turned to the right, they will not speak the truth to them, but on the contrary will bring them terrible confusion and will threaten them frightfully (31.7-11).

The same fate awaits the astrologers who do not know the new orbits and configurations of the celestial archons. They will be induced into error and fall victim to delusion (11-16). Also 'the archons' themselves 'that are in the eons and in their spheres and in their heavens and in all their places' become confused by the periodical change of direction, and do not know their own orbits anymore (31.26-32.4).

This may appear a slightly eccentric but generally clear account of how Jesus disarmed magic and astrology. But this is not the case.

---

[11] 'Eight-figure', ϣⲙⲟⲩⲛ ⲛ̄ⲥⲙⲟⲧ, also called ϣⲙⲟⲩⲛ ⲛ̄ⲥⲭⲏⲙⲁ, 'eight-aspect', in chap. 27. See below note 35.

Whereas Jesus' feats are, initially (chap. 18), recognized as the glorious fulfilment of Isaiah's prophecy concerning the astrologers and diviners of Egypt (see below), two serious reservations are made immediately afterwards (chaps 20-21). The first concerns magic. When straightforwardly asked whether magic is still effective or not, Jesus answers that it is certainly not effective anymore in the way it used to be. There is, however, an escape for the magicians:

> They may appeal to (?)[12] those who know the mysteries of the magic of the thirteenth eon and when they invoke the mysteries of the magic of the inhabitants of the thirteenth eon, they will execute them with flawless precision, for in accordance with the command of the First Mystery I did not rob any power from that place (29.21-30.2).

A second question (30.3-6) concerns the astrologers and the diviners: are they really now unable to forecast future events? Again, according to Jesus' answer, their impotence proves to be only relative and virtually limited to the periods when the first sphere and that of Fate rotate to the right. When 'the astrologers find Fate and the sphere turned left, according to their earlier disposition, their words come true and they will tell what is due to happen' (30.7-11). Worse, a clever astrologer may even be able to overcome entirely the problems posed by Jesus' intervention:

> He, however, who can find their computation (scil. of the astral configurations) from the moment that I reversed them (scil. the courses of both spheres) and made them spend six months looking to the 'parts' (μέρος) on their left and six months to the orbits on their right—he, then, who can observe them in that way, he will discover their influences (ἀποτέλεσμα) precisely and can predict everything they will effectuate (30.19-25).

Diviners are also not left entirely without resources: 'When they invoke the name(-s) of the archons and happen to find them looking left, everything they ask their decans about, they (scil. the decans) will tell them precisely' (30.25-31.3). Only during the other six months will they be misled and even threatened, because the names of the archons have changed. Even when the resulting confusion and error among the archons themselves are emphasized at the end of this chapter,

---

[12] Uncertain translation (MacDermot: 'will borrow from'; Schmidt: 'werden eine Anleihe machen bei'); the text has: ϲⲉⲛⲁⲉⲓⲣⲉ ⲛ̅ⲟⲩⲗⲟⲉⲓϭⲉ ϩ̅ⲛ̅ ..., but the word ⲗⲟⲉⲓϭⲉ means 'reason, pretext, blame'.

it is nevertheless clearly stated that, as far as the occult sciences are concerned, Jesus' intervention had only partial effects.

Jesus' victory over the archons, however, also had direct bearings on the salvation of the soul. These are discussed in a second digression, occupying chapters 22-27, which cannot be fully analyzed here. They are nevertheless important for their ideas about the origin and fate of the human and animal souls.[13] Only in chap. 29, following a brief summary in chap. 28, the story of Jesus' ascent is resumed.

Hostile worlds

The narrative of Jesus' heavenly journey is primarily a stepwise initiation of the reader into the author's cosmology and soteriology. It draws the map of the lower celestial world and gives a vivid depiction of the opposition between the divine light revealed by Jesus and the powers dominating that world. Their confrontation causes great disturbance and, eventually, a clash in which the evil tyrants of the eons are defeated and their empires unsettled. This unsettlement directly affects human trades, such as magic and astrology, which demand knowledge of the celestial powers or even their active cooperation. Although it is impossible to analyze every aspect of this rich text here, a brief discussion of two related questions is indispensable. These concern, first, the nature of the celestial world as it is described in this part of *PS* and, second, the modalities of the unsettlement of the archontic empire.

In the first three books of *PS*, the human world and the superior world of pure light, the divine world, are separated by a zone that consists of distinct superimposed layers, each characterized by an internal structure that involves spatial and moral elements arranged in a fixed hierarchical organization.[14] Both these layers and the powers that inhabit them, are hierarchized in an ascending scale on the complementary axes 'matter-power' and, particularly, 'darkness-light'. This entire zone is a world of 'mixture' (κερασμός), where darkness

---

[13] For which see Van Unnik, 'Zahl', esp. 218-19.

[14] For a general discussion, C. Schmidt, *Gnostische Schriften in koptischer Sprache aus dem Codex Brucianus*, Leipzig 1892, 378 ff., who also notes the divergences between the present chapters and the world view of the fourth book of *PS*, which has been purposely excluded from the discussion here.

and light co-exist in a state of permanent conflict. It can best be defined, from the point of view of human salvation, as a great, hostile machine that tries to withhold the fallen light and prevent its re-integration into the world of the divine. The world of humanity or 'perdition' as well as the στερέωμα and the two 'spheres' situated immediately above (the σφαῖρα proper, and the second sphere called Fate) are characterized as 'chaos'. Above the world of chaos, there are two layers of eons, that of the twelve eons and that of the thirteenth eon. The latter represents, within the world of κερασμός, the top level: it borders on the world of light but it is at the same time the scene of ongoing war over the fallen light or, in different terms, over the human soul.

The representation of these intermediate worlds is in its structuring principles and terminology strongly indebted to contemporary astrology. The first stage in Jesus' ascent is the firmament (στερέωμα), a term that is often loosely used (frequently in the plural) for 'heaven'. Here it denotes a distinct entity, the lowermost celestial zone, which apparently marks the boundary between the terrestrial and the astral world.[15] It does not play a specific role of its own here or elsewhere in *PS*.[16] This is different than the next two regions: the first sphere and the second one, identified with Fate. As their name indicates, these are conceived as celestial spheres revolving around the earth and carrying the celestial bodies. Indeed, *PS*'s discussion of astrology summarized above shows that it is these two spheres and their inhabitants that are the object of the mathematical observations of the astrologers and the invocations of the diviners. Both are distinguished only by the use of the term Fate for the second, uppermost sphere. From their relative position, it is logical to suppose that the first sphere is that of the planets and that the sphere of Fate carries the fixed stars. In the present context, the precise nature and structure of both spheres are not explained further beyond the general characteristics summarized above. As it appears from the following chapters (chaps 22-27), however, they play an important role in 'recycling' the superior light in the lower world and in producing the souls of the living beings inhabiting the lower

---

[15] See Schmidt, *Gnostische Schriften*, 401 (infra). For στερέωμα as a 'boundary' in Philo and Origen, see D.T. Runia, *Philo of Alexandria: On the Creation of the Cosmos according to Moses*, Leiden 2001, 174-8.

[16] Only *PS* 214.19-20, mentions, among celestial entities, 'the στερέωμα with all its veils (καταπέτασμα)'. It is nowhere the element of Satan, as in the *Ascension of Isaiah*.

world. *PS* subscribes to the widespread idea of an astral 'body' of the soul.[17] The 'ministers' (λειτουργοί) of the archons of both celestial spheres fashion the souls of all living creatures from an archontic material element in which a superior power is mixed up. The souls themselves are distributed by them 'in accordance with the circuit (κύκλος) of the archons of that sphere (scil. that below the eons, called Fate) and in accordance with all the aspects (σχῆμα) of its revolution (ⲕⲓⲛⲕⲱⲧⲉ)' (35.20-21) and then cast into the world. Through the soul, therefore, man is directly dependent on the stars and, in particular, on the stars of the uppermost of the two spheres, the one 'below the eons', where his nativity is established. Here, no doubt, the entirely negative concept of Fate comes in, the precise modalities of which are elaborated in terms of sin and death in the later books of *PS*.[18]

There may be a second reason why the uppermost sphere is associated with Fate; it borders directly on the world of the twelve eons. The two astral spheres are not only governed by these, but the number twelve also suggests that the world of the eons has been modelled on the zodiac and that an intrinsic link connects both. It is common practice in Gnostic writings to use the structural and numerological principles of traditional astrology and calendrical lore as a model for the organization of the archontic world. This is apparent, for example, in the widespread preference for seven- and twelve-tier systems and in the use of technical terminology, that assigns the archons to 'houses', 'places', 'spheres', etc.[19] Another Gnostic source that applies technical astrological terminology to its description of the archontic world is the *Trimorphic Protennoia* (NH XIII.1). In its chapter 'on Fate' (εἱμαρμένη), the panic caused by the arrival of the Redeemer ('the Voice') among the archons who govern the world is described in a way that is strongly reminiscent of *PS* in its use of astrological imagery (pp. 42-46; Turner,

---

[17] On the development of the concept of the astral body, see A. Scott, *Origen and the Life of the Stars: A History of an Idea*, Oxford 1991, 76-103 (93-103 deal with Gnostic sources).

[18] Particularly in the third (chaps 133-135) and fourth books (chaps 136-148), which, however, incorporate divergent traditions that cannot legitimately be projected upon the present chapters. Cf. Schröder, 'Fatum', 628-9; A. Böhlig, 'Zum Antimimon Pneuma in den koptisch-gnostischen Texten', in: *Mysterion und Wahrheit*, Leiden 1968, 162-74 at 167-9.

[19] For the important distinction between 'astrological reality' and 'astrological representation', see the cautious remarks in Scott, *Origen*, 93-6; Hodges, 'Gnostic liberation', seems insufficiently aware of this distinction.

416-424).[20] The fact, however, that this imagery is combined with imagery derived from the setting of the *descensus ad inferos* shows that the author's aim is a demonological interpretation of the archontic regime rather than a technical description of astrological realities.[21] In *PS*, the twelve eons, in spite of apparently being modelled on the zodiac, are at the same time distinct from and superior to the celestial bodies situated in the two spheres.[22] The archons of the eons use the latter as instruments in constructing what from the human point of view is Fate. Likewise, in the *Apocryphon of John*, the Chief Archon and his powers created Fate 'and fettered in measure and times and moments the gods of the heavens and the angels and the demons and humanity, so that all of them would be in its (scil. Fate's) bond (ⲙⲡⲣ) and it be master over everyone' (BG 72.4-11; Waldstein-Wisse, synopsis, 75-76). Time and space are a prison governed by Fate on behalf of the archons.

This is the cosmological framework in which Jesus' ascension and the ensuing triumph of light over the archons of the eons are set. Now we will take a closer look at the precise way in which Jesus manages to unsettle the archontic world. According to *PS*, he takes one third of the power of the archons and reverses the course of the spheres over which they rule. The fall of the archons who subsequently lose a third of their power was undoubtedly inspired by a combination of Rev 12. 7-9 (the fall of the Dragon) and 4 (the fall of one third of the stars) that was employed by Origen as well.[23] Jesus' second intervention is more elusive. An interpretation along purely astronomical lines would seem most attractive at first sight. Thus, H.J. Hodges proposed to connect the periodical inversion of the movement of the spheres with the precession of the equinoxes which was discovered by Hipparchus.[24] It is true that Origen, for example, used this discovery precisely to argue the inac-

---

[20] See Hodges, 'Gnostic liberation', 364-6.

[21] For the *descensus*-imagery: P.H. Poirier, 'La *Prôtennoia Trimorphe* (NH XIII,1) et le vocabulaire du *descensus ad inferos*', *Le Muséon* 96 (1983) 193-204, and J. van der Vliet, *L'image du mal en Égypte: Démonologie et cosmogonie d'après les textes gnostiques coptes*, Ph.D.-thesis Leiden 1996, 156-60, 319-34.

[22] Hodges, 'Gnostic liberation', 366, identifies the twelve eons and the zodiac without further ado; in my opinion, this view is not supported by the text. Note, however, that also PS itself has a tendency to lump the eons and the spheres together (e.g. in the brief recapitulation of chap. 28; 41.13-24).

[23] For its place in Origen's astro-demonology, see Scott, *Origen*, 138-40.

[24] 'Gnostic liberation', 369-73.

curacy and nullity of astrological predictions.[25] The precession of the
equinoxes, however, is a slow and progressive, almost unnoticeable,
fluctuating movement.[26] *PS* describes a sudden and radical inversion of
the movement of the astral bodies. Even if Hipparchus' discovery may
have provided Christians, such as Origen, with a scholarly argument
against astrology, thereby preparing *PS*'s argument conceptually, the
events described clearly do not match.[27]

Instead of Hipparchus' precession, it is far more attractive to refer
to a famous passage from Plato's *Statesman* (269 ff.).[28] In the cosmological myth that is reported by Plato, the cosmos revolves according to
two opposite movements that succeed each other. Divine intervention
periodically corrects the fatal course of the world. Plato's representation of a destructive course of the world that needs to be reverted
influenced later and, in particular, Christian concepts of Fate, which
links it to the astrological and soteriological discourse of *PS*.[29] The
Gnostic author clearly adapted Plato's myth of reversal to his own
purposes and made it part of Jesus' mission.[30] No slow natural process
is described, but rather a brusque and volitional act of power that
diminishes the impact of Fate and, simultaneously, deals a blow to
occult sciences based upon astrological calculations.

Evil practices

The incorporation of the Platonic myth into his account of Jesus'
mission situates *PS* within an ancient Christian tradition that considers
the breaking of astral Fate as a major achievement of the Incarna-

---

[25] See D. Amand, *Fatalisme et liberté dans l'antiquité grecque*, Louvain 1945, 314; von
Stuckrad, *Ringen*, 781.

[26] See e.g. D. Ulansey, *The Origins of the Mithraic Mysteries*, New York/Oxford
1989, 76-81.

[27] Pace Hodges, 'Gnostic liberation', 371-3.

[28] I owe this idea to R. Roukema. For a discussion of its original context, see
H.R. Scodel, *Diaeresis and Myth in Plato's Statesman*, Göttingen 1987, 74-89.

[29] See W. Gundel, *Beiträge zur Entwicklungsgeschichte der Begriffe Ananke und Heimarmene*,
Gießen 1914, 46-7; Schröder, 'Fatum', 628. Cf. F. Boll, C. Bezold, and W. Gundel,
Sternglaube und Sterndeutung, Leipzig/Berlin 1926, 93 and 201-2.

[30] This is even more evident in the chapters on its soteriological meaning (22
ff.). For another instance of rare Platonic imagery in *PS*, see M. Tardieu, 'La coupe
de l'oubli', in: C. Cannuyer (ed.), *Études coptes VIII: Dixième Journée d'études, Lille 14-16
juin 2001*, Lille/Paris 2003, 305-9 at 305.

tion. In early Christian literature this point of view had already found its expression in Ignatius of Antioch's *Letter to the Ephesians*, chap. 19 (Camelot, 74-76).[31] In a scene that plausibly alludes to the star of Bethlehem, God incarnate is revealed to 'the eons' as a dazzling new star. Ignatius' description of the manifestation of its surpassing light and its effects upon the other stars shows clear parallels to that of Jesus' apparition in the archontic world according to *PS*. The celestial bodies are unable to understand the origin and nature of this 'new star' (cf. *PS* 24.25-25.5). Its novelty and otherness cause disturbance among them (Ignatius: ταραχή; cf. *PS*: ϣⲧⲟⲣⲧⲣ) and, eventually, lead to the destruction of magic (μαγεία) and the abolition of 'every bond (δεσμός) of evil' (cf. Jesus undoing the 'bonds' of the celestial archons in *PS*). Both sources describe a similar process of liberation that opposes the divine light of Christ to the slavery of astral Fate.

Another second century source is the *Excerpta ex Theodoto*, extracts from the work of the Gnostic Theodotus assembled by Clement of Alexandria. Chapters 69-75 (Sagnard) deal extensively with astrology and the rule of Fate, broken by the descent of the Saviour. Theodotus, like Ignatius of Antioch, develops the association 'descent of Christ into the world—star of Bethlehem—abolition of astral Fate'.[32] Fate lost its impact thanks to the Lord who, rising as a 'strange and new star', appeared on earth 'in order to transfer those who have believed in Christ from Fate (εἱμαρμένη) to his Providence (πρόνοια)' (chap. 74). Conversion and baptism abolish Fate and grant power over the demons (chaps 76-78). Although the lavish mythological framework that is characteristic of *PS* is absent from the earlier Gnostic source, both make the stars subservient to invisible powers that control humanity (chap. 70). Moreover, they share a definite interest in the technical aspects of astrology. Thus, the *Excerpta* even contains a brief treatise on Fate and astrology (chaps 69-71). Astrology, for Theodotus, represents a neutral and even acceptable science (ἡ τῶν μαθημάτων

---

[31] My interpretation follows P.-Th. Camelot's, in the notes of his edition; see furthermore, J. Daniélou, 'L'étoile de Jacob', in: *Les symboles chrétiens primitifs*, Paris 1961, 109-30 at 119-20; W.R. Schoedel, *A Commentary on the Letters of Ignatius of Antioch*, Philadelphia 1985, 87-94; N. Denzey, 'A new star on the horizon: Astral christologies and stellar debates in early Christian discourse', in: S. Noegel, J. Walker, B. Wheeler (eds), *Prayer, Magic, and the Stars in the Ancient and Late Antique World*, University Park, Pennsylvania 2003, 207-21.

[32] Cf. Daniélou, 'Étoile', 120-1.

θεωρία, chap. 75) that may give an insight into and even proof of the mechanisms of astral Fate.[33]

PS shows a similar interest in the technical sides of astrology. Although no separate treatise is devoted to it, the author clearly demonstrates his awareness of what magic and astrology are about, also technically. Magic consists of 'mysteries' or esoteric rituals that derive their effectiveness from properly addressed and formulated 'invocations'. Such a representation is entirely consistent with modern descriptions of ancient magical practice.[34] Astrological predictions are based upon the observation of conventional geometrical relationships between the heavenly bodies, such as the quadrangles and triangles that are known from contemporary scholarly literature.[35] These configurations enable the computation of their ἀποτελέσματα. The author profusely uses technical jargon such as this and apparently considers astrology a real science.[36] Unlike the *Excerpta*, however, his judgment on the astrological practice is certainly not neutral.

Magic and astrology, throughout *PS*, meet with the strictures usually found in Christian sources of the period. Thus, the 'mysteries' of the sorcerers, which are explained as 'their magic' (ⲛⲉⲩⲙⲁⲅⲓⲁ), are derived from 'the angels who trespassed' (25.11-16, fully quoted above; cf. 27.4-10; 29.10-17). *PS* thereby adheres to the idea that the fallen angels revealed magic and astrology to primitive man. The origin of this idea is usually sought in *1 Enoch* 8, but it was commonplace amongst ancient Jewish and Christian authors.[37] It can also be found in a slightly adapted form in another Coptic Gnostic source, the treatise *On the origin of the world* (NH II.5), where the instructors of magic are the demonic angels of the seven heavenly archons who had been cast

---

[33] See F.-M.-M. Sagnard, in the commentary to his edition, 224-8; cf. von Stuckrad, *Ringen*, 650-5.

[34] See e.g. F. Graf, *Magic in the Ancient World*, Cambridge, Mass./London 1997, 97 (mysteries), 215-22 (magical prayer); A. Kropp, *Ausgewählte koptische Zaubertexte*, iii, Brussels 1930, 183-207 (magical epiklesis).

[35] E.g. Ptolemy, *Tetrabiblos* 1.13 (Robbins, 72-74); cf. Sagnard, in his edition of the *Excerpta ex Theodoto*, 226-227 (ad chaps 69-71). *PS* adds to these the 'eight-figure' or better 'eight-aspect', probably the octagon, which consists in a doubling of the quadrangle (see Geminus, *Elementa astronomiae* 2.15 [Manitius, 22-24]), and, in chaps 27-28, also the rare Coptic term for 'diametrical aspect' (ⲛⲉⲧⲙ̄ⲡⲉⲩϩⲟⲧ ⲉⲃⲟⲗ, 'their oppositions').

[36] Cf. Hodges, 'Gnostic liberation', 368-9.

[37] See M. Tardieu, *Trois mythes gnostiques*, Paris 1974, 72 note 157; F. Graf, 'Mythical production: Aspects of myth and technology in antiquity', in: R. Buxton (ed.), *From Myth to Reason? Studies in the Development of Greek Thought*, Oxford 1999, 317-28 at 318-22.

down from their heavens. Their angels initiated the human race into 'many kinds of errors and magic (μαγεία) and sorcery (φαρμακεία) and idolatry', and, with the assistance of Fate (εἰμαρμένη), trapped them in a permanent state of ignorance and error (chap. 124; Layton, 82).[38]

PS, too, links magic and astrology to the ascent of the archons over humanity. In an exegetic interlude, chap. 18, Mary Magdalene explains how Jesus' double action against the practices of magicians and astrologers had already been predicted by Isaiah in his vision of Egypt, which is quoted as: 'where now, Egypt, where are your diviners and your astrologers and necromancers and ventriloquists? Let them tell you from now on the things that the Lord Sabaôth will do!' (27.21-28.1). In Mary's following exegesis of this paraphrase of Isa 19.12 and 3 (LXX), the archons are identified as 'Egypt' on account of their association with matter (ὕλη; 28.9-10). Henceforth, they will be unable to predict what Jesus (cf. Isa 19.12: 'the Lord Sabaôth')[39] will do. The interpretation of Egypt as 'matter' is a conventional one in the allegoric tradition.[40] In Mary's exegetic commentary, the effectiveness of astrology and magic are seen as the expression of the rule of matter through the mediation of the archons. Their impotence reflects the defeat of the archons by Jesus' light.

As a corollary of this broad soteriological motivation, the author's rejection of magic shows strong moral and demonological accents. He rejects the occult sciences from a double ethical perspective that encompasses both their aims and their means.[41] Their aims, in particular those of magic, are evil by intent and their means are reprehensible since they assume some type of association with the demonized archons, with a spiritual 'Egypt'.[42] Those who 'through their mysteries, that is their wicked magic' (29.15) appeal to the power of the archons of the twelve eons are intent upon 'evil and criminal works' (27.7-8), by which they 'impede good works' (29.16). Magic is therefore not only condemned because of its association with demonic powers, but it is also seen as detrimental or, in modern terminology, as 'black' magic.

---

[38] Cf. Tardieu, *Trois mythes*, 71-2.

[39] This remarkable identification is explained in 28.11-16.

[40] See Tardieu, *Trois mythes*, 270-2.

[41] Compare Augustine's discussion of Moses and the magicians of Pharaoh: F. Graf, 'Augustine and magic', in: J.N. Bremmer and J.R. Veenstra (eds), *The Metamorphosis of Magic from Late Antiquity to the Early Modern Period*, Louvain 2002, 87-103 at 93.

[42] This is clearly implied in chap. 18, where *PS* concurs with mainstream patristic literature in identifying magic and astrology as the worship of demons; cf. Graf, 'Augustine', 96-8.

On the other hand, the formulae inscribed on Jesus' garment of light are not termed as magic, even though the nature of these *voces* and the way in which they operate would situate them technically within the domain of magic as it is understood both by modern opinion and *PS* itself. Magic is then taken as the use of 'mysterious' invocations that transfer the authority of higher powers onto those who are able to wield them. Ethically, however, the inscriptions on the garment do not fit within the author's negative definition of μαγεία, as they serve salvation, rather than evil. Therefore, in the condemnation of the occult sciences, soteriological, demonological and more strictly ethical motives all concur. In this light it is all the more remarkable that Jesus' measures against magic and astrology are so half-hearted. As was seen above, they were meant to score only a very partial success.

However negative the feelings of the author on magic and astrology may have been, his demonstration of their impotence is unhinged by a major paradox. At first, he meticulously points out how Jesus put an end to black magic and obstructed the work of the astrologers. Immediately afterwards, however, he provides an equally detailed exposition to explain how magic and astrology still do work in spite of everything. At first sight, an explanation along general pedagogic lines might seem attractive. Magic and astrology signify the continuing rule of the archons who remain in control of the human world until their realm finally collapses. Meanwhile, man stands in need of conversion and *PS*, like the *Excerpta ex Theodoto*, opposes conversion to Fate.[43] In the actual discussion about the effectiveness of astrology and magic, however, no trace of such reasoning is to be found, but rather very specific and technical arguments are used.[44] Magic still works because it is possible to ask for help from the thirteenth eon, an intermediate zone between the archontic world and the world of light. The traditional astrological calculations may fail during one half of the year, but still apply during the other half and very clever astrologers may even be able to adapt their calculations to the newly changed situation. Also, even if one concedes that the archons and their accomplices are still active and need to be overcome by each

---

[43] Schröder, 'Fatum', 629, on prayer and baptism (but note that the passages quoted are from the third book).

[44] In this respect the difference with the *Excerpta* is capital: there, the astrologers speak no more truth after baptism (chap. 78.1); in *PS*, after the turning of the spheres (30.11-15).

human being individually, this in no way excludes the possibility that, in the course of Jesus' combat against the powers, magic and astrology could have been disarmed decisively. This is, in fact, what Ignatius of Antioch appears to believe.

The paradox can only be resolved by accepting the terms and categories of the author of *PS* himself. At no point in his exposition does he show doubts about the virtual efficacy of magic, which he appears to understand as a certain type of 'mysteries' invoking the powers of the archons and enabling man to do harm. Nor does he ever doubt that precise mathematical calculations are in fact able to predict events that will take place on earth in some future time. The author condemns the astrologers' practices, but he does not query the essential validity of their procedures. He does not submit these to a rational criticism, but rather he applies ethical and demonological categories. The same phenomenon can be observed among some of his contemporaries. Origen may be quoted as a famous example of a Christian intellectual who severely criticizes the practices of magicians and diviners, but at the same time evolves a theory to account for the efficacy of magic.[45] In a similar way, the author of *PS*, in spite of his negative view of the occult sciences, does not preach against them, but rationalizes their (lack of) efficacy. His mode of discourse is not primarily parenetic, but technical. He explains mechanisms and, as was observed above, he partly does so in the terminology current in the occult sciences themselves. His rejection of these sciences is religiously motivated, but the models used in describing them are scholarly.[46]

Conclusions

The first book of the *Pistis Sophia*, by its paradoxical but nevertheless firmly negative attitude, represents an important chapter in the history of the early Christian debate about magic and astrology. The author adheres to a tradition that links the Incarnation with the abolition of

---

[45] See G. Bardy, 'Origène et la magie', *Recherches de Science Religieuse* 18 (1928) 126-42; cf. N. Brox, 'Magie und Aberglaube an den Anfängen des Christentums', *Trierer Theologische Zeitschrift* 83 (1974) 157-80 at 161-6; Graf, *Magic*, 74-5, 218-20.

[46] Scholarly, of course, in the acceptation it would have had in antiquity; see the interesting discussion by R. Gordon, '*Quaedam veritatis umbrae*: Hellenistic magic and astrology', in: P. Bilde et al. (eds), *Conventional Values of the Hellenistic Greeks*, Aarhus 1997, 128-58.

magic and the astral Fate. In describing this process, he uses mythical materials from various backgrounds in addition to consciously technical terminology. He is remarkably ambiguous, however, in the way he restricts the effects of this abolition. In conceding that magicians can still invoke higher powers and that astrological predictions may come true once the experts have grasped the new situation, he admits that magic, astrology and divination are still able to operate effectively. This is not because they are judged in any way favourably, despite the author's apparent interest in the mechanics of magic and astrology. He shows no sympathy for magicians and astrologers, treating them as distant 'others', as workers of evil and servants of the archontic world. His own use of 'powerful' formulae, those on the garment of light, does not fall within his negative definition of magic.

The author's technical appreciation of magic and astrology is balanced by ethical and demonological rejection. Against the background of this dilemma, his paradoxical attitude towards the occult sciences can be resolved. His astonishing concessions are meant to make room for a primarily technical understanding of magic and astrology, considered as scientifically or at least empirically undeniable facts. Instead of blaming Jesus with failure, he adopts a sophisticated though apparently contradictory attitude that accepts basic categories but nevertheless allows an ethically motivated distance. Thus he goes beyond many of the standard polemics against magic in negotiating a common ground where both the scholar and the Christian may tread.[47]

---

[47] Earlier versions of this paper were presented on May 17th, 2003, in a meeting of the Dutch Gnosticism Group, of which Gerard Luttikhuizen is one of the inspirers; during the XIe Journée d'études coptes at Strasbourg, June 12th-14th, and at the opening of the academic year, Department of Near Eastern Studies, Leiden University, September 2nd, 2003. I thank the members of the Gnosticism Group for much valuable discussion. T. Vorderstrasse kindly corrected the English version.

BIBLIOGRAPHY OF
GERARD P. LUTTIKHUIZEN

1. Scholarly publications

Forthcoming

Gnostic Revisions of Genesis Stories and Early Jesus Traditions (Nag Hammadi and Manichaean Studies 58), Leiden/Boston: Brill, 2005.

'The Elchasaites and their Book', in: P. Luomanen and A. Marjanen (eds), *The Other Side: A Handbook of Second Century Christian 'Heretics'*, Leiden/Boston: Brill.

'Waren Mani's Täufer Elchasaiten?', in: J. Tubach (ed.), *Die Inkulturation des Christentums im vorislamischen Persien*.

2004

De veelvormigheid van het vroegste christendom, Delft: Eburon, 2nd edn 2004.

'De oorsprong van het Kwaad volgens christelijke gnostici', in: B.J. Lietaert Peerbolte and E. Tigchelaar (eds), *Kennis van het Kwaad: Zeven visies uit jodendom en christendom*, Zoetermeer: Meinema, 2004, 89-101.

'Witnesses and Mediators of Christ's Gnostic Teachings', in: A. Hilhorst (ed.), *The Apostolic Age in Patristic Thought* (Supplements to Vigiliae Christianae 70), Leiden/Boston: Brill, 2004, 104-14.

'The Demonic Demiurge in Gnostic Mythology', in: C. Auffarth and L.T. Stuckenbruck (eds), *The Fall of the Angels* (Themes in Biblical Narrative 6), Leiden/Boston: Brill, 2004, 148-60.

2003

'The Critical Rewriting of Genesis in the Gnostic *Apocryphon of John*', in: F. García Martínez and G.P. Luttikhuizen (eds), *Jerusalem, Alexandria, Rome: Studies in Ancient Cultural Interaction in Honour of A. Hilhorst* (Supplements to the Journal for the Study of Judaism 82), Leiden/Boston: Brill, 2003, 187-200.

'Gnostic Ideas about Eve's Children and the Salvation of Humanity', in: G.P. Luttikhuizen (ed.), *Eve's Children: The Biblical Stories Retold and Interpreted in Jewish and Christian Traditions* (Themes in Biblical Narrative 5), Leiden/Boston: Brill, 2003, 203-17.

'The Suffering Jesus and the Invulnerable Christ in the Gnostic *Apocalypse of Peter*', in: J.N. Bremmer and I. Czachesz (eds), *The Apocalypse of Peter* (Studies on Early Christian Apocrypha 7), Louvain: Peeters, 2003, 187-99.

2002

'Traces of Aristotelian Thought in the *Apocryphon of John*', in: H.-G. Bethge, S. Emmel, K.L. King, and I. Schletterer (eds), *For the Children, Perfect Instruction: Studies in Honor of Hans-Martin Schenke on the Occasion of the Berliner Arbeitskreis für koptisch-gnostische Schriften's Thirtieth Year* (Nag Hammadi and Manichaean Studies 54), Leiden/Boston: Brill, 2002, 181-202.

'De pluriformiteit van het christendom', in: E. Noort and H. Zock (eds), *Trends in de Groninger theologie*, Delft: Eburon, 2002, 137-49.

De veelvormigheid van het vroegste christendom, Delft: Eburon, 2002.

2001

'Gnostic Hermeneutics', in: R. Kessler and P. Vandermeersch (eds), *God, Biblical Stories and Psychoanalytic Understanding*, Frankfurt am Main etc.: Peter Lang, 2001, 171-85.

'Veronderstellingen over het vroegste christendom in Alexandrië', in: J. Delobel et al. (eds), *Vroegchristelijke gemeenten tussen werkelijkheid en ideaal*, Kampen: Kok, 2001, 207-22.

'The Hymn of Jude Thomas, the Apostle, in the Country of the Indians (*ATh* 108-113)', in: J.N. Bremmer (ed.), *The Apocryphal Acts of Thomas* (Studies on Early Christian Apocrypha 6), Louvain: Peeters, 2001, 101-14.

2000

'The Creation of Man and Woman in *The Secret Book of John*', in: G.P. Luttikhuizen (ed.), *The Creation of Man and Woman: Interpretations of the Biblical Narratives in Jewish and Christian Traditions* (Themes in Biblical Narrative 3), Leiden/Boston/Cologne: Brill, 2000, 140-55.

'De uitleg van het Oude Testament in het Geheime Boek van Johannes en in het Ware Getuigenis', in: R. Roukema (ed.), *Het andere christendom: De gnosis en haar geestverwanten*, Zoetermeer: Meinema, 2000, 83-96.

'The Religious Message of Andrew's Speeches', in: J.N. Bremmer (ed.), *The Apocryphal Acts of Andrew* (Studies on the Apocryphal Acts of the Apostles 5), Louvain: Peeters, 2000, 96-103.

1999

'A Resistant Interpretation of the Paradise Story in the Gnostic *Testimony of Truth* (Nag Hamm. Cod. IX.3) 45-50', in: G.P. Luttikhuizen (ed.), *Paradise Interpreted: Representations of Biblical Paradise in Judaism and Christianity* (Themes in Biblical Narrative 2), Leiden/Boston/Cologne: Brill, 1999, 140-52.

'The Book of Elchasai: A Jewish Apocalyptic Writing, not a Christian Church Order', *Society of Biblical Literature 1999 Seminar Papers*, 405-25.

'Biblical Narrative in Gnostic Revision: The Story of Noah and the Flood in Classic Gnostic Mythology', in: F. García Martínez and G.P. Luttikhuizen (eds), *Interpretations of the Flood* (Themes in Biblical Narrative 1), Leiden/Boston/Cologne: Brill, 1999, 109-23.

1998

'Vroege tradities over Jezus in een niet-canonieke bron: Het Evangelie van Thomas', *Tijdschrift voor Theologie* 38 (1998) 120-43.

'Simon Magus as a Narrative Figure in the Acts of Peter', in: J.N. Bremmer (ed.), *The Apocryphal Acts of Peter* (Studies on the Apocryphal Acts of the Apostles 3), Louvain: Peeters, 1998, 39-51.

'De canonisering van vroege christelijke geschriften', *Met andere woorden: Kwartaalblad over bijbelvertalen* 17/3 (1998) 11-19.

1997

'The Thought Pattern of Gnostic Mythologizers and Their Use of Biblical Traditions', in: J.D. Turner and A. McGuire (eds), *The Nag Hammadi Library After Fifty Years: Proceedings of the 1995 Society of Biblical Literature Commemoration* (Nag Hammadi and Manichaean Studies 44), Leiden/Boston: Brill, 1997, 89-101.

'Gods onvolmaakte schepping: 'Wegens sterfgeval gesloten' van Jan Wolkers', in: G. Jensma and Y. Kuiper (eds), *De god van Nederland is de beste: Elf opstellen over religie in de moderne Nederlandse literatuur*, Kampen: Kok Agora, 1997, 128-37.

'De koptisch-orthodoxe kerk vanaf haar ontstaan tot 1900', in: H. Teule and A. Wessels (eds), *Oosterse christenen binnen de wereld van de islam*, Kampen: Kok, 1997, 200-14 [with H.W. Havelaar].

1996

'The Apocryphal Correspondence with the Corinthians and the Acts of Paul', in: J.N. Bremmer (ed.), *The Apocryphal Acts of Paul and Thecla* (Studies on the Apocryphal Acts of the Apostles 2), Kampen: Kok Pharos, 1996, 75-91.

'De veelvormigheid van het vroegste christendom: Diversiteit binnen en buiten de canon van het Nieuwe Testament', *Tijdschrift voor Theologie* 36 (1996) 331-47.

1995

'A Gnostic Reading of the Acts of John', in: J.N. Bremmer (ed.), *The Apocryphal Acts of John* (Studies on the Apocryphal Acts of the Apostles 1), Kampen: Kok Pharos, 1995, 119-52.

'Het evangelie van de nabije heerschappij van God', in: H.S. Benjamins et al. (eds), *Evangelie en beschaving: Studies bij het afscheid van Hans Roldanus*, Zoetermeer: Boekencentrum, 1995, 17-32.

1994

'Johannine Vocabulary and the Thought Structure of Gnostic Mythological Texts', in: H. Preißler and H. Seiwert (eds), *Gnosisforschung und Religionsgeschichte: Festschrift für K. Rudolph zum 65. Geburtstag*, Marburg: Diagonal-Verlag, 1994, 175-81.

'Early Christian Judaism and Christian Gnosis, and their Relation to Mainstream Christianity', *Neotestamentica* 28 (1994) 219-34.

'Vor- und nachösterliche Herrenworte in der 1. Offenbarung des Jacobus, NHC V,3', in: W. Beltz (ed.), *Der Gottesspruch in der koptischen Literatur: Hans-Martin Schenke zum 65. Geburtstag* (Hallesche Beiträge zur Orientwissenschaft 15), Halle: Martin-Luther Universität, 1994, 92-8.

'Roependen uit de woestijn: De Nag-Hammadigeschriften in de belangstelling', *De Bazuin* 77 (1994) 14-16.

1993

'The Poetic Character of Revelation 4 and 5', in: J. den Boeft and A. Hilhorst (eds), *Early Christian Poetry* (Supplements to Vigiliae Christianae 22), Leiden/New York/Cologne: Brill, 1993, 15-22.

1992

'Tekstsoort en taalniveau in het Nieuwe Testament', in: K.G. Pieterman (ed.), *Elementen van bijbelvertalen*, Haarlem: Nederlands Bijbelgenootschap, 1992, 67-83.

'De bijbelse en apocriefe voorgeschiedenis van de middeleeuwse hel', *Groniek: Historisch Tijdschrift* 117 (1992) 11-19.

1991

'Vroeg-christelijk jodendom', in: T. Baarda et al. (eds), *Jodendom en Vroeg Christendom: continuïteit en discontinuïteit*, Kampen: J.H. Kok, 1991, 163-89.

1990

Op zoek naar de samenhang van Paulus' gedachten: Rede uitgesproken bij de aanvaarding van het ambt van hoogleraar in de oudchristelijke letterkunde en de uitlegging van het Nieuwe Testament aan de Rijksuniversiteit van Groningen op 10 april 1990, Kampen: J.H. Kok, 1990 (Inaugural lecture Groningen).

1989

'Intertextual References in Readers' Responses to the Apocryphon of John', in: S. Draisma (ed.), *Intertextuality in Biblical Writings: Essays in Honour of Bas van Iersel*, Kampen: J.H. Kok, 1989, 117-26.

1988

'The Jewish Factor in the Development of the Gnostic Myth of Origins: Some Observations', in: T. Baarda et al. (eds), *Text and Testimony: Essays on New Testament and Apocryphal Literature in Honour of A.F.J. Klijn*, Kampen: J.H. Kok, 1988, 152-61.

'The Evaluation of the Teaching of Jesus in Christian Gnostic Revelation Dialogues', *Novum Testamentum* 30 (1988) 158-68. Also published in: J.-M. Sevrin (ed.), *The New Testament in Early Christianity / La réception des écrits néotestamentaires dans le christianisme primitif* (Bibliotheca Ephemeridum Theologicarum Lovaniensium 86), Louvain: University Press / Peeters, 1989, 363-72.

Gnostische Geschriften, i, *Het Evangelie naar Maria, het Evangelie naar Filippus* (Na de Schriften 2), Kampen: J.H. Kok, 2nd edn 1988.

1987

'The Book of Elchasai: A Jewish Apocalypse', *Aula Orientalis* 5 (1987) 101-6.

1986

Gnostische Geschriften, i, *Het Evangelie naar Maria, het Evangelie naar Filippus, de Brief van Petrus aan Filippus* (Na de Schriften 2), Kampen: J.H. Kok, 1986.

1985

The Revelation of Elchasai: Investigations into the Evidence for a Mesopotamian Jewish Apocalypse of the Second Century and its Reception by Judeo-Christian Propagandists (Texte und Studien zum Antiken Judentum 8), Tübingen: J.C.B. Mohr (Paul Siebeck), 1985.

1984

The Revelation of Elchasai: Investigations into the Evidence for a Mesopotamian Jewish Apocalypse of the Second Century and Its Reception by Judeo-Christian Propagandists (PhD thesis Groningen), 1984.

'Politieke macht in het licht van de heerschappij van God', *Schrift* 94 (1984) 132-5.

'Gnostisch christendom', *Theocreet* 16 (1984) 13-28.

1982

'Hippolytus' Polemic against Bishop Calixtus and Alcibiades of Apamea', in: E.A. Livingstone (ed.), *Studia Patristica XVII*, Oxford etc.: Pergamon Press, 1982, 808-12.

1979

'Wat betekent genade?', *Schrift* 63 (1979) 91-4.

'Het appèl van de tekst', *Theocreet* 11 (1979) 36-40.

1978

'The Letter of Peter to Philip and the New Testament', in: R. McL. Wilson (ed.), *Nag Hammadi and Gnosis* (Nag Hammadi Studies 14), Leiden: E.J. Brill, 1978, 96-102.

1975

'Χάρις. Een semantische verkenning', in: *Gratias agimus. Opstellen over Danken en Loven aangeboden aan Prof. Dr. W.F. Dankbaar* (Studies van het Instituut voor Liturgiewetenschap 2), Groningen 1975, 66-74 [with H. Schoonhoven].

1973

'De interpretatie van Marcus: op zoek naar het hermeneutisch uitgangspunt van Marcus' christologie', *Vox theologica* 43 (1973) 184-204.

'De theologische betekenis van de spijzigingsverhalen', *Getuigenis* 17 (1973) 217-23.

1971

'De toekomst van de theologie: vraaggesprekken met twaalf Nederlandse theologen', *Vox theologica* 41 (1971) 2-43 [with R. Oost].

2. Editorial work

(a) *Collective volumes*

Eve's Children: The Biblical Stories Retold and Interpreted in Jewish and Christian Traditions (Themes in Biblical Narrative 5), Leiden/Boston: Brill, 2003.

Jerusalem, Alexandria, Rome: Studies in Ancient Cultural Interaction in Honour of A. Hilhorst (Supplements to the Journal for the Study of Judaism 82), Leiden/ Boston 2003 [with F. García Martínez].

The Creation of Man and Woman: Interpretations of the Biblical Narratives in Jewish and Christian Traditions (Themes in Biblical Narrative 3), Leiden/Boston/ Cologne: Brill, 2000.

Paradise Interpreted: Representations of Biblical Paradise in Judaism and Christianity (Themes in Biblical Narrative 2), Leiden/Boston/Cologne: Brill, 1999.

Interpretations of the Flood (Themes in Biblical Narrative 1), Leiden/Boston/ Cologne: Brill, 1999 [with F. García Martínez].

Eeuwig kwetsbaar: Hedendaagse kunst en religie, Zoetermeer: Boekencentrum 1998 [with R. Steensma].

Text and Testimony: Essays on New Testament and Apocryphal Literature in Honour of A.F.J. Klijn, Kampen: J.H. Kok, 1988 [with T. Baarda, A. Hilhorst, and A.S. van der Woude].

Assistance to *Groot Nieuws voor U: Het Nieuwe Testament in de omgangstaal* (1972), revised edition *Groot Nieuws Bijbel* (1998).

(b) *Periodicals*

Co-editor of *Vox theologica: Interacademiaal theologisch tijdschrift*, 1969-73 [with R. Oost].

(c) *Series*

Studies on the Apocryphal Acts of the Apostles [since 1995], *continued as* Studies on Early Christian Apocrypha.

Themes in Biblical Narrative [1999-2005].

LIST OF CONTRIBUTORS

HENK BAKKER, PhD Groningen, Baptist minister, Katwijk aan Zee

JÁNOS BOLYKI, Professor Emeritus of New Testament Studies, Károli Gáspár University, Budapest

ABRAHAM P. BOS, Professor of Ancient Philosophy, Faculty of Philosophy, Free University, Amsterdam

JAN N. BREMMER, Professor of the General History of Religion and Comparative Religious Studies, Faculty of Theology and Religious Studies, University of Groningen

ISTVÁN CZACHESZ, Post-Doctoral Researcher of the Netherlands Organization for Scientific Research (NWO), Faculty of Theology and Religious Studies, University of Groningen

FLORENTINO GARCÍA MARTÍNEZ, Professor of the Religion and Literature of Early Judaism & Director of the Qumran Institute, Faculty of Theology and Religious Studies, University of Groningen, and Research Professor of Theology, Catholic University of Leuven

JOHN HERRMANN, Curator of Classical Art Emeritus at the Museum of Fine Arts, Boston, Massachusetts

ANTHONY HILHORST, Lecturer Emeritus in New Testament and Early Christian Studies, Faculty of Theology and Religious Studies, University of Groningen

ALBERT L.A. HOGETERP, Post-Doctoral Researcher, Faculty of Theology, Catholic University of Leuven

ATTILA JAKAB, Researcher, Public Foundation for European Comparative Minority Research, Budapest, and Lecturer in Geopolitics of Religions, International Centre for Geopolitical Studies, Geneva

ROB KUGLER, Paul S. Wright Professor of Christian Studies, Lewis & Clark College, Portland, Oregon

BERT JAN LIETAERT PEERBOLTE, University Lecturer in New Testament Studies, Kampen Theological University

JANNI LOMAN, PhD candidate, University of Groningen

MAARTEN J.J. MENKEN, Professor of New Testament Studies, Catholic Theological University of Utrecht

MARVIN MEYER, Griset Professor of Bible and Christian Studies, Department of Religious Studies, Chapman University, Orange, California

ED NOORT, Professor of Ancient Israelite Literature, Old Testament Interpretation, the History of Israelite Religion and Intertestamental Literature, Faculty of Theology and Religious Studies, University of Groningen

MONIKA PESTHY, Lecturer in Theology, Vilmos Apor Catholic College, Hungary

F. LAUTARO ROIG LANZILLOTTA, Post-Doctoral Researcher, Faculty of Philosophy and Arts, University of Córdoba, Spain

RIEMER ROUKEMA, Professor of New Testament Studies, Kampen Theological University

HERMAN TE VELDE, Professor Emeritus of Egyptology, Faculty of Theology and Religious Studies, University of Groningen

EIBERT J.C. TIGCHELAAR, Fellow of the Netherlands Organization for Scientific Research (NWO) at the Qumran Institute, Faculty of Theology and Religious Studies, University of Groningen

JÜRGEN TUBACH, Professor of Oriental & Byzantine Studies, Institut für Orientalistik, Martin-Luther-Universität Halle-Wittenberg, Halle

ANNEWIES VAN DEN HOEK, Lecturer in Greek and Latin, Harvard Divinity School, Harvard University

PIETER W. VAN DER HORST, Professor of New Testament Exegesis, Early Christian Literature, and the Jewish and Hellenistic World of Early Christianity, Faculty of Theology, University of Utrecht

JACQUES VAN DER VLIET, University Lecturer in Egyptology, Faculty of Arts, University of Leiden

HUUB VAN DE SANDT, University Lecturer in New Testament Studies, Faculty of Theology, University of Tilburg

JACOBUS VAN DIJK, University Lecturer in Egyptology, Faculty of Theology and Religious Studies, University of Groningen

JAN WILLEM VAN HENTEN, Professor of New Testament Exegesis, Early Christian Literature and Hellenistic-Jewish Literature, Faculty of Humanities, University of Amsterdam

GEORGE H. VAN KOOTEN, University Lecturer in New Testament and Early Christian Studies, Faculty of Theology and Religious Studies, University of Groningen

JACQUES T.A.G.M. VAN RUITEN, University Senior Lecturer in Ancient Israelite Literature, Old Testament Interpretation, and Early Jewish Literature, Faculty of Theology and Religious Studies, University of Groningen

INDEX OF SUBJECTS AND NAMES

INDEX OF ANCIENT AUTHORS AND WRITINGS

5, 282, 285, 292, 294, 299, 304, 306-8, 310, 319-20, 323-24, 360, 366-8, 370, 373-4, 378, 397, 400-2, 414, 449, 451, 452, 454, 459, 512, 531

Pseudo-Clementines (*Recognitions* and *Homilies*) 311-329

1 Corinthians 155, 235, 241, 268, 271, 274, 276-8, 383, 387, 402, 412, 435, 439

2 Corinthians 212, 267, 268-71, 273, 275, 278, 281, 392, 432, 435, 436, 439, 440, 447

Corpus Hermeticum 88, 107-8, 420, 445, 447, 450, 458

Cosmas Indicopleustes 320

Daniel, Book of 106, 186, 192-3, 198, 209, 230

Dead Sea Scrolls 18, 21-41, 43, 251, 355-6, 430

Deuteronomy, Book of 4, 8, 12, 16, 18, 19, 25, 136, 156, 161, 405

Dialogue of the Saviour (NHC III.5) 387, 392

Didache 227-45, 394

Didascalia Apostolorum 257

Didymus the Blind 165-6, 168, 170-1, 173-4, 401

Dio Cassius 93, 116-17, 119-20, 127, 129, 131-3, 178-80, 182-3, 188-92, 194-6, 199-202, 204, 206-7, 211, 338

Dio Chrysostom 180, 188, 192, 290-1

Diodorus Siculus 111-12, 158-9, 161

Diogenes Laertius 155, 289

Dionysius of Halicarnassus 207

Doctrina Apostolorum 251

Dorotheus of Sidon 315

End of the Work 423

1 Enoch 102, 357, 383, 396, 430, 489, 532

2 Enoch 396

Ephesians, Letter to the 95, 272, 277, 402, 407-8, 447

Ephrem the Syrian 32

Epiphanes 368, 372

Epiphanius 272, 366, 367, 449, 457, 459

2 Esdras 230

Eugnostos the Blessed (NHC III.3; V.1) 377

Euripides 93, 288, 291

Eusebius 30, 67, 119, 155, 162, 166-7, 171, 248, 319-20, 323, 331-45, 366-69, 374-6, 400, 446

Evagrios 353

Exegesis of the Soul (NHC II.6) 371-2

Exodus, Book of 3, 4, 8, 10-12, 14-15, 21, 24, 38, 43-65, 92, 135-7, 139, 153, 155-6, 161, 164, 168-9, 171, 172-3, 253, 256, 473

Explanation of the Secrets of the Ritual of Repulsing the Evil One 422

Ezekiel, Book of 6, 17, 156, 231, 256-7, 277

Ezekiel the Tragedian 59, 61, 63, 162, 165-6

4 Ezra 394

Firmicus Maternus 315-16

Florus 117, 129

Galatians, Letter to the 268-9, 278, 407, 432, 435-6

Gellius 319-21

Geminus 532

Genesis, Book of 3, 9-10, 15, 17-18, 21-41, 45, 55, 59, 67, 81-2, 86, 92, 95, 137, 156, 237, 250, 253, 276, 326, 356-7

Georgius Cedrenus 307

Georgius Monachus 307

Ginza 471-5, 478

Gospel according to the Hebrews 402

Gospel of Eve 457, 458

Gospel of Mary (BG I) 448-9

Gospel of Philip (NHC II.3) 409, 446, 457-8

Gospel of the Egyptians or *Holy Book of the Great Invisible Spirit* (NHC III.2; IV.2) 489, 503, 506, 510-17

Gospel of Truth (NHC I.3) 445, 451-4, 456-7, 459

Gregory Barhebraeus 279

Gregory of Nyssa 166, 168-72

Gregory Thaumatourgos 139

Hebrews, Letter to the 171

Heliodorus 92-4

INDEX OF HEBREW, GREEK, AND COPTIC WORDS

Ancient Judaism and Early Christianity

(Arbeiten zur Geschichte des Antiken Judentums
und des Urchristentums)

MARTIN HENGEL *Tübingen*
PIETER W. VAN DER HORST *Utrecht*·MARTIN GOODMAN *Oxford*
DANIEL R. SCHWARTZ *Jerusalem* ·CILLIERS BREYTENBACH *Berlin*
FRIEDRICH AVEMARIE *Marburg* ·SETH SCHWARTZ *New York*

Vergebungsvorstellungen in urchristlichen und frühjüdischen Texten. 1999. ISBN 90 04 11283 9

46 H. Leeming & K. Leeming (eds.). *Josephus' Jewish War and its Slavonic Version*. A Synoptic Comparison of the English Translation by H.St.J. Thackeray with the Critical Edition by N.A. Mescerskij of the Slavonic Version in the Vilna Manuscript translated into English by H. Leeming and L. Osinkina. ISBN 90 04 11438 6

47 M. Daly-Denton. *David in the Fourth Gospel*. The Johannine Reception of the Psalms. 1999. ISBN 90 04 11448 3

48 T. Rajak. *The Jewish Dialogue with Greece and Rome*. Studies in Cultural and Social Interaction 2000. ISBN 90 04 11285 5

49 H.H.D. Williams, III. *The Wisdom of the Wise*. The Presence and Function of Scripture within 1 Cor. 1:18-3:23. 2000. ISBN 90 04 11974 4

50 R.D. Rowe. *God's Kingdom and God's Son*. The Background to Mark's Christology from Concepts of Kingship in the Psalms. 2002. ISBN 90 04 11888 8

51 E. Condra. *Salvation for the Righteous Revealed*. Jesus amid Covenantal and Messianic Expectations in Second Temple Judaism. 2002. ISBN 90 04 12617 1

52 Ch.Ritter. *Rachels Klage im antiken Judentum und frühen Christentum*. Eine auslegungsgeschichtliche Studie. 2002. ISBN 90 04 12509 4

53 C. Breytenbach & L.L. Welborn (eds.). *Encounters with Hellenism*. Studies on the First Letter of Clement. 2003. ISBN 90 04 12526 4

54 W. Schmithals & C. Breytenbach (ed.). *Paulus, die Evangelien und das Urchristentum*. Beiträge von und zu Walter Schmithals zu seinem 80. Geburtstag. 2003. ISBN 90 04 12983 9

55 K.P. Sullivan. *Wrestling with Angels*. A Study of the Relationship between Angels and Humans in Ancient Jewish Literature and the New Testament. 2004. ISBN 90 04 13224 4

56 L. Triebel. *Jenseitshoffnung in Wort und Stein*. Nefesch und pyramidales Grabmal als Phänomene antiken jüdischen Bestattungswesens im Kontext der Nachbarkulturen. 2004. ISBN 90 04 12924 3

57 C. Breytenbach & J. Schröter. *Die Apostelgeschichte und die hellenistische Geschichtsschreibung*. Festschrift für Eckhard Plümacher zu seinem 65. Geburtstag. 2004. ISBN 90 04 13892 7

58 S. Weingarten. *The Saint's Saints*. Hagiography and Geography in Jerome. 2005. ISBN 90 04 14387 4

59 A. Hilhorst & G.H. van Kooten (eds.). *The Wisdom of Egypt*. Jewish, Early Christian, and Gnostic Essays in Honour of Gerard P. Luttikhuizen. 2005. ISBN 90 04 14425 0

60 S. Chepey. *Nazirites in Late Second Temple Judaism*. A Survey of Ancient Jewish Writings, the New Testament, Archaeological Evidence, and Other Writings from Late Antiquity. 2005. ISBN 90 04 14465 X